The Development of Education
in the
Twentieth Century

By
ADOLPH E. MEYER, Ph.D.
*Professor of Education, New York
University*

Second Edition

New York
PRENTICE-HALL, INC.
1949

PRENTICE-HALL EDUCATION SERIES

E. George Payne, Editor

Copyright, 1939, 1949, by
PRENTICE-HALL, INC.
70 Fifth Avenue, New York

PRINTED IN THE UNITED STATES OF AMERICA

Preface

When the present volume was originally planned some fifteen years ago, it was designed to meet the needs of a small number of education students pursuing a course in the history of developments of the twentieth century at the School of Education of New York University. Conducted since the late twenties, this course has sought to give a bird's-eye view of a number of salient points, approaching them comparatively rather than in strictly historical fashion. In the main this situation has not altered; hence in revising and rewriting the original edition, I have continued to adhere to my prime and original purpose. However, I have not been unmindful of the fact that *The Development of Education in the Twentieth Century* has drawn a far larger and a much more varied audience than I had ever dared to anticipate. It has found use not only in America, but in many other lands; it has served not only undergraduates, but graduates as well; and it has been employed not only as a text in the history of twentieth century education, but also in comparative education and in general introductory courses in modern education. During the forties the book was included in *A Reader's Guide to Education,* which is a list of "books about education for Americans," compiled by the National Education Association of the United States and the Book-of-the-Month Club, "to promote, through the medium of books, a more general understanding of American Education."

All these developments, though assuredly gratifying to any author, have unfortunately not been without their disadvantages. Thus, in revising the original edition, I have had to deal not only with the unusual effects of the passing years, but also with the diverse tastes and requirements of my readers. No light task in any event, the gauging and understanding of these needs was furthered considerably by the help of many colleagues, by the suggestions of parents, students, and teachers, but especially, of course, by the frank and honest criticism from scholars and professional educators everywhere. Although it has been impossible, and even undesirable, to heed all their counsel, yet a good part of its substance has made its way into the pages which follow. Specifically it has led to such matters as the following:

1. Since many readers may be only slightly acquainted with the roots of present-day education, I have gone into much greater historical detail. This is true not only of individuals like Rousseau, Pestalozzi, Herbart, Froebel and Parker, but also of the various national systems of education.

2. The cultural setting from which so many educational developments have sprung has been greatly amplified; indeed most of it was not included in the first edition.

3. Events and movements which fifteen years ago were in their early stages, but which have now assumed a certain solidity, have been treated in much more generous detail. Among these we find such subjects as the youth problem, workers' education, intercultural education, and education for international understanding.

4. The philosophical bases of American education have received far more attention than in the first edition. This holds not only for Dewey and other experimentalists, but also for their leading critics, such as the idealists, realists, Catholic scholastics, and neo-scholastics like Robert Maynard Hutchins and Mortimer Adler.

5. The pages dealing with Progressive Education have been considerably augmented with fresh material on the rise and development of the Progressive Education Association, whose role in American education has been important. The leading scientific appraisals of the Progressive movement have been

reported, as have the arguments of its leading critics, the Essentialists.

6. Naturally, the present edition has been brought as up to date as possible. The course of dictatorship in Italy, Germany, and Russia and its effects on education, the effects of the war in the victorious and vanquished lands, and the programs for reform and re-education have been considered.

7. Unlike its predecessor, the present volume has been substantially documented, not only in compliance with the canons of good historiography, but also to furnish leads for further reading. For the more advanced student references in French, German, and Italian have been included. The bibliography has been altogether rewritten, and, to facilitate its use, its listings have been classified under specific headings.

8. Even more than in the first edition, the emphasis has been on American education. This is necessarily so since the book is designed for American readers. I have always believed, however, that the study of education cannot be scientific if it is based on an attitude which is largely isolationist; hence I have sought to make my subject as inclusive as possible, and, like Horace Mann and Henry Barnard, I have approached it from the comparative viewpoint. The fact that I have restricted the present volume to the larger western nations should not be interpreted as any disparagement on my part of the educational developments in other parts of the world. China, Japan, India, Australia and other parts of the British Commonwealth, as well as Latin America are all important. But space in books is today a precious thing. To include them in the present study would involve a forbidding task of condensation; hence to do them the justice they deserve I have reserved for them a future day and a volume all their own.

A. E. M.

Contents

I

Modernizing Education

A. Introduction

THAT THE twentieth century has produced great material
progress is an obvious commonplace. Comparing our mode
of life with that of our forefathers, it is no idle vainglory
which prompts the assertion that we live better—if by better
living we mean that we enjoy superior communication and
transportation. We have greater control over disease and our
lives on the average are longer. Where even the nineteenth
century was a horse-and-buggy era, the twentieth has become
the streamlined period of the automobile and the airplane,
of technicolor, radio, and television. The twentieth century
is the Age of Machines and the Age of Science. Its scientific
achievements, in abstract theory as well as in practical application, have been enormous. The twentieth century is the
era of Einstein, of Planck, of Eddington, and of many other
giants of the laboratory. It is the century of relativity, of
quantum physics, of the galactic universe; but it is also the
century of nylon, plastics, synthetic rubber and wool, of sulfa
drugs, penicillin, and blood banks. Because of the great and
rapid strides of science and technology, more of the world's
goods have become available to more people than ever before.
There has been progress, too, in the extension and enhancement of individual security and in the reduction of poverty.
Perceptible dents have been made in the class system with its
inequalities and distinctions among people. Relatively rigid

1

in the nineteenth century, it was loosened considerably in the
twentieth, and in some parts of the world, such as the USSR,
it has been changed altogether. Moreover, with the growth
of social democracy, organized society has grown more energetic in its efforts to ameliorate the hardships and sufferings
of its less fortunate members. The twentieth century has
witnessed greater freedom of speech and of the press, greater
liberty of action and thought, and fewer overt religious
struggles than the past. In the field of education, too, there
have been gains. Education has been made broader in scope
and more varied in its offerings at the same time that it has
been extended, with the result that illiteracy has decreased
and people, on the whole, have become better informed.

Turning from the credit to the debit side of our cultural
ledger, we find that although we possess more exact knowledge
we have not been uniformly wise in our application of that
knowledge. Scientists have split the atom and developed new
physical phenomena only to have them turned into weapons
of terrible destruction. Though modern man has more
material gains than any of his predecessors, it is plain that
these riches are not universally enjoyed. The great bulk of
the world's wealth is still concentrated in the hands of the
very few; in a world of abundance one perceives entire populations in the grip of hunger. Democracy, so highly cherished
in some lands, has been assailed by foes on all sides, even in
the very lands that extol it. Its friends and defenders have
had to fight the bloodiest war in history against dictator-
controlled autocracies, where the state counted for all and the
individual for very little. Poverty and its ugly helpmate,
unemployment, still persist, despite man's battle to overcome
them. Equality, for which men have been willing to die, is
still considered in many places as an impractical, and even
undesirable, ideal. The idea that a man's worth is based on
his wealth or his political connection is, alas, found even in
democracies. True, in many lands—capitalist as well as
socialist and communist—socio-economic plans have been

developed to combat social and economic insecurity. But despite it all the social lag has continued. The concomitants of political democracy, such as freedom of speech and of the press and other civil liberties, have been under steady attack. In totalitarian states they were, of course, buried long ago. But even in a democracy like the United States they have had to be defended perennially. The tolerance of which Montaigne dreamed, and which the twentieth century thought it possessed —at least to a larger degree than ever before—went into eclipse in Nazi Germany. But elsewhere, too, minorities have suffered at the hands of the majority.

The conflicts and confusions of twentieth century culture have not been without their challenge. Philosophers and theologians have, as usual, sought to pilot men. Social scientists have emerged from their academic confines and, arming themselves with newer and more scientific procedures, have endeavored to come to grips with the great and baffling problems engulfing man in his everyday life. Some nations have tried to cope with recurrent economic crises by legislation. In the United States this was most recently attempted, with much opposition, under the New Deal, within the framework, of course, of capitalism. Fascism sought its solution by preserving capitalism under a dictatorship. Communism, for its part, destroyed capitalism altogether and substituted for it a workers' collectivism. What is known as the Middle Way was taken by Sweden, which reformed capitalism by means of state-capitalism and cooperative enterprise. The early twentieth century saw the creation of instrumentalities designed to preserve peace—the League of Nations, the Kellogg-Briand Pact, the World Court, economic sanctions, and the use of arbitration to settle international disputes. But these, as we well know, were feeble and impotent. Set in a world ruled by a passion for national sovereignty, enflamed with national rivalries and hostilities that were intensified by a fierce competition for foreign markets and raw materials, the agencies for peace were stifled and unable to prevent the second world war.

As for education, although the twentieth century has seen it extended to more people than ever, it has not always been dispensed in the interest of truth, better human understanding, and cooperation. Even in democratic countries it has been exploited time and again by self-interested groups to preserve a faulty, and in many respects unsatisfactory, *status quo*. In totalitarian states education and propaganda have become so interwined as to become one and the same. Finally, the twentieth century has been an era of bloodshed. In addition to the world wars there have been many other conflicts of a major scale—so many, in fact, that the years when the whole world has actually been at peace are the exception rather than the rule.

As might be expected, the new cultural forces of the twentieth century have affected educational theory and practice. Probably no other era has witnessed such prodigious educational activity, and none has been touched more markedly by its unrest and conflict. Twentieth century education, as the following pages will reveal, has re-examined and re-fashioned its aims. In harmony with the scientific temper of the age, educational philosophers have pitched their camp more and more in the field of naturalism and experimentalism. But they have been challenged all along the line by representatives of the older philosophies. Applying the findings of science on an ever-increasing scale, twentieth century education has overhauled most of its procedures. Not only has the modern schoolman profited by the contributions of the natural sciences, but he has made greater use of the products of science as well. His school buildings are better constructed, better lighted, better ventilated, with greater regard for health, and safety, and comfort. The twentieth century school makes use of the radio and the motion picture; its shops, workrooms, and laboratories would astonish our grandfathers. Thanks to psychologists, the twentieth century teacher has at his disposal valuable data relating to the behavior of man, his learning equipment and its operation, his feelings and emotions, his desires and drives. From the probings of psychoanalysts he has learned something of the significance of the subconscious and the part it plays in human action. From the anthropologists he has gained much and valuable information about mankind and his culture. Anthropology has made it clear beyond any doubt that the doctrine of the supremacy of the white race is a myth without any scientific foundation. From sociologists the modern educator has gained a newer and better understanding of the complex interrelationships which exist among men and the institutions and social forces working in our midst. He has learned about the effects of environment on society; the factors involved in social control; the tactics in social conflict; the domination of the group mind over the individual; and much more. It is clear that although the individual is important in education, his adjustment to society is even more important. Again, it is plain that the school does not operate in a vacuum, but that between it and the community and society at large there is a reciprocal relationship which must be understood and put to use.

Yet despite its immense and progressive transformation during the first half of the century, public education has not made full and honest use of its new assets. With a few salient exceptions, it has been the servant of an old and obsolescent order. It has been purblind to some of the most fundamental facts of society, economics, and politics. Though it is manifest, for example, that our economy has been unstable and precarious, that, as a system, it has cursed us with insecurity, inflation, and cycles of prosperity and collapse, a forthright study of such facts and the forces which produce them has generally been avoided by the public school. What is true in the economic domain is true also in other fields. Do we, for example, teach that this is One World and that the United Nations needs to be strong? We also teach that the United States is a sovereign power and that its rights are supreme and incon-

testable. Do we teach that the nations of the world should
cooperate for the common good? We also teach that atomic
energy must remain our secret. Do we teach that war is an
evil and a catastrophe? We also teach that wars are forced on
us and that we must be prepared. Do we teach that we
should support the efforts of the common people in every land
to rise in power? We also teach an uncritical acceptance of
our foreign policy when it thwarts such efforts in Spain, and
Greece, and China. And, finally, do we teach freedom,
equality, and brotherhood? In hundreds of schools throughout the country we also teach that the white race is superior
and that the Christian is better than the Jew, the Hindu, or
the Moslem.

The truth is that although the public school of the twentieth
century has advanced on many fronts, its advances have been
largely pedagogic. Culturally its outlook has been, in the
main, conservative. With rare exceptions the school has
played the role of reflecting the social order rather than of
reconstructing and improving it. Indeed, there are many who
hold that the latter is not a proper function of the school; who
insist that its mission is essentially that of transmitting the
so-called cultural heritage; who believe that to teach the
young to understand and deal with the frictions, tensions, and
conflicts which beset us on all sides is not within the province
of education. Of recent years, however, this traditional view
has been increasingly challenged. More and more, educators
are coming to the view that the function of the school is not
simply to reflect the cultural tradition, but also to contribute
to its improvement.

B.   Antecedents of Modern Education

Historically, modern education has been influenced by many
factors. The idea that the masses should be literate and that
the state should help to make them so originated in the
sixteenth century as a result of Martin Luther's dictum that
good Protestants must read the Bible. With the rise of the

national state the religious stress was superseded by a civic motive which envisioned the school's prime function as the making of acceptable and disciplined citizens. But whether the motive of education came from the church or whether it sprang from the state, its process was essentially to mold the child in the matrix of a preconceived culture. The school held the mirror up to the world of the adult and sought to model the child after the reflection. This it did by transmitting to him a cultural heritage and by imparting a body of facts and information as well as certain skills. Save for an occasional dissenting note from a protesting reformer, schoolmen gave virtually no heed to the individual interests and capacities of their pupils. These, in fact, were generally deemed to be the enemies of discipline, and for a schoolmaster to encourage them was something quite unthinkable. As a result, pedagogic practices became formalized and standardized, so much so, indeed, that differences in culture and environment were often almost imperceptible.

1. Jean-Jacques Rousseau

One of the first to castigate this formalism and to strike a significant blow for the rights of the individual in education was the rebellious Jean-Jacques Rousseau (1712–1778). Hostile to the conventionality of civilization, which he deemed artificial and depraved, Rousseau thought it necessary for mankind to start afresh. His vision of the new world he described in 1762 in the *Social Contract*, and he set forth the education designed to make mankind happy and good in the same year in *Émile*. Both works have been fiercely attacked by critics time and again. But since Rousseau's rebellion was at bottom a spiritual rebellion, it could not be quelled, and as long as men were willing to dream, the spirit of Rousseau continued to operate, a great and penetrating force in defiance of nearly every critical canon.

A good part of *Émile* was not original, as Rousseau himself was the first to concede. Behind many of his doctrines were the unmistakable shadows of John Locke, Michel de Montaigne, and the great Moravian educator, John Amos Comenius. From these men and from others Rousseau took what suited him; but to their views he also added some that were distinctly and at times, uniquely, his own.

In *Émile,* as in all his works, Rousseau expressed his tremendous faith in the goodness of nature. "Everything," he said, "is good as it comes from the hands of the Author of Nature; but everything degenerates in the hands of man." To be in accord with nature, education must respect the child; and since by nature children vary, education must respect the child's individuality. "Begin," he urged, "by studying your pupils more thoroughly, for it is very certain that you do not know them." He asserted that nothing should be taught a child until he could understand it, not even religion. He insisted that physical activity and health were of prime importance; that a child's natural interests, such as curiosity and play, should be harnessed to his education; that education should be less literary and linguistic and more sensory and rational. Rousseau believed that a youngster should learn directly from experience rather than indirectly from books. "Our first teachers," he proclaimed, "are our feet, our hands and our eyes. To substitute books for all these . . . is but to teach us to use the reason of others." Rousseau held that the child should receive more consideration on the part of adults than should the subjects he is to learn. He believed that the stress placed on memory was altogether too great, and finally, that education should be broad and many-sided so as to bring out a child's latent potentialities.

Few works on education have produced so many and so diverse reactions. Hardly had the book appeared when praise and blame began to fall like thunderclaps. Intellectuals like Diderot, Duclos, and d'Alembert poured enraptured eulogies upon it. The learned Immanuel Kant, far off in his Königsberg retreat, confessed that it was one of the few things which had ever kept him from taking his daily walk. But the sharp-minded Voltaire had little use for it: for him it was pap fit for babies, not men. The Archbishop of Paris, who assuredly was no friend of Voltaire, was also incensed and recommended Rousseau for the stake and the faggot. When Rousseau sought refuge in Calvinist Geneva, the city of his birth, he found the gates locked and *Émile* ordered burned in the public square. Put under the ban in a good part of continental Europe, the book, as usual, attracted readers in droves.

2. Johann Bernhard Basedow

It was in Dessau, a modest German city, that Rousseau's influence bore its first pedagogical fruit. There, in 1774, Johann Basedow (1724–1790) founded a school in which he hoped to apply some of Rousseau's more workable theories. A strange compound of sentimentalist and realist, Basedow was, like Rousseau, a caustic foe of formalism. Basedow espoused the cause of naturalism in education though in a different way. In his school, to which he gave the unalluring name of *Philanthropinum,* education was to be "according to nature." Powdered hair, rouged cheeks, and toy swords, the adornments of every fashionable boy in those days, were forbidden. Like the immortal Socrates, Basedow taught through conversation. He agreed with Rousseau that play was natural to childhood and that children could learn through play. Advocating universal education, Basedow opened his school to the poor as well as the rich, but the education he offered them was not alike. The rich were to be trained for social leadership whereas the poor were to become, he hoped, efficient and contented workers. True to *Émile,* Basedow based a good part of his teaching on the child's self-activity with a generous appeal to the senses. His methods were as up-to-date as he could make them. Arithmetic was mental; geography was taught from the local environment outward; grammar was studied for the sake of literature; and religion was nonsectarian. Basedow, moreover, believed that children should be taught the essential facts of sex; and this he did in a direct

and simple way, using anatomical charts and a language that
was plain and understandable.

Although the *Philanthropinum* lasted only a few years, it
was not without influence. The first school having *Emile* for
its inspiration, it served to give to some of Rousseau's educational visions the substance of reality; but in doing this it was
compelled to balance Rousseau's top-heavy stress on the individual with the counterweight of society. Basedow's pupils
were to learn how to realize themselves, but they were also,
as he put it, "to be citizens of the world."

If the *Philanthropinum* had a brief career, the fault lay not
so much with the principles upon which it was founded as
with Basedow himself. Vain, tactless, quarrelsome, a man
whom his colleagues openly called mad, Basedow was clearly
unfit for pedagogical robes. His doctrines, however, were not
without appeal. They were alluring enough, indeed, to receive
the consideration of men who were temperamentally much
better qualified than Basedow to put them into practice. Outstanding among them was Christian Salzmann (1744–1811).
Once a teacher in the *Philanthropinum*, Salzmann established
a similar school in 1784 in a place called Schnephenthal. Like
its prototype at Dessau, Salzmann's school was secular and
private. Though designed for the children of the rich and
courtly, the school had an exacting program. The youngsters
were made to rise at dawn and even before breakfast they
were busy in their gardens or on the farmlands. Eight hours
of their day were given to study; several went for play and
recreation; and at least one was devoted to gymnastics. There
was considerable stress on nature study and on the first-hand
observation of objects. Excursions were frequent, and on such
occasions the child was encouraged to observe people and
their occupations as well as the local *flora* and *fauna*. Salzmann accepted the greater part of Basedow's educational
credo, but in its application he was much wiser and far more
practical. His school prospered, and long after Salzmann's

death it continued to operate as a model of a better kind of education.

3. Johann Heinrich Pestalozzi

Out of Rousseau's stress on the necessity of understanding one's pupils came the "psychological movement." Taken up by school reformers—and in particular by the great triumvirate of "psychologizers," Pestalozzi, Herbart, and Froebel— the psychological movement flourished in the first half of the nineteenth century. The entire educational process, in so far as it involved learning and teaching, was scrutinized under the X-rays of psychology, and as time went on, the psychological approach to education became firmly established.

One of the first to relate psychology to education, albeit somewhat crudely, was Johann Pestalozzi (1746–1827). Born some two centuries ago in Zurich, Pestalozzi fell under the spell of Rousseau early in his life. He realized, of course, that the great Genevan was essentially a visionary, but he also felt that there was much wisdom in some of his teachings. Pestalozzi made his start as an educator when he undertook to raise his own son according to some of the more practicable theories in *Émile*. In doing this he kept a diary in which he carefully noted his observations. Subsequently, in 1774, he transformed part of his farm at Neuhof into a school where he hoped to educate a group of impoverished, neglected children. He taught them not only the usual three R's, but also such practical occupations as spinning, weaving, housekeeping, and farming. Through education he hoped to regenerate the underprivileged, or, as he expressed it, "to teach beggars to live like men." Unfortunately, a lack of capital made the venture precarious from the start and after a number of years it had to be abandoned. Pestalozzi's failure, however, did not divert him from education; on the contrary it seems actually to have spurred his enthusiasm. During the years which followed he wrote a number of books, notably *Leonard and Gertrude* (1781) and *How Gertrude Teaches Her Children* (1801), in which he expounded his educational views. These, together with his teaching in the towns of Stanz, Burgdorf, and Yverdon, an activity which occupied Pestalozzi for more than a quarter of a century, made him famous throughout the world.

As Pestalozzi saw it, education was "the natural, progressive, and harmonious development," of all the child's "powers and faculties." By this he meant that consideration must be given to the hand and the heart as well as the head. Like Rousseau, Pestalozzi rejected the religious motive in education, though he himself was a devout man. Again like Rousseau, he believed education to be, not the privilege of any single class, but the right of every child. But Pestalozzi tempered the stress on the individual with his insistence that in the end education must make for social progress. From *Émile* Pestalozzi extracted the idea of a return to nature, though he was never willing to leap completely into Rousseau's utopia of the natural man. He did urge, however, an education which was to be in harmony with the child's nature, one which would recognize that man's development depended upon natural laws, and one in which the school was to cease its stress on formalism and the "empty chattering of mere words."

Pestalozzi declared he wanted "to psychologize education." With this in view he took great pains to understand the child's nature and to develop teaching methods accordingly. To discover better methods of teaching he began by rejecting the findings of all previous educators. He and his co-workers were to "read nothing, but discover everything," and to test it in the laboratory of experience. "Prove all things," he exhorted his helpers, "and hold fast to what is good." His method, which was built on the belief that the senses are the reservoir of our knowledge, introduced real objects into the lesson, and hence became known as the object lesson. Relying on the spoken word rather than books, the object lesson proceeded analytically from what every child could perceive to what lay beyond the senses. Its end, moreover, was not simply an acquaintance with a vast catalog of facts, but rather the use of the facts acquired. Thus conceived, education sought to direct the learner toward mental, moral, and physical behavior.

In an age when a schoolmaster's success depended largely on a loud voice and a strong arm, very little attention was given to a teacher's training. But Pestalozzi soon came to realize that the best of all possible methods was no better than a teacher's ability to use it. Hence, both at Burgdorf and Yverdon, a good part of his work was devoted to training teachers. Students came to him from many lands. Indeed, some of the more alert nations, desiring to have teachers capable of instructing along Pestalozzian lines, granted governmental scholarships and sent their holders to Pestalozzi for training. In time his schools became a pedagogic Mecca to which teachers as well as laymen flocked from all over the world to observe the latest and most progressive educational procedures of their day.

Although many of Pestalozzi's teachings have long since been discarded, in at least one respect he will never grow obsolete—his great love for his fellow man. His respect for the human person, particularly for the humble and under-privileged, was at the bottom of all his labor. In his teaching it took the form of a deep and genuine affection for the child. Thus, where Rousseau had preached lofty theories about the rights of childhood only to violate a good many of them in his daily life, Pestalozzi not only did homage to them but also practiced them. He had no use for the brutal discipline which had, for ages, hung like a dark cloud over the schoolroom. Discipline, he felt, must be grounded, as in a civilized home, on sympathy and understanding; it must be strict when necessary, but it must also be humane and decent. Pestalozzi called it a "thinking love." His own schools reflected this spirit; in fact some observers have reported, in pleased amazement, that his was not a school at all, but a family.

Of Pestalozzi's host of disciples one of the most famous in his own right was Philip von Fellenberg (1771–1844). While he was still a young man, Fellenberg read *Leonard and Gertrude*. The book moved him deeply and he made up his mind to devote his life to the education of the underprivileged. A man of considerable fortune, Fellenberg was able to put his dream into actual being by establishing a school in the Swiss hamlet of Hofwyl. He called it the *Institute* and hoped to employ it as a means of improving society. The school was primarily for the children of the poor who were to learn the usual three R's and also to be trained industrially. Fellenberg felt that the poor and rich should be educated together in order to bring about, if possible, a mutual understanding. By 1828 the *Institute* had gained world renown. Composed of some six hundred acres, it possessed workshops for the manufacture of tools and clothing; an agricultural school for the education of farm labor as well as teachers of rural schools; and a lower school for the teaching of handicrafts and middle-class vocations. Fellenberg's work prospered and in time attracted substantial notice. As in the case of Pestalozzi, educators from all over the globe journeyed to Hofwyl to catch a glimpse of the Fellenberg experiments. Reams of learned reports about its virtues were printed both in the Old World and the New. Widely imitated in Europe, Fellenberg's plan of combining farming and schooling found many advocates in America. Schools patterned on the Fellenberg model appeared in a number of sections of the United States and not until the rise of machine labor and the opening of the rich farmlands to the west did Fellenberg's scheme begin to lose its appeal. Even so, about a generation later it appeared again in a new form in the Central West when people demanded the establishment of colleges specializing in agriculture and the mechanical arts, but this time without the feature of manual labor which had characterized the original Fellenberg plan.

As Pestalozzi's fame soared higher and higher, his methods began to be applied on a larger and larger scale. But, as often happens with prophets, Pestalozzi's homeland was woefully tardy in profiting by his experiments. Political and religious

diehards stood in the way, and it was not until their influence
had been broken with the advent of a more liberal government
after the Revolution of 1830 that Pestalozzi's methods began
to make any real headway in the Swiss schools.

In several other lands, however, Pestalozzianism soon became the reigning fashion. Especially was this the case in
Prussia. Both Herbart and Froebel, two giants of modern
education, visited Pestalozzi, and Froebel even studied under
him at Yverdon. The philosopher Fichte, who about this time
was striving to rouse Germans from the coma which had
enveloped them since their humiliating defeat at the hands of
Napoleon, perceived in Pestalozzi's doctrines at least one
means by which Prussia's social and political regeneration
might be accomplished. In 1808 the Prussian government took
cognizance of the significance of Pestalozzi's work by sending
him a group of teachers for special training in his methods.
They were not sent, however, simply to master the mechanics
of Pestalozzi's methods, but rather to warm themselves at the
" fire which burns in the heart of this man." In the same year
that Prussia sent its teachers to Pestalozzi the King of Württemberg invited August Zeller, a glowing advocate of the
newer theories, to come to his realm as a school inspector.
Before many months had elapsed the Prussians lured Zeller
to their land, where he was to organize a normal school and
introduce the Pestalozzian doctrines. From then on the
movement gained momentum and from Prussia it spread to
other German states.

In the United States, too, the new theories evoked a good
deal of interest. Pestalozzianism first showed itself in this
land in 1806 when Joseph Neef, one of Pestalozzi's teachers,
was engaged to teach in a Philadelphia private school; but
Neef's influence was only meager. A more important stimulus
to the development of the new pedagogy is to be found in the
numerous articles and reports written by Americans who had
observed Pestalozzi's work in Switzerland. A further spur to
the movement came toward the middle of the century when a

number of Swiss teachers, notably Arnold Guyot and Hermann Krüsi, Jr., a son of one of Pestalozzi's associates, accepted teaching positions in America. Most of these efforts were isolated and bore little general influence; until 1860 Pestalozzian doctrines had no substantial practice in the United States.

What firmly grounded the Pestalozzian movement in America more than anything else was the work of Edward A. Sheldon of Oswego, New York. Like Pestalozzi himself, Sheldon had entered the teaching ranks as a teacher of underprivileged children. In 1853, at the age of thirty, he became Oswego's first school superintendent. A man of progressive ideas, Sheldon devoted himself to the task of improving the Oswego schools. In the summer of 1859, while he was sojourning in Canada, he happened to see an exhibit of Pestalozzian teaching materials from the English Home and Colonial Infant Society which were on display in a Toronto museum. Though the exhibit represented the English or formalized variety of Pestalozzianism, it kindled Sheldon's interest, and on his return to Oswego he took steps to pattern his schools after what he had seen. The necessary books and materials were imported from England; a special training class was created to familiarize teachers with the new materials; and a special teacher was employed to direct the work. At the same time Oswego's course of study was modified with a shift in its emphasis from knowledge to observation. In 1861 the city paid tribute to Sheldon's reforms by establishing a normal school to train its teachers in the newer procedures.

The road to reform was studded with the usual criticisms; but whether these sprang from obscurantism or from a scientific basis, they failed to halt the Oswego movement. In 1862 a group of eminent educators publicly endorsed the Oswego work, and three years later the National Teachers Association, after careful study, gave the object method its blessing. Meanwhile the state of New York had become interested in the project, even going so far as to assist it with an annual grant of $3,000. Finally, in 1866, the state converted Oswego into its second State Normal School.

All these factors helped to advance Pestalozzianism, not only in and about the state of New York, but also throughout the nation. Visitors flocked to Oswego to observe the new practices, and students came from afar to learn how to use them. The demand for teachers trained in the newer methods grew steadily, and for more than a generation the Oswego State Normal School sent its graduates to every part of the country.

Important though Pestalozzi's contribution unquestionably was, it was not without its weaknesses. Taking his cue from Rousseau, Pestalozzi had stressed that all education must be based on the nature of the learner; that education was essentially an individual development and not something imposed upon the child from without; and that the method of teaching was to be sought empirically rather than constructed blindly and even dogmatically. Out of these doctrines emerged Pestalozzi's principles of observation and expression. These challenged the dominant role of the textbook and the remembering of mere words, stressing in their stead the use of the child's senses and his development of ideas about things. The psychological basis of Pestalozzi's pedagogy was the so-called "faculty psychology," which today is no longer accepted and which held education to be the "harmonious development" of the various mental faculties. At bottom Pestalozzi's teachings lacked a sound scientific basis. His infinite patience, his kindness, and his unbounded respect for the human person made Pestalozzi a truly great teacher, but as a contributor to educational theory and practice he was often in error. Even when he was sound, he had no scientific principles to guide him and to enable him to check and measure what he had done.

4. Johann Friedrich Herbart

The man who was to put modern education on a much sounder basis was Johann Friedrich Herbart (1776–1841). A warm admirer of Pestalozzi, Herbart was among the first in Germany to salute him, but he was also among the first to appraise Pestalozzi critically.

Although the two men labored in the same educational field, they were in many ways almost opposites. A practical teacher for most of his life, Pestalozzi derived most of his tenets from actual classroom experience. Herbart, on the other hand, spent only a small part of his life in teaching children. Temperamentally, Pestalozzi was a romantic, a man of the heart. He cherished simplicity, the charm of humility, and the treasure of little happinesses. Democratic to the core, he was interested above all in people, and he devoted his life to the enhancement of their happiness. Herbart, by contrast, was somewhat of an aristocrat, who, though he directed his thoughts to the advancement of society, had little first-hand contact with its problems. Intellectually, however, Herbart was clearly Pestalozzi's superior. In his thinking the latter was often wishful, illogical, and mistaken; but Herbart was a trained man of learning, with an eager and excellent mind, disciplined from childhood for scholarly excursions into the realm of knowledge.

What Pestalozzi had developed in the crucible of observation and experimentation Herbart hammered with reason and criticism. He worked on a far more elaborate scale than did the humble Swiss, and his findings were much more penetrating. As professor of philosophy, first at Königsberg, then at Göttingen, Herbart devoted most of his life to the careful study of education. He rejected Pestalozzi's aim, the "harmonious development" of the child's "powers and faculties." For Herbart the mind worked essentially as a unit and was not divided into faculties. Nor did Herbart have any use for Rousseau's unsocial emphasis in education. The aim of education, as Herbart conceived it, was to prepare the child to live in the existing social order; hence the stress was to be not mainly on knowledge, nor on nature, nor even on mental power, but rather on the development of character and social morality. "The term *virtue*," said Herbart, "expresses the whole purpose of education."

To understand the meaning of character and social morality Herbart, in his characteristic, systematic manner, analyzed man's interests and occupations as well as his social responsibilities. He found that the interests of man were many-sided; that they flowed from two main sources: man's contact with things and his relations with people. As for his social responsibilities, these were determined by the kind of society in which he lived.

It so happened that Pestalozzi, through his object lessons, had provided amply enough for the child's contact with things. For his dealings with people, however, Pestalozzi had relied solely on oral language, to which Herbart now added the tremendously important subjects of literature and history. Indeed, it was through Herbart that these subjects found their place in the elementary school.

Although Herbart rejected mere knowledge as the aim of education, he realized that proper knowledge was an essential ingredient of morality. Virtue in the individual and his understanding of his social responsibilities, Herbart felt, could only come from the right kind of knowledge; and this, he insisted further, had to be properly interpreted if the learner was to form clear ideas. To bring this about, good instruction was paramount.

Like Rousseau, Herbart believed that good teaching must start with the interests of the child. With Herbart, however, interest was closely connected with attention. In his analytical way Herbart divided this into two varieties: *spontaneous*, or the kind of attention which the child gave freely and of his own accord, and *forced*, which was the kind of attention he gave because he had been induced to give it. Time was when learning had been thought of largely in terms of overcoming obstacles; the more formidable the obstacles, the better since this would require effort and discipline on the part of the learner. Naturally, under such a scheme any attempt to

interest a child in what he was about to learn was deemed
undesirable since it would make learning easier and perhaps
even pleasant. Herbart had little use for this view. Not only
did he believe interest to be a prerequisite to learning, but
should it be lacking, he felt it was the teacher's task to create
it. Today, of course, there is nothing novel in this view.

Pestalozzi, it will be recalled, believed that learning proceeded most readily when it went from the known to the
unknown, and that the easiest way to accomplish this was by
the use of objects. These principles Herbart accepted, though
he garbed them in psychological terms. Herbart called the
process whereby the unknown is learned in terms of the known
"apperception."

Interest and apperception became the foundation of Herbart's method of teaching. Although he deplored the conventional memorizing of unrelated facts, he recognized that
the teaching of some facts was inescapable and even necessary.
However, when this was the case, the learning of the facts was
to be related to some definite purpose; furthermore, only the
facts which were pertinent to that purpose were to be taught,
and finally, the relationship of these facts was to be made
clear in order to establish the principle, which was the purpose
of the lesson. In time Herbart's method of instruction became
known as the Formal Steps. Originally there were four such
steps, but Herbart's followers employed five. (1) *Preparation.*
In accordance with the doctrines of interest and apperception,
the child was put in the proper frame of mind to receive the
new knowledge. (2) *Presentation.* This was simply the
statement and explanation of the material to be learned. (3)
Association. Here the new material was related to what the
child already knew; at the same time significant likenesses and
differences between the old and the new were pointed out,
(4) *Generalization.* This was the formulation of the rule,
principle, or definition derived from the facts considered in the
third step. (5) *Application.* Here the learner was expected

to test his understanding of the general principle he formulated in the fourth step.

Herbart devoted the greater part of his life to the careful study of education. It was he who suggested that a science of education is possible; he made education a field for university study. As a professor at the University of Königsberg he conducted a seminar in education and, during more than a score of years, he was in charge of a small practice school in which he and his associates worked out most of his educational doctrines. Yet when Herbart died in 1841, his ideas had not evoked much interest; indeed, it was not until another quarter-century had elapsed that Herbart finally came into his own. Then, as if to atone for their previous neglect, schoolmen everywhere vied with one another in their efforts to praise the forgotten Herbart.

The new interest in the Herbartian doctrines started, inauspiciously enough, in 1865 when Tuiskon Ziller, a German, published a book dealing with Herbart's views on education as a moral force. The work created quite a stir and three years later the tide of Herbartianism had risen sufficiently to cause the establishment of a scientific society for the study of the Herbartian pedagogy, with Ziller as its first president. The organization busied itself largely with the development and improvement of Herbart's doctrines. In 1874 the Herbartian movement received a substantial boost when the University of Jena dignified it scientifically with the establishment of a pedagogical seminary and a practice school. For the next generation Jena became the stronghold of Herbartianism. Here its tenets were studied and analyzed; here lesson plans were laboriously worked out; here novices from all over the world were trained in the use of the newer methods while their efforts were assiduously watched and criticized.

In time Herbart's doctrines found their way across the Atlantic. Like those of Pestalozzi in an earlier day, they were popularized through the reports of enthusiastic Americans who had observed the newer procedures at close range in Germany.

Some Americans translated their admiration for Herbartianism into textbooks to be used in the training of teachers. Three of these men, Charles de Garmo and the brothers Frank and Charles McMurry, towered above the rest; indeed, it has been said that their books did more to popularize Herbartianism in this country than all other influences combined. A further impetus was given to the movement in 1892 when a number of Americans who had studied at Jena founded the National Herbart Society. This organization concentrated on the study of Herbart's doctrines, such as interest, apperception, the Formal Steps, correlation, and education as a social and moral force. To disseminate a knowledge of its findings the society published a number of yearbooks. In 1902, when the Herbartian tide had begun to ebb, the organization broadened its scope to include a much more general study of education and at the same time it changed its name to the National Society for the Scientific Study of Education.

Once Herbartianism took hold it spread like a prairie fire. Normal schools everywhere reorganized their offerings, introducing courses in the newer psychology as well as in methods of teaching history and literature. The psychology has since been found faulty and is today outmoded; but in its heyday it served to throw new and significant light on the nature of the learning and teaching processes, and in this respect it was very useful. Nor can one overlook the Herbartian view that progress in education rested on experimentation. This stimulated the development of a more scientific approach to education. Under its influence more and more normal schools established practice schools in which the new teachings were applied and tested under more or less practical conditions. This spirit in time invaded the higher learning, with the result that American colleges and universities gave more and more time to a full and earnest study of education.

However, the fact remains that the emphasis of the Herbartians was largely intellectual. They acknowledged that man's interests are many-sided; their great and all-absorbing goal was moral. In their Formal Steps they recognized the need of creating an interest in what the child was to learn; and in the fifth of these steps, application, they caught a faint and partial glimpse of the child's need of self-activity if his learning was to be successful. Yet underlying all their work and thought was their purpose of imparting the social heritage; and to achieve this their stress was nearly always on knowledge and information. They did not, like Pestalozzi and Fellenberg, for example, help to improve the plight of the multitudes by helping them vocationally. Nor were they concerned to any significant extent, like Rousseau, with the nonintellectual phases of personality. They taught the three R's and also history and literature, but they neglected the use of the hands. They stressed the usual moral virtues, but they approached them largely through books and not through the experience derived from real situations. And in stressing of knowledge and discipline they gave little heed to the truth acknowledged by some of Herbart's forerunners that one may learn even in play.

5. Friedrich Froebel

The task of bringing these ideas into educational practice fell to another German, Friedrich Froebel (1782–1852). Unhappy in childhood, misunderstood by his parents, Froebel emerged into manhood shy and introspective. His sensitive and melancholy nature was touched by a deep spiritual longing, which at times almost overwhelmed him and which he could only still in the restful intimacy of philosophic pondering. He drifted for many years from one occupation to another, never finding what he sought, never even knowing what he wanted. Then, in his early twenties, he became a teacher in a small Pestalozzian private school at Frankfurt. Here at last his quest came to an end, for he had found what he had always longed for, but had always missed—it was, he said, as if his life "had at last discovered its native element."

Froebel's discovery fired his professional ambition and in

1808 he journeyed to Yverdon to study and teach under the renowned Pestalozzi. He was deeply impressed by the Swiss educator, but already his own genius was penetrating beyond the Pestalozzian bounds. What Froebel saw there was indeed a vision. It was an altogether new kind of education in which little children held the center of the stage, in which they were surrounded by kindness and understanding, and in which there were no stuffy, meaningless books, but instead there was the rapture of music, and play, and self-activity.

This was the vision Froebel brought back to Germany, but it was not to be realized at once. For a while Froebel studied at the University of Göttingen; then he went to Berlin to busy himself with mineralogy; finally, in its strange and ironic way Fate engulfed this shy and gentle spirit as a soldier in the wars against Napoleon. In 1816, at last, he was able to open a small experimental school. Its work was basically Pestalozzian, but music, play, and activity were in the forefront. Rich in ideals but poor in worldly assets, the school struggled through financial storms for ten arduous years. Finally, in 1826, the iron determination of its founder gave way and the project expired. It was obviously a financial failure; yet for Froebel's pedagogical thinking it had offered substantial nourishment. From it there evolved his book on education, *The Education of Man,* which appeared in 1826.

During the next few years Froebel's views gradually crystallized. He became convinced that "all school education was yet without proper initial foundation," and that "until the education of the nursery was reformed, nothing solid and worthy could be attained." It was not until 1837, when he was on the threshold of fifty, that Froebel was able to put his beliefs into practice. In that year, in the little Thuringian town of Blankenburg, he founded a school for youngsters between the ages of three and eight. He gave it the incredible name of *Kleinkinderbeschäftigungsanstalt;** in time, however,

---

* *klein,* little; *Kinder,* children; *Beschäftigung,* occupation; *Anstalt,* institution; hence, an institution for the occupation of little children.

the school became the *Kindergarten,* a name which has since found its way into virtually every civilized tongue.

At Blankenburg Froebel's work reached its full maturity. Here he and his associates developed plays, games, and songs for young children, and occupations designed especially to stimulate the child's self-activity. At the same time Froebel was busy with his pen, writing one of his most significant books, his *Mutter- und Koselieder,* which appeared in 1843 and which was subsequently published in English as *Mother and Play Songs.*

In money matters Froebel was no more practical than the idealistic Pestalozzi. Hence it should be no cause for wonder that his school, sound and noble though it was in purpose, was gradually devoured by debt. Froebel strove resolutely to ward off disaster through a series of lectures by which he hoped to make his ideas better understood. He addressed himself principally to women who might be sympathetic to his ideas, he felt, but his success was limited. It happened, however, that the Baroness Bertha von Marenholtz Bülow-Wendhausen (1810–93) was among those attracted to his views. Convinced that what Froebel was seeking was fundamentally good and that he was by no means the "old fool" his critics proclaimed him, she dedicated the best part of her life to making the work of this strange and retiring spirit better known to a world which seemed bent on ignoring him. She brought to her cause an adoration which was almost fanatical and an energy as amazing as it was boundless. To the end of her life she was the tireless advocate of the new education, pouring forth a flood of writings and lectures in its defence and traveling all over Europe in its behalf. In the end her indefatigable effort reaped a well-earned reward, for before she died she was able to enjoy the triumph of seeing the kindergarten acclaimed all over the civilized world.

Nowhere was the kindergarten more cordially received than in America. Its first enthusiasts in this country, however, were Germans who had fled from the Fatherland after the failure of the Revolution of 1848. Among the most liberal and the most industrious and independent portion of the German population, they were hospitable to all kinds of progressive ideas, among which was that of the kindergarten. The first of these newer schools opened its doors in 1855 in Watertown, Wisconsin. Founded by Mrs. Carl Schurz, a pupil of Froebel and the wife of a German who was destined to play a distinguished part in American affairs, the school was private and conducted in German. Through the influence of these early German kindergartens, and also through the eloquent praise bestowed on Froebel and his work by Henry Barnard and other American enthusiasts, the kindergarten idea spread swiftly. In 1860 the first English-speaking kindergarten was opened privately in Boston by Elizabeth Peabody. Largely at her suggestion a private training school for kindergarteners was opened in Boston some eight years later. This started the ball rolling and before very long similar schools had appeared in some of our larger cities. In 1873 what Froebel had wrought filtered at last into public education when, mainly because of the vision and pertinacity of Superintendent William T. Harris, the first public kindergarten was opened in St. Louis. By the end of the century the movement was rooted firmly in American soil, and everywhere kindergartens, both public and private, were bursting into vigorous bloom.

Froebel was a profoundly religious man. In an age which was to produce the revolutionary works of Marx and Darwin, the deep spirituality of Froebel is by contrast strange and almost medieval. In most of his thinking one finds the unchartered currents of mysticism, the vague, brooding, ecstatic states which in their simplest form soar at times to the sublimest heights. Froebel's educational writings, and even some of his kindergarten practices, reflect this mysticism. Today, of course, it is all but forgotten, and if the kindergarten has survived, the reason is to be found in the soundness of its sociological and psychological foundations rather than in the symbolism of its creator.

Education, Froebel believed, should develop the child's personality. Basically, however, this was to be self-development. Like Rousseau, Froebel held that the child is primarily an active creature and that he develops physically before he develops intellectually. Froebel felt education should build on these facts of nature. Hence, the kindergarten provided lavishly for the child's self-activity, which, however, was not to be indiscriminate or haphazard, but carefully directed. "To learn a thing in life and through doing," Froebel maintained, " is much more developing, cultivating, and strengthening than to learn it through the verbal communication of ideas." Not only was the child to be active, but his activity was to stem from his own interests. It was here that Froebel leaped ahead of his predecessors, and even some of his successors, for he was the first to recognize the immense educational value of the child's own world. Like Herbart, Froebel conceived of education as a social force. "Man," he said in one of his letters, "should develop in harmony, peace and joy within himself and with those around him, in accordance with human nature and destiny; and this should continue through all stages of development, and in all the various circumstances of life, in the family and school, in domestic and public life."

All these principles—self-development, activity, and social cooperation—are incorporated in the Froebelian kindergarten. Movement, play, song, color, the story, and all kinds of familiar human activities form the essence of the kindergarten, which, moreover, was to be a miniature society, "wherein the young citizen can learn to move freely but with consideration for his little fellows." In its work the kindergarten employed three sorts of special materials—the *Mother Play and Nursery Songs,* gifts, and occupations. Gifts and occupations were materials designed to stimulate the child's motor expression. Technically, gifts were materials whose form was fixed, such as cubes, cylinders. and the like. Occupations, for their part, were materials whose form changed while they were in use, such things, for example, as clay, sand, and cardboard. By the use of gifts and occupations Froebel hoped to develop the child's constructive and aesthetic powers. But the radiant jewel which set off the kindergarten was the story. Narrated by the teacher, it sparkled everywhere; it penetrated into the child's language, his songs, his play, and it showed itself even in things he made.

Froebel's constructive activities, such as needlework, paper-folding, weaving, and various kinds of work with sand, clay, and colors led in time to the manual training movement. The first country to organize courses in handwork as a part of its educational program was Finland. The idea had been proposed as early as 1858 by Uno Cygnaeus (1810–1888), an avowed admirer of Pestalozzi and Froebel and the father of the Finnish school system. Cygnaeus, however, envisioned a program which transcended that of the kindergarten. What he desired was a kind of training which would, as he explained, include "not only Froebel's gifts, but work suitable for older pupils," such as bench and metal work, basket-weaving, and wood-carving. Cygnaeus's advocacy of handwork as a form of educational expression made hosts of friends, and in 1866 the Finnish government gave his idea its official blessing by making some form of manual training compulsory for boys in the rural schools as well as in the training of its male teachers.

From Finland the movement crossed the border to its Scandinavian neighbor, Sweden. Here it had not only an educational basis but also an economic one. It so happened that as a result of that nation's expanding industrial development during the last quarter of a century, a good many of Sweden's home industries—for generations the backbone of its economy—were being hard pressed by the new and over-powering competition from the factories. In manual training the Swedish government believed, somewhat optimistically, that it had at last found the magic remedy to restore prosperity to its stricken economy. Consequently, in 1872, under

the name of *sloyd,* manual training was introduced into the
Swedish schools. The movement progressed swiftly and by
1877 it had found its way into the Swedish Folk Schools. The
fact that the new work seemed to bear economic benefits for
Sweden's little man no doubt helped to enhance its popularity.
But its growth was also furthered by the efforts of Otto Salomon (1849–1907), a Swedish schoolman. While he was tour-
ing through Finland, Salomon took the opportunity to
acquaint himself with that nation's experiments in manual
training. What he discovered impressed him and when he returned to his native land, he undertook a determined campaign to remodel Sweden's program of manual training after
the system of Finland. Salomon's faith in his cause was unconditional. Some of his views were sound enough, as, for
example, his belief that every student should do his own work
from beginning to end; that what he made should be useful
as well as ornamental; and that his modeling should be based
on real objects rather than patterns. But like most inspired
reformers Salomon also put forth some rather extravagant
claims. He asserted, for instance, that through the training
of the hand one would be inspired to respect the dignity of
honest toil, and that through the use of tools one would
acquire not only some specific skills, but also a "general skill"
which would be useful in all circumstances in later life. Under
the scrutiny of modern psychology such claims, which rest
largely on the theory of the transfer of training, have been
found substantially invalid. But these views were once quite
fashionable and as such they contributed in no small way to
the wide and rapid acceptance of manual training as an integral part of general education.

It was Russia rather than Sweden or Finland that brought
the manual training movement to the United States. At the
Centennial Exposition held in Philadelphia in 1876 the Russian government displayed some novel samples of metal and
woodwork turned out by pupils of the Imperial Technical
School at Moscow. The exhibit caught the eye of John

Runkle, President of the new Massachusetts Institute of Technology. Runkle, it seems, had been searching far and wide for ideas which might be incorporated in the work of rising M. I. T. His discovery at Philadelphia, and even more, his eulogistic reports thereon, not only provoked an interest in manual training, but also brought forth a spate of discussion on the nature of education in general.[1] An address which President Runkle delivered in St. Louis in 1878, some two years later, brought into being in that city America's first manual training high school, an institution which was destined before long to encourage similar schools in most of our larger cities.

6.   Francis W. Parker

It was only natural that the movement to improve American education should bring forth men whose accomplishments were of a high order. There were several such men, but one among them stands out, not only because of the high quality of his achievements but also because they foreshadowed principles and practices in education which we still accept. Regarded by many as the father of American Progressive Education, Francis Wayland Parker was born in New Hampshire in 1837, the descendant of a long line of Protestant divines. When he was six he lost his father; two years later he was apprenticed to a farmer. Between his labors on the farm he was allowed to attend the local district school and in due time he was able to make his way through Holy Writ and *Pilgrim's Progress,* the bulwarks of his employer's library. Young Parker devoted much of his spare time to exploring the wonders of the countryside; like Froebel he was fond of nature and at times he responded to it almost as ecstatically.

When he was thirteen, he bade farewell to the scythe and the plow and set out to acquire a fuller education. He must have achieved fair success, for three years later we find him

---

[1] Oddly enough, President Runkle overlooked another exhibit of equal or even superior merit—that of Cornell University's new Sibley College, an exhibit which embraced "a steam engine, power lathes, face plates, and various tools of precision, admirably finished, and each a model of its kind."

teaching in a village school at fifteen dollars a month and board. He was barely twenty when he became the principal of schools in Carrolton, Illinois, but the outbreak of the Civil War put an end to his work. For the next few years he soldiered as a private with the Union forces; he was wounded and taken prisoner, but emerged a colonel. With the termination of hostilities he resumed teaching, working in various places until 1872, when he went to Germany to study philosophy and education and to observe at close range the newer practices which had been pioneered by Pestalozzi, Herbart, and Froebel. On his return to America he resumed teaching, becoming the superintendent of schools at Quincy, Massachusetts in 1875, and eight years later the principal of the Cook County Normal School at Chicago. Just before the end of the century he was made the head of the Chicago Institute which had been founded especially for the purpose of educational experimentation. The Institute became a part of the University of Chicago in 1901, but Parker had hardly begun his new duties when he died in 1902.

The stamp of New England is plainly visible on Parker. Into the meshes of a lofty idealism he wove the strands of practical, common sense; democratic to the core, he was a determined individualist; a liberal in religion, he rejected the harsh theology of his forefathers for the humaner views of a nonconformist. Under the spell of Emerson, to whom he paid frequent tribute, Parker dreamed, almost as romantically, of progress and unlimited possibilities for human betterment. Like the sage of Concord, Parker was something of a transcendentalist, expressing many of his favorite apothegms in words that might have come from Emerson himself. Yet like William James and the pragmatists of a later day, Parker was wary of anything which claimed to be final or fixed. "O Lord," he prayed, "preserve Thou me from the foregone conclusion."

What did this man seek in his struggles to reform the American schools? He sought, in the first place, to change its dark spirit to one which would encourage the child's nature to soar to full expression. In a day when schoolmasters commonly believed in the necessity of hammering their desultory and unwanted facts into the human cerebrum Parker cast his vote for the child's creative activity. What counted in the school above all else, as he saw it, was not the learning of subject matter, neatly and logically arranged, but the child himself. The child's personality was the promising basis of whatever he might eventually become; hence, it should flow into all his work. The child's honest effort, be it only an amateurish and inscrutable scrawl on a piece of paper, was a thousand times better than the superb and flawless copying of a model from a drawing book. "Each child," he said, "has his own individuality, his stream of thought, his desires, his hopes and fears, his grief and joy." Parker, who had gained much of his own knowledge by hard and direct experience, took little stock in the claims made for book learning. With an assurance that was characteristic he held that "the best taught school in a densely populated city can never equal in educative value the life on a good farm, intelligently managed." [2]

It should be no cause for wonder that Parker, who had begun to earn his living before he was ten, should extol the virtues of work and activity. He believed that "the entire purpose of education consists of training the child for work, to work systematically, to love work and to put his brains and heart into work. . . ." [3]

It was at Quincy that Parker won his first great acclaim. Here he introduced ideas and practices which, though they reaped the usual denunciations from effete pedagogues, have since been recognized as the foundation of progressive education. He began by putting "the old-fashioned, stiff, unnatural order" under the ban. "The torture of sitting perfectly still with nothing to do was ruled out and in came an order of

---

[2] Parker, F. W., "The Quincy Method," *American Journal of Sociology,* VI, p. 117, July, 1900.

[3] Parker, F. W., *Talks on Teaching,* p. 161. Boston: A. S. Barnes & Co., Inc., 1883.

work, with all the whispering and noise compatible with the best results. The child began to feel that he had something to do for himself, that he was a member of society, with the responsibilities that accompany such an important position." [4] The newer practices which Parker had scrutinized in Europe now came into use. Geography, for example, was taught along modified Pestalozzian lines with an understanding of the local terrain more important than a knowledge of archipelagos, latitude and longitude, or the source of the Ganges. The Herbartian principle of concentration or correlation found its way to Quincy; thus, instead of teaching subjects for their own private sake, they were interrelated around a central core. Arithmetic was taught primarily through actual use rather than through strange and fantastic problems involving the areas of carpets, the number of ounces in a long ton, or the mythical profits of Messrs. A, B, and C. Language lessons were based on observation and valued for their practical social purposes; arts and crafts were introduced; and the sciences were approached through the laboratory. Behind it all beckoned the shadow of the gentle Froebel, for never before in America had the school child been bathed in such warm and tender respect. At Quincy he was, indeed, the center of the school. Here educational problems were approached, not from the viewpoint of an omniscient adult, but from that of the child himself. He flourished in his natural way, true to himself, busy and creative, using his brain of course, but also his arms and legs; his spirit unfettered, yet learning to understand something about the meaning of work and his responsibilities to others.

There were the usual and familiar criticisms. Not only were Parker and his associates personally excoriated but their methods were described in all sorts of low and dubious terms. The chief charge against them was that they failed to teach the fundamentals and that children would grow up more

---

[4] Parker, F. W., "The Quincy Method," *American Journal of Sociology*, VI, p. 118, July, 1900.

ignorant than their elders. However, when, in 1879, the Massachusetts Board of Education was persuaded to look into the matter, it found, to the disappointment of Parker's hopeful critics, that the Quincy children could read, write, spell, and figure better than the majority of children in the Bay State and that they were superior in their familiarity with history and geography.

What Parker had begun at Quincy he continued on an even grander scale at Chicago. At the Cook County Normal School, where he labored for eighteen years, Parker surrounded himself with a corps of excellent teachers, many of whom were destined to become famous in their own right. With them Parker initiated the practice of having weekly conferences in which supervisors, training instructors, and practice teachers discussed classroom problems. Continuing along the path on which he had started at Quincy, Parker assailed the mechanical, assembly-line methods of the traditional school. In their place he stressed "quality teaching" by which he meant such things as activity, creative self-expression, excursions, understanding the individual, the development of personality, the scientific study of education, the training of artist-teachers, and so on. Parker stressed the child's need of art, music, manual training, science, and physical training, even going so far as to employ special teachers in these domains. When parents expressed doubts as to the worth of such innovations, Parker helped to organize them into a Parent Teachers organization, the first in Chicago and one of the first in the state. At its meetings he threshed out his views, discussing them with puzzled and, at times bellicose, parents. In the end he converted most of them into energetic supporters. In his dealings with the Chicago politicians, however, he was not so fortunate. They hamstrung him at every turn, cutting down on essential appropriations, interfering with his work, and even slandering his good intentions. Consequently when, in 1899, Mrs. Emmons Blaine offered a million dollars to establish The Chicago Institute Academic and Pedagogic where she hoped Parker might work unmolested, he accepted. But in the midst of plans to erect a new home for the Institute the intrepid president of the University of Chicago, William Rainey Harper, proposed that the Institute should become a part of the university. Under Parker's directorship the Institute and three other institutions were merged into a School of Education. The new school came into being in 1901 and, as has been said, it was hardly on its way when Colonel Parker died.

Meanwhile the altruistic Mrs. Blaine had donated a second million dollars to help found a progressive elementary school on Chicago's northern side. It opened in 1901 as the Francis W. Parker School with Flora J. Cooke, one of his former faculty associates, as principal. Associated with her were sixteen men and women, most of whom had been trained under Parker. The school continued under her wise and benevolent leadership for more than thirty years, carving for itself an important place in the history of American progressive education. The young people who had been trained by Parker in the Normal School and by Flora Cooke carried on Parker's ideas. As a result a new generation of educational pioneers arose to perpetuate the Parker idea in all parts of the country. Many erudite pages have been composed to dissect that idea, but its philosophic essence is simple enough:

The training of children hitherto has had a sort of fatality behind it—a blind belief in traditional measures. We look upon multitudes of human beings on the crowded streets, we watch their faces, observe their forms and bearing. How few are strong and robust! How few thoughtful, reasoning men and women! We mourn over society, the state of politics, the dangers in self-government, but we have as yet little faith in possibilities of child growth, of the power and influence of possible character.[5]

[5] Parker, F. W., "President's Report," *Illinois Society for Child Study,* III, p. 63, April, 1898.

C. The Contribution of John Dewey

1. Background

Parker's successor as head of the new school of education was his friend and admirer, John Dewey. Born in 1859 in Burlington, Vermont, then a rising town of some ten thousand inhabitants, Dewey sprang from a rural background. He grew up an average lad, playing his full part in the free and energetic pastimes which delight the boyhood years, but excelling in none of them. His record in the primary school and high school was similarly undistinguished. When he entered the University of Vermont, he had no special ambitions; during the first years his scholastic attainments were unilluminated by any spark of potential greatness. But apparently the Fates had not overlooked him. A course in physiology, which he took in his junior year and in which he studied a textbook by Thomas Henry Huxley, put an unexpected edge on Dewey's intellectual appetite. Darwin's great contemporary and formidable ally in the fight for evolution proved irresistible. As Dewey pondered over this rare morsel, the mystery of its recipe aroused his wonder. As a punctilious churchgoer he had always believed that man's life was shaped by moral will; and now Huxley injected the idea that life was shaped largely by material forces.

The gap between these views was not only immense; for Dewey it was also alarming. Its impact ignited the young New Englander, and in the following senior year, the fire which Huxley had started burned ravenously in the young man's mind. To still it, he read and toiled far into the night seeking a way to bridge the chasm. In the process of searching, Dewey's scholarship assumed a new and extraordinary luster. Not only had he moved to the front of his class, taking the highest marks in philosophy on record, but, as he emerged from his college years, it was plain enough that at the age of nineteen John Dewey was a philosopher.

For a while he taught in the country schools; but his interest in philosophy was no less intense. Under the direction of his former philosophy professor, H. A. P. Torrey, young Dewey studied the philosophic classics and in a modest way he began to write some philosophy of his own. However, the spur with which Huxley and Darwin had prodded him was still there, and before long he enrolled at Johns Hopkins, a new kind of research university still in its infancy. In Baltimore Dewey studied under men whose names have since become famous in American intellectual history, for example, G. Stanley Hall and Charles Peirce. But the most wonderful teacher of all was a philosopher by the name of George Sylvester Morris. A follower of the German philosopher Hegel, Morris introduced his student to a system of thought which apparently was able to close the gap between the moral and the material sciences by the simple declaration that matter was after all nothing more than an illusion. The universe and everything in it, asserted Hegel, was really "spirit" and life is the eternal upward struggle of the Universal Mind of God. Dewey has long since discarded such a pious absolute, but at Johns Hopkins and for at least a decade after, Hegel's doctrines offered him a reassuring harbor in a culture which was agitated ever increasingly by tempestuous blasts from the natural sciences.

Soon after finishing his work at Hopkins, Dewey went to Michigan as an instructor in philosophy. Professionally, he advanced steadily, leaving Michigan for Minnesota, then returning to Michigan for a while, and finally going to the University of Chicago. Meanwhile he had published his first book, a volume on psychology, which was then still ruled by philosophers. Although Dewey was willing enough to envision a psychology which some day might be under the flag of the natural sciences, he was at that time still imbued with the conviction that the ultimate reality was God. The fact that life in the Middle West was swift and vigorous, full of kaleidoscopic change, was inevitably provocative to a man of Dewey's social temperament. However, in a world where things metamorphosed before one's very eyes it was no easy matter to bolster one's faith in a reality which never changed, which was spirit and not matter. During Dewey's sixteen years in the Midwest the region witnessed acute depression from which, however, it rebounded with elasticity. An amazing vitality pervaded Midwestern life, a vitality which contributed to rapid political, economic, and social changes. The universe, as William James so aptly put it, was wide open. It was a world of rugged individualism and free enterprise where men who were willing to take risks often bagged immense success and tremendous fortune. Although this system brought prosperity to some, it also took its heavy toll. For some were able to live more abundantly and according to a standard which was reputedly high, but there were, on the other hand, many more, especially in the large cities like Chicago, who lived wretched and exploited lives. Dewey's interest veered toward these social problems, and especially toward efforts aimed at improving the lot of the underprivileged and enhancing their opportunities for growth. Indeed, in the course of time his philosophy was to focus sharply on social reconstruction and on the social conflicts which come from the interaction of the forces of science, democracy, and industry. In such a philosophy there was no room for a Hegelian cosmos.

2. The Laboratory School

It was at Chicago that Dewey's interest in the new school became active. For one thing he sent his children, Fred and Evelyn, to the Cook County Normal School to study in the grades taught by the gifted Flora Cooke. In 1896 he founded what is officially known as The Laboratory School, but which today, fittingly enough, has been generally referred to as the Dewey School. Assisted by his wife Alice, Dewey piloted the school during the next seven years through waters which, at times, were very rough.[1] The new school was anything but

---

[1] The school opened in January with 16 pupils and two teachers in a private house on Chicago's South Side. Six years later it had 140 children, 23 instruc-

conventional. Few of the time-honored principles of educational orthodoxy graced its premises. There were no school subjects and even the familiar school furniture was prominently absent. Educational critics who came to observe it left shaking their heads and predicting that such innovations would never last. But the school continued, growing slowly amidst a welter of difficulties, and developing, nonetheless, a new kind of educational practice as it went along.

The school was intended for pupils from four to fourteen years of age. What its director sought was "to carry into effect certain principles which Froebel was perhaps the first consciously to set forth." At bottom Dewey's school sought "to train children in cooperative and mutually useful living." "The primary root of all educative activity," it was announced, lies "in the instinctive, impulsive attitudes of the child." Hence the Herbartian formal method, then the delight of the efficient schoolmaster, which stressed "the presentation of external material," was not looked upon with favor. Instead Dewey's procedure was on the basis of what is now generally known as the *activity program*. Even the traditional triumvirate of reading, writing, and arithmetic grew out of the child's "life activities" and not out of any foreordained set of studies. Active learning and the reconstruction of experience took the lead in the schoolroom. There was activity all along the line, including play, construction, contact with nature, self-expression, and so on. "The great thing to keep in mind," said Dewey, "is that through them [the activities] the entire spirit of the school is renewed. It has a chance to affiliate itself with life, to become the child's habitat, where he learns through directed living, instead of being only a place to learn lessons having an abstract and remote reference to some pos-

tors, and 10 assistants who were graduate students of the University. Dewey was Director and Ella Flagg Young was principal for several years. Mrs. Dewey was principal and director of Language Instruction from 1901. The most important literature on the work of the school is: J. Dewey, *The School and Society*, 1st edition, published in 1899 by University of Chicago Press, and *The Dewey School* by K. C. Mayhew and A. C. Edwards, published in 1936 by the D. Appleton-Century Company.

sible living to be done in the future. It gets a chance to be a miniature community, an embryonic society."

Not only was the child to be active instead of passive, not only was he to work rather than listen; he was also to learn how to become socially efficient. Cooperation rather than competition was the keynote. For

the school is primarily a social institution. Education being a social process, the school is simply that form of community life in which all those agencies are concentrated that will be most effective in bringing the child to share in the inherited resources of the race and to use his own powers for social ends.[2]

To bring this about the child's individual tendencies were to be "organized and directed through uses made of them in keeping up the cooperative living." Or, to put it in simpler terms, the school was to prepare its pupils for life *by being life*. It was to reproduce in miniature "the typical conditions of social life." Through production and creative use, Dewey argued, we secure valuable knowledge. In this way "modifications and abandonments of intellectual inheritance" were to be effected and society thus freed from the bonds of social heritage.

In many respects the Dewey School was not unique. If it was unconventional for its time, then so were the schools of Colonel Parker; and so were those of Froebel, Pestalozzi, and Basedow. In one sense, Dewey's school was a pioneer: it was the first genuine *experimental* school in this country. And in this sense it has remained to this day virtually without a rival. The Laboratory School was intended as a testing place for educational principles, its aim being

to test certain ideas which were used as working hypotheses. These ideas were derived from philosophy and psychology, some perhaps would prefer to say a philosophical interpretation of psychology. The underlying theory of knowledge emphasized the part of problems, which originated in active situations, in the development of thought and also the necessity of testing thought by action if thought was to pass over into knowledge. The only

[2] Dewey, J., *My Pedagogical Creed*. First set forth in 1897; reprinted by the Progressive Education Association, Washington, D. C., Article II, p. 6.

place in which a comprehensive theory of knowledge can receive an active test is in the processes of education.[3]

Dewey was concerned not so much with the testing of educational theories as such, as he was with certain theories of culture, philosophy, and psychology then shaping in his mind. Ideas, he felt even then, become valid only when put to the test in real situations. Among other things, Dewey was trying to reconcile and synthesize what seemed at first glance to be conflicting theories, as for example, interest and effort, school and society, individualism and collectivism, the child and the curriculum. Behind these antitheses he perceived intellectual and cultural chasms which had come into prominence with the change of society from an agrarian, homestead economy to one which was commercial and industrial. For the school, Dewey recognized, this cultural metamorphosis was of great significance. "The modification going on in the method and curriculum of education," he observed, "is as much a product of the changed social situation, and as much an effort to meet the needs of the new society that is forming, as are changes in modes of industry and commerce."[4]

3. Dewey's philosophy

Dewey began his philosophical reflections under the spell of Hegel, an idealist; then he became a pragmatist; and today he is commonly referred to as an instrumentalist or an experimentalist. He is the philosophical kinsman of William James, the author of pragmatism, and of Charles Peirce, the creator of the term and one of the profoundest philosophical minds to come out of America.[5] The task of philosophy, according to

[3] Mayhew, K. C. and Edwards, A. C., *The Dewey School*, Appendix II. New York: D. Appleton-Century Company, Inc., 1936. This is a summary of Dewey's "Plan of Organization," originally printed privately in 1895.

[4] Dewey, J., *The School and Society*, p. 4. Chicago: University of Chicago Press, 1916.

[5] Although Charles Santiago Sanders Peirce died in 1914, he has been unnoticed by the general public and, until quite recently, by the greater part of the learned world. Yet as Royce and Santayana have indicated, his philosophical thinking was far more penetrating and much more rigorous than that of

Dewey, is not to find out how we know the world, but rather how we can control and improve it. According to this viewpoint "philosophy is a study of social conflicts, especially those involved in the relations of the three alleged leading forces of modern society, namely, democracy, industry, and science." [6] Thus conceived, the problem of philosophy is "to clarify men's ideas as to the social and moral strifes of their own day." And to achieve such a result social problems must be approached experimentally. Unlike the older and more traditional philosophies, experimentalism, both as a philosophy and as a method, looks upon all things as experimental. Nothing, moreover, is fixed and nothing is permanent. The universe itself is in a state of flux and to set down neat and compact formulas about eternal and absolute truths is not only impossible but also futile. Denying a supernatural world, the experimentalist asserts that in the end, man must determine his own course. Only by harnessing the experimental procedure to his complex social problems can man hope to build an efficient social life. In his struggle to control the process of change man must rely on his creative intelligence. When philosophy thus ventures forth from its ivory tower, it does not mean, so Dewey insists, "the lowering in dignity of philosophy from a lofty plane to one of gross utilitarianism." It signifies instead "that the prime function of philosophy is that of rationalizing the possibilities of experience, especially collective human experience." [7]

All this, of course, depends in no small way on thinking. For Dewey, however, thinking becomes significant only when applied to life situations. It is, he has said, "an instrumen-

---

James. His essay "The Architecture of Theories," published in the January *Monist*, 1891, has been pronounced "one of the colossal contributions to the history of philosophy." "He was," says Charles Angoff, "the modern philosopher *par excellence*, a combination of scientist and logician." Angoff, C., "Charles Peirce," *American Mercury*, XIV, p. 337, 1928.

[6] Horne, H. H., *The Philosophy of Education*, p. 297. The Macmillan Company, revised 1927.

[7] Dewey, J., *Reconstruction in Philosophy*, p. 122. New York: Henry Holt & Company, Inc., 1920.

tality used by man in adjusting himself to the practical situations of life." Or to phrase it more simply, human beings think in order to live. Because of this stimulus, which has its basis in biology and sociology, it is impossible—it is absurd— to interpret life in a systematic and abstract way. Since, moreover, Dewey holds that life is in constant flux, it is impossible to solve problems with any degree of finality for the problems of tomorrow will be different from those of today.

As for the problem of knowledge, Dewey believes that knowledge is experience and that true experience is functional. What is a thing for? What is its use? Is a coal mine a physical deposit or does it have a function? And if so, what is it? Such are the questions that help to give meaning to one's experience; but such questions cannot be answered without antecedent action. Action must precede knowledge; there is no a priori knowledge. Whatever knowledge we possess has resulted from our activities, our efforts to survive, to obtain food, shelter, and clothing. Only that which has been organized into our disposition so as to enable us to adapt our environment to our needs and to adapt our aims and desires to the situation in which we exist is really knowledge.[8]

As has already been said, Dewey stresses the harnessing of the human intelligence to human improvement and the enrichment of life, the method to be employed being the experimental method. He would subject every belief, every tradition, every institution to the experimental test with its corollary of verification. The link here between Dewey and Peirce is plain enough. It was the latter who said: "The meaning of a concept is to be found in all the conceivable experimental phenomena which the affirmation or denial of the concept could imply."

The pragmatist is noted for his view of truth. Like the Sophists of ancient Athens he rejects the notion of absolute truth or reality. He asserts that all truth is relative, depend-

[8] Dewey, J., Democracy and Education, p. 400. New York: The Macmillan Company, 1916.

ing on time and place, and that what is apparently true in our own era may not be the truth of tomorrow. The pragmatic test of truth is: "Does it work?" By processes which range from simple trial and error to the elaborate and cautious steps of the experimental method people, interacting with their environment, arrive at some hypothesis which works. For the time being, or as long as it works, this is the truth. Such hypotheses remain truths only as long as they remain unchallenged by other true claims. "The opinion which is fated to be ultimately agreed to by all who investigate," declared Peirce, "is what we mean by the truth, and the object represented in this opinion is the real." [9] Truth, hence, is not eternal; nor is it a thing apart from human experience; it is simply a collective name for verification processes which may change from day to day. To paraphrase William James: We have to live today by what truth we can get today and to be ready tomorrow to call it a falsehood.

4. Educational philosophy.

For Dewey and his legions of followers philosophy and education render a reciprocal service. The one indicates what social values are desirable; the other seeks to promote them. Thus viewed, education becomes the laboratory of philosophy. Unlike those who assert that man is blessed with eternal verities, that absolutes exist, and that there are fixed and ultimate ends, Dewey holds no such view. Education, he declares, leads to no final end; it is something continuous, a "reconstruction of accumulated experience." The aim, such as it is, is identified with the process; and, like the horizon, it looms ever before us but can never be reached. But since, as Dewey

---

[9] In James this viewpoint took on another hue. For James the meaning of an idea became its practical results. "And from this naïve notion he leaped to the puerile doctrine that 'the justification of all ideas, like their meaning is to be found . . . in the service which they render to the will.' Truth, in this case, became 'one species of good. . . . The truth is the name of whatever proves itself to be good in the way of belief.'" Angoff, C., "Charles Peirce," *American Mercury*, XIV, p. 335, 1928. James, W., *Pragmatism*, p. 223. New York: Longmans, Green & Company, Inc., 1907.

insists, the reconstruction of our experience must be directed toward social efficiency, education must be a social process. The best school must be active and dynamic, one in which the child learns through his experience in relation to others. Here, to use the classic Dewey phrase, the child's education is life itself. Here his growth is cumulative, each state of development being the springboard for the next. The process of education is thus one of continuous adjustment. In this process two factors are fundamental and inescapable: the psychological, with its basis in the nervous system and with responses that range from the simple wink of an eyelid to the most complex, planned, and purposeful behavior; and the sociological, with its mores, attitudes, practices, and institutions.

Summarizing the foregoing, we note: (1) *education is life* and not merely a preparation for life; (2) *education is growth* and as long as growth continues education continues; (3) *education is a continuous reconstruction of accumulated experience;* (4) *education is a social process,* and to make this possible the school must be a democratic community.

Since the child is the center of education, the psychological factor must be carefully analyzed. The wisdom and knowledge of the elders may have conditioned what the child is to learn; nevertheless, every child must be regarded as unique, having his own life to live and being confronted with a future filled with new and unsolved problems. Education thus must start with a psychological insight into the child; his capacities, interests, and habits must be clearly understood. Four interests, according to Dewey, are paramount: "the interest in conversation or communication; in inquiring or finding out things; in making things or construction; and in artistic expression." [10] Since man has his roots in these activities, obviously they should be expected to play an important part in the making of the school curriculum. As the active core of

---

[10] Dewey, J., *The School and Society,* p. 45. Chicago: University of Chicago Press, 1916.

the whole learning process, however, the growing child must select and reorganize his cultural heritage, recasting it in the course of time to suit his needs in a new and changing world. To enable him to do this, creative activity must be encouraged, but not haphazardly; it must be guided and directed. Nor is this purely an individual proposition; at its best, it assumes the grand guise of discovery and adventure undertaken and shared with one's fellows.

As for the sociological, Dewey makes the point that inasmuch as man is not isolated and cannot be separated from society, education must provide those basic activities found in society as the starting point of the educational process. Through participation in activities involving social relationships, the individual powers are developed.

In education meet the three most powerful motives of human activity. Here are found sympathy and affection, the going out of the emotions to the most appealing and the most rewarding object of love—a little child. Here is found also the flowering of the social and institutional motive, interest in the welfare of society and its progress and reform by the surest and shortest means. Here, too, is found the intellectual and scientific motive, the interest in knowledge, in scholarship, in truth for its own sake, unhampered and unmixed with any alien ideal. Copartnership of these three motives—of affection, of social growth, and of scientific inquiry—must prove as nearly irresistible as anything human when they are once united. And, above all else, recognition of the spiritual basis of democracy, the efficacy and responsibility of freed intelligence, is necessary to secure this union.[11]

Regarding methodology, Dewey, like Rousseau, stresses direct, specific, impressive experiences. The child, he believes, must be confronted with concrete situations so that he may have something to do; yet he must be interested in what he is doing. Interest, for Dewey, provides the spark without which learning will not ignite, for it is only when the learner feels that an activity is valuable that he has any zest for learning. Yet for Dewey interest and effort are not antagonistic; they are essentially complementary, since all genuine

---

[11] Dewey, J., "Democracy in Education," *Journal of the National Education Association,* XVIII, p. 290, 1929.

effort springs from a deep, native interest in the task. In a word, if the interest is real, it means that a person has found himself in a course of action or has identified himself with it.

Closely connected with interest is Dewey's notion of purposeful activity. Not merely a casual or random response to a fleeting impulse, a purposeful activity, in the Dewey sense, becomes a controlled, experimental activity. Effective learning, he insists, can take place only when an activity means something to the learner. Or, as Dewey has suggested, desire, purpose, planning, choice—none of these can have meaning except in conditions where something is at stake—where action in one direction rather than another may result in creating a new situation which fulfills a need. Purposes, moreover, must not be divided but integrated so that intelligent action may be effected. The effective condition of the integration of all divided purposes and conflicts of belief is, according to Dewey, the realization that intelligent action is the sole ultimate resource of mankind in every field. Summing up his views on methodology Dewey believes that

processes of instruction are unified in the degree in which they center in the production of good habits of thinking. While we may speak, without error, of the method of thought, the important thing is that thinking is the method of an educative experience. The essentials of method are therefore identical with the essentials of reflection. They are first that the pupil have a genuine situation of experience—that there be a continuous activity in which he is interested for its own sake; secondly, that a genuine problem develop within this situation as a stimulus to thought; third, that he possess the information and make the observations needed to deal with it; fourth, that suggested solutions occur to him which he shall be responsible for developing in an orderly way; fifth, that he have opportunity and occasion to test his ideas by application, to make their meaning clear and discover for himself their validity.[12]

5. Dewey in relation to Froebel and Herbart

Inevitably the thinking of John Dewey has been influenced by that of previous thinkers, Froebel and Herbart in particu-

---

[12] From Dewey, J., *Democracy and Education,* p. 192. New York, Copyright, 1916 by The Macmillan Company and used with their permission.

lar. The cornerstone of education with Froebel was growth. This Dewey accepted, but he rejected the concept of growth as an unfolding of latent principles. As a pragmatist Dewey has discarded the Froebelian mysticism and symbolism, much of which is metaphysical and not at all essential to the practical operation of the kindergarten. Dewey reinterpreted Froebel's concept of "occupations," to which the founder of the kindergarten had attached strange and occult meanings. Froebel's teaching that a ball symbolizes the unity of all things and that a cube, because of its sharp, straight lines, represents individuality was discarded by later kindergartners who regarded occupations simply as a means for furthering skills and artistic capacities. Dewey went a step further when he introduced occupations which had some real meaning, such occupations, for example, as were necessary to provide people with food, clothing, and shelter. Froebel's great stress on the spiritual is of course unacceptable to the experimentalist. Froebel, being a philosophical idealist, accepted the idea of growth toward the Infinite and the Eternal. But for Dewey such things are meaningless, and developing toward any sort of a remote goal is impossible, since such a goal would be in the nature of something fixed or static. Education, as has been said, is for him a continuous process without any fixed goal. On several points Dewey and Froebel are at least in general agreement: both stress creative activity, but in different ways; both insist on learning by doing; and both conceive of the school as a living community wherein children participate in social activities.

Herbart's methods and practices, being much more formalized than those of Froebel, would naturally tend to draw greater criticism from Dewey. Thus the American educator has rejected the Herbartian type of recitation as being mainly deductive and allowing for too little pupil self-activity. For Dewey, Herbart's school is too teacher-controlled and not enough child-centered. It is too stiff, too authoritarian, and not democratic enough. That Dewey has rejected the Herbartian tendency toward abstract intellectualism should be no cause for wonder. On the points of more or less agreement between the two men, one finds that both stress the importance of interest in learning, though in different ways; both appreciate the significance of individual differences; and both recognize the need for studying the child before trying to teach him. Their methods of teaching are, of course, basically different. The Dewey Act of Thought and the Herbartian Formal Steps, stripped of their explanatory detail, may be characterized thus:

Essentials of Method

Dewey	Herbart
1. Activity	1. Preparation
2. Problem	2. Presentation
3. Data	3. Comparison
4. Hypothesis	4. Generalization
5. Testing	5. Application

The Herbartian procedure stresses the activity of the teacher; the Dewey steps focus on the child as an active learner. The latter method seeks to discover what is unknown to the child but known to the teacher. "The two methods," says Horne, "admirably supplement each other; they are usable in different fields. Herbart is effective in the linguistic, literary, historical, and ideational fields; Dewey in the fields of the manual arts and the sciences. Wherever the content of books is taught, Herbart is useful; wherever the manipulation of things is primary, Dewey is useful." [13] To this one must add, however, that Dewey's method is useful even in the realm of ideas, indeed, wherever the approach to learning is through problem solving.

---

[13] From Horne, H. H., *The Democratic Philosophy of Education*, p. 207. New York, Copyright, 1932 by The Macmillan Company and used with their permission.

6. John Dewey's influence

Dewey left the University of Chicago in 1904 to become professor of philosophy at Columbia. His direct influence on education during the next ten years was low. It is said that he had been disheartened by the seeming futility of his efforts to reconstruct American education. Time apparently has reversed this harsh judgment, for in most theoretic matters history has vindicated him. After his departure from Chicago, Dewey published virtually nothing on education. His *Democracy and Education,* acclaimed as one of the great educational works of all time, did not appear until 1916. His book on psychology, *How We Think,* had come out a few years earlier, in 1910; and his brief essay, *Interest and Effort in Education,* had appeared in 1913. His profound *Human Nature and Conduct,* in which he has set forth his social psychology, was not published until 1922.

Yet there is no question that John Dewey's influence on American education has been great. In a direct way through his own thinking and the testing of that thinking, and indirectly through the efforts of countless schoolmen and women who have been stimulated by his views, Dewey has contributed, probably more than any other American, to the reconstruction and redirection of our education. Taking Parker's theory of the school as a community, Dewey substantiated, developed, and amplified it in practice. He expounded and developed the principle of growth and gave new meaning to the conditions necessary for its fulfillment. An activist like Froebel, Pestalozzi, and Rousseau, Dewey was the first to ground the school life and program in the operational psychology of action. The focusing of his psychology on "problem-solving thinking," although admittedly inadequate today, even for many of its devoutest adherents, has nonetheless withstood most criticism. The same may be said of Dewey's use of man's social occupations of selecting subject matter, a principle which has found its way into countless progressive schools all over the country. As for Dewey's methodology, this too has left its mark, particularly in the rise and growth of the Project Method. (See p. 72.)

7. Philosophic critics of Dewey's theories

Despite Dewey's enormous influence on twentieth century education it must not be supposed that his theories have been universally accepted. His doctrines have been accepted in the main by the pragmatists and experimentalists, but have been rejected by the idealists, realists, and neo-scholastics.

For the realist the important thing is not to transform the world but to understand it as it actually is and to conform to it. To do this it is necessary to know nature's laws. There is for the realist an incontrovertible "scheme of things" to which we should be adjusted. The realist holds that in education the experience of the race is invaluable, as is the cultural heritage. There are indispensable facts and principles which must be mastered. Instruction in these cannot be left to chance; to assure their being learned they must be *required* of the learner. It is the teacher's task to see to it that they are learned—and the essence of that learning lies in the pupil's effort. For without effort, it is argued, there can be no real learning. To fulfill his task the teacher must exercise authority, he must pull youth into line when irrelevancies divert it from the path of learning; in short, the teacher must ever clasp the reins of discipline.

The realists have not contributed very substantially to educational theory, preferring to do most of their more solid thinking in the domain of pure philosophy.[14] The idealists, on the other hand, have been vigorous and productive in education. International in scope, their ranks embrace such names as Giovanni Gentile and Benedetto Croce of Italy, Paul Geheeb, once of Germany but now of Switzerland, Victor

---

[14] For an exposition of the realistic philosophy of education see Breed, F. S., "Education and the Realistic Outlook," *Philosophies of Education. Forty-first Yearbook,* National Society for the Study of Education, Part I. Bloomington, Illinois: Public School Publishing Company, 1942; Breed, F. S., *Education and the New Realism.* New York: The Macmillan Company, 1939.

Cousin of France, and May Sinclair of England. The American roll of idealists includes Josiah Royce, William Torrey Harris, and Herman Harrell Horne. Of these, Horne (1874–1946) has been Dewey's sharpest critic. Like Dewey, Horne has expounded his views in numerous writings, including *The Philosophy of Education* (1904), *Idealism in Education* (1910), *Free Will and Human Responsibility* (1912), *This New Education* (1931), and *The Democratic Philosophy of Education* (1932).

The center of Dewey's pragmatism is man; for Horne's idealism it is God. Dewey's philosophy has its roots in naturalism and humanism; Horne's springs from theism. "Truth is relative," says the pragmatist. "It is absolute," retorts the idealist. "Truth," asserts the pragmatist, "is simply a term we use to refer to ideas which work." "True ideas," counters the idealist, "are not just terms; they are real and they correctly represent facts and their connections." He adds that "ideas are not true because they work, but work, or will work when conditions are better, because they are true. . . . Truth does not change, though man's ideas of it may and do change." [15] Philosophy, as Dewey sees it, concerns itself with social conflicts, especially those which spring from the interaction of industry, science, and democracy. This the idealistic Horne accepts, but amplifies. Idealism, he points out, concerns itself not only with social conflicts, but with the "whole of reality." The intelligence which is to solve our social problems, as interpreted by Dewey, is strictly human, and in using it man must rely on himself alone. For Horne, however, intelligence is not just human: it is identified with the Absolute and hence it is super-human as well as human. For the pragmatist the basic principle of life and education is growth. This the idealist accepts, though growth, he hastens to explain, must relate to more than the individual life of the organism in this small world. "Growth in life," Horne believes, "is man's

---

[15] From Horne, H. H., *The Philosophy of Education,* p. 303. New York, Copyright by the Macmillan Company, Revised 1927.

finite way of approaching the Infinite." Longfellow expressed
the idealistic view in verse when he sought to improve each
shining hour by forever striving upward and onward—a view
which prompted the skeptical Morris Cohen to ask, "Where is
upward and why is onward?"

In their views on education Horne and Dewey, as might be
expected, are far apart. The former assigns a leading role to
the teacher who is cast as the inspirer of youth; the latter,
although not overlooking the worth of the personal relationship between pupil and teacher, sees greater educational value
in the activity produced by the impersonal relationship between the pupil and his problem situation.

With Dewey, Horne recognizes the value of interest, though
as an idealist he cannot follow Dewey in thinking of interest
and effort as complementary. Horne's stress is on effort, duty,
and discipline. Like Frederick the Great, he can never forget
that *Dienst ist Dienst* (Duty is duty) that, as he puts it, "some
obligations are binding, that duties must be done, that
right must be obeyed, that voluntary attention to the uninter-
esting but important is possible, that effort at times can and
must be put forth, that discipline in doing the disagreeable
that is necessary is worth while, so that effort may lead to
interest; that even if interest never comes as a result of effort
in such cases, still the obligatory thing must be done." [16]

Nor can Horne accept Dewey's stress on the practical and
the social. Criticizing it as being too narrow, Horne is convinced that such an education will produce the "cultivated
vocationalist" in the end. Horne believes that Dewey overlooks the other aspects of personality; that he underestimates
the importance of religious and spiritual experience; that he
fails to recognize the worth of aesthetic experience as a pure
delight to be pursued for its own sake.

The idealist does not believe like the realist that education
is necessarily conformity. However, he rejects the idea that
education is predominantly creative activity. For the idealist

---

[16] *Ibid.,* p. 313.

education is neither all of the former nor all the latter; it is partially both. The child conforms and creates. He accepts what seem to be plain and obvious truths; at the same time he must learn how to create new values. Unlike the pragmatist, the idealist rejects the view that education is a reconstruction of experience. What is reconstructed, he insists, is not experience but an ideal pattern of social and individual life antecedent to it. Man, as conceived by the idealist, is a free personality, and the function of education is to cultivate the free personality. Horne has put it this way: "Education is the awakening of life to the sublime realities and meanings of existence. Education is the awakening to the life of God in the soul of man, involving praise, prayer, and worship." [17] As viewed by the idealist, man's development potentially knows no bounds and therefore his education is ever incomplete. At the same time, however, education for the idealist does have a fixed and definite goal. As conceived by him, education is not simply growth, and constant adjustment, and readjustment; it is growth toward the Infinite. But that to the pragmatist is utterly vague.

Horne accepts the doctrine of an evolving society; but social evolution, he is certain, operates in accordance with universal principles. He does not find it necessary to ask the question directed by Henry Hazlitt at the pragmatists: "Unless we know where we want to go, or whether it is worth going there, what is the point in moving at all?" For the idealist such a query is irrelevant, since not only is he fairly certain of his direction, which he assures us is toward the Infinite, but at the same time he is piloted on his route by a number of constancies. Even in a changing world, Horne feels, there are changeless principles. The idealist's stress here is on the cultural heritage, on traditions and institutions, on moral and spiritual ideas, on organized subject matter. Horne's eyes are

---

[17] Horne, H. H., "Complete Living as the Goal of Education," *Education*, XLVIII, p. 342, 1928.

fixed on the solid mountain rather than on the snows melting on its sides.

Where Dewey's adherents and those of Horne glare at one another most menacingly is in their views of what the idealist calls the "whole of reality." Here the chasm between the two is unbridgeable. For his part Horne is convinced that the idealistic concept of education is more inclusive than the pragmatic since the latter is concerned primarily with the social life. "An idealistic philosophy," declares Horne, "touches earth with heaven, sees men as children of the Infinite, is nonpractical as well as practical, believes in knowledge for the sake of knowledge as well as for the sake of life, acknowledges an absolute goal for life and education in pursuit of which man finds himself most truly, accepts the divine origin and immortal destiny of man. . . ." [18] For the pragmatist this is unacceptable. For Dewey the term "social" is richer in meaning than the intangible Infinite; it is, indeed, the richest manifestation of reality attainable by human observation.

Opposed to the fundamental tenets of pragmatism as well as to those of most of its philosophic critics is the philosophy which underlies all Catholic education. This is the philosophy aptly styled scholastic, since it was during the later Middle Ages that it attained a synthetic character chiefly through the acumen of the great schoolman and theologian Thomas Aquinas. Theocentric in its viewpoint, Catholic scholasticism has God as its unchanging basis of action. Indeed, it insists that without such a basis there can be no real aim to any type of living, and hence there can be no real purpose to any system of education.

Catholic educational theory springs from its doctrine of man's nature and his supernatural destiny. It teaches that man is literally a personal creation of God; that he is body (material) and soul (spiritual); and that this dual elemental composition functions as an integrated unity. Catholic phi-

---

[18] Horne, H. H., *The Philosophy of Education*, p. 316. New York: The Macmillan Company, Revised, 1927.

losophy stresses too that man is endowed with free will or the power of self-determination; and that this, together with the fact that he possesses a mind which weighs and considers before choosing, sets him apart from all other living creatures. By nature man craves perfect happiness and to attain it he employs his mind and free will; yet since *perfect* happiness is attainable only in the next world, the method of attaining it is for man to lead a life based on the spiritual values and interpreted by the Church.

According to this view man is obviously not only a creature of nature: he also possesses a supernatural destiny. The Catholic Church holds that God teaches man directly or through Scriptures and His ordained agents and in this manner great truths have been made known. Through such divine revelation man has learned of his supernatural life of grace. According to this, God bestowed upon Adam not only his human nature but also a "destiny of supernatural union with Him." However, through Adam's sin and the Fall of Man, the gift of a supernatural life of grace was taken away. Yet this deprivation was not intended to be permanent and through Christ's atonement for the First Man's sin the gift was restored. God's plan "was that all men should incorporate themselves with the Second Adam, and thus, united with the very source of supernatural life, since He is God, be in a state even better than if merely restored to the position lost to them through Adam's sin." [19]

The supernatural is the essence of the Catholic system. It pervades its theology, its ethics, its practice, its view of life, and its education. The Church's "whole educational aim is to restore the sons of Adam to their high position as children of God. . . ." It insists that "education consists essentially in preparing man for what he must do here below in order to attain the sublime end for which he was created. . . ." Furthermore,

[19] McGucken, W. J., "The Philosophy of Catholic Education," *Forty-first Yearbook,* National Society for the Study of Education, Part I, p. 260. Bloomington, Illinois: Public School Publishing Company, 1942.

every form of pedagogic naturalism which in any way excludes or overlooks supernatural Christian formation in the teaching of youth is false. Every method of education founded, wholly or in part, on the denial or forget-fulness of Original Sin and of grace, and relying on the sole powers of human nature, is unsound. Such, generally speaking, are the modern systems bear-ing various names which appeal to a pretended self-government and un-restrained freedom on the part of the child and which diminish or even suppress the teacher's authority and action, attributing to the child an exclusive primacy of initiative and an activity independent of any higher law, natural or Divine, in the work of education.[20]

And again:

The true Christian does not renounce the activities of this life, he does not stunt his natural faculties; but he develops and perfects them by coordi-nating them with the supernatural. He thus ennobles what is merely natural in life and secures for it new strength in the material and temporal order, no less than in the spiritual and eternal.[21]

Such is the ultimate end of Catholic education and to it every Catholic educational institution, from the infant school to the graduate school, must address itself. Everything in education—content, method, discipline—must lead in the direction of man's supernatural destiny. And every agency playing a part in education—the school, the family, and the state—must heed this ultimate end. Any agency, therefore, which fails to impart or respect proper religious and moral instruction is fundamentally defective and inadequate, and unacceptable to the Catholic. Indeed, "it is necessary not only that religious instruction be given to the young at certain fixed times, but also that every other subject taught be permeated with Christian piety." [22]

From the Catholic standpoint "the main defect of Dewey's theory is the complete absence of religious belief. . . . Re-ligion would have shown him that the individual is, in the last

---

[20] Pius XI, Encyclical on the *Christian Education of Youth* (*Divini illius magistri*), p. 20. The America Press, 1936. (The original encyclical appeared December 31, 1929.)

[21] *Ibid.*, p. 33.

[22] Leo XIII, Encyclical *Militantis Ecclesiae*, August 1, 1897, as quoted in the above. *Ibid.*, p. 27.

analysis, the source and the end of social life; that society exists for the individual. Religion also would have made it clear to him that labor and toil are not the whole of man's life. Man must indeed work; but, if he would attain the peace of soul and happiness of life, he must also pray and meditate. . . . From religion, again, he would have learned that there are truths and intuitions, elements of human life, which, notwithstanding the most violent revolutions, remain unchanging and unchanged in the heart of man and likewise in his education."[23]

Another group to strike at Dewey's approach to education is represented by the neo-scholasticism of Robert Maynard Hutchins,[24] Chancellor of the University of Chicago, and his intellectual sympathizers—Mortimer J. Adler, professor of the philosophy of law at the same institution, Stringfellow Barr, former president of St. John's College, Annapolis, Mark van Doren, professor of literature at Columbia, and Richard McKeon and Scott Buchanan, deans at Chicago and St. John's respectively. Hutchins and Adler have been the most energetic in their criticism of Dewey's educational philosophy and its impact on American education.

Concerned in the main with the reform of higher education, Hutchins has repeatedly denounced it for its vocationalism. He has little sympathy for college and university courses in cosmetology, clog dancing, plumbing for women, and the like. He has deplored the "anti-intellectualism" of the American higher learning as well as its delight in minute and isolated specialization. Indeed, Hutchins has long been convinced that

---

[23] de Hovre, F. (Translated by Jordan, E. B.), *Philosophy and Education*, p. 115. New York: Benziger Brothers, 1931.

[24] For an expression of Hutchins' point of view see his *No Friendly Voice*. Chicago: University of Chicago Press, 1936; *The Higher Learning in America*. New Haven: Yale University Press, 1936; *Education for Freedom*. Baton Rouge, La.: Louisiana State University Press, 1943.

For a critical analysis of his views see Gideonse, H. D., *The Higher Learning in a Democracy*. New York: Farrar & Rinehart, Inc., 1937; for a biographical sketch see Meyer, A. E., "Hutchins of Chicago University," *American Mercury*, LVIII, pp. 450–457, 1944.

this trio—vocationalism, anti-intellectualism, and cultural isolation—have been largely responsible for the cultural chaos of modern America. Our love of money, our confused notion of democracy, and our adoration of whatever is new in the belief that change is identical with progress—all these, contends the Chicago chancellor, have their roots in the inadequacies and imperfections of American education. This, in essence, he sees in the grip of "cults"—the cult of skepticism, which decries the appeal to reason as vain; the cult of immediacy, which exalts the present and dismisses the past as unimportant and without value; the cult of science, which holds that science alone can cure the stupors and malaises of the modern world. "The essence of Mr. Dewey's position," declares Hutchins, "is that only science is knowledge; everything else is superstition. Only science is modern; everything else is out of date. History, philosophy, theology, religion, art and literature—almost everything, in short, that makes life worth living—are irrelevant and have no place in modern education." [25]

The anti-intellectualism of American education, Hutchins argues, leads to sentimentalism. It promotes an irrational and optimistic desire to help our fellow men. Naturally suspicious of the intellect, its devotees emphasize the all-importance of knowing *what* one wants rather than *why* one wants it, or, even more rarely, what one *ought* to want. At bottom, Hutchins feels this to be dangerous since it translates itself very readily into the belief that since one wants something one ought to have it, and to obtain it all that is needed is the necessary power. Thus "unlimited acquisition" becomes the human law and "success" the measurement of education.

To bring order to our cultural anarchy Hutchins and his followers recommend the cultivation of the intellect. "Our salvation," he asseverates, "lies not in the rejection of the

---

[25] Hutchins, R. M., *Education for Freedom,* pp. 35–36. Baton Rouge, La.: Louisiana State University Press, 1943.

intellect but in a return to it." [26]   Not that he is averse to physical and aesthetic education, nor even to the vocational, but their rightful place, he contends, lies outside the school. Holding that truth is absolute, that it is "everywhere the same," and "the same to all men," a doctrine which is denied by pragmatists and experimentalists, the Hutchins school contends that the ends of education cannot be relative and variable. Stating it syllogistically, as is his wont, Mortimer Adler has put it thus: *"Major:* Good habits (virtues) are the same for all men. *Minor:* Education should aim at the formation of good habits. *Conclusion:* Education should aim at the same objectives for all men." [27]   Under such an assumption there is of course no room for the view that youth should choose its own studies and that education should be adjusted to the needs and capacities of the individual. Instead, urges Hutchins, everyone between the ages of sixteen and twenty, except the obviously unfit, should be given the same general education.

The first steps in the direction of the training of the intellect Hutchins would make through grammar, rhetoric, and logic. Through this disciplinary trio the learner is to cultivate the arts of reading, writing, and speaking as well as whatever rational powers he possesses. As a reinforcement every

---

[26] The Catholic philosopher Jacques Maritain, who is fairly sympathetic to a good part of the Hutchins doctrine, sounds a warning at this point. Contending that the children of man are not made for aristocratic leisure, he cautions that the utilitarian aspect of education must not be disregarded. However, he feels that the ulterior specialized training which may be required must not imperil the essential aim of education. See Maritain, J., *Education at the Crossroads,* p. 10. New Haven: Yale University Press, 1943.

[27] Adler, M., "In Defense of a Philosophy of Education," *Forty-first Yearbook,* National Society for the Study of Education, Part I, p. 239. Bloomington, Illinois: Public School Publishing Company, 1942.

Whether this sort of logical demonstration impresses anyone but the unwary is questionable. Certainly the major premise, that good habits (virtues) are the same for all men, is disputable. Most formulas of this kind, the logician Ludwig Wittgenstein points out, "are not false but senseless. We cannot . . . answer questions of this kind at all, but only state their senselessness." Wittgenstein, L., *Tractatus Logico-Philosophicus,* p. 63. New York: Harcourt, Brace & Co., Inc., 1933.

student is required to study theoretic mathematics which "exemplifies reasoning in its clearest and most precise form." The special object of the Hutchins' program of general education, however, is the transmission of the accumulated wisdom of the ages. This is found in the so-called Great Books, "books which have throughout the centuries attained the dimensions of classics." A hundred in number, the Great Books become the gateway to man's great concepts or First Principles, which, Hutchins and his supporters insist, are the same for all men in all ages, and an understanding of which is essential if one is to dispel the cultural confusion that envelops the modern world.[28]

As for the higher learning, Hutchins continues in the same vein. He deplores the university's stress on the practical and the utilitarian and its neglect of learning for the sake of learning. He has repeatedly scored the experimentalist's stress on the laboratory, insisting that many of our problems can never be solved through the methods of science. Finally, he is at odds with the view that our contemporary industrial and technological society has little in common with the past, and that one can learn little or nothing from the past. Once again Hutchins puts reason in the curricular spotlight. Courses would be required of all students in the natural sciences in which man and nature are studied, without any vocational

---

[28] Three-quarters of the Great Books were composed before 1800; and two-thirds before 1700. Among the titles one finds many familiar ones such as the *Iliad* and the *Odyssey,* the Bible, the *Aeneid,* the *Confessions* of St. Augustine, Chaucer's *Canterbury Tales,* several of Shakespeare's dramas, Goethe's *Faust,* and so on. But one also finds Cantor's *Transfinite Numbers,* Riemann's *Hypothesis of Geometry,* Dalton's *A New System of Chemical Philosophy,* Grosseteste's *On Light,* Oresme's *On the Breadths of Forms.* At St. John's College, of which Hutchins is a trustee, the hundred Great Books constitute the basis of the four-year curriculum and must be read at a specific time for prescribed courses. As one would naturally expect, Hutchins' views have aroused considerable controversy. "Are we compelled to hold," John Dewey inquired, "that one method obtains in the natural sciences, and another, radically different, in moral questions?" For an analysis of the controversy between experimentalism and the Hutchins' neo-scholasticism see Gallagher, B. G., "Mr. Hutchins and Mr. Dewey," *Christian Century,* XLII, pp. 106–107, 1945.

purpose on the part of the student; the social sciences, which consider the relationships of man to man; and metaphysics and theology, without which, Hutchins believes, no unified university can exist. All teaching, moreover, must be grounded in metaphysical unity, which for Hutchins is, in essence, a synthesis of Aristotle, Plato, and Thomas Aquinas. Metaphysics is to be the binding thread which runs through all university work, giving it "constancy of direction and integrity of purpose." Basically the initial training of every future doctor, jurist, and pastor would be the same, with the effect, Hutchins believes, that they would have "ordered minds prepared for life because they have been educated in view of the purpose of life."

Although Hutchins and his fellow neo-scholastics have basked, rather pleasantly, in the nation-wide publicity of such journals as the *Saturday Evening Post, Harper's,* the *American Mercury,* the *Christian Century, Newsweek, The Nation,* and *The New Republic,* their net effect on the American public school has been slight. All schools of educational thought have discerned flaws in the Hutchins creed. Realists have denounced the neo-scholastics for their unwillingless to perceive the world as it really is; idealists have chided them for their neglect of the full personality; pragmatists and experimentalists, who have been their sharpest critics, have pounced on them from all directions, condemning them on many counts but particularly for their antiquated psychology, their lack of social understanding, and their disregard of the findings of educational experimentation of the last few decades. Catholic philosophers, however, have a friendly word for Hutchins. They admire, for one thing, "the lucidity and sanity of his theory." Nor does his respect for metaphysics as valid knowledge of both sensible and suprasensible being run counter to the Catholic grain. The Catholics, too, perceive cracks in the Hutchins' marble; and thus, while they salute him with one hand, they shake a warning with the other. Although they are no doubt pleased with Hutchins' stress on metaphysics, they cannot overlook that it is "a de-Christianized philosophy or metaphysic";[29] that "when he quotes Aquinas he quotes an Aquinas that never existed"; and, most damaging of all, that he fails to take into account the facts about man and his supernatural destiny.

At the University of Chicago, where Hutchins has been at the helm since 1929, none of his major philosophic tenets have found their way into general practice. Has Chicago purged itself of its practical, utilitarian courses? If it has, then how does one account for its offerings in business, finance, and banking? Is it any closer to the teaching of St. Thomas than the Univeristy of California, Massachusetts Institute of Technology, or Vassar? If it is, then how does one explain its doctoral theses in dishwashing methods, hosiery advertising, and the style cycles in women's undergarments?

It is true, there have been vast and important changes at Chicago during the years of Hutchins' presidency. The credit system has been discarded; attendance at classes is no longer obligatory; comprehensive examinations have replaced the traditional course examination; students may pick up their baccalaureate at the end of their sophomore years; and, most incredible of all, varsity football has been sent into exile. But these, in the main, are external changes; and none of them draws vital sustenance from the neo-scholastic doctrine. Only at St. John's, Annapolis, has this found a fitting and acceptable harbor. Here the educational theories of Hutchins have made great progress. Here one can see students bending over the Great Books, searching for great concepts and First Principles. Here all courses are required; here one finds no Commercial Spanish, no Public Speaking, no Personality I and II. The St. Johnnies, in short, are the answer to Hutchins' prayer. Yet, reviewed through the historian's eyes, they constitute but a drop in the vast stream of American education; so small,

---

[29] McGucken, W. J., *Forty-first Yearbook,* National Society for the Study of Education, Part I, p. 256. Bloomington, Illinois: Public School Publishing Company, 1942.

indeed, are they that for the moment at any rate their presence in that stream has been almost imperceptible.[30]

D. Progressive Education

1. Early stages

With the death of Colonel Parker in 1902 and the departure of John Dewey from Chicago in 1904, the pace of educational reform slackened for a time. There were, of course, some young fellows, then as now, who were at odds with the old ways and who were eager to change them. The young men and women who were excited about educational reform in the late nineties had been inspired by Herbart, especially by Charles De Garmo's book on *Herbart and the Herbartians*. With these young teachers, however, the stress was not on Herbart's "formal steps of the recitation," which they repudiated, but on the beguiling "doctrine of interest." This they found to be a powerful ally; indeed, with it they even got children through tricky and difficult examinations. But the number of such pedagogic rebels was quite small. They worked, moreover, largely by themselves, content to try out their newer ideas in the obscurity of their own little classrooms. Zealots rather than meticulous probers, they were delighted by what they were achieving, though they had little more to offer than their enthusiasm and strong convictions to support the claims they made for their accomplishments.

That ardor, fortunately, was never stilled. Though it glowed only faintly and sporadically during the century's first decade, it grew nonetheless. To it came the fortifying influence of Francis Parker. It came through the young teachers who had been trained by him and his co-workers in the Normal

---

[30] Recently various public libraries have promoted what are styled as "The Great Books Discussions on Basic Problems." The discussion leaders "have taken a special training course in leading book discussions." Based on the Hutchins' philosophy, the program seeks to stimulate "your appreciation of the basic ideas found in the Great Books." It is aimed at adults who "have the experience, maturity and sense of purpose necessary to deal with great human problems; only adults can become deeply possessed by ideas."

School. It came through a new generation of educational leaders, who, as children, had studied in the original Parker schools.[1] It came, too, through the work of the school which bore his name. Opened in 1901, with Flora Cooke as principal, the Francis W. Parker School continued under her enlightened leadership for more than thirty years. Like the progressive schools of a later day it was striving to eliminate the school's traditional stiffness. Like such schools it was seeking to break down hard and fast subject-matter boundary lines. It, too, was groping in the direction of the Project Method, though this had not yet been formulated in any precise terms. Under the auspices of the Francis W. Parker School there was issued, beginning in 1912, a series of *Year Books*. Seven in number, they contain many magnificent statements of the work and philosophy of the school. It is in the first volume that one finds expressed the credo of the teachers of this school:

that self-actuated work causes the greatest gain in the pupil; that training in initiative is the child's great need; that in his own interests we often find educative opportunity; that freedom with a balanced responsibility is the best condition of moral and intellectual growth; that real experience with actual material is an essential of learning; that opportunity for varied expression is necessary for right education; that for purposes of development children must be treated as individuals and not as a group; that one of the most effective and wholesome motives of work is the social motive.[2]

Such were the ideals that motivated the work of the school. In the lower grades—there were twelve grades in all—the compartmental subject setup was broken up and in its place came broad units of study, centering around the community, Greek life, colonial life, and the like. Curiously enough, experimentation in the high school curriculum was almost impos-

---

[1] Among them were Carleton W. Washburne, creator of the Winnetka Plan for individualizing the work of the school (see p. 492); Katherine Taylor, founder of the progressive Shady Hill School, Cambridge, Massachusetts; and Perry Dunlap Smith, director of the North Shore Country Day School.

[2] The Francis W. Parker School Year Book, Vol. I, *The Social Motive in School Work*, p. 11. Chicago: The School, 1912.

sible.   College and university domination barred the way to
change.   The same situation existed in many other countries
and, indeed, has continued to exist to the present.   Through
their entrance requirements, institutions of higher learning
have been able to exert a direct control over the secondary
school, with the result that educational experimentation, particularly with regard to the curriculum, has been exceedingly
difficult.   It is only in recent years, and particularly in the
United States, that the secondary school has been able to
break some of these fetters.

2.   Junius L. Meriam

While Flora Cooke and her teachers were developing their
splendid school in Chicago, two other educators in different
parts of the country established new schools.   The first was an
elementary school founded in 1904 by Professor Junius L.
Meriam of the University of Missouri; the other was the
School of Organic Education which Marietta Johnson (1864–
1938) opened in 1907 in the George Community at Fairhope,
Alabama.

In the practical work of modernizing educational theory,
the name of Junius L. Meriam is notable.   A pioneer like
Dewey, Meriam experimented with a radical curriculum for
a score of years.   He believed that education was not something to be imposed from without but something that
should draw the latent possibilities from within the child.
Like Dewey, Meriam was ready to break with convention in education.   To facilitate experimentation he did away
with the traditional school subjects and school furniture.
What he wanted was a curriculum that was related to the
child's life.   An activity program was installed, with excursions, constructive work, observation, and discussion playing the important parts.   After a while Meriam concluded
that, on the whole, it was impracticable to run a school day
without some sort of division.   Thus there gradually evolved
a fourfold organization of activities and materials: (1) ob-

servation, (2) play, (3) stories, (4) handwork. On the surface this is much more like Froebel's than Herbart's school. Meriam's program, corresponding to the school day, was divided into four ninety-minute periods. A far cry from the traditional school day, which scheduled its routine recitations at ten- to thirty-minute intervals, running them off very much as a railroad dispatches trains! The Meriam innovation not only broke with a long-standing tradition, but it also afforded teacher and learner considerable flexibility. Its significance lies in the fact that it established once and for all the idea that a school day is something more than a mere chronological proposition; that learning may, in fact, take place in a leisurely way under conditions which are actually pleasant.

3. Marietta Johnson's Fairhope School

Before organizing her School of Organic Education at Fairhope, Alabama, Marietta Johnson had been a teacher for some years in the elementary and secondary schools, and in the State Normal School of Minnesota. It was this experience that provided the stimulus for her doubts as to the value of conventional educational procedures for the general welfare of the child. When her own child was six years old, Mrs. Johnson moved to Fairhope where she established her school. What she was seeking was a more flexible method of instruction adjusted to the needs of the individual child. Beginning with a half-dozen children, the school subsequently extended from the kindergarten through the college.

Besides running her school, Mrs. Johnson lectured extensively, expounding her educational ideas in many parts of the country. Her main theories on education, and some of the experiences in her school, have been described in her *Youth in a World of Men,* published in 1929.[3]

The aim of the school "is to provide the right conditions of growth. Believing that education is life, it follows that the

---

[3] Johnson, M., *Youth in a World of Men.* New York: John Day Co., Inc., 1929.

school program must be life-giving to body, mind, and spirit."
What are the needs of the mind? What are the needs of the
spirit? These are the questions to which the school addressed
itself.

"The child," Mrs. Johnson agreed with Rousseau, "is not a
little adult." "The mother . . . who takes such pride in her
child's reading at an early age; who is so happy over the
thought that the child can sew; who boasts of her child's reliability and responsibility, is misguided." [4] At Fairhope, anything which violates the order of development is banned.
Reading and writing, consequently, have been postponed until
the ninth or tenth year. For the same reason formal work
has been delayed. Quoting the Fairhope authorities once
more, we note that they believe that "children should not *try*
to grow mentally any more than they should *try* to be heavier
or taller. . . . Learning at this age should be through wholesome experiences. There should be less teaching of facts and
more time for assimilation." [5]

At Fairhope, creative activity has always been stressed.
Several large rooms have been reserved for work in clay,
painting, drawing, sketching, metal work, woodwork, and
weaving. Folk dancing, singing, and nature study are other
popular childhood activities. Nature study has never been
taught at Fairhope simply to provide children with an array
of facts, but rather to stimulate their curiosity and to develop
their power of investigation.

The Fairhope youngsters begin formal work with reading,
writing, and spelling in the ninth or tenth year. Geography,
history, and literature are taught as literature. There are no
recitations, classes being conducted as an open discussion.
There are, of course, the usual creative subjects. At fourteen,
the young people "automatically pass into the high school."
The process throughout stresses the social, all work being conducted in the freest possible social atmosphere. "Wise control

---

[4] *Ibid.*, p. 32.
[5] Quoted from a Fairhope bulletin.

and guidance is needed at this uncertain stage of growth. Four years of the most serious, earnest work in science, history, mathematics, literature and language is given in the high school with folk dancing, music, arts, and woodwork."

In summing up the Fairhope Idea of Organic Education these points should be noted:

1. Fixed furniture in the school has been replaced by chairs and tables and movable furniture.

2. Fairhope consciously has tried to make all school work minister to the health of the child's nervous system. For this reason, formal reading and writing have been postponed until the child is eight or nine years old.

3. Specialization for the undeveloped child is not permitted.

4. External efficiency in any skill or learning is minimized.

5. To preserve the union of the intellectual and emotional life, "not only the creative handwork must be provided, but the purposefulness and initiative of the children be respected."

6. For the spirit, lack of self-consciousness is essential. All external demands, with external awards, are excluded.

7. Grading, marking, and promotion tend to develop double motives. The idea of grouping based on achievement is impossible.

8. Since children must be grouped for convenience, and since "grouping according to chronological age tends to eliminate selfconsciousness either of superiority or inferiority, this is the method adopted."

9. There is no do-as-you-please program. The new education controls and guides the child, but strives to have this guiding and controlling determined by the child's needs rather than the convenience of the adult.

10. "The new education believes that society owes all children guidance, control, instruction, association, and inspiration, through the primary, elementary, high school and college phases of growth. The whole question becomes, what are the needs of the body, the mind, and the spirit? . . . The new education identifies education and growth. It has small eye to the future, and no eye to the market. It is concentrated upon immediate human ends. Growth is for growth. The process and the end are one."

4. Other developments

The effect of the pioneer work of Mrs. Johnson and Professor Meriam, like that of Colonel Parker and John Dewey, was something of a shock to the average schoolmen. Not only were their schools pedagogically radical, but basically they seemed so wrong, so utterly opposed to what "sound education" had always stood for. At the same time, however, there were

unmistakable signs of a growing dissatisfaction with the traditional school. Here and there the rising discontent took concrete form in the establishment of a number of progressive
schools, such as the Play School, now the City and Country
School, organized by Caroline Pratt in New York City; the
Shady Hill School, opened in Cambridge, Massachusetts by
Professor and Mrs. W. E. Hocking; the Walden School,
founded by Margaret Naumburg in New York City; the Elementary School of the University of Iowa, a new type of training school under the direction of Ernest Horn; and the Oak
Lane Country School, which came into being in Philadelphia
under the direction of Frances M. Froehlicher.

New fuel was added to the reform movement when, in 1916,
the General Education Board published two important mono-
graphs on the subject of educational reform. One was
Abraham Flexner's *Modern School*, and the other, Charles
Eliot's *Changes Needed in America's Secondary Education*.
The two works were widely distributed, and since they were
critical and provocative, they caused a stir. The following
year the General Education Board gave the movement for
educational reform another boost when, with the help of
philanthropists and educational leaders, it assisted financially
in the establishment of the Lincoln School of Teachers College,
Columbia University. The new school was to serve a dual
purpose: it was, for one thing, to be a progressive school, "a
modern school," but it was also to serve, uniquely, as a laboratory for public school experimentation.

5.　The Progressive Education Association

The early efforts at educational reform, although they had
a great deal in common, were nonetheless quite diffuse. Scattered widely throughout the nation, the new schools worked
independently with no medium for exchanging ideas and experiences. To give the work of reform greater cohesion and to
make its results more generally known, a number of educators,
led by Stanwood Cobb, head of the Chevy Chase Country Day

School, met in the winter of 1918–19 in Washington, D. C., where they organized the Progressive Education Association. Predominantly child-centered, the viewpoint of the PEA embraced the following principles:

I. *Freedom to develop naturally*
The conduct of the pupil should be governed by himself according to the social needs of his community, rather than by arbitrary laws. Full opportunity for initiative and self-expression should be provided. . . .

II. *Interest, the motive of all work*
Interest should be satisfied and developed through: (1) direct and indirect contact with the world and its activities, and the use of the experiences thus gained; (2) application of knowledge gained, and correlation between different subjects; (3) the consciousness of achievement.

III. *The teacher a guide, not a taskmaster*
. . . Progressive teachers will encourage the use of all the senses, training the pupils in both observation and judgment, and, instead of hearing recitations only, will spend most of the time teaching how to use various sources of information, including life activities as well as books, how to reason about the information thus acquired, and how to express forcefully and logically the conclusions reached.

IV. *Scientific study of pupil development*
School records should not be confined to the marks given by the teachers to show the advancement of the pupils in their study of subject, but should also include both objective and subjective reports on those physical, mental, moral, and social characteristics which affect both school and adult life and which can be influenced by the school and the home. Such records should be used as a guide for the treatment of each pupil. . . .

V. *Greater attention to all that affects the child's physical development*
One of the first considerations of progressive education is the health of the pupils. Much more room in which to move about, better light and air, clean and well-ventilated buildings, easier access to the out-of-doors and greater use of it, are all necessary. . . .

VI. *Cooperation between school and home to meet the needs of child life*
The school should provide, with the home, as much as is possible of all that the natural interests and activities of the child demand, especially during the elementary-school years. These conditions can come about only through intelligent cooperation between parents and teachers.

VII. *The Progressive School a leader in educational movements*
The Progressive School . . . should be a laboratory where new ideas, if worthy, meet encouragement; where tradition alone does not

rule, but the best of the past is leavened with the discoveries of today, and the result is freely added to the sum of educational knowledge.[6]

From its feeble infancy the Progressive Education Association grew rapidly, its membership rising from several hundred in 1920 to its peak of some 10,000 in the late thirties. In its early days the Association was made up largely of parents and teachers connected with small private schools, but as time passed, the character of the membership became more and more professional. To give itself a national voice the organization held annual public conferences, the first two convening in Washington, and the others thereafter in one of the eastern cities. To disseminate its views even further, in 1924 PEA launched a magazine, *Progressive Education,* which soon won a distinguished place for itself in educational journalism both here and abroad.[7]

6. William H. Kilpatrick and the Project Method

The work of the Progressive Education Association helped to stir the awakening interest in the new education, but there were other factors, too, which contributed to its development. For one thing John Dewey re-entered the educational arena in 1916 with the publication of his *Democracy and Education.* Acclaimed as one of the most significant educational books ever written, the work set forth the pragmatic philosophy of education, a good part of which was readily acceptable to the proponents of the new, progressive school. But Dewey was too abstract for the average reader, and his involved and colorless style of writing made what he said appear even more difficult. What the sage of Columbia Heights needed for the wider acceptance of his views was expert interpretation in the country's Schools of Education as well as experimentation in new schools. Both came in time. By 1918 William Heard

---

[6] *Progressive Education Advances,* Progressive Education Association, pp. 5–6. New York: Appleton-Century-Crofts, Inc., 1938.

[7] Its first editor was Gertrude Hartman.

Kilpatrick had begun to write and lecture to his immense student audiences at Teachers College, explaining and clarifying the views of Dewey, and advancing the gospel of the new Project Method. Soon afterward Boyd H. Bode of Ohio State began his exposition of the experimentalist-progressive psychology and philosophy.

Once popularly designated as "the million dollar professor" because his lectures at Columbia had attracted such enormous crowds of students, Professor Kilpatrick achieved international renown for his lucid interpretation of John Dewey. But the fact must not be overlooked that Kilpatrick has himself contributed in a large way to the reconstruction of modern educational theory and practice. His plain and understandable writings, like his lectures, have familiarized thousands of teachers in America and elsewhere with the liberal trends in American education. Influenced by the psychology of William James, Edward L. Thorndike, and the newer *Gestaltists* (see p. 465), and convinced of the significance of a rapidly changing social order, Kilpatrick demanded that the school become "a place where actual experiencing takes place." Applying his psychology to the learning process, he pointed out that:

each significant learning experience in some measure remakes subsequent experience, in some measure gives a wider outlook as to the possibilities of life and deeper insight into its processes; gives also differentiated attitudes and appreciations with respect to the different new thing seen and felt; gives also increased technique, power of control over the experience process, to bring it more under conscious direction.[8]

Out of the thinking of Parker, Dewey, Meriam, and other leaders of the new education has come the Project Method, of which Kilpatrick was one of the first and outstanding advocates.[9] The term "project" had been employed in the field of

---

[8] Kilpatrick, W. H., "Statement of Position," *Twenty-Sixth Yearbook,* National Society for the Study of Education, *The Foundations and Technique of Curriculum-Making,* Part II, pp. 128–130. Quoted by permission of the Society. Bloomington, Illinois: Public School Publishing Company, 1926.

[9] For Kilpatrick's analysis see his article "The Project Method," *Teachers College Record,* XIX, September, 1918.

manual training as early as 1900 to refer to any practical problem which involved the physical making of a product. In time
the word found its way into the domains of agriculture and
home economics. After the turn of the century, however,
teachers began to speak of projects whenever they meant learning activities in which pupils had an opportunity to choose,
plan, and direct their work under conditions approximating
those of real life. Building a dog house, for example, was a
project, as was making a dress or a new hat, or raising chickens
for the butcher. When practical problems were launched and
worked out in the home, the term "home project" was sometimes used.

With the rise of progressive education in the second decade
of the century, the Project Method was given a new meaning,
largely through the influence of Kilpatrick. In essence, however, Kilpatrick's Project Method is much more than an artful
technique: it is a philosophy of education which has been
translated into a method. It has its roots in part in Kilpatrick's reaction to the misapplication by many teachers of
Dewey's "problem solving," which in some instances had
degenerated into a mechanical ritual for teaching the prescribed subjects of the conventional curriculum. What Kilpatrick proposed was to unite in one concept those elements
which seemed indispensable for true and worth-while learning.
Like Gaul, these were divided into three: (1) a hearty participation in the learning situation on the learner's part; (2)
the full application of the psychological principles of learning;
(3) provision for the ethical element and the sense of responsibility. This trio was to be interwoven in what Kilpatrick
described as "a whole-hearted, purposeful activity proceeding
in a social environment," or more simply, in "a hearty, purposeful act."

To carry out this idea, Kilpatrick recommended that the
school's work should be organized through activities which
would call forth the pupil's purposeful effort. Good projects,
he pointed out, would not eliminate or exclude the subject-

matter of the traditional school; at the same time projects should provide for intellectual and aesthetic activities as well as for those of a manual and motor caliber. To illustrate what he meant, Kilpatrick outlined four classes of projects:

Type I. *The construction or creative project:* where the purpose is to embody some idea or plan in external form, *e.g.,* building a boat, writing a letter, presenting a play.

Type II. *The appreciation or enjoyment project:* where the purpose is to enjoy some aesthetic experience, *e.g.,* listening to a story, hearing a symphony, appreciating a picture.

Type III. *The problem project:* where the purpose is to solve an intellectual difficulty, *e.g.,* why dew falls at certain times, why New York has outgrown Philadelphia.

Type IV. *The drill or specific learning project:* where the purpose is to acquire some item or degree of skill or knowledge, *e.g.,* learning to write a certain grade on a handwriting scale, achieving a certain standing in addition.

Ellsworth Collins, another educator who has contributed to the wider use of the Project Method, has arranged projects thus: Play Projects, Excursion Projects, Story Projects, and Hand Projects.

No longer an educational oddity, the Project Method has emerged from the realm of harangue and controversy and has found a fairly substantial support in the twentieth century school. The values which are claimed for it are several. In the first place, it is based on the current psychology of action which teaches that knowledge, ability, and character traits come from active participation in solving actual problems. Then it is lauded on the ground that inasmuch as the pupil chooses his project, it is begun with a purpose which is presumably his own and not that of his teacher. Furthermore, the project is an undertaking which is real and understandable to the pupil; it is something related to his experience, with goals that are clear and desired. The fact, moreover, that the pupil can plan and direct his own activity is considered good. When the project is an individual undertaking, it is a useful means of providing for individual differences, and when the

project is a group enterprise, it provides experiences in cooperation and social responsibility.

With all its allure, however, the Project Method has its
blemishes. For one thing a first-rate project is not easily and
quickly organized. Like an excellent dinner, it takes time, and
patience, and ingenuity to plan and prepare it. The old-style
recitation, like food that comes in cans, is so much easier to
serve. Moreover, even when hard-pressed teachers have been
willing to devote the extra time and labor that go into the
making of a good project, success has not always been their
reward. It has been found that despite the most careful planning, a curriculum based on the project procedure may omit
necessary content and needed pupil experience. Nor are
teachers so wrong when they lament that in the Project
Method there is a real danger of wasting time in useless and
unproductive activity. There is, indeed, often a lack of much
needed practice. Then, too, even when the knowledge gained
is vital, it has been found that in the project procedure it is
often isolated and fragmentary, leaving the pupil with no perspective of the integrated organization of the content of different fields—an accusation which, however, would be true to
some degree of almost any method.

Psychologically, Kilpatrick grounded his Project Method
on Thorndike's well-known Laws of Learning. These comprise
the *law of readiness,* which holds that since learning is a form
of selective response conditioned by the learner's attitudes,
moods, and mental set, to learn successfully one must be enthusiastic and motivated at the outset; the *law of exercise,*
which states that since learning involves the formation of a
connection between stimulus and response, the more frequently such a bond is exercised the stronger it becomes; the
law of effect, which asserts that since learning is helped when
accompanied by satisfaction, there must consequently be some
measure of progress so that the learner may enjoy his success
and derive satisfaction. These principles, Kilpatrick felt, were
inherent in the Project Method, which was described as "a

unit of purposeful experience . . . where dominating purpose, as inner urge (1) fixes the aim (or end) of the action, (2) guides the process, (3) furnishes its drive, its inner motivation for vigorous prosecution."

Out of his analysis of the Project Method, Kilpatrick developed his concept of *simultaneous learnings*. A very complex affair, learning, as viewed by Kilpatrick, does not take place singly. "The whole cat," he once said, "catches the mouse." Thus one never learns just one thing at a time; along with the acquisition of knowledge goes the development of habit, attitudes, and ideals. Learning, Kilpatrick holds, has three basic aspects: mental, physical, and dispositional. The first represents the *how* aspect—the solution of the problem; the second is the skill side; and the third constitutes the drive to do what is to be learned. The particular knowledge or skills set in a given learning situation are known as *primary* learnings; those that are derived from fields related to the primary learnings, as well as incidental knowledge acquired in the course of the learning, have been set down as *associate* learnings; finally, there are the *concomitant* learnings, which are those pertaining more to learning situations in general and involving the development of emotional attitudes, ideals, and standards. Since learning does not take place singly, Kilpatrick holds that teaching method must give adequate consideration to all the learnings going on simultaneously. Of particular importance are the social outcomes of learning and for these Kilpatrick believes concomitant learnings to be of special significance. For the development of character he prefers the Project Method to the "sit-alone-at-your desk" method, which he has described as antisocial. "A democratic society," he has declared, "should have a democratic social system and in this system a democratic method will play a most important part." Summarizing his views on the learning process, Kilpatrick has put it this way:

I learn each response in the degree that I feel it or count it important and also in the degree that it interrelates itself with what I already know. All that I thus learn I build at once into character. . . . The presence of interest or purpose constitutes a favorable condition for learning. Interest and felt purpose mean that the learner faces a situation in which he is concerned. The purpose as aim guides his thought and effort. Because of his interest and concern he gets more wholeheartedly into action; he puts forth more effort; what he learns has accordingly more importance to him and probably more meaningful connections. From both counts he is better learned.[10]

7. The spread of Progressivism

What had begun in the early twentieth century as a mood, as a protest against a conservative and antiquated sort of education, gradually solidified in the course of the next few years into a definite movement. Through the pionering work of teachers, through interpreters like Kilpatrick, through thinkers like Dewey, through the influence of the Progressive Education Association, the movement of Progressive Education slowly took shape. The few protest schools which had come into being during the first decade and which had increased slightly during the second, multiplied even more during the third. Nor was the movement confined to any particular part of the country. It showed itself everywhere: in California, where Cora Williams established her Institute for Creative Education in 1917; in Ohio, where the Downers' Grove School was organized in 1917; in Missouri, where the John Burroughs School was founded in 1923. By 1930 there were scores of Progressive schools all over the United States. Nearly all were private; nearly all were child-centered; and, with only a few exceptions, none of them were strictly experimental.

That the early Progressives should have stressed the child rather than the subject is hardly cause for amazement; after all such an emphasis was one of their prime reasons for being. The old school, with its hidebound curriculum, its stiff formality, its assembly-line procedures, had stifled self-expression and wiped out individuality. Whatever special talents a child

---

[10] Kilpatrick, W. H., "The Case for Progressivism in Education," *The Journal of the National Education Association*, XXX, pp. 231–232, November, 1941.

might have had were certainly not encouraged if they were noticed at all.

A number of teachers in the new movement saw in this situation a wonderful opportunity. Building their teaching on the child's natural desire to express himself, they evolved what is now commonly known as "creative education." They were of course not the dull and formal pedagogues familiar to us all. People of feeling rather than masters of facts, they were doers rather than rememberers; and instead of anesthetizing the human spirit, they encouraged it, enticing it into the open where it could unfold freely in the fullness of its nature. Temperamentally, they were artists and in their classes they became *par excellence* the artist-teachers.

8. Hughes Mearns and creative education

What the child could accomplish when he was properly guided was effectively demonstrated by Hughes Mearns 1875–). An antagonist of the conventional, uninspired education, Mearns became interested in the new education when it was just beginning. He was, in fact, one of its most energetic promoters. Educated at Harvard and Pennsylvania, in time he became absorbed in the creative possibilities of the young child. Here he found "a hidden individual spirit of surprising keenness and of stubborn honesty." When, subsequently, he worked with adolescents in high school he obtained a similar result, though the older children took somewhat longer to percolate. Later, as professor of Creative Education, in New York University's School of Education, Mearns discovered that what was true of the young was no less true of the adult. His experiences in creative education Mearns has recorded in three notable books, the first two, *Creative Youth* (1925) and *Creative Power* (1929), dealing largely with his work in the Lincoln School; the third, *The Creative Adult* (1940), came out of his experience with adults.

At the Lincoln School, where Mearns taught English, he started, as he said, with what he had—immature junior high school students relatively uninterested in good writing. To these youngsters he read, making comments as he went along. Slowly he lured the abler ones to do some oral reading to each other. Little by little the fact dawned upon them that they could be critical, that they had something to say, and that what they said was important. Out of these experiences grew the Robert Frost Club, which took the place of the literature class. Pupils were required to read—but what they read was entirely up to them. At the same time, fine writings were presented orally with comments that brought life into what had once been meaningless. Interest grew, and with it came keener and maturer discussions of literary values.

In his writing class Mearns followed a similar procedure. Here there was no required writing. With personal conferences, as well as helpful class discussions, Mearns nursed his protégés into a feeling of confidence. Gradually the children began to produce stories and poems. But Mearns constantly stressed the need of hard and strenuous effort. First, the child was to create; then came the labor of putting the finished production into its finest form. For Mearns this mechanical editing is of significance. "In its place," he has declared, "it is of high importance, this coldly intellectual stage; the value of a piece of created work is raised there in direct proportion to the intelligence of the creator." Under the spell of Mearns's guidance, the children wrote not only good prose but also lovely verse. A fifth-grade girl, for example, wrote the following:

Spring and Summer

On an evening soft with mist,
The moon shone on a silver brook;
Summer came out from the shadowed glade
And Spring came from the wood.
Summer stepped across the brook,
But Spring stood still.
They stayed together for one happy night—
Oh, the wonder of that night.

. . . . . .

Night had gone, and with it Spring;
Dawn found Summer all alone.

This bit of beauty was not a glittering exception. In his *Creative Youth* and *Creative Power,* Mearns has cited scores of others. Behind Mearns's success with creative youth lie many factors. To begin with, Mearns himself is a creative artist. For Mearns, moreover, children are essentially creative persons, not scholars. " They use language as the artist the world over and in all ages has used his medium, not as an end in itself, but as a means for the expression of thought and feeling. . . . The attention is never on the word, but on the force that creates the word." Above all, Mearns insists, the child must be spontaneous. There must be no interferences and no coercions. There must be no ridicule, no shame, no false standards.

But let it not be thought that Mearns stands for complete and unlimited freedom. "We knew . . . that we must teach them some of the rigorous and unchanging customs of the world." Naturalness, good as it may be, is, in other words, not everything. There are times for self-expression, and there are times for tact. "The secret of our results lies in the environment which we as teachers skillfully and knowingly set up day by day. Children do behave naturally, we trust, in the presence of influences that the school consciously brings to bear; they are not aware usually that our direction is important, but we are aware of it at every moment."

Creative education, as Mearns is forever reminding us, is not just another subject of study; it is an attitude toward all subjects. "It is," he said, "a way of using the mind, the feeling and the imagination while depending not so much on books as upon the student's own too much neglected mental and spiritual resources."

9. Mrs. Satis N. Coleman and creative music

That music should receive particular attention from the Progressives seems quite natural. Time was, and not so long ago, when only an hour or so of the school's weekly program was reserved for music. The form of expression was generally that of group singing, with special stress on the mastery of musical notation and sight reading. Like formal grammar, music tended to be abstract and intellectual. "In what key is this piece?" the teacher would ask. "How many flats are there? If it had sharps instead of flats what would it be? Is it a waltz or a march?" Thus taught, music was essentially a subject to be studied and not something to be experienced.

Contemporary educators are not in accord among themselves with respect to the place and purpose of music in education. Roughly speaking, there are two main schools of thought. On the one hand, there are those educators who are interested in music primarily as an art. Led by such eminent students of music as Seymour and Surette, this group looks upon music education chiefly as training in listening. Their aim, in the end, stresses appreciation rather than experience and expression. On the other hand, however, are those teachers of music who insist that the child should be creative in his musical education. Outstanding among this group of educators are such well-known teachers as Potter, Church, and Coleman. The original leader of the movement, Mrs. Satis Coleman (1878–   ), once likened children to "musical primitives." She feels that youngsters should experience music in all its phases, from its simplest beginnings to its highest and more complex forms.

In her book, *Creative Music for Children,* Mrs. Coleman has recorded her educational principles, chief among which are the following:

1. To keep the child's natural enthusiasm for music, *simplification* is necessary. A child's musical experience should be adapted to the child's development—i.e., his muscles, his vocabulary, understanding, etc. Music should be made so simple "that every child may be able to play."

2. There should be a succession of easy stages of musical development. This is to assure continuous growth. Music's whole history should be put within the reach of the child. It should be made practicable enough for him to live through it. There should be a carefully graded sequence of instruments—from rattles for the tiny tots in the kindergarten to stringed and wind instruments for the youngsters in the upper elementary school.

3. Musical experiences should be broad in variety. There should be one unified course of rhythmic activities, rich in content and wide in range. This should include singing, dancing, dramatics, rhythmics, making and playing on instruments, and so on.

4. Stress should be laid on creative activity and constructive doing.

5. Musical experiences should be integrated with other life experiences. Creative music should connect and relate the child's activities and rhythmic experiences.

In her studio and workshop Mrs. Coleman taught children of all ages. Here they danced and sang, making their own instruments and creating their own tunes. Beginning with simple instruments within the sphere of their abilities, they proceeded gradually to marimbas and flutes, trumpets and harps, and so on. Their musical experience grew steadily, and with it came understanding and self-expression.

Though Mrs. Coleman is somewhat of an innovator, her influence is marked, and the number of musical experimentalists in Progressive schools has grown steadily. Working closely with children, these teachers are interested first and foremost in the child's growth rather than in music as an art. Music, they feel, is for all, and not for the talented few.

10. Education and the social crisis

Progressive education in its early years focused its attention on the child: freedom for the child, respect for his interests, stimulus to his initiative, and a high esteem for his natural development were the dominant and recurrent notes in the progressive theme—a theme which was reechoed by the Progressive Education Association with its seven principles, not one of which, however, struck more than a very gentle note for society. In the movement's second decade, however, there was a palpable change in the Progressive's familiar refrain. The lean and tragic years of the Depression spurred a national interest in social and economic reconstruction, with the result that plans to regulate the American system poured down like a tropical cloudburst. Most of them were impracticable, or even foolish, but a few were scientific and seemingly practical.

Some found their way eventually into the governmental machinery from which they came forth in time as the New Deal.

That the new spirit should be reflected in the advanced thinking of American educators was only natural. One of the first to demand a stronger social role for the school was Kilpatrick. Declaring in 1932 that it was the school's function to apply the torch of criticism to existing and proposed institutions, Kilpatrick insisted that it was the school's task to help youth to think its way through to a defensible social program.[11] "All situations," said Kilpatrick, "must be open for study and criticism, all proposals for social improvement must be open for study in the light of democratic ideals." A few years later he added:

Recognizing grave evils in our industrial life, I favored for many years a great extension of "industrial democracy" into our economic regime but conceived this as continuing substantially within the framework of a *laissez-faire* competition for profits, only greatly reformed. Of late years, I have come to believe that no mere reformation of this framework will suffice. A fundamental remaking of our economic system seems necessary so that men shall no longer be compelled to work against each other but may rather be permitted and encouraged—and if a recalcitrant minority requires it, be compelled—to cooperate for the common good.[12]

Another schoolman to train his critical artillery on child-centered Progressive education was George S. Counts. A member, like Kilpatrick, of the Progressive Education Association, and an active and energetic advocate of a planned society for America, Counts publicly censured Progressive education for its apparent lack in social policy. Though he accepted most of its pedagogic tenets and lauded its past accomplishments, Counts felt that Progressive education had brought "into the picture only one-half of the educational landscape." Like American education in general, "it has elaborated no theory of social welfare, unless it be that of anarchy

---

[11] Kilpatrick, W. H., *Education and the Social Crisis.* New York: Liveright Publishing Corporation, 1932.

[12] Kilpatrick, W. H., "The Essentials of the Activity Movement," Vol. XI, p. 346. *Progressive Education,* October, 1934.

or extreme individualism." [13]   For the benefit of those Progressives who had anchored themselves in the position that indoctrination in the school was undesirable, Counts pointed out that

all education contains a large element of imposition, that in the very nature of the case this is inevitable, that the existence and evolution of society depend upon it, that it is consequently eminently desirable, and that the frank acceptance of this fact by the educators is a major professional obligation.[14]

As might be expected, Counts' unpadded declaration drew a number of counterblasts. One of his more conservative colleagues at Teachers College, Professor I. L. Kandel, poured ridicule on the whole business. For a score of years, he pointed out, the leaders of Progressive education had "been vociferous advocates of individualism, the new freedom, the child-centered school and the sanctity of the child's ego—in a word of *laissez-faire* in education," but now they were calling for "social reconstruction through the school with an emphasis on planning, cooperation and collective will." [15]

However, even before Kandel's broadside the Progressive Education Association had taken the bull by the horns by appointing a Committee on Social-Economic Problems, headed by Counts, to study the whole question. In *Call to the Teachers of the Nation* the Committee urged them to "recognize the corporate and the interdependent character of the contemporary order, and transfer the democratic tradition from individualistic to collectivist economic foundations." [16]

But the Committee soon encountered strong headwinds. Assailed by a substantial number of fellow Progressives and by laymen who saw no good in its collectivist economic founda-

---

[13] Counts, G. S., *Dare the School Build a New Social Order?* p. 6. New York: John Day Co., Inc., 1932.

[14] *Ibid.*

[15] Kandel, I. L., "Education and Social Disorder," *Teachers College Record,* February, 1933.

[16] John Day Pamphlets, No. 30, p. 21. New York: John Day Co., Inc., 1933.

tions, the Committee made no great gains for its program. Indeed, throughout the panicky thirties most Progressive schools continued to render obeisance to the child, and particularly to the little child in the grades.

As for the Progressive Education Association itself, during the thirties its interests and activities gradually assumed new expression. Although most of its members continued to devote themselves to the young child, the eyes of the Association had become sharpened to some of the newer developments in education. In 1936, for example, it established its first summer workshop at Ohio State University. To it came schoolmen and women from all over the country, with definite problems growing out of their experience, which, with the help of experts in the field and some intensive study, they hoped to clarify and perhaps solve. The enterprise proved so successful that in the next few years the number of workshops swiftly multiplied.

Somewhat more elaborate was the Association's research program which it carried on through a number of special committees and commissions, such as the Committee on Progressive Education in Rural Schools, the Committee on Community School Relations, the Committee on International Relations, and several others. Its Commission on Educational Freedom, created in 1935, was established "to give active and vigorous support to the protection of the educational freedom of teachers and students." Its Commission on Intercultural Education was formed in 1936 to study the "tensions and misunderstandings existing, and in some instances increasing, among the various cultural groups that are parts of American communities." There were, in addition, three other commissions, all concerned primarily with some phase of secondary education, as for example, the relation of school and college, the secondary school curriculum, and the nature and needs of American youth.

The Association kept on saluting the "importance of the individual," but also in 1938 it went on record to point out that "the individual is not visualized as separate from the group." "Man and society," it declared,

are conceived as interrelated. It is this concept which reenforces the belief that the curriculum of the schools should be developed in relationship to the nature of the community, and that education is not preparation for living but life itself. It is this concept which stresses the continuity of education and the belief that education goes on throughout life.[17]

A further departure from its earlier ways appeared in Progressive education's acceptance of the newer organismic psychology. Foreshadowed in Dewey's educational theories and in Kilpatrick's views of the educative process, as well as in some of the researches of the psychoanalysts and psychiatrists, the newer psychology upholds such basic and familiar principles as that: learning must be based on experience; it requires response to situations; it is a process of growth; it involves emotional concomitants; there are important by-products of learning which must be anticipated and considered; learning necessitates organization or integration; the personality acts as a whole. When this psychology is coupled to the notion that a person is by nature a social being, his education becomes a "cultivated response of creative adjustment to social situations." More, however, than mere mechanical adaptation, it calls for the application of intelligence which seeks on the one hand to change the situation itself, and on the other to facilitate the individual's adjustment to it. Or to put it another way, "education is the continuous and steady effort to act intelligently with regard to the immediate situation by bringing to bear upon it the results of past experience."[18]

During the first twenty years of its existence the Progressive Education Association had abstained from formulating any definite statement of its philosophy beyond its original seven principles. In the maelstrom of the changing thirties, with

---

[17] Progressive Education Association, *Progressive Education Advances,* p. 11. New York: Appleton-Century-Crofts, Inc., 1938.
[18] *Ibid.*

their clashing social and economic views, the original septette seemed to many of PEA's members quite inadequate. Finally, in 1938, the Association took cognizance of the situation by appointing a committee to draw up a statement of its philosophy. In its report, which it made three years later, the committee affirmed most of PEA's basic tenets. "Growth," it asserted, "is the richest reward for the individual when, in concert with all others, he brings intelligence and good-will to the shared task of creating the values for which his culture is to strive." [19] The transitional and confused nature of our culture was recognized. Our schools were urged to explore new ideas and to discuss controversial issues freely. Headlined were a "belief in the common man as a person of worth," "cooperative enterprise," and the "free use and extension of intelligence."

In an analysis of what this implied the committee named these essentials: (1) the ability and willingness to think reflectively in meeting the problems of living; (2) the desire and ability to cooperate in solving common problems; (3) the cultivation of the attitude of social sensibility. Finally, the committee emphatically refused to ally itself with "those who would begin with a social blueprint of the new society"; it preferred to dedicate itself, somewhat vaguely, alas, "to the ideal of the free play of intelligence in solving problems of human concern."

The social and economic stirrings following Wall Street's collapse found new expression in 1935 in the creation of the John Dewey Society for the Study of Education and Culture. An outgrowth of a small body of Teachers College professors who had been meeting more or less regularly for a number of years as a discussion group, the new society drew its membership from the nation's pioneer thinkers on social and economic questions. It believed that "education has an important, even strategic, role to play in the reconstruction of American so-

---

[19] *Progressive Education, Its Philosophy and Challenge*, reprinted from *Progressive Education*, p. 5, May, 1941.

ciety." Its views on various social questions found their way
into a series of important yearbooks.[20] Perhaps even more
important was its magazine, *The Social Frontier*. Founded in
1934, under the chairmanship of Kilpatrick and the editorship
of Counts, the periodical marked something new in the way of
American journalism. Instead of concerning itself with the
usual pedagogical minutiae, *The Social Frontier* assumed that

the age of individualism in economy is closing and that an age marked by
close integration of social life and by collective planning and control is
opened. For weal or woe it accepts as irrevocable this deliverance of the
historical process. It intends to go forward to meet the new age and to
proceed as rationally as possible to the realization of all possibilities for the
enrichment and refinement of human life,

which was a large order. In the first issue John Dewey led off
with "Can Education Share in Social Reconstruction?" to
which he naturally replied with a resounding "Yes." Other
articles dealt with such items as "Youth in a Confused
World," "Youth versus Capitalism," "Education *Is* the Social
Frontier," "Educational Ideals and the Profit Motive," " College Students React to Social Issues," "W. R. Hearst—Epit-
ome of Capitalist Civilization," "Our Revolutionary
Tradition," and so on. The circulation of the new periodical
rose rapidly though its till was generally empty. In 1939 the
Board of Directors of the Progressive Education Association
agreed to adopt the journal as the Association's social organ.
Significantly, however, it was rechristened, and now became
the *Frontiers of Democracy* with a new board of editors.
Professor Kilpatrick, however, continued to act as Chairman
of the Board. Considerably toned down, the magazine continued to appear until the end of 1943.

[20] The First Yearbook appeared in 1937 as *The Teacher and Society*. Subsequent titles included: *Educational Freedom and Democracy* (1938); *Democracy and the Curriculum* (1939); *Teachers for Democracy* (1940); *Workers'
Education in the United States* (1941); *Mobilizing Educational Resources
for Winning the War and Peace* (1943); *The Public Schools and Spiritual
Values* (1944); *The American High School* (1946); *Intercultural Attitudes in
the Making* (1947).

Actually its career had been meteoric. During the ten years of its existence it had played a formidable role in the effort to crack the schoolman's hitherto impenetrable social and economic complacency. Unfortunately its high voltage gave sleepless nights not only to implacable tories like Hearst and McCormick, and the usual defenders of the American System, like the Daughters of the American Revolution, the National Association of Manufacturers, and the American Legion, but it also scared a good many moderates. Its net effect on American education was therefore relatively slight.[21]

Although Counts and his sympathizers failed to make any appreciable dent in the American school, some of his collaborators, working through other channels, were somewhat more successful. Many of them were concerned by what they felt was an appalling inadequacy of the social studies. Though leading thinkers had been developing new approaches to the social sciences even before the first World War, America's schools in the twenties were for the most part unwilling to desert the familiar rut of academic tradition. Geography, history, civics, and, sometimes, economics were taught as separate subjects and were supposed to stay apart. They were, moreover, to concern themselves mainly with the facts of the dead past. Did they beckon to the present at all? Then it was in the spirit of reverence, with awesome hosannas to progress and faith in the grandeur of the *status quo*. Inflammable themes which brought sweat and wrinkles to the adult brow, which dealt with the realities of property, employment, labor, monopoly, socialism, strikes, and the cost of living, were kept out of the classroom as ruthlessly as discussions of glands and hormones. By the early twenties several groups of educators had begun to fix their searchlights on these

---

[21] The John Dewey Society is still operating. At the present moment it is seeking to "encourage, . . . initiate and support basic studies in the field of educational theory. . . ." It wants to "follow a positive line of action in its support of democracy by pointing out desirable values, forms and processes, and by encouraging constructive forces and agencies now operating in this field."

matters. The National Society for the Study of Education led off with a series of yearbooks wherein it offered valuable data on the facts and skills used by the average American in his daily life. If these did nothing else, they at least served the useful end of awakening the public school people to the need of studying the social usefulness of school materials. (See p. 439.) In 1923 the Society devoted its Twenty-second Yearbook to *The Social Studies.* With its underlying theme, "Problems of American Life as the Basis of the Curriculum," it hoped to bring the matter of reforming the social curriculum to the attention of educators. Four years later, in 1927, the Society brought forth its hefty two-volume *Foundations of Curriculum Making,* which was the first national report to grapple with the problems of curricular reconstruction in the light of the major cultural trends and problems.

To a small band of educators, however, it had become plain that reform in the social studies required direct and concentrated action. Consequently, led by Harold Rugg, his brother Earle, J. Montgomery Gambrill of Teachers College, and Edgar Dawson of Hunter College, in 1922 they founded the National Council for Social Studies. Out of its activities came the Social Science Pamphlets which, after considerable experimentation and much revising, comprised reading books, workbooks, and teachers' guides.[22] Their purpose was "to understand modern life and how it came to be." "To understand any institution or condition of life today," declared Rugg, "the mind must utilize facts, meanings, generalizations and historical movements that in the past have been set up in separate subjects."

For example, to understand the westward movement of the American

---

[22] In the evolution of the Rugg Social Science Course materials were used more or less experimentally in nearly all the states and in hundreds of schools. More than 50,000 tests were taken by pupils, in small towns, in medium-sized cities, in large cities. And the judgments of more than 1,000 teachers were obtained regarding needed revisions. The course itself, moreover, was based upon an elaborate research program. See Rugg, H., *Changing Governments and Changing Cultures,* p. x. Boston: Ginn & Company, 1932.

people one must see in close relationship the tide of immigration across the continent; the blazing of trails; the evolution of new land and waterways; the rapid development of new types of transportation; constantly changing forms of social life; the rise of cities behind the advancing frontier; the influence of mountains, deserts, climate, rivers and soil upon travel, transportation and communication; and where and how people live. All these factors must be tied closely together in their natural relationships. Hence the necessity of combining them into one general course instead of teaching them as separate subjects.[23]

The Rugg books were well written and effectively organized. Their influence was nation-wide. Thousands of teachers used them and millions of children read them. The attempt to integrate in one course what had hitherto been taught diffusely and reservedly in separate subjects has found swarms of imitators and seems likely to become a permanent practice. The inclusion in Rugg's books, however, of controversial issues brought down the usual howling and havoc. Lady patriots from the Daughters of the American Revolution and the Daughters of Colonial Wars, and high-pressured idealists from Kiwanis, the Advertising Federation of America, the American Legion, the National Association of Manufacturers, and dozens of others publicly denounced the books and yelled for their suppression. For a score of years the hurricane raged, and though, here and there, a frightened school board would ban them, elsewhere they would be saluted with cheers and high praise. As usual in matters pertaining to the forbidden, the detractors of Rugg and his books were their best advertisers, with the result that readers, who otherwise would never have peered into the books, flocked to them.[24]

As for the Progressive Education Association, although it accepted the principle that the school should play an active

---

[23] *Ibid.*, p. vii.

[24] Among other things Rugg was charged with being against religion, anticapitalist, opposed to the Constitution, and teaching "that our economic and political institutions are decadent." Harold McKinnon, of San Francisco, accused him of sowing the "seeds of class warfare" and of fulfilling "an earnest recommendation of Karl Marx." One of the Daughters of Colonial Wars declared that Rugg's books "tried to give the child an unbiased viewpoint instead of teaching him real Americanism."

part in the reconstruction of American society, its practical efforts were reserved and lukewarm. In the fall of 1943 the directors of the Association voted to discontinue publication of the *Frontiers of Democracy*. In 1944 the Association changed its historic name and became the American Education Fellowship.[25] At the same time it endorsed the following platform for the improvement of American education:

1. To give equal educational opportunity to every child, regardless of race, creed, or economic background.
2. To give "higher education"—college, professional, or technical training—to every student capable of absorbing or using it.
3. To make American schools so vital a part of our national life that they will attract and hold as teachers the most stimulating men and women of our time.
4. To establish a youth program for young people between 17 and 23 to carry them over from school to active participation in the adult community.
5. To make full use of school equipment in out-of-school time for youth meetings, community activities, adult education.
6. To cooperate fully with all community agencies and social agencies working toward a truly democratic society, but at the same time to keep education free from domination by any special group or interests.
7. To continue to expand educational research and experimentation.
8. To win community leaders toward making education a part of the community and the community a part of the school.

With the end of the war and its attendant unrest and disillusionment, the Fellowship harnessed itself to the task of reconstruction. "Inasmuch," its spokesmen declared, "as the forces that shape society are those that determine education as well, educators must understand what is taking place in the community, and must take stands as adult citizens on controversial issues of the day. It is their right and duty to

---

[25] Students of comparative education recognized in the new name at least an echo of the New Education Fellowship. Founded in 1921, with Beatrice Ensor of England as its first president, the NEF had operated internationally for the furtherance of progressive education in every part of the world. PEA had cooperated with the older organization, and many of PEA's members had participated in its conferences at which some of the world's most eminent men and women were present.

participate in active political life." First claims on the organization's active support were:

1. The reconstruction of the economic system in the direction of greater
social justice and stability; a system to be secured by whatever democratic
planning and social controls experience shows to be necessary; a system in
which social security and a guaranteed annual wage sufficient to meet
scientific standards of nourishment, shelter, clothing, health, recreation, and
education are universalized; a system in which the will of the majority
with due regard for the interests of all the people is the sovereign determinant of every basic economic policy.
2. The establishment of a genuine world order, an order in which
national sovereignty is subordinate to world authority in crucial interests
affecting peace and security; an order, therefore, in which all weapons of
war and police forces are finally under that authority; an order in which
international economic coordination of trade, resources, labor, distribution,
and standards is practiced parallel with the best standards of individual
nations; an order which must be geared with the increasing socializations
and public controls now developing in England, Sweden, New Zealand, and
certain other countries; an order in which all nations, races, and religions
receive equal rights; an order in which "world citizenship" thus assumes at
least equal status with national citizenship.

In putting these principles into practice there was, however,
to be "no attempt to indoctrinate for any political party or for
any given economic system." Instead the school was to be "a
center of experimentation in attaining communities of uncoerced persuasion."

11.   The community school

It was only natural that some of the social theories which
poured over American education in the thirties should, in time,
have produced something of promise. Such, indeed, were the
community schools which appeared in various parts of the
nation. Stressing society rather than the individual, they
have become known as "society-centered schools." Their
creators' proposal was essentially simple. "Let us use the
school," they suggested, "to improve the community life."
"We want," they continued, "to deal with the real and practical problems found in our community—every-day problems
of everybody." They beheld the community, not as something

divorced from the school, but as an actual part of it. The community, they explained, was like a laboratory, full of problems "which will serve as an immediate and practical program for every school system." On the other hand, the school's purpose was to help young people to grow by offering them real help in meeting the larger and inevitable problems arising beyond the fringes of the community—problems affecting the nation and even the world.[26]

Most community schools thus far have been of the public variety. They have been established in such diverse places as an overcrowded immigrant quarter in New York, on the slopes of Cumberland Mountain in Tennessee, in rural Michigan and Louisiana, and in Waialua, Hawaii. Despite the wide and glaring cultural differences of their people, these schools have been wrestling with the same general basic problem—the development of community living. For it makes little difference to the multitudes whether they happen to find themselves in a drab and struggling hamlet in Arizona or Oregon or in the thickly crowded schools of some big city's Little Italy or Little Poland, their needs and problems in the end are pretty much alike. The difficulties which beset them are as elemental and overmastering as the Sphinx's riddle. What they need to know is how to earn a living; how to stay healthy; how to read with understanding; how to get along with others; and how to put some fun into their lives.

It is on such realities that the community school has sought to throw light. To do it, it has had to transform the school from a place which catered to the very few to one which operates for all. Such education projects beyond the schoolroom into the community at large; it works on the grand scale as a process of which the adult is as much a part as the child. It deals with such involved and subtle complexities as matrimony, child care, personal hygiene, morals, and God, just as much as with the first ventures into written English, numera-

---

[26] See Everett, S., *The Community School*, p. 430. New York: D. Appleton-Century Company, 1938.

tors and denominators, and the oath of allegiance. In a word,
it is the community elements which comprise the school curriculum. In a community school among the Indians one finds,
for example, that

> children participated in many community activities with adults and carried
> on some community activities separately. They learned certain literate
> and other skills as a part of these and other activities. While the mothers
> and fathers were building the community oven, the children came along
> with them. The handy man and housekeeper went ahead with the oven,
> and for some of the time the children helped. They were there to see the
> frame of the oven set up. They patted some of the mud in place when
> the structure was being finished. They helped make the fire for the first
> baking. They saw the bread made, and made a few small loaves of their
> own to go in the first baking. . . .[27]

In New York's Benjamin Franklin High School the link
between school and community was forged through such committees as Parents' Association, Adult Education, Juvenile
Aid, Youth Guidance, the Old Friendship Committee, Housing,
Community Health, Citizenship, and the like. Moreover,
through a Service Bureau for Education in Human Relations,
the school undertook a study of racial problems, not as they
were presented in the learned books, but as they existed in all
their reality in the community itself. Through its study the
school hoped to nail down intolerance and to enhance fairness
and understanding among the people of the community.

The town of Monteagle, Tennessee, is a place where the
memory of feuds still lingers, where only a short time ago
"there was little unity and practically no native leadership."
Suspicion, jealousy, individualism were omnipresent and, like
the witches of *Macbeth,* they boded no good. To make matters worse, "old customs and new experiences were in conflict"
with a people "living in a rural area whose experiences had
been primarily those of industrial wage earners," but whose
labor couldn't be absorbed and for whom farming had become
unprofitable.

---

[27] *Ibid.,* p. 244.

To attack these problems the Highlander Folk School was established. The assumption on which it rested was that the town's changing economy could become the basis for a genuine democracy, and that the people could attain and protect their fullest rights "only through their economic and political organizations."

Slowly these principles were put to work. A farmer's wife, harried and puzzled by the antics of her unruly child, discussed the problem with her neighbor. The discussion expanded and in time involved other parents, some students, and a teacher. Out of this circle, at the request of neighbors and students, came a class in psychology for adults. In a similar way a class in cultural geography was born when people around an open fire began to talk about some snapshots taken in Europe. In the years of the Depression what could be more natural than questions about economics? And in a year of a presidential election who in America wouldn't want to talk about the men and the issues involved? In the same way, out of the needs and interests of the people themselves came classes in music, art, and dramatics. Within a year a community program had emerged and, as it took shape, it comprised not only classes for children and adults, but also the Cumberland Mountain Workers' League, with a program of forest conservation and a plan "to better the condition of the community by raising wages." [28] In time other labor organizations came into being, some of which later joined the ranks of the regular labor unions.

Side by side with this natural interest in politics, economics, and the social problems all about them, the people of the Highlander School developed a cultural and artistic program of the first order. Music lessons were provided for as many as a score of youngsters at a time. An energetic librarian gave reading a surprising boost. The recreation ground found children and adults at play, with room enough for baseball and an outdoor

---

[28] Everett, S., *The Community School,* pp. 147, 270–274. New York: D. Appleton-Century Company, Inc., 1938.

stage. There were talks, too, by teachers and others on the
subjects of war, race problems, the Bible, old and modern
Russia, on social progress in Scandinavia, and on the ever-
present questions about life and labor in the South. Once a
week there were informal gatherings for singing and dancing.
The old-fashioned square dance, outlawed as immoral before
the founding of Highlander, was now danced with zest by
young and old. Forgotten ballads and workers' songs were
revived and re-interpreted to suit the modern taste and tempo.
Their lilt and melody has made some of them famous far
beyond the confines of Monteagle; indeed, with the help of the
British Broadcasting Corporation, the Highlander Folk
School sent a program of ballads, workers' songs, and native
folk-dances over the air to England.

In addition, the Highlander Folk School has been experimenting with various phases of labor education. More intensive than the pleasant and easy-going community program,
this has been somewhat more formal. There are discussions
and workshops in such matters as workers' problems, the
history and organization of cooperatives, public speaking, parliamentary law, and labor dramatics. The stress, it should be
plain, is not on the accumulation of facts, but on learning to
work together creatively; and it is in this democratic spirit
that students and teachers together manage the school's life.

Has Highlander worked? There are no statistics to give the
verdict. But there is an eloquent answer, and I dare say a true
one. For it comes from those who really know—the people
themselves. Once torn in discord by their fears and social
tensions, the people of Monteagle think of the school as their
own, so much so that they have been willing to fight for it.
When the operators of a mining company and a hosiery mill
were allegedly plotting to demolish the school, the people
stood anxious guard in its defense. Later they did the same
when the American Legion threatened to "march on the
school." Certainly, no scientific appraisal of the Highlander
Folk School could tell us more.

Some of the finest examples of community education can be found in the most inconspicuous places, little atoms on the globe, like Arthurdale, West Virginia, and Jefferson County, Kentucky. There one finds a fascinating story of cooperation, of social planning of a great communal effort into which was woven the help and contribution of individuals, private agencies, local authorities, and government itself under the guiding genius in each case of Elsie R. Clapp. It is her belief that the community school is everybody's school; that people "make it for their children with your help"; and that "together you make it." [29] Such was the Roger Clark Ballard Memorial School, of Jefferson County, Kentucky, which ran from 1929 to 1934. It was, indeed, everybody's school—a school made and run by farmers, dairymen, shopkeepers, estate owners, truck drivers, business men, doctors, pastors, and lawyers. Teachers slipped out of their traditional robes and became the partners of fathers and mothers. Parents, for their part, pulled up their sleeves to share in the work of the school—running the lunch room, the lending library, and the movies. The Men's Club organized a fire brigade and did so well that in time it was promoted to the dignity of an official fire department. The Women's Club did its feminine part by taking care of school lunches, civic beautification, home adornment, art exhibits, and motion pictures.

As for the school itself, the life of the community became the subject matter of instruction. The school raised animals, from cows and sheep to hens, roosters, and baby chicks. It planted vegetable gardens; it ran the annual Ballard fair, exhibiting and selling crullers, jams, and other tasty morsels made in the school; and, with the cooperation of the school's cows and chickens, it displayed its riches in eggs, milk, cream, and cheese. Did the school need some better and stronger doors with creakless hinges? The older boys made them. Were the stairs decrepit? the plaster cracked and disreputable?

[29] Clapp, E. R., *Community Schools in Action*, p. 70. New York: The Viking Press, Inc., 1939.

the halls in need of paint? These were jobs for the boys who learned as they profited by the experience. Elsie Clapp's school was, in short, a place where "learning and living converged," a real and honest school of living. Its principles, which give it its aim as well as its method, are only five: a deep faith in democracy; a belief that democracy and freedom are challenges to self-realization; an affirmation in the child as a person of unlimited possibilities; a conviction that the best individualization comes only through one's harmonious adjustment to the community life; and a belief that pupils, through their activities, should at all times be lively and happy.

12. Modernizing the public school

On the whole, the advance of the American public school in the twentieth century does not present a picture comparable to that of the more or less independent Progressive school. Democratic living, with its stress on individual development, cooperative planning and working, and real functional activities, though on the increase, is still rare. The concept of education in most of the contemporary American public schools is to a large extent "schooling" in the traditional sense. Most public schools, of course, are subject to much more pressure than are the Progressive schools. The conservative nature and political complexion of public schools, operated under local initiative and control, usually preclude the sweeping innovations that are possible in the independent experimental school. Most reforms in the public school have been slow and piecemeal. And usually they have been the result of a cooperative leadership of farsighted and resourceful school administrators, supervisors, teachers, parents, and children. It is under such leadership that progressive communities have been able to emancipate their public schools from the fetters of tradition. The names of such communities are not too numerous, but they spread throughout the land from Los Angeles, California, to Bronxville, New York, from Winnetka, Illinois, to Raleigh, North Carolina. A study of the nation's foremost elementary schools reveals traces of an evolution in educational practice toward sound child growth and development. Curricular reports and articles in educational periodicals are ample evidence of this trend. Observation discloses that in many American cities education is going through a transition, a process which has been profoundly affected by the political, economic, and social tornadoes of the thirties and forties. As a result, systems are being scrutinized and evaluated. The prevalent social and political patterns of the localities and states are challenging education's purpose, scope, and range of service. As usual, however, the cost of public education is under constant fire, so that many desirable educational reconstructions have been slowed up or even completely stopped. On the other hand, many forward-looking Americans are questioning the cost of America's demoralized and misfit children.

13. Comparison of the traditional and the Progressive school

a. The traditional school. The old school tended to put stress on knowledge. From time immemorial, schools have emphasized the acquisition of facts. Educational reformers occasionally arose to protest, but on the whole, knowledge continued to be one of the school's main goals. At the turn of the century, youngsters in the state of New York were asked by their Regents to give an account of the Jugurthine War; to name the bones of the left upper extremity; to describe earthquakes, the drainage of South Africa, and the bed of the Atlantic Ocean. Schoolmasters, assuming that education is knowledge, concluded, logically enough, that the more you know the better educated you are. Hence their main task was to present to the learner an array of facts and to make sure that these were remembered. Drill, review, and frequent tests were inevitably necessary. Moreover, since the memorizing process happened to be chiefly of a mechanical sort, the knowledge which the pupil finally obtained was usually lacking in

the juices of life. In the end, subject matter assumed the un-
imaginative guise of a well-built outline, a skeleton of labeled
and classified parts. Such knowledge seldom stirred the
pupil's thinking nor did it move his creative impulses.
Because of its stress on facts, the traditional school sometimes
has been described as a *knowledge school.*

Fact accumulation, however, was not the only blemish of
the traditional school. There were, indeed, many other faults:
(1) Since instruction put a premium on knowledge, inadequate
consideration was given to other phases of personality. (2)
The fact that the normal child is an active rather than an
intellectual animal, though acclaimed by many educational
reformers since the days of Rousseau, nonetheless found little
application in practice. The child was expected to be quiet
and receptive rather than active and expressive. (3) Instruction was built mainly around the senses of sight and hearing,
and gave little consideration to the educational value of self-
activity. (4) The teacher, on the other hand, was very active.
He organized and presented his subject. He questioned and
expected answers. He drilled, tested, and gave marks. His
was a question-and-answer regime, and under it class discussions, socialized recitations, projects—all of which demand
greater pupil activity—could not flourish. (5) The teacher's
question was the kernel of the recitation. Questions, suggestions, or criticisms emanating from the learners were not welcome, and sometimes, indeed, were even deemed presumptuous.
(6) The usual relationship between teacher and pupil was
that of ruler and subject. His word was command. The idea
of pupil self-government was, of course, not cherished. (7)
Children were expected to accept authority. This rested either
in the teacher or in the textbook. Individual thought and
judgment on the part of the pupils were not fostered. (8)
The traditional school was not sufficiently socialized. Despite
the dicta of Froebel, Pestalozzi, and others, the school had
not developed into a dynamic society whose members were
conscious of any interrelationships. In the classroom much

was done to crush the communal feeling. Talking, unhampered locomotion, and mutual help on the part of pupils, as found in some modern schools, were forbidden. (9) Inadequate attention was given to individual ability. Performance requirements were standardized to meet the needs of the average. In demanding such a standardized performance from its students, the traditional school failed to take into account individual likes and dislikes. It failed to consider the multifarious experiences reaped by pupils outside of school. And finally, it failed to heed the many special needs of both the gifted and the dull pupil. (10) Education was looked upon mainly as preparation for adult life. To the child this represented something vague and far away. On this basis, education was not sufficiently connected with the child's own experiences.

Despite its numerous faults, the old-time school was not quite so bad as some of its modern adversaries would have us believe. Its virtues, however, are not as numerous as its faults. The former may be summarized thus: (1) One of its most valuable characteristics was its stress on the development of a moral personality in its pupils. Though the methods it used to develop character are today under heavy fire, its aim, nevertheless, was high. (2) Instruction in the traditional school on the whole was thorough—though often tyrannical. The youngsters who snared their diplomas, if they were normal in intellect, were usually proficient. Unfortunately, however, not all youngsters were normal, and hence were never reached by the traditional procedures. (3) The old school sought to develop some valuable attitudes, habits, and ideals—such as effort, industry, tidiness, and punctuality.

b. The twentieth century school. The new school began primarily as a protest against the old school. As such, many of its principles have been shaped by educational reformers rather than by the rank and file of practical schoolmasters. Although it is difficult to put the new education under the glass and analyze it, certain general characteristics still show themselves in virtually all the schools influenced by the movement.

Freedom. The new school favors pupil freedom. It would wipe out all kinds of superimposed and unnecessary restrictions. As a result, the pupils have gained such boons as the right to move about the classroom at will, to form natural groups, to talk, to choose their own subjects, to handle objects, to have a voice in student disciplinary matters, and to take a large and active part, in a general way, in class and school affairs. Behind this emphasis on pupil freedom lies the theory that liberty generates self-discipline and stimulates a sense of responsibility.

Activity. The late W. A. Lay, of Germany, named the new school an activity or doing school (*Tatschule*). The proponents of this school hold that "learning takes place in the response." According to this idea, a teacher at best can only teach, and what learning the child actually achieves is garnered through his own doing. Consequently what is important is not the gathering and storing of facts, but their use and application. As in the old school, pupils in the activity school are seeking knowledge—not as an end in itself, but as a means to something else. They gain their knowledge, moreover, not by passive absorption but by active participation or doing.

Experience the basis of the curriculum. The school curriculum's fundamental basis is centered in experiences which are typical of the community's living. Those activities necessary in meeting the daily needs of a group or several groups are provided, each age group shaping its plans and course to meet the needs and abilities of the children. Each child is expected to deal with vital things in successive and cumulative stages.

Socialization. The new school is looked upon as a living society, wherein typical life situations are reproduced. Thus we find schools with a bank, a post office, a school store, and a school newspaper, besides the usual congeries of clubs and teams. More than ever, classwork has taken on the mien of a cooperative enterprise. Children are allowed to discuss their problems with one another, and even to give and receive help. Student self-government is encouraged. The four walls of the school, moreover, are often disregarded to allow the children to gain social experiences by going to factories, slums, libraries, housing and welfare agencies, recreation centers, shops, and the like. Although the original Progressive schools were largely child-centered, and most of them still are, a few, known as society-centered schools, have tried to fuse the work of school and society.

Creative expression. Harnessing the child's creative urge to education, the new school stresses creative activities. Dramatics, including both the writing and production of plays, story-writing and story-telling, and pupil lectures are featured. Art, music, and dancing also are included—not for training but for self-expression. The same may be said for play, rhythmics, and handiwork. The aim is not to develop artists or dramatists, musicians or craftsmen, but to make education as rich and rounded as possible.

Recognition of the individual. Though the new type of school strives to socialize its pupils, each child is regarded as a unique person requiring special individual consideration. This is perhaps the only system under which freedom, self-activity, and creative work can properly flourish. In the new schools, consequently, there is much individual instruction, individual initiative, and self-education. Courses and methods are elastic, since they must be adjusted to the child's individual needs and abilities. The pedagogic recognition of the learner's individuality stands out sharply in contrast to the more conventional type of mass instruction.

Child study. The new school subscribes to Ellen Key's well-known statement that this is the "century of the child." Education in the new school has been called "child-centered." In essence this means that education should be shaped by the child's nature and needs. This being so, a thorough understanding of the child becomes imperative. It is this need that has stimulated the development of modern scientific child study. This, as is well known, seeks accurate and reliable data about the child's physical, mental, and emotional traits and his behavior. These findings the modern schoolman would harness to education.

All-around growth of the child. The new schools stress the all-around growth of every child. Accepting the principle that children function as organic wholes, they emphasize the importance of a child's growth in social, physical, and emotional power as well as in mental power. Under this scheme the school seeks to improve the whole life of every child as much as possible.

Slower rhythm of growth. The new school is sympathetic to a slower rhythm of growth. It realizes that real meanings do not spring into being over night and that their development is relatively a much more complex matter than the simple acquisition of facts. Learning experiences in the new school, to be worth while, demand considerable planning, experimenting, reflecting, and self-direction, as well as judgment and the assumption of responsibility by the pupils. At the same time, however, the pupils are developing the traits and habits that underlie good citizenship. They are slowly becoming aware of social relationships and gradually beginning to understand what is behind the rules and regulations, plans, and routines that govern a group. All this, of course, requires much more time than the simple routine of the old school.

Elimination of competition. Many, though by no means all, new schools frown upon competitive work. Some have eliminated marks as well as medals and prizes for excellence in school work. The child's progress is judged by the comparison of his own work and achievements. The pride of fine performance is considered reward and stimulus enough; just as disappointment and dissatisfaction follow poor work or the failure to accomplish the task to be done. The youngster who fashions a good play or poem has the reward of being appreciated by his fellows. The same applies to the child who helps and cooperates with his comrades.

Teacher participation. In the new school the teacher goes beyond the classroom. In some of them—usually the private institutions—teachers share in the making of the curriculum, the school's administration, the hiring and firing of the staff. Teachers are expected to function in the community and to contribute to its general education and progress. They are expected to take part in social, economic, and political movements.

Parental cooperation. There was a time when teachers regarded parents as a necessary evil in education. This notion the new school has abandoned. The modern educator seeks the active interest and cooperation of parents in the education of their children. In the new school every week is "Education Week," when the school doors are open to visitors. The new school realizes that home and school share a mutual interest and responsibility in the child's total living, and that without cooperation of home and school there can be no full success in educating the child. The result is that parents and teachers frequently meet in small or large groups to discuss their common problems. In some schools parents assist in the office and classrooms; they participate in trips and many other school and community undertakings.

E. Remaking Education Abroad

The movement to reconstruct educational theory and practice is not confined to America alone. The trend, indeed, has been international, having its advocates and experimenters in every part of the world. Chronologically, the pioneer schools of Dewey and Parker were preceded abroad by several others. In essence, Basedow's well-known *Philanthropinum* at Dessau was an effort to reconstruct education; as were the numerous schools of Basedow's imitators—men like Salzmann, Campe, and others. The efforts of Pestalozzi, Fellenberg, and Froebel were simply great attempts to bring about a better sort of education. Herbart, Ziller, and several of the Herbartians were all laboring to reconstruct educational theory and practice. In England Thomas Wright Hill, of the Hazelwood School, stressed educational practices which were essentially based on a utilitarian philosophy and on activist psychological postulates. What is often called the *first modern Progressive School* was established as far back as 1889 by Cecil Reddie at Derbyshire, England (see p. 135). This is the celebrated Abbotsholme School. It has had a colorful and inspiring history, with many ups and downs. Reorganized some years ago, Abbotsholme once again is actively contributing to the development of modern educational practice. The archetype of the country-home school, Abbotsholme inspired the establishment of similar schools, not only in England but also on the Continent, notable among them being the Country Home Schools of Hermann Lietz and the *École des Roches* of Edmond Demolins and Georges Bertier. (See p. 138.)

As in the United States, Europe's leading Progressives found it desirable to band together, and for this purpose they organized in 1921 the *Ligue internationale pour l'éducation nouvelle* at Calais. The new organization was international, with branches in many countries; in fact, as time went on the membership included not only the European lands, but many in Latin America and Australia. In England the society became the New Education Fellowship. Its first president and one of its most indefatigable contributors was Beatrice Ensor, a school inspectress at London. The new society published a periodical which was issued in various countries and in several languages. In its English version it is known as the *New Era*.[1] A feature of the association's work has been its convention. First held in 1923 in lovely Montreux in Switzerland, these conferences have grown steadily in interest and magnitude, attracting ultimately between 1,500 and 3,000 educators, philosophers, psychologists, and sociologists from as many as

---

[1] The *New Era* is published in London. The French version is known as *Pour l'ère nouvelle.*

half-a-hundred nations from every part of the globe.[2] During the war, as might be expected, the society was obliged to relinquish many of its activities; yet despite many obstacles it was able to keep going. With the end of hostilities in 1945, its work and influence needed more than ever, the Fellowship, which had been reinforced by the active collaboration of the American Progressive Association, resumed its activities on a scale which was reminiscent of its work before the war.

1. Maria Montessori

Maria Montessori's (1870–   ) first claim to academic distinction came at the turn of the century, when she became the first woman to receive the doctorate in medicine from the University of Rome.[3] She began her career in 1898 in Rome as a teacher of mental defectives. Subsequently, she applied her methods to normal children. Demanding complete freedom for the child, Montessori holds that such freedom is essentially biological, its chief requisite during the period of the child's growth being the absence of interference. No one, in the eyes of Montessori, is really free unless he is independent; and he is independent only when he is able to do things for himself without help from anybody else. For Montessori, worth-while education is "auto-education," that is to say, once the child is familiar with the general nature of his task, he is able to proceed by himself. Should he make a mistake, he is bound, in time, to discover and correct it. Should he fail to do this, Montessori believes, it is because he is not yet ready to do the task he chose. To assure her "auto-education," she has developed special materials known as didactic materials. In the Montessori school the child selects the activity that interests him, playing or working at it without interference,

---

[2] Prior to the second World War other conferences were held at Heidelberg (1925), Locarno (1927), Elsinore (1930), Nice (1933), and Cheltenham (1936).

[3] For a comprehensive discussion of Montessori's Method see her *The Montessori Method*. New York: Frederick A. Stokes Company, 1912; also Meyer, A. E., *Modern European Educators*. New York: Prentice-Hall, Inc., 1934.

unless he happens to disturb his companions. Sense and muscle training receive special attention. For Montessori, the goal is that the pupil "refine his senses through exercises of attention, of comparison, of judgment." Her belief that her sense exercises "are true intellectual exercises" has been challenged by those who see in this nothing more than another version of the theory of transfer of training. Through her special methods, Montessori achieved some excellent results, particularly in teaching reading and writing. It is felt, however, that her methods apply only to phonetic languages, such as Italian and German. Montessori herself, however, after considerable study, has decided that for children under six to read and write continually is not natural.

Montessori does not lack critics. In general, it is doubted whether her methods are as suitable to normal children as to the subnormal. Whether her didactic material is as suited to the needs of normal children as to others is also questionable. The most scientific criticism of the Montessori procedure probably was made by the late William Stern, an eminent child psychologist in pre-Nazi Germany. Convinced that Montessori's method was not in accord with the tenets of modern psychology, Stern held that the "emphasis laid upon learning or 'practice' . . . is unsuited to the character of the period. At this time everything the child handles or sees is the object of involuntary learning." Consequently it "is less necessary to make this learning the conscious aim of the whole of education in early childhood."

> It is a mistake not only to prepare the child's occupations in such a way that in each something quite definite must be practised, but even to arrange these occupations in a systematic sequence. That is premature transference of school methods to a period of the child's life which is not ready for the hard and fast system and the consciously fixed aims of school life.[4]

In most European countries the Montessori Method still flourishes. Of course, as a phase of the so-called New Edu-

---

[4] Stern, W., *The Psychology of Early Childhood*, p. 226. Translated from the German by Anne Barwell. New York: Henry Holt & Company, Inc., 1924.

cation, it is relatively old. Indeed, its success did much to stimulate the development of several other aspects of modern education. The Montessori achievement blew the breath of life into the belief that the usual recitation methods tended to be nothing more than a lock-step system, which actually retarded the educational growth of the individual members of a given class. Partly as a result of Montessori's renewed emphasis on individual learning, educators began once more to look for better methods of teaching classes with more consideration for the individual pupil's needs and abilities. The celebrated Dalton Plan and the Winnetka Plan are both pedagogical outcomes of this quest.

2. Jan Ligthart

Known as the Pestalozzi of Holland, Ligthart (1859–1916),[5] worked in a public elementary school in The Hague. Here he labored with new educational ideas and procedures, proving, incidentally, that many phases of Progressive education are workable even under adverse conditions in a public school. Ligthart concentrated on two problems: (1) the bringing about of greater pupil activity and (2) the better selection of subject matter. Like Montessori, he made a great deal of the child's spontaneity. Like Pestalozzi, he tried to make instruction objective. But unlike some teachers, Ligthart realized that, in instruction, words are indispensable.

"How," he once wrote, "can a teacher impart the facts of the past without the use of words? When this man tells his boys about Napoleon's march to Russia, so vividly that the lads participate with all their heart, then he is giving an object lesson, as beautiful as one can imagine." [6]

---

[5] Ligthart's works, unfortunately, are unavailable in English. For his life and work see Gunning, J. W. L. and M., *Jan Ligthart, Sa Vie et son Oeuvre.* Neuchâtel: Delachoix & Niestlé, 1921; also Meyer, A. E., *Modern European Educators.* New York: Prentice-Hall, Inc., 1934. One of Ligthart's books has been turned into German under the title *Pädagogik des vollen Lebens.* Translated by Hess, W. Weimar, 1931.

[6] From *Verspreide Opstellen,* p. 83. Groningen: Wolters, 1930.

Ligthart tried to make his pupils understand their environs, to show them the parts played by work, industry, gardening, and farming. During the first year, the child raised animals and studied plants. The next year he studied farming, including the raising of grain and potatoes, and food problems. In the third year, vegetables were studied; the following year came textiles and foodstuffs; and in the fifth year, starches were added to the list of studies. During these years, the school garden was the scene of much activity. In addition, the children worked as potters, carpenters, and glass blowers. Whatever man did and thought became—as far as the child's ability allowed it—a fitting subject for the school. It was in a very real sense a "doing" school.

For Ligthart school and life were, like the sun and the sky, one and inseparable. The world, he insisted, should be brought into the schoolroom. Nature, work, and man were the foundations of his method. Each of the six lower grades was to concentrate on a center of learning, these centers being: (1) the school neighborhood and the life of the peasant children; (2) food and shelter—sources of supply and the processes of preparation; (3) building materials and simple geology—maps and diagrams of the school garden, of Holland, and the world; (4) local vegetation, soils, and industries, and trade relations with the outside world; (5) geography, history, and natural science; (6) elementary biology, physics, and chemistry.

Like most Progressives Ligthart made pupil freedom the keystone of his method. Freedom he regarded as a privilege, through which the child learned the meaning of responsibilities. In a school, according to Ligthart, there may be two sorts of freedom. One may say: "You may do whatever I permit," or, "You may do everything—except what I am forced to forbid." More or less the traditional policy, the former assumes that we can make children do whatever we command. Ligthart did not believe in unadulterated freedom. The child's freedom, he averred, depended on two things, his own interest and that of the group. "It is necessary for us to show by our example that duty is not necessarily a disagreeable thing, for every obligation or restriction of liberty has its attractive side, which is the pleasure of work and the satisfaction of achievement."

The other extreme, namely, the imposition of unnecessary regulations on the child's freedom to force him into the paths prescribed by his elders, Ligthart felt to be unfair. "The health of the child's mind and the health of his body are at stake, for these can flourish only in an atmosphere of reasonable liberty."

A practical teacher, Ligthart stressed kindness in his treatment of children. For this Ligthart has been criticized; nonetheless, a fair part of his success with children had its roots in his ability to understand them. His pedagogy may have been "soft," particularly in the early twentieth century, yet Ligthart employed it most successfully.

3. Ovide Decroly

Belgium's outstanding twentieth-century educator, Decroly (1871–1932), like Montessori, began his professional work as a physician.[7] Again like Montessori, Decroly made his debut in education by establishing a school for mental defectives. In 1907 he established what was to become an internationally known school, the *École de l'Ermitage*. This, like so many other pioneering schools, was rich in ideals but poor in cash. The lack of money, however, was transformed into an asset, for the school was forced thereby to depend on the initiative, ideals, and ingenuity of its supporters. Launched with only a handful of pupils, the school grew steadily, and at the time of Decroly's death in 1932, approximately two hundred and fifty children were in attendance.

---

[7] For a comprehensive treatment of Decroly's work see Hamaïde, A., *The Decroly Class*. New York: E. P. Dutton & Co., Inc., 1924. For a contemporary summary of Decroly's work and influence see the *Congrès Decroly*, a report of meetings held in Brussels, in September, 1945, and published under the imprint of the *Université Libre de Bruxelles*.

Decroly never considered himself an innovator in education; yet, though his ideas were not original, he usually endeavored to test them in the laboratory of actual experience. His celebrated phrase, *l'éducation pour la vie par la vie*—"education for life by living"—summarizes his educational viewpoint.

Characterizing most of his educational principles as biosocial and biophysical, Decroly believed:

1. The child is a living organism which must be prepared for social living. Education should give him such preparation as will result in his happiness.

2. The child is a living, growing whole. Every moment marks growth. At every age the child is different.

3. Children of the same age differ from one another.

4. Certain interests are peculiar to each age, and these govern the child's mental activities.

5. The child's most potent activity is motor. If it has been properly encouraged, and if it has been controlled by the intellect, such motor activity is necessarily associated with all other activities.

These five principles form the keystone of what Decroly deemed a good school, with the following characteristics:

It is set in a natural environment—close to nature. Here the child lives in the midst of what he is studying.

The school is not too large. It should be coeducational and should include children between the ages of four and nineteen. In the larger schools, coeducation should be continued till the ages of ten or twelve. (In most of Europe coeducation is still a controversial matter.)

The rooms should be studios or laboratories. Here activity rules; and to stimulate it, the room is equipped with tables, workbenches, running water, artificial heat and lighting, shelves and counters for exhibits and collections, and so on.

The faculty should be composed of educators rather than teachers. Active, intelligent, possessed of creative imagination and ability, they should love children. They must be willing and eager to understand their pupils.

Groups should be as nearly alike as possible.

The morning hours should be used for number work, reading and writing, and spelling. Such exercises should be started through play or games. What is left of the morning is given over to various exercises: lessons of observation, comparison, and association; drawing, singing, and physical games.

The afternoons are to be used for manual work and foreign languages.

For some mornings special excursions should be planned. Hikes and visits are desirable. The children may go fishing; hunt bugs and insects for collections; inspect factories and museums.

The parent must be taken into the school's confidence. He should be acquainted not only with the problems involved in the education of his child, but also with the aims and hopes, the methods and procedures, of the school as a whole.

Informality should grace the school. The system should be understandable to the child mind. Only in this way can the child be expected to learn self-control and self-discipline.

To develop initiative and self-confidence, the children give lectures to their fellows. With the teacher's approval, the topics are selected by the children themselves. Usually the subject is related to the lessons of observation and association.

Individual and collective work is stressed, the latter being the way to cooperation.

The basis of Decroly's method is his "center of interest." Somewhat similar to the project procedure, this tries to break down the traditional recitation based on subject-matter. What Decroly was seeking was something that would be more in accord with the child's interest. Based on the psychology of childhood, each center of interest tries to awaken the child's interest by relating his learning to his needs. These Decroly has classified into four types: (1) the need for food; (2) the combat with the elements, such as heat and cold, and their influence on our ways of living; (3) the need of protection against our foes; (4) the need to work and to act. Each of these needs forms a center of interest for a year's work, the complete cycle being traced in four years. Like the project, the center of interest deals with a large problem from which come learnings and skills in arithmetic, language, history, geography, and so on.

By running his school with as few servants as possible, Decroly was able to give his pupils many opportunities in practical work. There was a Tidy-Up Club to keep the school clean; an entertainment officer to organize school meetings and parties. Many children worked in the garden. Every morning the youngest children set the table. Several groups cared for the school's pets and sold their young. Some of the older children tended the fowls, and bought and sold eggs and grain. Even the meals served in the school were prepared by the children. A group of the older pupils was responsible for the school's general organization.

One of Decroly's more lustrous achievements was his ability to enlist the active interest and cooperation of the parents. In 1926, a parents' association was formed to support Decroly in his work and to aid in establishing schools conducted according to his method in other parts of the country.

4. Roger Cousinet

Among those who have labored to reconstruct modern educational theory in France, the name of Roger Cousinet commands attention.[8] With Madame Gueritte, he organized an educational society, *La Nouvelle Éducation,* in January, 1921, an organization devoted to the furtherance of Progressive education throughout France.

Stated tersely, Cousinet's aim has been to find out whether children, when put in conditions similar to those under which they play by themselves, will be better able to work by themselves. Cousinet first tried out this idea in a single grade under one teacher in a girl's primary school at Arcis-sur-Aube. Interestingly enough, in this one class official regulations were practically suspended, while in the other classes they were relentlessly enforced. Twenty girls, aged ten and eleven, formed the group. Practically nothing was set in advance— no schedule, no course of study, no minimum standards. The room in which these girls worked was informally arranged, with benches around four or five tables. The children worked in groups according to their interests. Some might be writing poetry; others might be planning a play. Here and there an individual might be deep in a book; elsewhere, some girls tended the group's plants. And, of course, some might be

---

[8] See Cousinet, R., *La Méthode de travail libre par groupes.* Sedan, 1922; also Cousinet, R., "Experiments in French Primary Schools," Bulletin No. 12. Washington: Progressive Education Association, 1922.

doing nothing at all. At first glance, it might appear as if the teacher had nothing to do. Actually, the contrary was the fact. The teacher, indeed, was constantly responding to calls for help and advice.

There is no actual teaching; the students are merely set to work. The master does not teach; he helps the workers. The children observe, search, find, design, describe, classify, and by degrees explore the universe, not with the intention of knowing it, but for the joy of exercising their minds and learning to work. *They do not memorize or recite—they act.* They function just as they did before entering school, when they were investigating the world by themselves, gathering facts, comparing and classifying them, until they discovered a few general laws—very imperfect, it is true, but sufficient to guide their future activity and supply a basis for future experiments. They were learning by doing.

And again:

My method has the advantage of avoiding the continual repetitions which render scientific work so tedious for children—not to say for their teachers. What has been done in one year is not begun again the next. The repertoire is constantly enriched with new observations, and if one again takes up the index sheet, it is that he may supply notes that may be lacking, or to improve the classification by basing it upon more vital characteristics. The work is continuous, infinitely varied, and always interesting. It is like a game, always the same, yet always different. The role played by the master grows ever less, collective work insuring more and more mutual corrections and uninterrupted progress.[9]

Cousinet's group work is not altogether planless. At the beginning of the school year, the teacher tries to stimulate the pupils to bring materials to class and to make observations. They bring many things to class, including even animals, dead or alive. What impressions they gather from these materials they express in words and drawings. As the impressions increase in number, they are classified. Finally, the pupils synthesize their information by making charts and recording their main observations and illustrations. Through collective study, corrections are made by the pupils, cooperation and group authority fixing the standards of achievement.

---

[9] Cousinet, R., "Experiments in French Primary Schools," Bulletin No. 12. Washington: Progressive Education Association, 1922, p. 7.

Cousinet's group work is based on the theory that children can work together harmoniously and that they like to do so. Between the ages of nine and twelve, Cousinet feels, children naturally form into groups for play. Allowed to choose their activities just as they choose their games they are fairly independent, working as long as they care to, and stopping at will. As Cousinet has explained, the activities engaged in by his pupils are many. They include:

> manual work (drawing, painting, sewing, acting, gardening), concrete creative activity—literary work (writing and reading original stories, poems, plays), abstract creative activity—scientific work (observation, description and classification of plants and animals), work in history—observation, description and classification of documents relative to the history of civilization, work in arithmetic (solution of problems arising out of the other activities and invention of original problems).[10]

That Cousinet has been able to carry on his experimental work in France, which is notably conservative in education, is quite remarkable. Even more remarkable, perhaps, is the fact that despite all sorts of difficulties, particularly those emanating from the red tape of bureaucracy, Cousinet has been able to produce some tangible results. For one thing, the comradeship among the children appears to have been put on a genuine foundation. In general, the social tendencies of the girls have received an impetus, as is revealed both in their work and in their play. With Cousinet's group work, the division of labor begins early. Still another outcome of Cousinet's procedure concerns leadership, undesirable authority, based on mere physical superiority, having been minimized. Actually, free group work has allowed the child's personality to assert itself. The shyest youngster finds a willing audience in a group having a common problem. It should be noted that, though Cousinet has proceeded on the basis of a progressive sort of education, his pupils have had to face the same

---

[10] Boyd, W., Editor, *Towards a New Education*, pp. 163 f. New York: Alfred A. Knopf, Inc., 1930.

state examinations taken by those children who follow the conventional procedures.

5. Berthold Otto

Among the pre-Nazi German school reformers, Berthold Otto (1859–1933) must be classed with the more radical.[11] Reacting against the intellectualism of German education, Otto established a school near Berlin in 1906. Like many other educators, Otto felt that the essence of a good education lay in the development of personality; but for him this should stress individuality. Basically, he rejected what he called the "coercion and standardization of the old school." Like Marietta Johnson, of Fairhope, Alabama, Otto believed in education as "organic growth," which was to include the child's spirit and mind as well as his body. (See p. 68.) Instruction, he believed, should start with the child—it should be, as he frequently said, *vom Kinde aus*, that is to say, "child-centered."

Otto felt that the model for a school to follow was that of a happy home. He thought that the relationship between pupil and teacher should be patterned on that of parent and child. By nature, he held, children seek to adjust themselves to their world; their natural inquisitiveness leads them to explore their environs, and only when they reach snags do they turn to adults for help. This situation Otto wanted to reproduce in the school. What he disliked about the conventional school was the way it stifled the child's curiosity. Instead of harnessing the child's questioning attitude to his work, the traditional school fed him intellectual stuff for which he often had no appetite. Otto wanted to replace reading and writing, the conventional starting points of instruction, with objective language instruction on the child's own linguistic level, in

---

[11] Among Otto's more important writings are *Die Reformation der Schule*. Berlin: Lichterfelde, 1912; *Familienreform*. Berlin: Lichterfelde, 1912. For discussions of his work see Ferber, G., *Berthold Ottos Pädagogisches Wollen und Wirken*. Langensalza: Hermann Beyer & Sons, 1925; Meyer, Adolph E., *Modern European Educators*. New York: Prentice-Hall, Inc., 1934.

which his own elementary vocabulary—if necessary even his dialect—was to be used. Instruction, moreover, was to be generated by the questions of the children and the answers of their fellows and teachers.

This sort of procedure is the kernel of Otto's so-called *Gesamtunterricht* (integrated instruction). In its largest form it took the shape of a school assembly with some 50 to 80 children, aged from six to nineteen, as well as teachers and visitors in attendance. Three or four times a week this group gathered for an hour—outdoors if the weather permitted. The meeting was informal, the boys and girls sitting in an immense circle, with teachers amongst them—not as police guards, however, but as comrades and friends. The children were allowed to whisper and to move about, if they felt thus inclined. Some girls knitted or crocheted; here and there some boys perused books. In brief, the pupils had real liberty. Usually the assembly was launched with routine business of common interest, such as plans for a hike, or a play after which the assembly proceeded to the "order of the day." Any subject could be brought up, and whatever it was, it was discussed as long as it held interest. The discussions might emerge from a composition read by one of the group; more usually, though, they would be started by direct questions from the children. Someone might inquire about the nature of the eyeball, or the cause of wind, or what makes airplanes fly. In answering such queries, the youngest children were given the right of way; then came the older ones and finally the guests and the teachers. No attempt was made to enforce attention. In the average assembly, from three to four topics were usually discussed. Interestingly enough, a careful analysis of the topics considered during the school year has shown that not only did all the so-called "school subjects" come up for discussion, but also many other significant matters not usually considered in the classroom.

Besides this form of integrated learning, each class had integrated instruction of its own. Altogether there were four groups—beginning, elementary, intermediate, and advanced. Instruction was given in any subject the children wanted. Remarkable to say, some of the most popular subjects were mathematics and the classics. In all this work, formalism was reduced to its minimum. Indeed, formalism had been driven so far into the background that even progressive teachers of the most liberal brand were at times quite amazed on visiting Otto's school.

Another innovation introduced by Otto was his pupils' court—the *Schülergericht*. In the beginning, when Otto's school was small and the pupils were, so to say, a large family, no particular organization was necessary. However, as the school grew, the situation became more complex. Though the number of student disputes increased, still Otto refused to intervene. With the faculty thus on the sidelines, the pupils eventually took matters into their own hands, and out of this situation came an organization of justice which summoned student disturbers of the peace, then tried and punished them. At the outset, however, the organization was rather secretive about its work; nor was it democratic. Its verdicts were not always above suspicion. Often enough, moreover, it could not carry out its dictates. Gradually the youngsters became dissatisfied with their way of settling disputes. Finally, at a gathering of the whole school, in one of their *Gesamtunterricht* sessions, they came to grips with their problem. To settle their difficulties, they chose an arbiter, who was to be helped by a corps of assistants, composed equally of boys and girls. Next, laws were enacted. In the course of time there evolved a form of court trial, which in some respects imitated adult procedures but in others was strictly original. The severest punishment, incidentally, was the student's exclusion from school for several days.

So successful was this form of self-government that Otto was able to entrust all disciplinary matters to it. The whole organization and its work, it should be observed, had its roots in the soil of practical need. There was no attempt at teacher domination. The system was not "thought up" by an imaginative pedagogical mind; its sole sponsor was the real and living need of the pupils themselves.

6. Ludwig Gurlitt

Curiously enough, it was mainly chance that led Ludwig Gurlitt (1855–1931) to don the pedagogical robes. While out of work, he decided to make use of his license to teach in the secondary schools. He taught successively at Hamburg, Berlin, and Steglitz, a suburb of the Reich capital. His subject was the classics, and his success in teaching in this difficult field was instantaneous. Nonetheless, the seeds of revolt soon sprouted within him. A passionate devotee of untrammeled action, Gurlittt observed how unwittingly he had become a cog in a machine, grinding out "servile lackeys with the souls of vassals and job-seekers." Facts were what the visiting examiners sought from the pupils—such facts, for example, as: "How does Ode II. 7 begin?" and "How does the tenth poem in Goethe's *Liedersammlung* begin?" All this was rammed into the students, as one of Gurlitt's supervisors explained, "so that at least they shan't fail on account of any lack of information." Next to knowledge came the standard virtues of piety and obedience. "Above all," warned a schoolman, "guard the minds of those youths entrusted to you against doubt." Another pedagogue, according to Gurlitt, ably seconded him: "Before the age of fifteen youth is not to think its own thoughts, but rather it is to enter into those of great men."

Against all this Gurlitt went into battle. Launching his attack in 1902 with a monograph, *Der Deutsche und sein Vaterland,* Gurlitt ripped apart conventional and academic secondary education.[12] During the next few years, Gurlitt

---

[12] Interestingly enough it was at this moment that the German Youth Movement came to life. This, too, was a protest against the classroom intellectualism. (See p. 253.) It came, however, from the students themselves. It is probably only a coincidence that the movement came into being in the very

published several broadsides against the traditional school. He called for

a decrease in the number of hours, extermination of linguistic formalism, decided stress on local cultural values, a late beginning of foreign language instruction, elimination of learning-coercion in the lower classes, education in the outdoors, a student's right to question—in brief, a natural, local education from the near to the remote. The ancient languages were to be taught only to the adequately capable pupils and according to much more living methods.[13]

Traditional education, Gurlitt believed, places more stress "on limiting and holding down one's powers" than on liberating them, since education appears interested primarily in society and the state rather than in the individual. Gurlitt held that life's possibilities are so manifold that pedagogic theory cannot give final answers. All that it can do is to set up general principles which in individual instances are not inflexible. Gurlitt, moreover, was against indoctrination. With youth, he declared, "we do not have to set up ourselves as the custodians of untouchable and eternal truths. If only we can be of use to children and let them perceive our honest intentions to help them . . . then we can obtain the authority we desire." In his stress on individuality, Gurlitt put a high value on play:

Play hitherto has been condemned by all educators of correct dignity. It was believed that play in any case should end with the beginning of the school year, so that life's seriousness might start. It is odd that it was reserved for our own time to recognize just how serious nature was minded toward play; how important, how essential this impulse is . . . for the physical, spiritual, moral development of man.

The old pedagogical maxim which recommended the breaking of the child's will to secure obedience was flouted by Gurlitt. What he wanted was a free personality whose rights to its own

school where Gurlitt taught—indeed, some of the movement's most prominent apostles were students in Gurlitt's own class.

[13] Hahn, E., Editor, *Die Pädagogik der Gegenwart in Selbsdarstellungen,* Vol. II, p. 34. Leipzig: Felix Meiner, 1927.

temperament—including even hatred and passion—were to be respected.

In the midst of his struggle for educational reform Gurlitt's health deserted him and he was compelled to stop active work. Subsequently, however, he organized a new school along the lines of the country-home school. After the first World War he developed the idea of the school farm. When the Weimar Republic reconstructed its educational system, many of Gurlitt's once controversial ideas served as models.

7. Georg Kerschensteiner

The aim of education, for Kerschensteiner (1854–1932), was citizenship. He believed that the child develops through a process of internal growth, and that whatever he acquires is not really part of him until it has been absorbed through some sort of personal activity. "If the formation of character is the ultimate end of education," Kerschensteiner once said, "then the best school organization is that which gives character opportunity for development." And again, "character is developed only through action."

Kerschensteiner's emphasis on action made him the apostle of the *Arbeitsschule* or "activity school." Defining it as a school "which liberates the potential creative energy" of the child, Kerschensteiner introduced the activity principle on a large scale in the Munich public schools. At the outset he approached activity from the industrial and manual sides, but he subsequently broadened his concept to include the mental and moral aspects of behavior. True to Kerschensteiner's belief that education has for its main task the development of good citizenship, his activity school sought to make useful citizens, first by guiding the child to his proper life work; second, by planting in him the idea that each vocation has its place in serving society; third, by teaching the child that through his vocation he is to contribute his share in helping society to grow in the direction of a more perfect community.

Under Kerschensteiner's direction, and with the cooperation

of employer, teacher, student, and others, Munich developed a model program of continuation education. In this the student's occupation became the center about which the general subjects were clustered. If the youngster wanted to become a barber, he was given three hours of practical work, some elementary surgery, and trade knowledge, in addition to the usual subjects of religion, composition, arithmetic, book-keeping, and civics. If he aspired to be a tailor, then he was taught the main facts of his prospective vocation, in addition to technical drawing, information about wares and materials, and gymnastics—plus the general prescription. There were three classes of continuation schools: industrial, commercial, and general. The industrial schools were for prospective machinists, butchers, barbers, woodworkers, and printers. The commercial schools were organized in such groups as food and provisions; drapery and textiles; banking, insurance, and bookkeeping; porcelain, cutlery, and hardware. In all this work Kerschensteiner stressed citizenship, with the result that the subject of civics was lifted to a place of high importance. It included, among other things, personal and occupational hygiene, economic and industrial history, and civics proper.

In connection with training in citizenship, Kerschensteiner stressed self-government. "Education for citizenship," he declared, "stands or falls with the introduction of self-government in the conduct of the school. It alone is able to convert the school from a place of individual ambition into a place of social cooperation, from a place of theoretically intellectual one-sidedness into a place of practical and human many-sidedness, from a place of real acquisition of knowledge into a place of real application of knowledge. . . . We have schools for intellectual education and for technical education; but we have no schools for social education. Only with self-government will education become social." [14]

---

[14] Kerschensteiner, G., *Selbstregierung der Schüler*, p. 5. Vienna: Deutscher Verlag für Jugend und Volk, 1925.

8. Adolphe Ferrière

Among those who have served in a distinguished way to reconstruct modern education is the Swiss author and educator, Adolphe Ferrière (1879–). Once a teacher in one of Lietz's country home schools (see p. 140), Ferrière established the International Bureau of New Schools at Geneva in 1899. Subsequently this was organized on an international scale and was known as the New Education Fellowship. His most important book is *The Activity School*, published in 1927.

Like G. Stanley Hall, Ferrière upholds the theory of a parallelism between the development of the individual and the evolution of the human race, a theory which, under the Herbartians, gave the school the now discarded Culture Epochs Theory. To an extent, Ferrière also has been influenced by the psychiatric teachings of Jung, having drawn from him his "psychological types." From Henri Bergson, Ferrière has drawn the concept of the *élan vital*. With Dewey and others, Ferrière believes that education is life and that "life is a continuous growth . . . irregular no doubt in intensity and direction, but never at rest." Based on this general concept is Ferrière's activity school. It is in this domain that Ferrière has exerted his main influence on modern European education. The activity school, for him, is "not a collection of procedures." It is something to be lived. The activity movement has been considerably aided by the work of Edouard Claparède and Pierre Bovet, both of Geneva. The former, a psychologist and experimental educator, founded two important experimental schools. The latter helped to make the Jean-Jacques Rousseau Institute an outstanding center for educational research. It has been called the center of Europe's activity school program.

9. Bertrand Russell

Russell's (1872–) first full-length book on education was published in 1926 under the title "Education and the Good

Life," and the following year Russell and his wife decided to put some of their educational theories into practice by establishing the Beacon Hill School. Education, according to Russell, should produce men and women of courage, vitality, sensitiveness, and intelligence. Of these, vitality is related to one's power to do things; and it should promote happiness. "Vitality," Russell has declared, "promotes interest in the outside world; it also promotes the power of hard work."

By courage Russell does not mean the bull-dog sort, because this stems from ignorance. Found in several forms, courage is most significant in the absence of irrational fears. The courageous man is not only the fearless man: he is also the man with many interests; he is the man with an active intelligence; and he is the man who feels himself a small though not unimportant speck in an immense universe.

Concerning sensitiveness, Russell says that "a person is emotionally sensitive when many stimuli produce emotions in him. . . ." The goal, however, is not simply emotional intensity, but appropriateness of response. An important phase of sensitiveness is sympathy. Much of the world's unhappiness, Russell believes, has its roots in our stunted sympathy— the cruelty of our industrialism, the oppression of subject races, the savageness of war. Still another aspect of sensitiveness is that of our aesthetic emotions.

Believing that education, particularly in the United States, too often has neglected not only literary but also general aesthetic values, Russell wants the school to give more consideration to sense training and dancing, to music and singing. The school should be a doing school where the child can practice self-expression. Let each child discover for himself what colors, sounds and rhythms please him individually. Let there be cooperative activities to which each child can contribute according to his special talents.

Russell is an apostle of open-mindedness. He believes that one of the best spurs to intellectual interest is free discussion, and that the child in his later years should be encouraged to argue on every controversial question. The child should be allowed to make up his own mind on questions of religion, society and politics. In history, his view should be international rather than national or merely political.

Russell's views on morals and sex are well known in the United States. Briefly, he holds that we should impart knowledge solely for intellectual reasons, since to let moral considerations influence instruction is bad for both character and intelligence. The virtues Russell seeks in the cultured man are courage, sensitiveness, and love. The cultured man must have courage to stand up for unpopular causes when he believes they are right; he must be sensitive to the evils and injustices of the social and economic order; and he must love his fellow man.

In the good life, fearlessness is inherent, but too often prudish, or even obscene. Adults have wrought irreparable damage on the child by placing about him an unnecessary barrier of taboos. This is particularly true in the case of sex, where Russell urges complete and honest frankness. Questions about sex, he asserts, should be answered like all other questions. Sex, Russell believes, is neither horrid nor dirty, and it should be treated intelligently.

Unlike many twentieth-century educators, Russell is not hostile to "knowledge for the sake of knowledge." But he feels that the acquisition of such knowledge should not be a boring process. It should be an "intellectual adventure," and should be "related to real life" in such a way that its meaning is understandable to the child. Pure learning, Russell reminds us, has a very important place, "new knowledge being the chief cause of progress."

"Utilitarian knowledge," he says, "needs to be fructified by disinterested investigation, which has no motive beyond the desire to understand the world better. All the great advances are at first purely theoretical."

10. Stanlislas Shatsky

Born in Smolensk, in Western Russia, Shatsky (1878–1934), the son of a minor army official, was raised in strict military fashion from earliest childhood. When he entered school, he found it even more militaristic than his home. Full of coercion and formalism, it was spiritually empty, with the result that "students cheated, feared, and hated." The political revolution of 1905 served to make Shatsky detour from science to education. Under the spell of Tolstoi's work at Yasnaia Poliana, Shatsky determined to become an educator. He began his educational experiments in the country, emphasizing domestic work and agriculture, and economic and social cooperation. In time he began to feel that success was not possible through individual experimental institutions, but that they must be unified in a central body. By 1912 a plan was worked out for an Experimental Station for Children. In part, it was also realized in practice—in the kindergarten, secondary schools, clubs, libraries, workshops, and the children's labor colony. In 1915 a small subsidy was obtained from the Moscow municipal government. With the success of the October Revolution all the plans were unified into the first Experimental Station of Narkompros, the People's Board of Education. It was in this colony, which was subsequently called the "Colony of the Cheerful Life," that Shatsky worked out most of his educational theories. A detailed account of the experiment up to 1924 is set down in his book, *The Cheerful Life*.

Shatsky belongs to that legion of schoolmen who consider themselves disciples of John Dewey. Like Dewey, Shatsky subscribed to the pragmatic view of life. In education, he believed, it was the child that counted, the aims of education being as manifold as the child's periods of growth; what mattered was the child's growth and development, and not the superimposing of some extrinsic objective. Such a view, of course, did not harmonize with the official Communist philosophy of education. Yet, oddly enough, by 1930 Shatsky was one of the outstanding educators in the U. S. S. R. The fact is that his educational objectives, having undergone revision, now fitted in with the Soviet philosophy of politics and government.

Not that Shatsky had forsaken entirely his ideas of the individual child. He simply had discovered that, "ultimately, individual and society are one." He now believed that, on the one hand, the school should organize the child's life, endeavoring to develop those talents and abilities which are not provided for by ordinary living. On the other hand, the school also was to be a place where the requirements of contemporary life must be considered. The school, in other words, was to be child-centered, but it was to be for society. Shatsky's school was organized along progressive lines. Its program was not based on subject matter, but on the child's activities. In the school's work, the child was to be studied as thoroughly as possible. Furthermore, the school was a part of the environment, and the latter was to be interrelated economically, socially, and in every other possible way to the work of the school.

What was impressive about Shatsky's school was the stress it put on socially useful work. Indeed, the entire course of study was based on this. Work was organized in villages, classes were established for the illiterate, and there were lectures on all sorts of vital and important problems. Shatsky's school thus became a leading force in shaping the life of the whole village.

In breaking down the rigidity of traditional subject-matter lines, Shatsky developed what he called "the complex method," which, in its essence, is a broad interpretation of the project procedure. A complex is composed of several broad projects, the various parts of which are interrelated. Like the project, the complex flows from the child's interests. At one point or other, the complex, as developed by Shatsky, included the following content of the child's life: (1) his physical growth; (2) play; (3) art (the child's life in an artistic environment); (4) intellectual life; (5) social life; (6) emotional life; (7) work, labor, and activity.

11. Emile Jacques-Dalcroze

Modern Progressive education stresses the child's all-round development; not only is the youngster to grow mentally and physically, but spiritually and emotionally as well. To attain this goal a number of Progressives have given a great deal of attention to the child's rhythmic activities and experiences. The idea of rhythmics in education is, of course, quite old. The Athenian Greeks, in striving to develop an individual "harmoniously," clearly recognized the important part played by rhythmics. But Athenian education, after all, was for the élite and not for the masses; and up to only a short time ago schools for the masses—in the Western World at any rate— gave very little heed to music and dancing in the general education of the child.

A few decades ago Emile Jacques-Dalcroze (1864–   ), a teacher of music at Geneva, Switzerland, called our attention to the interrelationship of music and rhythmic bodily development. Musical training, Dalcroze found, could best be given by awakening our sense for tone and rhythm. Musical education, he felt, should develop not cellists, pianists, and singers, but "musically developed human beings." Before the student specialized on any instrument, he should develop all his musical faculties. Dalcroze found that pupils could not become creative musicians as long as their training was restricted to their ears and hands. What was essential before anything else was the freeing of the individual's mental, physical, and emotional capacities. What Dalcroze sought in his pupils was an integrated response, one in which there was a harmonization and coordination of the muscles and senses, the nerves, the will, and the emotions. This stress made it necessary for Dalcroze to give some attention to the education of the body. The result of his work and study was what he called *eurhythmics,* a systematic scheme of rhythmic bodily training.

What are the claims of Dalcroze and his supporters? To begin with, there is a positive physical development; there is a greater muscular control resulting in a feeling of physical self-mastery. Muscles and nerves are coordinated; and body and mind are harmonized. Dalcroze believes—and many psychologists agree—that only through the movements of the whole body can we really perceive rhythm. Dalcroze has gone so far as to assert that by the frequent repetition of exercises we can acquire a "muscular memory." Muscular and mental coordination are thus made automatic. After a year's training in eurhythmics, the pupil responds unhesitatingly to any kind of rhythm. With his body, mind, and emotions under control, he is ready to grow in an integrated way. Dalcroze has likened the body to a musical instrument, which can best be served through rhythmics and its handmaiden, music.

What distinguishes Dalcroze's rhythmic training from other forms of physical training is not only its musical aspects, but also its aesthetic value. Rhythmics, Dalcroze and his associates feel, may have a definite bearing on the development of aesthetic appreciation.

Dalcroze's influence has gone far beyond Geneva. There is a Dalcroze Institute in America, and many of our leading teachers' colleges conduct courses in eurhythmics. In Paris the influence of Dalcroze underlies two significant educational trends: "Education and Movement" and "Education and Rhythm." Both these movements have many supporters. One other significant contribution of Dalcroze is that he has awakened many contemporary educators to the general importance of rhythmics in the child's all-round education. Fundamentally, of course, Dalcroze developed his system as an approach to music. By transforming music into motion he hoped to enable the pupil to experience it *actively,* and thereby make him more directly conscious of it. Other teachers, many of whom have studied under Dalcroze or his followers, do not

always agree with their master. Some, for example, have felt
that for young children some of the Dalcroze exercises are too
complicated, and that as a result they sometimes inhibit a
child's natural rhythm. Others—particularly in America—
feel that rhythmic education of a less systematic sort would be
more desirable. Some critics, of course, have not yet been convinced of the value of rhythmics—either the Dalcroze variety
or any other kind. What they want is "objective evidence,"
and thus far this does not appear to be at hand. This lack,
however, has not dimmed the glow of the Progressive's enthusiasm.

12. Franz Cizek

Another pioneer in creative education is Franz Cizek (1865–
1947) of pre-Nazi Vienna. Through his work in art classes
for gifted children and the spread of his educational philosophy
among his students in the School of Arts and Crafts, Cizek
played a significant part in the school reform of the defunct
Austrian Republic. For a generation and a half, Cizek urged
the release of the child's natural powers through creative
expression. "The lid," he asserted, "must be taken off."
Every child, he believed, has a natural tendency to express
himself through some form of creation. This creativeness is
found first in the child's surplus energy, which craves an outlet
through creative expression; subsequently, when the energy
begins to ebb, the child draws on what Cizek has called "the
heritage of the ages"; finally, the child's creativeness is influenced by his environment. Some children, Cizek noted,
seem to develop spontaneously, "almost independently of circumstances." Others seem so bound to circumstances as to be
almost paralyzed in their capacity to create. In some cases
there are alternate periods of dependence and spontaneity.

Cizek's "soul heritage of the ages" is not always the same.
It may be latent, or it may be even lacking; in some instances
it may be confused. Is the heritage latent? Then consciousness of it must be aroused. Is it confused? Then it must be

clarified. Concerning environment, Cizek deplored the waning cultural and educative influence of the family. As for the average school, for Cizek it is essentially a mill which "manufactures children instead of letting them grow."

Cizek asserted that in the individual there are two egos—-the conscious and the unconscious. The latter is the one that stamps the child's work of art with its individual charm, but the conventional school has generally stifled the child's unconscious ego. This being the case, Cizek attempted to preserve for the youngster his child world—the unconscious ego. By informal suggestion and by praise discreetly bestowed, he sought to help each child to form subconsciously those ideas that are struggling within him for interpretation. According to Cizek, the impulse to create, to play freely with forms and ideas in the manner of an artist, is only a passing phase. If properly nurtured, he believed it would last through childhood —only to disappear in early adolescence. Thus it is essential to utilize this urge during childhood and to preserve it as long as possible. Then, in adolescence, pupils of ordinary ability should have at least a fertile basis of ideas and sensory experiences to put to work in the more formal crafts. Those rare souls who possess artistic talents will go on developing their creative powers, and will, in time, master those techniques and standards which constitute the necessary foundation for the highest artistic expression.

Cizek did not look too kindly on the usual type of art education. In school the usual teacher attempts to exert an influence over his pupils, and in this respect art as self-expression cannot flourish. For creative work the teacher's influence is bad; Cizek, in fact, asserted that his own influence was bad for his class— the best creative work being done by children when they are left to themselves. The teacher, Cizek insisted, "should be a cipher." Contending that he had no *method*, Cizek let himself be guided by his pupils. "We must let the children grow," and for this "there is no better method than the inner God." To this inner life of the child, educational technique can offer no magic key.   But to force forms upon him which are not natural to him, according to Cizek, is to strangle his individuality.

Cizek's class worked without any imposed discipline.   Order and routine had no place in his school—often, indeed, his groups raised considerable din.   The only external aid to discipline was music.   Rhythmics and singing were looked upon as important and valuable outlets.

13.   Some notable new schools

Abbotsholme.   With the establishment of Abbotsholme in Derbyshire, England, in 1889, the first modern experimental school was launched.   Its founder, Cecil Reddie (1858–1932), not only originated the so-called new school, but became, in the course of time, the spiritual sponsor of many similar institutions both in England and on the Continent.   The Germans subsequently dubbed Reddie the *Grossvater* (the grandfather) of the country home school movement.   Like all experimental schools, it was a protest against the traditional formalism then stalking particularly in England's secondary school.   Abbotsholme's aim was to develop personality through freedom, its motto being: "liberty is obedience through law."   What Reddie was seeking was a pupil who was "superior, fully developed in every respect," and capable of leadership, not because of the accidents of money or birth or influence, but because of ability.   After a rich and influential activity of many years, Abbotsholme gradually was eclipsed by other experimental schools.   Some years ago, however, new life was injected into it and once more Abbotsholme became an active new school.

Grouped into three divisions, Abbotsholme is a country home school for boys ranging in age from seven to sixteen. As in every typical new school, the aim of instruction at Abbotsholme is not primarily to impart knowledge.   The goals are character development and encouragement of reason and judgment.   The methods of teaching vary, but one of the favorite procedures is group discussion.   Instruction is less by book than by investigation; there is less stress on theory and

more on use and application. Since the school is in the country, there are splendid opportunities for work on the land.
Practical work, indeed, is compulsory. Problems of farms,
labor, supplies, seasons, and the like are studied from firsthand
experiences. A sharp difference between Abbotsholme and
the English public school [15] lies not only in its liberal curriculum, but also in its attitude toward games and athletics. At
Abbotsholme there is much less emphasis on team games,
creative activities and practical work receiving much more
attention.

Although Reddie was seeking to develop the individual
growing youngster, he was also mindful of the school's social
and civic functions. His school, indeed, was a family, empire,
and church all in one. It was a community where everyone,
including the school's director, the faculty, employees, and the
students, shared tasks and responsibilities. At Abbotsholme
there was a scheme of self-government, perhaps not as grand
as in some other schools, but effective just the same. Though
the school was born in an era stressing discipline and training,
it proceeded to break away from these bonds. It put its
liberalizing mark not only on curricula and methods, but also
on its teachers; they were not to be schoolmasters, but educators who understood and sympathized with their learners.

Bedales. One of England's best-known new schools is
Bedales. Founded in 1893, by John Haden Badley, the school
began its career with three teachers and three boys; today it is
coeducational, with some two hundred boys and girls.[16]
Badley (1865–   ), who retired in 1935, was once associated
with Cecil Reddie at Abbotsholme. Its emphasis on manual
work and physical activity impressed him immensely. Unlike
Reddie, however, Badley was convinced that sound education
must be coeducational.

---

[15] The English public school, unlike the American public school, is actually
a private preparatory school. Rugby, Eton, Harrow, Winchester are a few
examples. See p. 179.

[16] See Badley, J. H., *Bedales.* London: Methuen & Company, 1923; Meyer,
A. E., *Modern European Educators.* New York: Prentice-Hall, Inc., 1934.

Bedales is a country boarding school. Since 1900 it has been at Petersfield. It maintains a farm of more than a hundred acres and grows its own products. The gardens, orchard, and woodland provide outdoor work for the children throughout the year; and for those who want plots of their own, a special garden is reserved. Sports get considerable attention at Bedales, at least a dozen acres having been prepared for athletics of all sorts. The Bedalian boys and girls vary in age from four to nineteen. The younger children, numbering about 50, occupy what is known as the Junior School. For the older children there is the Upper School.

The aims and procedures of Bedales are of the progressive kind:

1. Freedom for normal and healthy development of body and mind, by the upbringing of girls and boys in an atmosphere that fosters understanding and co-operation.
2. Care for the mental, moral, and physical needs of each child, without neglecting the needs of the community. There is to be co-operation rather than competition, as is evidenced by the school's motto: "Work of each for the weal of all."
3. The creative urge is to have adequate opportunity for expression.
4. Through the observance and treatment of religious matters, free from any trace of dogma and acceptable to all, regardless of creed, a sense of things of eternal value is developed.
5. International goodwill is to be encouraged in every possible way.
6. Between pupil and teacher there is to be a relationship of trust. Discipline is to come from self-control rather than from any superimposed authority.

Coeducation is one of the features of Bedales. For a European school, distinction in this realm is rare; in fact, in the matter of coeducation the only other European school of great significance was Paul Geheeb's Odenwald School in pre-Nazi Germany, now the *École d'Humanité* in Switzerland (see p. 145).

Stressing cooperation, Bedales has banned competition as a spur to effort. Competition, it feels, is inherently selfish and ought to be discouraged; the cause of many evils, it is the root of much social and international misunderstanding. To obviate it as far as possible, Bedales gives no marks for daily classroom work, nor does it give medals or prizes for excellence in school studies, except when work is done under special conditions. The motive for good work is to be the pleasure derived from doing good work.

The accusation sometimes directed at the new schools, that they minimize or overlook the value of religious education, cannot be raised against Bedales. "Besides the life of the body, and beyond even the life of the mind, the life of the spirit is our chief concern," was Badley's point of view. But Bedales rejects any emphasis on creed. "To creeds and ceremonies and the varying tenets of which rival churches make so much, we attach little importance. A creed is a thing that each age must restate in its own language and in accordance of its own time." [17]

A visit to Bedales will reveal very few of the familiar marks of discipline. In the management of the school and its life as great a share as possible is given to the older boys and girls. The organization and direction of play, for example, is in charge of elected captains. Internal government is in the hands of prefects, appointed by the headmaster. A school council, comprised of a number of officials, such as the headmaster, the housemaster and housemistress, all form masters, and the head boy or girl, as well as a number of elected representatives from each of the classes in the main school, governs Bedales.

École des Roches. Inspired by both Reddie and Badley was a French sociologist, Edmond Demolins (1852–1907).[18] In 1897 Demolins published a treatise, *A quoi tient la supériorité des Anglo-Saxons?* ("Wherein lies the superiority of the Anglo-Saxons?"). He answered his query by saying that one of the causes of Anglo-Saxon superiority lay in their educa-

---

[17] Badley, J. H., *Bedales,* p. 210. London: Methuen & Company, 1923.

[18] For details concerning life at the *École des Roches* see its periodical, *L'Écho des Roches,* published before the war at Verneuil-sur-Avre, France; also Meyer, A. E., *Modern European Educators.* New York: Prentice-Hall, Inc., 1934.

tion, which was characterized by broader goals and more natural methods in England than France. One result of Demolins' publication was that a number of Frenchmen became interested in reforming education. Demolins continued his interest in education, and, in 1899, established the *École des Roches*. Eight years later Demolins died, but his work was carried on by Paul de Rousiers and Georges Bertier.

The *École des Roches* is essentially a boys' country boarding school of the progressive order. A few girls attend, but there has been no serious attempt at coeducation.

"Our first aim," says Bertier, "is to make of our students strong and generous personalities capable of solving tomorrow's problems in the best way." Stressing individual development, the school allows considerable individual freedom.

The *École des Roches* urges its boys to shoulder responsibility, the boys being expected to manage and direct their own activities. Individuals having special duties and obligations are in the classrooms, in the studies, in the libraries, and almost everywhere else. The school's main activities are entrusted to student committees. There is a committee in charge of the school paper, the *Écho des Roches*. Another manages athletics. There is a committee for manual work; another for charity and social work; and another in charge of the school grounds.

Everyone at the *École des Roches* must do something practical. Garden work offers opportunities in elementary agriculture; more advanced work in agriculture may be had in a near-by agricultural school. The shops for wood and metal work are well equipped; there is a department for bicycle repairs, where boys repair their own wheels; and a number of studios for arts and crafts. But the *École des Roches* stresses practical work, not only for the usual pedagogical reasons but also for social reasons. The pupils work for others—either for their fellows or for members of their family. A good deal of the practical work is cooperative, as in the making of a wireless set or an iron gate for the school. In some of the crafts, variations of the old guild system have been developed: a book-keeping guild, a pottery guild, and other guilds. Each of these organizations is headed by a master to whom the pupils apply for apprenticeship. After having served their probationary period, they are accepted as apprentices. They may be rejected, however, if they are found incapable of doing the guild's specialized work.

As is generally known, French education has been inclined toward the conservative. Through a relatively inelastic centralized organization, the nation operates its schools from Paris, controlling them even in small matters. (See p. 205.) The result is that educational experimentation and innovation have been difficult. Despite these difficulties, the *École des Roches* has flourished. True, it must meet the requirements of the state, and its students must take the usual examinations. The fact that the school is able to offer its broad progressive program of activities, and still meet the rigid requirements of the state, is significant.

Hermann Lietz's Country Home Schools (Landerziehungsheime).[19] Another school reformer inspired by Cecil Reddie was Hermann Lietz (1868–1918), who in 1898 established at Ilsenburg, Germany, the first of a number of schools. These he called *Landerziehungsheime* or country-home schools. The original school was crowded out of existence by the demands of expanding industry, but it was followed by six similar schools.

The keynote to Lietz's educational viewpoint is found in his early life. His boyhood on his father's farm, with its untrammeled freedom, led him to glorify the countryside as an educative force; and his unhappy schooldays made him the uncompromising foe of formalism.

---

[19] For a comprehensive account of Lietz and his work see Brickman, W. W., *The Contribution of Hermann Lietz to Education,* Ph.D. dissertation, New York University, School of Education, 1938; also Alexander, T. and Parker, B., *The New Education in the German Republic,* pp. 179 ff. New York: John Day Co., Inc., 1929; and Hilker, F., *Deutsche Schulversuche,* p. 58 ff. Berlin: Schwetschke and Son, 1924.

Fundamentally, Lietz's schools stressed the social and non-academic features of education. "We are striving to develop," asserted Alfred Andreesen, a successor to Lietz, "not only the one who knows, but the independent seeker and doer." The Lietzian schools wanted their pupils to be close to nature, away from the banalities of the city. The simple life of the peasant at its best, his industry and thrift, were absorbed by the pupils and shared in their own life and labor.

When the Lietzian schools were established, their founders gave special attention to the geographic environment, in the belief that this played an important part in the development of the child's nature. The site for each school was chosen with consideration for the age of the pupils who were to come there. The school for the youngest children, for example, was housed on a peaceful country estate in a slumbering German village, far from the rumble-bumble of the city. This charming countryside became the textbook from which the young Lietzians gathered their experiences. When classwork was over, the children worked in the fields and garden. They shared much of the community life about them, even celebrating the festivals that lend so much color and gaiety to the peasant life. These youngsters, in the words of Lietz, "are rooted in the native soil."

The Lietzian schools have always stressed a many-sided education, with the child's needs and interests as a starting point. The day's activities were balanced. There was intellectual work, manual work, and practical work. There was physical and aesthetic activity. There was individual and social work. Lietz's schools segregated children according to age. There was one school for the nine- to twelve-year-olds, three for the twelve- to sixteen-year-olds, and two for those between sixteen and eighteen. Those who organized the schools felt that individual self-development was hampered in a boarding school that had children of all ages. The development of individual talents and powers to the full, they believed, was often impeded by the human tendency to imitate. Younger pupils, they felt, liked to ape not only the doings and organizations of their older comrades, but also their mannerisms. Older pupils tended to overstimulate their younger colleagues; and the latter at times tended to hamper their older associates.

The Lietzian schools did not accept coeducation as fundamental. However, similar schools for girls arose although these were not in the Lietzian chain.

As might be assumed, the teacher in these schools was expected to play a significant part in his school's comprehensive educational program. His duties were never limited to the classroom. He was expected to have the rare capacity of being able to reduce to almost nothing the chasm separating teacher and pupil. Like the boys he was expected to educate, he had to be more than one who knows; he was also to be a doer.

The fact that these schools were private ventures of an experimental sort has led some to believe that instruction was not of a high order. This, as a matter of fact, is quite erroneous. Like the *École des Roches,* the Lietzian *Landerziehungsheim* was subject to state regulations and had to follow the course of study prescribed in the modern German secondary school. Thus bound to state regulations, the country home schools were unable to make many curricular changes. The best they were able to do was to make their program as flexible as possible, and to include many extracurricular activities. Still, the Lietzian schools were able to keep formalism and intellectualism from their midst. Not until the student entered the advanced group did examinations become significant—and then only in preparation for the final state examinations, the well-known *Reifeprüfung.*

The Lietzian schools were, of course, affected by the National Socialism of the Third Reich. Of all the experimental schools in Germany, they were the only ones to survive. They continued to enjoy a relative freedom, but, on the other hand, they had to adopt many Nazi innovations. Their teachers, for example, had to be Nazis. There was the usual Nazi indoctrination. And there were, of course, all the Nazi educational trimmings, including the activities of the Hitler Youth.

The influence of the original *Landerziehungsheime* has been considerable not only in Germany but in many lands, particularly in Switzerland. Lietz's influence, moreover, is discerned in the work of some of his teachers, who developed educational reforms of their own. Gustav Wyneken and Paul Geheeb organized a new school at Wickersdorf; and later, Geheeb established the famous Odenwald School. (See p. 145.) Adolphe Ferrière, one of the deans of the activity movement, was once associated with Lietz.

Gustav Wyneken's Wickersdorf. In 1906, Gustav Wyneken (1875–   ) and Paul Geheeb (1870–   ), both associated with Lietz, jointly established a new school of their own at Wickersdorf, Germany. Instead of being a country home school, the new school was to be a "free school community." Although the two types of schools had much in common, there were also some fundamental differences. On the whole, the latter were more experimental: they were less conservative, not only in education, but also in their social-political outlook. From its beginning, Wickersdorf had some form of coeducation, due mainly to the efforts of Geheeb, who is probably the Old World's warmest advocate of coeducation.

The foe of all indoctrination, Wyneken insisted that his school be a free community in fact as well as in name. The school was to be nobody's tool; neither the state nor church nor society, he felt, should dictate to the free school community. Wyneken's attitude toward the family is not too flattering. Too often, he believed, it counteracted the benefits of true education. It has forced, he said, "its young members to ape the parents"—and the older generation, Wyneken thought, was too materialistic. "As long as society and the nations are under the yoke of an economic struggle for existence," he declared, "just so long . . . the enslavement of youth will continue."

Wyneken's insistence on the noninterference of adults is closely related to a second doctrine. He himself has called it *Jugendkultur,* by which he meant that youth is to create its own world and culture. In the words of Wyneken:

Youth, hitherto only an appendage of the older generation, shunted out of public life, assigned a passive role in life . . . is beginning to think of itself. It seeks to shape its own life by itself in order to be free from the indolent habits of its elders and the dictates of an ugly convention. It seeks a new way of life which will correspond to its youthful being, but which at the same time will enable it to take itself and its creations seriously and help it to make itself a distinct factor with the work of civilization.[20]

On the whole, the work and life of the students at Wickersdorf resembled that of the children in the country-home school. There were, however, children of all ages at Wickersdorf. This and the fact that the school had girls as well as boys naturally affected the Wickersdorfer activities. Nonetheless, the daily program was much the same, with the same attempt to balance the educational diet. More attention, however, was given to music, art, and dramatics.

One of the features at Wickersdorf was its form of self-government. From almost the start students were encouraged to take an active part in shaping the school's policies. Pupils as well as teachers assembled to discuss common questions, all matters being finally settled by vote. Pupils had the same rights as teachers in these gatherings, which were called the *Schulgemeinde*—the "school community." The questions considered were real and vital. Such matters, for example, as those concerning pocket money, luxuries, betting, smoking, and drinking were considered and regulated by the school community.

Under the National Socialist scheme, Wickersdorf obviously could not continue. One of the first Nazi coups against the

---

[20] Wyneken, G., *Wickersdorf.* Lauenburg: Adolf Saal Verlag, 1922. See also Meyer, A. E., *Modern European Educators.* New York: Prentice-Hall, Inc., 1934.

free school communities came with the prohibition of the word "free." They were to be "school communities," but not "free school communities." Girls, moreover, were to be under the special supervision of married teachers. And the instrument of self-government was to cease.

Paul Geheeb's Odenwald School. One of Germany's finest experimental schools was the Odenwald School.[21] It was founded in 1910 by Paul Geheeb. Children came to Odenwald from many lands, about one-fifth of them, at times, being non-German. For many years the school was organized in families —that is, in groups of six to ten under a teacher or a married couple—and the family usually occupied one story of a house, each house being shared by some twenty-five to thirty boys and girls. Under the family system, every new pupil at Odenwald was tentatively assigned to a family; and after about six weeks he chose the particular family with which he wanted to be permanently.

Coeducation at Odenwald was very real. In fact, probably less than a half-dozen schools in the whole world could match Odenwald's achievement. Indeed, even John Badley, of Bedales, on a visit to Odenwald, saluted coeducation there as most remarkable. Like Wickersdorf, Odenwald had a genuine system of self-government, its school council being composed of students and faculty, but the latter had no dominating influence. Every member of the council—young and old—had a right to vote. The council was a sovereign body, its decrees and regulations being final. Not even Geheeb could set them aside. Interestingly enough, the council also concerned itself with disciplinary matters, and it had the exclusive right to punish. In individual cases, this authority might be delegated to others, though in no case to an adult. Losing his right to

---

[21] Geheeb, P., "Die Odenwaldschule im Lichte der Erziehungsaufgaben der Gegenwart," *Die pädagogische Hochschule,* III, p. 11 ff., 1931; Huguenin, E., *Paul Geheeb et la libre communauté scolaire de l'Odenwald.* Geneva, 1923; Meyer, A. E., *Modern European Educators.* New York: Prentice-Hall, Inc., 1934.

vote in the deliberations of the council was the severest punishment that could be inflicted.

Instead of putting the student into a program of studies for a year, or even a term, Odenwald offered all subjects for children over ten years of age in one-month courses. Every student was expected to pick two content subjects. He had the right, however, to elect nothing at all, and to concentrate instead on independent work. The children had virtually a free hand in selecting their work, the only limitation being the obvious one that they could not select work for which they plainly were not fit. Besides taking two content courses, every pupil took one practical or craft course. Here again the child was allowed his own choice. In the elementary classes there was more stress on play, and the four-week course was not followed.

At the end of every month there was a meeting of the school council, at which lectures and papers were presented by those who had completed their four-week courses. At such times also there was an exhibit of some of the work in the arts and crafts courses. Every pupil was expected to participate, though the precise form of contribution he wished to make was left to his own choice.

Drama and music were closely interwoven in the life of the children. The picturesque countryside was a first-rate setting for Shakespearean comedy. In music, every child was encouraged to play the instrument best suited to him. There were also large and small singing groups. One of the features of Odenwald's musical life was its music evenings, *Musikabende,* which usually were devoted to such immortals as Mozart, Beethoven, Bach, Haydn, Schubert, Händel, and Brahms.

Several times during the year, on the occasions of the birthdays of the great men for whom the various student houses were named, Odenwald celebrated on a grand scale. Months before the event committees worked on plans and preparations. When the day came, the entire school journeyed into the hills. Here, talks were given. Portions of the celebrity's works were read, and an open-air performance was staged. Some of the children's parents and visitors from the near-by villages also participated. Sometimes sports predominated: there was once a Schiller feast, which was completely devoid of any cultural smack. It was dedicated to physical training and featured intramural athletics.

Briefly, Odenwald sought to educate cultured, social human beings. It held that what counted in education was that man should be able to understand life and live it well. Much of the school's success was due, of course, to its founder and director. Now past his seventieth year, Geheeb has given the best part of his life to the reorganization of educational theory and practice. Odenwald, of course, was quite incompatible with Nazi ideology. After more and more interference from the National Socialists, and a steady rain of governmental prohibitions, Geheeb eventually succeeded in moving into Switzerland. There, in a locale situated some twenty minutes from Geneva, overlooking beautiful Lac Léman, Geheeb became associated—as a sort of co-director with J. W. Gunning—with the Institut Monnier. After a few years, however, this partnership was dissolved and Geheeb assumed the full direction of the school. Today it is known as the *École d'Humanité* and is located at Schwarzsee. (See p. 586).

F. Some Criticisms and Evaluations of Progressive Education

Like all breaks with tradition the new education has for years been subjected to the crossfire of criticism. The attacks have come from all sides, from idealists like Herman Harrell Horne; from psychologists like Guy Montrose Whipple; from job analysts like Werrett Wallace Charters and Ernest Horn; from college and university presidents and professors who stand firm for the old and trusted disciplines and standards; from scholastics, both of the Catholic and Hutchins variety; and from the vast army of parents and teachers who deplore what in general terms they have described as the inefficiency and excesses of Progressive education.[1]

The criticism of Progressive education are manifold. To begin with, the Dewey dictum that education should be life itself and not merely a preparation for it is attacked on the ground that, strictly speaking, this would mean that the school would have to imitate and include the outside world within its realm, and this, it is held, would mean that education is life in the raw. The Progressives, however, have returned the fire with a denial of such an implication in Dewey's words. The school, they contend, must furnish a special and rich environment, one which will stimulate the child's interests and liberate his capacities. To this the anti-Progressives reply that such, unfortunately, is not the situation in "real life." The discrepancy between the opposing views is not simply a verbal one, for the Progressives insist that the school must be part of civilization and the social order, which means that the school must deal with real and vital social needs and materials. In the past, the school has tended to deal primarily with formal and absolute questions.

Another question raised by the critics of the newer method is this: Can an integrated curriculum, based wholly, or almost wholly, on the child's interests, teach the formal skills needed in the tool subjects? Or in other words, can such a curriculum teach the complex skills involved in arithmetic, spelling, and the like? Can arithmetic, for example, really be successfully learned "as it is needed"?

1. William C. Bagley and the Essentialists

The sharpest adversaries of the New Education thus far have been the *Essentialists*.[2] A group of educators whose

---

[1] For Horne's criticism of the Progressive viewpoint see p. 52; for the Catholic point of view see p. 55; for that of Hutchins and his followers see p. 58.

[2] The name *Essentialist* was offered by the late Michael J. Demiashkevich to designate those who stress as the prime function of organized education the preservation and transmission of the basic elements of human culture. Demiashkevich himself was sympathetic to this point of view. For a sum-

views show much and amazing variety, who, as a matter of fact, are often in acute and emphatic disagreement among themselves, the Essentialists are united at least in their disapprobation of a substantial part of the Progressive theory and practice. They derive their name from their obvious stress on "essentials," by which they mean those human experiences, past and present, which (in *their* eyes at any rate) are indispensable to people living today. They hold that it is the main function of organized education to transmit these essentials to the young. Opening their attack on the Progressives at a convention of the National Education Association in Atlantic City in 1938, the Essentialists flung out the following question: "Should not our public schools prepare boys and girls for adult responsibility through systematic training in such subjects as reading, writing, arithmetic, history, and English, requiring mastery of such subjects, and, when necessary, stressing discipline and obedience?" The ensuing discussions generated a great deal of heat and no little drama, and, with the help of the ever eager newsmen, provoked a nation-wide controversy.[3]

The leading and most brilliant proponent of the Essentialist doctrine was William Chandler Bagley (1872-1946), onetime professor at Columbia, editor of the well-known educational periodical *School and Society,* and the author of several important books on education.

Philosophically, Bagley was not an idealist, like Horne; nor did he cast bouquets in the direction of the scholastics. He was probably more of a realist than anything else; certainly he did not hesitate to pay tribute to the new realism as compounded by Frederick S. Breed.[4] Rejecting the transcendental

---

mary of Essentialism's present status see Brickman, W. W., "Essentialism Ten Years After," *School and Society,* LXVII, p. 391 ff., May 15, 1948.

[3] *Time* Magazine deemed the controversy of sufficient general interest to feature the story in one of its issues. See "Progressivism's Progress," *Time,* XXXII, pp. 31–35, October 31, 1938.

[4] "The new realism offers an advantage in that it is a philosophy which has its source in the methods and findings of scientific inquiry. It recognizes at the same time that objective science has its limitations and that the essential

and metaphysical theorizing of the idealists, Bagley believed that one could "hold a thoroughgoing evolutionary hypothesis which links mankind structurally with the entire range of life from the simplest beginnings and yet recognizes in mankind a potential nobility without bringing in a metaphysical element." [5]   The theory of emergent evolution, Bagley felt, resolved the dualism of idealism and naturalism. The two, he asserted, "form a consistent whole when ideals are conceived of as emergent qualities of naturalistic integrations." [6]

Viewed in the evolutionary light, social development is perceived as "a progressive accumulation and refinement of learnings," and education "in the broadest sense is the process of transmitting these learnings."   Out of Bagley's theory of emergent evolution have sprung two of his major educational principles. Thus his stress on social evolution led him directly to his emphasis on the importance of the social heritage and the transmission of its essential values to the young. At the same time, however, Bagley committed no such naive folly as to overlook the need of recognizing the appearance of new emergents in the progress of the race. "He insists we must have both democracy and discipline," says Norman Woelfel, "if an emerging America is to run true to the institutional standards by which her course has been charted."

Bagley was probably the most articulate, the most indefatigable of the Essentialists. Though an acidulous foe of a good part of the Progressive doctrine, he tempered his criticism by an appreciative salute to some of its worth. The Essentialist, he conceded,

certainly would endorse the functional approach to the problem of teaching and learning; the effort to build lessons of race experience upon the

---

spirit of the philosophical disciplines must always play a fundamental role in human thought." Bagley in his introduction to Breed, F. S., *Education and the New Realism.* New York: The Macmillan Company, 1939.

[5] Bagley, W. C., *Education, Crime and Social Progress*, p. 122. New York: The Macmillan Company, 1931.

[6] Bagley, W. C., *Education and Emergent Man*, p. 64. New York: Thomas Nelson & Sons, 1935.

individual, first-hand experience of the learner; the condemnation always of stupid, parrot-like learning; the importance of the earlier years especially in the procedures that are reflected in such concepts as the project method and the activity program; and the efforts to make school life a happy as well as a profitable series of learning experiences.[7]

In a similar vein he had a few good things to say about the activity movement. The differences between Progressives and Essentialists, he felt, were "primarily differences in emphasis," but these differences, one might hasten to add, were as deep as the ocean itself.

Although Bagley aimed his shafts at the heart of the Progressives, he struck at much of American education in general.

American educational theory long since dropped the word "discipline" from its vocabulary. Today its most vocal and influential spokesmen enthrone the right even of the immature learner to choose what he shall learn. They condemn as "authoritarian" all learning tasks that are imposed by the teacher. They deny any value in the systematic and sequential mastery of the lessons that the race has learned at so great a cost. They condone and rationalize the refusal of the learner to attack a task that does not interest him. In effect they open wide the lines of least resistance and least effort. Obedience they stigmatize as a sign of weakness. All this they advocate in the magic names of "democracy" and "freedom." [8]

"Public education in the United States," declared Bagley, "is . . . appallingly weak and ineffective"—so much so, indeed, that standards of achievement in fundamentals in our elementary and secondary schools fall far behind those of other modern nations. Worse yet, our inept and enfeebling methods have contributed to "our appalling record of murder, assault, robbery, and other serious crimes."

Behind all this alleged deterioration Bagley beheld two causes. There are, for one thing, such social and economic factors as the growth of crowded cities, the swift increase and mobility of our population, immigration, the advancing

[7] Bagley, W. C., "The Significance of the Essentialist Movement in Educational Theory," *Classical Journal*, XXII, p. 334, 1940.

[8] Bagley, W. C., "An Essentialist's Platform for the Advancement of American Education," *Educational Administration and Supervision*, XXVI, pp. 241–256, 1938.

frontier, the widespread racial differences among the populace, the new vocational opportunities, and the tremendous expansion of mass education. The main blame for the American decadence, however, Bagley has placed on our emasculated educational theory which, he felt, has placed too high a premium on the beguiling doctrines of interest, freedom, personal experience, the satisfaction of immediate needs, popular initiative—all of which have become standard currency in the Progressive realm.

The theory that there should be a continuous change in the curriculum matching the social change evoked no bravos from Bagley. Nor was he enthusiastic over the doctrine that the elementary curriculum should reflect primarily the local community needs. His insistence, instead, was on a common core curriculum, one which was to be "the nucleus of a common culture for the children of the nation." [9] Without this, he feared our democracy would have no "social-binder." True to the Essentialist credo, Bagley wanted education to function as a stabilizing force in American society instead of hitching itself to the vicissitudes of changing fashion.

In their critical thrusts at the American school Bagley and the Essentialists have excoriated what they call its "debilitating" elements. They have deprecated the falling scholastic standards and the passing of the exacting studies. The practice, which prevails in some schools, of promoting all children regardless of their academic accomplishment gets no sympathy from the Essentialists. "We have graduates of our common schools, and even, I am sorry to say, of our high schools," Nicholas Murray Butler once lamented, "who triumphantly spell Caesar with an S and Xenophon with a Z, who think the Rule of Three has something to do with state politics, and that the Metric System is part of the human apparatus for digestion." To wipe out such ignorance the Essentialists demand

---

[9] Bagley, W. C., *The Twenty-sixth Yearbook*. National Society for the Study of Education, Part II, p. 33. Bloomington, Illinois: Public School Publishing Company, 1926.

a return "to the exact and exacting studies." Frankly favoring the "mental disciplines," they have given their blessing to Latin, algebra, and geometry, pointing out that although they don't put stock in such a thing as *automatic* transfer of training, there is, however, such a thing as a *conscious* transfer.

The Essentialists have been saddened, too, by what they deem an inordinate stress on the social studies. They grant them a part, but never a fat one, in the school's endeavor to make good citizens. At the same time they look askance at the efforts of such fellows as Rugg and Counts to make the school an active instrument for social change. To bring about a new and better social order, they would give the child not the elixir of more and more social studies, but an iron training in "basic fundamentals." And for this they have reserved a front place for the natural sciences. For no matter how useful the social studies may appear to be, in Essentialist eyes they cannot successfully compete with the natural sciences in the latter's requirement for thoroughness and precision.

Although a number of Essentialists, including Bagley himself, have conceded that there is some worth in projects and activity procedures, they have insisted that they be used sparingly. Certainly, say the Essentialists, they should not displace the tried and trusted subject-matter curriculum and those methods which stress systematic and sequential learning. The "opportunist school of thought," which caters to the immediate interest in curriculum content, draws only dark and menacing scowls from Bagley. "Gripping and enduring interests," he insists, "frequently, and in the respect of the higher interests almost always, grow out of initial learning efforts that are not intrinsically appealing or attractive. . . . To deny to the young the benefits that may be theirs by the use of this unique human prerogative would be a gross injustice." [10] In the matter of method and content, Bagley and

---

[10] Bagley, W. C., "Just What Is the Crux of the Conflict Between the Progressives and the Essentialists?" *Educational Administration and Supervision*, XXVI, p. 510, 1940.

the Essentialists have put effort above interest; subjects above activities; race experience above that of the individual; logical organization above the psychological; and the teacher's initiative above that of the learner.

The basis of most of these faults Bagley perceived in the educational theories of progressivism, its underlying pragmatism, and particularly its reliance on a utilitarian tradition and its mechanistic psychology. In this school of thought Bagley saw some formidable dangers. There was, for example, the notion that freedom is both an end and a means. To Bagley this was palpably absurd. Freedom, he felt, could be reached only through discipline. In a democracy self-discipline is the goal, but imposed discipline the necessary means. "Among individuals," declared Bagley, "as among nations, true freedom is always a conquest, never a gift." As for pupil freedom, what the learner really needs "is a strong tincture of iron." Incidentally, even the pragmatic Dewey found it necessary to point a warning finger at some of the practices masquerading in the New Schools in the guise of freedom. He has spoken out especially against the "deplorable egotism, cockiness, impertinence and disregard for others" on the part of some children attending some of the Progressive schools. In the actual world, freedom is, of course, a relative matter. In the final analysis, everything depends on the conditions under which the child is to be "free." On the one hand is the extreme restraint and repression of the old-style school; on the other is the egotistical brat described by Dewey. Plainly, neither of the extremes is desirable. In fact, the best of progressive practice, as exemplified in the better Progressive schools, would reject any such one-sided concept of freedom.

Another point of disagreement between Bagley and the Progressives is over the latter's "confusion of work and play." In his argument Bagley went to great length to explain that play "is the primitive, spontaneous, purposeless activity of the immature." Work, by contrast, is full of purpose and effort. It is the "controlled activity through which . . . volitional

maturity is achieved." When once that state is reached, the
dualism may be dissolved in the satisfaction one derives in
work. But, Bagley was quick to add, volitional maturity also
"means the capacity to sustain and control effort even if the
effort is not pleasurable," a capacity which obviously he felt
the Progressives with their play-ways did not encourage.

2. Boyd H. Bode's critique

Not all critical notes have been entoned by anti-Progressives.
Indeed, some of the more rousing ones have come from the
throats of the Progressives themselves. Somewhat in this
vein are the criticisms which have come from Boyd Henry
Bode (1873–   ) of Ohio State. Unlike Horne and Bagley,
the realists and the neo-scholastics, Bode has not been shooting at the Progressives from behind hostile fence corners. At
heart, in fact, he has been something of a Progressive himself,
and whatever discrediting comments he has made on the subject of Progressive education he has offered in the spirit of
furthering and improving it rather than in the hope of bringing
about its ultimate end.

Philosophically Bode stands close to the pragmatists and
their cousins, the experimental naturalists, cherishing with
them the view that democracy must be education's basic principle. In this respect he feels that the Progressives have a
unique opportunity. Indeed, Progressive education can
"become an avowed exponent of a democratic philosophy of
life. . . ." Unluckily, however, Progressive education appears
to be confused and full of contradictions.

It emphasizes freedom, yet it also attaches major importance to guidance
and direction. It plays up method, but it is also critical of the content of
the more conventional curriculum. It places the individual at the center
of the stage; yet it perpetually criticizes the competitive character of the
present social order, which indicates that it rejects the philosophy of
individualism. It insists that intelligence must be permitted to operate
freely; yet it seldom alarms its constituents, who, in the case of private
schools, are generally the more prosperous element in society. It commonly regards the college as the citadel of its enemy; yet its chief business

is often preparation for college. It holds that learning takes place through doing; yet physical activity tapers off sharply as we go up the educational scale. To the earnest observer all this is very confusing.[11]

These incongruities, Bode believes, have their source in our cultural discords which have sprung from the transitional nature of our era; to dispel them the purging flames of a well reasoned social philosophy are needed. But the Progressives, having made an idol of Rousseau's stress on the individual, have relied largely on the nature of the child to form their educational objectives, instead of deriving them from the social ideal of democracy. As a result, the great majority of Progressive schools have been shrines of individualism rather than cradles of democracy.

Despite the claims of the Progressives to the contrary, Bode is convinced that they still look upon the child's needs and interests as things having their abode in the child's immediate, individualistic desires and impulses. Not that Bode rejects the desirability of considering the child's needs and interests in learning; but to be valid these should bear the hallmark of the community life. To determine educational needs and interests by searching the individual rather than society, Bode feels, is like "fishing in the wrong pool." It would be better to forget about needs for a time, he counsels the Progressives; instead get on with the really important business of working out in clear terms the implications of a democratic philosophy of education.

Nor has the critical Bode been lulled by the enchanting perfume of the newer methods, particularly those which revolve around "projects," "centers of interest," "teaching units," and the like. Bode gives them their deserved praise, of course. He lauds them for establishing a closer connection between the pupil's daily life and his schoolwork. He commends them for having put to the challenge the school's stuffy bookishness, its adoration of memory, and its failure to kindle a serious interest in the pupil. At the same time he feels that the luster

---

[11] Bode, B. H., *Progressive Education at the Crossroads*, p. 10. New York: Newson & Company, 1938.

of the new methods is not without tarnish, since they have failed to give us clear and definite principles of organization akin to those of the logical and scientific method of organization underlying the traditional subject-matter curriculum. Like the Essentialists, Bode has pointed out that such logical organization is based, after all, on cultural principles which themselves have been accepted as indispensable educational values. How will the newer methods accomplish similar ends? In what way will they guarantee to the child the racial experience in knowledge and skills? Kilpatrick's leaning in the Project Method is disquieting to Bode, for it "is clearly toward letting the child determine his own curriculum"—and this is as undesirable as letting him pursue his own individualistic interests. The newer method Bode regards as "too discontinuous, too random, too haphazard, too immediate" to fulfill the school's basic purpose.[12]

When he turns to Dewey's view of education as growth, Bode again registers a critical frown. "Education for the sake of further education," "activity for further activity," "growth for more growth," are not his favorite dishes. Granting that such a view of education has struck a hard blow at the conventional mechanistic view of learning as well as the ancient notion that the purpose of education is to perpetuate the *status quo,* Bode is not convinced that it is an adequate doctrine. "Since growth is the characteristic of life," he has commented critically, "education is all one with growing; it has no end beyond itself." Bode, of course, is not unmindful of Kilpatrick's important proviso, namely, that teachers and grown-ups might interfere to bring about the "right kind of growth," and of Dewey's dictum that the "direction of growth must be social." But such declarations, Bode feels, are not enough. What do they mean? What is the right kind of growth? And whither is social direction? What Bode wants, in short, is more light and less wind; more meaning and less rhetoric.

[12] Bode, B. H., *Modern Educational Theories,* Chap. VII. New York: The Macmillan Company, 1927.

Bode's main complaint against Progressive education is its want of a clear and understandable philosophy of democracy as the source of its basic principle. The Progressives, he thinks, have paid homage largely to the verbalisms of democracy, to its trite and unctuous phrases, its meretricious and flamboyant trappings. What they need is to penetrate below the surface. The acceptance of the democratic principle means more than the movement of lips in its behalf: "it means the reconstruction of ingrained beliefs and habits, the reshaping of our entire way of life." It confronts us with disquieting moral and intellectual responsibilities. The method to be employed in such a reconstruction Bode sees in the procedures of modern science: a dispassionate and probing intelligence applied to the foundations of our civilization. To those who have suggested that he is merely replacing an old dogmatism with a new one, Bode has replied that he is doing nothing of the sort. His quest, he assures us, is not for a new absolute, but the development of clear workable concepts, which, he hopes, may serve as roadmarks to a more abundant life of the common man. For Bode two ideas appear to be of central importance in relation to education. One is that the meaning of liberty and democracy is linked with the question of the origin, content, and authority of moral standards: whether these rest on transcendental sanction on the one hand or on a purely social sanction on the other. The other is that our national tradition is ambiguous with reference to this question.[13]

3. Some experimental appraisals of Progressive education

While the philosophers were reacting to Progressive education, a number of trained experiments began to scrutinize the methods objectively. One of the first to make a scientific appraisal of Progressive education was J. Wayne Wrightstone. Probing a number of schools which were following, more or

---

[13] See Bode, B., "Education for Freedom," *Teachers College Record*, XLIX, p. 276, January, 1948.

The second proposition is discussed in a symposium which was published by the University of Pittsburgh Press under the title, *Modern Education and Human Values*, 1947.

less, the progressive line, Wrightstone sought to judge them by means of a series of objectives derived in the main from statements of schoolmen in various parts of the country. Wrightstone delved into such matters as whether the pupil manifested an understanding of desirable social habits, and whether he practiced them. Did he develop desirable individual habits? Did he appreciate and want to do worth-while things? Had he learned the three R's? Had he developed any particular skills? In his conclusions, which he published in 1930, Wrightstone revealed no vast difference between the results attained in the Progressive schools and the more old-fashioned kinds. It was clear, however, that when such matters as intelligence and home background were matched, children acquired the fundamentals as readily and as well under the newer methods as under the older ones. Progressive schools fared better when it came to reading; but they didn't do so well in arithmetic and spelling. Said Wrightstone: "An inspection of the test results for the primary pupils shows that in all the academic skills tested, the primary pupils in the experimental schools achieved scores on tests which were significantly larger than those of the conventional school pupils. In all subjects except arithmetic, the difference in favor of the experimental schools is statistically significant." [14]

Another study to cast some light on the worth and efficacy of the newer methods was made in the early forties by a committee which had been brought together by the Progressive Education Association. The body, which was known as the Informal Committee, was made up of administrators, professors of education, and research directors from various parts of the nation. The committee raised the questions often asked by parents. Are the children learning to read? Can they cipher and spell? Do they respect authority? Have they good manners? And so on. The committee's findings, all in all, were not unlike those of Wrightstone. "In general," the com-

[14] Wrightstone, J. W., *Appraisal of Newer Elementary School Practices,* pp. 203–204. New York: Bureau of Publications, Teachers College, Columbia University, 1938.

mittee reported, "the evidence shows convincingly that the
new methods do not result in a loss of academic proficiency
in the usual school subjects, and that, where any measures
have been applied, there is a definite gain in terms of initiative, skill in dealing with problems, knowledge of contemporary and world affairs, and social participation." Significantly, the Informal Committee suggested that "the
amount of formal recitation and drill can be reduced below the
traditional amount without any observable decline in scholastic achievement." [15]

Rather similar were the conclusions obtained in a study
conducted in New York City during 1935–1940. Focusing on
the activity program, the experiment covered some 70 schools
in each of which there was at least one activity class. What
the experimenters desired to find out was, for one thing,
whether the children in the activity classes lost any of the
values of the regular program, and, furthermore, whether they
gained in other values.

The results of the investigation, which were evaluated under
the direction of J. Cayce Morrison of the New York State
Department of Education, indicated that, as far as the usual
school objectives were concerned, there was no great difference
in the results attained under either of the two programs.
Children who had studied under the activity program were
more proficient in reading; they were more adept in the use of
simple research procedures; and they were superior in their
understanding of social relations and in their civic attitudes.
"The activity program," it was felt, "may be continued and
improved with reasonable assurance that children will gain as
thorough a mastery of knowledge and skills as they would
in the regular program." [16]

Regarding the objectives generally stressed by the Progres-

---

[15] *New Methods versus Old in American Education,* pp. 31, 33. New York:
Bureau of Publications, Teachers College, Columbia University, 1941.

[16] Morrison, J. C., *The Activity Program,* pp. 162, 163. New York: State
Department of Education, 1941.

II

National Systems

A. England

1. Historical background

At first glance England's educational system seems haphazard and unplanned. Within it there are public schools that are private; private schools with financial aid from the state; sectarian and nonsectarian schools; secondary schools with primary subjects; and primary schools with secondary school subjects. One perceives some local authorities with activities restricted to primary education and others completely free in the matter of setting whatever education they may offer. The powers of the national authority include no right to prescribe curricula, methods, or texts; and in the case of the local authorities there is again the same general loose relationship to the schools under their control.

a. The state and education. The reason for this apparently helter-skelter scheme lies in the piecemeal evolution of England's educational system which, in turn, is traceable to the English philosophy of government. Traditionally the English have been fearful of bureaucracy and centralized governmental authority. While the Prussian Hohenzollerns and the French Bourbons of the eighteenth century were perfecting their centralized autocracies, the English were strengthening their cabinet and parliament. In no other land had personal freedom attained such majesty. "Reason," Voltaire declared soon after his arrival in England, "is free here

163

and walks her own way. No manner of living appears strange. . . ." It was, he felt, "a nation fond of their liberty," a country where "people think freely and nobly, unrestricted by servile fear." English freedom and self-expression revealed themselves not only in the growth of parliamentary government, in which the lower chamber strode slowly but steadily to power, but in every town and hamlet, in every county and borough. Nowhere else among the larger European nations have local cultures received a more cordial respect and local government flourished more magnificently.

Attending the English esteem for personal freedom one notes a distrust of national regulation. Where a bureaucrat like Frederick the Great delighted in formulating codes and endless regulations governing the waking and sleeping hours of every subject, the British, by contrast, put their faith in *laissez-faire,* which meant a minimum of governmental control and interference not only in trade and commerce, but in every walk of life. Where Frederick believed passionately that the state was all and that the individual existed solely for it, England, even in the twentieth century, was afraid lest "the Juggernaut car of bureaucracy" might roll "over the liberties of local authorities." [1] Where Frederick proclaimed the credo *wie der Staat, so die Schule* (as the State, so the school), and held that all education, private as well as public, was subservient to the state and that its essential function was to mold its citizens in its own interest, the British feared that state action in education would produce this very result. "A general State education," declared John Stuart Mill, "is a mere contrivance for molding people to be exactly like one another; and as the mold in which it casts them is that which pleases the predominant power in government . . . in proportion as it is efficient and successful, it establishes a despot-

---

[1] Quoted from an address by Minister of Education, H. A. L. Fisher, in defending the government's educational bill which was subsequently enacted as the Education Act of 1918.

ism over the mind, leading by natural tendency to one over the body." [2]

Coupled with the English love of personal liberty and distrust of governmental action, one observes a reverence for traditional values and a hesitant acceptance of change. The reluctance to embark upon new and untrod highways has often been a check to reform. It explains in no small way why England lagged behind other European powers in modernizing her system of education. Thus, while Prussia had arrayed herself in the robes of a national educational system even before the end of the eighteenth century, and France was doing likewise under the direction of Napoleon, England continued to cling to private enterprise and *laissez-faire* in education. It was not until 1833 that England began to make some kind of provision for national grants to education. The sum of £20,000 was then voted "in aid of private subscriptions for the erection of schoolhouses for the education of the poorer classes of Great Britain." At best, of course, this was only a meager provision, a philanthropic gesture to help the more ambitious among the poor. However, since schoolhouses began to appear in ever-increasing numbers, the government was induced in time to convert its original grant into an annual one. As custom gave its sanction to the practice, the grants became steadily more substantial, until by 1945 the Ministry of Education was spending about £65,000,000 on the nation's schools. [3] The government's subsidizing of education gradually enhanced the state's interest in education, but it did not produce a national system of education nor a national program of education until many years after the practice of giving grants had started. In 1870 a modern system of elementary education came into being; and not until 1902 did a modern secondary school begin to emerge.

---

[2] Mill, J. S., *On Liberty*, p. 149. Boston: The Atlantic Monthly Press, 1923.

[3] The total annual expenditure of public money on education (excluding university education) was over £120,000,000. See *A Guide to the Educational System of England and Wales*, p. 52. London: Ministry of Education, 1945.

It was not, indeed, until that year that England may be said to have achieved a national system of education.

b. **School inspection.** As always, when a government is moved to extract a subsidy from its till, England became interested in the way her money was being spent. Thus it is not altogether a cause for wonder to note the rising demand for the supervision of these governmental grants. In the course of time various acts were passed tending to superintend parliamentary expenditures for the purpose of promoting public education. By 1839, however, public schools had not yet been established, the practice being to apportion national grants among organizations maintaining schools, such as the National Society and the British and Foreign School Society. All grants were made dependent on governmental inspection. Along the midway mark of the nineteenth century an important stride toward a national system was taken with the establishment of an Education Department. This was to take charge of the work of the Committee of the Council whose vice president was to be answerable to Commons in questions pertaining to education. In 1861 the much and hotly discussed payment-by-results system was introduced. Under this scheme, schools were to receive grants not according to their real needs, but rather on the basis of their attainments, particularly as demonstrated by their pupils' individual success in annual examinations.

c. **Elementary education.** Elementary education began its significant development in the nineteenth century. At the outset it was not a state enterprise at all, but the voluntary effort of a number of private organizations, mostly of a religious pattern—such as the British and Foreign Society and the National Society for Promoting the Education of the Poor in the Principles of the Established Church. These and other organizations provided schools for the poor, teaching them the three R's and religion and morals. For funds to maintain their schools they depended almost entirely on gifts from the philanthropically inclined. Not until 1833 did Parliament make its first grant to aid the elementary schools. However, it was from these simple beginnings that the publicly supported and controlled elementary school eventually emerged.

The cornerstone of the modern English elementary school was laid in 1870 when Parliament passed its well-known Elementary Education Act. The extension of suffrage a few years before contributed in no small way to the passage of the bill. A product of many conflicting ideas, the Act authorized the election of school boards and the levying of local taxes to establish elementary schools in such cases where the number of such schools was deemed insufficient. The voters of the community might elect the school board to maintain the elementary school. These were known as "board" schools, and the local rates which partly supported them were to be equal to the government's grant. In contrast to the board schools were the "voluntary" schools, that is to say, the church schools. They, too, were to share in the government grants, but not in the local taxes. All governmental grants, moreover, were dependent on the reports of the government inspectors. Board schools could give only undenominational religious instruction. In addition, all schools were required to put their religious instruction either at the beginning or end of the school session, so that any pupil whose parents might object to the kind of religious instruction being given could be withdrawn. It was the hope of the sponsors of the Act that education would now be "universal, gratuitous, compulsory." The Act, however, splendid though it was, had an Achilles heel. By permitting sectarian schools to receive governmental aid, the Act led to considerable rivalry and competition between the board and voluntary schools. The Act of 1870 did not eliminate the traditional prominence of voluntary agencies in the sphere of English education. On the contrary it provided for them specifically, recognizing what has since become known as the "dual system." Under this there are two types of grant-aided schools, one provided by the school boards and the other by the churches.

d. **Secondary education.** Although secondary education
has a venerable history, it is not until the latter part of the
nineteenth century that the state evinced any real interest in
this cultural domain. The initial step in the direction of
greater state action was taken in 1861 with the appointment
of the Clarendon Commission. Authorized to investigate the
nature of the endowments, funds, and revenues of the Great
Public schools and to inquire into the administration and
management of these schools, as well as their methods, curricula, and extent of instruction, the Commission reported in
1864. Four years later the Public School Act was passed,
providing for the administration and reorganization of seven
of the nine schools scrutinized by the Commission. Meanwhile another body, the Taunton Commission, had been appointed to make a study of the endowed secondary schools not
included in the study of the Clarendon group. The Taunton
Commission, or as it is sometimes known, the Schools Inquiry
Commission, issued its report in 1868. It revealed among
other things that the supply of secondary education was altogether inadequate; that the secondary school lacked a
clarity of purpose as well as an understanding of the needs of
pupils; that it was without recognized standards; and that
because of its inferior methods of teaching and its untrained
instructors, its results were unsatisfactory. In a more constructive vein the Commission recommended the creation of a
Central Authority empowered to study ways and means of
reorganizing educational endowments for subsequent parliamentary approval; to appoint inspectors of endowed schools;
to examine and audit the accounts of such schools; and,
finally, to determine whether or not certain charities designated as useless, or even "mischievous," might be converted to
educational uses. Furthermore, it was recommended that the
nation as a whole should be divided into administrative areas
under authorities entrusted with the task of coordinating the
secondary schools and developing plans for the consideration

of the Central Authority. Regarding the improvement of standards, it was proposed to establish an examining body for the purpose of examining pupils, of certifying candidates for the teaching profession, and of publishing annual reports. Significantly enough it was also suggested that various grades of schools should be established in order to meet the different needs of pupils of diverse social background.

However, despite the revealing light cast by the Clarendon and the Taunton Commissions on the inadequacies of secondary education, the state undertook no effective action. In fact, when the suggestion for some sort of local and national control was made, it was roundly denounced as being just another attempt at governmental interference. When Parliament legislated the Endowed School Acts of 1869 and 1874, therefore, it offered only a feeble makeshift for what should have been a comprehensive reform. Failing to deal with secondary education as a whole, it provided for the appointment of a Board of Endowed School Commissioners who were to devise schemes for reorganizing the Endowed Schools. No local authorities were created and no provision was made for the supervision and examination of secondary schools. In 1874 the powers of the Endowed School Commissioners were transferred to another body, the Charity Commissioners, who continued to hold the powers until 1900.

As might be expected, there was during all these years a growing demand for some sort of education above the primary level. In some instances this was met by the more efficient and ambitious boards with the establishment of the so-called higher primary schools. But in 1869 a new type of education was ushered in by the Technical Instruction Act. This made the county and county borough councils, established the year before, responsible for technical instruction. This, interestingly enough, was rather broadly defined as being the teaching of artistic and scientific principles applicable to industry and the special trades, but it failed to include the actual practice of such trades or industries. A year later the Local Taxation Act was embodied in the statute books, and by this provision technical instruction was to be aided by local taxes and governmental grants or the so-called "whisky money." The result of all this legislation proved a lusty boost not only for technical instruction, but for every realm of knowledge except Latin and Greek.

The disclosure of the lamentable deficiencies in secondary education, coupled with the disquieting possibility that the state might seek to establish its control over the secondary schools, was not without effect on a number of headmasters. Under the leadership of Edward Thring they joined forces in 1869 in the Headmasters' Conference, an organization which still flourishes today. The influence of the Conference was marked. Prompted by the organized headmasters, Oxford and Cambridge established in 1873 a Joint Board empowered to inspect and examine schools and to award certificates to successful pupils. In time other organizations came into being, and these, working in cooperation with the Joint Board and the Headmasters' Conference, contributed in a modest way to the improvement of the schools.

All this effort, good as it was, failed to strike at the heart of the problem. Nineteenth century England had undergone a rapid social evolution in which the nation's industrialization had forged ahead and in which there had been momentous changes in the national way of life. Parliament, not unmindful of the current of events, had enacted a mildly socialistic program in relation to health, housing, and labor conditions. Throughout the nineteenth century there had been a steady extension of political democracy so that by 1884 universal manhood suffrage had been virtually achieved. The Education Act of 1870 had created a national system of elementary education assuring the children of England at least the minimum educational essentials. But the nation's secondary schools failed to match this pace. Not only was their number quite inadequate, but the vast majority of them continued to stress the classics and to slight such newer subjects as the sciences and the modern languages.

In view of the government's procrastination, new approaches to the problem were adopted. With the help of grants from the Science and Art Department a number of elementary schools established advanced classes for pupils who were willing to continue their schooling beyond the compulsory age; special science schools giving evening as well as day instruction were organized; and a broad program of technical instruction was developed. However, none of these measures brought forth the desired solution. In fact, as the nineteenth century entered its last decade, England's secondary education was confused and chaotic.

Plainly, a scheme which had developed so planlessly would in time tend to become a legislative hodge-podge with duplication and overlapping. Cognizant of this deplorable fact, the government appointed a Royal Commission in 1894 "to consider what are the best methods of establishing a well-organized system of secondary education in England." The commission was headed by the celebrated James Bryce, and in its membership of seventeen there were three women. Slightly more than a year later the commission reported, and for the first time in England's history an outline for a national system of education was offered. Among other things it recommended the establishment of a central governmental authority for education under the direction of a cabinet minister; the creation of an educational council to act in an advisory capacity; and the adequate provision for secondary education on the part of the local educational authorities.

A few years after the appearance of the Bryce Report, in 1899 the government created the Board of Education as the Central Authority for Education.[4] The next step was taken in 1902 when, through the Education Act, counties and county

---

[4] By the Education Act of 1944 the Board of Education became a Ministry of Education.

boroughs were called upon to supply adequate secondary
education in their areas. Local authorities were, in the words
of the law, "to supply or aid the supply of education, other
than elementary, and to promote the general coordination of
all forms of education." Even so, the extension of secondary
education moved on very slowly. Economic necessity made
secondary schooling a luxury for most boys and girls and the
great majority of them continued to terminate their education
even before the end of the elementary school. In 1918 the
Fisher Act tried to make the secondary school more attractive
with the lure of scholarships. Three years later the Education
Act of 1921 pronounced it "the duty of the council of every
county and county borough so far as their powers extend to
contribute thereto by providing for the progressive development and comprehensive organization of education in respect
of their area."

By the outbreak of the second World War the number of
children attending the secondary schools had risen perceptibly
over what it had been at the dawn of the century. In 1900 it
has been estimated that not one child in seventy could ordinarily expect to enter a grammar school; just before the war
the figure was approximately one in ten. With few exceptions
the secondary schools charged tuition, but to be eligible for
grants from the Board of Education each year they had to
accept one-fourth of their children free of tuition. More eloquent, however, than the rise in enrollment is the fact that, in
the course of the twentieth century, secondary education was
made more and more accessible to children coming from the
elementary schools. Nor can the fact be overlooked that in
the progress of secondary education a larger proportion of
these children continue in the secondary schools than do the
fee-paying children, and that of those who eventually proceed
to the university, more than half took their first educational
steps not in the private preparatory school but in the regular
elementary school.

2. Administration of education [5]

The dominant characteristic of the English school system is its administrative decentralization, by which a large measure of autonomy is accorded the local school authorities. Generally speaking, the working relation between the national and the local authorities depends on consultation and cooperation, though both authorities are, of course, subject to Acts of Parliament. The central authority is the Ministry of Education of which the Minister of Education is the political head. Assisted by a Parliamentary Secretary, who sits in Parliament and is a member of the Government, the Minister exerts a strong influence on the development of a national educational policy. His department (1) inspects schools and reports on their efficiency; (2) acts as the Minister's local representative in administrative matters; and (3) advises the Minister in educational questions. By the Act of 1944 two General Advisory Councils, one for England and one for Wales, were created to make suggestions and recommendations to the Ministry.

Local administration of education was organized by the Acts of 1902 and 1903, by which the existing local governmental areas were made the units for educational administration. The instrument of local government is a locally elected council which, among other things, is required to establish an education committee to which is entrusted the work of education. Local education authorities must see to it that the full range of education is available within their areas. Although the local authorities are responsible in the last analysis to the ministry, their power and control are nonetheless very real. The money which finances public education is derived partly from parliamentary grants and partly from local taxes. For agricultural education, grants are made by the Ministry of

---

[5] Limitations of space preclude a consideration of the multifarious details of this subject. For a fuller analysis the reader is referred to *A Guide to the Educational System of England and Wales*. London: Ministry of Education, 1945.

Agriculture; for the education of delinquent or neglected children, by the Home Office. Grants to universities come from the Treasury.

3. Elementary education

a. **Provision of schools.** The Education Act of 1902 continued the "provided" and the "nonprovided" elementary schools. The essential difference between these two types is that the buildings of the former are built and maintained entirely by the education authority; whereas in the case of the "nonprovided" schools, the buildings are the property of the board of trustees, who rent them to the education authority. The trustees, moreover, are accorded certain rights in appointing teachers, with particular regard for their ability to impart religious instruction. Both "provided" and "nonprovided" schools are part of the public system of elementary education, and the local authorities are responsible for their maintenance.

b. **Private schools.** In addition to the regular public elementary schools there are a great many private schools. The precise number of children attending such schools is not known; but it is estimated that close to 400,000 children between the ages of six and fourteen are taught at home or in private schools.

c. **Compulsory school attendance.** By the Education Act of 1921 parents are responsible for the education of their children of not less than five nor more than fourteen years of age.[6] Although the law permits some exceptions, it requires compulsory education, which may be met by (1) attendance at any school, or (2) instruction at home, provided such instruction is efficient. By the Fisher Act of 1918 local authorities had been permitted to extend compulsory education to fifteen or sixteen years with the approval of the Ministry. The en-

---

[6] Subsequently the age was raised to fifteen, to take effect September 1, 1939, but this was postponed by the outbreak of the war. The Act of 1944 again raised the compulsory age to fifteen.

forcement of compulsory attendance is in the hands of the local authority.

d. **Infant and nursery schools.** The education of young children in England dates back to the early nineteenth century when Robert Owen organized a school "where children from two to six years of age were to dance and sing, to be out of doors as much as possible, to learn when their curiosity induced them to ask questions, and not to be annoyed with books." Owen's ideal, unfortunately, was not generally realized, and up to 1870 not much provision was made for the education of young children. The opening of kindergartens and the influence of Froebel injected some progressive streams into the movement. Early in the twentieth century (1905) the Board published a *Report on Children Under Five,* with recommendations for their education. What it "sought was a new school . . . for poor children," a place where "there should be more play, more sleep, more free conversation, storytelling, and observation." The Board's hope, however, was realized only very slowly. Under the influence of Montessori the education of young children received new attention. Another influence contributing to the development of a more progressive education of the young child was the Nursery School Movement.

By the Education Act of 1918 local education authorities were empowered to establish day nurseries for infants ranging in age from one month to three years, and nursery schools for children from two to five years old. For mothers who had to go to work such nurseries were a boon. Half the cost of these institutions was to be borne by the Board of Education. Unfortunately, the adverse economic conditions following the first World War interfered with the development of these schools.[7] Most nursery schools are of the open-air type. There is regular medical inspection, with records of the child's physical growth.

---

[7] By the Act of 1944 Local Education Authorities are obliged to provide nursery school facilities for children between the ages of two and three wherever there exists a reasonable demand.

Some schools also watch the child's general development, keeping records of his intelligence, skills, conduct, and so on. On the whole the work of the nursery school focuses on the development of good habits, with bathing, washing, dressing, social activities in preparing for meals, and the like. Much time, of course, is given to play and games. Sense training is stressed as well as the development of good habits of speech. Besides nursery schools there are also nursery classes whose work is fairly similar to that of the nursery school.

Formerly stressing the acquisition of the three R's, the best infant school of today emphasizes activities and experiences from which these fundamentals subsequently develop. There are games and play, story-telling and conversation, training in speech, nature study, drawing, music, dancing, manual work, and nature study. Just as the kindergarten helped to influence the work of the early years of American elementary education, the methods of the infant school are affecting the work of the early years of the English elementary school.

e. **The elementary school.** The annual *Code*, issued by the Board of Education from 1904 to 1926, asserted that "the purpose of the public elementary school is to form and strengthen the character and to develop the intelligence of the children entrusted to it, and to make the best use of the school years in assisting both boys and girls, according to their different needs, to fit themselves, practically as well as intellectually, for the work of life." The stress is on character development, with all its implications for an all-round growth of body, mind, and spirit. Liberal education is sought. In this respect the twentieth century English elementary school stands out in contrast to its nineteenth century predecessor with its emphasis on the thorough mastery of a few subjects. Chief Inspector of Schools of the London County Council, Dr. F. L. Spencer, declared that he was struck in visiting the schools

not merely by the changes in teaching methods and curriculum . . . but more than all, by the greater ease of discipline; by the fact that the relation between teacher and taught, once almost a condition of enmity, was now in the normal case, one of a friendly cooperation; and further by the almost uniform courtesy of the boys and girls. Discipline is as good as ever it was, but is achieved by vastly better methods.[8]

The Ministry of Education has steadfastly declined to prescribe the curriculum, insisting that "it is not possible to lay down the exact number of the subjects which should be in an individual school. The choice, indeed, cannot be in practice absolutely free. It is in part determined by public opinion as expressing the needs of the community. . . ." [9] The subjects ordinarily taught in the elementary school are religious instruction, English, writing, arithmetic, drawing and modeling, nature study, geography, history, singing and music, physical training and hygiene, manual work, and household subjects, including needlework, cooking, laundry work, and household management. The only subject wherein the Ministry has required its syllabus to be followed is physical training; and even here a local authority could employ its own syllabus, provided it has been approved by the inspectors.

Religious instruction [10] is given in all schools, but in the provided schools it is regulated by the Education Act of 1870 (Cowper-Temple Clause) which stipulates that "no religious catechism or formulary which is distinctive of any particular denomination shall be taught in the school." Applying this yardstick, this has meant that the Bible could be read, but without comment. In addition there are included the Ten Commandments, the Lord's Prayer, and the Apostles' Creed. Under the "conscience clause" of the Education Act, parents may have their children excused from religious instruction. In the nonprovided schools, which are mostly in the hands of the churches, religious instruction is, of course, sectarian.

Since the Ministry does not insist on curricular prescriptions,

---

[8] Wilson, J. D., Editor, *The Schools of England*, pp. 53 f. London: Sidgwick & Jackson, 1928.

[9] *Handbook of Suggestions for the Consideration of Teachers and Others Concerned in the Work of Public Elementary Schools*, p. 38. London: Board of Education, 1927.

[10] See p. 191 for modifications effected by the Education Act of 1944.

the local authority has considerable leeway in the matter. Such a situation has the advantage of allowing for freedom and elasticity, facilitating the adjustment of the school to the local needs. Under such a scheme, too, experimentation is possible. In its *Report on the Primary School* the Consultative Committee, for example, suggested an integrated curriculum for the early years of the child's schooling.

Although English elementary education is characterized by considerable liberty, there are some controls. Through its publications, lectures, conferences, and courses, the Ministry exerts an influence in determining educational aims and ideals. Another controlling force is the system of inspection, which, though not dictatorial, tends to unify standards. Though outside examinations for elementary school children are not encouraged, examinations are held to select eleven-year-old children for transfer to central or secondary schools. In some places all eleven-year-olds must take this examination; in others only those recommended by their teachers. At any rate the results of the examination, after all its shortcomings have been discounted, tend to indicate a standard of attainment.

f. **Intermediate education.** *Historical background.* The Education Act of 1870 stimulated the development of elementary education. Because of the lack of secondary schools, and to meet the needs of those pupils who wished to remain in school beyond the compulsory age, advanced elementary schools were established. With the creation of secondary education at public expense as a result of the Education Act of 1902, the need for advanced elementary education did not vanish. However, since these schools were required to be of a "predominantly scientific type," they were not satisfactory in meeting the diverse requirements of those boys and girls who could remain in school up to the age of fifteen. In 1910 the London County Council began to establish what were known as "central schools," which offered a four-year course to children selected from the elementary school at about the age of eleven. A number of other authorities, notably Manchester and Bradford, followed the London innovation. The Education Act of 1918 required advanced instruction and practical work in the last stage of the elementary school, and this requirement stimulated the development of a number of experiments. The result was that a number of types of organization came into being, as, for example, the selective central school, the nonselective central school, the partially selective central school, higher tops and senior standard departments, and various combinations of these.

Central schools. The central schools cater to those children who are able to continue their schooling for four years beyond the age of eleven. They are intended for practical-minded boys and girls rather than for the academic type. The work of the first two years at London includes English, algebra, geometry, science, history, geography, art, music, handwork, needlework, and domestic science. French is offered to those pupils who expect to go into the commercial course of the last two years. The second part of the course becomes more practical, with leanings to the commercial, industrial, or domestic subjects. Some central schools also continue the general course for the last two years.

Senior schools. The senior school may be the senior division of an elementary school with its own organization, or it may be a separate institution. Pupils are usually transferred to the senior school on the basis of age rather than academic achievements. Intended for pupils who have failed in examination to gain free admission to a selective senior or central school or to a secondary school, the senior school is nonselective. On the whole the senior school continues the work of the primary school, adding such practical work as is suited to the particular needs of the locality.

4. Secondary education

a. **The public school.** The oldest and most renowned of England's secondary schools are the so-called public schools, which actually are not public at all but private. Some of them have seen the centuries come and go: Winchester, which is the most venerable of them all, was founded in 1382 by William of Wykeham.[11] Nine of them—Charterhouse, Eton, Harrow, Merchant Taylors', Rugby, St. Paul's, Shrewsbury, Westminster, and Winchester—have been designated as the Great Schools.[12] Besides the vaunted nine there are more than 150 others, a few of which are very old, but most of which came into being in the nineteenth century. The vast majority are boarding schools whose fees range from $700 to $1,200 a year, though a number of scholarships are available. Admission to the public school is determined through the Common Entrance Examination for which the boy is generally prepared in a private preparatory school. There are more than five hundred of these schools. Ordinarily boys enter the preparatory school when they are eight years old; when they leave they are between thirteen and fourteen. Though in years they are on an elementary level, some of the studies which they pursue are traditionally secondary school subjects. Thus the prep school boy ponders not only over the usual elementary disciplines, but also over Latin, French, mathematics and, if he desires, Greek. Since the preparatory school's principal reason for being is to help its pupils past the Common Entrance Examination and into a public school, many of these schools have slanted their teaching more and more toward this examination. "In any case," asserts Sir Cyril Norwood, president of St. John's College, Oxford, and for many years Harrow's headmaster, "the

---

[11] Some of the characteristics of England's original public school have never entirely vanished and have found their way into other public schools. Thus Winchester's job was to prepare students for Oxford's New College with which it was closely connected. Winchester, furthermore, developed a prefect system by which eighteen of the more advanced boys gave instruction and exercised some control. At Winchester, for another thing, the school's communal life was stressed and extended to all activities. Finally, the all-engulfing aim was the development of character. See Wilson, J. D., Editor, *The Schools of England*, pp. 115–116. London: Sidgwick & Jackson, 1928.

[12] With the exception of Charterhouse, which was founded in 1612, all the nine Great Schools were established before the end of the sixteenth century.

object aimed at is to give a boy of thirteen the faculty of putting down knowledge in snippet form on all the subjects which he learns, in rapid succession during a space of two days, and he naturally regards this as the intellectual end of education. The end is not to learn Latin, or history, or mathematics, but to do a paper on them; hence drill has to be substituted for interest and cram for teaching." [13] Generally speaking, boys coming to the public school are about thirteen and a half years old and a little over eighteen when they leave. Most of their instructors come from Oxford or Cambridge, to which the majority of the boys who continue their studies will eventually proceed.

For generations, and even today, the public school has been the stronghold of the ancient classics. Stressing a general or liberal education, the public school has strongly resisted the demands for an increased consideration of vocational preparation. Its conservatism, however, has been affected inevitably by the shifting social and economic tides. With the change in the old order, particularly as seen in the twentieth century, the public schools have yielded more and more ground to the modern languages, to English and history, to science and mathematics. More has been done, too, to satisfy the aesthetic interests—though such activities receive their main stress outside the classroom walls. Traditionally, the public school has cast religion in a major role. Its chapel, in fact, has long been one of its distinguishing marks among English schools. In most public schools there is at least one sermon a week.

Although the public schools have been for the most part conservative and seemingly stress the development of a well trained intellect, they have not been oblivious to the other aspects of personality. Ever since William of Wykeham founded Winchester, English public schools have dedicated themselves first and foremost to the realization of his motto that "Manners makyth man." Their goal, indeed, has always

[13] Wilson, J. D., Editor, *The Schools of England*, p. 129. London: Sidgwick & Jackson, 1928.

been character—though their model has apparently been the English "gentleman." The public school's great stress on games and the playing field, the opportunities it offers for real experiences in the school community and its manifold societies and activities, which in a boarding school particularly are pervasive, all these contribute to the unfoldment and development of character. "The new boy," Sir Cyril Norwood has pointed out, "is a creature with no privileges and few rights, but little by little he is given his responsibilities and they are never artificial. . . . the boy has always to be thinking for others, and some of the positions to which he may rise, such as the captain of a game in a big school, or the head of a house, call for a good deal of organizing ability and the power to make and stick to decisions which are not easy." [14]

Although the public schools stand high in British esteem and have even been acclaimed as "the one great contribution of Britain to educational practice," [15] they have also been the target for a mounting criticism. There are those, for example, who deplore the schools' educational conservatism, their stress on the classics, and their adherence in the main to the obsolescent psychology of mental discipline. There are others who feel that the public school boy devotes entirely too much of his time to games and sports; still others censure the schools for their social exclusiveness, which they believe to be incompatible with democracy. The public schools obviously cater to the idea of an élite, but their élite, its critics assert, depends chiefly upon wealth and social class. The most serious charge directed at the public schools and their feeding stations, the preparatory schools, is that they are within the compass only of the well-to-do, and that even with scholarships the sons of the great multitude of Englishmen find the schools an impossible economic hurdle.

---

[14] Wilson, J. D., Editor, *The Schools of England,* p. 124. London: Sidgwick & Jackson, 1928.

[15] Wolfenden, J. F., "Public Schools and State Education in Britain," *The Educational Forum,* XII, p. 32, November, 1947.

Leaders in the public schools have not, of course, been insensible to these criticisms. On the contrary, they have often responded to them. More and more, modern subjects have come into the curriculum. Socially, attempts have been made to bring the public school boy into contact with the outside world through settlement work, Boy Scout activities, and activities shared with children of the regular elementary school. As for large social issues, and particularly those of a controversial nature, these have been zealously avoided.

It was at the request of the Headmasters' Conference and the Association of Governing Bodies that the Board of Education, in 1942, appointed a committee under Lord Fleming "to consider whereby the association between the public schools and the general education system could be developed and extended; also to consider how far any measures recommended in the case of boys' public schools could be applied to comparable schools for girls." The Committee's report, which was published in 1944, laid down the principle that "the opportunities in all public schools . . . should be made available to all boys and girls capable of profiting from them, irrespective of their parents' income." [16] To carry out this principle local education authorities were empowered "to provide a boarding school education for children, whatever their parents' means . . ." This was to be done, it was suggested, "either by paying the fees of a pupil at an existing boarding school, or by the provision by the local education authority, or by a group of authorities, of boarding schools of their own." [17]

b. **Day grammar schools.** There are besides the boarding secondary schools many hundreds of day grammar schools for boys and girls. Some of them are of ancient vintage—a few are as old as some of the more venerable public schools. They draw their pupils from the surrounding neighborhood and not

[16] *Report of the Fleming Committee on the Public Schools and the General Educational System,* Publication (H.M.S.O. 27–258) of the Ministry of Education, 1944.

[17] *A Guide to the Educational System of England and Wales,* p. 24. London: Ministry of Education, 1945.

from all parts of Britain as do the boarding schools. Because of their local connections, the day schools have been somewhat more in tune with social change; as a result they responded to the demands for curricular modernization somewhat earlier than the public schools. However, they have always emphasized a general liberal education, which is highly esteemed in England and is regarded by many not only as the best education for life, but also as the best basis for any eventual specialization. According to the *Regulations* of the Ministry of Education, secondary schools are required to offer instruction in the English language and literature, at least one foreign language, history, geography, mathematics, science, and drawing. If more than one foreign language is offered, at least one of them must be an ancient classical tongue. In addition, there must be provision for physical training, organized games, singing, and manual instruction. Girls' schools must provide instruction in domestic subjects, such as needlework, dressmaking, cooking, and the like.

In its scholastic organization the grammar school is not very different from the public school. Children are admitted to the grammar school, as to all secondary schools, on the basis of an entrance examination. Before the Butler Act of 1944 students usually came from an elementary or private school at about the age of twelve; most of them, however, left after passing their examination for the School Certificate, usually at the age of sixteen.[18] Those who continued to the end were generally eighteen when they left. Like the public school, the grammar school prepares its pupils for the universities and the professions; and stresses the school's corporate life, though in this respect it is obviously more limited than the boarding school which has command over the pupils' entire time. The grammar schools charge tuition fees ranging from about $50 to

---

[18] The examination falls into several groups of subjects: English, history, geography, and scripture; the foreign languages; mathematics and the sciences. The examination is important: It is the gateway to the universities; it opens the way to various professions; it is necessary, in normal times, for any youth who submits himself as a regular candidate for the Army.

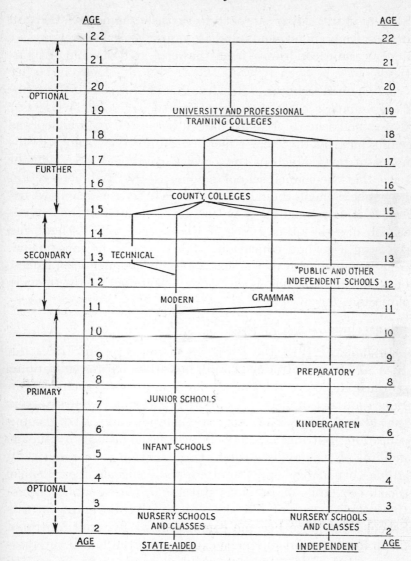

Fig. 1. Descriptive Chart of the Ladder of Education in Britian. (By permission, from *Education in Britain,* issued by the British Information Office, New York.)

$150 a year. Their support is further augmented through income from endowments and from grants which they receive under certain conditions from the local and national authorities.

c. Council schools. Besides the public schools and the day grammar schools there is a third type of secondary school, the council school. It is so named because it is provided and maintained by the local education authority which is in the hands of the Council of the Local Government Area. In the sense that the council school is operated by a public body it is a "public" school, though it, too, charges fees, which, however, are relatively modest. As for its curriculum, the council school, like the other types of English secondary school, put stress on a general education. Traditionally, however, it has been less enamored of the classics than the older schools; and on the whole it has been more hospitable to the modern subjects.

5. The Fisher Act of 1918

In January, 1918, the President of the Board of Education, H. A. L. Fisher, introduced a bill in Parliament for educational reform and before the end of the year it was enacted as the Education Act of 1918. More often it is simply referred to as the Fisher Act. The Act completely reorganized English education, putting it on a firmer national basis, although mindful of England's strong attachment to local liberty. It strove to equalize opportunity for all children regardless of social, economic, or religious status. Provision was made for the establishment of nursery schools for children under five. School attendance became compulsory at five and continued up to fourteen, but might be extended by the Local Authority for another year. In fact, children might stay in an elementary school up to and beyond sixteen if adequate provision were made for advanced instruction. Attendance at a private school was not accepted by the authorities unless such a school was open to inspection. A child might no longer leave school on the very day he became fourteen, but had to continue his attendance until the end of the term. The avenue to higher education was broadened. The number of scholarships were increased, and the Board made special provision for needy students. Up to the age of eighteen a child was to attend continuation school. However, for the first seven years of the new law's operation, at the discretion of the local authority, children were required to attend a continuation school only up to sixteen. In lieu of work at the continuation school, study at any other educational institution requiring high attendance was accepted.

The Fisher Act also totally abolished child labor up to the age of twelve, and partially up to fourteen. The so-called half-time system, whereby a child spent only half the required time at school, was wiped out. Medical attention in the schools was extended to include secondary schools, continuation schools, and such educational institutions as are provided by local authorities. With the approval of the Board, local authorities were privileged to support or maintain camps, gymnasiums, playgrounds, open-air schools, gardens, baths, and swimming pools. Provisions were made for the education of the physically and mentally handicapped. Concerning school inspection, all schools were required to furnish specific information about their organization and any other particulars specified by the Board of Education. Finally, the Board agreed to pay as much as one-half the cost of any worthy project undertaken by a local authority.

a. **Retrenchment** Though the Fisher Act met with the approval of progressive schoolmen everywhere, in its enforcement it soon struck a flock of snags. Because of bad economic conditions, budgets were cut sharply and, as usual, education came in for a generous share of economy. The result was that a substantial part of the Fisher Act was discarded.

Despite setbacks, however, some advances must be chronicled. Half-time was no more. Whole or partial exemption from school attendance was virtually stopped. A child could no longer leave school the moment he passed beyond the compulsory age; all children attended school at least up to the age of fourteen. Child labor, though still in furtive existence, was curtailed. The number of scholarships in the secondary schools became larger; and hygienic and medical facilities were extended.

6. The Hadow Report

In 1924 the Board of Education appointed a committee under the chairmanship of Sir Henry Hadow "to consider and report upon the organization, objective, and curricula of courses of study suitable for children who will remain in full-time attendance at schools other than secondary schools, up to the age of fifteen." Two years later the committee's report, *The Education of the Adolescent,* appeared. The Hadow Report favored (1) the expansion and enrichment of the upper years of the elementary school, that is, the years beyond eleven; (2) the development of senior schools of a less academic nature than the regular secondary schools; (3) the inclusion of commercial, industrial, agricultural, and domestic instruction as well as work in mathematics, science, and a modern language, besides the subjects begun in the lower years. Something like 75,000 children, it is estimated, annually enter the secondary schools from the elementary schools, and, as has been noted, this number is increasing.

7. The eve of the second World War

Just before the outbreak of the second World War England was spending slightly under $400,000,000 of public money a year on education—almost 5,000 times the original parliamentary grant of $80,000 in 1833. Whereas in 1870, the birth year of the nation's elementary school system, there were some 9,000 elementary schools providing for some 2,000,000 children, in 1938 there were 20,000 such schools taking care of 5,000,000 youngsters, besides 1,400 grant-aided secondary

schools catering to half a million boys and girls. As late as
1900 not one child in seventy entered a secondary grammar
school; by 1938 the number had risen to one in ten. Just
before the war, moreover, the compulsory attendance age had
been raised from fourteen to fifteen, though the outbreak of
hostilities forced a postponement of the new requirement.
Despite this obvious progress, there were a number of flaws
and inadequacies of which many of England's educational
leaders were well aware. It was felt, for example, in many
quarters that the number of nursery schools for children under
five was insufficient. In the elementary schools classes were
often too large. Nor were the additional services involving
health and guidance, the supply of school meals and milk, and
the like carried on on a broad enough scale. The "dual system," by which about half of the nation's schools were provided
by the local authorities and the rest by grant-aided voluntary
bodies, was attacked as being wasteful and inefficient. "The
dual system, with its divided responsibilities," its critics
asserted, "led to much complication in administration and put
a serious brake on educational progress." [19] The heaviest
blows, however, were generally reserved for education beyond
the elementary level. Though in the course of the twentieth
century England's secondary schools had been opened to more
and more children, they were still inaccessible to the great
majority. For too many boys and girls education ended at too
early an age, and for too many adolescents the opportunities
for further education, once they had left school and gone to
work, were inadequate. It was partly with an eye on such
deficiencies in England's system of education that a bill for
sweeping educational reforms was introduced in Parliament
under the leadership of Minister of Education Butler. When
it was finally adopted the bill became known as the Education
Act of 1944.

---

[19] *Education in Britain,* Bulletin, No. ID 606, of the British Information
Services, London, 1946, Revised, p. 7.

8. The Education Act of 1944

It seems odd that three of Britain's most significant educational acts should have been drawn up in periods of war. The Education Act of 1902, which laid the cornerstone of the educational system of England and Wales, came into being during the Boer War; the Fisher Act of 1918 was generated in the critical days of the first World War; and the Butler Act was passed in 1944. Foreshadowed a year earlier in an address by Prime Minister Churchill, the program for educational reform was sketched in a governmental White Paper, issued in 1943. Among other things this called for

1. A progressive decrease in the size of classes in the primary schools.
2. The adoption of a new and fairer arrangement for deciding on the type of secondary education to which children should pass after the primary stage.
3. The reform of the secondary school curriculum.
4. The expansion of the Youth Service.
5. The improvement of the facilities for enabling poor students to proceed to the universities.
6. The reform of the present methods of recruiting and training teachers.[20]

A little more than a year later (August, 1944) Parliament put most of these recommendations into law. Like its famous predecessor, the Fisher Act, the new law covered education "from the cradle to the grave." Somewhat more realistic perhaps than the older law in its attitude to the hard facts of postwar reconstruction, the Act of 1944 was conceived in many respects as a long-term program, some of whose principles, it is expected, will require at least a generation to fulfill.

What are the main provisions of the Act of 1944? To begin with, the law has spawned a number of changes in nomenclature, with which, of course, there has usually been an attendant change in purpose or function. Thus, what was once the Board of Education has become the Ministry of Education. Council schools have become County Schools. The program

---

[20] *Educational Reconstruction,* Publication (Cmd. 6458) of the Ministry of Education, 1943.

planned in 1918 by the Fisher Act for the Day Continuation School will be offered in time in modified and amplified form by the County College. The Elementary School will be referred to—in print at any rate—as the Primary School; and the denominational Nonprovided Schools will assume their former designation of Voluntary Schools.

Besides these modifications the Act has proposed a number of very substantial reforms. Regarding material conditions, for example, it has set the general standards with respect to buildings, school sites, playing fields, laboratories, work rooms, gymnasiums, lunchrooms, the minimum size and numbers of classrooms, and so on. Comprehensive regulations have been made which prescribe the general conditions under which the Ministry's grants are payable.[21]

Under the Butler Act school attendance has been made compulsory from the ages of five to fifteen, and eventually to sixteen. Moreover, by 1950 young people under eighteen who are not spending their full time in school will be required to spend part of their time at a County College. As for the very young child, local education authorities must provide nursery schools for youngsters between the ages of two and five whenever there is a reasonable demand. Elementary education, in the American sense of the term, is to embrace all children between the ages of five and eleven and a half.[22] Beyond this and up to the age of fifteen English boys and girls will have access to some form of free secondary education.

---

[21] Examples of their requirements are those governing the maximum size of classes—15 for children under three, 30 for children between three and five, 40 for children between five and eleven, and 30 for all children of secondary school age; and the requirements as to hours of school attendance and the maximum and minimum aggregate of school terms. See *A Guide to the Educational System of England and Wales,* pp. 21–22. London: Ministry of Education, 1945.

[22] English primary education includes children of the infant and nursery schools. It covers educational provisions for children between two and eleven and a half. Prior to the Act of 1944 the public elementary school was the only type of school which was not allowed to charge fees. It had to supply free education including books, stationery and apparatus for any child wishing to take advantage of it.

It is in the realm of secondary education that the Act of 1944 has proposed the most striking modifications. On the premise that every child should have the opportunity to receive the kind of education for which he is best fitted, free secondary education has been diversified in three ways, the grammar school, the modern school, and the technical school.[23] The grammar school, whose stress has been academic, offers a general education and leads to the universities and professions.

The modern school is a recent development in English education. It offers a four-year course of which the first half is devoted to a general education. During this period its curriculum and that of the grammar school have much in common, thereby facilitating the transfer of pupils from one type of school to the other, should they at a later time decide to make a change. In the third and fourth years the modern school gives increasing recognition to the pupil's interests and practical needs with special regard for the local environment with a view "to bridging the gap between the school and the employment available in the district." There are some modern schools, however, without this slant. Stressing, for the most part, a broad general education, they usually reserve the last year for some specialized work. The commercial curriculum seems to be a favorite with many boys and girls, although the industrial curriculum has its adherents too, especially among boys. Catering to the special needs and interests of girls are classes in cooking, home management, dressmaking, laundering, needlework, art, handicrafts, and hygiene. Boys' classes include wood and metal work, engineering, technical and machine drawing, physics, and chemistry.

Another type of secondary education is offered in the technical school. Its essence was anticipated even before the war, particularly by the Spens Report (1938), which proposed the creation of a technical high school to be based on the existing

---

[23] The private boarding school—or "public" school—is to be made accessible by the Local Education Authority to all competent children regardless of their parents' means. See p. 179.

junior technical schools, which provide a two- to three-year course for boys and girls graduating from the elementary schools. As envisioned by the Act of 1944, the technical school offers a general education related, however, to one or other of the main branches of industry, agriculture or business. Designed to meet the needs of boys and girls "with a practical turn of mind," the technical schools, through their relations with industry and business, "will give a sense of reality and objective which makes a direct appeal to young people of this kind and develops not merely their practical but their intellectual interests in a way that a more academic type of education cannot do." [24]

By 1950 all persons under eighteen who are not receiving a full-time education will be required to continue their schooling on a part-time basis in a county college. Attendance will be compulsory one whole day a week for a period of 44 weeks, or the equivalent. Though still in the blueprint stage, the program of the new school has been broadly conceived to meet the multiple needs of England's youth. The curriculum will include English, history, geography, citizenship, mathematics, and science; but attention is also to be given to various kinds of practical work which, it is hoped, will be helpful either as a hobby or in vocations. In addition, a broad and varied program of physical education is contemplated. This will include not only the usual gymnastics, but also such activities as athletics and team games, dancing, swimming, boxing, wrestling, fencing, and the like.

a. **Teacher training.** When the Act of 1944 raised the compulsory school age, it automatically created the necessity of increasing the supply of teachers. Before the war there had been some 200,000 teachers; under the new conditions this figure, it was estimated, would have to be increased by at least 100,000. To train its teachers England has relied in the past on two types of institutions: the training colleges and the

---

[24] *A Guide to the Educational System of England and Wales,* p. 23. London: Ministry of Education, 1945.

training departments provided by the universities. The former, of which many belong to voluntary bodies, offer a two-year course to students over eighteen years of age;[25] the latter give a one-year professional course to students who have completed at least three years' work toward a university degree. In 1945 there were more than 80 recognized training colleges and 22 university training departments. Prior to the war some 15,000 students were preparing to become teachers, and annually the training colleges and the university training departments would send forth some 6,500 trained young men and women. During the war this fairly steady flow slowed down considerably. Not only did thousands of men teachers join the armed forces and organizations of war service, but the influx of male recruits into the teaching profession slackened to a mere trickle. In fact, up to 1945 the number of women in training for teaching was below normal too.

England came to grips with its postwar teacher problem in a number of ways. In 1944 the McNair Committee made comprehensive recommendations for the improvement of the nation's system of teacher training. Several of the committee's proposals have since been adopted. Henceforth, for example, all teachers in schools publicly maintained are to be professionally trained; salary scales, the conditions of service, as well as the general status of the teaching profession have been somewhat improved; and by the Act of 1944 no woman may be barred from employment in any publicly supported school by reason only of marriage.

To help its hard-pressed teacher training colleges, the government raised the annual grant distributed to local education authorities maintaining such colleges to $400,000.[26] In addi-

---

[25] During the war the minimum age of admission was temporarily lowered to combat the growing teacher shortage.

[26] Steps were also taken "to widen the field of recruitment by asking Local Education Authorities to extend the educational opportunities for selected children in schools other than grammar schools with a view to the possibility of their becoming teachers." *A Guide to the Educational System of England and Wales,* p. 39. London: Ministry of Education, 1945.

tion, a number of emergency colleges were organized. Offering an intensive one-year course, these schools were designed for men and women of the armed services and other forms of national service. Upon completion of the course the student enters on a two-year probationary period. Although the emergency schools are organized under the local authorities, acting in essence as the agents of the ministry, their entire cost is borne by the Exchequer.[27]

9.   The religious question

Historically the elementary schools of England and Wales have a religious basis, about half of them having been established and supported by voluntary bodies, mostly churches. As might be expected, the church schools imparted denominational religious instruction. On the other hand, schools supported out of the public purse offered a purely nonsectarian type of religious instruction. In the course of the years this duality generated considerable controversy. There were those who felt that the system by which half of the nation's schools were supported by the public authorities and the other half by the churches should be abolished. The advocates of this viewpoint argued that the church schools should be taken over by the secular authorities and that public moneys should be provided for their general improvement. It was felt furthermore that all religious instruction should be nondenominational. Opposing this point of view were the Roman Catholics and some of the Anglicans who advocated financial support of the church schools to enable them to raise their standards to the level of those of the state schools, but who objected to any increase in public control over their school affairs or over religious instruction.

---

[27] The McNair Committee also recommended the extension of the training college's present two-year course to three years; but under the present conditions with its critical teacher shortage, this recommendation obviously could not be considered.

For the committee's study see the *Report of the McNair Committee on the Supply, Recruitment and Training of Teachers and Youth Leaders*. London: Ministry of Education, 1944.

Endeavoring to resolve this conflict the Education Act of 1944 took the church schools into the state school system as equal partners. The Act offered the church schools a 50 per cent subsidy to be used towards moving to new quarters. Schools able to furnish the remaining 50 per cent of the costs involved in bringing them in line with the state schools were to retain their right to appoint their teachers and to impart denominational religious instruction. Where a school is unable to provide the necessary money, it is to be supported out of public funds. In such an instance, however, its right to appoint its teachers has been restricted. As for religious instruction, such schools may devote two periods a week to sectarian religious instruction for those children whose parents desire it. For others, however, religious instruction is to be in accordance with an "agreed syllabus," which is a program devised by the local education authority.

Under the Education Act daily corporate religious worship is obligatory in schools. Religious instruction also is compulsory. However, if parents wish, they may have their children excused from these requirements. Prior to the Act the local authority was permitted to use its own judgment regarding the teaching of religion in its area, but the teacher could not. The new law has reversed the situation: now religious instruction is mandatory, but no teacher may be compelled to give such instruction.

To help local education authorities in compiling a suitable syllabus in accordance with the new requirements, a committee of Anglicans and Free Churchmen, the National Union of Teachers, and members of local education authorities drew up, in 1945, a national basic outline of religious instruction. Its content was based on the following principles:

1. The necessity for each child in Britain to become familiar with the Bible.
2. The need for moral and spiritual training to be based on the principles and standards of Christianity.

3. The influence of Christianity on the lives of men, on the social conditions of a country, and on the development of western civilization.[28]

10. The youth service

Like many other nations England, during the past generation and a half, has become more and more conscious of its youth problem. After the first World War the British government sought in various ways to cope with the problem by encouraging the development of facilities catering to the needs of young people, and especially by its time-honored method of subsidizing those projects it deemed worthy. Good as such efforts were, they were not adequate. The outbreak of the war in 1939 brought the problem to a new focus. Toward the end of the year the Board of Education, now the Ministry, was given the responsibility for looking after the special needs and interests of those young people who had left school and had begun to work. At the same time Parliament provided financial aid for voluntary organizations engaged in such work. To deal with the problem and also to advise the Minister of Education, a National Youth Committee and a Welsh Youth Committee were organized—the former of which has since been replaced by a Youth Advisory Council. At the outset the new Youth Service, as this branch of the Ministry's activity was called, was founded largely on the effort of voluntary groups. It took the form of encouraging the creation of special youth clubs for boys and girls, of broadening the activities of organizations like the Boy Scouts, Brigades, Guides, and the like, a great many of which were run under the auspices of the churches, and, to a lesser extent, the local educational authorities. During the war preservice organizations such as the Armed Cadet Forces, the Sea Cadets, and the Air Training Corps were especially popular.[29]

---

[28] *A National Basic Outline of Religious Instruction.* London: National Union of Teachers, 1945.

[29] Since the service cadet forces had no counterpart in the form of preservice organizations for girls, to meet their needs and interests the National Association of Training Corps for Girls was organized. Its membership was about

With the end of the war the Youth Service took on new force. Today the Ministry considers it "a normal educational service concerned with the leisure activities of young people between fourteen and twenty years of age who are no longer in full-time attendance at school. It is concerned with providing "increasing opportunity (without compulsion of any kind) for leisure time facilities of all kinds for young people." At bottom, however, the Youth Service is concerned with much more than the worthy use of leisure. It seeks "to provide for the training of young people in self-government and citizenship and as a means of continued education in the widest sense of the term." [30] Eventually, when the proposed county colleges materialize, the service of youth is expected to become an integral part of their program.

11. The postwar crisis and educational reconstruction

When the Education Act of 1944 was still in the realm of parliamentary debate, it was feared—even by many of its supporters—that the proposed law was too idealistic to be workable. The difficulties which beset the lamented Fisher Act were frequently recalled, for this too had come out of the idealistic, wishful thinking of a war-wearied Britain only to be found unworkable in the critical period following the first World War. Although it was realized that the second postwar period would throw up tremendous obstacles to the carrying-out of any far-reaching reform, it was felt that it was more important to put the law into the statute books while the public appeared sympathetic and to consider the problems of implementation later on. Unfortunately, as time went on it became increasingly clear that no one—not even the most pessimistic—had fully anticipated the nature and the formidable extent of the postwar problems and difficulties.

Like other war-scarred nations England has been troubled

100,000. Its purpose was to supervise and encourage the development of girls' preservice training.

[30] *A Guide to the Educational System of England and Wales*, p. 37. London: Ministry of Education, 1945.

by shortages which have seriously affected her educational program. The materials of instruction have been sadly inadequate; the number of school buildings has been insufficient for the rising number of students; and what has been true of buildings has been true of school equipment in general. Another difficulty confronting the English has been a serious shortage of teachers which, despite various emergency measures to replenish the ranks, has continued nonetheless. Aggravating the dearth of teachers more than anything else has been the raising of the school age and the reducing of the size of classes, both of which were required by the Act of 1944. Interestingly enough, postwar economic difficulties had no adverse effect on the nation's educational budget which has shown a steady increase each year since the war began.

Another difficulty to come out of the Act of 1944 has revolved around the question of clarifying the meaning of equality of educational opportunity. By the Act of 1944 secondary education was to be made available to all children between the ages of eleven and fifteen. To put this requirement into effect two plans have been proposed. The first would divide pupils at the age of eleven into three types of secondary schools—grammar, modern, or technical—with certain limitations placed on the numbers to be admitted to the grammar and technical schools. The second plan, accepted by the London County Council and several other local education authorities, provides for the establishment of multilateral schools, somewhat similar to the American comprehensive high school. In this all pupils follow a common core curriculum during the first years after which they will be assigned to the type of course for which they are seemingly best suited.

B.   France

1.   Historical background

a.   **National diversity and national solidarity.**   For ages France has been esteemed the great fashioner and disseminator of European culture and on occasion also its guardian. In the seventeenth century her language was the preferred language of every first-rank court in Europe, and her mode in dress, conversation, and polite manners set the standard throughout the civilized West. In the French Revolution she struck a blow for the "rights of man," for the ideals of enlightenment, for freedom and equality before the law. In the nineteenth century France became the great beacon for every European nation seeking to refashion its government on more democratic lines.

Like the English, the French prize their freedom. But with the English the love of freedom has evolved into a practical, working partnership, a companionate rather than a romantic attachment; whereas with the French it has had all the marks of a turbulent passion. Step by step from Runnymede in the thirteenth century to the epoch-making social and political enactments of the nineteenth and twentieth centuries, the English have advanced and solidified their freedom. They have done it slowly and pragmatically and, on the whole, peacefully. In France, by contrast, the history of freedom has been a gory chronicle, abounding in dramatic and violent outbursts against tyranny at home and stubborn and heroic stands against hostile incursions from abroad.

One would think the common experience of the centuries would have molded the people of France into a unified entity, a whole in which the parts serve the common cause. Yet such has never been quite the case. Unlike their practical neighbors across the Channel, the French have never been able to strike a neat and effective balance between individualism and collectivism. The civic spirit, so characteristic of the British, is ill at ease when garbed in Gallic raiment. And though Frenchmen may join hands against tyranny and invasion, in the moment of triumph they are apt to disperse. France, said Calonne in 1787, is so divided and so poorly administered that it was "impossible to govern"—an observation which, with a

few exceptions, might be applied to French history ever since.
For generations the spirit of France has been that of "frondeur"—the deep-grooved habit of resistance to authority,
rules, and regulations, regardless of source. The French, it has
been said, will die for their country, but they will not pay
taxes half so readily. French individualism has its roots in
history and geography. Even its grapes seem to have caught
the spirit, for though some of them grow only a few kilometers
apart, they will produce the most remarkably different wines.
The Basques and the Normans are Frenchmen, as are the
children of Brittany and Burgundy; yet despite their common
nationality they are marked by a diversity which sets them far
apart in their viewpoints.

The infinite diversity of the French has given their land its
genius and no little of its charm. It has taken its thinkers
and scientists and its inventors into new and unexplored
regions of knowledge and performance; it has revealed itself
in the exquisite objects fashioned by countless skilled and
talented craftsmen. At the same time, it has struck a divisive
note, one which has kept the French socially and economically
at effervescent odds and in a political turmoil which has been
a constant threat to their national solidarity. Thus, whereas
England has always been a monarchy, having evolved within
the royal framework from absolutism to its present democracy,
France has been a kingdom on several occasions, an empire
twice, and four times a republic.

France's battles against tyranny and despotism, though
graced generally by victory, have never attained a complete
and thorough finality. Although kings and emperors have
been removed and the monarchy uprooted, France still has
monarchists in its midst. Though the Church has been shorn
of its secular power, and state and church have long been
separate, in the embers of their former controversies the
ancient rivalries remain aglow. Indeed, there are in France
many millions of men and women who have clamored for the

return of Catholicism as the nation's established, official religion.[1]

For years the French have lived under the fear of invasion. The Industrial Revolution enhanced that fear, for France's resources of coal and iron lie within a few miles of her vulnerable eastern frontier. That fear, we well know, is no mere illusion; for three times within living memory France has been invaded and turned into a graveyard. It is the dread of German aggression, perhaps more than anything else, which has directed France's policy toward security, toward preserving intact not only her beloved soil, but also her cherished culture. France's desire for national solidarity has transcended even the great individualism of her people and has caused her to cling, through the vicissitudes of monarchy, empire, and republic, to the centralized bureaucracy developed by the first Napoleon. Though the republic rests on democracy, in which the state represents the will of the people who comprise it, that state nonetheless has been one of the most centralized known to modern civilization. Traditionally the French have accepted the concept of national control in education as the best guarantee of national solidarity. Hence, unlike England and the United States, France has been unwilling to make anything but a grudging concession to local cultures. Instead of encouraging local differences, it has sought instead to stress common ideals and common feelings through a uniform curriculum for the entire nation as well as uniform standards and requirements. The function of the elementary school, it has insisted, is to teach those things of which no adult Frenchman should be ignorant—and those

---

[1] Especially aggressive was the *Action française,* which waged an open campaign for the restoration of a Catholic monarchy, even at the cost of civil war. Its activities alarmed the papacy, which, by a series of decrees culminating in 1927 under Pius XI, put the movement under the ban of the Church, even though it was the strongest Catholic organization in France. By papal action the faithful were forbidden to support the *Action française* or even to read its paper. One reason, incidentally, why woman's suffrage was opposed in France was the fear on the part of anticlericals that women might vote for the restoration of Catholicism as France's official religion.

things include not only the common cultural heritage of *la grande nation,* but also the ideology of a democratic, secularized republic, in whose midst still lurk ancient foes and across whose frontier a beaten and battered Germany is potentially a danger to the peace and security of the republic.

b. **The early nineteenth century.** Almost to the outbreak of the Revolution in 1789, French education was dominated by a religious motive and was in the hands of the clergy. Between 1792 and 1795 the National Convention secularized the church schools, confiscating their property and at the same time considering the creation of a secular and national educational system. However, aside from the establishment of the Normal School and the Polytechnic School at Paris in 1793, relatively little was done. Napoleon concentrated mainly on secondary and higher education, reorganizing the secondary and higher schools and abolishing the independence of the universities, transforming them, with the exception of those in Paris, into groups of faculties whose main job was the granting of degrees. In 1806 he founded the so-called University of France, which was not a teaching body at all, but a corporate and state-controlled body of all secondary and higher institutions of learning. At the same time he divided the French nation into administrative "academies," each with a rector and administrative council, having supervision over its work. The centralized system which Napoleon created continued, with some modifications, to the outbreak of the second World War.

c. **Guizot's Law of 1833.** In the domain of elementary education Napoleon did nothing. In fact, the Church was allowed to re-assume its former control, with special concessions being made to the Christian Brothers, whose schools had been shut down by the Revolution in 1792.[2] Just before the second revolution broke out in 1830, elementary education was

---

[2] During the reign of Louis XVIII (1814–1824), members of the teaching congregations were allowed to teach without the formality of a state examination. All that was required of them was the presentation of a letter of obedience from the head of their order.

almost under the complete control of the teaching congregations. Meanwhile, the secondary schools had continued almost unchanged. Under the monarchy of Louis-Philippe (1830–1848) certain important changes were introduced. Through Guizot, the first Minister of Public Instruction in the new regime, the basis of a national system of education was laid. This sprang from the Law of 1833 which established a system of elementary schools, primary and higher primary, the former to be established in every commune, and the latter in the larger communes. Partially supported by fees, the schools were to get grants from the communes and the state, and were to admit the children of the poor without cost. Furthermore, provision was made for freedom in religious instruction. In addition, all teachers were to be certified and appointed by the state. Thirty normal schools were founded to provide for an adequate supply of trained teachers. As a result of the Law of 1833 the number of elementary schools, as well as the number of pupils attending them, increased considerably. Unfortunately, under Louis Napoleon this progress came to a halt. From 1848, when he was President of the Republic, to 1870, when, as Napoleon III, he wore the imperial purple, France went into a steady decline. Not only were many of her leading liberals sent into exile, but many who remained at home were under suspicion and closely watched. Like other crowned reactionaries before him, the third Napoleon made concessions to the clergy. Through his encouragement the number of religious schools almost doubled. Private schools, of which the greater proportion were denominational, were given inducements to compete with the state schools. These, by comparison, were hampered in several ways: their budgets were cut; the pay of primary teachers was decreased; and the number of courses in the normal schools was curtailed.

d. **The Third Republic.** After Napoleon's downfall, France concentrated on the task of clearing away the debris. During the first decade of its existence the Third Republic overhauled and renovated the French schools. Under the leadership of Gambetta it sought to create the basis of a system of universal education. Education gradually became a national enterprise, and to make it function, millions of francs were dispensed for the establishment of school buildings and equipment and the launching of technical and manual schools. It was not until 1881, however, that primary instruction was at last made completely free. One year later it was made compulsory for children between the ages of six and thirteen. To make available the teachers required by this increase in the schools, every *département* (county) was required to provide a normal school for teachers of each sex. A much more difficult task for the Third Republic to solve was the matter of school secularization. Here progress was slow but steady. In 1881 all teachers were required to have a license from the State. Five years later members of the clergy were forbidden to teach in the public schools. The heaviest blow fell in 1904 when the teaching congregations were suppressed. Thus, slightly more than a century after the French Revolution, France in its educational scheme had finally attained the Revolutionary ideals of a free, compulsory, and secularized system of schooling.

2. Administration of education

What strikes the eye at once when one examines the French educational system is its high degree of centralization—machinery has been created which is capable of dealing with every phase of the nation's education. Through this system the state has extended its control over every school in France, with the result that local autonomy and initiative in education, as they exist in the United States and England, are unknown to the French.[3]

At the head of the French school system stands the Minister of National Education, who is a member of the national cabinet and usually a member of the legislature. Charged with

---

[3] For a fuller treatment of this subject the reader is referred to Kandel, I. L., *Comparative Education*. Boston: Houghton Mifflin Company, 1933.

the direction of all the establishments and services of public education, the Minister is advised and assisted in the execution of his duties by a hierarchy of administrators, inspectors, and other officials. The largest and most important advisory body is the Higher Council of Public Instruction, which meets biennially, and a part of which has been organized into a Permanent Section. It is this group which does the Council's heavy work, reporting on questions of administration, studies, textbooks, and discipline which have been referred to it by the Ministry. In the actual administration of the educational laws and regulations the Minister's most important representative is the Rector, who is the chief educational officer in an administrative area known as an academy. There are seventeen such areas.

3. Elementary education

French elementary education comprises (1) the elementary school properly speaking, the *école primaire;* (2) the infant or maternal school, the *école maternelle* and the *classe enfantine;* (3) the higher elementary school, the *école primaire supérieure;* and (4) those institutions which prepare teachers for these schools, the *école normale primaire* and the *école normale primaire supérieure.*

a. **L'école maternelle.** In origin the French infant or maternal school is traceable to Jean Oberlin and Père Girard, and to the regulations of 1837, which sought "to provide maternal care and the early stage of education suited to the ages of the pupils." It was a decree and a regulation of January 18, 1887 which organized and defined the work of the school, and which laid the foundation for the infant school of today. Maternal schools may be established at the option of municipalities. For the school's support state aid is provided.[4]

Attendance at the *école maternelle* is, of course, voluntary,

---

[4] This regulation, however, applies only to communes with a population of at least 2,000, of whom 1,200 are in a town or village. In the case of smaller municipalities such schools must be maintained at their own expense.

children being admitted at the age of two and remaining until they are six. Particular attention is given to the child's health, no child being admitted without a medical certificate. Furthermore, a medical officer is expected to make monthly inspections. Maternal schools are restricted to 150 pupils; where the enrollment is more than 50 an assistant principal is appointed. Classes are restricted to 25 children, grouped into

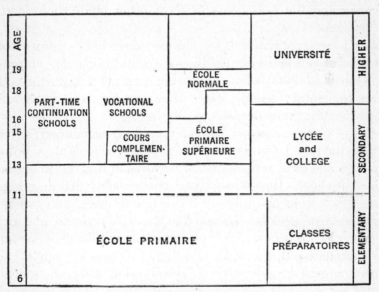

Fig. 2. The Schools of France in 1939. (From Myers and Williams, *Education in a Democracy*. Copyright by Prentice-Hall, Inc., 1937.)

two divisions according to age and intelligence. The curriculum is varied, consisting of (1) physical exercises: breathing exercises, games, and movements with songs; (2) sensory exercises, manual work, and drawing; (3) exercises in observation; (4) exercises for the development of moral habits; (5) exercises in language and recitation; (6) introductory exercises in reading, writing, and arithmetic. In the past the maternal school has been held down by a conservative scholastic tradition and by the insistence of ambitious parents that their children be taught the three R's as early as possible. Of recent years, however, there has been a trend toward more stress on play and free activities and less regard for formal school work and instruction. Freedom and spontaneity, health and happiness, physical and moral development, training in observation and thinking are aspects of the newer tendency. To some extent the *école maternelle* has been influenced by Montessori ideas (see p. 109). However, between the French *école maternelle* and the preschools of most other lands there is still quite a gap.

b. **L'école primaire.** In France education is compulsory for all children between the ages of six and thirteen. Founded by Guizot in 1833, when education was not compulsory, the state elementary schools used to charge fees, and it was not until 1882 that they became wholly free.

Every commune must provide a public elementary school. Where the population is over 500, separate schools are required for boys and girls, unless special permission is given to operate a mixed school. Boys must be taught by men; girls and mixed classes by women; only in exceptional cases may women teach in boys' schools. To teach in the *école primaire* one must possess the *brevet élementaire,* which is obtained by passing an examination in the work of a higher elementary school; the *brevet supérieur,* granted by examination after the normal school course; and the *certificat d'aptitude pédagogique,* obtained on examination after at least two years of service. Neither the *brevet élementaire* nor the *brevet supérieur* confers a permanent appointment. After two years' experience and the passing of an examination—and in the case of men, the completion of their military service—the teacher may become eligible for permanent appointment.

The elementary school's work is organized by courses rather than classes. Altogether there are four courses. The first is the preparatory course—*cours préparatoire*—and is for one year. The next three courses are each of two years' duration: the first is the elementary course—*cours élementaire*—for seven- to nine-year-olds; the intermediate course—*cours moyen*—for nine- to eleven-year-olds; and the advanced course—*cours supérieur*—for eleven- to thirteen-year-olds.

Theoretically conceived, the French elementary school seeks to give the learner what are generally accepted as fundamental facts, information, and knowledge. The child studies morals and civics, reading and writing, French, arithmetic and the metric system, history and geography with special stress on France, object lessons and elementary sciences, drawing, singing, manual work for boys with stress on agriculture, needlework for girls, and physical and military training.

What France expects, above all, of its elementary school is that its work shall be done thoroughly. Until recently the "new" education had made very little headway. On the whole, knowledge, facts, and information have been stressed. Through the influence of the crusading school reformers, *Les Compagnons,* the demands of regionalists, and the realization that rural education has not been successful because of its failure to adjust its program to local conditions, there has developed a growing tendency to allow adaptation to local conditions. Recent government instructions have, in fact, encouraged the normal schools to give some heed to preparing teachers for the small one-teacher school and elementary schools, to emphasizing the local environs and to giving some attention to the occupations of young children.

The methods of instruction found in the French elementary school have not the diversity of those found in many other countries.[5] Ordinarily, instruction falls into three parts: (1) exposition and presentation by the teacher, (2) discussions through questions and answers, (3) summarization in the form of an idea, a short statement to be noted in the pupil's exercise book and to be memorized. Every pupil must have an exercise book wherein is recorded the first task in each subject at the beginning of the month; if the teacher so decides, he may also have one in which he enters his daily work. Both these books

---

[5] The 1947 proposals made for the reform of French education recommended the activity method. See p. 225.

are used as records and are examined periodically both by parents and inspectors, to scrutinize not only the progress of the pupils, but also the work of the teacher.

The promotion of pupils is annual and is based on their records and the recommendation of their teachers. In the end there is a state examination for the certificate of primary studies—*certificat d'études primaires*. Pupils may take the examination if they are twelve years old in the year of the examination. For some time the examination has been under critical fire, and the authorities have tried to develop tests calling for observation and reflection. At the same time they have tried to discourage cramming and too much stress on preparation for the examinations. Thus far, however, they have not succeeded, and the examination continues to put a premium on bookishness and abstract methods. Although French elementary education is compulsory, its administration has not been too efficient. One explanation is the shortage of agricultural labor in the farming sections. The fact that up to a short time ago the school was not adapted to local conditions is probably another explanation of the problem. Then, too, in some instances parents have failed to cooperate with the authorities chiefly because of their indifference. Another cause, no doubt, lies in the Frenchman's natural individualism—his spirit of "frondeur," of resistance to regulation. The concomitant of poor school attendance is usually illiteracy, and France has been no exception. In 1924, for example, of 235,325 recruits called for military service, 13,838, or slightly more than 6 per cent, were unable to read and write.[6] Interestingly enough, in Alsace-Lorraine there is virtually no illiteracy.

One of the most difficult problems confronting French ele-

---

[6] "Despite the wide provision of primary education and the laws of compulsory attendance there was still a considerable number of illiterates, difficult to estimate and varying from region to region, but probably amounting to from 5 to 10 per cent." Henri Laugier in the chapter on France in Kandel, I. L., Editor, *Educational Yearbook 1944*. New York: Bureau of Publications, Teachers College, Columbia University, 1944.

mentary education has been the rural school. Time was when the authorities were not particularly concerned with rural education. But with the general increase in the population movement toward the city, French educators have become more aware of the immense significance of rural education. Attempts to adjust education to local needs are encouraged. Plans for the establishment of a rural school of an agricultural character have been proposed. In addition, agricultural societies have been asked with increasing frequency for suggestions with regard to the problems concerning rural education.

c. L'école primaire supérieure. Higher than the *école primaire*, but not the equivalent of the secondary school, is the advanced elementary school, the *école primaire supérieure*. Created in 1833 by the Guizot Law, the school offers a three-year course for boys and girls holding the elementary school certificate (*certificat d'études primaires*) and having been at least one year in the upper course of the elementary school. Students may also be admitted at times by examination or by having obtained a national scholarship.

Each school may decide on the number of curricula offering fields that are general, industrial, agricultural, commercial, or in home economics. The courses of study and the subjects are prescribed by the Ministry. However, principals may, with the advice of their teachers' councils, adjust them to local conditions. Since the advanced elementary school is generally established through the efforts of the local authorities, this freedom is of particular importance. The actions of the principal and the teachers' councils in administrative matters are subject to the approval of the Academy Inspectors.

The main purpose of the advanced elementary school is training for the country's administrative and economic occupations, for posts held in these domains by what might be designated as the intermediate grade of civil service official. The work is practical rather than academic. Indeed, it is this difference that marks the distinction between the advanced elementary and the secondary school. The *école primaire su-*

périeure is much more like the American high school than is either the *lycée* or the *collège,* the secondary schools of France. It is now possible for pupils to transfer from the advanced elementary school to the regular secondary school. National scholarships may be held interchangeably in one or the other.

An oral and written state examination must be taken by the pupil at the end of his three years of study. Success in the examination leads to the *brevet d'enseignement primaire supérieur.* Besides the written and oral test there is also a practical test, based on the vocational work of each section. The *brevet d'enseignement primaire supérieur* is a coveted certificate since it aids in securing certain appointments. It is required for entrance to certain schools and for elegibility to compete for scholarships for foreign travel.

Localities unable to establish advanced elementary schools sometimes organize a full-time continuation course—*cours complémentaire*—in connection with the existing elementary school. This generally offers a one- or two-year curriculum similar to that of the advanced elementary school.

4. Secondary education

a. **Historical background.**   Of venerable age, French secondary education can be traced back to the medieval era. However, it was the humanistic epoch which brought it into its present form. In the development of the secondary school and its traditions various religious orders wielded considerable influence. The Jesuits, the Oratorians, and the Port Royalists all left their mark on the secondary school. By the middle of the eighteenth century some one hundred *collèges* existed. Two main characteristics are discernible in these schools: they acknowledged the supremacy of the Church and they stressed Latin.

That period of political ferment which saw the French Revolution also witnessed a break in the classical tradition. The secondary school of the Revolution put mathematics and the sciences into its curriculum. This break, however, was only transitory, for under Napoleon the ancient ideals reappeared. Two types of secondary schools were developed—the *écoles secondaires communales* and the *lycées*. The former, which belonged to the communes or to private owners, form the nucleus of the present-day *collèges*. The *lycée,* then as now, was under the state. Political events of the nineteenth century did not greatly alter the tradition of classical instruction. There were, it is true, onslaughts on this tradition, and some of these attacks brought modifications.

In 1899 a commission, headed by Ribot, undertook to study the controversy between the advocates of the classics and the proponents of the modern subjects. Its findings led to the reform of 1902 under Minister Leygues. Under this the secondary school was to be for seven years, divided into two cycles of four and three years each. The first cycle was to be complete in itself, leading to a certificate. The second cycle had, during the first two years, a fourfold option: (1) Latin and Greek, (2) Latin and an advanced study of modern languages, (3) Latin and an advanced study of the sciences, (4) modern languages and sciences. At the end of each course the student could present himself for the first part of the baccalaureate examination. The seventh year offered a choice between specialization in mathematics and philosophy and was followed by the second part of the baccalaureate examination. Common to both courses were history and geography, mathematics, and the sciences. In the modern course, however, the last two groups of subjects received more time.

The Reform of 1902 brought down the curtain, for the time being, on an educational controversy that had raged for nearly a century. But the solution, at best, was an unsatisfactory compromise. During the first World War criticism grew more intense. Not only was the reform under fire, but it was held that secondary education should be available to all children of ability regardless of class, and that it should be general rather than specialized. It was generally agreed, however, that the purpose of secondary education should be to bestow a liberal education and to select the élite for leadership.

b. The Bérard Reform. After the war the demands for reform became stronger. Some would have substituted vocational and technical training for the traditional subjects; others preferred to retain cultural and general education, but wanted them more closely related to modern life. The proponents of technical and vocational preparation, however, were in a minority. The question which was really at issue hinged on the interpretation and meaning of general education: should this be modern or classical, and what should be the place of the sciences?

In 1921, after the appointment of Léon Bérard as Minister of Public Instruction, the problem came to a head. Secondary education, Bérard felt:

should form, by slow action of prolonged and disinterested studies, young people who, whatever specialty they take up later, will be distinguished by an eminent power to interest themselves in and to apply themselves to the varied creations of the spirit as well as of the industry of man.[7]

The best way to achieve this, Bérard believed, was by making the classics compulsory. He proposed a scheme requiring four years of Latin and two years of Greek of all secondary school students. Graphically, his system would appear as follows:

First Year: Latin
Second Year: Latin
Third Year: Latin and Greek
Fourth Year: Latin and Greek

Option: Latin-Greek	*Option:* Latin	*Option:* Modern Languages
Fifth Year	Fifth Year	Fifth Year
Sixth Year	Sixth Year	Sixth Year

The seventh year was to allow specialization in mathematics or philosophy.

---

[7] Quoted from the decree submitted by Berard to the President of the Republic. See also Kandel, I. L., *The Reform of Secondary Education in France.* New York: Teachers College, Columbia University, 1924.

The subject of modern versus classical training was debated in the French Parliament in 1922 and 1923. In 1923, a presidential decree announced that the Bérard system was to go into effect in the entering classes of the *lycées* and *collèges* the following fall. This much-discussed reform was introduced not by legislative enactment, but by a decree signed by the Minister of Public Instruction and countersigned by the President. The reform was not passed by Parliament until some time later. The decree had barely been in effect when there was a change in the government, and Bérard was succeeded by François Albert, who, by a decree of August, 1924, repealed the compulsory Latin and Greek, and restored the modern language option.

c. **Subsequent changes.** In 1925 a new course of study was announced. In the main the present system is based on this legislation, with subsequent slight modifications. Provision was made for a common course in the general subjects for the first six years, with an option, however, in the first four years between Latin and the modern foreign languages. Greek now became an elective subject for Latin students. In the fifth and sixth years the options are threefold: Section A being classical; Section A′ offering Latin and modern foreign languages; Section B offering modern foreign languages. The other subjects—French, history, geography, and the sciences— seek to effect a balanced curriculum by being the same for all. The aim is to give a liberal literary and scientific education and to delay specialization. The seventh year continues to be either philosophical or mathematical in emphasis.

d. **The baccalaureate.** The work of the secondary school is crowned with the baccalaureate which is awarded on the basis of written and oral state examinations. The first part of the test comes at the end of the student's sixth year; the second follows the work of the seventh year. The bachelor's certificate opens the way to most of the higher schools. From the standpoint of the educational authorities the examination serves to insure definite standards throughout the nation. At the same time it acts as a check on the private secondary schools.

The baccalaureate examination has been the subject of heated controversies. Believing that there are better ways of selecting students for higher education, some French educators are opposed to the baccalaureate examination. Paul Appel, for example, suggested in the *Revue Universitaire* in 1925 that those students receiving good grades in their written work from their fourth year on should be exempt from further examinations. However, the baccalaureate examination, besides being a tradition, is also a sturdy weapon enabling the state to keep its eye on educational standards.

e. Organization. There are two kinds of public secondary schools, the *collège* and the *lycée*. The latter is run by the state and is national; whereas the former is a local institution. However, the *collège* is partly subsidized by the state. Up to a few years ago the public secondary schools of France charged fees, but these now have been abolished.

With few exceptions, the French secondary schools are boarding schools. Their students are classified into several types: (1) boarders, residing at the school and leaving only during vacations or by special permission; (2) non-boarders, who fall into two groups, those attending school for their studies but living at home, and those who, in addition, do their homework at the school with the boarders and under the supervision of a member of the staff. In addition there are the semiboarders who take all their meals at school.

Strictly speaking, the French secondary school is more than a secondary school. At the lower end of the school, for example, pupils are admitted at a very early age. These classes were organized to give preparation for the secondary school proper which does not, as in the United States, articulate with the last class of the elementary school. In 1924, however, distinctions between these preparatory classes and the elementary school up to the end of the *cours moyen* were done away with. Furthermore, in 1925 provision was made for the admission of these sections of pupils from the elementary schools free of tuition, consideration, however, being given in the selection to the pupil's ability as well as the available accommodations.

Not only do the *collège* and *lycée* have elementary classes, but some also conduct advanced courses for students who have finished their secondary schooling and have obtained the baccalaureate. Some of the larger *lycées* conduct special courses for students wishing to prepare themselves for the competitive examination for the *école normale supérieure*. Advanced courses are also conducted in some schools preparing students for the competitive examination for St. Cyr, the military school for future French officers. In some schools there is an advanced mathematics course for those who wish to prepare themselves for a higher technical school as, for example, the *École Polytechnique*.

f. **Secondary education for girls.** It was not until the end of the nineteenth century that the state set up a definite form of secondary education for girls. Prior to this, girls' secondary education had been dominated by private organizations, mostly of a religious nature. Such education was meager, consisting of little more than elementary subject matter with a garnishing of singing, dancing, music, sewing, and the like. Various efforts on the part of the state to reform this situation had failed. However, in 1880 conservative resistance was swept away through a law sponsored by Camille Sée. This law provided for *lycées* and *collèges* for girls with five-year courses of three- and two-year periods respectively. Though the schools for girls corresponded in name to those of the boys, the curricula were different. These schools did not teach the ancient classical languages; nor did they prepare for the baccalaureate. The girls studied for the diploma of secondary education—*diplome de fin d'études*—which was awarded on the basis of an examination. Those girls who wanted to enter the universities needed private preparation for the baccalaureate.

With the changes in economic and social conditions, which took place in the twentieth century this type of secondary education became inadequate. More and more girls were seeking employment, and an increasing number desired the baccalaureate and access to the universities. In 1905, for example, the number of girls who took their baccalaureate in philosophy was 21; a decade later the number had risen to 447; in mathematics the number of successful candidates rose from five in 1905 to 55 in 1915. With the rising interest in the baccalaureate, and in response to pressure from parents, there gradually developed in the girls' *lycées* sections which sought to prepare them for the baccalaureate.

A decree of March, 1924 reorganized the system of secondary education for girls. By it the regular five-year course was converted into a six-year course. Girls were to be permitted to study for either the first part of the baccalaureate, with or without Latin, or for the *diplome de fin d'études secondaires*. The program included French, modern languages, science, history, geography, and drawing. Girls studying for the diploma were required to take courses in household management, handwork, music, ancient and modern foreign literatures in translation, psychology, and ethics. By an *arrêté* of July 10, 1925, the courses of study issued for boys' secondary schools were made applicable to girls' secondary schools, with such modifications of the time schedule as would be desirable because of their special needs.

Coeducation is not generally favored in France. Before 1930, girls were permitted to attend boys' schools only if no separate school was available for them. In no case were they admitted to schools having an enrollment of more than two hundred pupils, and never was the number of girls to be more than fifty. A ministerial circular of February 4, 1930 modified this by permitting girls to attend any secondary school regardless of the number of boys enrolled. Should the number of girls exceed 50 a special school must be built for them.

5. The école unique

For many years there has been a movement for the reform of public education. One of its prime purposes was to introduce the doctrine of the *école unique,* a common, unified school for all pupils. Strong advocates of the *école unique* are a group of World War I veterans, university men, who had organized under the title of the *Compagnons de l'Université Nouvelle.* Briefly summarized, their demands for reform include the following:

1. There should be more specialization in order to compete more successfully with foreign industry and commerce. Hence there should be more and better technical training. More attention should be given to local needs.
2. More attention should be devoted to schooling the masses.
3. The continuation school should be more efficient.
4. More and better education should be provided for girls.
5. All citizens of France should have an equal chance for higher education.
6. There should be free instruction in all grades: primary, secondary, and university.

Furthermore, the *Compagnons* demanded the introduction of the *école unique.*

To some extent the demands for reform have been realized. Thus, the curricula of the elementary classes of the *lycées* and the primary schools have been unified. For another thing, fees for day pupils in the secondary schools have been abolished. Furthermore, there is now a uniform system of awarding scholarships for secondary schools, postgraduate grades of the primary schools, and technical schools.

6. The second World War and after

a. **Under Nazi occupation.** As one might expect, the war left its devastating mark on the schools of France. Not only was there the usual deterioration and demoralization, but under the Nazi occupation a number of changes were wrought. In the first place, all Jewish teachers, and any others suspected of "political unreliability," were summarily discharged. Textbooks were subjected to the scrutiny of the lynx-eyed and touchy invader, and any statement exciting his displeasure was removed. In this process history books were accorded special attention and all references to German war-guilt and German atrocities in the first World War were deleted. On the other hand, the orations of Marshal Pétain, the literary value of which assuredly was dubious but the content of which was pleasing to the Nazis, became required reading for every French boy and girl. With the blessing of the Germans the demand to reintroduce religious instruction in the public school, an issue which had lived on scant rations for more than a half century, was carefully nurtured by the Nazis. One must not suppose, of course, that they had suddenly befriended religion. Their action was just another *coup de guerre* by which they hoped to divide the distressed and wartorn French still further. The same purpose prompted the Germans to insist that instruction in the French schools, and especially the teaching of history and civics, must henceforth be conducted in the spirit of "internationalism." Again spurred by the invader in their midst, the Vichy Government reclassified its civil service personnel, the traditional backbone of the republic, in which the public school teachers of France had always held a distinguished and respected place. The new scheme, reflecting the Nazi suspicion of the intellect, regarded teachers as potential trouble-makers and reduced their status to its lowest level in modern French history. Perhaps Vichy's fears were not entirely unfounded. Certainly the great majority of France's teachers were anti-Nazi and presumably anti-Vichy, and what they did to advance Hitler's New Order in France was, indeed, very little. And without the teachers' support and cooperation, the changes introduced by the Germans could obviously make little headway.

b. **After liberation.** With the coming of liberation the plight of France's teachers showed no improvement. On the contrary, under General de Gaulle's Provisional Government it sank steadily, for the most part because of the runaway franc, the general political unrest, and the inability of the government to restore to the teaching profession some of its former economic and social dignity. As might be expected, the schoolmaster's hard and distressful lot stripped his profession of the allure it formerly enjoyed. Gaining new recruits, a task which in happier times had never been too difficult, now became almost impossible; as for the older and experienced teachers, more and more they left for jobs which provided more amply for their pocketbook and for their self-esteem. The difficulties coming in the wake of the resulting teacher shortage were aggravated by two other factors: a perceptible rise in the birth-rate and a great scarcity of school buildings, many of which had been destroyed in the course of the war. Because of the shortage of materials, the rebuilding program could make no great progress, with the result that teachers, already hard pressed, were burdened even more by their inordinately large classes. One need hardly belabor the point that under such conditions the quality of education suffered perceptibly.

In the face of all these strains and stresses French educators were able, nonetheless, to lift their eyes to the future. Soon after liberation a commission was appointed to study the question of educational reform. Guided by the late Paul Langevin, a professor of the historic Collège de France, the Commission deliberated for two years. Its report, *La Réforme de l'enseignement,* which appeared in 1947, is notable not only for the grandeur of its vision, but even more for the boldness of its recommendations.[8]

Looking at French education with a cold and critical eye, the commission found many faults, the most glaring of which was that French education had not matched the pace of a changing democracy. The product of an historic past, during which diverse new institutions were established without being

---

[8] *La Réforme de l'enseignement, projet soumis à M. le ministre de l'éducation nationale par la commission ministerielle d'étude,* p. 47. Paris: *Ministère de l'Éducation Nationale,* 1947.

coordinated with existing ones, the French school system, despite its amazing centralization, had been vaguely conceived with no clear and definite plan of operation. New school laws were piled upon old ones without always replacing them; consequently the French educational organism had become sluggish with overlapping and duplication. In it, moreover, there were palpable gaps—so many, in fact, that instruction failed to meet the actual needs of living in a modern world. For the greater part of the twentieth century French education had been conservative—indeed, one might almost say reactionary. Meanwhile, the social order had undergone a rapid evolution. The increased use of machinery, the application of new kinds of power, the development of modern transportation and communication, the concentration of industry, the tremendous rise of production, the entrance of women into the nation's economic and industrial life, the spread of elementary education— all had a profound effect on the life and social organization of the French. The swift and widespread economic advance which, in 1880, had necessitated the extension of education to the working masses, produced in the twentieth century a need for an education which not only provided the fundamental knowledges and attitudes, but which, in addition, gave adequate recognition to the teaching of technical skills. Compared with Germany, Russia, and the United States, France had lagged appallingly in this respect—a state of affairs which the Langevin Commission plainly recognized. "The new needs of modern economy," it declared, "lay down the necessity of a remodeling of our instruction, which in its actual structure will be better adapted to social and economic conditions." [9]

A visible sign of the school's inadequacy under present social conditions was its almost complete lack of relationship to real life. This was true of every level of education, which seldom ventured beyond the outer fringe of reality; a cloistered microcosm, the school was shut off from the teeming and turbulent

[9] *Ibid.*, p. 8.

currents of the outside world. The divorcing of school and life was further accentuated by the static nature of France's educational institutions which, though supposedly an integral part of a rapidly changing society, were themselves apparently impervious to change. The school's isolation from society, the commission felt, robbed it of its educative function. "A reform," it was felt, "is urgently needed which will remedy this lack in the education of the producer and the citizen and which will permit it to give to all a training which will develop them civicly, socially, and culturally." [10]

In its recommendations the commission was guided by four basic principles. First, there was the principle of social justice, by which every child was to be assured an opportunity to achieve his maximum development in conformity with his personality and limited only by his capacity. No longer were economic and social barriers to stand in the way of such maximum development. In the second place there was to be what the commission called "a reclassification of real values" by virtue of which social tasks were to be on an equal footing—be they manual, technical, artistic or intellectual. Third was the principle of guidance; there was to be general guidance of the child in school, which was to be followed by adequate vocational guidance so that in the end "every worker and every citizen will be directed to the kind of work for which he is potentially best fitted." Finally, due recognition was to be given to the need of a general education, for "if education must yield a larger and larger place to specialized education, the training of the worker must nevertheless not jeopardize the development of the man." [11] General education, it was felt, should have the function of uniting men.

Putting these principles to work, the commission recommended a thorough overhauling of the entire school system. Education was to be compulsory from the age of six to eighteen. On the lower level, or as the French designate it,

[10] *Ibid.*, p. 8.
[11] *Ibid.*, p. 9.

"education of the first degree," the child's schooling was divided into three successive stages or "cycles." Preceded by an optional period of preschooling, which may begin as early as the child's third birthday, the first stage takes him through the age of eleven; the next goes as far as fifteen; and the last terminates at eighteen. As one might guess, each stage is dedicated to a special purpose. During the first (6-11), for example, the child is to master the basic skills and knowledge that will "enable him to understand and to be understood." [12] The second stage (11-15) is pre-eminently a period of guidance which, though it continues to deal in general culture and skills, is "to be devoted to a systematic observation of the children in order to discover their aptitudes and to facilitate their guidance." [13] In the third stage (15-18) education becomes diversified and specialized. Students of an academic bent, and hence potential candidates for the higher learning, will be grounded in the requisite theoretical subjects essential to the pursuit of university work. As for the others, besides their general education, they will receive specialized training leading to a career in agriculture, business, or industry. Significantly enough, the commission stressed that the work of the third stage be flexible, offering "a considerable diversity in order to provide combinations of studies, groupings of disciplines, adjusted to the various kinds of aptitudes." [14]

Beyond the eighteenth year—or the compulsory age—education enters upon its second level and is open to those, only to those, who have demonstrated the necessary competence. Amplified and diversified, it is to guide students more specifically in the direction of their fields of specialization. Technical studies will find their place here on an equal footing with the literary, scientific, and artistic. One of the important functions to be fulfilled by this level is the preparation of teachers, besides, of course, putting the finishing

---

[12] *Ibid.,* p. 9. Before the war the compulsory age terminated at thirteen.
[13] *Ibid.,* p. 10.
[14] *Ibid.*

touches on the academic preparation of the university student.

Recognizing that its proposed reform would be meaningless and certain to fail unless it was solidly founded on the rock of true social justice, the Langevin Commission recommended that public education must be free to all in fact as well as in theory. It must, furthermore, be made available on the higher level to every child who may profit by it. Free education, the commission asserted, can be effective only if a new and more realistic method of conferring scholarships is instituted, if provision is made for the payment of a salary in the third stage of the first level (15–18), and if, finally, the student is considered a worker, which in reality he is, and is granted a salary commensurate to the service he renders and is called upon to render to the collective group (*collectivité*).

Although the Langevin Commission stressed a reform in the organization of French education and advocated new principles upon which to base it, at the same time it offered general guide lines in other phases of education, such as administration and supervision, the preparation of teachers, education of the handicapped, adult education, and so on. Regarding method, the commission gave its blessing to the activity procedure, recommending it particularly in the elementary school.

Summarizing, one notes that the French have proposed to modernize and democratize their school system. By making it free and compulsory for all students up to the age of eighteen, they have eliminated their historic but undemocratic dual system which provided one kind of education for the vast multitude of Frenchmen and another kind for the élite. To make it possible for every child to go to school the French have gone so far as to propose a small salary for school children beginning with their fifteenth birthday. To bridge the gap between their modern industrial order and the school, the French have undertaken to reduce the latter's top-heavy intellectualism, and to put all curricula—manual, technical, artistic, and intellectual—on an equal footing. Not only is every French child to be guided and trained in harmony with his special aptitudes, but he is also to be grounded in the common core of a general education. As for education beyond the age of eighteen, it is to be for those of demonstrated ability in technical, literary, scientific, or artistic fields. Not only is it reserved for the competent, but the students, being workers and rendering a social service, are to be subsidized. Finally, the French have recommended that the activity method be given a front place in education, especially in the elementary school.

C. Germany

1. Background

It has become the fashion to say that the Germans display little individualism, that they are a disciplined people, who unquestioningly submit to authority. Their land has been depicted as one of law and order, full of *Verboten* signs which everyone readily obeys. Such descriptions are accurate enough, though they need the benefit of some explanatory footnotes. One should add, for example, a word about the Reich's political philosophy, a dominant and pervasive thing, which sought to instill and fortify these very qualities of docility and submission as the essential and basic traits of citizenry in a state bent on achieving what its leaders deemed to be its destiny. Certainly the Germans have not always been submissive. The peasants who revolted against their overlords in the days of Martin Luther were hardly docile; nor were the Germans who rose in arms against their government in 1848; nor were those Germans who fought against the old order in Berlin and Bavaria, in Hamburg and Saxony and elsewhere in Germany after the collapse of the Empire in 1918. The fact that the Germans of the Weimar Republic split into almost a score of political parties and that they were unable to achieve a common, working political accord for the sake of some sort of efficient national government is hardly testimony to substantiate their alleged lack of individualism.

The plain historical fact is that there are several Germanies.

There is, for one thing, the provincial, sectionalized Germany, the legacy of the Middle Ages, with its towering and beautiful cathedrals, its guilds of masters, journeymen, and apprentices, its variety of local usages, dialects, and folklore, and its colorful and distinctive costumes. This is the Germany of regionalism in which the *Landsmann* is conscious and proud of his homeland and thrills over his local heritage. There is another Germany, the Germany of lyrics, of enchanting music, of stirring philosophy, the Germany esteemed by civilized men everywhere, the Germany of Goethe, of Beethoven, of Kant. Finally, there is the Germany of Potsdam, the Germany of the Prussians and the Hohenzollerns, the Germany of cold and calculated efficiency, of trains-on-time, of martial airs and clicking heels, of soldiery and officialdom. This is the Germany of State Supremacy, of submission and obedience, of law and order, a Germany, as Voltaire observed, "full of moustaches and helmets of grenadiers."

All these Germanies exist, though since 1871, when Prussia assumed political control over all of Germany, it is the third Germany which has been in the forefront. The result has been a Germany which, though intrinsically as many-sided as its varying landscape, through the omnipresence of state control was cut to fit the garb of the dominant Prussian political philosophy. That twentieth century Germany was a police state even before the appearance of Hitler is a commonplace. Indeed, even in the relatively liberal political climate of the Weimar Republic, the government found a morals police (*Sittenpolizei*), a secret police (*Politischepolizei*), besides the usual police (*Schutzpolizei*) indispensable to its successful functioning.

Even more important for the operation and perpetuation of the State Supreme was its system of education. "As the state, so the school," was the maxim of Frederick the Great, who has been called the founder of German elementary education. In this system the state took priority over everything, insisting that it had the right to pattern the mind and behavior of its future citizens. Frederick, who was one of the so-called "benevolent despots," perceived an educated citizenry as the bulwark of a strong and prosperous state. Frederick believed in the improvement of his subjects—but never to the point where they might question the wisdom of the *status quo*. What he wanted—indeed, what Prussia has wanted ever since—was a system of education which would make the great bulk of its populace not only literate, but also pious and moral, vocationally and economically efficient, and above all, obedient and disciplined. As for the minority of citizens in the upper social and economic strata, for them a special education was reserved. Instead of attending the public elementary school, they went to fee-charging preparatory schools, which constituted the main road to the secondary schools and ultimately to the universities. By separating and differentiating the education of the masses from that of the "classes," the state assured itself on the one hand of a vast number of trained and subservient followers, and on the other hand of a small corps of an élite, especially prepared to fill the higher positions in the Reich.

2.   Evolution of the German school system

The German Empire was a combination of states (*Länder*) each of which possessed the theoretic right to manage its internal affairs. A few of the larger states even enjoyed a measure of control over their postal system, their army, and their railways. Unlike the United States, however, the component parts of old Germany were not equal in their rights and privileges. In various ways the Kingdom of Prussia, whose Hohenzollern monarch was also the Emperor of the German Reich, was able to assume a leading role. The principle of federation and the dominance of Prussia were reflected plainly in Germany's educational system. Autonomous in school matters, the German states had established school systems which in their details revealed considerable diversity, but despite such difference there was at the same time a large

to teach under them. The clergy looked askance at the growing state control. The upper classes looked with mingled contempt and fear on the idea of educating the masses. However, the regulations of 1763 became the foundation of the Prussian system.

The next significant step in the development of a state system of education was taken in 1787 with the establishment of the *Oberschulkollegium,* a central board of school administration intended to replace the local church boards. More important, however, were some of the educational stipulations embodied in the celebrated General Civil Code of 1794. The twelfth chapter is entirely devoted to education. Its most significant assertions read as follows:

Schools and universities are state institutions, charged with the instruction of youth in useful information and scientific knowledge. Such institutions may be established only with the knowledge and consent of the state. All public schools and educational institutions are under the supervision of the state, and are at all times subject to its examination and inspection.

Frederick William II, who succeeded the great Frederick, was by contrast an inept and colorless monarch. Under him Prussia steadily declined and, as might be expected, education was affected by the general deterioration. Afraid to risk the displeasure of the clergy, the king filled the *Oberschulkollegium* with pastors instead of lay experts, thereby thwarting that body's chief reason for being. The nadir of Prussia's power came during the reign of Frederick III (1797–1840), when the Prussians were overwhelmingly defeated by Napoleon in 1806 at Jena. By the Treaty of Tilsit, which followed, the Prussians were further humiliated: what had taken them almost a century to put together was now within a few months turned into a tattered memory. However, like the Treaty of Versailles after the first World War, that of Tilsit served to kindle an intense nationalism; and as in the case of the Nazis, education was harnessed to the Prussian state to a greater degree than ever. Relying on education, Prussian leaders sought to develop strong, patriotic, and efficient citizens.

"We shall and will gain in intrinsic power and splendor," divined Frederick William, "and therefore it is my earnest wish that the greatest attention be paid to public education." "We proceed," said the king's minister, Stein, "from the fundamental principle, to elevate the moral, religious and patriotic spirit in the nation, to instill into it again, courage, self-reliance and readiness to sacrifice everything for national honor and for independence from the foreigners. . . . To attain this end, we must rely on the education of the young."

To achieve these goals the whole system of education was overhauled and reformed. To eliminate ecclesiastic domination the *Oberschulkollegium* was abolished and replaced by another body, the Department of Public Instruction, a section of the State Department of the Interior. Subsequently, in 1817, the department was converted into the Ministry for Spiritual, Educational and Medical Affairs. The first to head the new department was Wilhelm von Humboldt, who, in the few years he held office, effected a series of educational reforms. Through his warm support, for example, the University of Berlin was founded in 1809. The first modern university in Germany, Berlin was to compensate in a measure for the loss of Halle, Göttingen, and other universities which the Prussians had been obliged to relinquish at Tilsit.

At the other end of the educational system, in the elementary school, the main reforms came in newer methods and content. More attention was given to the training of teachers. In fact, in 1808 the Prussian government sent seventeen teachers to Switzerland, paying their way for three years of study under the renowned Pestalozzi. The elementary schools of Prussia were infused with patriotism. Geography, history, and the mother tongue were limned in nationalistic hues. Religion, a compulsory subject, laid stress on catechism and doctrine, with lofty words on love of country, self-sacrifice, and obedience to authority. As might be expected, physical training, with its health and military values, came in for new prestige and emphasis.

In secondary education likewise there were numerous changes and reforms. In 1812 the classical secondary school, the *Gymnasium,* was required to meet standards determined by the state. The leaving examination—the *Maturitätsprüfung*—once denounced by the clergy, was revived. Controlled by the state, the examination became the determining basis for admission to the higher learning. Under the influence of men like Herder and Kant and with the benign encouragement of von Humboldt, stress was to be laid more and more on general culture, which was to be based on an understanding of the Greek and Latin classics. Though this neo-humanistic ideal was never fully realized, largely because of the German love for specialization and microscopic knowledge, nevertheless down to the seventies the *Gymnasium* continued to reign virtually unchallenged as the institution *par excellence* for the training of the élite.[1]

With the downfall of Napoleon the flickering lights of liberalism which had been lit so brilliantly with the outbreak of the French Revolution were extinguished all over Europe. Led by Prince Metternich, chancellor of the Austrian Empire and generally esteemed the astutest statesman of his time, the forces of reaction clamped the lid on liberalism, democracy, and the national yearnings of the small states. By espionage and censorship, by the use of secret police and *agents provocateurs*—even by the manipulation of the post office, the secret opening and copying of confidential letters and dispatches— the rulers of Europe, paced by Austria, sought to preserve their reactionary regimes. Especially suspect in that illiberal world were the Austrian and German universities. The ideals of freedom, which had flared so brightly among the students and professors during the wars of liberation against Napoleon, had never entirely gone out. Consequently the men of learn-

---

[1] Another reform required prospective teachers of the *Gymnasium* to pass a difficult examination grounded on university training in the secondary school subjects. The tests were given for the state by university authorities. To train prospective *Gymnasium* teachers, moreover, a number of universities established special pedagogical seminaries.

ing found themselves under constant surveillance. Governmental efforts to muzzle the intellectuals reached their climax in 1819 when Metternich issued the so-called Carlsbad Decrees. Striking against students and professors, against fraternities and secret societies, against journalists and clergymen—and in general against any manifestation of liberalism—the Decrees set the standard of German intellectual life for at least a score of years.[2]

The Carlsbad Decrees found their image all over Europe. In Italy revolutionary outbursts were brutally put down and were followed in 1820, with Austrian help, by a regime of repression. In the same year, becoming alarmed over the murder of the king's nephew, France not only untapped a policy of censorship, but also modified its electoral laws in favor of the conservatives. Again in 1820, Alexander I of Russia launched a policy of repression against the liberals in Poland. In the same eventful year insurrections broke out in Spain and Portugal, and a year later the Greeks took up arms against their Turkish oppressors. Even in England reaction and repression flared up. In 1819 Parliament, alarmed by the national discontent, passed the notorious Six Acts, the most repressive legislation known in England for generations. On four occasions from 1818 to 1822 representatives from the chief powers of Europe convened to survey conditions in the Old World and to ally themselves against any possible threat to their absolutism. The Concert of Europe, as this combination was called, became the Old World's political emergency squad, ever ready to put down liberal outbursts no matter where they occurred.

Nonetheless they were not successful. The clock of liberalism could not be stopped, nor even set back for any length of time. As the years ticked by, discontent erupted into revolu-

---

[2] What touched off the iniquitous decrees was the assassination of a Russian journalist by a student. The newsman happened to be a favorite of the Russian Czar Alexander I as well as of Prince Metternich. That he wrote favorably about their reactionary practices goes without saying.

tion all over Europe. Again and again the ideals of those who had fought against the Old Regime in France in 1789 re-echoed throughout Europe. Punctuated by revolutions in 1830 and again in 1848, liberalism and constitutionalism made slow but steady gains—though unfortunately not to the same degree in every land.

In Prussia, for example, the Revolution of 1848 came to an inglorious end. Its failure shaped a tragic course for Germany for generations to come. With the crushing of the liberal elements, the middle classes became submerged under the weight of a reactionary aristocracy. With the failure of the revolution, the forces of liberalism went into eclipse; in fact, many of Germany's most independent and most progressive citizens, disheartened by a desultory future, left their country to seek freedom elsewhere. The German middle classes thus lost the very leadership they needed most. That loss was never quite made up. The absence of experienced leadership showed itself tragically after 1919 in the struggles of the German Republic, and particularly in the early thirties when it was so sorely needed to stem the rising tide of fascism.

With the collapse of Prussia's liberals, the screws of reaction were turned tighter than ever. Blaming Prussia's teachers for having nurtured the revolution, Frederick William IV publicly censured them at one of their conferences in 1849. Said His Majesty:

You and you alone are to blame for all the misery which the last year brought upon Prussia. The irreligious pseudo-education of the masses is to be blamed for it, which you have been spreading under the name of true wisdom, and by which you have eradicated religious belief and loyalty from the hearts of my subjects and alienated their affection for my person. This sham education, strutting about like a peacock, has always been odious to me. I hated it already from the bottom of my soul before I came to the throne, and since my accession I have done everything I could to suppress it.

"I mean to proceed on this path," the king continued, "without taking heed of anyone, and, indeed, no power on earth shall divert me from it." The royal threat was soon turned into reality. In the following years all attempts at educational improvement became suspect. Even the kindergarten, in fact, was considered dangerous and put under the ban.

The tide of reaction gradually receded, but it was not until after the formation of the German Empire in 1870 that education was seriously re-examined and overhauled. In 1872 the elementary schools were given a new course of study. By this, instruction in religion was "to be in the center of the teacher's work"; at the same time, however, state control was reaffirmed. As for the secondary schools, as early as 1859 the so-called *Realschule,* which offered a nine-year course of study including Latin and the modern subjects, was accorded official recognition as a secondary school. The most significant changes, however, did not come until the last decade of the century. Meanwhile the rivalry between the classical disciplines and the newer cultures continued. The *Gymnasium* with its stress on Latin and Greek and on formal discipline, though assailed on all sides by the proponents of the modern languages and the sciences, continued to reign supreme. In 1890 Kaiser Wilhelm II threw his influence on the side of the modernists. "Whoever," he asserted, "has been in the *Gymnasium* himself and has caught a glimpse behind the scenes knows what is lacking there. Above all the national basis is lacking. We must take the German as the foundation for the *Gymnasium;* we ought to educate national young Germans and not young Greeks and Romans. . . ." This, the Kaiser said in Latin and most un-Germanically, was "the *punctum saliens.*" In 1901 all graduates of the three types of secondary schools—the *Gymnasium, the Realgymnasium* and the *Oberrealschule*— were to be admitted to the university on an equal basis. However, the latter two continued to be overshadowed by the prestige of the *Gymnasium,* and never quite attained its status. Requiring fees, Germany's secondary schools were inaccessible to the masses;³ and to make matters even more difficult, no articulation existed among them. As a result it became neces-

---

³ See p. 238 ff. for an analysis of the German secondary school.

sary for parents to decide whether their nine-year-old children should devote their next nine years to the study of the classics, the modern languages, or the natural sciences.[4]

3.   Elementary education in 1914

Given in the *Volksschule,* German elementary education in 1914 was universal, free, and compulsory. With minor variations, the compulsory period was eight years, beginning ordinarily when the child was six or seven. The school year lasted from forty to forty-two weeks, though in some rural sections concessions were sometimes made by the authorities. The weekly program comprised from twenty to twenty-two hours in the lower grades to about thirty hours in the upper grades. The usual fundamental subjects were taught, and instruction therein was efficient. This, combined with the rigid enforcement of compulsory education, made illiteracy virtually nonexistent. Gymnastics held an important place in the curriculum. So, too, did religion. In addition, there was instruction in drawing, nature study, and singing. In the more up-to-date schools boys usually received training in manual work, and girls were introduced to domestic science, with emphasis on sewing and cooking. Wherever economically possible, the sexes were taught separately. The teaching was done chiefly by men who had been excellently trained.

Not all German children attended the public *Volksschule.* Some went instead to the *Vorschule,* a three-year school charging tuition and preparing its pupils for the secondary school. Like many European lands, Germany had no educational ladder. Graduates of the *Volksschule* could not, without great inconvenience to themselves, enter the secondary school. One difficulty was due to the difference in the age of the graduate of the elementary *Volksschule,* which was generally around fourteen, and the age of the first-year pupil of the secondary

---

[4] Divinity students were required to know Greek, and hence they had to complete the gymnasial course. In the case of medical students, Latin being a requirement, they had to complete their work either at a *Gymnasium* or a *Realgymnasium.*

school which was nine. The fact, moreover, that the curriculum of the *Volksschule* made no provision for foreign languages or mathematics beyond arithmetic made it virtually impossible for the fourteen-year-old *Volksschule* graduate to fit into the secondary school, since secondary school students had been studying these subjects from their very first year; by the time they were fourteen, or the age of the average elementary school graduate, they had generally had some five years of these subjects. With truth it has been said that the young graduates of the *Volksschule* had no other destiny than work and the continuation school. To side-step this obstacle some children would attend the *Volksschule* for three years, and then at the age of nine they would transfer to the secondary school. This practice, however, was not relatively common. With the realization that something more than the ordinary form of elementary education was desirable for the masses, elementary education had been slowly extended. Gradually an intermediate system had evolved to provide an advanced elementary education and part-time vocational schools.

4. Secondary education in 1914

a. **Boys.** Designed for the mental as well as the social élite, the secondary schools of Imperial Germany were of several kinds. There was, to begin, the *Gymnasium*, which was a product of the humanistic era, and which stressed Latin and Greek. Then there was the *Realgymnasium*, a compromise between the humanities and the modern subjects. The *Realgymnasium* required Latin but not Greek. There was the *Oberrealschule*, which stressed the modern subjects, particularly the sciences and mathematics. Instead of Latin and Greek, the *Oberrealschule* required modern languages.

When, at the age of nine, a boy was about to enter the secondary school, he had to decide on one of the three types of curricula. A lad entering the *Oberrealschule* could not subsequently transfer to the *Gymnasium*, since in this school Latin was taught in the very first year; nor could he go from the *Realgymnasium* to the *Gymnasium* after his third year, since he would have had no Greek. To obviate these difficulties and others, a number of schools with a common basis had been developed, which aimed at delaying as long as possible the pupil's necessity for making a final choice. The reform idea was particularly attractive to some of the smaller communities, which it enabled to establish fairly good-sized secondary schools with a variety of courses. Besides the regular secondary schools there were a number of commercial and technical schools at the secondary level. With secondary education went a number of special privileges. For example, boys who completed six years of secondary schooling obtained a certificate entitling them to one-year military service instead of two. Not only did it shorten the length of their period of military service, but it also opened the road to certain careers. In practice, moreover, admission to the universities was possible for only those who, through their secondary schooling, had been able to pass the *Reifeprüfung* or the *Abiturientenexamen* ("leaving examination").

b. **Girls.** Secondary education for girls is a nineteenth century creation. In 1872 Prussia began to give real consideration to the problem with the establishment of a ten-year course, which a girl usually began at the age of six. Extended and improved in 1894, the courses offered to girls were virtually on a par with those given in the boys' schools. In 1908 Prussia once more recognized them. Again a ten-year course was set up, and, as before, the beginning age was six. The first three years were preparatory. The ten-year school was called the *Lyzeum*. Beyond it was the *Oberlyzeum*. Divided into two courses, this harbored the *Frauenschule* and the *Höheres Lehrerinnenseminar*. The former offered a two-year general course including household arts, kindergartening, needlework, languages, civics, economics, music, and art. The *Lehrerinnenseminar* offered a four-year course for prospective elementary school teachers. Girls who wanted a secondary school course similar to that of the boys transferred at the age of thirteen to the *Studienanstalt,* which offered courses of study similar to those of the *Gymnasium, Realgymnasium,* and *Oberrealschule.* Girls did not study Latin until they were thirteen, and Greek was postponed for another two years, but French was usually started at nine, and English at twelve. Secondary schooling for girls, as in the case of the boys, was not free.

    c. Criticism. Though the secondary schools had been reformed on several occasions, criticism continued. They were under fire for their heavy stress on the intellectual phase of education, as well as their continued emphasis on the classics. Secondary education was attacked by many who felt that it failed to give adequate consideration to modern life in an industrial technical age. Still others criticized the secondary schools because they failed to stress German life and culture. Another criticism was leveled at the schools' organization: what was wanted was a common school system, with better articulation with the elementary school. In addition there was also a movement for a common school—the *Einheitsschule.* Under the slogan "One Nation! One School!" the advocates of a common school system demanded the extension of educational opportunities with a common educational foundation for all up to the age of twelve, and the organization of diverse secondary school courses with enough variety to meet the needs and abilities of the pupils.

5. Other schools

    One of the features of German education before the first World War was the high enrollment of students in its continuation schools. Originating in the eighteenth century, these schools served at the outset to supplement the work of the regular elementary schools. Attendance therein was voluntary and they were conducted on Sundays. One of the first ordinances of any importance to deal with this kind of schooling came in 1869 in the *Gewerbeordnung* (trade regulation) which provided that "compulsory attendance at continuation school may be established by an ordinance of the community or local guild for boys under eighteen years of age and for girls under the same age if engaged in commercial pursuits." It was required, furthermore, that employers were "to grant the necessary time to all their employes, under eighteen years of age, who may be subject to attendance at a local or state continuation school." And instruction was to be dispensed "only at such hours on Sunday as will not interfere with the main church services. . . ."

Subsequently the features of these 1869 regulations found their way into the laws of the empire. In time, as German industry developed, the *Fortbildungsschule,* as the continuation school was called, made rapid strides. By 1914, either through state legislation or through local by-laws, it was virtually an accomplished fact throughout the Reich, though there was in this field of education no such thing as national uniformity. Bavaria, for example, required four years' attendance whereas Württemberg was satisfied with only two. Although there were many excellent continuation schools all over Germany, it was at Munich that they achieved some of their finest work. Here, under the capable direction of Georg Kerschensteiner, for many years one of Germany's outstanding schoolmen, a program of continuation education was developed with the cooperation of employers, teachers, parents, and pupils. The pupil's vocation was made the center around which the general subjects clustered. Was the youngster working as an apprentice barber? Then the school gave him three hours of practical work, some trade knowledge, and lessons in simple first aid, besides the usual prescription of religion, composition, arithmetic, bookkeeping and civics. Was he a tailor? Then it gave him a knowledge of his trade and taught him, for good measure, about wares and materials and technical drawing in addition to the general prescription. There were three types of continuation schools—industrial, trade and commercial, and general. The industrial school catered to prospective machinists, woodworkers, printers, butchers, barbers, and others. The trade and commercial schools were organized into such groups as those dealing with food and provisions; drapery and textiles; banking, insurance, and bookselling; porcelain, cutlery, and hardware. With Kerschensteiner the all-important goal of education had always been good and efficient citizenship; hence, as might be expected, the subject of civics became most important in the Munich schools. It included among other things such matters as personal and occupational hygiene, economic and industrial history, and civics proper. In addition to the regular continuation schools, Germany, of course, had most of the special schools found in other nations.

6. The German republic

Out of the first World War came the German republic. With Ebert, a former saddle-maker and the head of the Social Democrats, as its first president, the new government was based on a constitution, a document of 181 articles, drawn up at a convention at Weimar, a city famous in the history of German culture. Effective on August 11, 1919, the Weimar Constitution provided for a centralized republic, a bicameral parliament and a president elected for a seven-year term with wide powers, particularly in the event of an emergency. The new constitution established universal suffrage, guaranteed broad civil liberties, and made extensive economic and labor provisions. The Weimar Republic was inaugurated in the national capital of Berlin and by September, 1919, it began to function.

Its problems, as can be expected, were manifold. In its midst were many dissident elements, radical as well as reactionary, who were sworn enemies of democracy. By agitation and violence and by a series of armed insurrections culminating in 1933 in the triumph of the Nazis, they conspired to bring about the downfall of the republican regime. For another thing, there was the war's inevitable aftermath. The widespread national unrest, the vast unemployment, the prob-

lem of what to do with the millions of persons whose lives had
been shattered by the war, financial difficulties, the burden of
meeting the reparation payments, the problem of restoring
the nation's economic, business and social life—all made the
road back to normal conditions a hard one. Overshadowing
it, moreover, was the task of changing the German mentality,
of teaching a nation, so long accustomed to monarchy and the
doctrine of state supremacy, how to make democracy work.
For Germany—and, indeed, for the rest of the world—this
was the most important of its many problems, for on its outcome depended in large measure the course of world events for
generations to come.

The Republic endured for only fourteen years. During this
time there were three presidential elections in two of which
the idolized war hero, Paul von Hindenburg, was elected.[5] In
addition, there were twenty cabinet changes. Reflecting the
nation's restlessness and its general political instability, these
brought to the executive department a long line of politicians
of whom, however, only two—Gustav Stresemann and Heinrich Brüning—were of the first order. Despite its handicaps,
however, the republic was able to achieve a few major accomplishments. It succeeded in bringing about some mitigation of
the harsher clauses of the Versailles Treaty, particularly in
respect to reparations, the Allied occupation of the Rhineland,
and German relations to the League of Nations. It was able
also to resuscitate the Reich's shattered industrial and commercial strength. It triumphed, after a long struggle, over the
nation's fantastic and ruinous monetary inflation in 1923-24.
Finally, in spite of Germany's defeat in 1918 and its unconditional surrender, the Republic was able to maintain the Reich
as a major power in Europe.

These successes were offset by a number of palpable failures.
Thus the Weimar Republic could not withstand the crushing
force of the great economic depression which engulfed it after
1929, and which in a few short years left millions without jobs,

---

[5] Hindenburg was elected in April, 1925, and again in April, 1932.

in want and hunger. Nor could the new government make democracy palatable to the majority of Germans. In essence the republic was a democracy, but it was a democracy without democrats. Instead of taking a firm stand against its foes, it continued to put its faith in the constitutional bill of rights, thus giving free reign to those who had sworn to destroy those rights. Excessively idealistic at heart, the leaders of the republic continued to give balm to its former rulers, the war lords and the Junkers, even remunerating them lavishly for some of the losses they had sustained because of the war. Nor did the republic effectively challenge the militarists in its midst; the army, which had never been amicably disposed towards the republic, it permitted to operate as a free agent within the state, without the safeguard of parliamentary control.

In spite of the high hopes in which it was born, the Weimar Republic never matured. Hesitant in purpose, uncertain of its methods, it wavered between the ideals which brought it forth and the reality which confronted it. In the end it was no match for the shrewd and powerful forces which conspired to undo it. When the end came, in 1933, it passed on with no tears to honor it, unloved and unwanted, the victim of its own idealism and ineptitude.

7. Educational clauses of the Weimar Constitution

Devoting an entire section to education, the Weimar Constitution of August 11, 1919 laid the foundation of a new reformed system of education. Fundamentally, the general principle embodied in the new constitution's educational clauses is that art and science and the teaching thereof should have every liberty of action. Public school teachers were state employees with the rights, duties, and privileges of the same. School supervision was to be in the hands of lay and professional schoolmen. Education was compulsory for at least eight years, and was to be followed by attendance at the continuation school. A common four-year foundation school, known as the *Grundschule,* was established with attendance compulsory for all children. The *Vorschule,* the private preparatory school which some children attended before their admission to the secondary school, was to be abolished. Public moneys could be voted by the various states and localities to assist poor parents in sending their children to the middle and secondary schools. Civics and manual training were to be incorporated as a part of the school's work. A goal of education in all schools was "a moral education, a sense of responsibility to the state, individual and professional efficiency in the spirit of German nationality and of international reconciliation." Religion, as in the imperial era, was deemed part of the school curriculum. But it was no longer a required subject. Communities, as a matter of fact, were given the right of local option in the matter of religious education. They had the constitutional right to establish schools according to the particular religious creeds of the school patrons.

a. The Grundschule. As has been indicated, the Weimar Constitution provided for the establishment of a common four-year foundation school known as the *Grundschule.* This was to be a public school and attendance therein [6] was compulsory. By the federal decree of July 18, 1921, the aim of the *Grundschule* was:

The first four years of school have their own goal and unified sphere of activity. Their goal is the gradual unfolding of the child's abilities out of the instinct for play and movement toward a normal desire for work which manifests itself inside the school community.

The *Grundschule* was to give to its pupils not only the basic training for the work of the last four years of the elementary school, but also for that of the middle and secondary schools. Besides the three R's and religion, the child was instructed in drawing, singing, physical training, and manual work. During the first year instruction was organized on an integrated

---

[6] A subsequent amendment to this law permitted bright pupils to transfer to a secondary school after only three years of attendance at a *Grundschule.*

basis—*Gesamtunterricht.* Considerable attention was given
to studying the environment. Known as *Heimatkunde,* this
focused on such things as life and work in the home, school,
garden, market, the countryside, farm, factory, shop, and so
on. *Heimatkunde* furnished the content for nature study,
geography, history, local legends, customs, and traditions. In

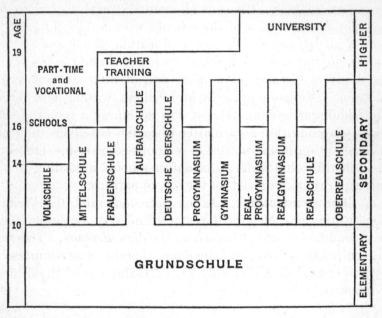

Fig. 3. The Schools of Germany in 1930. (From Myers and Williams,
Education in a Democracy. Copyright by Prentice-Hall, Inc., 1937.) The
Progymnasium, Realprogymnasium, and the *Oberrealschule* are schools cover-
ing the first six years of the regular secondary schools.

the *Grundschule* the child was to learn on the basis of activity.
Children were expected to learn how to observe, and how to
use their eyes and hands; for this purpose they participated
in simple manual activities. Physical training, incidentally,
was taught in the broad sense, and included games, gymnastics,
and walks, besides swimming, skating, and other things.

b. **The Oberstufe.** The four upper classes of the elementary school constitute the *Oberstufe,* which, together with the

Grundschule, forms a complete whole. The subjects taught were religion, German history and civics, natural history, arithmetic, geometry, geography, drawing, singing, gymnastics, and, in the case of girls, sewing. Wherever possible there was manual work for boys and household work for girls. Most elementary schools (the *Grundschule* plus the *Oberstufe*) had an eight-year course of study, though Bavaria and Württemberg had a seven-year course; Schleswig-Holstein, Brunswick, and Oldenburg had a nine-class system. In the *Oberstufe* self-activity continued to be stressed. In its instruction the school utilized the child's direct experience, supplementing it with the use of books, libraries, and museums. School excursions were no novelty in the prewar German school; but in Republican Germany they were more common, and took on a greater educational significance. Youth hostels had been established throughout Germany where, at a nominal cost, youthful hikers and their teachers could be accommodated. Interestingly enough, there were no examinations in the Prussian elementary school either at the end of the year or at the end of the course, promotions being made on the class teachers' recommendations with the approval of the teachers' council.

8. Intermediate education

Like most European countries, Germany established intermediate schools for children who wished a longer and more advanced elementary school course. The standard of work was higher than that of the elementary school, but not comparable to that of the secondary school. Prussia offered intermediate education in the *Mittelschule*, an advanced elementary school charging tuition, and the *Latein-* or *Rektoralschule*, lower secondary schools, charging fees, and maintained in the smaller localities.

Admitting children who had completed the *Grundschule*, the intermediate schools offered a six-year program leading to the *mittlere Reife* or intermediate qualifying certificate. In some smaller localities the middle schools took the place of the lower and middle classes of the secondary schools. The intermediate school's first three years were common to all pupils, but the last three offered differentiated programs, including (1) a general program for boys, (2) a general program for girls, (3) a specialized program for boys, with stress on commerce and trade, or industry, (4) a program for girls with special consideration of trade and commerce, domestic economy, or social service, and (5) a program of secondary studies for boys and girls. Localities that could not provide this variety of work were expected to provide the general course only. Those intermediate schools designed to lead into the secondary schools included a second foreign language in their work, and their curriculum in general followed that of the regular nonclassical schools. In many respects the middle school resembles the American high school.

9. Secondary education

Republican Germany kept its prewar division of secondary schools, the *Gymnasium, Realgymnasium,* and *Oberrealschule.* In addition, the *Aufbauschule* and the *Deutsche Oberschule* grew in popularity. The *Aufbauschule* was a six-year school, following the completion of the seventh year of the elementary school. The *Deutsche Oberschule,* a nine-year school, required two modern foreign languages. True to its name it stressed German culture. Normally, a child entering a nine-year secondary school would be about ten years old; when he entered the *Aufbauschule* he was ordinarily about thirteen. The normal age for finishing secondary school was nineteen.

There were several types of secondary schools for the girls. However, in all cases the first three years had the same program and included one foreign language. Differentiation took place in the intermediate and upper classes. Like the boys, girls studied in nine-year schools. The school comparable to the *Gymnasium* was the *Gymnasiale Studienanstalt.* This required six years of Latin, four of Greek and French. The

Oberlyzeum gave more attention to the modern languages. Also there was the *Oberlyzeum der Oberrealschulrichtung,* which like the boys' *Oberrealschule* focused on the sciences. In addition to the foregoing institutions, there was also the *Deutsche Oberschule,* whose work corresponded to that of the boys' school by the same name. In all German states, girls could be admitted to a secondary school for boys when it was too difficult for them to attend a girls' school. Particularly was this important in those cases where girls wished to prepare for higher education and there was no girls' school within their locality. Secondary schools could be either public or private, but they were subject to state control. The schools were not free, though there were numerous scholarships.

In contrast to the system of secondary education existing in 1914, that of the republic was inclined to be more liberal. The prewar system had been intellectually and socially selective. In the absence of articulation with the elementary school, the prewar secondary school had relied on the private preparatory school—the *Vorschule*—to prepare the children for admission. Not only was there a gap between the elementary and secondary schools, but there was a marked tendency for each type of secondary school to cultivate its own specialized identity, without any consideration for the development of a common foundation. The opportunities for transfer from one type to another were not readily available. The demands failed for a reorganization of the entire secondary school system after the war; as did the movement for a common elementary school for all up to the age of twelve. However, a common four-year *Grundschule* leading to the secondary school was adopted. To some extent opportunities to attend the secondary school were augmented by provisions for maintenance grants, scholarships, and the reduction of fees.

Another charge against the pre-republican secondary school was that it had put a premium on mental work of a narrow sort rather than on a broad liberal culture and the development of personality. Under the republic, however, liberal education continued to be interpreted as before the war; nor was there any attempt to make the schools more practical, or vocational, or technical. Foreign languages, the mother tongue, history and geography, science and mathematics were still deemed the essence of a broad general culture. However, though the general cultural ideal remained practically unchanged, there was a perceptible change in the organization of subjects for national and social purposes. To promote a sense of national solidarity the principle of *Heimatkunde*—a study of one's environment—was used as a basis for curriculum construction in the elementary school and, as far as feasible, in the secondary school. In the latter instance *Heimatkunde* was approached broadly, including national and foreign factors that had entered into German culture. Then, too, there was a marked trend towards *Deutschtum*—a greater stress on German culture and civilization.

10. The religious question [7]

Ever since the Reformation the Germans have thought of religion as an essential part of the school curriculum. This was true even in Prussia where, as we have seen, the state asserted its primacy in education. The Weimar Constitution preserved this religious tradition. In several articles it guaranteed freedom of conscience, the undisturbed practice of religion under the protection of the state, the right of free assembly for religious purposes, protection against coercion for religious reasons, and the like. As in the days of the empire, religion was regarded as a part of the curriculum, a subject which every school was required to teach. However, no pupil could be compelled to study religion; nor could any teacher be forced to teach it. On parental demand, moreover, communities were accorded the right to establish schools in accord-

---

[7] See Meyer, A. E., "Germany's State and Church Struggle for School Control," *Current History*, XXIII, 817 ff., 1926.

ance with the particular religious beliefs of the pupils, provided, of course, that the regular school program would not be jeopardized. Such were the guiding principles by which the various German states were to enact their individual school laws.

As a result, a variety of schools came into being. There was, for example, the out-and-out secular school—the *Weltliche Schule*—the child of socialist ideology, wherein no religion was taught. There was also a *Weltanschauungsschule* (Free Thought School) where ethics was taught in lieu of denominational religion. The reverse side of this picture was represented by the denominational, or confessional, school where teachers and pupils belonged to the same denomination, and where religion, like arithmetic and the mother tongue, was taught as a regular subject. Between these extremes there was the so-called *Simultanschule*, or interdenominational school. In this compromise creation children of all creeds were taught the regular subjects together, but received separate religious instruction in their respective creeds. When the constitution was being drawn up, it was hoped that the *Simultanschule* might ultimately emerge as the established school. Unfortunately, in trying to please everyone the school ended by pleasing nobody. Socialists were against it because it was not entirely secularized. The clergy, for their part, were dissatisfied with it because it didn't go far enough—though it met their demands by providing denominational instruction, on the other hand it did not teach the regular subjects from the denominational point of view.[8]

Nor did the constitution's vague generalizations help the situation. In Saxony, for example, where the socialists were in power for a time, religion was eliminated entirely for a while from the curriculum, until, with the coming of reaction,

---

[8] The concern manifested by certain churches in the secular subjects is well illustrated in the anti-evolution laws in effect in a number of states in the U. S. Prohibiting the teaching of the theory of evolution in biology, these laws have the backing of the Fundamentalists.

it returned. Whether a child should have religious instruction was, in accordance with the constitution, to be left to the decision of the parents. But, as sometimes happens, parents couldn't always agree. In such an event the law of Saxony required the court appointment of some disinterested person to make the decision. Should the child happen to be between the ages of ten and twelve, his own opinion in the matter was to be considered; if he happened to be beyond the age of twelve, he was to be permitted to decide the issue for himself.

In contrast to the freedom found in Saxony was the conservatism prevalent in Bavaria, which was predominantly Catholic. Before the war its clergy had managed to retain a number of rights and privileges in the realm of school control, especially in the rural schools. Shorn of their traditional powers under the constitution, they waged a vigorous campaign against the new provisions. The *Simultanschule* especially aroused them. They even advised parents to keep their children at home. In 1922, as a protest against the *Simultanschule,* a number of priests requested parents to keep their children out of school. The strike, however, was unsuccessful.

On a national scale several attempts were made by ecclesiasts of various sects to bring about a change in the law. Supported by Catholic and Protestant clerics, bills were introduced in parliament by which teachers, curricula, and texts would have been controlled less by the state and more by religious associations. Educational supervision would have passed to a large extent into church hands, Catholics under the authority of Catholic superiors and Protestants under Protestant superiors.[9] But none of these proposed laws were enacted; and though the republic's path between state and church was a hazardous one, it managed to hold off these groups.

---

[9] Provision was also made that in school districts where 40 or more children requested religious instruction, a school was to be established by the state with Protestant or Catholic religious instruction, as requested by the majority, without concern for the minority.

11. The Youth movement [10]

The English historian, Professor George P. Gooch, has declared the Youth movement to be "an exclusively German phenomenon." The germ of the movement is found as early as 1896 in a classical *Gymnasium* at Steglitz, a suburb of Berlin, when the magnetic Karl Fischer brought together a number of students who were anxious for a larger freedom than that offered in their conventional classical school. Some eight years later Fischer organized the *Wandervogel,* forming at the same time a council of parents to help him in his work. Moved somewhat by a back-to-nature idea, these young people spent much of their free time in the open, trekking into the country, making acquaintance with the peasants, learning folk songs and folk dances. Gradually the movement developed from an experiment in living into a philosophy of life—a *Weltanschauung* which reacted against the banalities of a mechanized and materialized industrialism. Power and pleasure, wealth and social prestige were cast aside. The *Wandervogel* and other associations of youth believed above all in the spiritual freedom of the individual.

Just before the first World War several thousand young people were organized as the *Freideutsche Jugend* (Free German Youth), a body which was nonpolitical, and had no religious commitments. Bound by common ideals, these youths shunned tobacco and alcohol; they substituted the open air for the dingy tap-room; and above all they were convinced of their right of self-determination. Not that they were windy pacifists, avoiding their patriotic responsibilities. Quite the contrary is demonstrated by their war record: some ten thousand members of the *Wandervogel* served in the war and of these two thousand were killed. Before and during most of the war the movement had been seared neither by religion nor politics. True, the young people were opposed on

---

[10] Förster, F. W., *Jugendseele, Jugendbewegung, Jugendziele.* Erlenbach-Zurich: Rotapfel, 1926; Messer, A., *Die freideutsche Jugendbewegung.* Revised, Langensalza: Hermann Beyer & Sons, 1924.

the whole to the Empire's super-nationalism; but beyond that their ideals transcended the national. But the revolution after the war planted the seeds of politics, resulting ultimately in the organization of the *Jungdeutscher Bund*, a nationalistic group of the *Freideutsche Jugend*.

Much criticism—some deserved and some undeserved—has been pointed at the *Jugendbewegung*. Because of its stand against the conventional, the Youth movement has often seemed something immoral to the old generation. Its lack of reverence for authority aroused hostility; as did its scant interest in creed and dogma. The comradeship between the sexes favored by some sections of the Youth movement drew intense criticism. As the movement progressed, the German churches became interested in it. At several universities a number of Protestant branches were organized. In the Catholic Church the movement took hold, due, among other things, to the Church's independence from the state, its deep antipathy for the stiff Prussian tradition, and also its own rich and colorful past. In time Catholic youth organizations outnumbered others. The various members were organized into groups, such as the "Quickborn," "Grossquickborn," "Hochland," and "Jungborn." Quickborn sprang from a temperance organization and was for boys and girls from the secondary schools. Grossquickborn was intended for those entering the industrial world, while Hochland was for those entering the university. Jungborn was for the working youth. Each local group strove to have its own home, a humble and broken-down mill or a tumbling castle, or something of similar romantic nature.

There was also a socialist Youth movement which was interested primarily in internal politics. Launched in the early twentieth century as a branch of the party, the socialist Youth movement had attracted some one hundred thousand members by 1914. With the coming of peace the organization split, and a rival organization, *Die Freie Sozialistische Jugend*, was formed.

Separated from its trivialities, the Youth movement left a significant mark. Begun in part as a protest against the school's intellectualism, it struck a keynote for greater educational liberalism. It sought the realization of spiritual liberty, the assertion of an individual's worth, and a return to the simplicities of life. It focused on the cultivation of *Deutschtum* of a genuine sort based on experience and contact with things, rather than through classroom memorization and drill.

12. The Arbeitsschule [11]

In Article 148 the Weimar Constitution injected *Arbeitsunterricht*—the activity program—into the republic's school system. Unfortunately, there was considerable difference of opinion as to what such a program should be. There were those, like Kerschensteiner, who saw in the *Arbeitsschule* a doing- or activity-school, which, through its methods and organization, developed good citizens. There were others, like Hugo Gaudig, who were more concerned with the pupil himself than with his relationship to the state. Contending that learning by doing should not be restricted to physical activity, they envisioned the classroom as a workshop where the child acquired knowledge and abilities through self-activity and participation.

As might be expected, the vagueness of the constitution with regard to *Arbeitsunterricht* furnished a splendid grindstone for the whetting of political axes. After considerable talk, a statement was issued by the Ministry of Public Education wherein it was explained that a merely external acquisition of knowledge was not desirable if there were no inner reaction on the part of the learner. All instruction was to stress the relationship existing between the child and his home. Self-activity—mental as well as physical—was to be a recognized part of the republic's school system.

---

[11] See Meyer, A. E., "The Doing-School in Germany," *School and Society*, XVII, 360 ff., 1923. For the history of the activity movement in Germany see Meyer, A. E., "The Arbeitsschule in Germany," *Pedagogical Seminary*, XXXIII, 508–520, 1926.

13. The Einheitsschule

Opposed to the Empire's dual system of education, the *Einheitsschule* demanded common instruction, fairly uniform in content, for all children through most of their elementary school career. Unfortunately, little was done in republican Germany to realize such a system. An approach was made by the establishment of the four-year *Grundschule* which was compulsory for all children. At the end of this common instructional period differentiation began.

14. The republic's educational weaknesses

Although the Weimar Republic had injected high ideals into its contemplated educational reforms, in the course of a little more than a decade most of these ideals became frayed and tattered. It is true, of course, that the German republic itself lived precariously and that it was engulfed by a sea of problems. Its economic troubles and political vicissitudes, together with the widespread national discontent, made the realization of the Weimar program a formidable undertaking. There were other factors which played an even stronger hand in undermining the aspirations of the new Reich. The republic, for one thing, had never taken a firm stand against its most natural enemies, the adherents of the old regime, such as the landed Prussian Junkers, the big industrialists, the militarists, the nationalists, and reactionaries in general. As the republic floundered more and more in political chaos, its foes became increasingly vocal, and in various ways, but especially by means of artful propaganda, subtly implanted in the movies and the press, they undertook to sabotage the new Germany.[12]

---

[12] Organized by a group of German industrialists towards the end of the first World War, Germany's leading film company UFA made no secret of its hostility to the republican regime. Among its first offerings after the war were such historical films as *Henry VIII, Madame Dubarry,* and *Anne Boleyn,* which were frankly anti-English and anti-French. These were followed by a stream of out-and-out nationalistic showings such as the *Nibelungen* and *Fridericus Rex.* In 1922 UFA came under the control of the avowed national-

In the schools, strangely enough, their strongest allies were the teachers. As a class, Germany's schoolmen had stood high in the days of the Kaiser. As civil servants of the mighty and respected state, they had been entrusted with the responsibility of making acceptable citizens for it. For this they had been well trained and to help them achieve their end they were cloaked with adequate authority. They earned a good salary and faced a future secured with the assurance of an adequate pension. All in all theirs was an important calling, one which enjoyed an enviable prestige throughout the Reich. With the advent of the republic this pleasant world came to an end. Not only were teachers expected to reconstruct their old loyalties and to relinquish their faith in the defunct imperial order, with its sharp and convenient class cleavage, its distinction between the handful of the privileged élite and the vast servant multitudes, but in the inflation they, like the middle classes to which they belonged, were financially wiped out. Consequently they looked upon the new regime with a sour face, and though the republic needed their cooperation desperately in carrying out its new educational program, they were generally cold to its ideals. Not only did the Reich's older and more experienced teachers hamstring the good intentions of the new government, but in their classrooms they openly indoctrinated for the old order; and when Hitler eventually beckoned, many of them gladly clasped the hand of Nazism.

Another flaw in the republic's educational program lay in its inability to break up the isolation of the secondary schools. Though attempts had been made to develop a German curriculum, the secondary schools, with their stress on the classics, the foreign languages, and the natural sciences, continued to be out of step with the needs and interests of the vast majority of Germans. As in the days of the Empire their stress was intellectual and their essential purpose to prepare their charges

---

ist millionaire Alfred Hugenberg. A German version of William Randolph Hearst, Hugenberg controlled a substantial part of his country's press, advertising, and national and international wire services.

for the higher learning. Among the middle classes the secondary school had always borne a mark of high prestige, and although many parents might have preferred an advanced cultural or a vocational education for their children, nonetheless many of them went to great lengths to give their sons and daughters a secondary schooling. Under the new regime the luster of the secondary school was undimmed. Indeed, because of the fact that secondary education had been made more accessible to the masses, they attracted more students than ever. For them, however, no new curricular provisions were made. Like the generations of youths before them they were offered the traditional academic wares, and if, after nine years of study, they passed their state examinations, they might, if they chose, enter the university.

Once the pride of Germany and the envy of many other lands, the universities could not withstand the tide of cultural deterioration which inundated the new Germany. Staffed on the whole by competent scholars with a great zeal for truth, the German university of prewar days had enjoyed a high degree of intellectual freedom. The number of its students, moreover, had been carefully restricted, in the main, to those of ability who were admitted only after having had a thorough grounding in basic subjects.

Under the republican regime all this rapidly changed. Before the war Germany's higher learning had enrolled some 80,000 students, but by 1923 the number had risen to 132,000. With their larger rosters and their increasingly hard-pressed facilities, the universities found it more and more difficult to maintain their prewar standards. These, in fact, began to slide so badly that some professors openly objected. In 1928 the Philosophical Faculty of the University of Berlin took even bolder steps by requiring its prospective students to pass special tests. Regarding the educational situation in the Reich the professors felt that it

emphasizes too much general dabbling in experience, too much for the *Weltanschauung* side—emotional side. . . . Power is not developed to overcome obstacles, to grapple with matters according to their nature, and to submit oneself with that objective devotion and unselfishness . . . to the firm discipline which is characteristic of scientific work.

As in America, moreover, Germany's higher learning began to attract more and more students whose goals were vocational rather than cultural. The fact that swarms of young Ph.D.'s were standing in breadlines and that hundreds of others were toiling as janitors and park attendants did not seem to deter multitudes of others from entering the university. In response to the newer demands the universities gradually yielded their old neo-humanistic ideals and increasingly gave way to vocationalism and specialization. Leipzig, for example, went in on a large scale for physical education; and some of the large universities, like Berlin, and the more romantic ones, like Heidelberg, catered to visiting American students by organizing special short courses for them which counted for credit in their various American colleges.

With their swollen enrollments and their requirements becoming progressively easier, the republic's universities found themselves conferring more and more doctorates. So important had degrees become that special private tutoring bureaus sprang up in nearly every university town. Specializing in helping their clients to cram for their final examinations, some of them boldly advertised themselves in the newspapers. Some went so far as to guarantee success, and a few actually offered to ghost-write a student's doctoral thesis. Though the professors denounced these doings, they apparently could not obliterate them.

Before the first World War honorary degrees had been a rarity, and when bestowed they were for distinguished service in the world of the intellect. Successful financiers and businessmen, if honored at all, were converted into *Geheimrat* (privy councilor) or *Kommerzienrat* (councilor of commerce) by the government and not by the universities. Under the republic this tradition was cast aside, and honorary degrees were handed out in growing number. As in the United States, moreover, they were not infrequently awarded to men whose wealth and good will was their main distinction.

If the republic's higher learning deteriorated in these many respects, its cowardly surrender of academic freedom was even sadder. Once intellectually free and judged largely on the basis of their academic competence, Germany's professors became increasingly shackled. Oddly enough, the pressure on them was exerted not so much by the state but by the students. When professorial utterances displeased them, both within and without the university, they resorted to strikes, general disturbances, and fisticuffs. On at least four occasions students compelled the authorities to discharge a professor. One was the celebrated case of Professor Gumbel, a Heidelberg statistician and a pacifist. Another was Theodor Lessing, a professor of philosophy and also a pacifist. Guenther Dehn's crime was his belief that in war man had the right to choose between God and country. Professor Nawiasky of Munich made the mistake of telling his classes that the Allies at Versailles had done to Germany, in more gentle manner, what the Reich had done to the vanquished Russians at Brest-Litovsk. The fact that each of these men had been a competent and productive scholar did not save them. Naturally this student pressure was hailed and encouraged by the Nazi leaders. It served them splendidly as a fascist block and helped to make the higher learning increasingly nationalistic, reactionary, and antisemitic. In time it became more militant, and when the Nazis rose to power, it became the party's strong right arm in the German universities.

15. The Third Reich

When Adolf Hitler became the German Chancellor early in 1933, he assured the German people unity, prosperity, and equality among the nations. The promised unification, however, turned out to be nazification. By means of an efficient and ruthless police, aided by an army of Nazi storm troopers, and by wholesale arrests, imprisonments, and killings of those who dared to oppose them, the National Socialist German Workers Party transformed the Reich into a totalitarian state under its undisputed mastery. By decrees in March, 1933 and in January, 1934, Germany's historic provinces—Prussia, Bavaria, Baden, Saxony, and the rest—lost their identity as governmental subdivisions. Under the new scheme they were subjected to centralized control from Berlin, and their local and regional autonomy, which in the past had always been vigorous, was vastly curtailed. Soon after Hitler's rise to the chancellorship, he was voted dictatorial powers and became the nation's Führer. Shortly after, only Nazis were allowed to hold jobs in the civil service. Trade unions, long the backbone of Germany's social democracy, were put under the ban, their funds confiscated, and all strikes prohibited.[13] Under the Ministry of Public Enlightenment and Propaganda, directed by Paul Josef Goebbels, virtually every form of expression—the radio, the theater, the cinema, the fine arts, the press, even the churches and the schools—were made the instruments of Nazi propaganda.[14] By July, 1933 all political parties except the National Socialists were forbidden even to exist in Germany. In 1936 the capstone was put on the Nazi edifice when the People's Court was permanently constituted as a five-man body, three of whose members were to be laymen selected from the roster of Nazi worthies.

The Nazi rule, though ushered in and maintained by force and terrorism, was sanctioned and supported by the vast majority of Germans. It was made possible by the psychology of a defeated nation, aggravated by Germany's chaotic postwar

---

[13] To replace the unions the Nazis created the Labor Front through which workers secured some benefits, such as rent rebates, a modicum of social insurance, reduction in tickets for entertainment, etc. The Labor Front was of course a travesty on a free labor union. The privileges accruing to the worker were paid for by his own money, something like 13% being deducted from the average pay of all German workers.

[14] Goebbels announced that he would play on the press "like a piano." To effect his ambition more than 1,300 "uncooperative" newspapers were suppressed during the Nazis' first year in power. Those editors who objected were warned and if they continued to be "uncooperative," they were imprisoned.

conditions and the inability of the republic to cope with them. But it was also made possible by the Germans' acquiescence and it was bolstered by their willingness to trade their freedom, such as it was, for stability and security. The fact that the Führer gave the Germans what they wanted most, and that in a short time he wiped out not only all traces of Weimar but even of Versailles, swelled their national pride and made them accept, and even justify, his wildest dreams.

Hitler's promise of prosperity was swiftly translated into actuality. In fact, in the course of only five years the number of jobless persons in the Reich was reduced from some six millions to less than 100,000. This seeming miracle was wrought by an enormous public works program, involving projects of slum clearance and town planning. Blocks of workers' homes were erected, as were town halls, post offices, and railway stations. Under the direction of Fritz Todt four-lane super highways, a network of some 2,000 miles connecting Germany's far-flung cities and substantial enough to support the heaviest military machines, had been built by 1939. Even more significant was the Third Reich's colossal rearmament program. This not only enrolled millions of men in the armed forces, but it also required the efforts of an even larger force to produce all the things they needed. Under the direction of Hermann Goering two Four-Year Plans [15] were put into operation, calling for the expansion of agriculture and industry and the production of raw materials, such as rubber, wool, oil, and the like, for the purpose of making Germany entirely self-sufficient. All this meant work and this in turn meant employment. Moreover, under an ingenious system of international barter and state control of currency and credits, a

---

[15] The Plans required the strictest "cooperation" on the part of both labor and capital. The former had of course been regimented along Nazi lines through the Labor Front, which toward the end of the '30's comprised some 30,000,000 members. As for the businessman, he had to submit to such controls as a managed currency, price stabilization, profit limitation, government priorities, rationing of all raw materials, state credit, and gigantic state cartels. This was one of the most thorough-going forms of state capitalism ever devised.

system developed by Finance Minister Schacht, Germany's economy was given new life.[16] Thus, by the end of the thirties the Nazi revolution emerged in triumph; but that triumph, alas, boded no good. For, as the next decade was to disclose, what the Nazis had sought was not jobs and bread and contentment for an industrious German people, not the creation of a vast Germanic New Deal, but preparation for an aggressive second world war.

a. **Race and Soil.** Hitler's philosophy was set forth at length in his *Mein Kampf,* a good part of which was written during 1924 while its author was in prison. From its pages emerge the Nazi doctrines of Race and Soil. Put briefly, Hitler's racial theme went somewhat as follows: The Nordic or "Aryan" race is superior to all others.[17] Not only is it endowed with an abundance of the noblest virtues, but it is also the most gifted in war and the most fit to rule. Hence, the task of the German State must be first to unite all Germans under one flag to insure ample space for the expansion of their master race, and then to fulfill the natural mission of that race, which is to assume the leadership in world civilization. Though palpably absurd, Hitler's racial views became one of the most important articles in the Nazi faith. From them flowed a brutal and determined policy of antisemitism. In a series of laws and decrees Germany's Jews were stripped of their civic and political rights, their property was confiscated, and thousands of them were thrown into concentration camps.

---

[16] Dr. Schacht prohibited the export of all capital. Foreigners selling to Germany had to leave their credits in the Berlin bank. In exchange they had to accept receipts which they sold to buyers from Germany at a different rate for each country. Schacht bought large quantities of agricultural produce from the Balkans which, however, could get little but German arms in exchange.

[17] Hitler's racial views had been set forth earlier by the Frenchman Gobineau and Houston Stewart Chamberlain, an Englishman who became a German citizen. Anthropologists generally scoffed at them. In fact even Nazi apologists and propagandists submitted that only a small fraction of the German populace were blond, blue-eyed, long-headed, and tall—the characteristics of the pure Nordic. Not even the Führer himself could have qualified on this basis. In such cases the creative imagination of the propagandist came to the rescue. Thus even the Japanese found themselves "honorary Aryans."

By 1939 the Nazis had reduced Jews to the appalling condition of the medieval ghetto.

A concomitant of Hitler's theory was that Germans should reproduce abundantly. To fulfill her Nordic role, the German woman was expected to resume her place in the home. To encourage early marriage, young people were granted state aid, and if they produced four offspring, the loan was entirely canceled. In addition, parents of large families were accorded special boons, such as rent allowances, preferences in public employment, reductions in a number of taxes, reduced prices on certain amusement tickets, and so on. Moreover, "to honor the German mother and to thank her for the children she presents to the nation," the Führer created a special Cross of Honor of German Motherhood, which was awarded to mothers blessed with extra large families.[18] To insure "racial purity" sexual intercourse between Jews and "Aryans" was made a punishable act by the Nuremberg Laws of 1935. To prevent the perpetuation of heritable diseases, sterilization was authorized for a number of causes.

The companion of the race doctrine was soil—*Blut und Boden* the Nazis phrased it. The Aryans supposedly were lovers of the soil and nature. Hence the peasant was superior to the city dweller, a situation which was reflected in Nazi law by which the rural populace was accorded special benefits. To gratify the "Aryan's" love of nature, the Nazi state provided its devotees with opportunities to travel in the country at specially reduced rates. Known as *Kraft durch Freude* (Strength through joy), the program offered Germans a choice of some 250 domestic tours and fifteen sea trips.

16. Education under National Socialism

a. Beginnings. Long before Hitler and his party rose to prominence, the National Socialists were planning far-reaching educational changes. Some of these had been hinted at in the

---

[18] Vonolfen, W., Piel, E., and Seifert, P., *Der Weg zum Reich*, p. 214. Berlin: Deutscher Schulverlag, 1944.

Führer's book, *Mein Kampf.* One of the first educational decrees under the Nazi regime was issued March 17, 1933. Significantly, it held that "Germanic culture must be treated thoroughly." The fact that "in the school of the Marxist system (i.e., the republic) German pre-history found no fitting place" was to be remedied by an increased attention to the early Germans. In its subsequent instructions concerning history texts, the Ministry of the Interior reaffirmed this stand, holding that German pre-history was "pre-eminently national learning (*Wissenschaft*)," than which "no other is better suited to counteract the traditional undervaluation of the cultural heights of our ancestors." Stress was to be put on "the national idea in contrast to the international, whose lingering poison for more than a hundred years has been threatening to destroy the German soul."

b. **Race.** The same ministerial instructions gave considerable attention to the question of race: "From primitive times through all later millennia to the present the significance of race must be given a fitting consideration." Also: "The history of Europe is the work of Aryan peoples. . . ." Furthermore: "Not until the work of the originally Aryan Hindus, Medes, Persians, as well as the Hittites, was the history of western Asia definitely influenced. The pupil must experience the fates of these peoples as those of his own blood, who in the end are destroyed because of the predominance of foreign racial blood, but only after they (i.e., the Aryan Hindus, etc.) had created high civilizations in India and Persia." In studying the ancient Greeks "once again it should be stressed that we are dealing with our closest racial brethren."

Rassenkunde (race science) was given a place of the first order in the school curriculum. In fact, a major part of what used to be biology now became *Rassenkunde;* nor did health education and physical training escape the racial stress. A good part of it was, of course, dubious in a scientific sense. One commonly used text asserted that ". . . the mixture of people of German stock with foreign races must be rejected unconditionally. . . . The mixture of Germans with Jews is disastrous. . . . Jewish traits are wholly opposed to the most valuable German traits. . . . No poem of Heinrich Heine can be read without perceiving that only too clearly!" [19]

c. **Modern history.** Naturally, the Nazis assigned a significant place to modern history. "The last two decades of our own times are to be a leading chapter in the study of history. The monstrous experience of the World War with the heroic struggle of the German people against a world of foes, the disintegration of our power of resistance through forces hostile to the Fatherland, the humiliation of our people by the Versailles dictate, and the subsequent breakdown of the liberalistic-Marxian philosophy are to be treated just as thoroughly as the nation's nascent awakening from the Ruhr struggle to the penetration of the National Socialist concept of freedom and the restoration of the German nation on the Day of Potsdam."

The Hamburg pupils were taught about the rise and achievements of Hitler and his party. The leaders, symbols, program, and organization of the Nazi party were to be studied. Special consideration was to be bestowed on the fundamental Nazi tenets of "nation, race, culture, state and church." Although a limited number of dates was still to be learned, the memorization of slogans was preferable—such as: "We need colonies!" (*Wir brauchen Kolonien!*) and "One People, one Nation, one Führer!" (*Ein Volk, ein Reich, ein Führer!*).

That history taught this way was national and political propaganda is plain. As a matter of fact, the Nazis were quite frank about admitting this, as the following sentence from the Hamburg syllabus indicates: "The primacy of politics, in history especially, must come to the relief of pedagogy.

---

[19] Heinrich Heine (1797–1856), one of Germany's great lyric poets, was the author of the famed *Lorelei*. His satirical thrusts at the Prussians and his warm feeling for the French brought upon him the disapprobation of the Prussian ruling classes. The fact that he was a Jew was sufficient cause for the Nazis to disown him.

Propaganda and education today operate together. . . ." And again: "Since the contemporary themes serve particularly to educate the German nationally and politically, the teacher must lead his pupils to take definite positions, which from an external as well as internal political standpoint will clearly contrast friend and foe. At the same time the educational authorities expect every teacher to become positively identified with National Socialism." [20]

   d. **Geography.** Almost as significant as history in the German's national and political education was geography or, as it now became, geo-politics. Thus the decree of March 17th lamented that German children often knew more about foreign lands than about the Fatherland, and that too often they were inclined to overrate the former at the expense of the latter. To attend to these matters the decree of June 7, 1933 was promulgated. This regulated study-trips in Germany and abroad. The latter could be "undertaken only by such students who have previously participated in trips through their native land . . . and who have acquired an adequate understanding of their own Fatherland, and who possess the requisite maturity to consider foreign peoples critically." Pupils were to be encouraged to travel in Germany "to gain an impressionable picture of the German native land."

   The fact that something like a third of the Germans lived outside the boundaries of the Reich received constant stress. Every child was to contribute to the fund for the *Auslandsdeutschtum* (German culture abroad), and numerous detailed pamphets suggested methods of working the *"koloniale Gedanke"* (the idea of colonies) into every subject. To bring the German to a closer relationship with his national kinsmen abroad, a series of texts was published under the title "The

---

[20] In *Der Weg zum Reich,* a history text used in the *Volksschule* as late as 1945, by far the greater part of the book is devoted to the glorification of war and particularly to the part played in wars by Germany. By contrast the Weimar Republic is dismissed in a half-page footnote under the caption "Germany under Jews and Marxists." No direct mention of Japan's attack on Pearl Harbor is made.

German in Foreign Lands" (*Der Deutsche im Auslande*).
Some of the titles in this series were "The German in Peru,"
"The German in Mexico," "The German in the Volga Land,"
"The German in Transcaucasia," and so on. The final goal
of any study-trip "was an increased national consciousness."

e. **Physical training.** During the republican regime the
schools had stressed physical training as a phase of a well-
rounded education. In the Nazi educational scheme the body
came first; character next; and the intellect last. Before
Germany rearmed, the Nationalist Socialist school gave substantial attention to physical training as a form of premilitary
training. What is known as *Geländesport* was made compulsory for all. This was a form of athletic activity in the
open country, and included marching, running, leaping over
obstacles, and so on. In the universities student dueling, prohibited during the Weimar regime, was re-established and encouraged. The ideal in physical training, as indeed in all
Nazi education, was the soldier. "The soldier and the worker
demand struggle. . . . His origin is blood, iron, and fire. . . .
The citizen is the type of a past age. . . . The fundamental
law of the soldierly man is fighting. . . . A state that can
demonstrate hardness and brutality is . . . racially sound."
"A youth will grow up," proclaimed Hitler, "before whom the
world will shrink."

f. **Secondary education.** Several decrees affecting secondary education were issued. As in the lower schools, the stress
was to be on things German. "The national will is to receive
that strengthening which he [the student himself] has so long
desired, but which he never dared to display openly," commented the *Pädagogisches Zentralblatt* in its analysis of the
new orders. State-operated secondary schools were to be run
as National Socialist *Erziehungsstätten* (places of education).
In Prussia the former cadet schools were re-established even
before the Reich announced its rearming. During the republican regime these schools had been transformed into up-to-date,
progressive boarding schools.

An innovation in German secondary education was the *Arbeitsdienst,* or labor service. Originally on a voluntary basis, the *Arbeitsdienst* was made compulsory. It was required of all secondary school graduates before they began their higher studies, or before they entered on a vocation. In the main the student's labor took the form of land reclamation projects. At least a month and a half were devoted to concentrated physical training which included "exercises of all kinds as well as shooting weapons of small calibre." Originating before the Reich's reinstitution of compulsory military service, the *Arbeitsdienst* was intended in the main as a form of premilitary training. The students lived together in barracks, were subject to military discipline, and wore a special uniform. By 1939 labor service had become an integral part of Nazi education, the rule being that every physically able boy or girl in his or her nineteenth year had to serve six months in a labor camp.

Under the Nazis the humanities received less stress. In the classical *Gymnasium* English, however, was given more stress than before. In February, 1937, Minister of Education Rust announced that English would be the leading modern foreign language in the *Mittelschule.* Latin, curiously enough, was not immune to Nazification. Thus, the aim of instruction in ancient languages was set down as: (1) to make the pupil conscious of the physical and spiritual powers of the Nordic race in all forms and expressions of the kindred Greeks and Romans; (2) to arouse the will of the race from the knowledge that the loss of racial consciousness caused the downfall of the Greeks and Romans.

g. **Restriction of enrollment.** One of the most significant laws affecting German education came into being on April 25, 1933. This restricted enrollment in all schools. At the beginning of the school year the authorities were to decide "how many pupils may be admitted to each school and how many students to each university faculty." To check the overcrowding of professions the number of students was to be decreased. The law applied to both public and private schools. Through the law, it was simple to regulate the number of non-Aryan students attending school.

h. **Teachers.** To assure itself of a body of teachers able and willing to teach in the Nazi spirit, the Third Reich overhauled its training of teachers. By ministerial decree the Republican normal school, known as the Pedagogic Academy (*Pädagogische Akademie*) was rechristened the Higher School for Teacher Training (*Hochschule für Lehrerbildung*). The discarded name, consisting as it did of two words of non-German origin, was not looked upon with favor. More important, however, was the fact that "the teacher is no longer to be trained as a citizen of the world who was to educate youth for the international ideals of humanity, but instead he is to become a genuine teacher, bound to the Fatherland, who will lead youth to a real German national consciousness." Though the teaching profession was crowded, the Nazis opened several new normal schools. One of the first was at Lauenburg, Pomerania. It was to become a cultural-political bulwark against the Corridor.[21] In his address at the ceremonies opening the new school, Minister of Education Rust epitomized the Reich's new policy in teacher training. " Teachers," he asserted, "must know that their pupils are to be judged according to race. Our teachers will learn something about our boundaries, study races and military geography instead of social and industrial sciences and novelties." The contemporary German elementary school teacher was "not to grasp at cultural forms which must be rejected by National Socialism as unsuitable." Furthermore, the teacher was to be prepared for a German school which "is to function in the spirit of our great . . . army and is to see that a whole people in its totality is brought up with this thought in mind." These future

---

[21] By the Treaty of Versailles Germany ceded to Poland a strip of land 260 miles long and 80 miles wide lying between the province of East Prussia and the rest of Germany. This strip of territory, splitting Germany in two, became known as the Corridor.

teachers, in the words of Minister Rust, were "the Storm Troop leaders of German national education." The Hessian Ministry of Education was one of the first to transform these words into reality by declaring that "only he may become an educator who up to his 35th year . . . has served in the ranks of the Storm Troops. Unless this requirement is fulfilled no one may expect to be called into the service of the State." Subsequently all candidates for teaching posts had to have served as *active* National Socialists. All teachers had to be "politically reliable." They were, of course, all regimented as cogs in the totalitarian machine and had to belong to the National Socialist organization for teachers.

i. **Youth and the party.** Nazi education laid considerable stress on the "heroic." The personality of the Führer, omnipresent in the Reich, was in particular evidence in the school. Every classroom displayed his picture—and each one was different; his bust was in every school vestibule, in every corridor, and every auditorium. Passages from *Mein Kampf* struck one's eyes everywhere, as did familiar Nazi slogans, such as "Führer command, and we will follow!" They were painted on the school walls; sometimes they were even carved into stone. That they were often the basis for written essays goes without saying. They were even used for themes in the *Reifeprüfung,* the examination which is traditionally taken after the completion of one's studies in the secondary school. The Nazi salute was everywhere, every class from the kindergarten to the university being started and ended with the class standing at attention and shouting "Heil Hitler!" [22] Every time a pupil or teacher left or entered a room he was required to use this greeting. Eulogy for the Führer poured forth constantly. The following *Prayer for Grace Before Meals* was to be taught in all German kindergartens:

---

[22] The Hitler greeting had become the vogue as the customary way of saying *hello* or *good-bye.* It was used to conclude a letter instead of *yours truly,* and it was even used to terminate a telephone conversation.

> Fold your little hands,
> Bow your little head,
> Think of him who gives us
> Our daily bread.
> Adolf Hitler is his name
> Him we as our Savior claim.[23]

Prominent in the training of Germany's youth and an integral part of education, were the Hitler Youth organizations. Known as the *Hitler-Jugend* (the HJ), the movement was under the official direction of Baldur von Schirach, whose views on youth may be epitomized in his oft repeated phrase *"Die deutsche Jugend gehört dem Führer!"* (German youth belongs to the Führer). Membership in the Hitler Youth was compulsory, and by 1939 it comprised some 7,000,000 boys and girls between the ages of ten and eighteen. Unlike the original and historic German Youth Movement, that of the *Hitler-Jugend* was not an attempt to help youth to unfold its individual personality,[24] on the contrary, the virtues it strove to instill were the Prussian ones of Frederick the Great: duty, obedience, discipline, and the willingness to sacrifice everything for the Fatherland. The boys and girls of the Hitler Youth were to be fashioned into 100 per cent dynamic Nazis. Their credo was summarized for them by Robert Ley, head of the Labor Front, when in 1937 at Berlin he addressed an assembly of 15,000 young people thus:

We believe on this earth solely in Adolf Hitler. We believe that National Socialism is the sole faith and salvation of our people. We believe there is a God in Heaven who has created us, led us, and publicly laid his blessing upon us. We believe that God has sent us Adolf Hitler so that Germany may receive a foundation for its existence through all eternity.[25]

Boys and girls of the *Hitler-Jugend* wore their own distinctive uniforms and they played a real and active part in many of the government's enterprises. They collected funds for the

---

[23] See *The Journal of Education* (London), LXXVII, 525, 1945.

[24] The girls' branch of the Hitler Youth was known as the *Bund Deutscher Mädchen,* the BDM.

[25] As reported by the Associated Press.

national winter relief campaigns and they participated in the Reich's drives against waste, collecting old metal, bones, rags, and paper. Psychologically this stirred their ego as well as their communal feeling and helped to make them think of themselves as indispensable factors in the development of a bigger and better Reich. The program of indoctrination, so relentlessly carried out in the school, was supplemented in the *Hitler-Jugend*, particularly along military and political lines. The doctrines of Race and Soil were reinforced not only with propaganda, but with exercises for health and strength, with marches into the country, and with extended sojourns in the Youth Hostels, many of which were located in some of the most beautiful spots in Germany. What was known as the *Landjahr* was a period of time spent by fifteen-year-olds in the country. During the daytime they worked in the fields, assisting farmers with the planting, the plowing, and the harvesting, with an occasional interlude for physical exercises; in the evenings they received their lessons in National Socialism.

For boys excelling in the Nazi virtues whose Nordic physique approached perfection and whose record in the Hitler Youth was flawless, special schools were established to train future Nazi leaders. Among them were the *Nationalpolitische Erziehungsanstalten*, the so-called "Napoli," and the *Adolf Hitler Schulen*, both of which offered a secondary education. From the cream of Nazi youth a small group of young men of twenty-five was picked for special training at the *Ordensburgen* (Castles of Knights) where they were to be molded into Germany's future Hitlers, Goerings, and Goebbels.

j. Reduction of schooling. The National Socialist government steadily reduced the number of years of instruction of children taking the complete elementary and higher courses which prepare for entrance into universities. In the fall of 1936 Minister of Education Rust declared that the thirteen-year course required for preparatory school graduation would be reduced to twelve. Previously the Ministry had issued a ruling abolishing the sixth school-day in each week, which was to be used instead for training in athletics and in learning National Socialist ideas. Spread over twelve years of the child's schooling this decrease added up to about two years, so that with the cut of one year, the child had in effect lost three years. In view of the time and energy that Germany's youth had to devote to athletics and political activities, both in and out of school hours, the reduction of time inevitably led to a deterioration in scholastic standards.

17. Re-education

Even before the Third Reich's downfall in 1945 it was recognized that something would have to be done to counteract the effects of Nazi education on German youth. Based on the notion that the child was the father of the man, Nazi education had taken the child in his youngest years and subjected him over a period of time to a thorough and relentless conditioning. So efficiently had this been administered that even in defeat young Germany continued to glow adoringly for the principles of the Führer. These precepts had the force of a religion. From them sprang the Nazi moral code which, though abhorrent to civilized men, became the basis of the Nazi ethic. The National Socialists were certainly not cynical when they preached the doctrine of the master race and when they asserted that might makes right; they believed these things with a fanatical fervor. With Spengler they affirmed time and again that "socialism means power, power and again power" and that "plans and thoughts are nothing without power." Indubitably, strength was moral and war its noblest expression. Hence, it should be no cause for wonder that young Nazis were ready to march to all corners of the earth singing *"heute gehört uns Deutschland und morgen die ganze Welt"* (Today we own Germany, tomorrow the whole world).

Nor can one ignore the damaging effects of Nazist racial theories. The belief that the German Aryan was of the *Herrenvolk*, destined to rule over all others, was cherished long before the advent of the swastika; but under Hitler this doctrine was implanted in every boy and girl, and today its roots run deep.

A formidable weapon of fascism was its disparagement of the intellect. "I will have no intellectual training," vociferated the Führer; for the intellect, he was convinced, was a "disease of life." "Knowledge," he went on to say, with unwitting accuracy, "is the ruination of my young men" and "universal education the most corroding and disintegrating poison." Consequently, the Nazi policy was to destroy the intellectual basis of education, and particularly higher education not only in Germany, but in the occupied lands as well. So thorough and far-reaching was its triumph in Germany that it will take years to repair the damage—if, indeed, it can ever be repaired.

Defeated Germany, a nation of some 63 million people, has been divided into four zones governed respectively by the United States, Russia, France, and Great Britain, with joint control of Berlin and with machinery for cooperative planning for all zones in the Allied Control Council. Pending the establishment of a unified administration of all Germany, each of the occupying nations has been made responsible for developing the governmental policy, including the educational policy, within the zone assigned to it.

Educational experts were sent to the Reich to study the problem of remaking the German mind. In addition, the help of German emigrés was utilized. Even before the war's end a group of such men and women had organized in England as the German Educational Reconstruction, a society dedicated to furthering and developing a democratic system of education in Germany. From them came a number of writings setting forth the various aspects of the German educational problem and offering suggestions for its eventual solution.[26] Moreover, under the auspices of the United States Department of State

---

[26] Among these one might note Specht, Minna, *Education in Postwar Germany*. London: International Publishing Company, 1944; Zink, H., *American Military Government in Germany*. New York: The Macmillan Company, 1947; Richter, W., *Reeducating Germany*. Chicago: University of Chicago Press, 1945.

and the War Department, a special mission went to the Reich "to observe and evaluate the educational program of the United States Military Government in Germany." Based on the Potsdam agreement, that program was premised on the idea that "German education shall be so controlled as completely to eliminate Nazi and militaristic doctrines and to make possible the successful development of democratic ideas." The first step in this direction was the campaign of "denazification," which was carried on throughout Germany and by which the schools were shorn of teachers known to have been Nazis.

Much more difficult was the more positive task of developing and carrying out a democratic educational program. Not only did this mean the creation of new texts and study materials in harmony with the purposes of the new program, but at the same time it required the cooperation, and hence the cultural and moral regeneration, of the German adult. To rewrite German school books in the new spirit was not too difficult—indeed, with the help of German emigrés in the United States a new supply of texts soon became available. But remaking the ways of the German adult has proved a much more formidable task, in fact, there are many who despair of its achievement. Materially, the task of re-education has been handicapped by obstacles such as a lack of school houses, a dearth of teaching materials, a shortage of teachers, and, of course, the appalling malnutrition existing among Germany's children. Yet in spite of these titanic difficulties, most elementary schools and a fairly large number of secondary schools were open in the fall of 1945. Subsequently, some universities began opening their doors.

The experience of the British has been much like that of the Americans. When, in 1945, the late Ellen Wilkinson, then Minister of Education, visited the British Zone in Germany, she found the same material shortages, the same problems of supplying young Germany with denazified textbooks, new equipment, and schools, and of providing them with non-Nazi teachers.[27] Everywhere there loomed the same problems of food and housing, of clothing, of disease and immorality. On the whole the British program has been similar to that of the Americans, and by the fall of 1945 they, too, had succeeded in reopening the elementary schools as well as some of the secondary schools. The University of Göttingen was the first of the universities to resume its academic activities with an enrollment of some 4,000 students.

In the French zone of occupation the Germans number only six million, which is less than one tenth of the population within the present confines of Germany Aside from the coal-producing Saar, which in effect is now a French province, the segment of Germany under French rule is relatively insignificant. However, having found themselves without any allies in the East, the French have come to the unwelcome realization that the West includes Germany. Whether the Teuton is weak or strong makes little difference to the Gallic mind. Experience has conditioned the French to regard the Germans as a potential threat. Consequently, the French in their present situation have undertaken the task of creating a new German mind, and of orienting it toward France. For this purpose they have given less consideration to the material rehabilitation of German education than have the Americans and the British. Instead they have stressed education itself. Like the Americans and the British, they have rewritten the former textbooks of the Nazi Reich, and have issued more than two million new copies. Unlike the Americans and the British, however, the French have not been favorably disposed to our denazification policy. Criticizing it as "unjust and unconstructive," they have employed former Nazi teachers, keeping them of course under some degree of surveillance. The French have been proud especially of their accomplishments in the field of German higher education. Under the occupation, the Univer-

---

[27] For an account of Miss Wilkinson's findings see *The Journal of Education* (London), LXXVII, 528, 1945.

sity of Mainz, which had been closed for more than a generation, has been reopened.

Russia's iron curtain has enveloped its re-educational activities in obscurity; a few facts, however, have been disclosed.
Unlike the French, for example, the Russians have given a
front place to mass education, including the theater, the
movies, the radio, and the press. Russia's policy of re-education, moreover, appears to be closely related to the basic principles of Communist educational doctrine. Thus, we find a
program of compulsory education for all children between the
ages of six and fourteen. All private schools have been
abolished, including parochial schools. As in Russia, the
Russians have established an educational ladder to replace the
former dual system, thereby making secondary education more
accessible than heretofore to the qualified children of the
masses. Following the compulsory elementary school are several types of secondary schools with differentiated curricula.
Children who do not continue their schooling after the compulsory period are required to attend some kind of vocational
school for at least eight hours every week over a period of
three years. As one might expect, the Russians have separated
church and state, and in accordance with this principle, have
abolished religious instruction in the schools. Assigned to the
churches, religious instruction is now given to children whose
parents desire it. Following the pattern existing in the
USSR, the Russian Occupational Government has encouraged
teachers to organize and to hold regular educational conferences. Characteristic of these meetings is the fact that attendance is obligatory, and that administrators and supervisors
as well as university professors are required to be present.

D.   Italy

1.   Background

Though Italians point with pride to their ancient Roman
beginnings and a history stretching back for more than two
and a half thousand years, modern Italy, united in one

economic and political whole, did not unfold until 1871. A frail and precarious creature, the new state took its place among the nations, a land half the size of France but with more than 25,000,000 inhabitants. Italy was poor, bereft of colonies, and unblessed by natural resources. To uphold and defend the young state an army and a navy were needed; and to speed the national progress a large and realistic program of public works was essential. All this required financing which, in turn, necessitated high taxes. Under the resultant economic pressure discontent and discord grew, and many Italians, yearning for greener pastures, left their homeland. In fact, by 1914 between five and six millions of them had trekked to other lands, especially to the United States, but also to Argentina and Brazil. Offset by the high Italian birth rate, the losses in population were cancelled to some degree, and just before the outbreak of the first World War, some 35,000,000 persons were crowded into the boot-shaped peninsula.

From the time of its inception in 1871 to 1914 and even thereafter, Italy has been harassed by three persistent problems, none of which it ever fully solved and all of which released torrential political, economic, and social antagonisms. Specifically, these problems were concerned with (1) the attempt to bring about better relations between the state and the papacy, now shorn of its ancient sovereign temporal powers, but still the spiritual mother of the vast majority of Italians; (2) the endeavor to create national unity among a people disrupted by a welter of inner dissensions; and (3) the satisfaction of its desire to be a great nation playing a leading role in the drama of international affairs.

To appreciate the nature of the problem involving the relationship between the Italian state and the Catholic Church, one must bear in mind that the years immediately before and after the birth of the Italian State were in the nature of a second Counter-Reformation. During this period the Church took an iron stand on many of the trends resulting from the advance of nineteenth century science and technology. In the

encyclical *Quanta cura* and the *Syllabus of Errors,* both published in 1864, Pope Pius IX condemned and challenged the
new ideas of "naturalism," not only in biology, but in their
major social, economic, and political aspects as well. Also in
1870 the doctrine of papal infallibility—when the pope speaks
ex cathedra on matters of faith and morals he is infallible—
was formally stated. Such was the theological climate in
which the Italian state was born. Obviously at odds in many
of their basic interests, Church and state were bound to
collide.

In its relations with the Catholic Church, the Italian government was confronted by two questions, both of which were
rooted in the remote and moss-covered past. One of these
hinged on the Church's claim to independent territorial sovereignty as a prerequisite to the proper discharge of papal
functions; the other related to the Church's support through
public moneys, the activities of its religious orders and
monastic organizations, and its role in education.

To the first of these questions the state replied in a resounding negative, declaring its opposition to any temporal
powers for the Vatican. With equal resolution Pope Pius IX
held that his historic sovereign rights were essential for the
well-being of the Church. When the Papal States were seized
by the Italian government, Pius IX became a voluntary
"prisoner in the Vatican," to which his sovereignty was restricted, refusing thereafter to have any official relations with
the Italian government. His successors followed suit until
1929, when the Lateran Treaty resolved the situation.

Regarding the second question, the results were less unhappy. Though Pius IX had forbidden Italian Catholics to
accept the rights and duties of citizenship, Pope Pius X re-
laxed the prohibition, thereby permitting Catholics to participate formally in Italian politics. On the whole the state's
attitude toward the Church was neither harsh nor unsympathetic: it made generous provision for the Church's support out of the public treasury; it accepted the Church's views

on divorce by refusing to approve it; at the same time, however, it reduced the number of monastic establishments, taking over large slices of ecclesiastic property. In essence the relationship between Church and state was strained and delicate, and required every ounce of diplomacy and tact.

With the achievement of Italy's unification in 1871, there came into being a national consciousness which profoundly affected age-old customs, traditions, and institutions, and which reflected itself in the nation's arts and sciences and in education. Under the impact of modern industrialization and the accompanying economic transformation, Italy's antiquated feudal structure gave way. Particularly affected were northern and central Italy, where, in cities like Milan, Turin, Genoa, and Naples, commercial and manufacturing enterprises made swift headway. Banks and mutual loan associations, co-operative organizations of producers and consumers, labor unions, and other bodies designed in one way or other to improve the lot of the industrial worker and the small farmer developed with the emergence of the new industrial order.

Behind the façade of unity, however, were signs of division. Indeed, the word "unrest" might well epitomize the history of Italian politics during this period. Political cliques, a hangover from Italy's feudal past in which petty and absolute states vied with one another for political gain, survived to hamper the growth of strong and effective political parties with clearly delineated doctrines. With the rise of industrialization, socialism began to gather political force, and although attempts were made in the nineties to suppress it, it continued to attract adherents. But feuds and dissensions among anarchists, syndicalists, socialists, and organized Catholicism kept the political pot in a constant bubble. It was not until after 1912, as a result of a general reform in the franchise, that peasants and workers were in a position to exert any direct political influence,[1] and it wasn't until after the first

---

[1] As a result of the new suffrage laws the number of voters rose from 3,500,-000 to 8,000,000.

World War that Italy was to witness the rise of three major political parties with doctrines more or less clearly defined. They were the Catholic People's Party, the Socialist Party, and the Communist Party.

Meanwhile the fires of nationalism which had wrought the Italian state continued to burn. They were fed by a small group of chauvinistic thinkers and politicians, by ambitious army and naval officers, and by colonial-minded merchants and industrialists. Italy's envy, moreover, of the great imperial powers, such as Britain and France, her need for more land to house and feed her expanding populace, the inadequacy of her supply of raw materials—all were seductive lures to imperialistic adventuring. To gratify her colonial yearnings Italy supported a large army and navy, and from the eighties to 1912 she engaged in a number of costly wars in Africa, emerging from them with Eritrea, Italian Somaliland, and Libya. But her march to empire faltered ingloriously in Ethiopia where Italian forces were defeated in 1896. Worse yet was the effect of these undertakings on Italy's economy which, immature and underdeveloped to begin with, creaked distressfully under the added strain.

Undaunted by the costliness of their dubious African ventures, Italy's nationalists set their eyes on other goals. Giving their full and active support to the movement of *irredentism*, they called for the liberation of their compatriots living under Austria-Hungary in Trieste and Trent and on the northeastern Adriatic. Not only must they be freed, but it was demanded that their lands be incorporated in the Kingdom of Italy. That such an accomplishment could only be brought about by force was obvious, and in the years before the first World War the Italian people were contributing heavily to provide the machinery for such a venture.

When the first World War broke out, Italy's attitude was indecisive. Though bound by treaty to the Central Powers in the Triple Alliance, she declared her neutrality. Her active support continued to be implored by both of the warring sides and, after teetering hesitantly between the two for almost a year, she finally threw her lot in with the Allies. She entered the conflict laden with the promise of rich territorial rewards in Dalmatia, Albania, the Near East, and Africa, a promise confirmed in a secret treaty at London. These aspirations were never realized, and Italy emerged from the war, disappointed and resentful. Economically battered, politically in turmoil, and nursing a psychology which boded no good, she faced a dark and turbulent future.

2. Evolution of education

With the enactment of the Casati Law in 1859, the Kingdom of Sardinia laid the cornerstone of the peninsula's educational structure. Under this law which was subsequently applied to the Kingdom of Italy, the provision of elementary education was left to the municipalities which were provincial or local capitals and to districts having a population of more than ten thousand. The law, however, required compulsory school attendance for only three years. Since the localities did not receive state aid, they were not keen about enforcing the law. The Casati Law also laid the foundation for the secondary school system which included the classical *ginnasi-licei* and technical institutes which prepared for the normal schools and the universities. In 1877 the Coppino Act extended the period of compulsory attendance to four years. It was not until 1904 that the period was extended to six years in the larger communities. The fact that there was considerable illiteracy induced the state to grant aid.[2] At the same time it bestowed privileges, such as the suffrage, the right to carry arms, and to secure work in the public services, upon those who had completed the elementary course. In 1906 schools with two or three daily sessions, as well as traveling schools, were estab-

---

[2] The Orlando Law (July, 1904) extended compulsory education to the age of twelve and provided state aid. In addition it required illiterate adults to attend evening school. Those failing to conform to the law were to lose certain privileges, such as the franchise, public employment, and permits to hunt and carry arms.

lished in an endeavor to bring elementary education to the scattered population of southern Italy.[3] Five years later the Daneo-Credaro Law was passed to improve the bad conditions revealed by examinations—the inferior preparation of teachers, and the shortness of the courses. Because of the general ineffectiveness of the local educational authorities, provincial bodies were created and authorized to establish schools at the cost of the state in impoverished or backward communities. Taking advantage of the proffered aid of the state, the majority of localities relinquished their right to provide elementary education.

Despite these legislative attempts at educational improvement, progress, particularly in the realm of elementary education, was slow. School attendance was poor; of those attending school, moreover, only some sixty per cent completed their courses. The usual companion of poor school attendance is illiteracy, and in this respect Italy was no exception, the percentage of illiteracy ranging from 11 per cent in Piedmont to 70 per cent in Calabria. School administration on the whole was inefficient; teachers were poorly prepared; classes were unevenly distributed in size; teaching was inefficient; and public opinion was not particularly interested in the development of an up-to-date and efficient public school system.

3. Administration of education before World War I

Italy's educational administration was centralized, resembling that of France rather than that of England. At the head of the system was the Minister of Public Instruction who was assisted by a hierarchy of inspectors and officials.[4] A member of the national cabinet, the Minister had charge of the nation's public education. He was also entrusted with the supervision of private schools. Also under the care of the

---

[3] The Sonnino Law (July, 1906) authorized the establishment of state schools in scattered districts.

[4] In 1929 under the Fascist regime the title was changed to Minister of National Education.

Ministry were the nation's libraries, its fine arts and museums, and its learned societies. Next in importance to the Minister was the Under Secretary of State for Public Instruction, who, in a general way, served as the Minister's assistant and on occasion even substituted for him. Assisting the Minister was the *Consiglio Superiore,* an educational advisory body, some of whose members were appointed by the Minister, who was also chairman of the body. Although it met only twice a year, the council played an important part in Italian education. At the request of the Minister, for example, any bill on education might be referred to it for consideration and advice. Within the council there was a committee of 15 members, officially known as the *Giunta.* Meeting regularly once a month, the *Giunta* concerned itself with higher education and with matters not considered by the *Consiglio Superiore.*

For the purpose of local administration Italy was organized into a number of provinces each of which was administered by a superintendent, a *provveditore agli studi.* Appointed by the Minister, the superintendent was responsible to him, executing his orders and submitting data and information to him. In his region the *provveditore* enjoyed large powers. He supervised all public and private education; approved the selection of textbooks; approved standards for examinations for teachers; transferred, retired, or dismissed them on the advice of the educational committee; heard appeals against decisions of inspectors; exercised disciplinary authority over teachers and imposed penalties upon them when necessary; appointed bodies to examine cases involving negligence on the part of localities in complying with the educational law; and ordered the closing of schools in cases of emergency. Assisting the *provveditore* were a number of bodies, such as the *consiglio provinciale scolastico,* which concerned itself with the elementary school. Secondary education was under the *giunta provinciale.* In addition, there were the *deputazione scolastica,* which was in charge of the budget, and the *delegazione governativa,* whose task was the revision of accounts of the council.[5]

4. Elementary education before World War I

Before the first World War elementary education was divided into two levels: in the lower stage children learned the conventional three R's; in the later years they also studied geography, national history, current national events, and the simple elements of the natural and physical sciences. Religion was not taught in the public schools. On the whole the emphasis was on the acquisition of factual information, and the methods employed to attain such a goal were formal, with stress on memory and drill.

Before entering the regular elementary school a child might attend a preschool. Of such schools the *asili infantili* (kindergartens) were the oldest, having been founded early in the nineteenth century by Father Aporti (1781–1858), who had drawn much of his inspiration from the Swiss Pestalozzi. Subsequently, two Catholic nuns, Sisters Rosa and Carolina Agazzi, opened a kindergarten at Mompiano, where they developed new methods in the education of the young child. Influenced somewhat by Froebel, they stressed play and self-activity, devising special methods for teaching singing, and, in general, sought to further the child's moral, mental, and physical development. Their methods created quite a stir and in 1910 were adopted by the city of Turin. Meanwhile Maria Montessori had begun her experiments in the education of young children in Rome, where in conjunction with the Association for Good Building she had established her famous children's house (*casa dei bambini*) for children between the ages of three and seven. Her methods of sense and motor training and her stress on the development of freedom and

---

[5] The state, the provinces, and the localities (communes) shared in the financing of education, but under conditions that varied considerably for elementary and secondary education and from commune to commune. For a succinct analysis of Italy's educational finance see Kandel, I. L., *Comparative Education,* pp. 305–306. Boston: Houghton Mifflin Company, 1933.

spontaneity in the education of children attracted followers not only in Italy but throughout the entire world.

5. Secondary education before World War I

The foundations of Italian secondary education were laid by the Casati Law of 1859. Seeking to break the monopoly of the ancient classics, this law established diversified courses, reorganized the classical school, and founded technical institutes and normal schools. However, the highroad to advanced study was open only to pupils from the classical *ginnasi-licei* and to those who had completed the work of a special section for mathematics and physics given in the technical institutes and preparing for the university faculties of mathematics and the physical and natural sciences. During the last part of the nineteenth century, six *licei moderni* were established as an experiment. In these, German and French were added to the classical curriculum. Not until after 1904 were modern sections organized in the classical schools.

Prewar secondary schools fall into three types. Of these the classical *ginnasi-licei* were traditional, and the most esteemed. An eight-year course was offered, of which five years were spent in the *ginnasio*, and three in the *liceo*. More modern were the newer secondary schools without Latin and Greek and the technical schools. Of these, the *scuola tecnica* with its three-year curriculum prepared students for the lower civil service and commercial positions. French was the usual foreign language. On the whole, the course of study leaned to the more practical side, and for this reason the *scuola tecnica* made rapid strides toward greater public esteem. Upon completion of the three years of the *scuola tecnica*, students continued in a higher technical institute, known as the *instituto tecnico*. Here a four-year course of study, divided into three sections, was offered. The third type of secondary school was the normal school, the *scuola normale*, which offered a three-year course of study to prepare the student for teaching. There was also a two-year preparatory course known as the *corso magistrale*.

As in other countries, secondary education in Italy during the first three decades of the twentieth century was marked by considerable unrest. Not only were its aims and curricula under fire, but several other of its aspects were criticized. For one thing, it was decidedly the intellectual side of education that was stressed. Everywhere encyclopedic knowledge seemed to be the chief goal; and drill and cramming the means to the end. Teachers were generally poorly paid and over-burdened. They tended, moreover, to be narrow specialists in their own particular subject. As far as examinations were concerned, pupils were examined by their own teachers without any outside check; only those pupils who had failed to obtain a minimum mark of six out of a possible ten were examined. Pupils of private schools had to turn to the public schools for their examinations and they were questioned on their entire school program.

6. The reform program

Accentuated during the course of the first World War, the defects of Italian education loomed large. More than ever, serious thinkers became aware of Italy's educational in-adequacy. With the advance and spread of the movement for school reform numerous programs were set up; among which one of the most far-reaching was that proposed by the National Union of Italian Teachers, which recommended: (1) a decrease in the length of the elementary school course with a thorough revision of the curricula; (2) a curtailment of the number of pupils under one teacher, the number being fixed at twenty-five; (3) an increase in teachers' salaries; (4) an improvement in the elementary school teacher's professional preparation; (5) more stringent enforcement of compulsory education; (6) better adjustment of the school to local needs and conditions.

In 1918, by royal decree, a commission was organized to study the type of education best fitted to meet the nation's postwar problems. Its recommendations advocated: (1) the establishment of at least one compulsory school of four grades in every commune; (2) the fixing of eighteen years as the leaving age of pupils; (3) the lengthening of the school year; (4) the organic inclusion within the state system of nursery school and kindergarten education; (5) the raising of the teachers' minimum salaries; (6) the establishment of special secondary schools for the preliminary professional training of teachers; (7) the creation of compulsory schools for illiterate adults up to the age of forty-five.

7. The Fascist state

The Italian people came out of World War I frustrated and disillusioned. The rich territorial prizes which Italy had been led to expect had failed to materialize. For them she had sacrificed the lives of some 700,000 men. Financially she was in ruins, with a budget deficit of more than 12,000,000,000 lire; meanwhile taxes were soaring, as were the costs of living and unemployment. Worse yet, the nation's political leaders, greedy for power and bickering among themselves, were unable to take effective steps against the threatening disaster. Feeble and impotent financial measures, political ineptitude, strikes, riots, and bloodshed—such was the situation in which Fascism unfolded. To it, in fact, Mussolini and his followers contributed no little, for it was their considered policy to stir up trouble and to contribute to the national chaos as much as possible; at the right moment they planned to assume control over the government.

That moment came in 1922. Taking advantage of a cabinet crisis in the fall of that year, Mussolini and his followers, including numerous army officers, industrialists, and business men, staged a *coup d'état*. King Victor Emmanual gave it his sanction when he appointed Mussolini to the premiership. Proceeding cautiously, almost *pianissimo,* the new premier included only four Fascisti in his first cabinet of fourteen members. It wasn't long, however, before we find the am-

bitious premier demanding a free hand from the Chamber of
Deputies for the carrying out of his somewhat nebulous
program. The request was granted with little opposition, and
thus the regime of Mussolini possessed at least a legal basis.
It was used, of course, to demolish the very system which had
made its legality possible. Step by step Mussolini destroyed
what remained of Italy's liberal democracy. By 1926 the
Fascists were the only legal party in Italy, and though parliament continued to exist, it was little more than a docile and
obsequious audience for the Duce. The Senate, or upper
house, which had always been appointive, was converted in
1928 into the Fascist Grand Council, a body which soon superseded the national cabinet. As for the lower house, after
various changes in its structure designed mainly to lessen its
power, in 1938 it gave itself the final and merciful *coup de
grâce* by voting itself out of existence.

Italian Fascism was in many respects the colossal echo of
Mussolini's temperament. Vigor and strength were the Duce's
household gods, and war man's crowning glory. *"Combattere,
combattere, combattere!"* became the first of Fascist watch-
words. Disdainful of democracy, which he called decadent, the
Duce promised the future to Fascism. For Italy he proclaimed the role of empire, a nation which was, he said, "like
ancient Imperial Rome to be respected and feared" throughout the world. The methods employed were the familiar ones
of a totalitarian police state.

Like their Nordic counterparts in the Reich, Italy's Fascists
instituted a gigantic program of public works, designed not
only to create jobs, but also to make Italy self-sufficient. The
cultivation of wheat, Italy's basic food, was stimulated by
every device known to agriculture and propaganda. Tremendous land reclamation projects were undertaken besides
ambitious programs of reforestation. New motor highways
were built, old railways repaired and new ones constructed.
To glorify Fascism to the eye, lavish public building projects

were carried out in the nation's chief cities—especially in Rome.[6]

Socially, the Fascist program called for bigger families; it offered stimulants to early matrimony and bonuses for an abundance of children. Old-age, disability, and sickness insurance were increased and extended. During 1926 and 1927 "order" was brought to the realm of labor by the banning of unions and the prohibition of strikes and by the enforced "cooperation" of management and labor. In 1934 Italy became a "corporative state" in which a system of economic "corporations" became the basis of the nation's business life. Organized in every domain of economic endeavor, these corporations, of which there were twenty-two, all of which were under the state, had large powers in advising the government, in planning and controlling production, distribution, and prices, and in arbitrating labor disputes.[7]

In its relations with the papacy the Fascist State succeeded in terminating its ancient dispute with the Vatican. By the Lateran Accord of 1929 the Church gave official recognition to the Kingdom of Italy, and the state, for its part, recognized the authority of the Pope in his own state of Vatican City.[8] The Catholic faith was accepted as the state religion and was to be taught in the public elementary schools. In addition, the state agreed to pay all clerical salaries, and the clerics swore loyalty to the state as far as temporal affairs were con-

---

[6] Mussolini's object was to make Italy a modernized self-sufficient state. During the first decade of Fascism the output of electric power was quadrupled; 6,000 kilometers of highways were built; 11,000 schools and 50,000 tenements constructed. Millions of lire were put into the building of new aqueducts and ports.

[7] For a critical analysis of the corporative system see Salvemini, Gaetano, *Under the Axe of Fascism*, pp. 116 ff. New York: The Viking Press, Inc., 1936. A fairly cordial résumé is presented in Schmidt, C. T., *The Corporate State in Action*. New York: Oxford University Press, 1939.

[8] A dwarf among the sovereign states of the world, Vatican City comprises a little over a hundred acres with about a thousand inhabitants. Over it the Pope is absolute ruler. The state issues its own coins, stamps, and passports, has its own police force, radio broadcasting station, and daily newspaper, the *Osservatore Romano*.

cerned. Furthermore, the state undertook to pay the papacy
some 92 million dollars to indemnify it for the destruction of
its historic temporal rights in 1871 and the seizure of the
16,000 miles of Papal States. Thus the Church emerged victorious from its controversy, but it was a dubious triumph,
for the Fascists violated a number of their solemn pledges.

Fascist Italy was of course imperialistic. Not only did it
demand the "redemption" of Italians in the neighboring lands
of Austria, Albania, and Yugoslavia, but it cast covetous
glances at Africa. To appease its imperialistic appetites, it
developed a huge military program. It struck in 1935 in
Abyssinia, which it quickly subdued and, in less than a year,
annexed to the Italian crown. Once the die of military expansion had been cast, the game continued lugubriously, first
in Spain and finally in 1940 when Italy struck at France in the
second World War.

That the Fascist program consumed a prodigious amount of
money should be plain. In the first decade of Fascist rule
18,000,000,000 lire were spent on public works alone. The
rearmament program ran into another fortune. All this of
course put a terrific burden on the Italian taxpayer, who, while
he toiled more assiduously than ever, after the state had extracted its toll in taxes, actually earned a pathetically small
amount. At the price of becoming a Great Power, the Italians
had surrendered their freedom of thought and action, had
burdened themselves with an ironclad dictatorship, and had
embarked upon a highroad which led inevitably to peril and
disaster.

8. The Gentile reform

Born in 1875, Giovanni Gentile, after studying law at the
University of Pisa, became professor of philosophy in the
secondary schools at Campobasso and Naples. His first philosophical work of note was *The Rebirth of Idealism* (*La
Rinascita dell' Idealismo*). With Benedetto Croce, another
exponent of philosophic idealism, he published *La Critica,* a

periodical devoted to philosophy and expounding ideas for the reform of Italian education. Subsequently Gentile became professor of philosophy at the University of Palermo, then at Pisa, and later at Rome. A prolific writer, he wrote copiously on philosophy and education, his most noted work in the latter domain being *La Riforma dell' Educazione,* a study which has been translated into English.[9] Politically a conservative liberal, Gentile belonged to those who, in 1922, favored the granting of discretionary powers to the rising Mussolini government. Appointed Minister of Public Instruction in the first Mussolini cabinet, Gentile was granted unconditional powers, and with the help of Giuseppe Lombardo-Radice, he undertook the reform of the Italian school system. The reform was effected in 1923 and the following year Gentile retired from the ministry.[10] Hailed grandiloquently by Mussolini as the "most Fascist of reforms" (*piu fasciste delle riforme*), it stands out as one of the most important developments in twentieth century Italian education.

Philosophically, Gentile was under the spell of the neo-Hegelians. He favored nationalism and imperialism. He scoffed at the attempt to create an international body seeking to bring about an enduring peace. The national state was his ideal and its schools, he asserted, should be used for national ends.

The State is not a system of hindrances and external juridical controls from which men flee, but an ethical being which . . . manifests its personality and achieves its historical growth in human society. Thus it is conscious not of being hedged in by special limits, but of being open, ready, and capable of expanding as a collective and yet individual will. The nation is that will, conscious of itself and of its own historical past, which, as we

---

[9] Gentile, G., *The Reform of Education.* Translated by Bigongiari, D. New York: Harcourt, Brace & Company, Inc., 1922.

[10] Giuseppe Lombardo-Radice, sometimes called the Italian Pestalozzi, was noted especially for his work with children and for his contributions to teacher training. Opposing the materialistic nature of Italian education as well as the stilted formalism of its methods, Lombardo-Radice encouraged the child's self-expression through play and activity. Among his important works are his *Nuovi Saggi di Propaganda pedagogica* (1922); *Educazione e Diseducazione* (1923); and *Vita nuova della Scuola del Popolo* (1925).

formulate it in our minds, divines and delineates our nationality, generating an end to be attained, a mission to be realized. For that will, in case of need, our lives are sacrificed, for our lives are genuine, worthy, and endowed with incontestable value only as they are spent in the accomplishment of that mission.

The State's active and dynamic consciousness is a system of thought, of ideas, of interests to be satisfied and of morality to be realized. Hence the State is, as it ought to be, a teacher; it maintains and develops schools to promote this morality. In the school, the State comes to a consciousness of its real being.[11]

Frankly antagonistic to socialism and democracy, Gentile, like his fellow idealist Croce, had little sympathy with the aspirations of the Italian people, especially the common people, to larger and better opportunities in their country's educational system. Thus Gentile supported the traditional caste system in education which, by keeping the vast majority of Italians out of the secondary school, effectively closed the door for them to the better civil service jobs and the professions. "Secondary education," Gentile declared, "is aristocratic by its own nature. It is made for a few and has to be imparted to a few." [12] As for higher education, it "is not, and cannot be, for everybody. . . . The State must open a door to higher education, but a small rather than a large door, to prevent the crowd from rushing in." [13]

Formative education and moral personality furnish the key to Gentile's educational aims. Opposed to the pedantry and intellectualism which had hung themselves on Italian education, Gentile felt that neither abstract learning nor a vast knowledge of facts led the way to true education. Accordingly he favored a complete overhauling of the entire educational system, from the course of study itself down even to the textbooks. By a decree of March 11, 1923, interestingly enough, textbooks not on the official list could be used under certain

---

[11] Circular dated November 2, 1922. *Cf.* Gentile, *Il Fascismo al Governo della Scuola,* p. 9. Palermo, 1924. Quoted and translated in Schneider, H. W. and Clough, S. B., *Making Fascists,* p. 85. Chicago: University of Chicago Press, 1929.

[12] *Il Messaggero della Domenica,* June 15, 1919.

[13] *Ibid.,* August 27, 1918.

conditions, but all pedantic books were barred. Popular literature and folk traditions were stressed. Bestowing a broad
autonomy on private schools, Gentile encouraged their growth.
As for the national organization of education, the government
replaced the school provincial councils and their deputies by
19 regional administrative bodies, each appointed by the government and headed by a regional superintendent. To offset
the overintellectualistic emphasis found in the Italian school,
more attention was to be given to hygiene and physical training. Although Gentile had been labeled as antireligious and
anti-Catholic, and had at one time expressed his opposition
to the confessional school, yet he was instrumental in bringing
religious instruction into the public elementary school.[14] In
harmony with Mussolini's pronouncement that there can be
no morals without religion and that Italy is Catholic, the
Gentile regulations recognized religious instruction as "the
basis and the crown of all grades of elementary instruction." [15]
It was to be imparted by lay teachers, but it was agreed that
"the Royal Inspector for schools will conform to the views of
the local clerical authorities in judging the fitness of teachers
or other persons to impart religious instruction." It was not,
however, until 1929, when Gentile was no longer in the ministerial office, that religious instruction was introduced in the
secondary schools.[16]

9. Elementary education

At the outbreak of the second World War attendance at the
elementary school was compulsory. Divided into levels, ele-

[14] In 1907, for example, Gentile had declared, "Confessional teaching coarsens
the spirit and bestows a new harshness upon it. Brotherhood is replaced by
division, collaboration by intolerance; an instinctive resistance to the free
development of scientific thought in the broadest sense. The confessional
school is thus no school; it is the negation of school." *Cf.* Matteotti, G., *The
Fascist Exposed,* p. 54. London: Independent Labour Party Publishing Department, 1924.

[15] Decree of October 1, 1923, signed by Gentile as Minister of Public Instruction.

[16] This came about as a consequence of the Concordat signed by the Church
and state. See p. 291.

mentary education comprised a preparatory, lower, and higher section. Up to 1930 these divisions were supplemented by a prevocational course of two years, but in that year such work was transferred to the domain of lower secondary education. Compulsory education began at six and continued to fourteen, the length of the school year being fixed at ten months. Private schools could be established by persons who had the same qualifications as teachers in the public schools. Such schools, needless to say, were subject to the control of the state. For children between the ages of three and six there were pre-schools, which were recognized as the preparatory stage of elementary education. Such schools in the past had generally been private. Because of the intense interest of the Fascist regime in the early education of children, it is not surprising to note a rapid increase in the provisions made for the education of children between the ages of three and six.[17] Divided into thirty-five short weekly periods, the course included prayers, singing of nursery and patriotic tunes, gymnastics and rhythmics, work in plastic and manual activities, gardening, care of animals, elementary general information, reading, recitation, and dramatization.

The work of the lower stage in the regular elementary school included religion, reading, writing, arithmetic, the metric system, oral translation from the local dialect into standard Italian, geography, general information with particular provision for experiences in industrial and agricultural work, and a knowledge of works of art, records, and monuments. In the higher grades the pupil studied the work of the lower stage in greater detail. He also studied the history of the Catholic religion. In addition there was history, some simple geometry, elementary science, applied design, and physical education.

10. Secondary education

Very few children continued their education beyond their

---

[17] In 1915 there existed some 4,500 kindergartens; in 1922 the number had risen to slightly less than 6,000; in 1930 official statistics put the number at 7,076.

first five years. Of those who did go on, some entered the so-called *corsi integrativi,* and others attended post-elementary school. Those who continued their education on a full-time basis usually entered the *scuola complementare,* a complementary school comparable to the English central school, the French *école primaire supérieure,* and the German *Mittelschule.*

As designed by Gentile, the complementary school was to replace the older technical school. This, it will be recalled, offered a three-year course. After completing it a pupil might continue in the regular secondary school; or if he chose to terminate his schooling, he was eligible for the school-leaving certificate. The technical school had been especially popular with the lower middle classes, for it offered their children both a practical and a broad, general education. It prepared the way to a vocation without, however, closing the road to the university. Under the Gentile scheme some of these features vanished. Though officially recognized as a secondary school, strictly speaking the complementary school was nothing of the sort since it did not lead to the higher learning. It was simply an advanced elementary school leading to an educational terminus.

The complementary school met with scant favor. Instead of becoming, as Gentile had prophesied, "one of the fundamental nerve centers of Italy's public instruction," it encountered criticism and protest. In fact, when the new schools were opened in 1923, they attracted some 40,000 fewer pupils than the technical schools had drawn a year earlier. The continued disfavor accorded the complementary school led in time to some modification. In 1929 the various types of post-elementary and trade schools were merged into the vocational secondary school (*scuola secondaria d'avviamento professionale*). By passing an examination students were to be allowed to continue their education in a normal school or technical institute. In 1930 a further modification of secondary education was effected when a two- or three-year technical school

was established, the purpose of which was to "complete the
specific practical preparation for the graduates of the vocational school, and by training suitable skilled workers, to
contribute to the development of the national economy.[18]

Thus the ambition of many Italians to have something
more than an advanced elementary school for their children
was realized to some degree. But Fascist spokesmen continued to disparage the idea of secondary education for the
multitude, an aspiration which obviously was not in accord
with the Fascist view of the subordinate place assigned to the
masses in the Corporate State. The popular ambition for
secondary education, declared Giuseppe Bottai, Minister of
National Education, was "sterile and dangerous in any case."
"The vocational schools," he went on to say some time later,
". . . today gravitate toward the secondary schools. They
must be integrated with elementary education and must give
the people's education a more concrete character." [19] Italians,
he went on to explain, must not forget that they "live in a
corporate order, which requires very definite attitudes." [20]
Speaking before the Senate in the spring of 1938, Bottai said
that "the vocational school has lost its original character and
that, on the inclined plane of its aspiration toward the secondary school, it has lost the living and tough characteristics of
a school of the people and for the people. We will bring it
back to the elementary school." [21]

11. The Bottai reform

Such were the basic views from which flowed the Educational Charter of 1939 [22] and the Bottai Reform. Aiming
among other things to make the Italian school more than ever

---

[18] Law No. 889, June 15, 1931.

[19] An address on the Budget for Public Instruction, March 17, 1937.

[20] An address before the Senate, March 22, 1937.

[21] An address before the Senate, March 26, 1938.

[22] Submitted to the Fascist Grand Council in January, 1939, the Charter was
approved by Mussolini within a few days. For an analysis of the Charter see
Bottai, G., *La Carta della Scuola*. Milan: 1939.

a tool of Fascism, the reform was "to be put into effect gradually." Italy's entrance into the war in June, 1940 made even
this difficult. Nonetheless, some of the features of the reform
were of significance. All elementary schools, for example,
were required to use a single series of textbooks prepared by the
Ministry of National Education. All in all there were ten
books, beginning with the First Reader, or "*sillabario*," and
including in the end material in arithmetic, grammar, history,
geography, religion, and science.[23] Well printed and attrac-
tively illustrated, the books were of course harnessed to Fascist
ideology and propaganda. Even arithmetic problems and
grammatical exercises were thus constructed, the child, for
example, memorizing "I obey the Duce, thou obeyest the
Duce, he obeys the Duce," and so on.

Regarding the reorganization of the schools, the Bottai
Reform proposed a three-year common school to be known as
the *scuola media unica*. Obviously an echo of the French
école unique, the new school was to follow five years of elementary education and was designed for those children who
desired to continue in the secondary school. By replacing the
lower technical institute and the lower normal school, the
scuola media unica offered a common base to all upper secondary schools of whatever type, thus enabling a student to post-
pone the choice of his ultimate vocation until he was fourteen
instead of eleven years old.

As for those children whose families could not afford to
send them to the secondary school—and they were legion—
two choices remained open to them. Those dwelling in the
rural sections and in the smaller towns would follow their
elementary schooling with a three-year course in the "artisan
school." Those living in the large cities would go either to a
three-year vocational school or a two-year technical school.
The artisan school, Bottai explained, was not to provide "even

---

[23] The second and third readers appeared in special editions for use in the
rural schools.

unwittingly an incentive to change one's social position." [24]
Rather it was "to implant in the boys and girls an attachment
to the traditions of honesty and industry of the Italian family." As for the schools organized for the city youngsters,
their task was to "prepare the small classes of employes and
the best skilled workers for industry."

Although these schools led to an educational dead end, some
slight provision was made for pupils of special ability. For
them the state provided free "colleges" of a "military and
Fascist character." Intended for a very small élite, such a
school, Minister Bottai felt, would never become the "fomenter
of ambitions, creator of unemployed and dissatisfied masses, a
continuous element of disorder and of disturbance in the productive and moral life of the State." By contrast Italy's new
school was to be "a school of the Fascist people and of the
Fascist State: of the people who may be able to attend it: of a
State which may make use of it for its cadres and aims." [25]

Stripped of Bottai's rhetoric, however, the "school of the
people" was intended to preserve the *status quo*. By the
artisan school the rural classes were to be kept from going to
the cities: peasants were to stick to the land, tilling the soil,
contended to be upholding the "traditions of honesty and
industry of the Italian family." The city vocational and technical schools for their part stratified the city's lower classes
and effectively barred their way to social and economic betterment. As for the few of "special aptitude," the free education
offered them in the "colleges" was intended to make them the
faithful servants of the rulers of the corporate state.

12. Opera Nazionale Balilla

Like Nazi Germany and Soviet Russia, Fascist Italy developed a vigorous youth movement to supplement the work of

---

[24] Bottai, G., *La Carta della Scuola*, p. 29. Milan, 1939. What was wrong
with Italy's vocational schools according to Minister Bottai was that it
"nourished with its crumbs of culture, deceptive ambitions, which offer an
escape from manual labor as a price of social elevation."

[25] *Ibid.*

the schools. The movement was known as the *Opera Nazionale Balilla,* the ONB. Its name *Balilla* referred to the nickname of an Italian youth who, in 1746, distinguished himself at Genoa in the Italian campaign against the Austrians.[26] The organization itself had its beginnings in the *Avanguardia Fascista,* a group of party militiamen who in the early days of the party's struggle for power actively combated Fascist opponents. Subsequently a *Gruppo Balilla* was formed for boys between eight and fourteen, and in 1926 the ONB was given official and legal recognition as an integral part of the Fascist party organization with direction and financial subsidies from the state. Two years later, in 1928, all competing youth organizations, among which the Catholic Boy Scouts were the most important, were dissolved, thereby giving the ONB a monopoly in its field. By 1940 some 5,000,000 young Italians were members of the organization.

The *Opera Nazionale Balilla* comprised both boys and girls between the ages of six and seventeen.[27] The youngest boys (6-8) were known as *Sons of the Wolf;* from eight to fourteen they were called *Balilla;* and thereafter they were the *Avanguardisti.* For girls there were similar groups, the *Piccole Italiane* for girls between the ages of eight and fourteen, and the *Giovani Italiane* for those between fourteen and eighteen. On becoming eighteen, members of the *Avanguardisti* and the *Giovani Italiane* were taken into the *Fasci Giovanili di Combattimento,* the organization of Young Fascists. This constituted the last rung on the ladder of Fascist training before one could, at the age of twenty-one, become a member of the Fascist Party.

The aim of the ONB was the making of a healthy and disciplined Fascist, one who would be ready to play an active part in the preconceived social and political order. Stretching its

---

[26] The lad's full name was Giovanni Battista Perasso. Eventually the *Opera Nazionale Balilla* became the *Gioventù Italiana del Littorio* (GIL).

[27] In 1936 a campaign to organize boys under six into Fascist units in order to indoctrinate them in the fundamentals of Fascism was begun.

influence over virtually every domain affecting the life of the
future citizen, including his mind, body, and spirit, the ONB
stressed obedience and discipline as well as loyalty to the Duce.
Major emphasis was laid on physical training, including sports
and athletics of all kinds. Every local organization had its own
athletic field, or the use of one. A high point in the physical
program was an annual national athletic meet. During the
summer the *Balilla* continued their training in special camps
or on ocean cruises. Special training was offered in aviation,
skiing, cycling, and naval exercises.

From the beginning the *Balilla* had a military complexion,
being organized along ancient Roman lines into squads, com-
panies, centuries, cohorts, and legions.[28] Members of the
Balilla had their own distinctive uniform, consisting of black
shirt, green-grey trousers, and a black fez, which they wore
whenever they attended some important event, when they
went on their hikes, or even while attending school. As time
went on more and more stress was put on military training.
"The basis of the organization of the ONB," declared one of
its official handbooks, "is purely military; at the age of eight
years the *Balilla* begins to practice his first military exercises.
. . . The *avanguardist* is a perfect soldier. He knows how to
handle a gun, is accustomed to march long stretches . . . to
salute his own commanders and those of the army with military correctness." [29] The military spirit was omnipresent not
only in salutes and marches, but also in a rigid discipline, any
infraction of which was punishable by military law. The older
boys learned how to use rifles and machine guns, and to spur
them on, competitions in machine-gun maneuvers were held.
At the tenth anniversary of the *Opera Nazionale Balilla*,
50,000 boys and girls participated in the celebrations at Rome.
Their equipment included gas masks.

---

[28] Eleven boys comprised a *squadra;* three *squadre* formed a *manipulo;*
three *manipuli,* a *centuria;* three *centurie,* a *coorte;* and three *coorte,* a *legione.*
[29] See *Il Capo Centuria,* p. 292. Rome: *Opera Nazionale Balilla,* 1931. This
is a handbook for commanders of the *centurie.* Of interest in this connection
is the chapter on "Training for War," pp. 75 ff.

In their stress on military training for the young, the Fascists were not unmindful of the needs of the navy and the air force. A half-dozen schools for seamen were put at the disposal of the ONB. Their emphasis, as might be expected, was on the art and science of naval warfare. As for air training, the ONB not only trained pilots in flying planes and gliders, but it also gave training to thousands of *avanguardisti* in the techniques of air defence.[30]

The moral code offered Italy's youth was the Fascist Decalogue. It taught him that he should "know that the Fascist and especially the militiaman must not believe in everlasting peace." And also "the rifle and the cartridge box have not been entrusted to you to be damaged, but to be kept for war." The final authority in all this was the Duce himself, for as one of the ten commandments said, *"Mussolini ha sempre raggione"* ("Mussolini is always right").[31]

Girls in the ONB received a training which, except for the omission of military drill, was in the main similar to that of the boys. They too were garbed in distinctive robes—white blouses, black skirts, white stockings, and black berets. Like their brothers they were taught to believe and obey. Physical fitness was of the first importance, and like the boys they were sent to camps in the summertime. Their patriotic ardor was kindled by harangues from Fascist bigwigs, by movies, and by special pilgrimages to war monuments and patriotic shrines. The Fascist girl was expected "to serve the Nation as her other and greater mother, the mother of all good Italians." She was "to obey her superiors with joy"; she was to "abhor stupid vanity," "to love work, which is life," "to repulse those who give evil counsel and deride honesty." Most important of all, she was "to love the Duce who has made the Nation stronger and greater." [32]

---

[30] For the use of members of the ONB special model machine guns were constructed. Cf. *Bulletino del Opera Balilla,* Supplement to No. 1, November 1, 1932.

[31] *Il Capo Centuria,* p. 76. Rome: *Opera Nazionale Balilla,* 1931.

[32] From an address by Augusto Turati, Secretary of the Fascist Party in 1928.

13. Making Fascists

In the Fascist state the supreme task of education—at bottom, indeed, its only task—was the making of Fascists. It was to mold "the Fascist conscience and the Fascist will." [33] Under Italy's totalitarian rule, education became the instrument of propaganda and indoctrination. As in Nazi Germany and Soviet Russia, the purpose of Fascist education was to bend the individual to the will of the state, to condition him permanently for obedient submission and unquestioning acceptance. Italian children, as the Fascists tersely put it, were to be trained to "believe, obey, fight" (*"credere, obbedire, combattere"*). Every aspect of life and every form of expressing it was subject to the control of the state. Under the Fascist regime education became more and more centralized until, in the end, every phase of it was under the full and complete control of the state. In it, moreover, the traditional distinction between formal and informal education gradually vanished. Indeed, since the carrying out of the Fascist program depended more on an appeal to the emotions than on reason, it is not surprising to see more and more stress given to the activities of outside agencies, such as, for example, the *Balilla*, and to great public festivals the movies, the theater, and the press, all of which, of course, were under the strict control of the state.

Under the Fascists the school's first stress was on national patriotism; but this love of country, chauvinistic and military to the core, was identified with Fascism. Its reminders, moreover, were ubiquitous. Every classroom displayed pictures of the king and Mussolini. Local Fascist heroes who had died in battle received special admiration, and their memorial tablets were expected by the government to be perenially honored by schoolchildren bringing fresh flowers. The rods of the ancient lictors, once the symbol of authority in ancient Rome and now adopted to express the same idea for Fascism, were to be con-

---

[33] Starace, A., in the *Europäische Revue,* p. 705. Berlin, November, 1932.

spicuously worked into the architecture of every new school building. By ministerial decree the day's schoolwork was begun with a prayer, followed by a patriotic tune, such as the national anthem or *Giovinezza*, the official hymn of the Fascists. Every teacher was exhorted to hammer home the idea that "if our country is today great, respected, and feared, we owe this to the thousands of heroes who laid down their lives on the field of battle." [34]

All texts of course had to be in strict accord with Fascist ideology. "Italy," one of them observed, "seems to have inherited the mission of teaching beauty, justice, and science to other races." [35] "Religious principles," asseverated another, "are not discussed because they are truths revealed by God. Fascist principles are not discussed because they emanate from the mind of a Genius, that of Benito Mussolini." [36]

Secondary school children began their school year with a parade, followed by salutes to the flag and a political harangue by one of the teachers. For those pupils distinguishing themselves along the line of Fascist ideology, pilgrimages to the "redeemed" provinces, or to national shrines such as the tomb of the unknown solier were recommended by the government. By ministerial decree (1929), secondary school teachers were required to urge their protegés to join the Fascist youth movement. Teachers were expected to be propagandists for Fascism at all times, both in and out of school.

One should hardly have to be reminded that under Fascism there was no academic freedom. Not only did the state try to eliminate those teachers who were politically unacceptable, but in making new appointments it gave preference to those who had actively served the Fascist cause. To keep the teaching ranks pure and undefiled of anti-Fascist elements, the government created the necessary legal machinery to facilitate the

---

[34] Renda, Umberto, *Cività Fascista,* p. 487. Turin: G. B. Paravia, 1928.

[35] Brocchi, V., and Gustarelli, A., *Allegretto e Serenella,* p. 90. Milan: A. Mondadori, 1925.

[36] Campogrando, V., *L'Ordinamento dello Stato Italiano Fascista,* p. 6. Turin: S. Lates & Co., 1928.

dismissal of teachers already in the service. With its characteristic suspicion of the intellect, it imposed an oath of loyalty to the crown and the Fascist state upon all university professors.[37] Finally, holding that women were not physically able to perform the special tasks required of the Fascist teacher, the government sought to exclude them as teachers in the secondary and higher schools. Ironically enough, however, because of the flight of men from the teaching profession under Fascism the number of women teachers steadily increased.

14. Re-education

Like its partner, the Nazi Reich, defeated Italy was put through a process of re-education. On the whole, this assumed a pattern which was similar to the one which had developed in Germany. Thus, the Allied Governments undertook to reopen schools, universities, and other cultural institutions and to get them functioning on a non-Fascist basis as quickly as possible. As in Germany, though to a lesser extent, there were the familiar shortages in buildings, equipment, and school materials in addition to the general scarcity of the necessities of life. To give Italian education a fresh start it was purged as thoroughly as possible of all Fascist elements. All elementary textbooks were rewritten along non-Fascist lines; and all others were scrutinized before being approved for use in the schools. Teachers suspected of having been loyal Fascists were dismissed.[38] To break the regimentation imposed by the corporate state on Italy's school system, school administration was decentralized. Fascist youth organizations were liqui-

---

[37] The oath ran as follows: "I swear to be loyal to the King, to his Royal Successors, and to the Fascist Regime, loyally to observe the Statute and the other laws of the State, to fill my office at the university and all other of my academic duties with the intent to train industrious, upright citizens devoted to their country and the Regime. I swear that I neither belong nor will belong to associations or parties whose activies are not in accord with my official duties."

[38] Only about 4% of all classroom teachers had to be removed. On the other hand more than 90% of the *provveditori* were found to be unacceptable, as were about one fourth of the school principals and other school heads.

dated, their properties put under the jurisdiction of the provincial superintendents, with the stipulation, however, that they be reserved exclusively for the use of Italy's youth. Besides this primary work in the remaking of the Fascist mind, the Allies encouraged the furtherance of any activity which appeared to be in harmony with their general purposes. Thus they gave their approval to such organizations as the Boy Scouts and the Girl Scouts, Youth Hostels, Summer Camps, the Junior Red Cross, and so on.

E. Russia

1. Background

Russia entered the nineteenth century as a geographic entity embracing almost one sixth of the earth. Although her cultural roots were imbedded in the East, she had become an important European power. With England, Prussia, and Austria she had helped to crush Napoleon and, after the Corsican's banishment, she joined her former cobelligerents in the Quadruple Alliance (1815).[1] The Russian populace was made up largely of landowners and peasants. Until 1861 most of the latter were serfs bound to the soil, eking out a bare and toilful existence in the service of the landed proprietors. Even after their liberation they continued to be impoverished and underprivileged, dominated by the power of a self-interested clergy and aristocracy.

Agriculture continued to be the nation's leading enterprise until the end of the century, when the government embarked upon a policy of industrialization. Treaties, negotiated with

---

[1] The four allied powers pledged themselves to meet regularly during the next twenty years to consider any measures which "shall be judged most salutary for the repose and prosperity of the peoples and for the maintenance of the peace of the State." Thereby was launched the principle of the "Concert of Europe," an ideal which in some form or other has agitated the European breast ever since. Despite the Quadruple Alliance's lofty words, however, the course of European events after Napoleon's exit was anything but peaceful. The Alliance, in plain fact, was a reactionary force of the first order. See page 233 for further details.

Britain and France in 1906, brought the needed capital from those lands to expedite the Russian program of industrialization. In the course of the ensuing years mines and metal works were developed in the Ukraine and the Donetz region, and in the environs of Moscow and what is now Leningrad light industry came into being. In 1904 Russia grappled with Japan in war, and although this ended in ignominious defeat for Russian arms, it was a spur to the nation's war industry. Two years later Russia was, in fact, producing most of the material it required for its expanding railways.

On the eve of the first World War some two and a half million workers were engaged in industry and in mining. Even as late as 1914, however, the conditions of labor in Russia were almost primitive. The laboring Russian's hours were long and arduous, his pay small, and his housing abominable. Unlike the workers of most of the western industrial nations, the Russian could turn to no governmental authority for relief and assistance; the state, apathetic to his woes, refused to exert itself in his behalf. Consequently, as year followed year and conditions failed to improve, the Russian proletariat turned its mind more and more to self-help, and in these thoughts revolution loomed in the foreground.

The plight of the Russian worker stimulated an interest among a small number of intellectuals and contributed to the formation, in 1897, of the Socialist Party.[2] But in Czarist Russia the way to reform was hazardous. Since there was neither freedom of speech nor of the press and no right of assembly, those who would agitate for reform were deprived of the normal means of making themselves heard. Over their head, moreover, hung the ever-present shadow of the Czar's

---

[2] The Russian Socialists affiliated themselves with the Socialist and the Social Democratic Parties, operating in some of the western industrialized nations, which had organized an International Working Men's Association under the guidance of Karl Marx in 1864. After the failure of the French workers to establish a Commune in 1871, the First International broke up, but it was soon succeeded by another, somewhat more moderate, the Second International.

police, the Ochrana, which was dedicated especially to the discovery and apprehension of liberals and radicals.

Yet the Russian agitators operated nonetheless. Driven underground by their foes, they gathered clandestinely behind bolted doors, holding their meetings and laying their plans, and creating their armament of revolutionary tracts and pamphlets which they brought forth from printing presses carefully concealed from the prying eyes of the law. When such men were caught, as, indeed, they often were, their punishment was death or banishment to Siberia. Lev Davidovitch Bronstein, known to the world as Trotsky, was exiled at the age of eighteen for having organized a party of Odessa workers. Vladimir Ilytch Ulianov, whose pen name was Lenin, was sent to Siberia in 1896 for three years, and later went to Europe where he remained in exile until 1917. Josef Djugashvilli, or as he is known, Stalin, was jailed at least a dozen times for his radical and revolutionary activities; but since he was adept at escaping, he was finally sent away for four years to the bleak wastelands of eastern Siberia.

Japan's swift and easy triumph over Russia in 1905 raised the hopes of the peasants and the workers. Throughout the land spontaneous insurrections flared up. In the countryside the peasants stormed the manor houses, looting them of their valuables and destroying farm machinery. In the cities strikes erupted everywhere. In Leningrad, then known as St. Petersburg, the strikers organized a Council of Workers or Soviet, and elected Trotsky, who had suddenly emerged from his European retreat, to be its president. Moscow became the scene of a general strike and fierce fighting in which the workers gradually won control over the greater part of the city. But these triumphs were shortlived. By the end of the year, the Czar's troops returned from Manchuria, were pitted against the insurrectionists, and before long the uprising came to its fatal end. In the heat of the fighting, the Czar's government, frightened by what was going on and by the possibility of even graver events, pledged itself to a number of reforms;

but in the course of time reaction resumed its role and the Czar's promises, if not forgotten, were repudiated.

2. The evolution of Russian education

Of the large European nations Russia was dilatory in developing an up-to-date national system of education. Educational progress was closely related to the political and social philosophy of the ruling czar. If the country happened to be in the hands of an enlightened sovereign, there was usually some form of educational advance; if, on the other hand, the czar happened to be a reactionary, there was invariably some kind of educational retrogression.

The earliest impetus to Russian education came through Peter the Great (1689–1725). Barbarous and often brutal, more of an Asiatic than a European, Peter nonetheless was susceptible to the blandishments of western culture.[3] Perceiving therein the secret of European strength and progress, the Russian ruler set himself the task of Europeanizing his country, whose culture was then still predominantly of an Asiatic hue. Peter was an ardent admirer of learning; so much so, in fact, that on his private seal he had engraved the words "I belong to those who seek knowledge and are willing to learn." Quite properly he might be called the father of Russian education, for it was during his reign that elementary as well as secondary schools were organized. When Peter died, there was almost one of each kind in every provincial town. It was during his reign also that a naval and a clerical academy was organized and the Academy of Sciences with an attached university and a preparatory school came into being.

During the century which followed the reign of Peter, only

---

[3] Voltaire, who was Peter's biographer, saw in his subject a man who was "extraordinarily wise." "The Russians," wrote Voltaire, "ought certainly to regard Peter as the greatest of men. . . . But ought he to be a hero to ourselves? Was he comparable in valor to our Condés and Villars? And in knowledge, intellect, morals, was he comparable to a crowd of men among whom we live today? . . . He was an architect who built in brick, and who elsewhere would have built in marble."

two Russian rulers showed an interest in the development of their country's education. The enlightened Catherine II (1762–96), who corresponded with Diderot, Rousseau, and Voltaire, and who, no doubt, had an excellent mind, espoused a number of theories on education. She believed, for example, that the most important step toward an improved system of education was the rearing of a "new breed of new fathers and mothers," with special stress on the education of girls. It should be no cause for surprise that she gave her blessing, in 1764, to the establishment of special boarding schools for young ladies of quality. These institutions, although admitting the daughters of the higher middle classes, had special classes for the daughters of the nobility. By the educational plan of 1782 there was provided a "main" public school in each of the government's chief cities, or capitals, a "small" public school in the smaller district seats, and four universities. Unfortunately this scheme came to grief because of the government's lack of money.

The next ruler to evince more than a cursory interest in the development of adequate schools was Alexander I (1801–25), who through his contribution to the rout of Napoleon had gilded the prestige of Russia in the eyes of Europe. During Alexander's reign education was to be not only free, but in certain cases it was even to be rewarded with a small income: students of Russia's higher schools received a small remuneration for their academic efforts and were considered the equivalent of state officials in the service of the Romanovs. It is sad but true that the Russians responded languidly to the educational ideals of their more benevolent rulers. Not until the end of Alexander's reign was there any change in this general insensibility to education.

Alexander's successor, Nicholas I (1825–55) was not antagonistic to education. In fact his educational policy might be said to have been one of encouragement, tempered, however, with caution. Set in an era when the common people of Europe were protesting—at times with guns and bloodshed—

against post-Napoleonic tyranny, education, even in countries with a more liberal tradition than that of Russia, was often looked upon with suspicion. Hence, it was perhaps only natural that Nicholas should have perceived possible dangers in education and that he should have subjected it to stringent regulation, but despite his natural fears, Nicholas carried on the work of his predecessor. During his reign technical schools, military academies, and teachers' colleges were opened in several places; colleges for women were established; and special schools were founded for the children of noble blood. Here the classics were introduced. Children of the merchants and the bourgeoisie had special schools but they were discouraged in various ways from attending the classical schools. Not to be denied, however, many commoners sought to still their thirst for learning by penetrating into these select institutions. Unfortunately this alarmed the governing classes and led to repressive measures. Fees began to be charged. The universities' freedom of teaching, hitherto guaranteed, was abrogated. The teaching of philosophy, which sought to give clarity to men's thoughts, was deemed dangerous and consequently was abolished. Military discipline, which seemed more useful than philosophy, was introduced in the universities and in the upper classes of the secondary schools. What further aggravated the tension were the various uprisings which were exploding all over the continent. Their impact on Czar Nicholas was unmistakable. By the end of his reign his early interest in education had paled considerably, and throughout his realm reaction was rampant.

With the coronation of Alexander II (1855–81), known to posterity as the Emancipator for his liberation of the serfs in 1861, there began what is known in Russian history as the epoch of great reforms.[4] Local government was reformed so

---

[4] Russia's emancipation of the serfs involved some 47 million human beings. Interestingly enough, it was effected by the simple signing of an imperial ukase. Also of interest is the fact that it occurred within 60 days of the outbreak of the American Civil War.

as to afford localities a greater degree of self-government. The administration of justice was overhauled: the English jury system was introduced for criminal cases; judges were put on a salary basis; trials were to be public affairs; and appeals to higher courts were authorized.[5] In 1865 newspaper censorship was liberalized, permitting the printing of material without first having it approved by government officers. If, however, the printed words proved subsequently to be unacceptable to the authorities, punishment might still be meted out. The reform wave finally reached the army. In 1874 military training was decreed for all men, with no special favors for those of social rank or financial position; modern methods of training were ushered in; and an elaborate system for eliminating illiteracy among recruits was introduced.

As might be expected, a man of Alexander's liberal stripe was inclined rather hospitably toward the improvement of education. At the commencement of his reign the Czar set aside most of the repressive measures of his predecessor. The universities' traditional freedom of teaching was restored; but students, largely because of their penchant for political discussion, were forbidden to organize faternities. This was also the time when secondary education was reorganized. Convinced that the natural sciences, which had received a tremendous stimulus in the western world through the publication in 1859 of Darwin's *On the Origin of Species,* were the cause of materialism and nihilism, the Minister of Public Instruction sought to undo their nefarious influence by bestowing his blessing on the humanistic and safely classical secondary school. The so-called *"real gymnasium,"* whose name had been imported from Germany and whose stress was on the sciences, was reduced in status to that of a "real school." Only graduates of the classical secondary school were now accepted by the universities. Besides these innovations, steps were taken

---

[5] The fact should not be overlooked that many of these reforms for a long time existed only on paper. Nonetheless, they mark the beginning of modern juridical procedures in Russia.

to improve the education of girls. It was made less exclusive and more adaptable to the needs of those girls in whose veins coursed no noble blood. In 1863 schools for the training of women teachers were established, and several years later a medical school for women was organized. In addition, several women's colleges were founded at St. Petersburg and other university towns, thus consummating the interest which the second Catherine had manifested in the education of the members of her sex. Finally, the program of educational reform included a number of new primary schools which were established throughout the country. Unfortunately, however, in the minds of the governing classes lower education was of no great concern, and during the last quarter of the nineteenth century Russian education was weakest where it should have been the strongest.

Alexander II was assassinated in 1881 while riding through the streets of his capital. The fatal shot not only put an end to a memorable reign, but it also snuffed out the spirit which pervaded it. The procession of reform and social progress halted abruptly; in its place came one of recrimination and murder. A policy which had been fairly positive was traversed by one which was emphatically negative, and progress was edged into the background by reaction.

3. Elementary education in 1914

Although Russian schools were state-controlled, only a small number were state-maintained. Indeed, had it not been for the initiative of the *zemstvos,* the provincial organs of self-government, the maintenance of primary public education would have been virtually impossible. Interestingly enough, the church schools, of which there was a goodly number, were recipients of some aid from the state treasury, but even they had to depend on additional local funds.[6] Compulsory educa-

------

[6] In 1905 the Russian *duma* voted 10,000,000 rubles as an additional sum to the state's annual expenditure on education. Considering, however, what was really needed, this expenditure was anything but adequate.

tion was almost nonexistent. In the wake of this general educational apathy there was, as usual, a high degree of illiteracy.

Russian primary education consisted of higher and lower schools, of which the majority were of the former kind. Free and coeducational, the lower primary schools offered a course which in some localities lasted three years, and in others four years. Even so, peasant children, obliged to help their parents on the farm, seldom attended school during the full year. Classes, generally speaking, were large. Legally, the number of children in one class under a single teacher was fixed at 50; actually, however, the number was often as high as 70, and sometimes it was even higher. Most elementary schools devoted their efforts to the traditional curricular trio—reading, writing, and arithmetic. Some time was also given to the fundamentals of geography and history. Where there was sufficient demand, instruction was also offered in practical subjects, such as gardening and needlework. Religion was obligatory in all schools and was taught by the local priest, who introduced the young Russians to parts of the Old and the New Testament and the creed and initiated them into church singing, important prayers, and the Ten Commandments. Only one examination was held throughout the entire lower course—when the child left school; and even this was usually not written but oral. Probably the greatest boon to the boy's happiness lay not in his completion of the work required for graduation from the lower elementary school, but in the fact that the completion of this work substantially reduced his term of compulsory military service.

Higher primary education catered to boys. Usually offered in the district and urban schools, the regular course generally comprised five or six years. Of these, the first two were usually little more than a review of the work of the lower primary school—in fact its curricular fare was on the whole not very different. Religion was again required, and the three R's were also present. In addition, the pupil received instruction in Slavonic, elementary geometry, history and geography, penmanship, drawing, physics, and natural history. Sometimes commercial and technical subjects were taught. Because of their location in the larger towns, the higher primary schools were practically inaccessible to the peasant children.

Not all children attended the free state primary school. Some went, instead, to the synod school, whose work was not very different from that of the public school. Naturally the church school gave a great deal of attention to religion.

As for the teachers in the public elementary schools, about two thirds were women. Their monthly salary was about thirty rubles, in addition to which they were usually provided with rooms, "fires and lighting." For every five years of service their salary was raised five rubles a month; never, however, was the teacher to draw more than fifty rubles a month. After twenty-five years of service, teachers were entitled to a pension equal to their full salary.[7]

4.   Secondary education in 1914

Similar to the systems of secondary education prevailing in the larger continental nations, Russia's system shared the defect of not being connected with elementary education. Like the secondary schools of France, Germany, and several other European lands, those of Russia were designed for the élite. In addition to the classical gymnasium, there was the "real school," which was an outgrowth of the scientific schools, discontinued during the reign of Alexander II. Both the gymnasium and the real school were under the control of the Ministry of Public Instruction. In addition, there were two other types of schools, the ecclesiastial schools and seminaries, both of which were under the holy synod, and the cadet corps, which were military boarding schools kept and controlled by the War Office.

Maintained either by state or by private initiative, the gymnasium charged fees, about 15 per cent of the student body

---

[7] In 1914 the ruble was worth about fifty cents.

being admitted free. Even though the gymnasium was seldom attended by the poorer classes, it was not quite exclusive enough for the upper class nobility. Their children were usually sent abroad to expensive private schools. The greater part of the student body attending the gymnasium was made up of the sons of professional people or of clerks in the civil service. Beginning his secondary schooling usually at the age of ten, the Russian boy was offered an eight-year course at the gymnasium and a seven-year course at the real school. At the gymnasium he studied religion, Russian, Slavonic, Latin, Greek, mathematics, physics, history, geography, either French or German, penmanship, drawing, and logic. No classical languages were taught in the real school, instead the modern tongues were compulsory. As usual in schools of this kind, more time was devoted to mathematics and physics and less to history and literature. In certain real schools students in the upper classes were allowed to elect commercial subjects.

Virtually similar in their organization, the gymnasium and the real school were in charge of a director (principal), appointed by the curator of the district. The director was in turn assisted by an inspector. It was customary for both the director and his assistant to participate in the teaching. Appointed by the curator, teachers of the secondary school were required to possess a university degree or its equivalent. In the gymnasium teachers were paid from about 1,800 rubles to 2,200 rubles ($1,100) a year. Teachers employed in the state schools were considered civil servants of the crown. Theoretically, if not always in practice, they were exempt from military service. Like the teachers of the lower public schools, those of the secondary schools were entitled to a pension after the completion of twenty-five years of service.

Supported by funds collected locally, the ecclesiastical schools and seminaries were designed for children of the clergy. Such youngsters were admitted free, although provision was also made for the admission of others, who, however, were required to pay a fee. A six-year course preceded by four years of preparation was offered at the seminaries. Students of the seminary usually took holy orders and then entered the ranks of the evangelical clergy. The more gifted seminarists were encouraged to continue their training at the ecclesiastical academy where they were prepared for the higher church positions. A few entered one of the three universities open to seminary graduates.[8] The curriculum of these religious secondary schools was fairly similar to that of the classical gymnasium, although greater stress was placed on religious subjects.

True to its name, the cadet corps was a military institution intended for boys who desired to prepare themselves for a career in arms, or for one of the higher military colleges. A seven-year course was available. Resembling that of the real school, the curriculum of the cadet corps closed its doors to the classics. All the teaching, moreover, was done by the military.

Of the various secondary schools the gymnasium alone qualified the student for the university, and a diploma from the real school opened the way to the higher technical schools. Graduation from either the gymnasium or the real school reduced the term of compulsory military service to one year.

5. Secondary education for girls in 1914

Secondary education for girls before the first World War comprised institutes, gymnasiums, and diocesan schools. Institutes were exclusive boarding schools offering a seven-year course to the daughters of the upper classes. The gymnasium was a day school, supported by the state or by private persons; open theoretically to all classes, but appealing especially to the well-to-do middle class, the gymnasium offered a seven- or eight-year course. The diocesan school was a seven-year day school designed especially for daughters of the clergy, but open also to other students. Like the seminaries and the ecclesiastical schools for boys, the diocesan schools were supported chiefly by local funds. Graduation from any one of these three

---

[8] These were at Dorpat, Tomsk, and Warsaw.

schools entitled one to teach in the primary schools. To teach in the secondary school, however, a girl was required to have more education. On the whole, the curriculum of the girls' schools was similar to that of the boys'. One salient difference, however, may be noted in the absence of the classical disciplines in the girls' curricula. Some time also was devoted to such special subjects as needlework, education, and the like. Besides these general types of secondary schools there were also a number which provided special education, such as the training of primary school teachers and the preparation of doctors' assistants.

6. Technical and commercial schools in 1914

Toward the end of the reign of Russia's last czar, Nicholas II, provision for technical and commercial schools, though far from adequate, was increasing. There were some 200 schools offering a three- or four-year course for the training of artisans; these schools, however, were not state-supported. Generally speaking, they were open to adults who had worked in a factory for at least two years and also to boys between the ages of eleven and fifteen who had completed the regular primary course. There were also a few higher technical schools intended for the training of engineers and chemists. Such schools were open only to the graduates of the gymnasiums and the real schools.

With only two exceptions the commercial schools were under the control of the Ministry of Finance. They were supported by local funds, and for this reason were as independent as any school might be in czarist Russia. Commercial education consisted of four kinds: (1) commercial schools, (2) business schools, (3) business classes, (4) courses in commercial knowledge. Commercial schools offered a seven-year course and did almost the same work as the real school; but during the last two years they concentrated on commercial training. Such seven-year schools were intended primarily for those who expected to enter the technical higher school. The so-called business schools, however, were designed to train clerks and office workers. Primary education was a prerequisite for entrance. Business *classes* were held at night. They were designed in the main for office workers and were fairly elementary and usually nontechnical. The most advanced type of commercial instruction was offered in the courses in commercial knowledge. Intended mainly to train teachers of commercial subjects, these courses gave advanced instruction in special fields. They were open only to persons having a secondary education.

7. The educational situation in 1914

In the late nineteenth century, with the rise of industry, schools began to be more generally established. The revolution of 1905 brought about some educational changes. Three years later large grants were made to elementary education, with the result that the number of schools rapidly increased. From this time to the outbreak of the first World War efforts to improve Russian education were increased. At the beginning of the war Russia had more than six million children attending school. There were over 100,000 free primary schools, some 1,600 intermediate, and 2,500 secondary schools. The number of vocational schools was approximately 2,800, and they were attended by something like 250,000 pupils, outside of commercial students.

Despite the authorities' efforts at educational reconstruction, they came too late to do much good. It is true that Russia had a centralized school system which outwardly possessed the hallmarks of efficiency, yet upon close scrutiny many of the more commendable features of Russian education vanish into air. The departed empire, for example, made provision for elementary education; yet its provision never carried with it the mandate of enforcement. There were secondary schools—but only for a selected few. The chasm between primary and secondary education was deeper and wider in Russia than in France and Germany; for in both these nations primary education was at least effective enough to provide a thorough grounding in the fundamentals and to come to successful grips with illiteracy. In Russia, on the other hand, illiteracy flourished. It has been said that "the Imperial Government, far from trying to stimulate educational activities, did everything in its power to hamper the work of enlightenment." [9] Russian education was the embodiment of the principle formulated by the Minister of Education Shishkov during the reign of Alexander I. "To teach the mass of people," declared the Minister, "or even the majority of them, how to read will bring more harm than good." Besides being shackled to the deadweight of reaction, Russian education was tied to clericalism. The fact that the primary school devoted more time to the study of religion than to writing and arithmetic is eloquent testimony of the successful pressure exerted by the church. In one respect, however, the educational officers of the czar were thoroughly efficient. Familiar to the last detail with the intricacies of bureaucracy, and versed in the first principles of espionage, the swarms of government inspectors served their masters excellently. From a good many teachers, however, they gained little more than contempt and hatred; and when the worn out educational machine was dismantled under the Communists, the ministerial inspectors were among the first to go.

8. Marxism

The collapse of the Revolution of 1905 did not extinguish the hopes of liberals and radicals. Indeed, the fact that the czarist government repudiated most of its promises for reform and became instead solidly reactionary, spurred the revolutionary leaders to new plans and efforts. Their aspirations drew much of their sustenance from Karl Marx's monumental work *Das Kapital*. Published in 1867, a few years after Darwin's *On the Origin of Species*, Marx's book was destined

---

[9] Pavolsky, L., "Education under Communism," *Educational Review*, LXII, 210, 1921.

to become even more disquieting. The intellectual wellsprings which poured into the thinking of Marx,[10] and especially into his 2,500-page *Das Kapital,* sprang from the philosophy of Hegel, from the science of Darwin, and from the writings of the "utilitarian" economists. Marx had been impressed by Hegel's ideas of state evolution and by Darwin's theory of biological evolution. To these he added his own philosophical idea of "must." Arguing that inasmuch as certain social and economic events had taken place in the past, Marx insisted that certain further developments must necessarily occur in the future. At bottom this was something of a stimulus-response formula applied to social and economic events, but growing out of historic and cultural antecedents. Since to Marx's mind these developments were altogether inevitable, the author of *Das Kapital* addressed himself to the task of giving us a blueprint of tomorrow's better society, and what is more important, to fashion the formula for attaining it.

Marx's analysis of the good society was hardly novel, since in essence it had been attempted several times by utopian socialists. But the Marxian formula for attaining that society, a formula which involved strategy, tactics, and methods, was without doubt a significant contribution to nineteenth century thought. It calls for the rise to power of a small but rigorously disciplined party of communists. In Marx's realistic language, this group must establish itself by force, seizing control of the entire population and of their resources, which it will dispose in accordance with the philosophy of the leaders. In time, Marx predicted, economic classes would vanish; social in-

---

[10] Born in 1818 in the Rhenish town of Trier, Karl Marx was the son of a well-to-do lawyer. After an uneven career in the higher learning, Marx turned to journalism for the leftist press, opposing the existing Prussian government and especially the post-Napoleonic reactionary system as applied by the Austrian Prince Metternich in the German Confederation. In 1843 Marx went to Paris where he participated in the activities of the radical intellectuals. There with the German exile Friedrich Engels, he wrote, in 1848, the epoch-making *Communist Manifesto.* Soon after, the two men took part in the ill-fated liberal revolutionary movement in Germany during 1848–49. After its collapse, Marx and his family settled in London where they remained until his death in 1883.

equalities would level off; and the organized state would "wither away," leaving in its place a classless society. With the overmastering passion of an evangelist, Marx proclaimed that the collapse of Europe's prevailing capitalistic order was close at hand. When that day came, Marx argued, if the workers of the world were organized as well as bold and intrepid, the keys to power would inevitably be theirs. Spontaneous revolutions—as those in Russia during 1905—were of no avail, for they would be put down; the eventual revolution, asserted Marx, must be made by a disciplined revolutionary party acting through the workers' own organizations.

Such was the gospel of Karl Marx. From the day it was first enunciated to the present, it has set men in turmoil wherever their minds have turned to the nature of social organization. It has evoked bitterness, denunciation, and worse; at the same time it has given hope to millions and has been called the fairest creed the world has ever seen. On Marxian premises communist parties have developed in every land; and on Marxian premises Soviet Russia came into being. On the other hand, lined up against Marxist theories have been strong arguments which have come from modern psychology and organized religion, phases of thought and life with which Marx was altogether unfamiliar, from newer economic developments, and from a maturer interpretation of historical events. Still the conflict between Marxism and its opponents rages; in fact during the twentieth century the gains of the former have been great; and it may well be that the antagonisms developed between East and West after the second World War may be a significant part of that conflict.

9. Revolution and ideology

World War I opened the door to revolution in Russia. Following the military breakdown of the czarist armies and the separate peace with Germany, signed at Brest-Litovsk in 1918, Russia passed through three of the goriest years in its history. Warring among themselves at home and obliged, in the midst of domestic struggles, to defend themselves sometimes against the assaults of foreign foes on no fewer than fourteen fronts, the Communists managed to emerge in battered triumph. Their program, which was based in its fundamentals on the doctrines of Marx, called for the swift and complete communization of every important aspect of Russian life.

As launched in Russia, the ideology of Communism consisted of about a dozen general conceptions, all closely interrelated. First there is the acceptance of the principle of dictatorship. "We are not liberals," Stalin has declared. "We put the interests of the Party above the interests of formal democracy."

Acceptance of dictatorship has for its handmaid the rejection of multiparty rule. Many parties, the Communist believes, are nothing more than a smokescreen set off to blind the masses and credulous and unrealistic liberals, while behind the scenes real dictatorship under the control of vested interests actually exists.

The Soviet citizen must be militant. He must be ready to fight for his principles. Until the class foe has been permanently routed there can be no permanent peace; whatever peace exists is but a fleeting lull in the total picture of "worldwide revolution."

The good Communist must be an activist. The toga of passivity which enfolded prerevolutionary Russia was discarded, and "all citizens . . . must labor for the common welfare as the dictatorship directs."

Ultimately Russia is to be classless; but obviously until capitalist and bourgeois classes, inherited from the capitalistic regime have been eliminated, classlessness must wait. Eventually, when they have slid down the chute into their predestined obscurity, classlessness will become a reality. Meanwhile, there is work to be done: class prejudices must be enflamed to prepare the proletariat for the coming and inevitable struggle.

In Communist ideology a high place was given to labor.

The backbone of the soviet system, the worker, was recognized as the nation's producer, and as such he alone was entitled to eat. Nonproducers, which in the Marxian catalog include the bourgeois, the capitalist, the merchant, the priest, and others, are regarded as exploiters who live by the labor of others.

Ideologically, Communism beholds a world which is entirely secular. The church, which for generations had been the helpful co-worker of the Russian state, was shorn of its power. The school, as an arm of the Communist state, was rid of clerical dominance. Freedom of religious and antireligious propaganda was assured to every citizen. Actually, however, this was largely a theory; in practice the priest's sphere of influence became smaller and smaller. His sole function, asserted the Communists, was to deal with the immaterial world —and in a world which was so utterly and and so pervasively materialistic in its outlook this was palpably not much of a concession.

The new Russian was to be political. Since there was only one accepted political creed, the task of making the Russian political-minded was not so forbidding as one might at first imagine. Harnessed to the job, for example, were to be all the agencies of education, from the lowest kindergarten to the university. Such secondary agencies as the radio, the press, the screen, and so on were all to be put to work in politicizing the Russian.

In Communist ideology freedom of the individual is rejected. Wherever it has been allowed free rein, the Communists argue, it has degenerated usually into the satisfaction of selfish ends, in the exploitation of the weak by the strong. For individualism the Communists substituted collectivism. Ideologically, Marxist communism preaches non-nationalism. Within the vast stretches of Russian territory there are all sorts of nationalities accepting all kinds of customs and speaking a babble of languages. Instead of insisting on a common language for all, as do nearly all the national states, the Soviets permitted their heterogeneous nationalities to use their native tongues in their schools. If there are enough Tartars or Jews or Germans in a locality, schools were to be opened for them. Hand in hand with the non-nationalistic principle goes that of the international mind. Communism perceives itself as world-wide. Through it the thought of workers throughout the world is to be molded and unified for the purpose of advancing the class struggle.

In its stripling days Communist Russia preached the principle of absolute sex equality. In education this meant the elimination of sex discriminations. From the nursery schools to the higher professional schools coeducation was to be the style. Only in Southeast and Central Asia, where the populace is heavily Mohammedan, were concessions to be made to the old taboos by the establishment of separate elementary schools. In the course of Communist history, however, this principle, like so many of the other ideological canons, has undergone drastic modification.

In the Russian credo, finally, a prominent place was assigned to health, for obviously only a healthy citizen can be all the things that have been envisaged by Communist ideology. Only the healthy Communist can be of any use in the successful prosecution of the class struggle.

10. Political organization

To bring about the new order, Communist leaders brooked no opposition and with the aid of their secret police, the dreaded Cheka, which later became the Ogpu, they ferreted out their opponents, frightening them into submission and acquiescence, or jailing or liquidating them entirely. On July 6, 1923 the Union of Soviet Socialist Republics, the USSR, was proclaimed.

Politically, the USSR was built around the basic unit of the soviet, or workers' council. All in all there were some 70,000 of these. Organized in hierarchical order, the great majority were local soviets, and over all of them stood the Congress of the Supreme Council of Soviets. With the adoption of the new constitution in 1936, the Supreme Council was transformed into a bicameral legislature, composed of the Council of Nationalities and the Council of the Union.[11] Candidates for membership in these soviets are picked by the Communist Party, which is the only legally sanctioned party in the USSR. The Congress of the Supreme Council is not a legislature in the ordinary sense, its chief function being to discuss and approve governmental acts. In effect the real legislative body in Russia is not the Council of Soviets, but the Congress of the Communist Party. All legislation "enacted" by the Council must first be drawn up by the Communist Party and then endorsed by the Council's executive committee, which is the highest executive body within the state.

11. The Communist Party

By the Constitution of 1936 membership in the Communist Party alone was recognized, thus making it the sole legal party in the USSR. Relatively the Party is small, enrolling about two million members, or an average of one for every 80 of the population. Members are recruited from adult workers, but a good many come from the ranks of the youth organizations. In any case the recruit is subjected to a careful preliminary examination and before being accepted as a full-fledged member, he must pass through a period of probation. Party discipline is strict, requiring a high standard of personal behavior. Self-sacrifice, low compensation, and obedience to the Party's dictates are insisted upon. Members' records are frequently scrutinized, and anyone found weak or wanting in essential qualities is expelled. Although it is a small minority, the Communist Party is the only group possessing real political power in Soviet Russia.

---

[11] In 1939 the Supreme Council was composed of 1,143 members, of whom 465 were workers, 330 peasants, 65 soldiers; of the total 187 were women. Moreover, 870 were members of the Party.

12. Stalin's rise to power

With the death of Lenin in 1924, the Communist leadership became the object of violent dispute. Trotsky, who had been Lenin's chief collaborator in the early stages of the revolution, found himself opposed by several rivals of whom Stalin was the most powerful. The struggle for leadership was intensified not only by the usual personal ambitions and interparty rivalries, but also by a wide cleavage of opinion regarding party policy. However, by 1927 Trotsky found himself out-maneuvered by his foes and was ousted from the country. Though the feud between Trotskyites and Stalinists continued unabated until 1940, when Trotsky was murdered in Mexico, Stalin established himself as the head of the Communist Party and the master of the USSR.

13. The Five Year Plans

Soon after Stalin's triumph, Russia instituted the first of a number of Five Year Plans. Calling for a rigidly planned economy, this took stock of Russia's needs for the ensuing five years and at the same time organized the nation's agriculture, industry, transportation, and education to fulfill the blue-printed requirements.[12] The results of the plans were many, but four of them stand out. In its efforts to become self-sufficient, Russia enlarged and accelerated its industrial development; huge enterprises involving heavy industry, power plants, and mines were inaugurated. Not only was the development of industrial projects given a tremendous impetus, but in the course of the years there was a steady and perceptible increase in the nation's industrial output.

To guide and direct Russia's new industrial program, the country needed numerous trained technicians and engineers. When the first Five Year plan was introduced, the number of

---

[12] The first Five Year plan ran from 1928 to 1933; the second began in 1933 and the third in 1938. In 1946 the fourth Five Year plan was inaugurated "to rehabilitate the devastated regions of the country, to recover the prewar level in industry and agriculture, and then considerably to surpass that level."

such experts was far from adequate, and consequently Russia had to depend largely upon the help of experts from foreign lands. However, as Russian education was harnessed to the country's technical needs, the supply of trained specialists steadily increased. In 1933, for example, there were only 6,000 technical graduates in all Russia, but a half decade later the number had swollen to more than 25,000.

One of the significant outcomes of Russia's various Plans was the redistribution of its industry. Seeking to decentralize Russian industry and manufacturing and to shift it from the west where the dangers from any possible European war were relatively great, the Russian planners, directed by Stalin, developed industrial enterprises toward the east in Asiatic Russia. Thus, the policy which Peter the Great had initiated when he sought to bring his country closer to European influence was reversed. East of the Urals, the low mountains ranging north and south to mark off European from Asiatic Russia, a flock of new industrial centers came into being, places like Magnitogorsk, which was noted for its iron and steel; Berezniki, famous for its chemical output; Cheliabinsk, for its tractors; Sverdlovsk, for its farm machinery; and several others.[13]

An integral part of Russia's economic planning was the collectivization of its farms. Some peasants, called the kulaks, had profited materially by the Revolution, having acquired actual possession of the farms which they operated. When, in 1930, the government announced that it planned a program of collective farms, these kulaks vigorously objected. Their opposition was put down with even greater vigor, in fact at times with an appalling brutality. By 1938 the collectivization of the farms was well on the way to success;[14] in that year

---

[13] In 1939 Russia was producing 33% of its coal, power, and iron in or east of the Ural Mountains. At the same time 80% of its copper output came from these regions. When Russia and Germany went to war in 1941, however, more than 60% of her heavy industry and most of her oil production were still west of the Volga, as was the bulk of her manpower.

[14] To bring the kulaks into line the government executed many thousands

Russia boasted of some 245,000 collective farms. Owned by
the state, they were operated by hired hands and were producing more than 90 per cent of Russia's grain and foodstuffs.

14. Communist economy

The pattern of Communist economy is reflected in Russia's
various Five Year Plans. Founded on what is known in the
Marxian vocabulary as the "dictatorship of the proletariat,"
the Soviet state owns all the principal means of production.
All new capital construction is financed by the state, and
whatever profits accrue therefrom go exclusively to the state.
In its economic operations the Russian state had a monopoly
of all foreign trade, enabling it thereby to prevent any influence of world prices on internal prices. A further safeguard
was devised by keeping the Russian ruble, the basic monetary
unit, off the foreign exchange; it was against the law either to
import or to export the ruble. At bottom, Russian economy
is based on the idea of price control, all prices being fixed by
the state planning authorities. Where the fixed prices were in
excess of the cost of production, the profits went into the
coffers of the state; where the reverse happened to be the
situation, the state made up the difference.

15. The evolution of the USSR

Notwithstanding Marxian predictions, as Communism unfolded the state did not "wither away." On the contrary, the
Communist state was omnipresent, projecting itself into every
phase of Russian life. By the end of the thirties it was one of
the most elaborately and extensively organized states in existence. It possessed not only the ministries common to most
countries, such as those concerned with foreign affairs,
finances, war, and the like, but also it had many special ones,

---

and systematically starved millions more, mainly in the Ukraine. The same
drastic treatment was accorded to any others who dared to disagree with the
official policy. From 1934 to 1938 there was a series of "blood purges" and
"treason trials" followed by executions or long prison terms for some of
Russia's foremost Communists.

such as the Ministry of the Automobile Industry, the Ministry of Cinematography, the Ministry of the Grocery Supplies Industry, the Ministry of the Machine-Tool Industry, the Ministry of the Medical Supplies Industry, the Ministry of the Fish Industry of the Eastern Areas, and the Ministry of the Fish Industry of the Western Areas, and so on. As in totalitarian Germany and Italy, civil liberty in Russia existed mainly on paper; and as in the case of the departed fascist states, refugees who managed to escape from the Soviets told of sad and often harrowing experiences. The Russian state, like the fascist dictatorships, employed the familiar methods of intimidation, concentration camps, torture, and death for those who opposed it. Nor was Russia unlike other totalitarian states in its use of propaganda in the school, radio, movies, and press to mold public opinion and to effect public action.

Although Communistic Russia was presumably a dictatorship of the proletariat, in actual practice it was a dictatorship of the Party; and though in theory the worker was to be favored, in practice the choicest benefits went to the Party's higher potentates and to the army. Compared with the lot of the average worker, that of those who served in the armed forces was better. The army was favored with the best food and the best living, and it got better pay than any group in the land. Although Russian ideology bathed capitalists and their methods in the acid of denunciation, still it employed some of their favorite devices, some of which it introduced in 1935 in the Stakhanov system, a system for speeding up production.

There is no doubt that in thirty years of history the USSR has made great and even astounding progress, especially in medicine, science, and public welfare, and also in some of the arts; yet it may be doubted whether its most notable attainments were superior to those of the non-Communist world. It is, indeed, even doubtful whether its achievements in some of these domains were on a par with the best of Russian efforts in the old regime. In the sphere of letters certainly the Soviets have produced no one to rival Tolstoi, Dostoievski, Gogol, or

Goncharov. As for music, their greatest composers, of whom Shostakovich, Prokofiev, and Khachaturian are well known in America, undoubtedly possess the attributes of genius which might put them in a class with Russia's great composers of the past. Yet under the hammer and sickle, what genius needs most, the freedom of self-expression, is lacking. Fettered to the Marxist ideology it cannot really soar.

The great accomplishments of the Russians have been largely in the realm of the material, where, cutting through hoary and unrealistic traditions, they have made good headway. Their challenge to democracy has at least served to compel its upholders to examine its meaning, to question its values, and to scrutinize and criticize its prevailing shortcomings. The Russian criticism of capitalism, particularly when presented against the backdrop of world depression, against the strange and tragic spectacle of people in dire want in a world of abundance, has brought forth an examination of the whole capitalistic system.

The Russians, however, have not marched forward in a straight line. Their shifts from their original ideology have been many and often amazing. Where once they preached an absolute equality of the sexes, they now make reservations, where once they espoused easy marriages and no less easy divorces, they now apply the brakes; where once abortion was as permissible as an appendectomy, it is now for the most part outside the law. Did the Soviet leaders formerly decry the influence of religion and call for the elimination of priests? Then today they permit churches to be open. Did Trotsky and Lenin, and even Stalin, once extol a non-national scheme of things? Then today Russia has succumbed to the national fever and has become as nationalistic as the states its leaders once denounced.

In one respect, however, the Marxian Russian has remained immutable. Though the vicissitudes of internal and external politics may have caused shifts and even reversals in policy, Communism still clings to the idea of world revolution.

Although that revolution did not materialize in 1918, as most Communists had confidently anticipated, their leaders still hold that the logic of history makes world Communism inevitable. Inasmuch as the movement has been somewhat tardy in its arrival, the Communists believe in prodding it by agitation and propaganda. For that purpose the Third International was organized in 1919. Although supposedly apart from the Soviet state, this body had its blessings, holding its biennial meetings in Moscow, where the so-called "party line" was developed and adopted and funds appropriated and apportioned among the delegates for putting it into effect. From the late twenties to the mid thirties, the years of the world's great economic depression, the Third International worked zealously, seeking through agitation, the promotion of strikes, and the fostering of civil strife wherever possible, to hasten the "inevitable" world revolution. Only when the peril of Fascism began to alarm Communists everywhere, did the activities of the Third International come to a halt. With the initiation in 1935 of the so-called Popular-Front policy, Communist hopes for a world revolution were momentarily dispelled to enable Communists and liberals in all lands to work together against the Fascists. With the signing of the Russo-German alliance in 1939, the party line had to be revamped afresh, only to be revised again when, in 1941, Russia and the Reich grappled with one another in war. With the end of the second World War, the idea of world-wide Communist revolution has reappeared and with it the former activities of the Third International have once more become discernible.

16. Education in Soviet Russia

With the advent of the new order in Russia, education was completely overhauled. In a general way the new communistic state harnessed the school to the needs of the state. In October, 1917 it proclaimed that education must include (1) the liquidation of illiteracy, (2) free, universal, secular, and compulsory schooling, (3) a maximum educational opportunity for all, (4) preparation of a trained body of teachers, and (5) adequate support of education. That it was not easy to carry out these ideas should be obvious. Particularly was this the case from 1917 to 1921 when the Communist state was fighting for existence. Still, progress, though at first somewhat slow, was steady nonetheless. Today the U.S.S.R. has an

Age						
ABOVE 22 yrs	RESEARCH INSTITUTES / HIGHER COURSES					
17-22	UNIVERSITIES / HIGH SCHOOLS					COMMUNIST UNIVERSITY
	TECHNICUMS					
15-17	SECOND DIVISION SECONDARY SCHOOLS SPECIAL COURSES				WORKMAN'S FACULTIES ADULT SCHOOL SECOND GRADE	SOVIET PARTY SCHOOL SECOND GRADE
						SOVIET PARTY SCHOOL FIRST GRADE
12-15	FIRST DIVISION SECONDARY SCHOOLS SPECIAL COURSES	VOCATIONAL	WORKING APPRENTICE-SHIP	PEASANT YOUTH	ADULT SCHOOL of FIRST GRADE	SCHOOL of POLITICAL LITERACY
8-12	PRIMARY SCHOOLS					
3-8	KINDERGARTEN and PRE-SCHOOLS				LIQUIDATION of ILLITERACY	
UNDER 3	NURSERY					

Fig. 4. The Schools of Russia in 1937 (From *Education in a Democracy*, by Myers and Williams. Copyright by Prentice-Hall, Inc., 1937.)

educational ladder. For youngsters under three there is a nursery. Up to the age of eight come the kindergarten and other preschool institutions. Primary education is given in a unified labor school offering a four-year course for children eight to twelve years old. Primary schools are referred to as schools of the first grade; they are followed by schools of the second grade, which may be attached to schools of the first grade, continuing for three additional years, or may be independent. In addition to this, some schools offer two-year courses, which may be vocational—preparing the student for factory or office work—or they may prepare the student for higher education. Besides these schools there is another system by which the children from the primary schools may continue their schooling for three years in institutions connected with factories, trades, or workshops. In 1927 schools for peasant youths were established. These are seven-year schools; they may include the primary school, or the last three years may be separate.

For students who have completed a seven-year course further training is available in three- and four-year specialized technicums. These offer courses leading to industry, agriculture, business management, arts and crafts, music and the theater, nursing, social service, teaching, and so on. Finally there are the universities and higher institutions of a specialized character.

The Communist regime has given considerable attention to the problem of adult education. For grownups several types of education are available. Most important of all is the attempt to eliminate illiteracy. In addition, there are adult schools dedicated to vocational education, and to what is known as a cultural-political education.

a. **The reconstruction of curricula and methods.** Starting with a clean slate, Communist educators undertook to revise education along progressive lines. Briefly stated by the Russians themselves, education was to mean (1) active participation in the building of their own lives; (2) stress on socially useful labor; (3) establishment of intimate connections with contemporary life; (4) the study of nature and the development of a materialistic outlook. Education was to be on the basis of activity, with the "complex method," a form of the project method, receiving special stress. In addition the Dalton Plan was adopted in many places. Furthermore, student self-government was installed on a generous scale. American educators, visiting Russia to view the reconstructed schools, although often flatly disagreeing with the Soviets' political and economic ideals, were often most enthusiastic about the "progressiveness of Russia's new education."

When the Soviets first began to install their reconstructed education, there were numerous objections; but in any educational tilt the government had the final say, and so it was usually possible to brush conservative objections aside. Thus, while controversies rage over the various aspects of Progressive education, the authorities continued to apply many of its principles. Their attitude in the main was experimental, and whenever anything was found not to be producing the desired communistic results, it was scrapped.

Despite what the authorities decreed, however, protests against some of the newer practices did not cease. Not only did teachers here and there voice objections to some of the new doings, but even in important Party conclaves doubts were increasingly cast on various aspects of Russia's new education. The Dalton Plan and the Project Method in particular seemed to be suspect. The latter, wrote Bubnov, a noted Communist authority, was, after all, an American method "designed to educate an individualist who is able to stay afloat in a society based on competition." Doubt was also raised over the results produced by the newer methods. In the Don region, for example, official investigations revealed that more than half the children of a given school were wholly unable to copy a simple dictated passage. In fact, one third of the pupils could not write even one sentence without making a mistake. The first official blast against the newer procedures came in 1931 when the Central Committee of the Communist Party decreed that "no one method should be accepted as fundamental." A few years later the use of standard textbooks was made obligatory. In line with the new requirement, physical geography was to be taught "systematically" and in history facts were to be stressed. They were to be taught in chronological order instead of in the form of "abstract sociological schemes." Furthermore, the commissariats of education in the various Soviet republics were ordered "to liquidate the perversions of the laboratory method," which was obviously a blow at the Dalton Plan as it was being applied in Russia. In addition, the committee announced that hereafter "the accepted form of teaching in both the elementary and secondary schools must be classroom recitation based on a strict schedule and designed for a definite group of pupils." The teacher was no longer merely "to guide and advise." Instead, the committee now directed him to present his subject "in a systematic and sequential way, the pupils to be trained in the use of the textbooks."

If the Dalton Plan and the Project Method were subjected to these attacks, then so was the idea of pupil freedom. Not only was the child to attend classes according to a fixed schedule, but he was to master fundamentals thoroughly. To insure this, the committee decreed that "a final examination at the end of the year is compulsory for all pupils." Pupil self-government was also restricted. Principals and teachers were once more made "responsible for the maintenance of discipline among the pupils." Furthermore, "incorrigible pupils who insult the school personnel, violate the school rules, and are guilty of destroying school property," may be expelled.

Another change wrought in Russian education during this time resulted from a dispute over the status and value of certain applications of scientific child study. Known to Russians as pedology, the science of child study as defined by one of its Soviet practitioners, Professor Blonsky, is "the science of the child's chronological development under conditions of a definite social environment." Biological factors stemming from heredity, and social factors from environment, Blonsky identified as the "two interactive forces conditioning the child's development." [15] During the first decade of its unfoldment the Russian school had accorded a front place to the pedologist. Addressing himself to the task of studying the child through tests and other devices employed the world over

---

[15] For a fuller analysis see P. P. Blonsky's *Pedology*. Moscow: 1936.

by child psychologists, the Soviet pedologist was empowered to make recommendations calling for special educational treatment of those children who were in need thereof on the basis of his findings. Although in many lands this was not at all an unusual practice, in Russia it generated a great deal of friction. Many teachers disliked it because they felt that it subordinated their work to that of the pedologist. By the early thirties the role of the pedologist and his science was being subjected to a relentless fire. Calling pedology a pseudo-science, Professor Voskressensky excoriated it for having "appropriated the methods of bourgeois psychology" and for being "contradictory to Marxism." In 1936 the Central Committee of the Communist Party condemned "the theory and practice of the contemporary, so-called pedology" as having been "founded on pseudo-scientific, anti-Marxist theses." It decried especially pedology's "main 'law' . . . of the fatalistic conditioning of the child's destiny by biological and stationary social factors and a sort of unchanging environment." [16] Denouncing pedologists for their "harmful intelligence tests" and for having "grouped masses of children in the category of the 'backward,' transferring them from normal educational institutions to special auxiliary schools," [17] the Central Committee played up the part performed by Soviet education in molding the character and behavior of the child. "The educator," declared one of its defenders, "can direct in any direction the consciousness and behavior of men; he can nurture new traits of behavior, character, and not only develop those already present." [18] Finally, in 1936, the controversy was edged into the background when the Central Committee decreed the removal of the pedologists from the schools and at the same time accorded teachers a priority right in the management of the schools.

---

[16] "On the pedological distortion in the system of the Narkomprosov," a discussion of the decree of the Central Committee of the Communist Party, July 4, 1936, *Izvestia,* Vipusk III, p. 5, Irkutski Gosudarstvenni Pedagogicheski Institut, 1936.

[17] Medynski, E. M., *Istoriya Pedagogiki,* p. 101. Moscow: 1938.

[18] *Izvestia,* p. 13.

b. Educating the young child. Soviet Russia has made the early education of the child an integral part of its educational system. Preschool education carries the child through his eighth year. It is given in three types of institutions: crèches or nurseries, kindergartens, and hearths. The crèches, which are attached to factories where women are employed, are nurseries caring for young babes while their mothers work. The care of children under three is a duty of the People's Health Commissariat. The work is essentially practical, emphasizing health, hygiene, and the development of social and personal habits. The hearths and kindergartens supplement the work of the nursery. They care for children between the ages of three and eight, and lay great stress on cleanliness, health, and habit formation. They are open the whole day, receiving children as early as six o'clock in the morning.

In the preschool the child is initiated into the elementary forms of self-service and gradually is led into more social types of labor. Children help to keep things tidy and clean; they assist at the tables, care for animals, work in the garden, shovel snow, and participate in dozens of other activities. Much stress is laid on nature. In their studies the children make their own collections, and on their hikes and excursions they search for flowers, insects, stones, and all sorts of things which not only appeal to the childish eye and heart but are also instructive. Children are taught to note the relations between the things they see growing and their actual use in everyday life. The children themselves grow things—often vegetables that the kindergarten requires, and usually they raise animals. Every kindergarten has some kind of a workshop, which is often built by the children themselves.

As far as possible the child's education is related to the actual living world. The children make frequent trips to places of interest and importance. Shoemakers are visited; blacksmiths' shops and farms are inspected. If a carpenter or an electrician comes to the school, the children are encouraged to observe him at work.

Of predominant influence in the school is the stress put on collective activity. In conformance with this, the older groups hold meetings, elect a school soviet, select committees, and confer jointly with their parents and teachers. Every effort is made to prepare the children for a cooperative life.

Creative and aesthetic expression are also stressed. The older groups record their impressions and their daily activities in drawings; and, as in other new schools, these drawings are sometimes placed on the walls, where they become a sort of mural newspaper. Music, singing, dancing, and rhythmics are other notable features of the curriculum.

At the age of seven the child begins his work with grammar and arithmetic, which are taught as part of other activities, not as separate subjects. Much attention has been given to the development of a child literature that does not restrict itself to any particular educational level, but covers the child's whole life. Classified under five heads, the contents of the Russian child's literature comprise: (1) the child's environment; (2) the world of machines and inventions; (3) stories from far and near, old and new; (4) riddles and stories to test and direct perception; (5) imaginative entertainment. Books reflecting the child's world consider such matters as plant and animal life, health and hygiene, toys and their makers, pets, and children's organizations. Most of the books, of course, serve as vehicles of indoctrination. In arithmetic, for example, the child wrestles with problems of the Five Year Plan, of prices charged in cooperative stores, and so on; nor are numerous direct and subtle jibes at the clergy lacking.

Realizing that education flourishes only in the soil of cooperation and understanding, the Russian government has been striving to familiarize parents with the problems involved in the rearing of children. For mothers there is a formidable amount of publications dealing with all phases of a child's life. Written in plain language, these pamphlets present their material in from 15 to 30 pages and cover such topics as: How to Protect Little Children from Diseases; What Toys are Necessary for Children?; Playthings in the Preschool Age; What Kind of Diversions Do Children Need?

c. **Communist Youth.** The motif predominating in education in the Soviets is political. Theoretically, education by itself or for itself for the Communist is meaningless; education is for the social order. On all levels it is identical with propaganda and indoctrination.

To train future members of the Communist Party special organizations have been created. There are the Octobrists for children from six to ten; the Pioneers for ten- to fifteen-year-olds; and finally there are the Young Communists for those between the ages of fifteen and twenty-five. Something like one fifth of the population within the age groups mentioned are members of these three organizations. All these youngsters are trained in the meaning of Communism with special reference to the class struggle and the meaning of Leninism. All are grounded in Communist ideology: they are expected to be activists, materialists, and nonreligious in addition to being productive workers. They are taught to be ready at all times to further the Communist cause. They must be healthy and keep physically fit. Members of the older groups act as advisers to those belonging to the next younger group. To be admitted to full membership in the Pioneers and Young Communists, the youngster must go through a period of probation and study. As in the case of the Communist Party itself, there are frequent purges of the youth organizations, and only those members whose activity, interest, and loyalty are beyond any doubt are retained. The Pioneers and young Communists are the preparatory schools for membership in the Communist Party.

17. The war and Russian education

In Russia, as in all the war-ravaged lands, the conflict left its mark on education. In the wake of the terrific destruction wrought both by the enemy and the Russian "scorching the earth" there could be little thought of genuine schooling.

Where education was able to function, it was completely immersed in the national emergency. Relating itself fully to the country's struggle with the Nazis, the school not only taught its usual subjects in terms of war, but it also put the school children to work on the country's many patriotic enterprises, drives, and campaigns. As for the older children, those between fourteen and seventeen were in many instances sent to specially created craft and railway schools and to factory schools, where they were trained as skilled technicians and factory workers. In some places they were drafted for agricultural work or put into the labor reserves. Despite all the government could do, however, there was a perceptible moral let-down among Russian youth, with the usual toll in increased school truancy, juvenile delinquency, and civil crime.

As the fortunes of war turned more and more to the Russian favor, important educational improvements began to be made. More schools were opened as Russian towns were liberated. Whereas in 1942 some 9,500,000 were attending school, two years later the number had risen to 15,000,000. Even in 1942, when Hitler's armies were deep in Russian territory, the Russians saw to it that children in industry could continue their secondary schooling if they so desired. For those unfortunate youngsters whom the war had scarred in mind or body the government opened special schools. Russian schools also provided meals for the children, special canteens being established for the children of soldiers. Office and factory canteens were required to provide children with two daily meals when the schools themselves were unable to do so. In addition to food, clothing and shoes were issued.

It was during the war that Russia altered its stand on the question of coeducation. Originally, the Soviets, in their stress on the equality of opportunity among the sexes, had inaugurated coeducation thereby dramatizing the educational implications of the emancipation of the Russian woman. Yet, even before the outbreak of the war, the desirability of coeducation had aroused some speculation among Russian educators. In

1943 the controversy was given its quietus with the establishment on an "experimental basis" of separate elementary and secondary schools for boys and girls. In explanation of the new policy the People's Commissar of Education declared that "coeducation makes no allowances for differences in physical development of boys and girls, for variations required by the sexes in preparing each for their future life work, for good practical activity, for military activity, and it does not insure the required discipline among the pupils." [19]

a. **Educational reconstruction.** In 1946 Russia launched its fourth Five Year Plan. Its general purpose was to rehabilitate and reconstruct devastated Russia and to bring it up to its prewar level. For education the new plan included a number of tasks. Most important of these was the creation of facilities for the contemplated extension of education to the "working city and village youth." It was estimated that by 1950 the number of the former would reach some 480,000 and the latter were expected to total about 587,000. According to the Plan the number of children enrolled in kindergartens in 1950 would probably be more than double that of 1940, or in actual figures a register of some two and a quarter million children. In its drive for a general compulsory education the Plan envisaged some 190,000 elementary and secondary schools by 1950 with an aggregate attendance of some 32,000,000. By 1950, moreover, there were to be accommodations for 1,280,000 students in specialized secondary schools and for some 674,000 in higher educational institutions. Up to 1940 higher education had been free; in that year, however, fees began to be charged.

In addition to Russia's educational blueprint for 1950 as outlined in its fourth Five Year Plan, a number of curricular changes have been proposed. Generally speaking, "formalism" has been under assault. More stress is to be given to "real knowledge" and higher standards. For the secondary

---

[19] *Cf.* Ivanov, S., "Separate Education for Soviet Boys and Girls," *Voks*, p. 22 ff., November-December, 1945.

school, dialectics, psychology, and what is known as the "foundations of Darwinism" have been proposed. Marxian dialectics is to be taught to stimulate clear thinking. Psychology is intended to bring about better human relations and to assist the student in his practical task of learning. In Darwinism Soviet educators perceive not only the study of organic evolution in the usual sense, but also its relation to Marx's prediction of the inevitability of the world proletarian revolution.

18. Education and Communist morality

In 1946 there was published in Moscow a textbook on Russian education. Its title was *Pedagogika* and its authors the Russian educators, B. P. Yesipov and N. K. Goncharov. A part of the volume has since been translated into English by George S. Counts and Nucia P. Lodge, both of Teachers College, Columbia University.[20] Inasmuch as the book has been officially approved as a textbook on education, one may assume that it speaks with a measure of authority and that, in the main, its views are in harmony with the views of those who direct the fortunes of contemporary Russian education.

What are those views? They are, in the first place, that Russian education "is directed toward the strengthening of the Socialist State." To bring this about one must form "the new man" who is "characterized by his attitude toward labor" for the state. That attitude, we are told, "is most intimately related to the *Communist attitude toward public ownership.*" It becomes the duty of every Soviet citizen "to safeguard and strengthen public, socialist property." He is the patriot who strives "to contribute as much as possible to society, to the State," and is ready to give his life for his Motherland. To

---

[20] The English translation deals only with the sections on "Moral Education." Its American title is *I Want to Be Like Stalin. An Authoritative Statement of the Principles of Education in the Communist Morality.* New York: John Day Co., Inc., 1948. Neither the subtitle nor the main title is part of the original book. However, the translators did not create the title out of thin air, for the book is filled with hero worship. "Comrade Stalin," one learns from it, "watches over every Soviet person."

cultivate such patriots is "the most important task of moral education in our country." Furthermore:

Soviet patriotism is expressed in devotion to the Communist Party and supreme readiness to serve the cause of Lenin and Stalin. . . . To educate a member of our Soviet society means to educate a person to understand that he has no personal interests opposed to the collective interests, that with us there are no contradictions between individual and society. . . . Pupils must come to know that in our Soviet country the interests of the people are inseparable from the interests of their Government. . . . We must instill into our youth the knowledge that our truth is the truth of all toiling mankind. . . . Children associate with the concrete images of Lenin and Stalin, the Party created by the great leaders . . . our Soviet state, . . . to see the relation of their work and their study to the tasks of the entire society, to the tasks of the State.[21]

The identification of morality with service to the Leader and to the state is of course a familiar characteristic of totalitarianism. It was not Stalin, but Mussolini, who insisted on "everything for the State; nothing against the State; nothing outside the State."

The handmaiden of fascist totalitarianism was nationalism, and the same is true of Communist totalitarianism. Gone certainly is that article of Russian ideology of some three decades ago which laid stress on the non-nationalistic. Today's child of Russia is to be inoculated with the conviction that his Motherland is "the largest country in the world . . . the richest country in the world . . . the most powerful country in the world . . . the most advanced country in the world."

The cultivation of Soviet patriotism begins early in the child's life. Indeed, it is found in the kindergarten with its three- to six-year-olds. Here one is to instill "discipline, love of our great Motherland, love and respect for the Red Army." In their games the Russian tots are to "play Red Army soldier." To enable them to do this one puts little flags into their hands while "on their uniforms and caps are the insignia of infantry, tankmen, sailors and aviators." Naturally, they "march in formation to the tune of a martial song."

[21] *Ibid.*, p. 36 ff.

As for the primary school, its work is carried on to equip pupils "with those elements of general knowledge which are closely related to the military preparation of future warriors." Children no longer merely play at soldiering; now they "are to become acquainted with the types of arms used in the Red Army." And, once again, as in the demolished fascist states of Hitler and Mussolini, geography is recognized as "an essential part of military study," and the study of mathematics becomes "important for the mastery of military technique."

Not only is the mind to be imbued with military knowledge, but the child's senses are to be sharpened for war. Children are to be trained so that they may "hear the faintest sounds even to a barely perceptible rustling," since "in modern warfare the future defenders of the Motherland, and particularly the scout, must possess such powers."

Nor are the emotions to be overlooked, especially love of country and hatred for the enemy. Soviet children are to realize "that the feeling of Soviet patriotism is saturated with irreconcilable hatred toward the enemies of our socialist society." But hatred is not enough. One must learn "not only to hate the enemy, but also to struggle with him . . . to unmask him . . . to destroy him." In short, it is the school's task to instill "class revolutionary vigilance" and to create "a feeling of irreconcilability toward the class enemy."

Accentuating the militaristic tone of contemporary Soviet education are the recurrent notes of order, obedience, and discipline. "Discipline," the Russian teacher is told, "is one of the basic conditions of the Communist attitude toward labor." Why is this necessary? It is necessary to prepare "for organized disciplined labor in higher schools, in production, and in the service of the Red Army." How can discipline be inculcated? It can be inculcated if teachers remember that "children imitate before they understand." In its opposition to behavioristic conditioning, Soviet education has rejected the doctrine of developing unconscious and automatic habits of obedience; instead it has proposed "a feeling that honor means to get him [the pupil] to value the good opinion of people in authority." For the Russians it is not just a question of insuring discipline during school hours; it is fundamentally a question of "the cultivation in children of a *state of discipline*" and this means "unquestioned obedience and submission to the leader, the teacher, or the organizer." The identifying mark of discipline as it is to be developed in the child is his submission to the will of the leader.

Notwithstanding Communist ideology, after 30 years Soviet society gives no evidence of being classless. Actually it is one in which there is a marked cleavage between those who lead and those who follow. It is a society in which the thinking and the planning have been entrusted to a small and privileged group and in which the multitudes of people have been cast in the role of acquiescent and obedient robots. For them the taste of initiative is indeed a luxury. Nor is it an initiative that may serve merely to satisfy man's inner creative urges. "The citizens of the Soviet Union," one is reminded, "are expected not only to execute the will of their leaders, but also to show personal resourcefulness of their own." But this, one must ever remember, is always to "be directed toward the welfare of the Motherland. . . ."

Obviously there can be little room in such a society for the innovator, since in such a preconceived order "habits have a tremendous power." To disturb the habitual order is to arouse "a sense of perplexity on the part of the collective and is followed by resistance." In such case the innovator is in essence a "violator," who, "feeling the disapproval of the majority, submits to the established regimen." Such a system Communist rulers applaud for it "gives a certain style to the social life of the institution and constitutes what is known as *tradition*." And that tradition, derived substantially from Marx and Engels, Lenin and Stalin, appears to have been endowed with the qualities of an inexorable absolute.

F.   The United States

1.   Background

Rooted in the culture of the Old World, early American education reflected the characteristics of its European parent. Thus, wherever the colonists established schools they patterned them after Europe's traditional dual system by which an elementary schooling was available to the common people, but anything beyond that was reserved for a small élite. Hence, although the colonists generally desired an elementary education for the children of the masses, especially in reading, they did not think it necessary for such youngsters to go any further.   Moreover , wherever education beyond the primary level was established, it was of the traditional classical variety and was intended largely for lads who hoped some day to be pastors.   This educational dualism is clearly discernible in the famed Massachusetts Law of 1647 which required towns of 50 families to provide primary schooling for all boys and girls and, in the comparatively few large towns of 100 families, required the establishment of a Latin grammar school "to instruct youth so farr as they shall be fited for ye university."

In the south, where class cleavage was sharply drawn, the educational dualism was even more marked.   For there the wealthy land-owning aristocracy satisfied its educational requirements by private instruction and by sending its sons to the English motherland for secondary and higher education. For the children of the poor there were practically no educational facilities except such as were provided by philanthropy. Eventually there came into being a number of private schools, and, before the close of the seventeenth century, the College of William and Mary was established.   But such institutions of course were designed for the élite and were not accessible to the common people.

In the course of a relatively short time, however, American

education developed characteristics which were uniquely its own. In the climate of the rising American democracy the dual system found its existence precarious, and although it continued to flourish in Europe even after the first World War, in the United States it withered and died. Contributing no little to its undoing was the westward push of the American people. Among frontiersmen class differences evaporated—certainly there could be no aristocracy. The school which emerged under these conditions quite naturally was a school which recognized no class differences: it was the same school for all, the so-called common school. The single means of education of all the people, the common school took to itself everybody's children, in some instances when they were still tiny tots of four, and allowed them to come to its sessions year after year until they were ready to wed and assume the responsibilities of mature men and women. From its modest beginnings the common school grew in time to the stature and dignity of a single system of articulated schools, one system for all, stretching from the kindergarten to the college.

From its early days in seventeenth century Massachusetts American education has enjoyed a substantial measure of local autonomy. Although the Puritan theocracy, and later the state, enacted laws requiring localities to maintain schools, the details of carrying out such statutes were left almost entirely to the discretion of the community. As the country expanded and more settlements came into being—often at scattered points and at a distance from the older communities—school districts were established to minister to the educational needs of the new localities. Out of these arose the district school system, which still has its lingering survivors in many parts of the nation. Under the conditions that produced the district school, the local government enjoyed a virtually unhampered freedom of action in education, and it was not until after the War of 1812 that some of the states began to assert a greater authority in this domain. However, despite the tendency toward greater centralization, the educational system which evolved in America never became a province of the national government as it did, for example, in France and Prussia and many other European lands. In our country education has become the function of the individual states.

The War of 1812 has been called the Second War of Independence. In its wake one may perceive the unmistakable signs of a nation becoming conscious of its prowess. With the help of embargoes a substantial boost was given to the development of American manufacturing and to the furtherance of the nation's self-sufficiency. With the growing national consciousness came an enhanced interest in social improvements of all kinds. It was in such a cultural climate that some of the states began to scrutinize their educational facilities.

To direct and supervise the schools, a number of states created state boards of education, launching thereby the first major offensive in the struggle to improve education. When Massachusetts organized its State Board of Education in 1837, it appointed Horace Mann (1796–1859), a lawyer and a member of the state legislature, to be its Secretary and chief executive.[1] For 12 years Mann worked sedulously in what he called "the sphere of mind and morals." Through personal inspection of the schools, an inspection which carried him into every part of the Commonwealth, and through his writings in the *Common School Journal* and his *Annual Reports,* Mann sought to arouse the public on behalf of educational reform. From his capable pen streamed the whole dismal educational gallery as he had observed it in the state: sectarianism, incompetent teachers, obsolete equipment, decadent schoolhouses, a lack of educational opportunity for the masses, inadequate supervision, and so on down to a lack of standards

---

[1] For the life and work of Horace Mann see Mann, Mary T., *Life of Horace Mann.* New York: Lee and Shephard, 1865; also the more recent Williams, E. F., *Horace Mann Educational Statesman.* New York: The Macmillan Company, 1937. See also Mann's own *Annual Reports* and his excellent material on education in the *Common School Journal.* For the influence of Europe on the development of American educational theory see pp. 15, 21, 25.

and general inefficiency. Mann's criticism produced a torrent of rejoinders and no little personal abuse. Nonetheless during Mann's 12 secretarial years school appropriations almost doubled. Two millions were put into the construction of better school buildings. Teachers were made happy with substantial increases in salary; but in return they were expected to render better service. To help them the state established a number of public normal schools. A full month was added to the school year. Supervision was elevated to a plane of greater professional efficiency. Public high schools increased in number and gradually they edged the private secondary schools into the background. Textbooks were rewritten and improved; teaching methods were brought in line with newer theories; discipline was mellowed and humanized; school libraries were established. In short, during Mann's years in office, education in the Commonwealth was transformed from a feeble and insignificant thing into a public and secular system of the first order.

Mann's efforts to reform education in Massachusetts found their counterpart in other states. In Connecticut and Rhode Island Henry Barnard led the way. In Ohio it was Calvin Stowe; in Indiana, Caleb Mills; in Michigan, John Pierce; and in North Carolina, Calvin Wiley.

It was not until after the Civil War that the reform of the American public school system moved into high gear. Like every other large-scale conflict, the war between the North and South profoundly affected the nation's social and economic structure, and education inevitably felt the impact. The decades following the Civil War witnessed the tremendous increase in the use of coal and iron, which in turn became the blood and muscle of the machine. The development of a mechanized industry brought with it the factory system, the concentration of population in cities, the rise of the labor movement, and the usual concomitants of the industrial revolution.

Industrial mechanization and urbanization have left their

marks on education in a number of ways. Machine labor produced more goods and made more services available than had been possible with the older hand methods. Increased production in turn led to a rise in the nation's standard of living. Less and less was it necessary for families to depend on the labor of their children to maintain a satisfactory standard of living. Instead of having to send their youngsters to work, parents increasingly found it possible to send them to school. When the national occupation was largely agricultural, the work of the school had been organized so as to make it possible to release children to help their elders during the busy seasons of planting and harvesting. In the city there were of course no such seasonal phenomena, and schools could be kept open for longer periods of time. Thus, where in 1870 the average school year comprised only 78 days, by 1926 it had risen to 136, and in the cities it approached the 200-day mark. With their more abundant means and the greater compactness of their populations, cities could afford more elaborate facilities and equipment and could maintain services which smaller towns would have found physically and economically beyond them. But the cities' advantages were not unmixed; for, as they became larger and larger, their budgets often failed to match the pace. Educationally this reflected itself in a flock of problems, such as overcrowded classes, a dearth of proper housing facilities for the school population, a growing difficulty in providing an adequate corps of properly trained teachers, and so on.

The nineteenth century witnessed the growing emancipation of women. For a woman to work in an office in the days prior to the Civil War would have been to run the risk of social ostracism. From her status of social and economic dependence and political sterility, the American woman has advanced to a position where she participates in every phase of the national life. With her assumption of an active role in affairs which once had been the monopoly of the male, woman has devoted less and less time to what was formerly her exclusive province—the home. Educationally this has been of momentous consequence. Time was when the home was an educational institution of no minor significance, one in which woman played a leading part and in which she enjoyed a sense of personal value.[2] Not only did she direct and guide her children's moral and religious progress, but she helped them with the three R's besides imparting training in a host of skills. With the passing of the old-style home, the school has had to assume many of the functions which formerly devolved upon the family. As we look at the world about us, with its mills and warehouses, its office buildings, its schools and churches, we perceive in them the result of something abstracted from the traditional home.

Looking at the schools of 1850 one observes that some 45 per cent of the nation's young between five and twenty years of age were in attendance; a similar glance in 1920 would have revealed some 65 per cent of them going to school. Behind this increase lie a number of factors. For one thing, the nineteenth century showed a rise in humanitarianism. Its voice, though still faint in the turmoil of industrial struggle, was nonetheless audible. Increasingly, and with more and more success, humanitarians like Robert Owen, Johann Heinrich Pestalozzi, Ellen Key, and scores of others exerted themselves on behalf of children, fighting against their exploitation and for their right to an education in at least the fundamentals. Much more powerful, though less noble, were a number of factors which stemmed from our industrial transformation. Not only did our improved economic status make it possible for more and more parents to give their children the advantages of an education, but at the same time young people were finding it increasingly difficult to get employment. Where formerly it had profited employers to hire the young, in a

---

[2] An excellent discussion of the early American home may be found in Earle, A. M., *Home Life in Colonial Days*. New York: The Macmillan Company, 1898. For the changing activity of the home see Ogburn, W. F., *The Changing Family*. American Sociological Society, 1929.

mechanized industry such profits shrank. Obviously it requires skill and training and no little maturity to handle the more intricate machines of today—machines which incidentally involve a considerable capital investment.[3] Where young people have been put to work under such conditions, the rate of accidents in the factory has tended to rise; therefore, when manufacturers have employed the young, the cost of insurance has inevitably gone up, thus increasing the cost of production and cutting into profits. All in all, it has become unprofitable for manufacturers to hire the unskilled young; and when children can't find jobs, it is most likely that they will turn to the school.

In the rise of school attendance no less important than the manufacturer's profit motive was the attitude of labor, which has always been hostile toward the employment of youth. Competition for jobs obviously becomes more intense with the young in the employment market and organized labor has favored restrictions on the employment of youths. Besides seeking and obtaining legislative curbs on the employment of children, organized labor has throughout its history worked vigorously on behalf of public education and the extension of its opportunities to more and more children.

The cultural changes that took place in America after the Civil War, and especially after 1870, affected the development of American education in many ways. Not only was education characterized by a general expansion of its facilities, an overhauling of its administration, supervision, and financing, and an effort to improve its general effectiveness, but, as the nineteenth century moved on, the demand for education steadily mounted, until it contributed to the organization of the public secondary school.[4] Originating in the nineteenth century, the

---

[3] "Employers generally realize that child labor is not profitable. . . . Immature children are not capable of handling to advantage expensive and complicated machinery." Edmonds, R. H., "Introduction to Facts about Child Labor," *Manufacturers' Record*, XC, 1926.

[4] Under the common school system, which provided for the needs of all children from the very young up to the age of twenty-one, there was no need

public high school had been designed to enable graduates of the eight-year elementary school to continue their education at public expense. In an age when secondary education was commonly regarded as a privilege rather than a right, the public high school was the response to the desire of those Americans who wished to extend education beyond the elementary school for the multitude. There were some, of course, who opposed the use of public moneys for such a purpose, but their challenge was effectively halted in 1874 by an epoch-making decision of the Supreme Court of Michigan. In what is known as the Kalamazoo Decision, the principle was established that the high school is an essential part of our public school system. "We content ourselves," wrote Judge Cooley in rendering the Court's decision, "with the statement that neither in our state policy, in our constitution, or in our laws, do we find the primary school districts restricted in the branches of knowledge which their officers may cause to be taught, or the grade of instruction that may be given, if their voters consent in regular form to bear the expense and raise the taxes for the purpose." [5]

Although sanctioned by law, the American public high school did not attain full blossom until the twentieth century. A glance at the enrollment figures for 1900 reveals some 696,000 boys and girls attending high school. In 1920, the number had risen to some 2,495,000. A decade later the number had almost doubled, and in the mid thirties it passed the 6,500,000 mark.

Whether formal education could have soared to its present enormous figures without the impact of the industrial revolution is doubtful. Certainly the widening scale of machine

---

for a high school. The existing academy, which was private and which in the main prepared one for college, was, of course, not intended as a school for the masses. With the rise of a graded eight-year elementary school, however, the need for a school ministering to the needs of those youngsters who desired an advanced education began to be felt.

[5] *Stuart, et al.* v. *School District No. 1 of the Village of Kalamazoo,* 30 Mich. 69.

production created a demand for better educated and specially trained persons. There was not much room in the factory for the unskilled worker, nor was there much place for the illiterate, for if he couldn't read the factories' varied signs and instructions, its rules and regulations plainly, he couldn't function efficiently. In the office, too, literacy was indispensable. Hence, in the competitive struggle for employment schooling was palpably an asset. Moreover, as the age of machines progressed, the need for skilled operators and technicians increased prodigiously. Schools were harnessed to the task; as the nineteenth century moved into the twentieth, the American school was called upon more and more to impart not only the traditional fundamentals, but also to prepare young people for their role in industry and business.

Thus emerged the American school system. A product, in part, of our democratic idealism, which has its roots in our English heritage and in ideas of the French Revolution, it is also, and perhaps even to a larger degree, the product of our industrial, technical civilization.

2.   Underlying principles of American education

As is well known, the contemporary American educational enterprise is vast, engaging in one way or another something like one fourth of the nation's population. Obviously, the cost of running such a gigantic undertaking is tremendous. From 1930 to 1945, for example, the cost of public education has averaged well over two billion dollars a year and sometimes it has approached the two and one half billion mark. Adding to this sum the moneys spent to maintain private institutions, the figure runs to more than three billions.[6]

In the strict sense the United States does not have a national system of schools. There is, for one thing, no national

---

[6] It should be observed that despite the seeming hugeness of our expenditure on public education, it represents but a fraction of the national income. In 1946 the United States spent about 1.5% of its total estimated income of 160 billion dollars on education. At the same time impoverished England spent some 3%, and the Soviet Union averaged around 8%.

authority as in many other countries. There is not, as in France, a national organization of schools uniform throughout the nation with identical curricula, methods, teacher training, and so on. There is not even, as in England, a minimum national uniformity in such a matter, for example, as a common compulsory attendance age throughout the country. But if there is no national system in the strict sense, there is nonetheless an American system, with definite and recognizable characteristics, based upon generally accepted principles, of which the following are some of the chief ones:

1. *Decentralization.* As in England, our schools are nationally decentralized with a large amount of local control and freedom. There are, as a matter of fact, 49 school systems, one for each of the 48 states and the District of Columbia. Although the control of education is vested in the states, the federal government aids in supporting public education.

2. *Free, compulsory, universal education.* America believes that education is fundamental for the continued existence of a self-governing democracy. The length of compulsory education varies from state to state. In some of the more progressive states there is a growing trend to extend compulsory education to adolescents.

3. *The educational ladder.* America believes in one system of articulated schools from the kindergarten to the university. It is opposed to the so-called dual system of schools.

4. *Private schools.* Although the state may compel parents to send their children to school, the state cannot select the school. The state has no right to compel parents to send their children to the public school—as in Germany from 1919 to 1945 and in the Russian zone of occupation in Germany at present.

5. *Parochial schools.* Religious denominational schools may exist, and parents have the right to send their children to such schools. However, public moneys are not to be used for any sectarian purposes.

6. In principle, there is to be *equality of educational opportunity;* in practice, however, this principle is not generally realized.

7. *Separation of church and state.* Under the Constitution, church and state are separate. Hence, the public school may not offer religious instruction in the school building and on school time.

3. Federal participation in education

By virtue of the Tenth Amendment, which reserves to the states those "powers not delegated to the United States by the Constitution, nor prohibited by it to the States," the con-

trol and administration of education has become a function of
the states rather than of the federal government. However,
even though the national government exerts no direct control
over the nation's schools, it has been neither inactive nor
without influence in the realm of education. There is, for
example, the United States Office of Education in Washington,
D. C. Established by Congress in 1867, originally as a Department of Education, the Office subsequently was converted into
a bureau in the Department of the Interior, only to be recon-
verted, in 1930, into the Office of Education. In 1939, under
the general governmental reorganization plans, the Office of
Education became part of the Federal Security Agency. In
charge of the United States Commissioner of Education, the
Office of Education is essentially a fact-finding body, conducting researches and investigations, and concerned with the collection and dissemination of information related to education.[7]
Aside from its supervisory powers over the schools for Indians
and Eskimos in Alaska, the Office exerts no authority over the
nation's school systems. Like all governmental agencies, it is
supported by annual Congressional appropriations, none of
which, however, has been very large. Even so, the Office has
performed admirably. Through its publications, its reports
and bulletins, and especially its *Biennial Surveys of Education,*
it has made available a mine of educational information.
Moreover, at the request of state and local authorities, it has
promoted a number of important researches and investigations
and reported thereon. In 1932, with the help of educators
throughout the country, it supervised an extensive survey of
the nation's secondary education. Similarly, it has conducted

---

[7] Since the establishment of the commissionership in 1867, eleven men have
held the office. Appointed by the President, they hold office for an indefinite
term. The first Commissioner was Henry Barnard, who was in office for only
three years. He was followed by John Eaton (1870–86); Nathaniel H. R.
Dawson (1886–89); William T. Harris (1889–1906); Elmer E. Brown (1906–
11); Philander P. Claxton (1911–21); John J. Tigert (1921–28); William J.
Cooper (1929–1933); George F. Zook (1933–34); John W. Studebaker (1934–
1948); Earl J. McGrath (1949–).

national surveys in Negro education, teacher education, and school finance.

The Children's Bureau of Education, which was created in 1912 as a part of the Department of Commerce and Labor, but which has since been put under the Department of Labor, has performed a similar though somewhat more specialized function. Concerned with the welfare of children, the Bureau has investigated and reported on such matters as infant mortality, delinquency, children's diseases, accidents, child labor, and legislation pertinent to the welfare of children.[8]

In 1917 Congress established the Federal Board of Vocational Education for the purpose of cooperating with the states in the furtherance and development of vocational education. To the Board was entrusted the power and responsibility of administering the funds provided by Congress under certain laws, such as the Smith-Hughes Act (1917), the George-Reed Act (1929), the George-Dean Act (1937), and other related legislation seeking to promote vocational education in schools below the college level. In 1920, the Board was charged with the administration of the Civilian Vocational Rehabilitation Act (Smith-Bankhead), which appropriated money to the states for the training of handicapped persons.

Oddly enough, the Department of Agriculture has duties and powers which directly affect education in several significant ways. Under the Morrill Acts (1862 and 1890), the Department was entrusted with the supervision of the so-called land-grant colleges which had been established by these laws; under the Hatch Act (1887), and subsequent supplementary legislation, control over agricultural experimental stations was vested in the Department; and by the Smith-Lever Act (1914) supplemented by the Capper-Ketcham Act (1929), the Department was given certain powers in carrying on extension work in home economics and agriculture.[9]

---

[8] In 1921 the Bureau was empowered to administer the Sheppard-Towner Maternity Act, which provided funds for cooperation with the states in "promoting the welfare and hygiene of maternity and infancy."

[9] Beginning with the first Morrill Act (1862) each state received 30,000 acres

In addition to the foregoing enterprises, the federal government, through its other executive departments, carries on a number of educational programs, most of which relate to the training of specialized personnel.[10]

During Franklin D. Roosevelt's first term, the federal government began to assume larger responsibilities in the nation's education. Under the New Deal a number of emergency agencies were organized to combat the depression, and although relief was one of their essential purposes, at the same time several of them developed important educational programs. The first of the relief agencies, the Civilian Conservation Corps (CCC), was organized in 1933 "for the purpose of providing employment as well as vocational training for youthful citizens of the United States who are unemployed and in need of employment. . . ." The young men who participated in the CCC generally enrolled for a period of not less than six months during which they lived away from home in camps and helped to carry out a program designed to conserve and develop our national parks, forests, and other resources. (See p. 499.)

In 1935 the National Youth Administration (NYA) was inaugurated.[11] Like the CCC, the NYA was designed to help unemployed young people. Its specific purpose was to assist needy students by means of small grants which they earned while working at various projects under the general super-

---

of land for each Senator and Representative then in Congress. The proceeds from the sale of such land were to be invested at 5% interest and were to be used by each state for the endowment, maintenance, and support "of at least one college . . . where the leading object shall be . . . to teach such branches of learning as are related to agriculture and home economics." The original act was supplemented by further grants in the second Morrill Act (1890), the Nelson Amendment (1907), and the Bankhead-Jones Act (1935). All in all, 69 land-grant colleges have been established.

[10] There are also several agencies with an educational function under the Federal Security Agencies. Under the Tennessee Valley Authority (TVA) the federal government has contributed to the carrying out of an educational program of the first order.

[11] The precursor of the NYA was the Federal Emergency Relief Administration (FERA)

vision of the institutions they attended. Besides these features the NYA carried on projects which were connected with defense activities and a guidance program which included placement.

Despite their obvious merits, the CCC and the NYA drew considerable critical fire, particularly from those forces which were hostile to the New Deal, and in 1942 and 1943 the two agencies were terminated.

Two other emergency bodies created during the depression years left their mark on American education. Under the Works Progress Administration (WPA) the federal government provided funds for work-relief payments for unemployed teachers. By these means an extensive educational program was made possible in a variety of fields, such as nursery education, workers' education, adult education, vocational training and rehabilitation, and the development of American citizenship programs for aliens residing in the United States. The Public Works Administration (PWA) offered loans and grants to states and communities desiring to erect school buildings.

As the United States moved from the depression toward the second World War, the government began to support educational measures related to national defense. Thus, in 1938 the Civil Aeronautics Authority (CAA) was established to develop programs for the training of pilots, and two years later federal funds were appropriated for the training of defense workers in schools and colleges. In five years some 12,000,000 persons were trained under this program at a cost of about $500,000,000.

With victory on the horizon, the government turned to the large army of prospective veterans. In 1944 Congress enacted the Serviceman's Readjustment Act, or as it is popularly known, the GI Bill. By it ex-servicemen and women were granted $500 for tuition and supplies for an academic year of study in school or college. Veterans with three months' service were entitled to a year's education, besides additional time equal to the period of service, up to a maximum of four years. Furthermore, besides tuition and fees, veteran students were to be allowed a subsistence of $50 a month if single and $75 if they had dependents. With the end of hostilities in 1945, thousands of veterans began taking advantage of these benefits. In fact, so great was their response that before long colleges found themselves hard pressed to cope with the enormous demands for an education. Because of the general rise in the cost of living, Congress in 1948 increased the subsistence allowance to $75 a month if single, $100 if one dependent, and $120 if more than one dependent.

Although the Constitution of the United States does not specifically mention education as a province of the national government, in practice the federal government has obviously displayed an educational function.[12] Nor has its activity in this sphere been merely advisory. In fact, from its earliest days as a republic, it has encouraged education, first by grants of land, and then by financial subsidies. With the admission of Ohio into the Union in 1802, the practice was inaugurated of granting the incoming state the sixteenth section of land for the maintenance of schools. In the course of the years the amount of land thus conveyed was increased. Moreover, various legislative enactments, beginning with the First Morrill Act and continuing to the present, sought to encourage certain kinds of vocational education, creating for this purpose not only the necessary machinery to implement the law, but also providing special monetary grants to the state. Not until 1911, however, were states required as a condition for obtaining federal aid to match the subsidy received with an

---

[12] The national government's concern for education was manifested in the Ordinance of 1785, which provided for a survey of the Northwest Territory, and contains a provision reserving the sixteenth section of every township for the purpose of education. The Ordinance of 1787, which provided for the government of the Northwest Territory, expressed the government's attitude toward education, thus: "Religion, morality and knowledge being necessary to good government and the happiness of mankind, schools and the means of education shall be forever encouraged."

equal amount, and also to pass acts of assent to the provisions
of the federal acts. On the whole the history of federal grants
seems to reveal a gradual tightening of federal control. Thus,
whereas the first Morrill Act imposed very few restrictions,
the Smith-Hughes Act by contrast went to great lengths in
specifying the details of the program of vocational education
to be pursued by the recipients of federal grants.

Ever since the early twenties there has been a movement to
enlarge the federal government's participation in education.
Many believe that the cause of American education would
benefit by the creation of a Department of Education with a
Secretary of Education in the President's cabinet. Such an
organization, it has been argued, would elevate American
education in dignity and renown as one of the government's
major enterprises, and would bestow upon it the power and
influence which it properly should wield. On the other hand,
there are probably just as many who oppose the establishment of such a central body on the ground that it would
endanger the states' traditional rights in education; that it
would serve to interfere with the educational liberties of
certain minority groups, especially parochial schools; and
that on the whole it would tend to standardize and bureau-
cratize American education. During the Hoover administration, in 1931, a presidential committee recommended the
establishment of "a Department of Education with a Secretary of Education at its head." However, a minority report,
presented by two committee members, opposed the recommendation. Several bills have been introduced in Congress
seeking to establish such a secretaryship, but so far they have
all met with defeat.

During the last score of years there has been a growing
demand for increased federal aid. Heretofore such financial
assistance has been for education of a specified nature, such
as for colleges teaching agriculture or the mechanic arts, for
vocational aid and home economics, for military training, for
relief purposes, and for veterans. General education, as

carried on in the thousands of American schools throughout the land, has had to rely on the resources of state and locality. Unfortunately, these are not equally distributed, with the result that the quality of education and the opportunities related thereto vary tremendously in different parts of the country. The depression and the war aftermath, moreover, have played havoc with public finances and have aggravated economic discrepancies so that education, particularly in the poorer states, has suffered—and even deteriorated alarmingly. To ameliorate these conditions federal aid has been proposed on the ground that education is after all a matter of national concern and importance. Only by combining our national resources, it has been asserted, and by distributing them equitably can educational opportunities be somewhat equalized throughout the nation. Bills seeking such an end have been introduced in Congress ever since the early twenties, but they have never come to fruit. The truth is that although they have been heartily endorsed, and that states no doubt would gladly accept money out of the federal till, these bills have also engendered a number of fears and objections. The feeling that federal aid will lead inevitably to federal interference, or perhaps even control, in matters which are of local concern has led many to oppose the proposal. There has been a division of opinion, too, as to how federal moneys should be apportioned, one group holding that such funds should go to public schools exclusively, and another maintaining that it should be distributed among private and parochial schools as well as public schools. Bills introduced by Senator Taft of Ohio (1947 and 1948) have tried to meet these objections by authorizing federal funds of more than a quarter billion dollars a year to assist schools in the neediest states; by apportioning the money on the basis of need, as determined by the wealth of the state and the number of its children; by guaranteeing a minimum educational expenditure for every child in every school community in every state; by safeguarding the local control of public education; and by providing for a fair distribution of federal moneys.

4. State and local control of education

Participating in a relatively small way in education, the federal government has no direct control over the conduct of education in the various states and localities. Education, in other words, is a state function. So jealously has this right been guarded that the fear of possible federal encroachment upon it has prompted opposition in many quarters to suggestions that the federal government should play a greater and more influential role in American education.

The largest unit of governmental authority in education is the individual state. Autonomous in educational matters within its own domain, the state has generally permitted localities freedom in carrying out their educational responsibilities. All but a few states have a body such as the state board of education to serve mainly as a policy-making group charged with the general oversight of the school system. A number of states have established a system of multiple boards, each with special functions. Like city boards of education, the state board makes appointments recommended by the superintendent and approves budgets prepared by him. As for the board members, in some states they hold office *ex officio;* such persons hold other state offices which automatically confer membership on the board of education. In Louisiana, Michigan, and Nevada board members are elected. In the majority of states, however, the board members are appointed.[13]

The chief executive of the board is the state superintendent, or, as he is known in a number of states, the commissioner of education. Historically, the office came into being in New

---

[13] The first state school board to be established in this country was the Board of Regents for New York. Founded in 1784, it was charged with the supervision of collegiate and academic education in the state. The institutions under its control became known as the University of the State of New York, a name which is still employed.

York in 1812. By mid-century, the office had been created in most of the northern states and in a number of those south of the Potomac. In the majority of states the state superintendency is an elective office, a condition which has been subjected to no little criticism, since at least part of the superintendent's efforts will presumably be devoted to political maneuvering to keep himself in office. In some states the superintendent is appointed by the governor, and in others he is appointed by the state board of education. The duties which devolve upon the state superintendent vary from state to state. Generally speaking, it is his function to carry out the laws and regulations passed by the legislature and the state board of education. Part of every superintendent's work is statistical, involving the compilation of data on the schools of the state. The superintendent is expected to keep the governor and the legislature posted on needed educational legislation. It is his duty to advise local school boards and to interpret the school laws. There have been occasions when he has acted as a court of appeals in cases involving the hiring and firing of a teacher. As might be expected, the superintendent exercises a supervisory function, the inspection and rating of schools maintained by the various localities being one of the prime duties of his office. A good part of his work is administrative, including such responsibilities as the certification of teachers and the allocation of state moneys among the various localities.[14]

Usually the state educational organization is divided into smaller administrative units, such as county, township, town, and local school district. In New England, local school organization is on a town or township basis; in most of the southern states the county basis prevails. In the west and middle west one usually finds the district type. Delaware has

---

[14] The superintendent is assisted in his manifold duties by a corps of professional and nonprofessional personnel, generally known as the State Department of Education.

abolished the local units, substituting for them a state unit.[15]

Originally the nature of the local unit depended no little on geographic and cultural factors. In the colonial south, for example, with its immense estates and far-flung towns, the unit of local government was naturally large. In early New England, by contrast, where settlements lay much closer together and where population was fairly compact, the town unit for school administration was the more practical. However, as the population dispersed to remoter areas, and as the distance between towns became greater, the district replaced the town as the unit for local school control. Under the district system a one-room school usually sufficed to teach some 10 to 40 pupils of varying ages. The fact that such education seemed cheap made it attractive to the economy-minded; hence the district school system persisted long after the factors which had brought it into being had vanished. It was not until such men as Henry Barnard and Horace Mann waged their war upon it that the district school lost its grip in New England.

The factors which more or less necessitated the maintenance of small administrative units in rural sections have largely disappeared. With the coming of good roads and modern facilities for transportation, it has become possible to organize on a larger and more efficient scale. Thus the old one-room school with its single teacher for all the children is being superseded by the consolidated school serving several areas. Yet, despite their savings to the taxpayer, their greater efficiency, and the better opportunities they offer the children, such schools have been stubbornly opposed.[16] Local pride and provincialism have stood in the way of consolidation.

---

[15] Some states, it should be observed, have combined types. Thus, in any county of Oregon and Montana, and in certain ones of Minnesota, Nebraska, and Texas, qualified electors may establish the county unit of school administration, even though these states are district states.

[16] In some states the number of school officeholders exceeds the number of teachers. Naturally loath to lose their offices, they represent a vested interest that is difficult to remove. Conservative to the core, they are for the old-fashioned ways by which they benefit.

In charge of the local school system is the board of education, a body of laymen who generally serve without compensation and whose qualifications and term of office vary from place to place.[17] In some cities they are appointed either by the mayor or by the city council or board of aldermen; in others they are elected by the voters.[18] Whatever the manner in which they are chosen, members of the board of education are the direct representatives of the people. Essentially they are a policy-forming body; their function is to devise policies for carrying out the wishes of the citizens in their community, consistent, of course, with the educational laws of the state. The specific powers of boards of education vary considerably. Among some of their more common duties are the appointment of the teaching, supervisory, administrative, and other personnel; the acquisition of school sites and the building of schools; the purchase of supplies and equipment; the levying of taxes, or in lieu thereof, the submission of estimates to some other body; the adoption of courses of study; the framing of regulations for the management of the schools; and the enforcement of the school attendance law.

The chief local school officer is the superintendent.[19] Appointed by the board of education, he serves as its executive agent in the management of the school system. His duties are manifold, especially in the larger cities. In fact, to fulfill them all successfully he must be not only an educator, but also

---

[17] An example of the lack of national uniformity in American education is revealed in the variety of names we have for what is probably one of our most important educational agencies. Thus in various places the board of education is referred to as the school board, the selectmen, the board of trustees, etc.

[18] Boards of education vary in size from a one-man board to as many as forty members. Terms of office range from two years to life. The most common seems to be a four-year term.

[19] Historically, the city superintendency came into being in 1837 when Buffalo, New York, and Louisville, Ky., created the position. It was not, however, until after the seventies, with the nation's growing industrialization and the growth of cities, that the superintendency came into its own. The National Association of School Superintendents was organized in 1865. Today it has become one of the largest divisions of the NEA. Its present name is the American Association of School Administrators.

something of a business man, a fiscal expert, a student of law, a psychologist who has mastered the art of getting along with all kinds of people, and an active participant in the community life. By way of monetary reward the superintendency offers some of the richest plums in the field of American education, but it is also an exacting and difficult office, with many headaches and no little grief. So important has this position become in the American school system, and so intricate and involved are its duties and responsibilities, that special training for it is almost necessary. In fact, training students for this position has become an important part of the work of every first-rate school of education. Generally speaking, the superintendent recommends the appointment—and at times the suspension or dismissal—of personnel. He assigns and transfers personnel. With the advice of teachers and others, he selects textbooks, supplies, and equipment, supervising purchases and distribution. He prepares, or has prepared for his approval, all courses of study. He directs the supervision of instruction and extracurricular activities. He grants permission for the use of classrooms, gymnasiums, and auditoriums for community functions, subject to such terms as the school board may see fit to impose. The superintendent is general overseer over the maintenance and operation of the school plant. He keeps the board informed about the community's educational and school requirements, recommending the erection of new buildings, the repair and alteration of old ones, the installation of new equipment, and so on. He makes monthly and annual reports to the board regarding educational conditions in the community. In many of the smaller towns, moreover, the superintendent also teaches. Through his activities the superintendent is drawn into relationship with the board of education, the administrative and supervisory personnel, the teaching personnel, the pupils, and his fellow citizens. In the nation's larger cities, where education has become an enormous enterprise, obviously no one person could by himself successfully discharge so many tasks. Under such circumstances the superintendent is usually provided with a corps of assistants to whom he delegates the actual performance of many of his functions. Thus one may find the busy superintendent helped by a staff including such specialists as a business manager, a plant manager, attendance officers, assistant and associate superintendents, directors and specialists in the various subjects, and research directors, as well as an army of clerks, accountants, lawyers, and the like.

5. Independent bodies with educational functions

Besides the state and local agencies legally entrusted with the responsibility of carrying out the educational program in their respective areas, there are a number of independent bodies actively engaged in a variety of educational enterprises. Some of them, it is true, are, in the main, nothing more than pressure groups seeking in one way or another to grind their special axe. Many others, however, have been established to work within the framework of the existing educational system for the purpose of carrying on activities and services which ordinarily lie beyond the capabilities of the usual governmental educational agencies. There are, for example, numerous organizations characterized as "accrediting agencies," whose purpose it is to inspect and rate educational institutions desiring such a service and to extend membership to those found to be of satisfactory merit. Originating toward the close of the nineteenth century, the accrediting movement came into prominence in the following century with the publication of Abraham Flexner's report on the nation's medical schools.[20] Exposing the fact that the standards of our medical education varied considerably and that many of our medical schools were nothing more than trade schools with standards that were appallingly low, Flexner's study prompted the American Medical Association to rate the country's medical schools, classifying them as A, B,

---

[20] Flexner, A., *Medical Education in the United States and Canada*, Bulletin 4. New York: Carnegie Foundation for the Advancement of Teaching, 1910.

or C institutions. Since no medical student in his right mind would obviously care to receive his degree from an inferior institution, schools of low rating were compelled to improve their educational standards and facilities or pass out of existence altogether. The result was that the C schools swiftly disappeared; the B schools lingered for a while, but in the course of the years they, too, came to an unlamented end.

Somewhat akin to the accrediting role played by the American Medical Association is that of the American Bar Association. Composed of the country's practicing lawyers, the American Bar Association has established standards which law schools desiring its approval must meet. The American Association of Teachers Colleges has acted in similar fashion in the realm of teacher education, and other professional groups operate in more or less the same way in the fields of architecture, business, journalism, and the like.

The Association of American Universities has been concerned largely with the realm of graduate study, its chief task being the inspection of colleges to ascertain whether they have adequate facilities to prepare their students for competent graduate work. Those schools which meet its requirements are put on the Association's approved list. Graduates from colleges on this list may enter any graduate school in this land and in most foreign lands with full recognition of their undergraduate work.

Playing a significant role in the furtherance of education are numerous professional organizations. Some of them are relatively specialized in purpose and scope, as, for example, the American Historical Association, the American Philosophical Society, the American Vocational Association, and so on, including societies devoted to virtually every phase of American education. Other bodies, such as the American Education Fellowship (formerly known as the Progressive Education Association) and the National Education Association, have a much wider scope. The largest professional organization in America is the National Education Association, the NEA, which in 1948 had approximately 400,000 members.[21] Established in 1857 in Philadelphia as the National Teachers' Association, the NEA sought "to elevate the character and advance the interests of the teaching profession and to promote the cause of education throughout the country." Today the NEA platform comprises several printed pages involving matters relating to the child, the teacher, the adult, organization, educational finance, and public relations. Through its national conventions, its various councils and commissions, and its numerous publications, the NEA has played a role of major significance in furthering the cause of American education.

The twentieth century saw the rise and development of the teacher-union movement. Founded in 1916, the American Federation of Teachers enrolled slightly less than 3,000 members during the first year of its existence. Today its membership is estimated at something like 25,000. Generally speaking, the American Federation of Teachers has concerned itself with the extension and protection of teachers' rights. It has devoted itself especially to such matters as salaries, tenure, retirement, and the defense of academic freedom. An outspoken propagandist in favor of progressive social and labor programs, the American Federation of Teachers has lobbied vigorously, both nationally and locally, on behalf of a child labor amendment, federal aid to the schools, antidiscrimination measures, and so on.[22]

---

[21] There are seven commissions and councils: Educational Policies Commission, Legislative Commission, National Commission for the Defense of Democracy through Education, National Commission on Teacher Education and Professional Standards, National Commission on Safety Education, National Council of Education, and the National Council on Teacher Retirement. The leading publication of the NEA is the *Journal of the National Education Association,* which is published monthly during the school year. In addition the NEA has contributed significantly to educational writings through its bulletins and especially through its yearbooks. In 1945–46 the Association printed and distributed 376,519,658 pages of material.

[22] Another teachers' union, more recent in origin than the American Federation of Teachers, is a CIO affiliate. Though it has no great national strength, it is quite strong in the vicinity of New York City, where it claims a member-

Familiar to many Americans is the Parent-Teachers' Association, commonly known as the PTA. Organized in Washington in 1894, the movement was known as the National Congress of Mothers at first and was interested in "little children, the home, the school, and the community." In 1900 the body obtained a formal charter and became the National Congress of Parents and Teachers. PTA's operate locally and nationally and some of them have even crossed the frontier to participate in international programs. In 1940 about two million fathers, mothers, and teachers belonged to some 26,000 PTA's. At bottom the purpose of parent-teachers' organizations is to advance the welfare of the child through a better cooperation between home and school. Carried on in this spirit, the work of the PTA has served a magnificent cause. Occasionally, however, some local PTA, forgetting the limitations placed on its rights and powers, has sought to dictate policies and actions to the school authorities. Sometimes, too, a PTA has allowed its real reason for being to become obscured in a welter of social activities which, though pleasant for the participants, have essentially little to contribute to child welfare. All in all such lapses have been incidental, and to generalize from them would be to do a great injustice to the large majority of PTA members whose efforts on behalf of education have been of a high order.

In the United States, perhaps more than in any other land, philanthropy has played an immense part in the promotion of education. Indeed, the amount of money donated annually for this purpose runs into more than a quarter billion dollars. The administration of these huge sums has become

---

ship of some 7,000 members. As for the membership of the AFT, this has fluctuated a good deal. Its high point came in 1941 when it had some 35,000 members.

Amid the wide demoralization among American teachers in the years following the second World War, an increasing number of teachers began to turn to teachers' unions as an effective means of obtaining a satisfactory settlement of some of their grievances. In contrast to some of the older professional organizations, teachers' unions endorse the strike as a weapon to secure the teachers' goals.

the special province of endowed foundations [23] which are usually directed by a self-perpetuating board of trustees with the power of deciding how the income, and sometimes part of the principal, of a given fund shall be spent. Generally speaking, foundations have concerned themselves largely with privately controlled education rather than with the public variety, and with the college, university, and professional school, rather than with the lower educational levels. Flexner's study of America's medical education was made possible with foundation money. On the lower academic level, foundation funds made possible the experimental work of the Lincoln School and the Eight Year Study, both of which had immense implications for public as well as private education. Occasionally the findings of a foundation investigation have attracted the public eye. Such, for example, was the case a number of years ago when the Carnegie Foundation published its study of intercollegiate athletics. The fact that this investigation revealed some highly dubious practices not only aroused the public interest, but in a number of colleges even brought forth some reform in the conduct of their athletic programs. All in all, endowed foundations have served American education most usefully, facilitating the conduct of studies and researches which ordinarily could not have been financed out of the public treasury, and the results of which have helped to give no little direction to the American educational system.

6. Our articulated organization

Of the larger nations the United States was the first country to provide free, universal education through the elementary and secondary schools. Even today few nations have an

---

[23] Among some of the foundations are The American Foundation, The American Foundation for Mental Hygiene, the Barnes Foundation, the Carnegie Foundation for the Advancement of Teaching, the William T. Carter Child Helping Foundation, the Commonwealth Fund, the John Simon Guggenheim Memorial Foundation, etc. For a full list see *American Foundations for Social Welfare,* compiled by the Russell Sage Foundation Library, New York.

educational ladder comparable to that of the United States, a scheme in which every unit is articulated to that above and below it, and in which all levels are integrated in a continuous educational program from the lowest class to the highest.[24] Historically the idea of the educational ladder goes back at least to the seventeenth century to the educational thinking of Comenius. In practice, however, the ladder system was evolved in the United States in the early part of the nineteenth century. By the end of the first decade of the twentieth century, the scheme was arranged as follows:

High School	Grades 9–10
Grammar Grades	Grades 7– 8
Intermediate Grades	Grades 4– 6
Primary Grades	Grades 1– 3

Today one still hears of *primary* and *intermediate* grades, but the term *grammar* grades is vanishing. Since the rise of the junior high school, the term *secondary education* seems to be increasingly favored to indicate the high school; and the term *elementary education* is replacing the *grades*. Before 1910 the elementary school was generally an eight-year institution, and was followed by a four-year high school. This is known as an 8–4 system. About 1910 the so-called 6–3–3 system was introduced whereby the elementary school was shortened, and the secondary school extended downward to include what were once known as the grammar grades, the seventh and eighth grades of the eight-year elementary school.

The seventh, eighth, and ninth grades now became the junior high school, and the following three grades comprised the senior high school. In some communities the reorganization combined the junior-senior high school, a scheme generally referred to as the 6–6 plan. The next change in the

[24] Before World War II, Soviet Russia was the only large European nation with an articulated school system comparable to that of the United States. However, if and when the Education Act of 1944 is fully carried out, England, too, will boast of an educational ladder. By the proposed Langevin Reform France also is to have a system of articulated schools. See p. 190 and p. 221.

A Age	B Year	C Before Re-organi-zation	D Re-organization including Junior High School	E Re-organization including Junior College	F Projected Re-organization of the Future	G
25						H
24		PROFES-				I
23		SIONAL	PROFESSIONAL	PROFESSIONAL	PROFESSIONAL	G
22						H
21	Sr.	**4**		**2** COLL.		E
20	Jr.					R
19	So.	COLLEGE	COLLEGE	**2** JUNIOR COLL.	TECHNI-CAL VOCATION-AL PART TIME	**4** COLLEGE / S E C O N D A R Y
18	Fr.					
17	12	**4**	**3** S.H.S.	**3** S.H.S.		
16	11		**6**	**6**	TIME	COLLEGE
15	10	HIGH			**4**	
14	9	SCHOOL	**3**	**3**	HIGH SCHOOL	
13	8		SECOND-ARY	SECOND-ARY		
12	7		J.H.S.	J.H.S.		
11	6	**8**				E
10	5		**6**	**6**	**6**	L E M E N T A R Y
9	4					
8	3					
7	2	GRADES	ELEMENTARY	ELEMENTARY	ELEMENTARY	
6	1					
5	Kg.	Kg.	KINDERGARTEN	KINDERGARTEN	KINDERGARTEN	

Fig. 5. Chart Showing Changes in Organization of the Schools of the United States. (From Myers and Williams, *Education in a Democracy.* Copyright by Prentice-Hall, Inc., 1937.)

American schools introduced the junior college into the public school system on the basis of a 6–3–3–2 or a 6–6–2 plan.

7. Religion and the public school

The child of the Reformation, early American education had its beginnings for the most part in religion. Often the servant of the church, the colonial school devoted itself to teaching not only the usual three R's, but also religion and morals, the singing of psalms, and the practice of church worship. In such a religious culture parochial schools naturally stood high in popular esteem; so warmly were they regarded that in some places they were even favored with grants from the public funds. However, as the American culture shifted to more material acres, the American school, reflecting the change, moved with it from a sectarian to a secular bias. Signs of the new order were evident even before the end of the eighteenth century; for it was in 1792 that New Hampshire invested its constitution with a provision which forbade public sectarian instruction.

Reflecting the principle of the separation of church and state, the twentieth century American public school is secular and does not teach religion. There is no unanimity among the states as to what constitutes religious instruction, however. Is reading Holy Writ in the public school, for example, an act involving religious teaching and hence contrary to the principles of secularized schooling? A few states say that it is and have taken measures against it. With equal assurance, however, others have asserted the contrary. Still others have banned certain portions of the Sacred Writ, while endorsing others. Finally, there are some states—about a dozen—where the Bible has been made required reading.[25] The question of

---

[25] Delaware and New Jersey require as a minimum the reading of five verses from the Bible; Pennsylvania and Tennessee demand ten; Idaho, from twelve to twenty; and Georgia, at least an entire chapter. In the public schools of New Jersey and the District of Columbia the Lord's Prayer must be recited daily. In Idaho "the standard American version of the Bible" must be used; in New Jersey all readings must be selected from the Old Testament.

what is permissible under the secular principle seems at times a bit enigmatic and has evoked a stream of contradictory responses. Some states, for example, have specifically forbidden teachers from wearing religious robes while working in the public schools; others have not only accorded it legal sanction, but have even permitted members of religious orders to teach in the public schools. Some localities have questioned the legality of the use of the Lord's Prayer in the public school and have banished it from the premises; others have forbidden the singing of Christmas songs of religious nature; and some have banned the performance of Christmas playlets depicting the nativity.

Concerning the matter of religious instruction the churches are by no means in accord. The Roman Catholic Church quite naturally is for it. Indeed, in harmony with its traditional conception of education, it holds that the very essence of all education is, and must be, religion; and that its control is the historic and indisputable right of the Church. In practice, however, the Church has recognized that these claims are not applicable to the non-Catholic.

Among Jews and Protestants several views are espoused. Some favor the complete separation of church and state. In a nation of so many diverse religious affiliations, they feel that this is necessary if the principles of democracy are to be upheld. To a good many Protestants, however, such a rigid split between church and state is disquieting. To bridge the gap they have supported the idea of offering some form of nonsectarian religious instruction in the public school. Their argument concentrates on the point that American culture in its origin was substantially of Christian making; and in this common religious background, so they assert, we have the basis of nonsectarian religious instruction. Its most common form has been that of reading the Bible in the schools. Found in the main in states which are predominantly Protestant,

Rivlin, H. N. and Schueler, H., Editors, *Encyclopedia of Modern Education*, p. 677. New York: Philosophical Library, 1943.

Bible reading in such cases has generally employed a Protestant Bible, a practice which has been decried by zealous non-Protestants as one which is fundamentally sectarian and hence unacceptable.

A practice which appears palatable to all faiths, and one which has made persistent progress during the last quarter century, is that of "releasing" pupils during certain periods of the school day so that they may obtain religious instruction in their faith. Such instruction is generally imparted off the school premises and is conducted under the churches' auspices, with the schools providing attendance checkups and other active cooperation. All in all, it has been figured, about 2,000,000 children in more than 2,000 communities were attending some kind of religious classes during school hours in 1947.[26]

Released time, however, has not been without opposition. Its opponents have lashed out against it on the ground that it violated the principle of separation of church and state; that it discriminated against those children whose parents did not want them to have religious instruction; and that it caused such youngsters a feeling of embarrassment and inferiority when others were excused from their regular classes. To counteract these objections some religious leaders have supported what is known as "dismissed time." Under this scheme children are simply dismissed for one period a week with no school checkup to ascertain whether they actually attend classes in religion or not.

The skirmishes between those favoring religious instruction and those opposed to it have resulted in numerous legal battles, and a few of them have even ended in the chambers of the United States Supreme Court. Such was the case of Mrs. Vashti McCollum versus the Board of Education of

---

[26] During 1947 in New York City some 111,600 pupils were excused for a half-hour every week to go to church classes. In Chicago the number was around 25,000.

Champaign, Illinois. In the Champaign plan the school board cooperated with the local Church Council on Religious Education by making available the needed facilities. The Council, for its part, provided outside teachers representing the Jewish, Catholic, and Protestant faiths. With the parents' consent a child could attend classes taught by any of these groups. Mrs. McCollum, an avowed atheist, brought suit against the Champaign school board on the ground that its plan of religious education discriminated against her child. Declaring that she did not want her son to receive religious instruction, Mrs. McCollum contended that when he did not attend the classes he was made conspicuous and subjected to ridicule by other pupils; consequently she asked the Illinois courts to put an end to the whole project as a violation of the historic concept of separation of church and state. When the jurists ruled against her, Mrs. McCollum appealed to the United States Supreme Court which, in March, 1948, overruled the state court's action by an 8-1 decision. Speaking for the majority, Justice Hugo Black said the Champaign practice had "beyond all question" been using tax-established and tax-supported schools "to aid religious groups to spread their faith." "It falls," he added, "squarely under the ban of the First Amendment." This, the Justice elucidated, "rests upon the premise that both religion and government can best work to achieve their lofty aims if each is left free from the other within its respective sphere."

Analyzing the court's decision one finds that it rests on three fundamental points: (1) the Champaign public school buildings were used for religious purposes; (2) the school authorities cooperated in the program; and (3) the compulsory school system was used to assist religious sects in carrying out their program of instruction. Under the high court's ruling any plan of religious instruction involving any of these points becomes unconstitutional. In fact, Justice Stanley F. Reed, in dissent from the majority finding, felt that the decision "threw into doubt all forms of religious instruction connected in any way with school systems." [27]

Private and parochial schools. The needs of those children whose parents believe that religion is the indispensable basis of morality and knowledge cannot, of course, be adequately met in the secular school. To cater to such special desires churches and religious groups have established their own schools. Several million children attend them—in fact, it has been estimated that slightly more than one-tenth of America's school population is enrolled in private and parochial schools. Of these, the great majority—more than 90%—is of the Roman Catholic faith.[28] Stressing religion, such schools usually offer courses in the Bible, and history, practices, and traditions of the particular church in addition to the subjects usually found in the public school.

Although nonpublic schools are subject to certain state controls, their legal status has the sanction of the courts. The rights of the state in the realm of private education, as well as the limitations of its powers, rest largely on the decision handed down by the United States Supreme Court in 1925 in the celebrated Oregon Case. Three years earlier the state of Oregon had enacted a statute which required every child between the ages of eight and sixteen to attend public school. To test the constitutionality of the law two private institutions brought suit. When the case came before the Supreme Court, the Oregon statute was invalidated on the ground that it had violated the due-process-of-law clause of the Constitution.[29] Affirming the principle, moreover, that

---

[27] Legal experts of the National Education Association suggested that the system of "dismissed time" might turn out to be the only fully constitutional technique of religious instruction for public school children.

[28] *The Official Catholic Directory, 1947.* New York: P. J. Kenedy & Sons, 1947, cites the following figures: Diocesan and parochial high schools, 1,653; students, 315,424; private high schools, 778, students, 187,543; parochial elementary schools: 7,637, students, 2,115,006; private elementary schools, 528, students: 71,559.

[29] The Court held that the business and property of the private schools were "threatened with destruction through unwarranted compulsion" which the state was endeavoring to exert.

the child was the creature of his parents rather than of the state, the court declared that the Oregon law unduly interfered "with the liberty of parents and guardians to direct the upbringing and education of children under their control. . . ." "The fundamental theory of liberty," the court went on to state, "upon which all governments of this Union repose excludes any general power of the state to standardize its children by forcing them to accept instruction from public teachers only." As for the rights of the state in the education of its citizens, the court declared that it was within the province of the state to require all children to be educated; and that in order to ascertain whether or not minimum educational requirements were being met, the state might supervise and inspect all schools, private and parochial as well as public.

The use of public funds in education. Another question which has embroiled the partisans of state and church in volcanic controversy relates to the use of public funds for education. Historically, the question erupted violently in various states in the nineteenth century when the process of secularizing the schools was in full swing. In accordance with the principle of keeping state and church separate, most states at that time enacted legislation outlawing, or drastically restricting, the use of public moneys for sectarian purposes.[30] To the present, most churches have been cold to this principle and have worked assiduously to effect its end, or at least to bring about some benevolent modification. Insisting that religion and education are inseparable, they have taken the position that inasmuch as the public school may not teach religion, they are obliged to support a dual system of schools: the public schools by virtue of the taxes they pay and the church schools to which they send their children. This, they maintain, is a form of double taxation and is unjust to them; for, so they argue, the civic and social objectives of the church

---

[30] Maine is a notable exception. Borrowing the phraseology of statutes in force in its mother state of Massachusetts, Maine in 1820 did not forbid the public support of private schools, a condition which still prevails.

schools are the same as those of the public schools, and the state can achieve its ends quite as well through the parochial schools as through the public schools.

To remedy this situation they have proposed the allocation of public funds to support the church schools, at least as far as the secular phases of their work are concerned. While this question has remained largely in the realm of controversy, it has frequently penetrated into the sphere of practical reality. Thus, there have been legal rulings and court decisions authorizing the expenditure of public funds for health services for children attending church schools, the argument being that since health services must be regarded as apart from education, the restricting constitutional clauses do not apply. In other cases courts have upheld the use of public moneys for the transportation of children to parochial schools.

The question of whether or not public moneys should be made available to private and parochial schools has made its appearance in Washington, where, just as in the states, it has plagued the lawmakers no little. Senator Taft's bill for federal aid to education, which was passed by the Senate in 1948, encountered tempestuous debate when it came to this particular issue. The bill originally introduced by Senator Aiken of Vermont would have permitted all states to apply the federal moneys to parochial schools.[31] However, in its final form the bill allowed federal funds to be expended on private and parochial schools only in those states which already permitted such expenditures of state funds. Whether this conforms to the letter, if not the spirit, of the law as expressed in the decision of the United States Supreme Court in the Champaign Case (1948) in the sense that it keeps "the wall between Church and State . . . high and impregnable" is of course debatable. Its ultimate disposition will probably rest once more with our highest court.

---

[31] Subsequently Senator McMahon of Connecticut sought vainly to amend the Taft bill to the same effect.

8. Elementary education

Although the child's compulsory schooling does not begin until he is old enough to enter the first grade of the elementary school, it has been increasingly felt that some form of pre-elementary education, either in the form of the kindergarten or of nursery school, has distinct advantages. Historically, of course, both these institutions constitute an old and familiar chapter in the story of education.[32] The kindergarten, transplanted from Germany in the nineteenth century, took firm root in our country and by 1940 there were some 625,000 children attending public kindergartens and some 40,000 more in private ones. The nursery school was received less enthusiastically. In fact, even in the early twenties there was still considerable disagreement among educators as to its values. Those favoring it hailed its social, psychological, and health advantages; those opposed to it asserted that the school took the child from the family at too early an age and that it institutionalized him prematurely. In the early thirties, while the nation was rocking from the depression, the nursery school movement gathered force, and, with the help of federal money, schools designed for two- and three-year-olds were established under the auspices of the New Deal in various parts of the country. Most of them, of course, were of an emergency nature; nevertheless, by 1939, they had

---

[32] The educational significance of the period of early childhood was first called to our attention in an important way by the seventeenth century John Amos Comenius. Near the end of the eighteenth century (1790) Robert Owen established an "infant school" in connection with his cotton mills in New Lanark, Scotland. But these schools were very different from the modern nursery school. Not only did they include children as old as seven, but they also included some intellectual content in their teaching. In France it was Jean Oberlin who established the first school for young children in 1769. Notable modern pioneers in the movement were Grace Owen and Margaret Macmillan, who organized a nursery school in the poor districts of London and Manchester. In 1920 specialists from Miss Macmillan's school introduced similar work at Teachers College, Columbia University. A year earlier Harriet Johnson had founded her Nursery School in New York. A typical nursery school of the modern variety, the Johnson school was also partly experimental in nature. For the kindergarten see p. 25. For Montessori's work in this field of education see p. 109.

enrolled some 300,000 children. The great response to the movement prompted some educators to propose its continuation and extension as a permanent feature of our public school system.

As one might expect, the majority of nursery schools and kindergartens are located in cities. Their rise in popularity has been due in a large measure to the industrial nature of our twentieth century culture in which more and more mothers have shifted their main activities from the home to business and the factory. Once a luxury for the children of the well-to-do, the nursery school, under the impact of industrialization, became a haven where the working mother could leave her child without worry while she was away from home. Today these reasons for being are no longer of prime importance. Sociologically the preschool is today endorsed as a place where a child, associated with children of his own age, shares their interests and experiences and thus gets his first practical lessons in social behavior. Psychologists have declared that inasmuch as many of the mental and nervous disorders of adults spring from unfortunate conditions which surround the child during his early formative years, an institutional organization such as the nursery school can not only discover such undesirable factors, but also counteract them. The modern nursery school, moreover, is much more than a place for small children. Interested in the welfare of the child in the broadest possible sense, it concerns itself also with the problems of maternity care and parental education.

If the American public school is the foundation of its democracy, then the elementary school is its cornerstone. Not only is the elementary school the cradle of democracy, but it continues to teach the basic skills, the celebrated three R's, without which intelligent citizenship would be impossible. In teaching these fundamental subjects the elementary school in recent years has tended to shift its emphasis. Oral reading, for example, has given way to silent reading. Instead of reading and re-reading a single reader, moreover, the pupil reads widely, sometimes including in his reading a dozen books or so. Formal grammar has been superseded by emphasis on the development of correct written and oral speech habits. In handwriting the prime goal is legibility rather than the formation of perfect letters or the adherence to some particular system of penmanship such as the Palmer or Spencerian scheme. Up-to-date schools, moreover, do not compel their left-handed writers to use their right hands. Spelling has been harnessed to the everyday, practical vocabulary. In arithmetic the emphasis is first on the social and practical values. The old idea of arithmetic as an aid to mental discipline is no longer in good standing. In fact, many authorities have begun to doubt the advisability of teaching any arithmetic formally before the seventh grade.

The curriculum of the modern elementary school is, of course, not restricted to the three R's. Ever since the days of Herbart it has been gradually enlarged. First came such subjects as history and geography and literature. Could the schoolmaster of 1776 visit a contemporary American elementary school he would find that the three R's which he strove so laboriously to impart have been joined by a host of companions. The roster of what is taught in the up-to-date elementary school would surely amaze him. For on it he would discern not only the familiar quartet of reading, writing, spelling, and arithmetic, but also such items as citizenship, the social studies of history, geography, and civics, literature, physical training, health and hygiene, safety, arts and crafts, music, and shopwork. The methods he employed he would still find here and there. But in much greater evidence would be procedures he never knew. Could such old-timers as Comenius and Pestalozzi revisit us, how astonished they would be by the use we make of visual aids, the beautifully illustrated textbooks, the posters, charts, and drawings—yes, even the words themselves have been garbed in letters so alluring as to bewitch the eye.[33] What would they

---

[33] John Amos Comenius (1592–1670), a Moravian educator and pastor, has

say could they observe how we have put their theory of learning through the senses to use in the film which by the mere pressing of a button unveils before the pupils' eyes the great treasures of mankind everywhere, and does it all so magnificently as to make one forget that this, after all, is just a vicarious experience!

Even the duration of elementary education has undergone a change. Though slightly more than half the nation's lower schools are still on an eight-year basis, the length of the elementary school period is now generally looked upon as six years. The number of years is of course not the all-important factor; increasingly the tendency has been to recognize goals in the form of accomplishments. The pupil's actual growth and development is accordingly more significant than his grade placement.

9. Secondary education

a. **Historical development.** When, in 1635, the first American secondary school—the Boston Latin School—was founded, its purpose was relatively simple. Like its prototype in England, it sought to impart the ancient classics to youths who, for the most part, were destined for the ministry. We know very little about the school's early history. We do know, however, that in 1642 there was a general meeting of Boston's richer inhabitants and that subscriptions were taken "towards the maintenance of a free school master for the youth with us." Before long public maintenance was provided and the school continued on a career which has extended to the present. The kind of education offered by the Boston Latin School became the model for our early colonial secondary schools, the so-called grammar schools. Established

---

earned a high place for himself in education's Hall of Fame. Styled sometimes as the "first great modern educator," Comenius stressed the principles inherent in sense realism. Among his many writings on education was his illustrated Latin text, the *Orbis Pictus*. Although this was not the first illustrated text, as is sometimes claimed, it was, nevertheless, the first illustrated schoolbook of far-reaching significance.

by the more populous towns under colonial law, they were theoretically free though, except in the case of the poorest students, they did charge fees. They were never large; indeed, most of them were staffed by one or two teachers. Since most of their pupils expected to enter college, they concentrated on Latin and Greek, which were then the indispensable keys for college admission. Moreover, since their ultimate mission was to prepare their protégés for positions in the church or the state, the schools were impregnated with a strong religious spirit.

As the emphasis in our culture shifted to more material spheres, especially toward trade and manufacturing, the classical disciplines lost some of their appeal. Latin and Greek, it is true, continued in the curriculum since they were necessary for college. On the other hand, there was a perceptible demand for courses which might be more practically related to the everyday world, and which would be of use especially to such youngsters who had no intention of going to college. Benjamin Franklin reflected this viewpoint when he proposed education along these lines for the youth in Pennsylvania. "It would be well," he argued, "for them to be taught everything that is useful and everything that is ornamental. But art is long and their time is short. It is therefore proposed that they learn those things that are likely to be *most useful* and *most ornamental;* regard being had for the several professions for which they are intended." [34] In 1751 Franklin's proposals came to partial fruit in the establishment in Phila-

---

[34] "All intended for divinity," Franklin went on to say, "should be taught the Latin and Greek; for physic, the Latin, Greek and French; for law, the Latin and French; merchants, the French, German and Spanish; and though all should not be compelled to learn Latin, Greek, or the modern foreign languages, yet none that have an ardent desire to learn them should be refused; their English, arithmetic, and other studies absolutely necessary, being at the same time not neglected." Franklin, Benjamin, *Proposals Related to the Education of Youth in Pennsylvania,* reprinted in Woody, T., *Educational Views of Benjamin Franklin,* pp. 158, 173. New York: McGraw-Hill Book Company, Inc., 1931.

delphia of a new kind of secondary school known as the academy.

Born in the spirit of dissent, the new institution at first was less under the spell of the college than the older grammar schools had been. The classics, of course, had to be taught, for to potential college students they were "useful as well as ornamental." But the academies also taught English, science, geography, and many other nonclassical subjects; and because they responded so satisfactorily to the needs and demands of the people, they soon put the traditional grammar schools into the background. By the outbreak of the Revolution their number had increased substantially, and by 1830 some 500 academies graced the land. Meanwhile their offerings had continued to increase. In 1837, for example, a curricular inventory of the subjects taught by New York's academies included not only the ancient Greek, Roman, and Hebrew languages, but the modern ones as well, besides English in all its aspects from grammar to orthography and pronunciation, to rhetoric, composition, reading, and literature. In addition, the list included the following:

arithmetic, algebra, architecture, astronomy, botany, bookkeeping, Biblical antiquities, biography, chemistry, conic sections, constitution of the United States, constitution of New York, elements of criticism, declamation, drawing, dialing, evidences of Christianity, embroidery, civil engineering, extemporaneous speaking, geography, physical geography, geology, plane geometry, analytic geometry, Grecian antiquities, general history, history of the United States, history of New York, law, logic, leveling, logarithms, vocal music, instrumental music, mapping, mensuration, mineralogy, mythology, natural history, navigation, nautical astronomy, natural theology, natural philosophy, moral philosophy, intellectual philosophy, penmanship, political economy, painting, perspective, physiology, Roman antiquities, stenography, statistics, surveying, topography, technology, and the principles of teaching.

Not only did the academies strike a blow for a broader culture which might be of some direct use in one's daily life, but they believed that this practical kind of secondary education should be open to all classes. Most of them, moreover, admitted girls as well as boys. In this respect they were far more liberal than their classical predecessors which, nurtured in the Reformation, conceded that girls, having souls, needed to become literate to read Holy Writ, but beyond that their intellectual needs were at an end. With all their democratic preachments, however, the academies were private schools, supported by fees, subscriptions, and endowments. Therefore they were necessarily selective, and since they were operated as private enterprises, they entered into no organic liaison with the public elementary schools.

The first public high school was established in Boston in 1821.[35] Four years later New York followed suit with a High School for Boys, and in 1826 one for girls.[36] Springing from a culture which differed vastly from the early colonial and pre-Revolutionary civilizations, the new school reflected the rising American democracy, its trade and manufacturing interests, its new middle classes. To the unfolding demands of the new order neither the grammar schools, with their sights on the college, nor the academies, with their expensive tuition fees, were suited. What was wanted was a school which would be free and under public control and which, at the same time, would offer courses akin to those found in the academy. Such an institution the high school started out to be. Its growth at the outset was slow; indeed, it was not until after the Civil War that the battle for free public secondary education emerged victorious, a triumph which was bolstered by the decision rendered by the courts in the Kalamazoo Case. In the course of time, however, the high school shed its original purpose of catering mainly to those who had no desire to go to college. Indeed, it was not long ere the free schools succumbed to the lure of college preparation. In the end the high school which came forth possessed the functions of both the grammar school and the academy. In the guise of the

---

[35] Known originally as the English Classical School, in 1824 the school became the English High School. Historically, this marks the first use of the term "high school."

[36] These schools were discontinued in 1831.

former it stressed the subjects which prepared for college; in
that of the latter it emphasized a cultural and practical course
of study.

The fact that college preparation became one of the functions of the American high school was not without significance.
Asserting that what was good preparation for college work
was likewise good preparation for life, the colleges exerted
powerful pressure in favor of the college preparatory course.
Thus conceived, the primary function of secondary education
became the training of the mind. It is true that after the
middle of the nineteenth century new degrees began to be
offered to compete with the B.A., then the hallmark of a
classical education. The new degrees afforded high schools a
little more leeway in their precollegiate offerings, enabling
them to introduce a number of new courses as electives. In
any case, however, it was what the college would accept for
entrance credit that shaped the academic destiny of the bulk
of the high school population. Not until the twentieth century, after the American high school had developed a social
philosophy which was clearly its own and the psychologists
had exploded the validity of the theory of mental discipline,
was the high school able to free itself from the grip of the
college.

From Europe the American secondary school had inherited
the tradition of exclusiveness. As originally designed, the
grammar school was for a social and intellectual élite. The
academy, although opening its doors to all classes, was nonetheless private. Despite the impact of America's emerging
democracy and the effects of the industrial revolution, the
notion that the high school was the people's school and that it
should serve all manner of men regardless of status grew very
slowly. In fact, as late as 1893 the Committee of Ten in its
Report on Secondary School Studies declared that the high
school should be for "that small proportion of all the children
in the country—a proportion small in number, but very important to the welfare of the nation—who show themselves

able to profit by an education prolonged to the eighteenth year, and whose parents are able to support them while they remain at school." [37]   Although this view still lingers in scattered nooks and crannies, it is no longer of reputable standing. Generally speaking, in America secondary education is no longer regarded as a privilege, but as a right.   In those states where compulsory schooling extends to the age of sixteen, attendance at the high school, or at least the junior high school, is virtually inevitable.

At the turn of the century America's public high schools enrolled some 500,000 pupils; a half century later the figure had risen to more than 5,500,000.   A number of factors had contributed to this remarkable rise as, for example, the increase in the national wealth, a rising standard of living, the difficulty experienced by untrained and unskilled youths in getting employment, and the great economic value of a high school education.   Of no little consequence also was the fact that in the twentieth century the high school at last discarded the idea of mental discipline.   As a result of public pressure the high school has been harnessed to the multiple needs of life in a democracy.   Where the traditional high school stressed the requirements of an intellectual élite, the modern counterpart seeks an education which is much more comprehensive, which contributes to health, which develops a command of the fundamental processes, worthy home membership, vocation, citizenship, the worthy use of leisure time, and ethical character.[38]   Under the conditions of our contemporary culture the American high school no longer endeavors primarily to prepare its pupils for college.   In fact, where in 1900 some 75 per cent of the nation's high school graduates entered college, today only some 25 per cent continue their studies in the institutions of higher learning.

The high school which, at the beginning of the century,

[37] *Report of the Committee of Ten on Secondary School Studies,* p. 51. New York: American Book Company, 1894.

[38] These are the well-known Seven Cardinal Principles of Secondary Education as promulgated in 1918 by the Commission of Secondary Education.

stressed the academic subjects and threw a few crumbs to music, drawing, and gymnastics, and occasionally to shorthand, typing, and bookkeeping, has become much more varied and generous in its offerings. Although high schools continue, of course, to teach the subjects which colleges accept for entrance credit, yet to meet the extensive and diverse needs of the great majority of their students the secondary schools have gone far beyond the old academic frontier. Focusing on the functional requirements of their young charges, high schools have introduced instruction in fields which not so long ago would have been summarily rejected as having little or no connection with secondary education. Thus, as one scrutinizes the curricula of high schools throughout the nation, one will find not only the older and familiar disciplines, but also courses in automobile driving, aviation, in personal problems and human relations, in mental and personal hygiene, in home nursing, in playwriting, dramatics, and radio, and in the practical, everyday phases of democratic living. One will find attention bestowed upon the great occupations of men and women: agriculture, industry, business, homemaking, the arts in all their aspects, and the applied sciences. The up-to-date high school, where facilities and budgets permit, will have forges as well as labs, a kitchen, nursery, and sewing room as well as a music and an art room, and a gymnasium, an auditorium, a playing field in addition to the usual array of classrooms.

There has been a tendency of recent years for some of our high schools to get away from the highly specialized subject fields and to merge related areas. Biology and the physical sciences have been fused into general science; similarly, history, civics, geography, and sociology have become the social studies; and arithmetic, algebra, and geometry have developed into general mathematics.

It is true, of course, that the practical and vocational slant of the modern high school has received sharp raps from critics, especially from upholders of the traditional subject-matter curriculum, and their allies who continue to insist that the prime function of the high school should be the training of the mind or the preservation of the cultural heritage. Perhaps a common ground between the old and the new may be found in time to come in the recommendations that have been put forth by some of our colleges in favor of a "general education." The most publicized of these has been the report of the Harvard committee, published in 1946 as *General Education in a Free Society.*[39] General education, says the Harvard report, "has somewhat the meaning of a liberal education." It is "that part of a student's whole education which looks first of all to his life as a responsible human being and a citizen." With this in view Harvard has offered the high schools a basic plan which, so it is hoped, will provide the student with a fair measure of general education before he gets to college or begins to specialize vocationally. Eight basic units—three in English, three in science, three in mathematics, two in the social studies—would be a fundamental part of the four-year high school program. Specialization, moreover, would be in the form of an extension of one of these avenues.

Among the schools of the world those of America have long stood out for their student activities. Their games and sports, their varied club activities, the social and recreational programs carried on during and after school hours invariably amaze the visitor from abroad. Once assigned only a small and modest part in the school's educational program, and at times even suspected of being inimical to the interests of the intellect, student activities have come into lush and vigorous bloom. Not only have they been recognized as an important phase of everyone's education, but great effort has gone into stimulating and promoting their development in sound and effective programs. Thus, what was once a sideline of education has now become a partner; and some schools, recognizing the educational legitimacy of student activities, have

[39] Harvard University Press.

even set aside definite periods in the daily schedule for club meetings and other noncurricular doings. Obviously, the carrying out of such a program demands no little wisdom from teachers. How to stimulate and provide desirable activities, how to guide and direct the participating children, and above all how to avoid being paternalistic and to insure that student activities really reflect the wishes and expressions of the children themselves and not those of the faculty—these are no light problems. Indeed, the person who is qualified to solve them is eagerly sought; and just as schools once looked for specialists in French and music and gymnastics, they now seek teachers who are especially competent in giving leadership in the sphere of student activities.

b. **The junior high school.** The American high school emerged from the nineteenth century with a twofold purpose: it served, on the one hand, as a link between the elementary school and the college; on the other hand, it also offered an opportunity for advanced elementary education of a general nature as well as some kind of industrial and commercial training. Before 1910 pupils between fourteen and eighteen years of age pursuing either of these goals were generally regarded as high school students. Since then, however, this term has become much more inclusive.

As early as 1888 President Eliot of Harvard had suggested the desirability of reorganizing the secondary school, and some cities, like Springfield, Massachusetts, had even before that time undertaken a partial reorganization. In the last decade of the nineteenth century, reports issued by the Committee of Ten (1893) and the Committee on College Entrance Requirements (1899) suggested a reorganization of elementary and secondary education into six-year periods. About 1910 the new unit came into being in Columbus, Ohio, and Los Angeles and Berkeley, California. However, there is some doubt as to where the idea originated. Since then the movement has gained considerable momentum, there being more than 2,300 junior high schools and something like 6,200 junior-senior high schools today.

Sometimes the junior high school consists of two grades, the seventh and the eighth; the more orthodox variety, however, is a three-year school extending from the seventh through the ninth years. The purposes of the junior high school are several. For one thing, there is its *exploratory* nature: general science and prevocational courses are frequently offered. Then there is the matter of *guidance*: frequently looked upon as the cornerstone of the junior high school, this seeks to help the pupil to find and realize his own possibilities and limitations. In addition, attempts are made to provide for the *individual differences* of the pupils, particular attention being given to the individual pupil's needs and interests. Finally, there is the matter of *socialization,* the trend being to stress the natural social tendencies of the adolescent.

The fact that the junior high school movement has spread is significant, for it reveals a trend toward a less academic interpretation of secondary education than that which prevailed in the conventional American high school. The general growth of secondary school attendance, together with the reorganization of the secondary school, has brought us to the place where we consider the secondary school as the school for all adolescents. The old subject specialism has been replaced in the newer secondary school by much broader motives. In this new school, youth is prepared to live in a complex world; and his preparation bestows attention on his health, his social, civic, and domestic efficiency, his vocational and economic adjustment, his leisure interests, and the development of a healthy view of life.

c. **Intermediate secondary education.** From the junior high school the pupil usually goes to the senior high school. This, like its predecessor, is a three-year school with grades ten, eleven, and twelve. Together with the six-year elementary school and the three-year junior high school, the senior high school forms part of the 6–3–3 system.

Despite the growth of the junior high school and its complement, the senior high school, the traditional four-year high school is still the prevailing type. Often its existence has been dictated by local conditions, such as the availability of buildings and other facilities, the economic status of the community, its social outlook, and so on. Sometimes, as in Illinois, the high school is administered by a separate board of education and has no connection with the elementary school district. In such a situation the 6–3–3 plan would obviously be impossible. But even where a high school is of the conventional four-year type, in its inner operation it need not be conventional. As far as its goals are concerned, its curriculum and methods, the spirit of its teachers and pupils, and the philosophy which guides them—in these vital matters the four-year high school may be as liberal and advanced as any of the newer types.

Some communities, especially the larger cities, have organized secondary schools of a specialized nature. In New York City one finds the High School of Music and Art and the Brooklyn High School of Automotive Trades, and in Miami, Florida, there is the Technical High School. In addition, there are the usual vocational and industrial schools.

d. **The junior college.** The junior high school was a movement to extend secondary education downward, and the junior college movement projected it upward. The idea of turning over the work of the first two college years to the high school was proclaimed as early as 1852 by Henry Tappan, of Michigan. In its essence, however, the junior college is a twentieth century development. Nor must it be thought of merely as the first two years of the usual college work. There are such junior colleges, it is true; but like the junior high school at its best, the junior college has developed features which are its own. As such it seeks to respond to the peculiar needs and problems of students who find themselves in what is regarded as a transitional period between the exploratory experiences of the secondary school and the more serious accompaniments of professional study or adjustment in the occupational world. There are several kinds of junior colleges, some being public or tax-supported institutions, others being private and often denominational.[40] Some are parts of larger universities, and others have been added to secondary schools. Originating in Illinois and Texas, the movement has made its greatest advance in the west and middle west. In the eastern states the movement progressed somewhat more slowly. During the depression a number of junior colleges were established under the auspices of the government's educational program. The years after the second World War witnessed a further spurt in the movement. Because of the great upward surge in their enrollments, due to the influx of men and women returning from the service, the existing colleges found themselves unable to meet all the demands put upon them. As a result many states and municipalities began to establish junior colleges. It is true, of course, that in many instances the newly created institutions were essentially of an emergency nature and were, in fact, nothing more than an abbreviated version of the orthodox four-year college. However, in a number of places, notably in Illinois and California, where the movement had previously been well established, the new schools were of the first order.

What are the arguments in favor of the junior college? There are several. In the first place, the advantages of two years of college work are extended at a relatively low cost to all high school graduates in the community. In many cases a student would find it too expensive to leave home for a college education; for him the junior college has been a boon. Then again, the transition from high school to college and its consequent adjustment is not so abrupt. Furthermore, the junior college has absorbed many adolescents who have not been able to find employment, and hence have found their postsecondary

---

[40] Publicly supported junior colleges may be supported by direct state appropriation for every pupil in average daily attendance, as in the case of California; or they may be supported through the general school levies, as in the case of Texas and some other states.

school adjustment extremely difficult. In many junior colleges, moreover, instruction has been of the highest order, being carried on by more experienced teachers than those found so often in the first and second years at some of the larger universities. Although it is possible for graduates from the junior college to continue their education on a higher level, for the great majority it is the end of formal learning. For this reason it has been urged that the junior college should devote itself more particularly to the development of curricula which are terminal in nature, but which are marked not only by subjects of a vocational and semiprofessional bias, but which also give adequate attention to general education of civic and social value.[41]

There are, of course, also some arguments against the junior college: it has increased the cost of public education, occasionally it has absorbed funds which should have gone to the furtherance of elementary and secondary education; moreover, it competes with the small college, and in some instances it would eliminate such institutions.

As we approach the midway mark of the century, the junior college is still in a state of flux. No longer, however, is it on the defensive. Growing visibly in strength, it has become in many places a definite part of the public school system. Its numbers have increased from slightly more than 200 in the early twenties to more than 600 in the early forties and during the same period its enrollment has grown from some 16,000 students to more than 236,000. Its right to support from the public treasury has been legally approved. When that right was challenged, as it was in 1930 in Asheville, North Carolina, the supreme court of that state held that the city had the right to tax itself to maintain a junior college out of the public school funds. In the majority of states the maintenance of

_____

[41] The longer period of secondary education provided by the unit extending from the junior high school through the college, a period of eight years, resembles the European practice of offering a long secondary school course.

public junior colleges has been sanctioned by special legislation.

10. Vocational education and guidance

The history of curricular development in the public schools
reveals a steady increase in the number of vocational and
quasi-vocational courses. From the early courses in accounting in the old academies and the commercial courses in the
public high schools, vocational education has grown in scope
to the many specialized courses found in such public high
schools as the Textile High School of New York City or the
Brooklyn Technical High School. Most up-to-date teachers'
colleges have given recognition to vocational education by
developing special curricula to meet the needs of teachers in
this particular field. Under the traditional secondary school
curriculum, with its neglect of manual and industrial activities,
the student's opportunity to discover himself and, through the
guidance of his teachers, to find his vocational place in society
did not exist. The old curriculum, at its best, was designed
for those youngsters who were eventually to enter business or
the professions; it was not organized for those children who
were destined for the trades or for technical work. The fact
that this need is today generally recognized is at least one
explanation for the growth of vocational education. Despite
the recognition of the general need of the various types of
vocational education, it was not until the second decade of
the present century that significant progress in the vocational
domain was made in the public schools. In 1913 Congress
authorized a Presidential Commission to investigate the
matter, and this brought to light the fact that the United
States lagged behind the other great industrial lands, particularly Germany, in vocational education. In 1917 the Smith-
Hughes Act created a Federal Board of Vocational Education
and authorized federal appropriations for vocational education. This act, incidentally, is the first example of legislation
whereby a federal agency received the right to accept or reject

state educational programs and to grant or withhold funds. The Smith-Hughes Act and several other Congressional enactments provided for appropriations to further the vocational rehabilitation of disabled civilians, for cooperation with the states in the promotion of special education for agriculture, industry, and the trades, and for the training of vocational teachers. Generally these Congressional appropriations have stipulated that the states must appropriate money to supplement the federal funds. The Smith-Hughes Act was followed by several other Congressional enactments, such as the George-Reed Act (1929), increasing the appropriations, and the George-Ellzey Act (1934) and the George-Deen Act (1936). More than doubling the amount of former federal appropriations to the states for the purpose of vocational education, the George-Deen Act discontinued the practice of requiring federal funds to be matched dollar for dollar by state and local funds. The new law, moreover, broadened the field to which federal help might be extended. Formerly only four fields— agriculture, trades and industry, home economics, and training of teachers in those fields—had been recognized, but the George-Deen Act included the fields of distribution, such as selling, and indirectly gave recognition to certain spheres of public service, such as the work of school janitors. The George-Barden Act, passed in 1946, introduced the idea of grants to be used for vocational guidance.

Another milestone in the history of vocational education was laid in 1938 when, in line with the program of national defense, Congress established the Civil Aeronautics Authority, which was designed to develop programs for the training of pilots. Two years later (1940) the government began to distribute funds through the United States Office of Education for the purpose of training defense workers in schools and colleges. In the course of the next five years this program provided vocational training to some 12,000,000 men and women at a cost of approximately $500,000,000.

Accompanying vocational education have been the rise and

growth of psychological and vocational tests and measurements. Today there are numerous special aptitude tests of all sorts. Vocational guidance in the public schools is still another development. Beginning in Boston in 1910 with the establishment of a bureau to advise on the choice of a vocation, the guidance program has since then undergone a somewhat uneven development. Some schools, for example, still have virtually no effective guidance program, whereas others have a most comprehensive program. In general, guidance is becoming increasingly recognized as an essential part of the modern public school, with the result that a number of states and cities have developed broad programs for vocational guidance.

Although vocational education has shown a magnificent development in this country during the twentieth century, the recent years have revealed the need for a vocational education capable of equipping the individual with a wider scope of activity, which will, at the same time, enable him to grasp the social implications of his work. No doubt the new economic and industrial readjustments have contributed to this broadening trend. In our rapidly changing industrial world vocational flexibility appears to be desirable. On the other hand, narrow vocational specialization seems less desirable, with the consequence that there is today a shift away from it. Some highly specialized vocational schools, like engineering schools, have begun to supplement the more conventional and technical subject matter with subject matter from the field of the social sciences. The same trend, incidentally, is beginning to manifest itself in the domain of teacher training, where state and municipal authorities appear to be favoring more cultural work and less professional work in the training of prospective teachers.

11. The preparation of teachers

The great diversities and variations which are so characteristic of American education are especially discernible in our divergent practices in the preparation of teachers. Here are reflected our regional differences, our multiform cultural backgrounds, our wide social and economic discrepancies, as well as our varying attitudes toward education. All kinds of institutions are engaged in the task of preparing teachers, institutions which vary from high school training classes and county normal schools to teachers' colleges and graduate schools of education. The wide variations that prevail in the realm of teacher education are due, however, not only to our divergent regional cultures, but also, in significant measure, to the historical evolution of the teacher training system.

Originally, when the preparation of teachers was given any attention at all, it was carried on in the academies and the liberal arts colleges. As such it was generally based on the assumption that teaching was essentially an art the successful pursuit of which depended mainly on the thorough mastery of one's subject. Hence the focus was on subject matter with little attention to teaching itself. However, when American education started to expand, institutions for the training of teachers began to be established in various places. These were not directly subjected to the influences which were shaping the rest of the school system. To begin with, because of the decentralized nature of our school system, the control and administration of the teacher training schools fell to local bodies, which naturally varied considerably in their basic philosophy. For another thing, because of the lack of secondary schools, the normal schools which came into being had to assume the double function of supplying not only a professional training but also an academic education. The result of these factors, as might be expected, was a wide divergence in the purposes, scope, and content as well as the quality of the work of these institutions. Still another factor which tended to contribute to the immense variation in the preparation of teachers was the lack of any general standards in certification. Not only did this vary from place to place, but in actual practice many states were reluctant to enforce whatever standards they may have had, with the result that many localities appointed their teachers on the basis of a very simple examination given by the local school board. Not until the twentieth century was there any forceful effort to bring order to this chaotic situation and to establish certain minimum requirements for the preparation of teaching.

The first normal school [42] in the United States was private and was established by a minister, Samuel R. Hall, in 1823 at Concord, Vermont. Soon thereafter, in 1827, James G. Carter founded a similar school in Lancaster, Massachusetts. The first state normal school was established in the same state at historic Lexington in 1839. By the middle of the century cities and counties had begun to establish normal schools. They appeared in all parts of the country, from Boston and St. Louis to Philadelphia and San Francisco; by the end of 1898 some 170 public normal schools had come into being.

Contributing to the early progress of teacher training in this country were a number of European influences, which came especially from Prussia and France.[43] Both these nations had reorganized and modernized their systems of teacher training and their work in this sphere caught the eye of some of our leading educators, men like Horace Mann, Calvin Stowe, Charles Brooks, and others. From Switzerland came still another influence, that of Pestalozzi, whose work and methods made an enthusiastic convert of Edward Sheldon who was instrumental in developing the Oswego Movement in teacher training. (See p. 404.)

In its initial stage the normal school was little more than a secondary school admitting students directly from the elementary school. Its low entrance requirement was often attractive to students whose qualifications for teaching were

---

[42] The term "normal" came to us from the French. It means a model or a rule; hence, a normal school suggests a school which imparts rules.

[43] The translation from the French of Victor Cousin's *Report on Public Instruction in Prussia* (1834) obtained a wide circulation in the United States and was of more than ordinary influence in spurring the interest in teacher training.

at best dubious.[44] Moreover, since professional training was not generally necessary for certification, a great many teachers received no special training at all. The course of study in the normal school varied in duration, the most common requirement being two years, though many students failed to complete even this training. Since most of the students had had little more than an elementary education, the curriculum of the early normal school included both academic and professional studies. Often, however, the former entailed little more than a review of the common branches, and the latter, which consumed by far the greater portion of the student's time, comprised the principles, methods, and practice of education. In its earliest phases this sort of teacher preparation was essentially in the nature of training.

In the course of time, however, it became apparent that the adequate training of teachers required something more than the mastery of subject matter and the acquisition of a number of pedagogical tricks, and that an elementary education followed even by two years at a normal school was not enough to insure a high professional quality in our teachers. The first recognition of this situation came in 1857 when the Illinois State Normal University was established. After the Civil War the movement to raise the level of teacher preparation gained momentum. Several liberal arts colleges, notably New York University, Brown, and Michigan, instituted lectureships in what was then grandiloquently referred to as the "art of teaching" or "pedagogy." To the University of Michigan, however, goes the credit for establishing the first full-time chair in education (1879). Graduate instruction was offered by New York University in what was destined to become a graduate School of Pedagogy (1888). In the same year the New York College for Teachers, under the presidency of Nicholas Murray Butler, came into being. Four years later its name was changed to Teachers College, which it retained when

---

[44] As late as the early twentieth century the common requirement for admission to a normal school was only two years of high school work.

subsequently (1898) it became affiliated with Columbia University.[45]

The twofold function of the early normal school—of stressing the common school branches, and of putting a major emphasis on the professional courses—projected itself into the early twentieth century. Indeed, as late as 1910 the greater part of teacher training carried on in this country was still restricting itself academically to the subjects of the elementary school, and giving its major emphasis to the development of teaching techniques as derived from the so-called professional subjects.

By the end of the first quarter of the century, however, the preparation of teachers had assumed more and more the nature of a broad professional training. By 1920 the normal school and the training school were making their exit, their place being taken increasingly by the four-year teachers' college. When 1920 came to an end there were some 45 of these colleges; 20 years later the number had almost quadrupled. Not only were the old normal schools being edged into the historic past, but even old established colleges and universities began to readjust themselves to the newer trends. Thus, in 1922 New York University, converting its School of Pedagogy into the School of Education, instituted a change in its policy by which it sought to broaden the school's professional nature and thereby bring it in line with the modern stress in the preparation of teachers. In a similar way other institutions established centers of teacher education. Paralleling the movement was a tendency to establish standards for the preparation of teachers. In this the American Association of Teachers Colleges played an important part. (See p. 409.)

---

[45] By far the most influential of American teachers' colleges, Columbia University's Teachers College has attracted students from all over the world. The names of its faculty include some of the most eminent ones in American education. Oddly enough, when Teachers College first petitioned Columbia University to become affiliated with it, its request was rejected on the ground that ". . . there is no such subject as education, and, moreover, it would bring into the university women who are not wanted." Verily, the old order changeth and giveth place to the new!

Following the depression, when there was an oversupply of teachers, there was a perceptible movement in several states toward raising the minimum requirements for teacher certification for both elementary and secondary school teachers. Indeed, several states now require four years of preparation from their prospective elementary school teachers and a master's degree from those who desire to teach in the high school.

To the fathers of the normal school movement teacher education in its full modern regalia would appear strange. Not only has it been elevated from a secondary school to a college level, with an emphasis that has shifted from training more and more to professional education, but its work now embraces "preservice" as well as "in-service" stages. Replacing the older conception of training, teacher education has been broadened to include a general education, some specialization in one's teaching field, a professional education, and an introduction into the actual practice of teaching.

General education is intended to provide a rich academic background in organized knowledge and human activities. In a number of teachers' education institutions the trend toward general education has taken the form of general or integrated courses (1) in the subject-matter departments of the social, natural, and physical sciences and in the arts and humanities; and (2) in the departments of education themselves.

Subject-matter specialization, for its part, involves the process of becoming familiar with what one expects to teach. The trend has been to specialize not so much in individual subjects but rather in fields such as the social sciences, the humanities and language arts, the arts, the natural sciences and mathematics, and so on.

As for the prospective teacher's professional education, this centers on the so-called foundations of education, which generally include the philosophy or principles of education, the history of education, educational psychology, and educational sociology. Led by Columbia University's Teachers College, a small number of institutions have tried to fuse the essential elements of these subjects into a unified and integrated offering known as Educational Foundations.

What is probably the high point in the teacher's education comes when he is inducted into the actual practice of teaching. Known as the period of student teaching or practice teaching —in some regions it is known as cadet teaching—this generally comes in the latter part of the student's career. It is intended to provide experiences in the application of the theory which he has been studying in his other courses. Carried on under the watchful eyes of a supervising or critic teacher, student teaching has become a most important phase of the total process of becoming a teacher.

Although the twentieth century has witnessed great changes in the preparation of prospective teachers, it has also seen the development of new ways of stimulating the professional growth of teachers already in service. A potent factor in this sphere has been the newer approach to supervision. Once thought of primarily as an administrative check upon the teacher's classroom efficiency, supervision in recent years has moved in the direction of professional guidance. Today's superintendent, if he is not of the older vintage, no longer limits his field of operation to classroom teaching but deals rather with the entire field of learning and teaching. Less authoritarian than in the past, supervision at its best is today less concerned with criticism than with the stimulation of the teachers' professional development. The means of fostering professional growth among teachers in service are varied. One of the most common is further study, either in summer school or in some form of extension work or adult education. Many institutions of teacher education have made special provisions to enable teachers to attend courses in the late afternoon or evening, or on Saturdays. One of the most recent developments is the workshop. This differs from the courses conventionally offered by colleges and other institutions in that its members come with definite problems growing out of their school work. Those who direct workshops give no courses, at least in the strict sense, but discuss with the members of the workshop their individual problems and give whatever help they can in their solution. The workshop is a cooperative effort to solve practical problems with the help and guidance of experts.

Contributing considerably to the general professional advance of the American teacher has been the immense amount of research carried on during the last half century. This has been conducted not only by professional educators connected with the country's leading colleges and universities, but also under the auspices of professional organizations, such as the National Education Association, the American Education Fellowship, the National Society for the Study of Education, the John Dewey Society, the National Society of College Teachers of Education, the American Association of Teachers Colleges, and others. To throw light on the multifarious aspects of teaching in America, several noteworthy nation-wide surveys have been conducted. One of the first of such studies was made by W. C. Bagley and W. S. Learned under the auspices of the Carnegie Foundation for the Advancement of Teaching; its results were published in 1920. One of the most comprehensive surveys ever to be made was the National Survey of Teacher Education. Authorized by Congress, it was conducted under the leadership of Professor Evenden of Teachers College, Columbia University, from 1928 to 1931. Its findings comprise six large volumes and were published in 1933 by the United States Office of Education. In 1938 the American Council of Education began a five-year study of teacher education in America. Some 35 institutions were invited to cooperate on the improvement of teacher education. By means of consultative services, institutes of various kinds, workshops, and other agencies, those conducting the study sought to develop ways and means by which institutions would be enabled to improve and evaluate their own programs.

12.   The teaching profession

A teacher's lot in the early days of American education was anything but lustrous. Poorly paid, professionally unrecognized, socially an underling, such, in the main, were the salient characteristics of a teacher. With the unfolding of the American public school system in the nineteenth century, there came a change in this tawdry picture. Slowly the qualifications and requirements for teaching grew more exacting, and with their rise came a gradual improvement in the teacher's general status.

Today teaching in America has all the attributes of a profession. Numerically, in fact, it is the largest in the land, with about one million men and women in its ranks. Every state in the Union now requires a certificate or license to teach in the public schools, and the standards for certification have been steadily rising.

The twentieth century has seen improvement in matters involving the teacher's general welfare, such as sick-leave, sabbaticals, tenure, pensions, and academic freedom. Some states have enacted laws to protect teachers from unwarranted dismissal. Ordinarily, however, the matter of tenure has been left in local hands, with the usual ensuing diversity throughout the country. Some places—especially the larger cities—have put their teachers on a civil service basis with permanent tenure. On the other hand, we find most localities appointing their teachers on an annual basis, or on a basis of a permissive contract for more than one year, or on a continued basis, none carrying any assurance of permanent tenure.[46]

As for retirement, time was when teachers, like fire horses, were expected to work until old age overcame them. Whatever security they might enjoy in their declining years was strictly their own concern. Today, however, such views have become obsolete. In harmony with the philosophy that the

---

[46] Especially active in promoting teacher tenure and retirement has been the National Education Association. See its *Handbook of Teacher Tenure* (1936) and its *Teacher Retirement Systems and Social Security* (1937).

protection of old age is a responsibility of society, states as well as cities and smaller localities have adopted retirement schemes of various kinds. The first state to do so on a state-wide basis was New Jersey (1896). Since then the majority of states and Puerto Rico, Alaska, and Hawaii have followed the example.[47]

There has also been some improvement in teachers' salaries. In 1900 public elementary and high school teachers drew an average annual salary of $325, but 40 years later their pay averaged about $1,350. Within this average, however, there were wide variations. In the early forties, for example, New York's teachers averaged some $2,600; at the same time their less fortunate professional brothers in Mississippi were earning only an average $525 a year. Some 200,000 teachers, it has been estimated, were earning less than $1,200 annually, and some 25,000 were receiving less than $600. Relatively, the pay of teachers has lagged behind that of most other professions. In 1935 the nation's average lawyer earned three and a half times as much as its average teacher. In fact the average teacher received less than the average worker in the skilled trades.

The paltry pay America offers its teachers has been explained in a number of ways. Teachers are paid less than dentists and pastors and, in some instances, truck drivers and barkeepers because, for one thing, the supply until recently has generally exceeded the number of available jobs.[48] As a

---

[47] Retirement plans vary considerably; usually, membership in a teachers' retirement system is optional. Generally, teachers contribute a fraction of their salary—about 5%—to an annuity fund; to which the state, or other authority, contributes a similar, or sometimes larger, amount. Upon the teacher's retirement, he receives payment based on the accumulated principal. Provisions are also made for payment in the instance of a teacher's withdrawal from the service or in the event of his death. In certain plans provision is also made for a reserve fund to be available for use in unforeseen contingencies.

[48] An excellent study of this subject may be found in Clark, H. F., "Life Earnings in Selected Occupations." New York: Harper & Brothers, 1937; also "Salaries of School Employes, 1938–1939," *Research Bulletin* of the National Education Association, XV, March, 1939. See also Fine, B., *Our Children Are Cheated*. New York: Henry Holt & Company, Inc., 1947.

rule teachers have been recruited from the farming and lower middle classes. By and large they have not sprung from a wealthy background which would have enabled them to overcome their low income; nor have they been conscious to any extent of the organized labor movement, which might have spurred them to work for higher salaries. Moreover, since teachers are paid out of the public purse, efforts to increase their salaries have generally encountered the stiff resistance of organized tax-paying interests. Sometimes it has been argued that, inasmuch as most teachers are women—some 80 per cent at the present moment—their salaries should not be comparable to those of the other more mannish professions.

Whatever the reasons for the teachers' low pay, the effect thereof has been marked. It has shown itself in the reluctance of men to enter the teaching profession, and it has contributed directly to a national teacher shortage. With the coming of the war thousands of teachers left the classroom for the office and the factory, where in many cases they earned more money in a week than they had formerly received in a month. Once having tasted the satisfaction of adequate wages, many never again donned their pedagogic robes. With the swift rise in the cost of living after the close of the war, teachers' salaries were generally raised, but unfortunately not always sufficiently to offset the shrinking buying power of the dollar. So critical did the situation become that in several places teachers resorted to strikes in order to gain adequate wages.

In the cities the private lives of teachers have been pretty much their own, and as long as they comport themselves no worse than the average moral citizen, they may do as they please. But in the smaller communities, where all walls apparently have eyes and ears, teachers may not always indulge in the normal joys of other people. Indeed, with the exception of the clergy no other profession has been so subject to social pressure.[49] "I promise to abstain from dancing,

---

[49] For an analysis of these and other prohibitions imposed upon teachers see

immodest dressing, and any other conduct unbecoming a teacher or a lady," are words which were written into a teacher's contract in a Southern community not so long ago. The same teacher agreed "not to fall in love, become engaged or secretly married. . . ." Smoking, even in the Southern tobacco belt, is a frequent thou-shalt-not for teachers; and what goes for smoking applies also to drinking, card-playing, and dating. Worse than these taboos have been discriminations of a more sordid kind. Reflecting usually the local *mores,* these vary according to time and place. Some boards of education, for example, will not hire Catholics; others have put the ban on Jews or Negroes. Some localities have laws against the employment of divorced or married women teachers. Elsewhere pacifists have a difficult time, as do political leftists, liberals of all kinds, and teachers with pro-labor sympathies.

Closely related to the social pressures which have been put upon teachers is the matter of academic freedom. A teacher's right—nay, his duty—to present all sides and alternatives of a question has been frequently challenged and at times even prohibited by law. Two states, for example, have laws which make the teaching of the doctrine of biological evolution an illegal and punishable offense. Several states have required teachers to swear oaths of loyalty, though the same states have not generally required similar affirmations of allegiance from persons in other professions. Before the thirties many communities inserted clauses in their contracts forbidding teachers to join a union. This attitude still exists in many places, but of recent years it has apparently begun to recede.

The varying and conflicting currents which stream through our culture have reflected themselves in many heated and bitter controversies. In the clash of opposing views some educators have proposed that controversial issues have no place in the classroom and that teachers should teach what is

---

"Unreasonable Restrictions on Teachers' Activities," *Elementary School Journal,* XXXVII, 92 ff., October, 1936.

generally accepted by the community. Rejecting this point of view, however, other educators have held that controversial issues should be discussed, but that teachers should be impartial and express no convictions of their own. Still others have urged that not only should a teacher present controversial issues, but, as an informed and presumably intelligent person, he should also present his own convictions, though not foisting them upon students. From this point of view the school is not a depot of indoctrination, but a place of experimentation in developing communities of uncoerced persuasion.

13. Depression and World War II

The last decades have not been easy for American education. The impact of the depression and after it the war both left their damaging marks. By 1931 the influence of the collapse of 1929 had begun to be generally felt in schools throughout the land. Most seriously affected were the Southern Atlantic and the South Central states. Interestingly enough, the schools of the United States appear to have suffered more than those of France and England. Forced to reduce their budgets, school boards and administrators naturally had to cut their expenditures. At the outset this reduction took the form of eliminating what might be called miscellaneous educational services and of delaying anticipated improvements. Subsequently, however, current school expenses were lowered by drastic cuts in teachers' salaries. At the same time classes were enlarged and special teachers and supervisors assigned to regular teaching work. The general economy wave poured into the area of the so-called special subjects, such as art, music, shopwork, and physical education, which were in many instances not only curtailed in scope but even eliminated altogether. Moreover, while teachers were being dropped, other persons, unable to get employment in their own field, began to turn to teaching, with the result that there developed an oversupply of qualified or partially qualified teachers.

In many places the school term was shortened by as much as 20 days. In fact, in hundreds of rural areas schools failed to open at all. Obviously only a small number of new buildings were opened, and even necessary repairs and improvements were drastically neglected. The kindergarten and education of handicapped children disappeared in many places, and in others the work was seriously curtailed. By the spring of 1933, it is estimated, some ten million boys and girls had been seriously interrupted in their educational development as a result of the depression.

Not only did the depression halt and retard the educational labor and progress of half a century, but at the same time it was seized upon as an opportunity by those who were inhospitable to public education. Groups of citizens, in many cases heavy taxpayers, launched unbridled criticism of the educational program. The schools, they argued, had gone too far; education was full of "fads and frills"—such as the kindergarten, vocational guidance, special education of the handicapped—and teachers were overpaid.

Others, though not so acidulous in their attacks on the schools themselves, were convinced that the schools represented a disproportionate item in the various budgets. What was necessary, they argued, was economy of an efficient and sensible sort. In their search for a method of financing public education it was eventually realized that our method of making the schools dependent in a large way for revenue drawn from taxes on real property was unsatisfactory.

In 1936 the nation's public schools began to rally from the depression; but in 1939 the backlash of the so-called "recession" struck them. Not only was there another wave of economy and retrenchment in many states and localities, but in some places financial difficulties were immense and serious. In Ohio, for example, the state school fund was reported to be some $17,000,000 short. School funds were also low in other states: Georgia, for example, owed its school teachers some $5,000,000. In Pennsylvania, the Pennsylvania Property

Owners Association warned that their state's public school system was "doomed to early collapse," unless something could be done to replenish the special state fund for schools in distressed areas. Under the leadership of an economy administration Connecticut undertook to close most of its state teachers' colleges and to diminish many of its educational services.

The damage caused by the depression was further aggravated by the effects of the war. Although America escaped the material havoc caused by actual combat, the harm done to its schools directly and indirectly by the war was nonetheless immense.[50] Throughout the country, school buildings, plants, and equipment have deteriorated to such an extent that it has been estimated it would require some five billion dollars to bring the situation back to normal. Inflated prices and shortages of vital building materials have further hampered programs of reconstruction. In addition to buildings, the nation's schools lack an adequate supply of textbooks. In fact, many of the school books in use in the postwar American public school are of ancient vintage, badly battered, and often sadly out of date. It is no simple matter to replace them since that would involve the expenditure of mountainous sums of money. The war's worst effect on our schools was not of a material nature: America came out of the war in the grips of a nation-wide teacher shortage. Of the thousands of qualified teachers who, during the war, had left the school for better paying jobs, many never returned. Unfortunately, the lot of those who did remain was not always alluring; in fact, during the forties the morale of the American teacher struck its nadir.

14. At midcentury

As America approaches midcentury, its schools bear the scars of war and depression. At close range there is no doubt that the picture is dark; at the same time, however, one may

---

[50] For an account of the postwar crisis in American education read Fine, B., *Our Children are Cheated*. New York: Henry Holt & Company, Inc., 1947.

perceive unmistakable surgings toward something better. One does not have to look below the surface to observe it, for it is all about us. It has been given its fullest rein in the formulation of plans and programs, of countless suggestions and blueprints, all of which seem to aim toward the same ultimate end—better schools available to more and more Americans to live and work in a world in which the Four Freedoms will be something more than a lovely dream.

One of the first to cast eyes over the American educational panorama was Benjamin Fine, the education editor of *The New York Times*. In a series of a dozen articles Fine probed the national crisis in American education, presenting with specific examples and statistics, the whole remarkable picture, so lugubrious and withal so promising. His recommendations, which represent the consensus of some of America's foremost educators, have been summarized:

1. Increased salaries for teachers.
2. Higher certification standards.
3. Higher caliber teachers—improvement in training and selection.
4. Increased state supervision and aid.
5. Improvement and additions in school buildings.
6. Reorganization of school administration districts to increase efficiency.
7. Equality of educational opportunity for all children.
8. Assistance from the federal government.
9. Better school transportation.
10. Better health programs.
11. Smaller classes.
12. Removing politics from the schools.
13. Improved working conditions for teachers.
14. Improvement of curriculum.[51]

In the spring of 1948 the Commission on Educational Reconstruction of the American Federation of Teachers made public the results of a two-year study.[52] The major de-

---

[51] Fine, B., *Our Children Are Cheated*, p. 222. New York: Henry Holt & Company, Inc., 1947.

[52] The Commission's report was prepared by Floyd W. Reeves of the University of Chicago, Irvin R. Kuenzli of the American Federation of Teachers,

ficiencies it found in American education stressed, once again, the fact that teaching has become an unattractive profession to competent persons, and that young people are turning to law, medicine, dentistry, and engineering rather than to teaching. Not only do these professions bring larger economic rewards, but with them also goes a greater social prestige. The classroom teacher, the report declared, is still at the bottom of the list of professions. According to the report, moreover, our curricula and methods have lagged behind the demand of our times. Too many school curricula "are still geared to the agrarian community of a century ago." What is recommended is that they "be modernized to conform to the new scientific and psychological developments of the day." Regarding school organization, the Commission found thousands of school districts with fewer than ten pupils, and yet financially so poor that they were unable to do an adequate educational job. Like many other investigations, that of the Commission revealed once more the immense inequalities of educational financing and opportunity throughout the country. So great was this divergence that states like California, New Jersey, and New York were able to spend from four to five times as much as Arkansas, Alabama, and Mississippi. To correct these and other deficiencies the Commission recommended that:

1. The American educational system must be made more democratic in its organization and practices.
2. Between the schools and the community there should be an interacting relationship of mutual value.
3. The curriculum should be more carefully organized to embody the objectives for which American democracy is striving.
4. Teacher education must be given a place of the first importance in an expanded educational program.
5. Personnel policies should be improved so as to strengthen the educational profession and build a stronger morale among teachers.
6. A planned building and equipment program should be developed.

and Lester A. Kirkendall, director of the Association for Family Living in Chicago.

7. School programs should be designed to extend educational advantages to increasing numbers of American youth.

8. For efficiency and progress school administrative and attendance units should be reorganized.

9. An educational program which will strengthen rural life should be developed.

10. An adequate program of financial support, including federal aid, is necessary.

More concerned with the crisis aspect of contemporary civilization and the part education should play therein were the "two great constructive purposes" adopted by the American Education Fellowship at its national conference in Chicago in the fall of 1947. As written by Theodore Brameld of New York University, these involve:

1. The reconstruction of the economic system in the direction of greater social justice and stability; a system to be secured by whatever democratic planning and social controls experience shows to be necessary; a system in which social security and a guaranteed annual wage sufficient to meet scientific standards of nourishment, shelter, clothing, health, recreation and education are universalized; a system in which the will of the majority with due regard for the interests of all the people is the sovereign determinant of every basic economic policy.

2. The establishment of a genuine world order, an order in which national sovereignty is subordinated to world authority in crucial interests affecting peace and security; an order, therefore, in which all weapons of war and police forces are finally under that authority; an order in which international economic coordination of trade, resources, labor, distribution and standards is practiced parallel with the best standards of individual nations; an order which must be geared with the increasing socializations and public controls now developing in England, Sweden, New Zealand and certain other countries; an order in which all nations, races and religions receive equal rights; an order in which "world citizenship" thus assumes at least equal status with national citizenship.

In putting these guiding principles to work, educators must not only understand what is going on in the community, but they "must take stands as adult citizens on controversial issues of the day." Furthermore, "it is their right and duty to participate in active political life." As for teaching practice, however, "there should be no attempt to indoctrinate for any political party or for any given economic system." The task is "to experiment with techniques of learning through social agreement, not by superimposing prejudgments." For only thus can there be rule "by an informed majority who understand what they want and how democratically to get what they want." As for the school itself, it "should become a center of experimentation in attaining communities of uncoerced persuasion."

III

Some Other Developments

A. The Scientific Movement in Education

1. Background

The idea that education should be studied scientifically is
a bewhiskered creature, more than a hundred years old.
Its germ is plain to see in the work and utterances of the
renowned Herbart. Not only did he call for the application
of psychology to the art of teaching, but he also did some of
the important work of excavation which led in time to the
creation of modern educational psychology. Through his
efforts, the study of education, especially in its psychological
aspects, was raised from the teacher training school to the
scientific chambers of the higher learning. However, it was
not until the last few laps of the nineteenth century that the
scientific study of education and educational psychology began
to quicken its stride. In the almanac of modern psychology
the year 1879 is marked with a star, for it was then that
Wilhelm Max Wundt, a Leipzig professor, established the
first psychological laboratory. Its purpose was to rid psychology of its mystical, philosophical trappings, and to invest
it, as far as possible, with the robes of experimental science.
In the Wundtian laboratory an army of pioneers in modern
psychology received its basic training, and among them were
not a few Americans, notably James McKeen Cattell, who

had been Wundt's first assistant, G. Stanley Hall, Edward Bradford Titchener, and Charles Hubbard Judd.

Each of these men contributed to the development of education and psychology in America. In 1884 G. Stanley Hall established a center for applied psychology at Johns Hopkins for the purpose of studying the child's mental development. A few years later, in 1887, he brought out 3,000 subscriptionless copies of the first issue of the *American Journal of Psychology*, the first periodical of its kind in English. Subsequently, Hall helped to found and direct Clark University—indeed, he was Clark University. It was here that he created the child study movement. Its methods, however, leaned heavily on the questionnaire by which parents and teachers were asked to report their observations of children and their behavior. Unfortunately, many of the observers were utterly lacking in the essentials of sharp and objective discernment and what they recorded on their questionnaires was often quite unreliable. As for the questionnaires themselves, they were too loosely constructed to be of much scientific value. Consequently, a good deal of the material that they brought forth was dubious and did not contribute effectively to the establishment of a science of education. To Hall's credit, however, let it be noted that he gave a great lift to child psychology. Moreover, though today it has become the fashion to disparage Hall's experimental work, the laboratory psychologists generally submit that it was due largely to Hall that their research was able to attain the status of an independent science. Hall's greatest contribution, however, was his bulky volumes *Adolescence* and *Senescence*. In the former he assembled an immense array of data on the nature of the adolescent's physical and mental developments. A good part of these findings, it is true, have disintegrated under the impact of modern psychology. Even so, Hall did uncover many significant items; and more important still is the fact that he helped to make a serious study of adolescence and to give it a permanent place in educational research.

From Hall's first attempts to tunnel his way into the nature of the child has developed a much more scientific method of child study. Not only is our technique of observation more careful, accurate, and systematic than Hall's discursive questionnaire method, but we now possess measuring rods which have produced determinations of the stages of the child's mental and physical development. Centers for scientific child study, once the dream of men like Hall, have become the commonplace of the twentieth century.

While Wundt was hammering psychology into the first stages of an experimental science, other German scholars, notably Ernst Heinrich Weber and Gustav Theodor Fechner, were busy at work on a series of psychophysical measurements. The former developed a number of "laws" and the latter glorified them with intricate mathematics, thereby giving psychology an impressive mathematical complexion. Meanwhile, in England Francis Galton and Karl Pearson had injected statistics into the study of biology, eugenics, heredity, sociology, and psychology. They were not interested in educational research; yet the statistical methods and principles which they fashioned have put them in the vanguard of the statistical movement in educational research. Out of their distinguished labors came the science of biometry or anthropometry, which in the United States attracted the interest of James McKeen Cattell. From this source and from his earlier work at Leipzig with Wundt, Cattell drew the inspiration which was to make him a master of exact laboratory and statistical methods, and which, in 1890, sired his path-breaking *Mental Tests and Measurement*. The real originator of educational statistics, however, was not to be Cattell, but one of his graduate students at Columbia, the gifted Edward Lee Thorndike.

Despite the fact that mental testing had the enthusiastic support of the American Psychological Association, its development was relatively slow. In fact, for a time, interest in mental testing died down almost to zero. Not until America suddenly discovered the work of Alfred Binet among the Parisian school children did the interest in mental testing once more show its head.

Binet had started his pioneer work in 1895. What he was seeking at the time was some reliable way of distinguishing the bright pupils from the stupid ones. In 1905 Binet and his co-worker, Simon, set out to measure what they termed "general intelligence." Their work produced a scale intended to measure general intelligence. Far from satisfactory, even to its creators, the original Binet-Simon scale was twice revised, once in 1908 and again in 1911. In the United States Dr. H. H. Goddard and Dr. Lewis Terman contributed significantly to furthering the development of intelligence testing. The former had, by 1910, classified 400 inmates of the Training School for Feeble Minded Children at Vineland, New Jersey, according to the Binet-Simon tests. In 1916 Terman published the Stanford Revision of the Binet-Simon tests, a twelve-page brochure with examinations for most of the years from three to what Terman called a "superior adult." Terman also provided instructions for estimating the child's "Intelligent Quotient," by dividing his "mental age," as revealed by the mental tests, by his chronological age. In this, however, Terman was not strictly an innovator, since the idea of the intelligence quotient had previously been suggested by William Stern, then of Germany. The world war gave mental testing another boost, producing the Army Alpha and Beta group intelligence scales. Employed to test large groups, these tests at least indicated the possibility of measuring large numbers at the same time. After the war, Terman, Otis, Haggerty, Thorndike, and others devised group tests to be used in schools. Since then the intelligence test has become a regular part of the twentieth century school, being used in all parts of the world for all sorts of purposes.

2. The measurement movement

Just as the nineteenth century was approaching its end, a new note was heard in the study of education. It came from Dr. Joseph M. Rice, who, as editor of the *Forum,* had been giving his impressions of the American school. Noting that his personal observations and evaluations weren't worth a row of beans, Rice asserted that what was needed was objective evidence. "Before pedagogy can be recognized as a science," he wrote, "it will be necessary to discover at least some truths in regard to the educational process. . . ." To start the ball rolling Rice undertook to make a comparative study of the spelling abilities of children taught by different methods in various cities. For this purpose he drew up a list of common words which the children were asked to spell. Before he was through, Rice had noted the spelling achievements of some 30,000 pupils. He found, interestingly enough, that those pupils who had devoted 15 minutes a day to spelling could spell as well as those who had given 40 minutes a day to the subject. Rice's undertaking, astounding and even heretical in its day, was destined to open the door to the measurement movement. His use of measured results instead of personal judgment to appraise education marked a new step in the advance of the science of education. To Rice's concept of measurement, moreover, was coupled a technique which gave promise of becoming an instrument of the first caliber in the study of educational results.

Rice's excursion into the study of spelling made him the target for the usual critical outbursts. But since then, time has dissolved most of such skepticism; indeed, in 1915 the same association of school superintendents that, a generation earlier, had poured its disapproval upon Rice and his method devoted 57 addresses to tests and measurements of educational efficiency. They bowed to the same general doctrine, namely, that the effectiveness of the school, its methods, and its teachers must be measured in terms of the results obtained. Truly, the times bring different customs!

Although Rice has been justly credited with the invention of the first comparative educational test, the scientific study of education received its first real impetus in this country from Edward L. Thorndike and Charles H. Judd. The two had been college mates at Wesleyan in the nineties. Both had made psychology their major academic love, Judd specializing in it for his doctorate under Wundt at Leipzig, and Thorndike working under Cattell at Columbia. The two men were at times in acute disagreement over the issues of education— they fought over the question of transfer of training for almost three solid decades. Yet they both were animated by the same great and inexhaustible devotion to their science. It was the underlying spirit of their being; and, as they labored in the enclosures of their mechanistic psychology during the century's first two decades, Thorndike and Judd inspired quantitative investigations into every phase of education, from marks to methods, from the curriculum to adminis- tration. Thorndike laid the groundwork when he devised a scale unit for the measurement of educational achievement. In 1908 Cliff W. Stone, working under Thorndike's direction at Columbia, issued the first objective arithmetic reasoning test. A year later, Thorndike presented his scale for the measurement of handwriting before a meeting of the American Association for the Advancement of Science, and in 1910 the scale was published. Generally speaking, the publication of Thorndike's scale has been recognized as the beginning of the movement for measuring educational products scientifically. During the ensuing years, scales and tests appeared rapidly and in increasing numbers. From Thorndike's students came the Hillegas Composition Scale, the Trabue Language Scale, the Buckingham Spelling Scale, the Woody Fundamentals of Arithmetic Scale, and many others.

Meanwhile Judd had taken over Dewey's reins as head of the School of Education at Chicago. But the eternal shade of Wundt must have been there too, reminding his former student, as he once had in a more earthly form, that *"a priori ist garnichts!"* (a priori is of no value). For, like his one-time Leipzig professor, Judd was all aglow for the methods of science, and in the course of the next three decades he was to make Chicago one of America's great centers for the scientific study of education. Like Thorndike, Judd had an unquenchable thirst for facts which lured him into every phase of education. Again like Thorndike, Judd ignited the spark of inquiry in the student mind, and some of the young men who came from his classes were destined to play prominent parts in the advancement of American education.

The first article in Judd's intellectual credo was "Get your facts," the second was "Be exact." These ideas he tried to implant in his students. Pervading his own activity, his high principles followed him into the laboratory where they unfolded in the work of his students. Some of the young men who labored under his guidance in the psychological laboratory performed meritoriously indeed—C. T. Gray's *Types of Reading Ability* (1917), F. N. Freeman's *The Handwriting Movement* (1918), and G. Buswell's *Experimental Study of the Eye-Voice in Reading* (1920).[1]

From the seeds planted by Judd and Thorndike grew the measurement movement. Its basic text was enunciated by William A. McCall who proclaimed that "whatever exists, exists in some amount," and "anything which exists in amount is measurable"[2]—provided, of course, that the essential measuring stick is at hand. In the first quarter of the century the measurers and testers were in the center of the educational spotlight. With questionnaires, with tests, scales, and measurements, with statistics, they explored and sought to evaluate

---

[1] Among Judd's students were such front-rank educators as F. N. Freeman, who became dean of education at the University of California; W. S. Gray and G. T. Buswell of the University of Chicago; W. A. Brownell of Duke University; G. S. Counts of Columbia University; H. T. Rainey, president of Stephens College; and William H. Burton of Harvard University.

[2] McCall, W. A., *How to Measure in Education.* New York: The Macmillan Company, 1922.

every phase of American school practice. At the same time they endeavored to sharpen their tools in the desire to make their technique as objective, scientific, and useful as possible. Annually professors of education and their graduate students turned out scores of statistical studies, many of which, it is now all too plain, were of flimsy worth.

In addition, a number of professional journals, such as *The Educational Measurement Review,* published by the Southern California Educational Research Association, the "Review of Educational Research," the *Encyclopedia of Educational Research,* and the *Journal of Educational Research,* the official organ of the Educational Research Association (a department of the National Education Association), gave much space to the movement and its findings. Not only did the number of standardized tests multiply prolifically during the century's second decade, but the area of investigation also widened. Not only were formal achievements in the three R's and other school subjects put under the investigator's inquiring eyes, but also such things as ability in artistic creativeness, reasoning, and the like were considered. Even emotion, personality, and interest were examined, as were religion and morals— though not always with satisfactory results.

Testing and measuring have become an integral part of the twentieth century school. There is no longer any doubt that there are some things in education which can be measured. Measurement, however, has been chiefly American, and though there are measurers in England, the movement is not so popular nor so widespread in most other lands.

What can we measure? We know of course we can measure physique; we have a remarkable collection of gadgets to test our senses and our muscles. But we can also measure the more elusive thing known as temperament; every school child knows that we have tests for intelligence. We can also measure attitudes, be they related to the sphere of ethics or economics, race, politics, religion, or society. We can test for attitudes involving emotional characteristics, stereotypes, or opinions on current issues. As for aptitudes, whatever they are, we can measure all kinds, from the simplest mechanical variety to the more subtle kind that makes up musical talent, to the very intricate sort that constitutes a first-rate flyer in the Army Air Force. As for character, we have the Lewin measurements of psychic tensions and a number of tests for honesty, will, temperament, moral standard, and several other things as well. We can measure, too, some of the products of education; we have fair yardsticks to measure knowledge, skill in, and interpretation of problems and situations.

We can measure all these things with a fair degree of reliability, though not to the same degree in all cases. When, however, we deal with the personality of the whole person, with the efficiency of the teacher, with the school as a whole, we rely on methods of evaluation involving judgment rather than measurement. To study personality, we get help from many directions. We call in the psychoanalysts and the psychiatrists who use techniques suggested by the studies of Drs. Freud, Jung, and Adler. We use the ink blot tests of Rorschach, rating scales of several kinds, and we even use the questionnaire.

Measurement has also left its mark on teaching. Through the use of objective test questions, teachers began to construct their own informal objective tests. True-false, completion, matching, multiple-choice, identification, and vocabulary tests are widely used. Many colleges now regularly employ objective tests of various sorts in selecting their students, and it has become a common practice to subject candidates for graduate degrees to batteries of objective tests. Another outcome of the measurement is the so-called workbook, which is being used in almost all subjects in the contemporary American school. Indeed, in 1940, there were over 500 different workbooks in use in the American schools, and today there are even more.

EXAMPLES OF NEW KINDS OF TESTS

TRUE-FALSE:

True False   Columbus discovered America in 1492.

True False   Columbus was a Spaniard.

True False   Modern educational research utilizes the scientific method.

MULTIPLE-CHOICE:

Richard Wagner is famous as a (1) poet (2) painter
(3) composer (4) statesman.

The result obtained in addition is called the (1) product
(2) sum (3) quotient (4) remainder.

Wooden houses are painted because:
they look nicer.
paint protects the wood.
paint makes the house warmer.

MATCHING:

Match the following: .... Defoe   (1)   English

 .... Swift   (2)   American

 .... Irving   (3)   English

 .... Shakespeare   (4)   English

 .... Mark Twain   (5)   English

 .... Dreiser   (6)   German

 .... Goethe   (7)   French

 .... Huxley   (8)   American

 .... Diderot   (9)   American

COMPLETION:

Complete the following thoughts:

The process by which starch is produced in green plants is called...............

The honor of fathering the modern measurement movement is generally
accorded to.............................who in.....................suggested
that before education can be recognized as a science it will be necessary to

VOCABULARY:

Der Hund ist:
(1)   ein Buch   (2)   ein Tier   (3)   eine Feder.

Erbsen und Bohnen sind
(1)   Mineralien   (2)   Gemüse   (3)   Bilder.

IDENTIFICATION:

Identify the following:

.... Acute angle
.... Chord
.... Diameter
.... Hypotenuse
.... Arms
.... Obtuse angle
.... Right angle
.... Radius
.... Vertex
.... Secant
.... Segment
.... Tangent

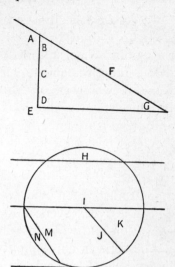

3. The survey movement

Closely related to the "get-the-facts" idea was the origin of the survey movement. Born in the sociological studies of family, housing, food, income, and the like, the survey came into being when it was realized that social facts can only be understood when they are studied broadly and comprehensively in relation to their total setting. One of the first social surveys of large dimension was undertaken in Pittsburgh in 1909. Directed by Paul U. Kellogg and Edward T. Devine, and fortified financially by the Russell Sage Foundation, the Pittsburgh quest was in the nature of

a rapid, close-range investigation of wage-earners in the American steel district . . . a demonstration in social economy made graphic against the background of a single city . . . an attempt to throw light on these and kindred economic forces not by theoretic discussion of them, but by spreading forth the objective facts of life and labor which should help in forming judgment as to their results. . . .[2]

[2] Kellogg, P., *The Pittsburgh District: Civic Frontage*, p. 493 ff. New York: Russell Sage Foundation, 1914.

Credit for the first school survey in America is generally given to Calvin N. Kendall, who in 1910 was summoned by the public school authorities of Boise, Idaho, to appraise their school practices and to suggest how they might be improved. Kendall, who was superintendent of schools in Indianapolis, Indiana, spent several days in Boise scrutinizing the schools, and some time later he issued a report which was printed in the local newspapers.[3]

The survey movement rooted quickly and by the second decade of the twentieth century it had grown to formidable magnitude. Men who were in the educational forefront— Judd, Strayer, Ayers, and Cubberley—recruited professors of education and went forth with them to examine and appraise public schools throughout the land. Some of the country's larger school systems in cities like New York, Baltimore, Portland, Oregon, Salt Lake City, and Cleveland came under their eyes. In 1913 Boise treated itself to a second helping of the survey, this time on a more ambitious and extensive scale. In 1914 the National Society for the Study of Education gave over Part Two of its Thirteenth Yearbook to a discussion of surveys. Since then there have been thousands of surveys in every part of the nation. Not only have city school systems been put under scrutiny, but states too have been surveyed; there have even been some national surveys, which, however, have generally concerned themselves with more limited searches into education, such as a study of teaching personnel or a study of secondary education. Much more ambitious was the survey undertaken in 1938 by President Roosevelt's Advisory Committee. Buttressed by 19 supplementary staff studies, this was by far the most comprehensive analysis of educational conditions ever undertaken by any nation.

---

[3] Although the modern educational survey is the child of the sociological survey, reports dealing extensively with school conditions are an old story in American education. There comes to one's mind almost at once the celebrated reports of Horace Mann which he issued in the late thirties and early forties of the last century. Comprehensive and informative, and written at times with dash, Mann's reports on the conditions he observed in the schools of Massachusetts might very properly be called surveys. They differ, of course, very substantially in the technique which produced them.

Compared with its Boise parent, the modern survey is, indeed, a very different creature. Kendall's original exploration had been a simple affair, requiring only a few days and depending largely on personal judgment. The early surveyors sat in classrooms and appraised teachers; they pored over syllabi and courses of study; they took a glimpse at the school records and reports, the financial and pupil accounting, the business management. But their judgment was seated largely in their own being; it came out of their beliefs, their opinions, their experience—and sometimes, alas, out of their preconceived notions. In time they began to "objectify"; and instead of appraising a school system by itself, they began to rank it in comparison with others. They determined their yardstick with a good deal of care. At the same time their method was essentially descriptive; it set forth clearly *what was,* but it seldom revealed very much about *what might be.* The early surveyors missed their chance to point out unused capacities and what might be done with them.

The surveyors who examined the New York City schools in 1912 were the first to employ a standardized test—the Courtis Arithmetic Test—to gather a part of their data. Since then, tests, scales, and other measuring devices have become standard. During the thirties, for example, the Cooperative Study of Secondary School Standards presented a graphic contrivance that it called "Educational Temperatures" whereby any school could determine its standing from a ranked list of 198 schools. In the course of six years the Cooperative Study used some 300,000 standard tests, though in the end these were given a relatively small weighting. The survey movement was actually a spur to the measurement movement; indeed, a number of the early standardized measuring rods owe their being to the fact that they were created for specific use in surveys.[4]

---

[4] Note, for example, the Strayer-Englehardt Score Card for Junior High School Building, the Bruner Criteria for Evaluating Teaching and Learning Materials, and the Mort-Cornell Guide for Self-Appraisal of School Systems.

Few surveys, even the most simple, would today be conducted by one person. Generally a full-strength survey requires the services of a battalion of experts. Assembled from many special fields, they include professors of education, sociologists, psychologists, statisticians, management experts, efficiency experts, tax experts, and public accountants. A number of agencies have engaged extensively in conducting school surveys. Among them the United States Office of Education is probably the most important. Several significant surveys were made possible largely because of the assistance of one of the endowed foundations, as the Russell Sage Foundation, the Carnegie Foundation for the Advancement of Teaching, and the General Education Board. A few universities, too, have established special surveying bodies. Among them are such pioneers as the Bureau of Field Studies at Columbia's Teachers College, the Bureau of School Studies at the University of Kentucky, and the Bureau of Field Studies at the George Peabody College for Teachers in Nashville, Tennessee.

Why bother with an educational survey? After all, it does run into money. It takes time and toil, and now and then there are even tears. There are two main reasons for the survey. First, there is the obvious desire for an accurate interpretation of what's what. What are we doing? Are we accomplishing our purposes? How can we improve our work and service? These are some of the basic and omnipresent questions prompting a survey. The other factor is economic. With school enrollments on the rise, and with the cost of school maintenance ascending like a balloon, hard-pressed school authorities, prodded by equally hard-pressed taxpayers, are quite naturally interested in squeezing every bit of value out of the gasping dollar. Ever since the depression fact-finding expeditions into public school financing have been common.

All these have the imprint of the Bureau of Publications, Teachers College, Columbia University.

Surveys range from the very simple to the most elaborate. They may concern themselves with the efficiency of teaching in a single department, or they may turn their searchlight on an entire system in a whole city, or state, or more. They may examine not only teaching, but also administration, supervision, the pupils' background, health, and habits. They may concern themselves with the school plant. its lighting, heating, and ventilation, the cafeteria, the janitorial service, and so on down to the last relevant jot and tittle.

The Regents' Inquiry into the Character and Cost of Public Education in the state of New York, organized late in 1935, undertook "to find out what the educational system of the State is accomplishing, how well its total program fits present-day needs, and what the costs and cost elements of that program are and should be." Less interested in the usual statistical portrait of every phase of education, the Regents' Inquiry cruised in the waters of "major issues." It found among other things that in the state of New York

1.   The educational system has not yet adjusted its program to carry the new load imposed by the coming into the schools, particularly into the secondary schools, of all the children of all people, with their many new and different needs.

2.   The school work for boys and girls has not been redesigned to fit them for the new and changing work opportunities which they must face in modern economic life.

3.   The school program does not sufficiently recognize the increased difficulties of becoming and being a good citizen.

4.   The educational system has not caught up with the flood of new scientific knowledge about the natural and the social world which has been made part of life in recent decades, and fails to give boys and girls a scientific point of view and an understanding of the world.

5.   The educational system has not been replanned to meet the new conditions of modern life and the new ways of living, in which the family, the church, and early work now exercise less influence and in which increasing leisure in later life calls for, and makes possible, a rich and growing inner life.

6.   The citizens and the school leaders of the State of New York do not have a specific, agreed-upon goal. Both groups are going ahead in many

directions, but without a destination toward which all may bend their energies.[5]

More specifically, the Regents' Inquiry delved into such matters as the high school and its relation to life, the preparation of school personnel, adult education, the youth problem, education for work, the school health program, motion pictures and radio, the school and the community, and the inescapable and ever-present problem of state aid and school costs.

The survey is as typically American as baseball and the banana split; it is not found to any extent in any foreign lands. That it has helped to highlight school conditions is fairly plain; certainly it has put its finger on faults and weaknesses. It has also helped to promote more up-to-date and progressive practices. A thorough-going survey not only gives meaning to elusive details, usually by way of careful standardization, but it also gives a clearer perspective of the entire educational organism—the school, the plant, the curriculum, and so on. A well executed survey should, moreover, bring forth the philosophy of the school: it should clarify its purposes, objectives, the nature and needs of the pupil, the nature and needs of the community of which the school is a part and which it serves. Thus a well-rounded and penetrating survey not only discloses what is and what goes on, but at the same time it offers guidance and direction toward a better education.

4. Curricular reconstruction

Changing the curriculum is an old practice; it is probably as old as the school itself. In the past, however, curricular changes were generally slow. They usually represented a gradual, and more often a dilatory, adjustment on the part of the school to social and intellectual changes. Pressure from

---

[5] By permission from *Education for American Life,* p. 5, by L. H. Gulick. General Report of the Regents' Inquiry. New York: McGraw-Hill Book Company, Inc., 1938.

outside the school was sometimes instrumental in adding new subjects, but once such subjects had been added, they tended to become traditional fixtures. Latin, for example, was once a very practical subject since all educated men spoke it. But with the rise of the vernacular, the practical reason for teaching Latin vanished. The same is true of geometry which, like Latin, was once taught for practical reasons.

Up to the 1890's curriculum construction was commonly entrusted to an individual, or to some single agency. By the end of the century, however, curriculum-making came into the hands of specialized committees. Impetus to the new approach came from the work of the Committee of Ten. Organized in 1892 by the National Education Association, it was headed by President Charles W. Eliot of Harvard, and was comprised of leading men of learning from the liberal arts colleges. Specifically, the committee's task was to define the function of the American public high school and to establish recognized national standards for it. The committee took a long and careful look at the secondary school's content; it pried into Latin and Greek, English, the modern foreign languages, mathematics, physics, astronomy, chemistry, natural history, biology, history, civics, economics, physical geography, geology, and meteorology. For guidance it asked itself such questions as: How much instruction is needed in a given subject in the four-year high school? When should the subject first be introduced? Should it be accepted for college entrance? Should it be treated differently for those pupils going to college and for those not going to the higher learning?

From its ponderings the committee emerged in time with a number of suggestions. It came out for a six-year elementary school and a six-year high school, a recommendation to which most American schoolmen at the time turned a deaf ear. The committee reasserted the belief that the high school's primary function was to prepare American youth for practical life. It made suggestions in regard to college entrance requirements as well as the quality of high school instruction; it gave its blessing to the elective system in the high school; and it invented the notion of the unit system by basing a unit of instruction on the number of recitation periods during a week.[6]

The fact that the first committees to give their attention to refashioning the curriculum consisted almost entirely of liberal arts professors is not unimportant. For at bottom they were not only trail-blazers, they were also molders; and although their recommendations were often by-passed, the values they stressed left a perceptible mark. The professors leaned heavily on a content which was mathematical and linguistic. Although the Committee of Ten saluted the practical aspect of secondary education, somehow the practical and the academic were closely intertwined. By and large, the professors paid homage to the notion that the chief task of the secondary school was to furnish the college with a well-prepared intellectual élite; the modern idea of the school and the community being one and having reciprocal functions and obligations was not even considered.[7]

In the early twentieth century the make-up of curricular committees slowly changed. Teachers, principals, and superintendents gradually replaced the men of higher learning; and after the first World War professors of education began to appear in larger numbers on more and more committees.[8] The late twenties saw several committees of the NEA's Department of Superintendence coming to grips with the curriculum, and several of their yearbooks reported thereon. With the financial help of some of the educational foundations, three learned societies undertook national studies.[9] In their

---

[6] A normal program for a high school boy or girl was put at four subjects, each having four periods a week.

[7] In 1893 the National Education Association appointed the Committee of Fifteen to make a study of the elementary school. Its report, promulgated in 1895, raised important questions about the elementary school curriculum as it then existed.

[8] As for example the Commission on the Reorganization of Secondary Education (1918).

[9] Note the National Committee on Mathematical Requirements organized

basic viewpoints these expeditions into the curriculum were very much like the earlier ones: they continued as before to be subject-centered, linguistic, and mathematical.

Not until 1926 did the old subject-matter stronghold show any signs of vulnerability. In that year the Curriculum Committee of the National Society for the Study of Education published its report, the *Foundations of Curriculum-Making*. No liberal arts professors and no school superintendents graced the membership of this committee; instead its 12 members were professional students of education, including Progressives like William H. Kilpatrick and Essentialists like William C. Bagley. Though they hailed from different philosophic camps, the members of the committee found themselves in agreement on a number of important points. For one thing, they accepted the concept of social change as basic to curriculum-making; moreover, they recorded themselves in favor of a society-centered emphasis, thereby laying the foundation for an integration of the child-centered and society-centered principles.

The social foundations concept was given another boost in 1930 when America's historians reported on the teaching of history and other social studies. The report was the work of a committee of the American Historical Association, and was financed by several foundations. Led by George S. Counts, the committee included some of America's most eminent students of society—Charles A. Beard, Howard Odum, Charles E. Merriam, and Carleton Hayes. The social slant of its investigation is revealed in the titles of some of the sixteen volumes published by the Committee: *A Charter for the Social Sciences in the Schools, Citizens' Organizations and the Civic Training of Youth, Geography in Relation to the Social Sciences, Social Foundations of Education, The Social Ideas of American Educators,* and so on.

---

by the Mathematical Association of America (1920–1923); the Classical Investigation of the Classical Society of America (1921–1925); the Modern Language Study of the Modern Language Association of America (1924–1927).

The social forces which were unchained by the depression and the second World War produced another period in the evolution of the school curriculum. Socially, there were such factors as the important changes taking place in production, employment, and government; the influence of planned enterprises like the TVA and the New Deal; the emergence of the one-world idea and its challenge to the concept of the national state; the American reaffirmation of the democratic way of life as against the totalitarian form. Educationally, there were such factors as the growing acceptance of Dewey's educational philosophy; the advance of the psychology of experience; the influence of the Progressives; the revelations of the testers and the measurers; the findings of the Eight-Year Study of the Progressive Education Association (see p. 161).

It was in the thirties and the forties that the weight of these forces began to make itself felt. After several decades under the sway of the liberal arts professors, curriculum-making now came more and more under the direction of professional experts on the curriculum. By the mid-thirties there were enough experts to form an organization, the *Society for Curriculum Study*. Most of them were of progressive leanings and many of them had participated in some phase or other of the Progressive movement.[10] Of even greater importance was the fact that they were professional students of education and of the curriculum in particular. However, there was among them no professional psychologist or sociologist; no full-fledged student of the culture; and only an infinitesimal minority with a truly philosophic orientation.

Under their leadership curriculum-making assumed a new form. At first it had been entrusted to an individual, more or less competent, next, to a committee of scholars versed in the liberal arts, now it drew upon the services not only of special-

---

[10] Among its founders were Herbert Bruner, Hollis Caswell, Ruth Cunningham, Henry Harap, Laura Zirbes, Gordon Mackenzie, Prudence Cutright, Harold Hand, and Paul Hanna—to mention only a few.

ized students of the curriculum itself, but also of teachers and intelligent citizens interested in the improvement of education. Every parent and every teacher now became a potential contributor to the curriculum; in one place after another they were given an important share in remaking the curriculum. This was true of a town like Little Rock, Arkansas, as well as of an entire state like Virginia. "The curriculum revision program which fails to carry editors, civic leaders, and other intelligent laymen along with it," astutely observed the NEA, "will encounter active opposition or lukewarm support." [11]

When a body of parents and teachers goes to work on a new curriculum, it may or may not operate scientifically.[12] Generally speaking, a substantial part of its judgments has sprung from the personal opinions of its members. This has been true especially where the curriculum-changers have veered away from the traditional subject-matter emphasis and have gone instead in the direction of newer and less conventional values.

Where the stress has been subject-centered, however, several objective approaches to content have developed. One of the first was the so-called "analysis of frequency of use." Accepting as its basic assumption that the school's function was to prepare a child for life, the frequency-of-use technique determines its instructional program by presenting to the pupil situations requiring the use of definite knowledge and skills. It assumes, for example, that every youngster must learn how to spell. But what words should he learn? Should the choice be left to the individual teacher? Or should it be

[11] *Research Bulletin,* National Education Association, III, 121, 1925.

[12] The material on the curriculum is, of course, enormous. Note especially the following: Caswell, H. L., and Campbell, D. S., *Curriculum Development.* New York: American Book Company, 1935; Norton, J. K., and Norton, M. A., *Foundations of Curriculum Building.* Boston: Ginn & Company, 1936; Gwyn, J. M., *Curriculum Principles and Social Trends.* New York: The Macmillan Company, 1943. Valuable also are such studies as North Carolina's *Suggested Procedures for Curriculum Construction and Course of Study Building* (1934–1935); Virginia's *Organization for Virginia State Curriculum Program* (1932); Texas's *Handbook for Curriculum Study* (1934). The latter three are issued by the respective state boards of education.

left to the textbook? Not so long ago seventh-graders were expected to master the intricacies of words like *daguerreotype, erysipelas, abutilon, mnemonics, trichinae* and dozens of others. In 1914 Leonard P. Ayres, while surveying the Springfield public schools, made a scientific study of the spelling curriculum. He made two basic assumptions: (1) that the spelling taught a child should have some relation to the words he was going to use as a grownup, and (2) that the most common form of spelling activity of the ordinary adult took the form of letter writing. Accordingly, Ayres scrutinized thousands of business and personal letters, tabulating the words most frequently used therein. When Ayres examined his list he found, as one might expect, that the average mortal was able to correspond quite satisfactorily without ever using words like *mnemonics* and *daguerreotype*. Instead, he employed generous doses of the common prepositions, some adjectives and adverbs, and the simplest of verbs.[13] Putting all this together in a published list of spelling words, Ayres earned the distinction of being the first to devise such a list on an objective basis. His venture was followed by others, though some of these were based on different premises.[14] It was from such investigations that Edward L. Thorndike was able to compose his list of the 20,000 most common words in the English language. Since 1920 every first-rate speller has been made up by means of such a word list.[15]

What has been the case in spelling has also been the case in other subjects. The children who had been made to spell *erysipelas* and *trichinae* were expected to know the length of South America, the location of the desert of Atacama, and the

---

[13] That the spelling needs of the great proportion of adults are relatively simple should be obvious. It is possible, however, that a person might deliberately avoid using certain words simply because he doesn't know how to spell them.

[14] Ayres, L. P., *The Public Schools of Springfield*, pp. 86–89. Illinois: Russell Sage Foundation, 1914.

[15] Thorndike, E. L., *A Teacher's Word Book of the Twenty Thousand Words Found Most Frequently and Widely in General Reading for Children and Young People*. New York: Teachers College, Columbia University, 1931.

Pamir Plateau. "Italy," they were told, "uses the time of 15 degrees East and Illinois that of 90 degrees West." "When it is noon in Italy," asked their arithmetic teacher, "what time is it in Illinois?" They were told to calculate "the area of the base of a cylindrical gallon can 10 inches high," to "express 150 degrees Centigrade in terms of Fahrenheit," and to figure out the specific gravity of alcohol if 2 liters of it weighed 1.58 kilograms. Besides knowing all these things they were expected to be familiar with the historical significance of October 17, 1781, September, 1901, as well as the year 1,000.[16]

Because of the newer approach to content, historical and geographic references were determined on the basis of the frequency with which they were referred to in print. However, since such references tend to vary with the shifting current of events, the use of the newer method in these fields was not as satisfactory as in the case of spelling. As for arithmetic, Guy Mitchell Wilson made a study of the arithmetic used by the parents of the pupils of several school systems. He found that the calculations made by the elders were of the simplest kind, that, as a matter of fact, they used arithmetic processes only slightly.[17]

Another approach to the study of curricular content was the so-called job analysis, a technique which has found favor particularly with those who give courses in preparation for vocations. As developed by Werrett Wallace Charters, the job analysis began by dissecting the operations carried on in a given vocation, and then developing and organizing instructional materials which would develop in the student the requisite knowledge, skills, and habits for the successful execution of these operations.[18] Thus, instead of accepting the moss-covered assumption that to be successful as a

---

[16] Ayres, L. P., *The Public Schools of Springfield*, pp. 86–89. Illinois: Russell Sage Foundation, 1914.

[17] Wilson, G. M., *A Survey of the Social and Business Usage of Arithmetic*. New York: Teachers College, Columbia University, 1919.

[18] Charters, W. W., *Analysis of Secretarial Duties and Traits*. Baltimore: Williams & Wilkins, 1924.

pharmacist one must devote at least three years to the study
of Latin—a study which involved Caesar and Cicero and
formidable brigades of syntax and grammar—Charters pried
into the Latin actually used by practicing pharmacists. After
examining many hundreds of prescriptions filed in apothecary
records he found, as one might readily suspect, that the
language of Caesar and Cicero was hardly like that of the
average medico. The number of Latin words embalmed in
doctoral prescriptions was meager, to say the least. Quite
logically, Charters drew the conclusion that for vocational
purposes, the study of Latin could be considerably curtailed;
and that, as in the case of spelling, it might be better educationally were the student to concentrate on the words common to pharmaceutical practice.[19]

It should be plain that the approaches to curricular reconstruction have been varied. Not only has content been
reorganized within the subjects themselves; there has also
been correlation of subjects. Early in the century many
secondary schools chose to organize their curriculum around a
core of subjects which were regarded as "constant" and required of all pupils; the remainder of the program was
"variable" and elective. Historically this has been set down
as the core curriculum, though there are those who speak of it
as the "constants and variables plan of organization." A
more recent plan of curricular organization builds broad fields
of general, integrated subjects. What is known as the "multiple curriculum with variables" sets up type curricula, each
with a core of prescribed subjects. In each of such curricula,
what remains beyond the core is elective. Generally the
electives have been designed to develop certain groupings or
sequences of subject matter commonly known as majors and
minors.

Although the approaches to curricular reconstruction have

---

[19] Charters, W. W., *et al.*, *Basic Materials for a Pharmaceutical Curriculum*.
New York: McGraw-Hill Book Company, Inc., 1927.

been diverse, there are a few points on which most authorities appear to agree:

1. Curricular objectives must be formulated, and all subsequent steps must be taken in accordance with these objectives.
2. The formulation of such objectives demands a consideration of (a) the world in which we live, (b) the kind of world in which we should live, and (c) our philosophy of the educative process.
3. Materials of instruction must be selected, organized, and administered in accordance with the formulated objectives.
4. The preceding steps should be tested, and the results should be evaluated.
5. Since curricular reconstruction is a perennial task, the preceding procedures must be continued.

But there are also disagreements. These are rooted mostly in basic philosophic differences. Broadly speaking there are two contending views: for one thing, there are the traditionalists whose first stress has always been on subject matter. In their ranks we find men like Bagley, Horne, and Judd; devotees of the Great Books like Adler, Barr, and Hutchins; the legions of Catholics, scholastics, and otherwise; and also analyzers like Ayres, Wilson, and Charters. Opposing the subject-centered traditionalists are those whose main stress has been on experience, and among whom the Progressives have played a leading part. Thus far, however, their main effectiveness has been outside the nation's public schools. As for these, though no doubt their curricular offering represents a great improvement over that of a few generations ago, they still refuse to come to grips with certain great and significant phases of living, as for example, sex, love, and home living; personal and social work; religion; controversial issues relating to the economic and social system, issues dealing clearly and honestly with questions of race, religion, property, labor, and the like; the relationship of freedom and discipline in democratic living; the fusing of the community life with education. Despite its advances, the curriculum of the American public school as it now stands is still not adequately geared to life.[20]

[20] Late in 1947 the Commission on Life Adjustment Education for Youth publicly declared itself in favor of a "much broader type of education to

5. Child study

Though Rousseau, Pestalozzi, and Froebel had clamored for recognition of the child's rights in education, small children were not generally admitted to schools until about a century ago, with the establishment of the kindergarten and the nursery school on something more than a private basis. The early attempts to study the child, his nature and behavior, were necessarily crude. Pestalozzi, for example, kept a diary of his son's growth. Another early study of a child was made by Charles Darwin, who in 1877 published his "Biographical Sketch of an Infant," in *Mind*. One of the pioneers in modern child study is William Preyer, who wrote *The Mind of the Child*. Generally speaking, the founder of the movement of child study in the United States is considered to be G. Stanley Hall, who published his study of the "Content of Children's Minds on Entering School" in 1883. As editor of the *Pedagogical Seminary* Hall published numerous articles in the field of scientific child study. With the development of psychology as a science, the field of child study naturally made rapid strides. It was just a few years after the turn of the century that Thorndike published his *Notes on Child Study* (1903). In 1904 appeared William Stern's *Psychologie der frühen Kindheit* (Psychology of Early Childhood), probably the first comprehensive study of the child up to the age of six. With the advent of behaviorism and psychoanalysis, child study received fresh impetus, being approached from new angles.

Child study has been greatly interested in the "growth concept," investigating those factors that stimulate or retard the child's growth. Physical examinations throw light on such

reach an estimated 6,000,000 to 7,000,000 youths now preparing for college or skilled professions." What is sought has been explained thus: "The youth adjusted to life is adjusted to his job, has good health habits, is a good citizen, knows how to use his leisure time well, has a high standard of ethics and morals." Francis L. Bacon, principal of an Evanston, Ill., high school, representing the National Association of Secondary School Principals, named algebra, foreign languages, some of the older courses in history, and "any compendium of facts that have no appeal" among the subjects having little attraction for youths not interested in preparing for college.

matters as physical defects, malnutrition, defective teeth, poor vision or hearing, or bad posture. Armed with a knowledge of such defects, the educator, assisted by experts in the various fields concerned, can devise a remedial program to help the youngster to overcome his weaknesses and, if possible, to grow healthfully and normally. As far as the child's mental growth is concerned, of particular interest are his ability to learn, his achievements, and those factors which impede or retard his progress. Here again, a program is organized which is adjusted to the special needs of the individual; nor is the child's moral development overlooked.

The twentieth century school has harnessed child study to its complex work. Most closely associated with the movement is the growth of the modern nursery school. Ordinarily, this institution accepts young children between the ages of two and four, though in many instances there is much variation in this respect. Both England and Soviet Russia have given considerable attention to the promotion of this type of education. Notable in the development of the movement in England are Grace Owen and Margaret Macmillan, who organized nursery schools in the poor sections of London and Manchester. In 1920 specialists from Miss Macmillan's school introduced similar work at Teachers College, Columbia University. Today there are several hundred nursery schools throughout the land. Sometimes they are connected with institutions specializing in the study of children; sometimes they are organized by charitable organizations and churches; in some instances they are included in the regular public school system. Stated briefly, the nursery school is really a nursery, run on up-to-date scientific lines, and catering to the child's all-around growth.

Outstanding in the field of child study is the Clinic of Child Development which has been conducted by Yale University for years. Under the direction of Dr. Arnold Gesell, it has been observing and studying children while they ate and talked and learned and played—even while they slept. The

facts about children which the Yale Clinic has unearthed have
been made available not only in the usual learned reports, but
also in a number of books written especially for laymen, as
well as in action photographs and films. As a matter of fact
Dr. Gesell's *Infant and Child in the Culture of Today* has
become something of a handbook on child care for many
hundreds of American fathers and mothers.[21] Of interest and
value also is *Life with Baby,* which was filmed at the Clinic
and which has been viewed by many thousands throughout
the country. Despite the useful generalizations about children
and their development which Dr. Gesell has made, his scientific reserve has made him issue the caution that "every child
has an individual pattern of growth, unique to him," and
that "he travels by his own tailor-made time schedule."

B.   The Development of the Psychological Movement

1.   Background

Though psychology can be traced to Aristotle, it was not
until the nineteenth century that it donned the proud robes
of an exact science. Through the experimental toil of physicists and physiologists, men like Johannes Müller, Ludwig von
Helmholtz, Ernst Weber, Theodor Fechner, and others, psychology gradually emancipated itself from metaphysics and
from its speculations about the soul. It remained for Wilhelm
Max Wundt (1832–1920), while professor of physiological
psychology at Heidelberg, to draw for us the first portrait of
psychology as a true and respectable science amenable to the
rigorous requirements of experimentation. The first conceptions of psychology as a science of any considerable scope
appeared in Wundt's monumental work, his *Grundzüge der*

---

[21] Dr. Gesell has written more than 20 books. One of his recent works,
written in collaboration with Dr. Frances L. Ilg, *The Child from Five to Ten.*
New York: Harper & Brothers, 1945, gives a composite picture of 50 children
of "high average or superior" intelligence from homes that are economically
well fixed. Most of these children went from the Clinic's nursery to the public
school.

physiologischen Psychologie. Published in 1874, it eventually passed through a half-dozen editions, the last one appearing in 1911.

Wundt did more than to declare that psychology was a science as exact as physics. He went so far as to argue that, of the two, psychology was the fundamental science. Unlike the physicists, said Wundt, the psychologists are not limited in their researches to realities which, though measurable, are nevertheless abstractions since they are intangible or invisible. By contrast, Wundt thought, the physiologist can always observe the consciousness which he studies. However, it must be investigated in the spirit of the laboratory—nothing was to be taken for granted. Such doings, he explained, may be all right in the natural sciences where "it is possible under favorable conditions to make accurate observation without recourse to experiment." But, he cautioned his colleagues, "there is no such possibility in psychology," a pronouncement which, however, many a modern psychologist has been prone to ignore.

From the lecture halls of the bewhiskered Wilhelm marched a long line of students, many of whom were, in time, to become prominent psychologists in their own right. Among them was young William James (1842–1910), the same James who subsequently wrote *Pragmatism.* James left Heidelberg, after only a brief stay, to return to Harvard, where, after taking his M.D., a degree he never used professionally, he began to instruct in anatomy and physiology. Meanwhile he yearned to "work at psychology." Though he often professed an intense dislike for the ardors of experimental work, it was James who unwittingly gave psychology its experimental beginning in America. The precise time has escaped the historians, but it must have been in 1874 or 1875 when he brought his metronome and horopter chart and other strange gadgets to a deserted little room beneath the stairway of the old science building where, quite unobtrusively, he went to "work at psychology." A few years later, in 1877, he inscribed his name in psychological history once more when he offered the first course at Harvard in what its catalog tersely described as "Psychology."

Meanwhile James had met the great and fertile genius of Charles Santiago Sanders Peirce. The son of the noted mathematician, Professor Benjamin Peirce, he was graduated from Harvard in 1859. Except for a brief period at Johns Hopkins, Peirce never taught at any university. His chief interest was always in the natural sciences and it was his boast that he had been raised in the laboratory. Peirce and James had much in common. They were, indeed, close friends until, in their later years, they became estranged. In Cambridge both belonged to the Metaphysical Club, where they wrestled intellectually with the gifted Chauncey Wright and others. The role played by the Metaphysical Club in the advancement of American thought must have been enormous, but it is only in recent years that this fact has begun to be appreciated. How James and Peirce influenced one another's ideas is of course hard to estimate. Of the two, Peirce was clearly the more brilliant, the more original—he was, in fact, one of the most original thinkers ever to come out of America. A scientist to his very marrow, Peirce was forever insisting on experimental verification of all ideas, including even the sacred ones of theology. "The spirit of science," he asserted, "is hostile to any religion. . . . Let the consequences of such a belief be as dire as they may, one thing is certain: that the state of the facts . . . will surely get found out, and no human prudence can long arrest the triumphal car of truth. . . ." James, on the other hand, was a humanist, and although he had a consuming interest in what he called "stubborn and irreducible facts," he was not nearly as scrupulous in the logic with which he approached the foundations of human belief.

Though Peirce's interest lay in natural science, his passion for truth drove him inevitably into the area of philosophy. He was never really a psychologist, certainly not in the accepted modern sense, but in a day when the frontier between philosophy and psychology was elastic, it was almost certain that his thinking should cross the line. It is to him that modern psychologists owe what has been called, a bit glowingly, "the most profound psychology of ideas the world has ever known." It was Peirce who first caught a glimpse of what is now known to psychologists as "the operational principle." In a series of articles published in 1877 and 1878 in the *Popular Science Monthly,* Peirce led the way in pointing out the relation between thought and action. He held that "beliefs are nothing more than roles of action." "The whole function of thought," he explained, "is to produce habits of action." What the habit is, he went on to say, depends on when and how it causes us to act. "There is no distinction of meaning so fine as to consist in anything but a possible difference in practice." There is, for example, no difference between a heavy object and a light one so long as they are not brought to the test. "Our conception of any object," said Peirce, consists of "the practical effects we conceive the object to have."

Another important contribution of Peirce to education's psychological foundations was his interpretation of what is now spoken of as the "psychology of the act." This he viewed as a sequence in which the conceptual processes of thinking and reasoning took place in a setting created by feeling and the active response of the body. The first element in the sequence of the act was *feeling*: "To be conscious," Peirce declared, "is nothing else than to feel." And again: "The whole content of consciousness is made up of qualities of feeling, as truly as the whole of space is made up of points of a whole of time of instants." Next there is the *sense of action*: "Besides feelings, we have sensations of reaction; as when . . . we make a muscular effort." "The sense of action and reaction . . . is plainly connected with the discharge of nervous energy through the nerve fibres." Finally there is the *concept*: "The one primary and fundamental law of mental action consists in a tendency to generalization. Feeling tends to spread; connections between feelings awaken feelings; neighboring feelings become assimilated; feelings, by being excited, become more easily excited. . . . The consciousness of such a habit constitutes a general conception." He adds that "the starting point of all our reasoning is not in sense impressions, but in our percepts."

The world at large is just becoming aware of Charles Peirce. Yet among American thinkers he was a colossus. He was the groundbreaker of modern American philosophy, the unearther of the first principles of pragmatism—the very name of which was his invention. Peirce's theory of the "experimental method of knowing" flowed into the thinking of James, and thence into that of Dewey, where we encounter it in such tributaries as "thinking as problem solving," "experience as doing and making," and "learning as an active process."

In 1890 William James again made psychological history when he published his two-volume *Principles of Psychology* which, despite its 1,200 pages, its more than 2,000 footnotes, and its fill of technical quotations, nonetheless soared to the heights of fame. James McKeen Cattell called the book "psychology's Declaration of Independence." James had devoted 12 years to the composition of the book, and though he lived to disparage the idea that there was such a thing as a science of psychology, he also lived to see his study spur a generation of younger Americans to embrace the scientific method of inquiry. Hailed as a literary and scientific masterpiece, the *Principles* exerted a powerful effect on the currents that were to course through American psychology during the next few generations. With Dewey and Angell, who came in his wake, and with his contemporary, Charles Peirce, James charted the course for the psychology of experience.

Although the progress of psychology has antiquated a number of James's teachings—as his theory of instincts—others have withstood the severest critical onslaught. James, like Peirce, stressed experience and action as the determinants of meaning. In fact, James went so far as to hold that experience was the sole valid source of psychology. "Experience as it is immediately given, the stream of consciousness as it flows before perception," was his starting line for the study of psychology. What concerned the thinking man was the "practical business of reacting to his environment." True to his pragmatic credo, James never lost sight of the fact that people are primarily creatures of action; that they are compellingly motivated by feelings and purposes; and that they are creatures of reason and intellect only in a subordinate degree. James believed that psychology must deal with the activities of the living organism with the body as its basis. Thus he related his psychology to the living, growing human being, emerging and developing in his environment and slowly learning how to control it. That a physiologist like James should harness his psychology to physiology is understandable; his stress, however, was not, like that of Wundt, on physiological *structure* but on *function*. The question for him was not how the brain is built and looks, but how it operates. What are the functions of the brain? What are the general conditions of brain activity? James turned his attention to man's day-by-day activity; life, as he saw it, was an ever growing network of habits. Man was "a walking bundle of habits." Every day he was habitually fashioning his character. Long before the psychologists of a later day began to talk about conditioning human behavior, William James was teaching the theory of acquired reactions (see p. 462). "Every acquired reaction," he said, "is as a rule either a complication grafted on a native reaction, or a substitute for a native reaction, which the same object originally tended to provoke."

The core of James's psychology is the "stream of conscious thought," the continuous onward-flowing current of which the Self is forever a part. "Every thought tends to be a part of personal consciousness." The Self, however, is focal: it launches, stimulates, directs, and, at times, inhibits behavior. The stream of thought, which is in constant flux, is not only personal, but discriminative; even the functions of the organism, its sense organs, operate selectively. "Consciousness," James wrote, "does not appear to itself chopped up in bits. Such words as 'chain' or 'train' do not describe it fitly as it presents itself in the first instance. It is nothing jointed: it flows. A 'river' or a 'stream' are the metaphors by which it is most naturally described. In talking of it hereafter, let us call it the stream of thought, of consciousness, or of the subjective life." And so, ever since, it has been called not only by psychologists but by historians, sociologists, and men who create with pen and paper.

With Peirce, James held that "knowledge about a thing is knowledge of its relations." Most relations, he believed, are feelings. Thus, he explained, a "line is a relation; feel it and you feel the relation." Central in every response are the felt relations of the body. Asserted James: "Every possible feeling produces a movement" and "the movement is a movement of the entire organism and of each and all of its parts."

Though the *Principles* generated a torrent of eulogiums, they met with a round of sharp criticism, too. Edward B. Titchener, a thorough Wundtian, agreed with G. Stanley Hall that what James had composed was not a comprehensive system of psychology at all, but a theory of knowledge written from the standpoint of psychologist. Perhaps their ungracious comment was not altogether unjustified. Yet for the rising generation of psychologists the *Principles* became a lodestar. Certainly it shifted their attention from structure to function. It unfolded to them a portrait of the living being in action on a scale that was truly immense. It became the broad foundation on which they were to work.

In time James's interest in psychology lagged, and as his years descended to their inevitable end he gave himself almost exclusively to philosophy. But the subject to which he had devoted so many years of labor moved on. Since 1889, when Harvard made William James a professor of psychology, what was once a rarity has become a commonplace. Today no self-esteeming university would be without a chair in psychology any more than one in chemistry. Many cities, both here and abroad, have established psychological clinics whose work they have often related to educational problems. One of the chief scientific glories of Hamburg, before the rise of the Nazis, was its magnificent psychological institute, where all kinds of educational and sociological perplexities were explored. Though psychology had its scientific beginnings among the Germans, it is in America where it has flourished most luxuriantly. Psychology has in fact become an everyday word in the American idiom and it is spoken as glibly by salesmen and poets as it is by men of learning. America, even before the war, had more psychological laboratories of serious and scientific nature than any other country, and what it expends in staffing and keeping them runs into lofty figures. It is in America that the Gestaltists got their large hearing; and it is in America, too, that Sigmund Freud gave his first popular lectures—in Massachusetts—many years before Europe responded to his doctrine. Many lands, of course, recognize the important role played by psychology in education, but it is in the United States especially that psychology has entered into such a close partnership with education— where, indeed, the job of school psychologist is becoming more and more common.

2. Diverse types of psychology

Over modern psychology float many banners, for, as in the case of medicine, psychology works in diversified ways. Among the established schools of psychology—to cite only a few—are structuralists, functionalists, behaviorists, and Gestaltists.

Structuralism. During the last quarter of the nineteenth century and for a brief part of the twentieth, structuralism was the leading academic psychology in American universities. Its chief proponent was the English-born Edward Bradford Titchener (1867–1927), for more than 30 years Cornell's chief claim to psychological glory. Titchener had studied under

Wundt and to the end of his days he remained deeply loyal to his master's scientific ideals. Titchener's works have been translated into more foreign tongues than those of any other English-speaking psychologist. When Russia built its first independent school of experimental psychology, she followed Titchener's recommendations. For years one of his books was the standard and official psychology text of France and Japan. And yet, despite his far-flung fame, the plain and remarkable fact is that Titchener's influence on American thought has been relatively small. Aloof, conservative, devoted to the strictest code of science, Titchener immersed himself in the solitude of the laboratory. Unlike the energetic and effervescent James, with his boundless interest in the doings of men and women, Titchener was by comparison almost monastic, deliberately isolating himself from the rest of American life.

Unlike James, Titchener was determined to preserve psychology as an impersonal science. "The concept of psychology," he proclaimed with a meaningful look at James, "is the morphology of the mind—what is there and in what quantity, not what [it] is for." It is, in other words, structural and not functional. The study of the living organism, Titchener believed, was the task of the biologist, not the psychologist. As for harnessing psychology to the problems of life, he would have no truck with such heresy. "Science," he was convinced, "deals not with values, but with facts."

Like functionalism, structuralism has traditionally concerned itself with the study of consciousness; but it is not the turbulent stream of thought popularized by James's classic description. Consciousness is simply "the sum-total of human experience considered as dependent upon a nervous system." Like the functionalist, the structuralist has identified mind with consciousness, but unlike his rival, he does not accept it as a biological function of the brain. Instead, he prefers to view it as an intricate formation of psychic elements. Structurally perceived, every phenomenon of experience has its site in the nervous system.

For its method, structuralism has relied almost entirely on self-observation; but this is not the soul-searching of an agonized Hamlet or a Rousseau, nor is it the leisurely self-examination employed by James and his followers. For Titchener introspection meant a very rigorous, precise, dispassionate, impersonal description of one's mental processes produced by the excitation of the nervous system, with no consideration at all of the meaning or worth of these processes. It was Titchener's unshakable belief that introspection was the only method by which the mind could be studied scientifically.

In recent years the magnet of structuralism has lost much of its strength. Partly this has been due to its strict academism, its unwillingness to come out of the cloister and tell the multitude what it wants to know. To the national pragmatism such an attitude makes no appeal, even though it be in the name of science. Certainly in this respect it is no match for the psychology of experience and action, which after all can readily be hitched to service. But structuralism had inherent weaknesses, too. It was impractical—purposely so. It was also artificial. Though its adherents labored assiduously for years to analyze consciousness, to break it up into its elements, they deliberately closed the door to the study of personality. Their view of consciousness as "the sum-total of mental processes occurring *now* at any given 'present' time," is today under heavy fire. Many critics of structuralism contend that consciousness is a continued, ever changing thing—a stream of thought, if you will—leading to action and consequences. The structuralist views mental life "atomistically"; that is to say, he seeks to understand it by breaking it up into its component parts and analyzing and scrutinizing the action of each one separately. This view, too, is being cannonaded by those who think of mental life not simply as the sum-total of its component parts, but as an organic whole. They reject the notion that the complex, integrated behavior of a living organism can be explained by studying the action and reaction of the organism's separate parts. Another weakness in the armament of structuralism is its technique of introspection. Although the structuralists concede that self-observation can only be effective as a method when it is executed with the utmost objectivity and exactitude, and that training is necessary for this, as a primary and reliable source of scientific data the method is generally rejected today.

Though structuralism is being assailed on many fronts and though it is obviously on the wane, its adherents are by no means inconsequential. Despite the heavy conversions made by some of the newer psychologies, structuralism is still the reigning psychology in many of our leading colleges and universities. Nor can the historian lightly dismiss its influence. It did its part in emancipating psychology from philosophy. Its zeal for an impersonal science is certainly laudable as is its desire for a meticulous, scientific methodology. The findings which have come out of its researches have, on the whole, held their ground. But they are narrow, even microscopic, and when viewed against the great and breathtaking totality of human behavior, they seem as foreign almost as the dodo and the dinosaur.

Functionalism. On the roster of functionalism will be found such lustrous names as James and Dewey, and many others. Like the structuralists, the functionalists have employed introspection to a great extent; but they have bolstered their findings with accurate and objective observation; moreover, they frequently admit that a complete experimental control of mental functions is thus far only a noble aspiration. Starting with the premise that man is a living organism, a product of heredity and environment, the functionalist is interested not merely in what the phenomena of consciousness are, but in *what they do*. Our mental life, as reflected through our feelings, sensations, and thoughts, is the functionalist's main sphere of interest. Since he is primarily concerned with use or function, the functionalist obviously must give some attention to human behavior; in this respect he has occupied himself considerably with instincts and habits. Functionalists are not averse to studying life in its natural setting. They do not agree in the least with Titchener that the science of human behavior should deal only with facts and not with values. Thus they see no reason why psychology should not contribute to the improvement of the human lot. It was Dewey, a functionalist, who, as president of the American Psychological Association, in 1900 made a plea for the application of psychology to social practice. With their pragmatic background, functionalists have taken kindly to applied psychology. Vocational guidance, industrial psychology, social and abnormal psychology—indeed, the vast congeries of man's practical affairs—they deem as their rightful sphere of operation. They are by no means reluctant to relate their psychology to human needs and problems. The horror which once overwhelmed Harvard's Professor Hugo Münsterberg, lest psychology might some day concern itself with what men prefer in cigarette-holders and meerschaum pipes, is no horror at all for the modern functionalist. He is as much concerned with them as he is with the three R's, the selection of competent switchboard operators, and with one's taste in comics. As a matter of fact, Münsterberg himself was able in time to overcome his horror and he helped no little in the development of vocational guidance and industrial psychology.

Unlike structuralism, functionalism is indigenous to America; in fact, it has been called "the most characteristic American psychology." Functionalism has stressed a more objective methodology. It has helped to clear away many of the fantastic notions once held about the successive steps involved in the development of our mental function from birth to maturity. It has yielded some valuable clues to our understanding of the psychology of learning. It called attention to the part played by motivation and goal-seeking in our lives. It was in the vanguard in discerning the importance of behavior and dynamics—two fundamental principles of virtually every up-to-date psychological school. The fact that the functionalists have been willing to relate their researches to individual and social needs and practices has of course greatly extended the scope of psychology.

Rooted in functionalism, of which it is really a part, is the connectionist psychology of Edward Lee Thorndike.[1] Thorndike was a student of William James, but he took his doctor's degree at Columbia under James McKeen Cattell. In time he became a professor at his alma mater's Teachers College, and in this capacity his influence on American school practice was enormous. Thorndike's important spade work in the development of psychology is of the first order. He pioneered in the development of animal psychology; he was the first to present us with an exhaustive quantitative study of learning and of transfer of training; and he was in the front ranks of those who developed the measuring movement.

Thorndike's psychology is mechanistic. It is commonly referred to as a connectionist psychology. He himself has described it thus:

We ask the reader to adopt . . . the vocabulary of what may be called a situation-response or connectionist psychology, in which the word *situation* or the symbol S is used to mean any state of affairs outside or inside an organism; the word *response* or the symbol R is used to mean any state of affairs in some organism which is, or seems to be, related to some S by sequence at least and perhaps in more dynamic ways; and the word connection or the symbol —> is used to mean the fact that S is followed by R or the probability that S will be followed by R, other things being equal. A situation may be as minute and definite as a pinprick on a certain spot, or as large and vague as a thunderstorm. It may be short . . . or long. . . . A response may be any real event in an organism—a movement, an idea, a mood, a liking, a craving, or any part or feature of any such real event. It may be as little and short and unitary as the knee-jerk or as big and elaborate as writing an encyclopedia. A connection may be as direct as that between the tap on the knee and the jerk of the muscle, or as meditated as that between the receipt of a bill and the writing of a check. It may be as single as that between thinking *a, b, c, d* and thinking *e,* or as multiple as

[1] For Thorndike's part in the measurement movement see p. 426.

that between the impression of tennis court, opponent, and balls and the position, timing, force and direction of one's return stroke. Situation, response and connection are terms used here to help describe and prophesy what an animal does, not to make any assumptions concerning how or why the animal does it.[2]

As with James and Dewey the stress with Thorndike is on behavior.

Thorndike's connectionist psychology reached its high mark in the twenties; since then, however, the S–R psychology has slid down the hill; and today in the light of the organismic wholeness concepts it appears no longer to be quite adequate. Nonetheless, the name of Thorndike is written large in the history of educational psychology. His versatile pioneering opened immense new vistas in psychology at the very time when modern conceptions and techniques were taking shape. At Teachers College Thorndike taught many hundreds of students, injecting into them not only his views but instilling in many of them a real esteem for the scientific spirit, although his emphasis, it is true, was essentially quantitative and statistical. His own researches took him into many fields. He, with others, confirmed the activist psychology of experience; he explored and documented the nature of individual differences and of mental abilities; he added copiously to our knowledge of the psychology of skill and the psychology of growth; and in his studies of adult learning he put the scientific quietus on the notion that only the young can learn successfully.

Behaviorism. The behaviorists are of more recent origin than their structural and functional brethren. Registered as behaviorists are John Broadus Watson and Karl Lashley. Watson is generally regarded as the sire of the movement, though Lashley, his student at Johns Hopkins, anticipated some of the theories which Watson later expounded and popularized. Behaviorists have not always been in accord about

---

[2] Thorndike, E. L., *The Psychology of Wants, Interests and Attitudes and Human Learning*, pp. 17–18. New York: Appleton-Century-Crofts, Inc., 1935.

their beliefs, with the consequence that there have occasionally been feuds in their midst. Indeed, there have been several varieties of behaviorism. Like the biologist, the behaviorist regards man as an animal. He is *homo sapiens,* chief among the primates. What distinguishes him from his comrades in the animal world is simply, say the Watsonians, the number and fineness of his manual, laryngeal, and visceral habits. These are the three classes of responses recognized by the orthodox behaviorist, and on them he has focused his observation. Consciousness, so dear to the older psychologies, has been discarded by the behaviorist; also introspection as a method of study. Behaviorism has reserved its investigations for such activities as are observable to an outsider, aided, if need be and if possible, by scientific instruments. In the language of the behaviorist, life is simply a set of psychological responses resulting from physical stimuli. Behaviorists have made much of the responses of the body, though they apparently have ignored James's stress on the mechanism of the feelings in body response.

Behaviorism came into the psychological limelight for its exaltation of the conditioned reflex. The layman was almost as cognizant of conditioning as he was of Freud and suppressed desires. Actually the experiments which laid the foundation for the conditioned reflex were performed by the noted Russian physiologist, Ivan Pavlov (1849–1936). Like other students of the human body, Pavlov had observed that the eating of a savory morsel causes the flow of not only saliva, but also the stomach's gastric juices. Pavlov had noticed that a dog's glands would begin secreting before the actual eating began. Not only would the taste of the food untap a flow of juices, but also its odor and sight, or, for that matter, even the sudden appearance of the animal's attendant. Pavlov knew of course that there was no direct connection between the dog's salivary glands and the dinner-bearer. This caused the physiologist to wonder whether he could produce other stimuli, not ordinarily associated with the dog's food, which might cause a food response from the dog's glands. Accordingly, while the dog was drooling in anticipation of a tasty morsel, Pavlov would stimulate him in diverse ways, such as ringing a bell or flashing a light. After many trials he rang the bell or flashed the light—but with no food in sight—with the result that the dog's mouth would begin to water nonetheless. Pavlov summarized his conclusion thus: "Any ocular stimulus, any desired sound, any odor that might be selected, and the stimulation of any part of the skin, either by mechanical means or by the application of heat or cold, have in our hands never failed to stimulate the salivary glands. . . ." Such were the beginnings of our knowledge of the conditioned reflex.[3]

For his contribution Pavlov was awarded the Nobel Prize for Medicine in 1904. Before the end of the first decade the significance of the conditioned reflex was beginning to become apparent to a number of American psychologists. By 1908, for example, Morton Prince, with Pavlov as his inspirer, was seeking to establish that the psychic powers of animals were not essentially different from those of humans. A few years later, Karl Lashley, experimenting in the Johns Hopkins laboratories and using his teacher, Watson, as one of his subjects, proved definitely that human glands could be conditioned. Watson himself carried on a number of experiments on very young infants. He found that humans came into this world with only three undefiled emotions: fear, rage, and love; and that these are evoked by only a limited number of stimuli. A babe whose age was reckoned by a few days is afraid, it seems, of nothing but loud sounds and losing its support; if subsequently, as an adult, it is afraid of the dark or snakes, or anything else, that fear, concluded Watson, has been acquired. Watson asserted furthermore that there were no instincts. He

[3] The official English version of Pavlov's experiment appeared in 1902, though G. Stanley Hall, perceiving its possible significance for psychology, had obtained a private translation even before that date. As for John B. Watson, the subsequent popularizer of the conditioned reflex, as late as 1914 he was convinced that there were "inherent difficulties in the method" and that it was decidedly limited in its "general range of usefulness."

denied that "slight differences in body and brain structure . . .
make a difference in the way the newborn starts out." Admitting that some people begin life without good eyes or ears,
that some may come into this world without fingers, and that
some are deficient mentally, Watson held these things to be
of minor significance when "contrasted with what the human
infant must learn." Conditioning, in other words, became all-
important. The talismanic effects Watson claimed for conditioning made him go so far as to insist that, given any
healthy infant and allowed to rear it in the specified Wat-
sonian environment, he could make it become the adult he
chose it to be—or as he put it, "doctor, lawyer, artist, mer-
chant-chief, and, yes, even beggar-man and thief, regardless
of his talents, penchants, tendencies, abilities, vocations, and
race of his ancestors."

The heyday of behaviorism was in the early twenties.
Today one no longer characterizes it as a movement. Its
recession in popularity has been due in no small degree to the
extravagance of its claims. However, it would be false to
suggest that behaviorism has been discredited or that it has
been without influence. Actually, few of its doctrines have
been *scientifically* disproved, though some of them have undergone modification. That conditioning, for example, is possible,
and that it may be turned to valuable use in the development
of a person's behavior, no first-rate psychologist would dispute.
What has been done in this respect has been demonstrated all
too well, alas, by the Nazis. But to put behavior on a purely
mechanical, stimulus-response, conditioning basis has not met
with universal applause from American psychologists. Behaviorism's great claim to distinction is its emphasis on
strictly objective investigation. In its quest into the mysteries
of human behavior, it has consistently held itself to a consideration of only those factors capable of observation and
analysis. In restricting themselves to the rigorous techniques
of the laboratory scientist, the behaviorists have necessarily
circumscribed the scope of their operations. The findings of

the behaviorists, although admirable for their painstaking technique, have been confined relatively to a fractional part of that complex phenomenon known as human behavior. The behaviorists delivered the *coup de mort* to introspection as a satisfactory scientific method in psychology. Moreover, their caustic criticisms of some of the ancient and flyblown assumptions of the more conventional kinds of psychology have tended to bring new growth and development to psychology as a whole.

Gestalt. Gestalt psychology is the child of structuralism, even though it hotly rejects mental elements. Its pioneers were the Germans, Max Wertheimer, Kurt Koffka, Wolfgang Köhler, and Kurt Lewin; in America the new psychology was fathered by R. M. Ogden, George Hartmann, and Raymond Wheeler. Gestaltism was first seen in 1912 when Wertheimer, then at Berlin, reported some new views in the field of perception, presenting at the same time the theory that movement is actually sensed and not re-interpreted by the higher mental processes. The new doctrine was antagonistic to the atomistic teachings of Wundt, then still a power in German psychology; however, after a lapse of several decades, Wertheimer's views are still in the realm of debate.

Two years after Wertheimer's disclosure, his associate Wolfgang Köhler was studying the mentality of apes on the Canary Island of Teneriffe when the outbreak of the first War caused him to be interned. Out of his enforced sojourn came his important study, *The Mentality of the Apes,* which probably did more than any previous book by a Gestaltist to advertise the new psychology in the United States. Opposed to Thorndike's explanation of animal learning, particularly his trial-and-error explanation, Köhler undertook a series of graded experiments on the chimpanzee on the hypothesis that the animal's successful response was due to a mental process which Köhler called insight. To reveal such a power Köhler believed that it was futile to put the animal into "blind situations," such as mazes and puzzle boxes, to which he can only respond at random. Instead, the animal must "see the whole situation." To make this possible Köhler put his chimpanzees into a large open cage where he left them with the stimulus in the form of a basket of food, together with sticks, and strings, and other material in plain sight. One of the subjects, after having learned how to obtain food which was out of reach by means of one stick, was given two sticks, neither one of which, however, was quite long enough to reach the food. After more than an hour of trial-and-error behavior, it suddenly occurred to the chimpanzee that he might reach the food by fitting the two sticks together. Was the ape's successful response an accident? Was it random behavior? Köhler was certain that it was not; for when the solution came, it came like a flash; it was accompaied by excitement and a new liveliness; and furthermore it was well remembered the following day. Koffka, who was Köhler's associate, has pointed out that the animal must see all the significant parts of the situation together. The ape's behavior Koffka has interpreted thus:

it is not merely a matter of seeing or noticing an object such as a stick, because before it is employed the object must cease to be an isolated neutral thing to the animal and become a member of the situation at hand. The object must, in short, become a "tool." As a necessary condition for a correct type of behavior an alteration must occur in the object of perception. What at the beginning possessed only the character of "indifference" or "something to bite upon," etc., now obtains the character of "something to fetch fruit with." . . .

What the animal has actually learned is to make an irrelevant object relevant to the situation. . . .

Only one conception of the performance is possible: that the animal has acquired an ability to introduce "tools" into certain situations. Nor is this ability limited to the particular thing with which it was acquired; on the contrary it is an acquisition of a much more general nature.

A transfer of learning from one thing to another results, therefore, from the sensible application of a certain principle of configuration.[4]

---

[4] Koffka, K., *The Growth of the Mind,* pp. 191 ff. New York: Harcourt Brace & Company, Inc., 1924.

In explaining Köhler's studies, the American psychologist R. S. Woodworth has said:

The stress of Gestalt psychology is on the perceptual factor in learning. Learning means doing something new. The newness cannot be understood by examining the motor performance alone, for the newness consists in a reorganization of the situation, so as to bridge the gap between the situation as it is and the goal. The gap is bridged by seeing the situation as a pattern and leading to the goal.[5]

Gestalt is the German word for "form," "figure," or "shape," though in psychological English it has generally been translated as "configuration," or "pattern." For the Gestaltist this is the basic attribute of the mind. All mental life—indeed, all existence—consists of organized segregated wholes, having their own unitary structure and operating in 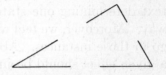 accord with their own laws. Everything one experiences has a definite and inherent pattern, or as it is sometimes called, a *configuration*. The phases of any experience in their sum at any moment are integrated. Does a man attend a play? Then clearly his overloaded stomach, his aching feet, and his boring companions attend with him. Whatever his reactions, they are affected by consciousness and environment.

The central teaching of the Gestalt psychology can be readily understood from one of their own illustrations. Although the three sides of the figure have been broken, on beholding it one has an inescapable tendency to complete the triangle. One reacts thus to the total situation, to elements which are not wholly apparent as well as to the fully apparent ones. In the whole pattern of experience some elements will assume a leading and dominant importance, and others will be reduced to the ground for the stressed factors. Essential for the pattern, these ground elements are said to act somewhat

[5] Robert S. Woodworth, *Contemporary Schools of Psychology,* p. 101. New York, Copyright, 1931 by The Ronald Press Company.

in the manner of the background of a portrait in lending it its characteristic tone. The pattern of experience is not necessarily permanent, nor is it always the same. At another time it may assemble itself with a new set of elements playing the lead, now thrusting the former dominant ones into the background. The factor behind such changes, according to Gestalt theory, is the goal of the moment. Configurations, it should be noted, are not looked upon by the true-blue Gestaltist as mere mechanical events; on the contrary, they form themselves "towards a definite end." Holding that man knows what he is going to do and how he is going to do it, Köhler has asserted that "we experience the live and dynamical context determining one state this way and that change another way. Moreover, we feel where they come from and where they go in those instances. Above all we may experience *why* . . . a given effect should be just the one growing out of it." Thus the stress of Gestalt seems to be on purpose as the integrating element in any experience.

The early work of the Gestaltists lay in the field of perception. In time, however, their activity led them almost inevitably into other domains, such as learning and memory, growth and development, thinking and feeling, intelligence and personality. As for learning, Gestaltists say that it is more in the nature of perceiving and patterning than doing and drilling. As has been indicated, they are generally opposed to the concept of trial and error, as they are to the idea of stimulus-response, and use and effect. Instead, they stress the *total organization,* involving insight, perception, and understanding. Remembering and forgetting they describe as "a meaningful reorganization of total phenomena and fields." As for growth and development, they stress heredity and maturation as against environment and learning. In intelligence and personality they prefer to scrutinize qualitative factors and unique central characteristics rather than quantitative scores and traits. Regarding will, it "is the energy of the total human system consciously conditioning the

activities of its parts." The same wholeness of view is evident
in the Gestaltist's interpretation of emotion. This is not a
"special discrete kind of behavior. . . . It is an aspect of
whatever the person is doing at the time, when, in the
approach to a given goal, the tension is increased and
maintained through intraorganic stimulation. . . . Emotive
behavior . . . is an intentional, intelligent behavior, *ener-
gized*." [6]

To the Gestaltists, and particularly to the late Kurt Lewin
(1890–1947), we are indebted for the development of a number of new and promising theories.[7] Lewin began his psychological career in Germany before the first World War. During
the Weimar political interlude he taught at Berlin, occasionally visiting and lecturing in the United States. When
Hitler's Aryan Reich made life intolerable, he migrated to the
United States where he taught at various universities. In
1926 Lewin published his monograph *Purpose, Will and Need*,
wherein he rejected the view that behavior was caused by
neural connections, as expounded by Behaviorists and S-R
Connectionists. Behavior, contended Lewin, is the result of
tension energy systems which spring from the organism's
needs or wants (*Bedürfnisse*). Lewin held the release of
tension to be the leading factor in determining human behavior. He illustrated his abstraction by the example of what
takes place when one tries to remember to mail a letter. As
long as the epistle is unmailed, tension remains within the
physical system; but once it is posted, equilibrium is established, and one proceeds to forget about it. Lewin sought to
relate psychic energies to the organism's needs. He described
the latter as psychic forces which drew upon reservoirs of

---

[6] Wheeler, R. H. and Perkins, F. T., *Principles of Mental Development*, pp.
201, 207. New York: The Thomas Y. Crowell Company, 1932.

[7] Among Lewin's more important writings in English note particularly the
following: *A Dynamic Theory of Personality*. New York: McGraw-Hill Book
Company, Inc., 1935; *Principles of Topological Psychology*. New York: Mc-
Graw-Hill Book Company, Inc., 1936; and his monograph "The Conflict
between Aristotelean and Galilean Modes of Thought," *Journal of Psychology*,
pp. 141–177, 1931.

energy; as the organism's need changed, bodily tensions changed likewise. Lewin's stress on the dynamic, motivating factors behind human behavior led him and his students to investigate such problems as the dynamics of play, the behavior of children in new and strange situations, the structure and the state of the whole person, the relation of tension to fatigue and effectiveness, the speed and discharge of tense systems on different levels of reality and unreality, and so on.

In the thirties Lewin offered the first glimpse of what is now commonly known as the force-energy psychology. By structuring psychology in space-time concepts—somewhat along the line of the new physics—Lewin endeavored to devise the basic theory of a force-energy psychology. He rejects the traditional assumptions of the atomistic-mechanistic schools and seems to have gathered a considerable amount of evidence in support of the wholeness, integrationist interpretation of human behavior. The question of prime importance for Lewin is not some statistical average derived from the study of a few thousand cases. Lewin is concerned with the profounder problem of *why?* "Why," he asks, "does a person at a given moment, in a given state and environment, behave precisely as he does?" "Why, at such a moment, does a situation have precisely this structure?" "Why does the person have precisely this state or condition?" The answer to these questions, Lewin believed, can come only through the actual study of human behavior in actual and concrete situations and not from any statistical average. It was Lewin's contention, moreover, that the study of behavior causes can be approached satisfactorily only when we know something about the "form of a definite structure in a definite sort of environment" and that this is possible only when the dynamics of the processes have been derived "from the relation of the concrete individual to the concrete situation." In their new approach to the causes of behavior Lewin and his co-workers insisted that psychology must be structured in space-time concepts.[8] Their

---

[8] For a "workable representation" of their "field of force" concept, Lewin

theory was that "whenever an organism behaves psychologically, it is said to be behaving in a psychological field." Organisms, moreover, are said to move toward goals "under the propulsion of forces"—though precisely what the nature of these forces is, is not yet clear.   In recasting their theories in terms of energy concepts, American Gestaltists have been led by Raymond Wheeler who has summed up the Lewin psychology in eight "organismic laws." [9]

Like their psychological brethren laboring under different hypotheses, the Gestaltists have not escaped criticism.   Their psychology has been accused of vagueness.   Its generalizations have been assailed on the ground of being largely qualitative and hence of no specific predictive value.   It has been charged with being unscientific in its treatment of mental life, since its stress on the uniqueness of mental phenomena precludes a repetition of events, a condition deemed essential for experimentation.   Finally, the opponents of Gestalt attack the overstressing of its central principle, its wholeness point of view.

The Gestaltists, for their part, have not taken these crit-

_____

and his associates have made full use of the mathematics known as topology, "the science of place," originated by Listin in 1883. It is defined as "the geometrical theory of situations without respect to size or shape." See Lewin, K., *Principles of Topological Psychology*. New York: McGraw-Hill Book Company, Inc., 1936.

[9] As summed up by Wheeler, the organismic laws are: the Law of Field Properties: "A whole is more than the sum of its parts" . . . "properties pertaining to the complex wholes are known as field properties"; the Law of Derived Properties: "Parts derive their properties from wholes"; the Law of Determined Action: "the whole determines the activities of its parts"; the Law of Individuation: "parts of wholes come into existence through an emergence process called individuation, or structurization, or differentiation"; the Law of Field Genesis: "wholes evolve as wholes"; the Law of Least Action: "energy interchange takes place through the shortest spatio-temporal interval"; the Law of Maximum Work: "any influence affecting a system of energy affects it throughout . . . in an energy system a maximum amount of energy, for any given set of conditions, will be expended in the course of maintaining balance"; the Law of Configuration: "energy systems function as units; they adjust themselves to multitudes of disturbing influences, known as total situations; "the unit that adjusts itself is called a configuration . . . the laws of least action and maximum work explain why a configuration must behave as a single unit." See Wheeler, R. H. and Perkins, F. T., *Principles of Mental Development*. New York: The Thomas Y. Crowell Company, 1932.

icisms sitting down. They have pointed out, for example, that some of their views have been partly confirmed by such exacting experimenters as G. E. Coghill, K. S. Lashley, and several others. As for the charge that their treatment of mental life has been unscientific, they have asserted that since, in their view, mental life is unique and cannot be satisfactorily studied with any existing methodology, it is not at all unscientific to devise a more workable methodology.

Without doubt, the Gestaltists have caused re-examination of many of the traditional teachings of psychology. They have amassed a good deal of evidence against the mechanistic stimulus-response interpretation of behavior. Certainly their stress on the unity or integratedness of an experience is significant; nor can its emphasis on the monetary background lying behind human behavior be lightly dismissed.

Psychoanalysis. Psychoanalysis is another importation from the continent. Teaching that the key to human behavior is to be found in unconscious motivation, the psychoanalytic doctrines have played a more significant part in medicine than in education. The reason is easy to find, for psychoanalysis concentrates on abnormal rather than on normal behavior. The efforts to attach psychoanalysis to education have been more deliberate and determined in the Old World than here. The Swiss city of Zurich has brought forth a scientific magazine, *Zeitschrift für psycho-analytische Pädagogik*, dedicated to the study of psychoanalysis in education. Significantly enough, most of its contributors display the M. D., and most of its discussions deal with the behavior disorders of children.

The father of modern psychoanalysis is Sigmund Freud (1856–1939). Active in Austria before the Nazi deluge forced him out, Freud bestowed a threefold classification on the human psyche. There is first the *id*, which is instinctive and unconscious; then there is the *ego,* which is largely conscious and rational; and finally there is the *super-ego,* which is moral and corresponds to ethical conscience. In the unconscious are seated the primal human urges. Some of these, no longer accepted as "good" in modern society, have been *repressed* or inhibited. That is to say, they have been consciously rejected or disowned. According to the Freudians, the force of erotic instinct, or as they prefer to call it, *libido,* is on hand even in human babyhood, when it is manifested toward the mother. She, in Freudian parlance, is the infant's first love. Where such impulses are subsequently not directed toward other objects they are said to be *fixated.* In their integrated form they become the much publicized Oedipus complex. These resulting complexes reveal themselves especially in dreams. Interpreted in the Freudian manner, dreams are the revelations of repressed desires. Where erotic impulses have turned toward nonsexual objects, they are said to have been *sublimated.*

Re-interpreting and modifying the Freudian doctrines, Carl Jung has insisted that beyond the personal unconscious of Freud, there is a collective *super-personal unconscious* composed of racial images. Every man has an unconscious feminine nature, the *anima;* and every woman a corresponding *animus.* The followers of Jung impart a much smaller role to sex, preferring the theory of psychological types to explain personality. According to this, one is either *introverted* or *extraverted.* In the former event, the whole force of one's psyche focuses itself inward on one's own self; in the latter case it reaches outward to other persons and things. If one is in the first group, one is shy and retiring; in the second case, one is more forward, perhaps a joiner and a backslapper. In attempting to work out his theory in an experimental way, Jung has further classified his extraverts and introverts into several special categories.

Taking still another tack, Alfred Adler deemed the inferiority complex the great motivating force of human nature. Such a complex is acquired in early infancy. Its cause, according to Adler, is the feeling of weakness, inadequacy, or helplessness that is experienced in trying to cope with one's world. A physical or mental deficiency, real or fancied, will augment it. It is the inferiority complex, so Adler teaches, that makes its holders lust to dominate their environment.

The critics of psychoanalysis stand divided. There are those, for example, who lift it and its founders to the stratosphere, and who perceive in its teachings the philtre which will cure all our ailments. Then there are those who see in it nothing but a dangerous pestilence. In Hitler's Third Reich, the Nazis burned the writings of most of the psychoanalysts, and arrested or exiled most of the psychoanalytic practitioners. Most of the dicta of the psychoanalysts have been derived from case studies of individuals, who in most instances were neurotic, mentally sick, or emotionally deranged. What general conclusions can be drawn from these cases is still a matter of debate. However, as one of several ways of exploring the intricate mazes of human behavior, the psychoanalytic technique has excellent uses. Particularly does this appear to be so in the study of emotions and personality.

3.   Some aspects of educational psychology

Instincts. During the past generation the rafters of the psychological arena have been charred by heated controversies over instincts. A good part of these disputations has been academic and ultimately, no doubt, of little significance. The roots of the debate are imbedded partly in an unsatisfactory definition of the term *instinct,* and partly in the elusive and often incomplete nature of the instinctive tendencies of most members of the human race. The fact is that most of the available psychological evidence regarding instincts is empirical rather than experimental. As might be anticipated, the listings of instincts vary considerably. Turning from one authority to others, we find some who hold that there are no human instincts, that there are two basic ones, that there are so many as to be uncountable.

Thorndike has cast instincts into three groups to include those reactions (1) related to food and self-preservation, (2) those concerned with tendencies to respond to the behavior of others, and (3) those dealing with bodily movements and cerebral activities. From Woodworth has come another inventory, again with three classifications, thus: (1) satisfaction of bodily needs, (2) social responses, and (3) play activities. Still another tripartite grouping has emerged from Gates: (1) responses to bodily or organic conditions, (2) responses to objects or events in the environment, (3) responses to the presence or activities of other human beings. Among the more eager of modern champions of instincts, the late William McDougall in 1908 listed seven major instincts: revulsion, curiosity, flight, pugnacity, self-abasement, self-assertion, and the parental instinct. Subsequently he added laughter. Then came distress, food-seeking, acquisitiveness, pairing, and mating. Some of McDougall's lists also have construction. In contrast to McDougall's large roll of instincts, that of Watson has shrunk almost to nothing: fear, love, and rage.

Emotions. Our knowledge of emotions, as in the case of instincts, has been undergoing revision. Not so long ago it was accepted that we inherit patterns of hatred, love, fear, sympathy, humor, and pathos. But again, based largely on empirical data, this belief has been found unwarranted by some of the newer experimental psychologists. Led by the studies of Watson, many now lean to the view that children under the age of three possess only three primary emotions of fear, anger, and love. These very likely are innate, but the more complex emotional reactions are held to have been acquired through experience. Biologically, emotions, inherited and acquired, are organic, manifesting bodily changes in the form of glandular secretions, blood pressure, digestion, and respiration. Whatever the final verdict as to which emotions are inherited and which acquired, all of them are intricately commingled with our daily living. Emotion is the stream that runs through our prejudices and enthusiasms, our likes and dislikes, our interests and attitudes. That there are educational implications in our direction of emotionalized behavior is obvious.

Capacities and differences. Like his scientific kinsmen engaged in other spheres, the psychologist is concerned with finding and formulating laws and principles. Because such laws must possess general validity holding for the rank and file of all men, psychologists and educators have tended in the past to study groups rather than individuals. Underlying such efforts was the notion that people are more alike than different. More recently, however, the realization has dawned that people vary just as much psychologically as they do biologically, or perhaps even more. Not only are such variations present, but a proper understanding of them is today deemed essential for sound educational procedure.

Inspected at random, an ordinary class of school children will display vividly not only the usual observable variations in height and weight, but also in teeth and eyes, tonsils and adenoids. There will be differences that are largely social, so that one may perceive liars and bullies and leaders of genuine fabric. Psychologically, one will discover I. Q.'s covering the whole mental scale. One will note special talents of high caliber in music, art, and mechanical skill. There will be some for whom mathematics is simple and a delight; others who excel in reading comprehension or reading rate; and still others who shine in putting their ideas into the written word.

So significant for education are these individual capacities that much effort has gone into their study. Not only have psychologists produced interesting works of purely academic importance, but they have also created many first-rate aids for the practical schoolman. It is today possible not only to detect particular capacities, but also to gauge them quantitatively (see pp. 425 ff.).

Diversity in human ability in the acquisition of knowledges and skills has been treated well and thoroughly by contemporary educational psychologists. On the other hand, concerning the more imponderable differences in human temperament, emotions, and sensitiveness, we are still in uncertain darkness. The truth seems to be that, temperamentally and emotionally, children are no more uniform than they are physically. In the past, teachers, unfortunately, have been either ignorant or unmindful of this elementary matter. Uniformity has generally been their yardstick of justice. Thus the thick-hided, whose complacency could not be rippled by a cannon, were accorded the same treatment as the sensitive and gentle-minded. It has become clear that such a procedure is not only unfair but often quite harmful. It has been found, for example, that a child's dislike of school often is caused not so much by coercion or possible dullness, but by the torture that has been done to the child's inner self. Educational psychology, unfortunately, has not yet been able to find a foolproof method for dealing with such manifold perplexities; but on the other hand, it has uncovered sufficient serious facts to make educators cognizant of these matters.[10]

Racial differences. It was during World War I that the first comprehensive data regarding differences between whites, Negroes, and Indians were compiled. Through the Army Alpha tests it appeared that whites were superior in their ability to do abstract thinking. Subsequent studies by others seem to have substantiated this conclusion. But it should be noted that in no case do the differences appear large enough to warrant any general claim for racial superiority. Ferguson, as a matter of fact, has demonstrated that, despite lower averages, there are relatively few whites with an intelligence superior to that of the highest of the Negroes; and again, there are correspondingly few Negroes with a lesser intelligence than that of the dullest of the whites. There seem to be important temperamental differences, but to what extent these are innate and peculiar to the race and to what extent they are due to environmental factors is still uncertain. Likewise, there seems to be no real evidence to warrant the conclusion

---

[10] For an excellent study of these problems see Schohaus, W., *The Dark Places in Education.* New York: Henry Holt & Company, Inc., 1932.

that the white man is superior to the other races in his capacities for manual dexterity of any sort. Anthropologists who have applied themselves to the problem of racial differences are still far from any solution. On one thing, however, they seem more or less agreed, and that is that it is utterly rash to talk about a pure Aryan race, and even more absurd to laud its alleged superiority.

Interest and learning. The idea that interest is essential for effective learning is of ancient vintage. Not until recently, however, have educational psychologists put the proposition under their experimental lenses. Their studies, both here and abroad, have tended to substantiate what heretofore has been only an assumption. Interest, it has been found, is not only important in efficient learning—it is almost indispensable. Yet despite all this, educators are still far apart when it comes to determining the actual role to be played by interest in education. Indeed, the old feud between the advocates of interest and the proponents of effort has never ceased. The same factions are still peppering away at one another, the only discernible difference being that they are campaigning under new flags. On the one hand are the so-called *progressives,* who proclaim interest to be of dominant importance, with all ,questions of curriculum, organization, and methods related to it. On the other hand are the *essentialists* who, though they concede the general theory in favor of interest, yet would subordinate it to the rank of a contributing factor. (See p. 148.)

Different views of learning. Traditionally, learning used to be viewed as the acquiring and piling up of knowledge. This, interestingly enough, is still the common view of the layman. There were, of course, many ways of imparting knowledge. Where the process was directed by a teacher who had risen to a high craftsmanship, such learning was usually launched through the senses, including, as it proceeded, the building of images and concepts. In the hands of a less gifted teacher the process was generally nothing more than mind-stuffing.

With the coming of the behaviorists, learning was looked upon more as a form of habit formation, of conditioning, than the building up of ideas. Given a stimulus, there would be a response; and to get the desirable response, what was essential was the right stimulus. Learning thus conceived, as some of the critics of behaviorism have pointed out, is still mechanical.

Today this view of learning is no longer quite so fashionable; and even its adherents have tended to become somewhat more judicious. If learning, thus conceived, tended to be piecemeal and fragmentary, under Gestalt direction its stress has been altogether different. The Gestaltist interprets learning not simply as a response to a stimulus, but rather as an organization and reorganization of behavior, flowing from the interaction of a growing organism and its world. Memorized facts are no longer the substance of learning, nor are conditioned reflexes. Learning, as seen through Gestalt eyes, is not so simple. For the Gestaltist, the whole organism is participating in an act of learning—and not just part of it; learning involves not fragmentary responses, but responses organized into patterns.

Transfer of training. In the nineteenth century it was generally believed that the study of such subjects as Latin or mathematics "trained the mind." Traditionally, the mind was thought to be comprised of *faculties* of various kinds. Certain subjects, it was felt, would best develop certain faculties. Geometry, originally a very practical subject, continued to be taught after it had lost its original reason for being, on the ground that it trained the reason. History, it was argued, trained the memory. Drawing polished the power of observation. Turning to the other subjects, even newer ones like sewing and manual training were often advocated and defended because of their alleged special qualities to train and develop our various powers. Once a certain subject had trained a particular power, that power was held to be usable in any other subject or field. Accordingly, the accuracy manifested in the workshop when a pupil built a table was thought to carry over to a general habit of accuracy. This is the doctrine of transfer of training.

It was not until the present century that this theory was seriously questioned. One experiment after another was run off to test the doctrine of transfer, and in no case was it completely upheld. Where once transfer had been vigorously affirmed by the practicing schoolman, it was now just as vigorously denied. But psychologists, continuing their labors, were inclined to be more restrained in their conclusions. Following Thorndike, some began to assert that all learning was specific, and that transfer, if it took place at all, did so only on the basis of *identical elements*.[11] The study of arithmetic, for example, should be of some help in algebra, because of a basic similarity of content. If, in addition, the habits of reasoning and of making applications have been developed, very likely the transfer may be still more potent. Other psychologists, following Judd, have maintained that transfer occurs only in so far as our experiences have been generalized in the act of learning. Still another view regards learning as widespread, affecting broad patterns in functional organization. It considers the mind as an entity within itself and with the whole organism.

C. Educating Exceptional Children

1. Atypical children

Twentieth century education seeks for each child an education which will be in harmony with his native capacities. There are, unfortunately, many thousands of youngsters who, by virtue of their inheritance or the influence of their environment, are so constituted that they can profit very little from what the average school has to offer. Among them are the undernourished, the physically handicapped, and the mentally defective, as well as those who excel in mind and body. Society seeks, wherever possible, to build up in such children

---

[11] See Orata, P. T., *The Theory of Identical Elements,* Ohio State University, 1928, for a discussion of the various theories.

a feeling of confidence and self-respect and to increase their individual contentment, besides, of course, making them as self-supporting as possible. To meet their varying needs, many forms of special education have been developed. There are, for example, something like 125,000 blind persons in this country. For them the federal government annually makes a special appropriation to print books in Braille to be distributed to state schools. Each state, furthermore, is financially responsible for the education of the blind, providing for their education either in its own schools or subsidizing their education in outside institutions. Most school systems in the larger cities make special provision for the teaching of the physically handicapped. Such education includes not only reading and writing, but, as in the case of the deaf, it also includes vocational training. The old "sign language," or method of communicating ideas by finger movements, is being replaced by the "oral" method, by which the deaf pupil is taught to read lip movements and to use his vocal organs in speech.

It has been estimated that about 2 per cent of America's children of school age are mentally too retarded to do ordinary school work. Their retardation varies from that of the borderline case to the hopeless. Obviously, such children cannot profit from the work of the average school. The modern movement to educate the feeble-minded has its origins in the work of Jean Marc Itard (1775–1838) and Edward Seguin (1812–1880), two Frenchmen of the nineteenth century. Both men influenced Maria Montessori, and many of her educational principles were derived from their pioneer work. Seguin stressed manual work for mental defectives, seeking through it to appeal to the mind. He emphasized sensory and motor work and made considerable use of concrete materials, such as pictures, patterns, papers, clay, sand, etc. With the development of psychology as a science, the education of mental defectives has made significant advances. Psychological tests to select and classify the feeble-minded have been of particular value. Most up-to-date school systems have organized special classes for the feeble-minded. In addition, many clinics for studying proper methods of teaching the defective have been established.

2. Delinquent children

With the establishment in New York City in 1825 of the House of Refuge, a reformatory for juvenile offenders, the problems involved in child delinquency began to draw serious attention. Similar institutions soon were established in other parts of the country. Some states, in fact, created special State Industrial Schools. In 1899, the first juvenile court was organized in Chicago. This, among other things, marked the recognition that, in the case of juvenile offenders, special and modified court procedure was desirable. From the United States the idea of the juvenile court spread to other lands, and today it is found in virtually every civilized country. Not only has the work of the juvenile court made rapid strides during the last quarter of a century, but even more significant have been the various studies of the causes of youthful delinquency. Today it is generally recognized that in the case of delinquency, as in the case of disease, prevention is far more desirable than cure. Significant also is the trend to put the delinquent in as normal a social environment as possible instead of secluding him. In promoting the child's welfare, the cooperation of all the agencies affecting him is sought. For this purpose, coordinating councils have been established in some states. Generally, this is made up of representatives of the juvenile court, the parent-teacher organizations, and such groups as are interested in child welfare.

3. The intellectually superior

Background. Time was when the many particular needs of the mentally gifted child were completely unknown. Indeed, frequently the mentally superior youngster was regarded as something odd. Various attempts were made to obtain an accurate understanding of the nature of intelligence, but it was not until Binet began work in his Paris laboratory that any really scientific foundation was laid. But Binet was looking for a method which would select the mentally inferior rather than the superior. Consequently, for a period of years Binet's original purpose remained the paramount aim of his army of imitators. Educators were then focusing their attention on the intellectually subnormal, in the hope of reclaiming mental derelicts. Since those days, we have come to realize the significance of individual differences in the mentality of school children. More and more, schoolmen have become aware of the importance of uncovering those unexplored regions of the child psyche wherein lie untapped treasures applicable to a solution of the needs of the gifted child. Writing in the *Journal of Educational Psychology* some four decades ago, William Stern, then active in Breslau, Germany, was one of the first to call attention to the educational needs of the gifted. By his call for an about-face in our traditional treatment of the gifted, Stern became the pacemaker for a movement which, during the last few years, has gathered considerable strength in America as well as abroad.

Terman's study. Careful and reliable studies of superior children are, unfortunately, still not too numerous. A number of American investigators, however, have done some meritorious preliminary work. G. M. Whipple, Helen Davis, and Lewis M. Terman are particularly noteworthy in this territory. One of the most extensive studies of gifted children is that undertaken by Professor Terman and his California associates. As a starting point for his investigation, Professor Terman relied on the teacher's judgment, requiring the teacher to nominate her brightest and her youngest pupil. Some 1,400 more or less exceptionally bright children were thus selected. Subjected, however, to the more discerning judgment of a mental test, this battalion eventually shrank to some 650. All these, however, possessed an intelligence quotient of at least 140, which, in the Terman language, is "genius." Besides this selected group there was also a control group of some 600 unselected youngsters.

Studying these children from several viewpoints—anthropological, sociological, physiological, psychological—Terman was able to make some significant conclusions. His results showed the exceptionally bright child to be much above the average in general health and physical growth. This discovery, although not new and more or less suspected by psychologists, runs contrary to the general popular belief holding that those who were strong in the head were perforce frail in body or delicate in health. Interesting also was the fact that in the character tests administered, the mentally exceptional children rated above the average. Says Terman in this connection: "Trait ratings and social data give no evidence that gifted children tend more often than others to be lacking in social adaptability or leadership. However, they are probably less superior in social, emotional, and psychophysical traits than in intellectual and volitional traits." Another finding was that the gifted child showed a potent play interest and possessed a greater knowledge of games than did the unselected children. That the superior child is inclined to play less than other children seemed to be true, but this was due to competition between the play interest and a vast colony of other interests. In studying the various intellectual interests of the gifted child, Terman found that he is very much interested in books and that these are generally much more difficult than those preferred by the child of average intelligence. History, biography, travel, and informational fiction constitute the main ingredients of the gifted child's reading diet. Terman found that a large number of the children selected were related to prominent individuals, living or dead. Concerning the educational opportunities offered these bright children, Terman observed that, on the whole, they enjoyed no special program of instruction. Indeed, usually they had not even been promoted any more rapidly than the average child.

In the wake of their original studies Terman and his

associates carried out a number of systematic follow-up investigations. Of these an over-all report was published in 1947 in a volume, *The Gifted Child Grows Up.* Now averaging 35 years of age, the gifted child of Terman's first study has shown himself to be healthier than the average American. Near mid-life he "may be expected to show normal, or below normal, incidence of serious personality maladjustment, insanity, delinquency, alcoholism and homosexuality." Of the 1,400 subjects in the study, thus far three have become alcoholics and four have landed in jail. As for vocational achievement "the gifted child rates well above the average of college graduates, and as compared with the general population is represented in the higher professions by 8 or 9 times its proportionate share." [1] Their incomes are above the average, but not very much. Their matrimonial incidence "is above that of the generality of college graduates of comparable age . . . and about equal to that of the general population." Their marital adjustment as measured by the marital happiness test appears about "equal or superior to that found in groups less highly selected for intelligence." In sexual adjustment the gifted were found to be as normal as "a less gifted and less educated group of 792 couples." In fertility the gifted group was reported "as probably below that necessary for the continuation of the stock from which the subjects came." In ability, character, and personality traits as measured either by tests or by ratings the Jewish subjects of the gifted group differed very little from the non-Jewish, but they displayed a somewhat stronger drive to achieve, formed more stable marriages, and were less conservative in political and social attitudes.

Some of these generalizations no doubt will have to be modified in the course of the coming years. Thus, although

---

[1] Thus far 85 of the 1,400 have become college professors; 69 are lawyers; and 44 are doctors. There are 25 writers among them, and 7 are composers or artists. Seven have become policemen and one is a truck driver. They have written more than 1,200 magazine articles, some 100 books and have taken out 150 patents.

Terman reports that "we see no signs of a prospective statesman in the group" and that "it contains . . . no mathematician of truly first rank . . . and that it gives no promise
of contributing any Aristotles, Newtons or Tolstoys" at least
another quarter-century will have to elapse before any final
judgment may be made. It is still too early, declares Terman,
"to estimate accurately the ultimate contribution of the group
to science, scholarship, literature and social welfare, or its
ultimate fertility, longevity, insanity rate and divorce incidence." [2]

William Stern. The late William Stern (1871–1938), formerly of Hamburg—who many years ago tried to rouse
educators to an understanding of the needs of the intellectually superior children—was opposed to a hit-or-miss method
of selecting gifted children. Boiled down to a few words,
Stern's contention was that in the selection of the gifted a
decision often is made concerning the child's whole future.
No source of information, however small, should, therefore, be
left untouched; and no criteria unsought. Parent and teacher,
physician and psychologist, should work together in an attempt to reach the wisest, most correct, and most satisfactory
decision.

Acting merely as a sort of scout, the teacher, according to
Stern's plan, was requested by the Hamburg educational
authorities to observe his students carefully throughout the
school year and to note characteristics which might indicate a
superior mind. Lest the teacher's watch be too unsystematic,
he was required to fill out for each of his students an observational record. The data thus gathered were mostly qualitative, but used in conjunction with the quantitative scores
obtained through the mental test, they offered a picture of
the child's personality. In the final decision, the observational
record played as prominent a part as the mental test. In
addition, there were other criteria, such as the child's health,

---

[2] Terman, L. M. *et al., The Gifted Child Grows Up,* p. 379. Stanford, California: Stanford University Press, 1947.

extracurricular activities, scholastic attainments, and general school record. The latter included a consideration of the child's school habits, such as attendance, punctuality, behavior, and so on. What was most important was the fact that when the mental test was given it was so constructed as to test not only *reactive* but also *spontaneous* intelligence. It sought to find out something about the kind of intelligence as well as its degree. The test, moreover, was given by a teacher especially trained for such work by the municipal psychological institute. The test was woven into the ordinary school work so superbly that the children did not even know they were being tested. The actual procedure was somewhat as follows: shortly before Easter, the children to be selected were transferred into trial classes where, while receiving their usual instruction, they were also given several mental tests in an unobtrusive way. "The children," Stern reported, "do not notice at all that they are being tested; one test gives the impression of being a composition; another looks like a new kind of work in arithmetic." In the main, such conditions tend, of course, to spare the child emotionally as much as possible.

Criticisms. The common objections to the Hamburg and similar methods are that they are too complicated; they require too much time; too much depends on an assumed cooperation among the various persons involved in the test; the methods cannot be applied on a large scale in any large urban school system; and finally, the simpler methods employed elsewhere arrive at conclusions that are just as reliable as those attained at Hamburg. To these arguments Stern replied as follows: "Selection is such a difficult and such a responsible undertaking that no available help may be refused. . . . A decision is often made concerning the child's life and destiny. . . . Therein lies a responsibility which cannot be left . . . to any one single factor. . . ." Whether the Hamburg procedure is accepted or not, the scientific basis on which the method is grounded is sound. Measured, moreover, by the ineffable yardstick of practice, the Stern method actually seemed to work.

Trends. In 1919 Professor Guy M. Whipple, after much study, regretfully announced that classes for the mentally superior were not being maintained in many places. Although often reported as existing, such classes, on closer examination, usually turned out to be something quite different. Professor Whipple found, for example, that one city "had a room for dull, but never for bright children; one had a 'mixed' room for both dull and gifted; and two gave individual coaching for special promotions." Such conditions, unfortunately, still can be found.

On the whole, however, this state of affairs has changed. Evidence of this fact is contained in another report by Professor Whipple in 1924. Now the professor could write more enthusiastically, for "during the past ten years a variety of plans for handling gifted pupils have been instituted." The most common among such plans was that of special promotion or skipping. Usually based on the child's scholastic attainment rather than on his inherent mental ability, and determined ordinarily by the teacher's judgment, special promotion was the traditional way of helping the supernormal. Not infrequently, however, special promotion was used not so much to help the gifted child as simply to speed him along on his way to graduation in order to make room for other pupils in an overcrowded school. This tendency has been particularly common in some of our larger cities where the funds for new schools have not been able to match strides with the growing school population.

D. Individualizing Education

1. The Dalton Plan

Early history. Early in the century, when the ideas of Maria Montessori first attracted attention, one of those interested was a young woman, Helen Parkhurst. Like Montessori, though in different ways, Miss Parkhurst believes in allowing pupils opportunity for individual development. It is her belief that children should be permitted to concentrate on their activities over longer periods of time, in accordance with a strongly motivated interest under conditions of a flexible schedule which varied from day to day.

Pondering over these views as early as 1911 Miss Parkhurst continued to test their possibilities until 1920, when she was afforded a chance to put them into practice in the high school of Dalton, Massachusetts.

Underlying principles. The Dalton Plan has been portrayed as "a piece of machinery for putting into operation the principle of individual work. . . ." Says Miss Parkhurst: "It is a simple and economic reorganization of the schools whereby pupils and teachers function to better advantage. . . ."

Three principles grace the Dalton Plan. The first is *freedom*. However, freedom does not mean that the pupil may do as he likes. A child with no restrictions on him, Miss Parkhurst feels, "is likely to be arbitrary and unwilling to cooperate."

Her second principle Miss Parkhurst has explained in the words of John Dewey: "The object of a democratic education is not merely to make an individual an intelligent participator in the life of his immediate group, but to bring the various groups into such constant interaction that no individual, no economic group could presume to live independently of others." This principle has been identified as that of *group interaction*.

Her third principle Miss Parkhurst has described as the "psychology of a point of view." "A child," she has explained, "never voluntarily undertakes anything that he does not understand," but he does launch "pursuits which he can understand" and "in initiating his own pursuits he looks at a thing from all angles and he plans to carry out his objectives." This *"psychology of a point of view"* is the underlying motive force of the stress on individual work.

The laboratory. Miss Parkhurst's scheme is known some-times as the Laboratory Plan. The old-time classrooms have been converted into laboratories with children as the experimenters. Properly furnished, a laboratory would enable a child (in literature for example) to have access to complete editions, "be permitted to discover that Milton wrote more than one sonnet and to learn that authors differ in opinion on the same subject." The laboratory is in charge of a teacher who gives counsel and information regarding the use of laboratory equipment. He is expected to offer suggestions regarding ways of attacking problems. The conventional situation, it seems, has been reversed, for under the Dalton scheme the pupil and not the teacher asks most of the questions.

Plainly, in the laboratory the rules for the traditional classroom cannot be applied. When the pupil begins his work in the morning, he may select any laboratory he desires. Once he has begun work he is not thrust into the usual strait jacket of a superimposed classroom decorum. He may talk, move about at will, request and give help, and when he wishes he may stop work and go to another laboratory. In the original Dalton Plan about two hours of every morning absorbed such individual work.

The conference and the contract. The recitation has not been completely discarded. Its usual form now is the *conference,* by which provision is made for meeting fixed groups several times a week. True to its name the conference is more of a discussion than recitation, its chief aim being to throw light on common difficulties encountered by the pupils in their individual assignments. The conference also is intended to furnish some social ballast to an education which tends to emphasize individualization.

With the elimination of the conventional recitation, the nature of homework has also changed. Instead of preparing definite work for a definite class at a definite time, the Dalton pupil is given a mimeographed guide sheet with an assignment for an entire month. This is known as a *contract*. It seeks to adjust the work to the individual's capacity.

To meet individual differences some schools using the Dalton Plan allow their pupils complete liberty in the working out of the monthly assignment. Accordingly, a student may distribute his time as he deems fit, concentrating on his weaker subjects and easing up on his stronger ones. In doing his assignment a pupil may work in all his subjects at an even pace; or he may do it in a few sittings at a time.

Group activities. The Dalton Plan, as has been said, is trying to meet the learning speed of the individual. But this is obviously only one phase of the child's all-around education. Accordingly, the original Dalton scheme called for fairly liberal group activities besides the regular Dalton program. English, for example, was to be enriched by literary meetings, debates, public speeches, and histrionics, in all of which the pupils were to assume a large share. In history there were to be discussions of present-day politics, the customs and manners of another era, and so on. For uncontrollable reasons, the Dalton originators had to scrap their socialization scheme. But among the hosts of Dalton followers, many have set aside afternoons for the so-called group projects, which include all the activities mentioned and also such diversions as games, gymnastics, and other doings which are to stimulate the child's social nature.

The Plan abroad. Curiously enough, the Dalton Plan has attracted more followers in foreign lands than in the United States. Miss Parkhurst herself has helped to organize it in England, Japan, and China. In various forms, it is found in Germany, Switzerland, Austria, Holland, and Russia. In 1929 Dr. Lucy Wilson of Philadelphia was invited by Peru to introduce the Plan in that country. The rise of Dalton in England is due, in part at least, to the efforts of Rosa Bassett, who for a time studied the new scheme at Dalton itself. Later, Miss Bassett's Streatham Hill School became one of the leading exponents of the new plan. Today, England has some 2,000 Daltonized schools.

Criticism. Among the most challenging criticisms directed at the Dalton Plan are those which attack the "unsocial nature" of the Plan. Thus, Dr. Philip W. L. Cox has held that the Dalton Plan fails "to provide socialized behavior outcomes for those boys and girls whose important contributions must be behavioristic rather than purely intellectual."

"The Dalton Plan," he says further, "is highly inadequate for social education. Unless it is subordinated to the truer objects of education, any plan that seeks chiefly the individual mastery of subject matter must result in the failure of the school to accomplish the purposes for which the community supports it." Somewhat along the same tack are the criticisms of the Communist educator, Pinkevitch, who pleads thus:

> In spite of the insistent statements of Miss Parkhurst regarding its significance for social education, we cannot but express the fear that it [the Dalton Plan] will be instrumental in developing individualistic tendencies in children. Under the Dalton scheme every pupil is busy with his own assignment and with the completion of his own work. Since each is absorbed in a different matter, what one's neighbors are doing is unfamiliar and foreign. In laboratory recitations . . . there is always some work in common. In the studios of Miss Parkhurst there is almost no collective work of any kind.[3]

Both criticisms, however, hold only when applied to the original Dalton Plan, which, through no fault of its inventress, was constrained to omit much of its group work and activities. But in the many up-to-date Dalton schools now flourishing throughout the world a balanced educational diet of socialized and individualized dishes is offered.

2. The Winnetka Plan

Somewhat akin to the Dalton Plan is that of Winnetka, sponsored by Carleton Washburne (1889–   ). Like Miss Parkhurst, Washburne opposed the old-style recitation, sub-

---

[3] Pinkevitch, A., *The New Education in the Soviet Republic*, p. 285. New York: John Day Co., Inc., 1929.

stituting for it a system of individual instruction. Launched in 1919, the Winnetka Plan applied an Individual Technique, revealing at the same time, however, that group activities need not be sacrificed for individual progress.

Spelling. Winnetka's campaign for individual instruction began with spelling. An examination of every child at the beginning of the term in the words he was to learn during the term revealed that the average child already could spell about two thirds of these words. Under the old procedure all the children would have had an identical spelling lesson every day. But at Winnetka, the child's work in spelling was adjusted to his needs. To begin with, the teacher checked in each child's spelling book those words he had missed, and these he was expected to master before the end of the term. He was free to study them as he pleased. The result was revealing. A few youngsters actually completed their entire term's spelling in a single day. Even the slowest student did not have to study as many words under this scheme as under the traditional plan.

Reading. The next attack was made on reading. Once more the children were tested and after each child's reading ability had been determined, books were bought for each individual. The class recitation was discarded, pupils reading to the teacher one at a time while their classmates studied. This was a benefit for all. For the retarded reader, it meant that he was reading something he could understand at a pace which was not beyond him. The same applied to the average and the better readers.

From spelling and reading, Winnetka proceeded to arithmetic, language, history, and geography. Individualizing these subjects was by no means simple, since the class size could not be curtailed, and the teacher's work was not to be increased.

Tasks and goals. Under the original Dalton Plan, a pupil could not go on in any subject until he had completed his whole monthly assignment. At Winnetka, however, no such academic stoplights blocked the way. One bright pupil was "one year and one month advanced in reading, one year and six months ahead in arithmetic, two years and two months ahead in language." At Winnetka, studies are divided into *tasks* or *goals*. Each goal is planned by the teachers, and every pupil is equipped with simple directions enabling him to proceed by himself. When a goal or, in some cases, part of it is reached, the pupil undergoes a self-administered test by which he knows whether he has actually mastered his task and whether he is ready to face a test given by his teacher.

Group activities. In the Winnetka schools, half the morning and half the afternoon sessions are devoted to individual work. The remaining half is reserved for such social activities as open forums, plays, self-government meetings, school journals, excursions, shopwork, music, art, and the like. During this time the magic of socialization weaves its spell. "It is during this freer part of the day that the children learn how to fit their interests and abilities in with those of others, to cooperate, to participate in the activities of the group."

E.   The Platoon School Movement

1.   William Wirt

In 1908 William Wirt (1874–1938) was made superintendent of schools at Gary, Indiana. Like many other schoolmen, Wirt held that the school should educate not only intellectually, but also physically, manually, scientifically, and artistically. To achieve this all-around purpose, the school must be equipped with playgrounds, gardens, swimming pools, science laboratories, machine shops, music and drawing studios, and so on. But even such an institution, Wirt believed, would not of itself insure the child's development unless his school activities were bolstered with activities outside the school.

Equipped to bring about a *varied education*, the ideal Wirtian school included (1) play and exercise, (2) special work in shop or laboratory, (3) social and creative activities in the school auditorium as well as in the community, and (4) the standard academic subject matter. Work and play were deemed an indispensable part of education. Not "mere trimmings of the regular work," participated in once or twice a week, this balanced program of study and play *is* the "regular work."

In one of his first statements at Gary Wirt said that "the main business of the school is to utilize to the best advantage the time that the child spends in school," and added that "the greatest problem of the school is to counteract and overcome the demoralizing influences of the child's life in the streets and alleys and unfortunately in many homes, so called." [1] Five hours of a child's average daily routine, it appeared to Mr. Wirt, were passed fatuously, and often even dangerously, in the Gary streets and alleys.

"We try," he went on, "to provide a school seat in a classroom for the exclusive use of each child. Then we try to have an auditorium large enough to seat all the children, which is the same thing as providing an auditorium seat for each child's exclusive use. All children play at one time, which is the same thing as providing a playground for each child."

2. Multiple use and balanced load

The thing to do, Wirt argued, was to apply the principles of "multiple use and balanced load." Specifically, this meant discarding the idea of providing a school seat for the exclusive use of each child. Load distribution now became the maxim. Each morning half the student populace was to be seated in classrooms; one fourth was to be found in special workshops for manual training, music, art, science, geography, and history; one eighth would occupy the auditorium; and the remaining pupils would be on the playgrounds and in the gymnasiums. Two or three hours a day was the limit of time to be bestowed on the tool subjects. The classroom was to be used alternately by two groups—since neither required such a

---

[1] Report on the Gary school, 1908.

room more than two or three hours daily. Later named
platoons, these groups were to alternate between the classroom
and the other activities already mentioned. Economically the
application of the multiple use and balanced load principles
proved successful. Since under Wirt's plan the number of
required classrooms was cut in half there obviously was a
corresponding saving in money. These savings were used to
purchase such additional facilities as playgrounds, gardens,
gymnasiums, workshops, swimming pools, and so on, thereby
making possible a richer education.

3. Balanced load on a large scale

Wirt's effort to wring the maximum use out of a school
building brought with it not only the platoon scheme but
many other things. The school day, for instance, was lengthened, beginning in the higher grades at 8:30 a. m. and
continuing till five. The motive behind this was not only to
promote economy and efficiency, but also "to utilize the pupils'
leisure time for wholesome recreation or supplementary work."
Not only was the school day lengthened, but evenings and
Saturdays were put into harness. This was optional, yet some
three fourths of the pupils registered for Saturday work.
Today an ancient tale, particularly in the cities, the idea of
evening activity was then a daring novelty. To a goodly
number of its evening students Gary proffered "instruction in
the gymnasium, swimming pool, football, basket ball, etc."

If the maximum use is to be had from a building, bolting its
doors in the summertime becomes absurd. "Many children,"
Wirt declared, "are unavoidably absent during the school term
under the old form of organization. Under the four-quarter
(all-year) arrangement, the allotted vacation of such children
can be so arranged as to include such absence, thus insuring
36 weeks of schooling." Older children, moreover, were able
to take their twelve-week vacation in any quarter of the year
during which they could get the most profitable employment.

4. The complete school

Described as "a playground, garden, workshop, social center, library and traditional school under the same management," the Gary School is the so-called *complete school* where under one roof are found children of all ages—from the kindergartner to the high school senior. Specifically, this means that the familiar cleavage between the higher and lower schools has been disrupted. Although not all Gary schools were organized as complete schools, those schools that were established took care of the vast majority of the Gary youth.

5. School and society

Like many other American schools, those of Gary have been influenced by John Dewey. Thus one finds children doing "the things that have meaning to them as children." This puts a premium on the project or similar methods in which the community often plays a part. Since education tends to be socialized and practical at Gary, special stress has been put on vocational training. However, instead of hiring the usual special teachers Gary employs skilled professionals. Expected to keep the school plant in repair and first-rate condition, these workingmen are also asked to assume the teacher's robes. When active thus they teach their craft to the Gary students, who, like the apprentices of another day, learn their jobs by working with their masters. Naturally enough, the number of trades thus represented is large. Besides cabinet-makers, printers, and plumbers, there are carpenters, painters, sheet-metal workers, electricians, foundrymen, machinists, and many others. In their shops the student is put to work. Here he makes and repairs school furniture, and becomes familiar with his alma mater's clocks, bells, lights, and motors, the secrets of paints, their mixture and application. The same procedure prevails in domestic science. Here the students help to prepare actual meals, serving them in the school lunchroom to fellow students and teachers.

Most efficient in the platoon school's socializing program is the auditorium which is devoted to such group activities as choral singing, dramatics, movies, concerts, debates, orations, and the like. The auditorium stage is large—large enough in some instances to accommodate a basketball game or a folk dance. Every day the Gary youngster spends at least an hour in the auditorium.

6. The development of the work-study-play idea

Since its inception at Gary the work-study-play program has appeared in numerous cities. As early as 1915 it came to Kalamazoo, Michigan. Three years later Detroit adopted it. In 1928 Ohio State University, recognizing "the demand for trained platoon principals, supervisors, and teachers," gave special summer courses. Lending added potency to the Gary idea and its many modifications is the National Association for the Study of the Platoon or Work-Study-Play Organization.

F. The Youth Problem

1. Significance

In essence the problem of youth is as old as civilization. Whenever a society enjoyed a fair degree of stability, the problem, to be sure, was never poignant; but as soon as the cultural tides began to shift, it revealed itself. This was the case in the time of Pericles when the swirling currents of social and economic change raced over Athens; and it was the case again in the succeeding eras when the western world moved from a relatively simple agrarian culture to one which was increasingly industrial and technological. Two world wars with their wake of social and economic unrest have aggravated the problem all over the world.

There are in the United States more than twenty-one million young people for whom the period between their exit from school and their entrance into vocations has become critical. Styled in the jazzy twenties as wild and flaming, as the Lost Generation, they were struck head-on by the depression. In the early thirties more than 4,000,000 young people, or about a fifth of those out of school, were jobless. In 1940, on the eve of Pearl Harbor, about 22 per cent of our employable population was under twenty-five; yet 35 per cent of the total unemployed were young people under twenty-five.[1]   Briefly, the problem was as follows:

Recent social and economic changes in the United States have given rise to difficulties in the care and education of young people with which existing institutions are quite unprepared to deal adequately. The changes not only have greatly intensified the problems which confront the schools, but also have created an urgent need of protection and further education for millions of youth whom the schools are not now reaching. Without some provision for basic planning to meet this situation, there is serious danger that present conditions may constitute a fundamental threat to the national welfare.[2]

2. The New Deal

With the coming of the New Deal the federal government took definite steps to remedy this serious situation. Thus in 1933 it created the CCC, the Civilian Conservation Corps, and two years later it organized the NYA, the National Youth Administration. The former offered young men full-time employment on projects involving land reclamation and re-forestation, with compensation and housing near their work. The NYA offered part-time work to young men and women residing at home and "living their normal community lives." The work itself was diverse and ranged from the building of schools and community centers, the construction of airfields and parks, to clerical and service work in schools, hospitals, libraries, and social agencies. Men and women of the NYA made clothing and household articles; they constructed school furniture; they produced playground equipment, hospital supplies, and scores of other items.[3]

---

[1] For an eloquent and clear account of the youth problem see Bell, H. M., *Youth Tell Their Story*. Washington, D. C.: American Council on Education, 1938.

[2] Reeves, F. W., *et al. American Youth and the Future*, p. x. General Report of the American Youth Commission. Washington, D. C.: American Council on Education, 1942.

[3] The CCC's yearly cost per worker was about $1,200; that of the NYA, $225. By 1940 the CCC had provided work for some 2,500,000 young men,

3. The American Youth Commission

To study the youth problem in its complex aspects, the American Council on Education formed the American Youth Commission in 1935.[4] Within a few years this body offered its first tangible contribution—its "Study of the Conditions and Attitudes of (13,528) Young People in Maryland." Translated into national terms for the year 1940, this revealed that there were some 21,000,000 Americans between the ages of sixteen and twenty-four. Of these, 7,000,000 were attending high school; 2,500,000 were going to college or the equivalent; more than 10,000,000 belonged to families of the "working classes" and lived in homes of less than an adequate standard of living and diet; and about a third of these were the fragments of shattered homes. Low-income and large-family homes were the capstone of the youth problem. Growing social stratification, it was found, discriminated against millions of young people in their quest for jobs and increasingly restricted their opportunities in their march to adulthood. Economic factors drove the young out of school and put them prematurely into the hard and difficult race for jobs; eventually they married and raised families and thus continued the evil and appalling "circle of economic determinism."[5] To dissolve the circle, the Commission recommended

---

more than 80% of whom were under nineteen. In the CCC's eight years of activity, 1933–1941, some 80% of its participants worked for one or more terms of six months. The value of their labors totaled some $1,500,000,000. The NYA, for its part, gave work to some 1,750,000 out-of-school youth and a student program for some 1,800,000 in-school young men and women. A typical program totaled about 60 hours a month and earned the worker about $16.

[4] Members of the Commission included Newton D. Baker, Owen D. Young, and Henry L. Harriman. Its educational directors were Homer P. Rainey (1934–1939) and Floyd W. Reeves (1939–1941). The Commission's most important publications comprised *Youth and the Future,* by Reeves and others; *Youth Tell Their Story,* by Howard M. Bell; *What the High School Ought to Teach,* by the Commission's Staff; *Color, Class and Personality,* by Robert L. Sutherland; *Youth Work Programs,* by Lewis L. Lorwin; and *Youth-Serving Organizations,* by M. M. Chambers. These reports appeared between 1938 and 1948.

[5] Bell, H. M., *Youth and the Future.* Washington, D. C.: American Council on Education, 1938.

that the state and the community must somehow equalize youth's economic opportunities; and that furthermore young people must be educated in the effects of large families and continued poverty. The Commission concluded that an effective educational, vocational, and recreational program for all young people of America was essential; but these, it warned, must serve more than an ideal; they must be plainly related to the basic needs of youth, and in the end they must help to equalize youth's economic opportunities.

The key to the youth problem in the eyes of most discerning students is economic. Headlined, it is expressed in *Work for Youth.* Of the 9,000 young Marylanders, two thirds felt economic security to be their most pressing personal problem, with vocational guidance and educational opportunity the runners-up. "There are said to be many things," one investigator declared, "that a democracy must have, or die. One of these things, we suspect, is a social order enriched with enough generosity and foresight to provide all its youth with opportunities to grow, and endowed with enough wisdom and courage to make these opportunities worth the taking." [6]

4. The PEA Commissions

It was in the disturbed thirties that the Progressive Education Association turned its floodlights on the youth problem. The work of its Commission on the Relation between School and College has already been mentioned. This not only showed that the traditional college requirements for admission were not necessary in order to select first-rate college students, but it also threw open the gates to the development of an education suitable to the needs of youth, thereby enabling the secondary school to build a better quality of young men and women.

The peculiar nature of these needs was looked into by two special PEA commissions—one to deal with the secondary

---

[6] Bell, H. M., *Youth and the Future,* p. 48. Washington, D. C.: American Council on Education, 1938.

school curriculum and one to come to grips with the intricacies of "human relations." Of significance in the work of these two groups was the labor of the late Dr. Caroline Zachry who led the subcommittee on "The Study of Adolescents." With her co-workers Dr. Zachry explored "four crucial areas of needs."

Studies of adolescents suggest that their needs group themselves roughly into four areas: immediate social relationships, wider social relationships, economic relationships and—closely related to all these—personal living. . . . Needs are phrased in terms of the individual's functioning relationships primarily because they are conceived as both personal and social in nature. The personality of the individual is formed only through functioning relationships with others and its needs cannot be met without them.[7]

In other words, the commonplace that man is a social animal and that he cannot grow properly unless his relations to others are suitable and satisfactory was reaffirmed. Becoming a person, the Commission on the Secondary School Curriculum found, was made difficult in the school by "the preoccupation with pecuniary rewards," "the halo of prestige of outmoded ideas of 'personal culture,'" "the neglect of the esthetic quality of experience," "the feverish quest for obliviousness, to 'lose oneself in the crowd,'" and "the lack of a valid philosophy of values."

To combat these adverse conditions and attitudes the Commission suggested three guiding principles. The first related to our "sense of the dignity and worth of ourselves as Persons." "Any pursuit, conception, or preoccupation," declared the Commission, "that robs the individual of worth in his own eyes or in those of his fellows is unworthy of the personal life as it is of social, civic or economic relationships." For its second principle the Commission asserted that "those activities are worthy which further mutually responsible and enriching relationships between the individual and the group." The Commission's third principle advocated the free play of

---

[7] Thayer, V. T., Zachry, C. B., and Kotinsky, R., *Reorganizing Secondary Education*, p. 44. New York: Appleton-Century-Crofts, Inc., 1930.

intelligence. In answer to the question, How can the school contribute to the building of the Person? the Commission recommended that the school should rid itself of its academic and economic stress; that it should eliminate its emphasis on standardization; that it should reduce the weight given to problem-solving; that it should consciously build the health of its students; that it should value the student's *personal life;* that it should encourage a democracy of interests; and that it should help the student toward a personal philosophy of life.

Led by Dr. Alice Keliher, the Commission on Human Relations sought to uncover the "unspoken tensions and psychological distortions which are today leading so directly into intolerance, hatred, vindictiveness and eagerness to judge and condemn others," in order to create in the end "a new view of human nature and society . . . to deflect these turbulent currents." [8] Prying into anthropology, psychology, psychiatry, sociology, child study, and literature in its quest for clues to the perennial questions which perplex youth, the Commission found that what young people wanted most was "understanding friendship."

They want to know how to attract friends of their own age, of their own sex and of the opposite sex. They are tremendously concerned about the application of standards of behavior to their social lives. They want help in clarifying confusions which come about inevitably because their parents live with a set of ideals and ideas different from those of their own age groups. Young people in their concerns about personal relationships are also looking forward to the place marriage will play in their life design.[9]

A good many of youth's problems have their roots in the adult world, in its attempt to dominate and impose, and in its own uncertainty and befuddlement. All around him the young person beholds adults adrift in a changing world. He perceives a lack of integrity in American life; he sees the efforts of the cheap and the shoddy pluck high rewards; he

---

[8] *Progressive Education Advances,* p. 49. New York: Appleton-Century-Crofts, Inc., 1938.
[9] *Ibid.,* p. 50.

sees people turning aside "human considerations for business success, for economic security, for political prestige." If he happens to be the offspring of foreign-born parents, he is confronted by the additional problem "of deriving his values from two distinct cultures in which he must live, the culture of his parents and the culture of his community." [10] When the youth does break emotionally with his family, he finds himself "afterwards feeling guilty about their behavior."

Most baffling to youths "is the vastness and complexity of our social organization," and the difficulty of satisfying "their natural need to have a recognized place in society." As seen by one of its own, youth

> . . . goes about in still alarm,
> With shrouded future at his arm,
> With longings that can find no tongue,
> I see him thus, for I am young.[11]

Underlying the complexity of the youth problem is the inescapable biological factor of sex. The Commission recognized the fairly obvious necessity for a frank and honest attitude toward sex problems in lieu of the traditional and, alas, still common, hush-hush approach to questions about natural growth and the physiological processes. Something must be done to banish the "feelings of shame coupled with ignorance" and the tensions resulting therefrom. What the Commission recommended was a realistic education which would "deal not only with the facts demanded by questioning youth," but which would also give them "an interpretation of the flow of ideas, prejudices and superstitions which envelop them in their culture." [12]

---

[10] *Ibid.*, p. 52.

[11] Sargent, N. B., *Younger Poets: An Anthology of American Secondary School Verse*, p. 351. New York: Appleton-Century-Crofts, Inc., 1932.

[12] *Progressive Education Advances*, pp. 52–53. New York: Appleton-Century-Crofts, Inc., 1938. Also considered by the Commission on Human Relations were ways in which the school can bring about a closer and more effective relationship between young people and the community. It studied the question of how the various disciplines—science, language, the social studies, mathematics, the arts and letters—can help youth to a better understanding of himself.

G. Modernizing the College

1. The new college

Of American educational institutions, the college probably has been the most severely censured. Proclaimed an idolizer of tradition, it has been accused of being unadjusted to the needs of modern society. College graduates, some pedagogical wiseacres have maintained, are "unprepared for participation in the life of a social democracy." Probably the truest criticism, from a pedagogical viewpoint, is the ancient claim that the college always has tended to lag somewhat behind the times. Thus, while the lower and secondary schools were employing the newer progressive methods based to some extent on the results of educational research, the college cruised in old and familiar waters. Of recent years, however, the college of old appears to be fading. A new college is supplanting it. One of the most striking aspects of this new college is its amazing enrollment. Statisticians have noted, for example, that for one student attending college in 1890 there were five in the heyday of Coolidge prosperity, and today the number is, of course, even larger.[1] The flood of registrants has brought with it a cargo of perplexing problems. The numbers of students have gone up, but the means of providing for them, alas, has not been able to match the pace. Educational costs, like nearly every other cost, have been on the rise. But endowments have tended to remain relatively stationary. With the growth of mass education, moreover, the individual student and his needs tend to be lost in the crowd. Social and economic conditions have changed so vastly as to make the traditional college curriculum inadequate. The new membership of the college has been making new demands, and the college of tradition has been unprepared to meet them.

---

[1] In the fall of 1947 enrollment in 1,753 collegiate institutions was 2,338,226 which was 12.5 per cent higher than in 1946.

2. The survey

One indication of the transformation which has come over the college is the fact that it studies itself. Many colleges, driven by public demand to justify their reason for being, have undertaken what are known as self-surveys. The object of a self-survey is not so much to arrive at any definite conclusion as it is to clear the field for further study. Self-surveys may be either general or special. In the former case every possible phase of college education is investigated. Where the survey is special, it is restricted to some particular aspect of college education, such as the study of the undergraduate instruction in Harvard's department of economics made by the department of education.

One of the most comprehensive surveys ever conducted by any higher institution of learning was undertaken at Wisconsin in 1914. This was a general survey ordered by the state legislature for the purpose of finding out the truth about the university's work so as to "clarify some of the doubts in the minds of the tax-paying public of the state of Wisconsin." An attempt was made to obtain the cooperation of the faculty, the students, and the alumni. Every member of the teaching staff was expected to answer in detail the questions set forth in an elaborate questionnaire. Covering nearly every phase of the teacher's relationship to the university, this sought light on such matters as the professors' teaching qualifications and experience, methods of grading students' work, faculty and departmental meetings, committee assignments, summer and outside employment, measures of teaching efficiency, and so on. The alumni and former students tackled another sort of question-sheet. They were expected to divulge information about courses—especially about the kind of courses preferred and the kind slighted. There were also plenty of questions about efficient instruction, faculty advisers, extracurricular activities, secret societies, honor system, student government, etc. Besides Wisconsin's self-study others have been made at Colorado, Iowa, Maryland, Miami, Minnesota, New York,

North Dakota, Ohio, Oregon, Washington, and in many other places.

The findings of a survey are helpful as a means to an end. Based on the questionnaire method, such a survey at best is only semiscientific. The survey is only a searchlight: it illuminates problems, but it doesn't solve them. To be efficient, a survey, naturally enough, should be conducted by properly qualified persons. If made exclusively by members of a given college, a survey is rarely satisfactory, largely because of the absence of an objective critical attitude. The ideal group of surveyors should be independent, thoroughly familiar with the local and special conditions of the college to be studied, and possessed, moreover, of a working knowledge of the principles and practices of modern education.[2]

3. Reorganization of entrance requirements and methods of admission

Under the pressure of the vast registration growth, many colleges have found themselves compelled to revise their admission requirements. The usual requirement for admission to college is the equivalent of graduation from a standard four-year high school. A candidate must present evidence, either by certificate or by examination, that he has completed fifteen units or so of high school work. Some of these, like English, are definitely fixed; others are elective. Some institutions also use psychological tests to determine admission. The general tendency seems to be to demand a higher standard of work on the part of the candidate. To that end the average grade required for admission is being raised, and the type of entrance examination is being changed so as to make it, as far as possible, a test of power and ability rather than of memory. There is a growing tendency to stress the candidate's high school record, both academic and otherwise. In many colleges personal interviews are held with the prospective matriculant,

---

[2] In 1940 a two-year survey of higher education of Negroes was begun with authorization and financial aid from Congress.

and some colleges even require their prospective students to have the recommendation of some competent adult, such as the high school principal, a prominent citizen, or an alumnus.

Most of the trends just cited are healthy, at least in so far as they make the sorting of college material less haphazard. Examination results are now only one means of determining who is fit for college. Factors of personality are being given greater weight than ever. Selection is becoming much more rigorous by means of these revisions, but at the same time a more flexible and much broader method is being developed. When a nascent collegian is to be judged not alone by the results of a single examination but also by his general high school career, a mental examination, a personal interview with a responsible representative of the college, and a confidential report made by the high school principal, the chances are that the college ought to be in a better position to choose students who are qualified for the work. That the traditional college entrance requirements are unwarranted was well demonstrated by the Progressive Education Association's Eight-Year Study on the Relation of School and College, which has been described elsewhere (see p. 161).

The system of having prospective students get the recommendation of their high school principals or of some prominent citizen has been inaugurated in a number of colleges. The college for women at Bennington, Vermont, requires a confidential report from the principal and two teachers of the school attended by the candidate. At Oberlin the intending matriculant must present a recommendation "by a prominent citizen who vouches for the candidate's character and ability." Dartmouth asks its prospects to show the endorsement of an alumnus who is to sign a certificate whereon he rates the candidate according to intellectual interest, native ability, individuality, faithfulness, originality, integrity, straightforwardness, clear-mindedness, fair play, interest in fellows, and leadership.

4. Curricular readjustment

Because of the rapid and extensive growth of the natural sciences and the application of human knowledge to everyday practical affairs, as well as the growth of democracy in America, the aristocratic ideal of the college perpetuated since the Renaissance is no longer adequate. Indeed, the idea is being expressed increasingly that a college education should be available to every qualified youth. "The American people," President Truman's Commission on Higher Education recently declared, "should set as their ultimate goal an educational system in which at no level—high school, college, graduate school or professional school—will a qualified individual in any part of the country encounter an insuperable economic barrier to the attainment of the kind of education suited to his aptitudes and interests." That these interests are not exclusively nor even primarily academic has of course become increasingly plain. Not only have they produced and given strength to colleges whose purpose is essentially vocational, such as schools of commerce, education, and the like, but even the liberal arts colleges now commonly include practical courses ranging from accounting and short-story writing to methods of teaching. The Washington Square College of New York University offers a four-year course in radio. A number of colleges give courses in marriage and family life. At Stephens College sex education is taught to every woman student as a part of a comprehensive program of junior college education. And thus one might continue with scores of similar examples culled from the work of colleges all over the country.

The multiplication of courses, moreover, has increased the tendency on the part of students to treat subject matter in compartments, to look upon education as just so many courses taken or credits received, without regard to their interrelationships. This lack of adequate organization among the student's several courses is beginning to be seen as a problem of the first magnitude. Indeed, some college educators have become convinced that entirely too much stress is put on the snaring of credits and the passing of courses, and too little emphasis on the development of the student's ability to think through new problems. It is felt that too often the student carries away from college only a scattering of knowledge which hasn't been presented to him as a unit. To remedy this situation various *quasi*-experiments have been made. For one thing, there has been an increasing cooperation between the high school and the college in determining courses. In the second place, a reaction against the free elective system as inaugurated by Charles W. Eliot at Harvard in the latter nineteenth century has set in. For another thing, a movement has been developing to give the college student the elements of a "broad, fundamental training combined with a limited amount of specialization." Furthermore, some colleges have been experimenting with what has been called a general final examination. Finally, there are some attempts to meet the special needs of the exceptional student by allowing him greater latitude and freedom in the working out of individual problems.

5. College and high school rapprochement

The twentieth century has seen a slow but increasing rapprochement between college and high school. The principal's recommendation of his protégés for college admission has already been mentioned. Some colleges have adopted the practice of reporting to the high school on the quality of the work done by its graduates, at least during their freshman year at college. The purpose here has been to throw greater responsibility on the high school. Knowing that their recommendations are going to be watched, principals don't dare to become too glowing in their eulogies. There has also been a rising tendency on the part of some colleges to adjust their requirements for graduation to what a student brings with him from the high school. At least one college of major repute, for example, allows college credit in mathematics and foreign languages to a student who presents more than the entrance requirements in those subjects and has more than the necessary total number of units needed for admission.

6. The elective system

When Charles W. Eliot inaugurated the elective system at Harvard, he was reacting against the prevailing idea that college students of and by themselves would attempt nothing worth while in education. Eliot's move was a blow against curricular prescriptions which included generous slices of the classics and mathematics, and which gave the student very little opportunity to try his hand at self-direction. After years of tinkering on the machinery of the elective system, however, many colleges finally have come to the viewpoint that although the elective system may have excellent virtues, in the hands of the average student it refuses to perform with complete satisfaction. Most contemporary educational leaders are convinced that the student's choice of subjects needs to be controlled. There has been, as one educator has phrased it, "too much intellectual vagrancy on the part of the student." Some, as for example Alexander Meiklejohn, are convinced that the elective system is chiefly responsible for the incoherence and confusion in college teaching today. The antithesis of the free elective system prevails in St. Johns College at Annapolis, where all subjects are required.

7. Survey courses

To give the student a background for his advanced work, many of our higher institutions have established what are known as general survey courses. At the University of Iowa the survey course evolved from a series of freshman lectures. The aim there was "to give the freshman student information and guidance in his college life" and "to give a vision of the world of knowledge and skill as it appears in institutions of higher learning . . . to waken [in the student] a desire to learn." Columbia requires its freshmen to take a course in

"Contemporary Civilization." Here the purpose is "to give the student early in his college course objective material upon which to base his own further studies." This survey tendency has also manifested itself in the senior year. Here, obviously, such a course serves no longer as an introduction but rather as a summary and review. Not so long ago a committee of the American Association of University Professors put into print some warnings against the survey courses. For one thing, it was felt that such courses tend to be superficial, leaving the student with a "false impression that the treatment of the subject dealt with is definitive." For another thing, as usual, it is difficult to get competent instructors to teach a survey course effectively. In some quarters, however, the survey course has reaped abundance of praise. Dr. George Boas, while active at Johns Hopkins, felt that the survey course "was successful in making students more aware of the means by which thought becomes coherent and intelligent. . . . What has been most noticeable is that as the year progressed the students showed themselves more capable of asking good questions. . . . [They] began to show a realization that some questions were enlightening and others were simply time-killers."

8. Culture and service

Many colleges of recent years have shown a marked tendency to organize their work so as to lay the foundations of "general culture" and at the same time offer the student some means of preparing for his life work. Thus there have developed such combination courses as the college-commerce, college-education, college-journalism, college-music, and so on. The aim is "to make the college prepare for life." It is in this spirit that Vassar has created its celebrated Department of Euthenics which deals with "the direct application of the sciences to the betterment of living conditions." The field includes a vast congeries of knowledge, ranging from horticulture to heredity, from the family to physiology.

9.   General education

To counteract the tendency toward premature specialization
on the part of undergraduates as well as to make sure that
their education will not disregard "those common spheres,
which, as citizens and heirs of a joint culture, they will share
with others," a growing number of colleges have introduced
programs calling for some sort of required general education.
At the University of Chicago, for example, students are
required to pass comprehensive examinations in the humanities, the social sciences, the physical sciences, and the biological sciences before they are permitted to specialize.

The most publicized of the various plans for a general
education is that which Harvard introduced in 1945, and the
basis of which has been set forth in an elaborate report of one
of its committees, published in a volume entitled *General
Education in a Free Society*.[3]   Toward the end of the nineteenth century Harvard, it will be recalled, introduced the
free elective system.   Under President Abbott Lawrence
Lowell, however, the free elective scheme was modified so that
a student was required to concentrate a number of courses in
what most colleges generally call a "major."   In addition he
was required to "distribute" a number of his courses in a
variety of fields.   Even under this plan students had considerable choice of curriculum.   In 1941, for example, a freshman could select from some 48 different courses; when he
became a sophomore, he could choose among 30 different
fields of concentration.   To curb this freedom which, for
various reasons, was felt to be undesirable, Harvard in 1941
required its freshmen to take four "courses of distribution" in
three fields of knowledge—the humanities, social studies, and
the sciences.

The program of General Education, which was put into
effect in 1945, was started on an experimental basis by which
it was hoped that methods and materials would be developed

---

[3] *General Education in a Free Society,* p. 4. Cambridge: Harvard University
Press, 1945.

and perfected and the necessary teaching staffs assembled. Briefly, the new scheme envisages a requirement of at least six courses of the sixteen needed for graduation in the field of general education—that is to say, in the humanities, social studies, and the sciences. The humanities are courses which "might be called the Great Texts in Literature"; the social sciences are those "which might be called Western Thought and Institutions." As for natural science "there would be two to four closely related alternative courses concerned with the principles of physical science and a similar group dealing with the principles of the biological sciences." Eventually all students in Harvard College will be required to take one course in either one or the other group. The trio comprising the humanities, the social and the natural sciences is expected to furnish "the common core, the body of learning and of ideas which would be a common experience of all Harvard students."

Another group to declare itself in favor of general education was President Truman's Commission on Higher Education for American Democracy. Holding that "present college programs are not contributing adequately to the quality of students' adult lives either as workers or as citizens," the Commission in its report (1947) asserted that this was true "in large part because the unity of liberal education has been splintered by overspecialization." The college graduate of today, it went on to say, may have acquired professional or technical training in one field or another, but is "only incidentally, if at all, made ready for performing his duties as a man, a parent and a citizen." Although often enough he has acquired competence in some particular occupation, he falls short "of that human wholeness and civic conscience which the cooperative activities of citizenship require." To remedy this situation the college, it was felt, should provide a unified general education for American youth by which the right relationship between specialized training and the transmission of a common cultural heritage toward a common citizenship will be effected. A general education, however, was not to be thought of "in terms of mastering particular bodies of knowledge." Rather it was to be thought of "in terms of performance." Its objects were:

1. To develop for the regulation of one's personal and civic life a code of behavior based on ethical principles consistent with democratic ideals.
2. To participate actively as an informed and responsible citizen in solving the social, economic and political problems of one's community, state and nation.
3. To recognize the interdependence of the different peoples of the world and one's personal responsibility for fostering international understanding and peace.
4. To understand the common phenomena in one's physical environment, to apply habits of scientific thought to both personal and civic problems, and to appreciate the implications of scientific discoveries for human welfare.
5. To understand the ideas of others and to express one's own effectively.
6. To attain a satisfactory emotional and social adjustment.
7. To maintain and improve his own health and to cooperate actively and intelligently in solving community health problems.
8. To understand and enjoy literature, art, music and other cultural activities as expressions of personal and social experience and to participate to some extent in some form of creative activity.
9. To acquire the knowledge and attitudes basic to a satisfying family life.
10. To choose a socially useful and personally satisfying vocation that will permit one to use to the full his particular interests and abilities.
11. To acquire and use the skills and habits involved in critical and constructive thinking.[4]

10. Honors courses

In his inaugural address at Swarthmore College in October, 1921, President Frank Aydelotte declared that:

the most fundamentally wasteful feature of our educational institutions is the lack of a higher standard of intellectual attainment. We are educating more students up to a fair average than any country in the world, but we are wastefully allowing the capacity of the average to prevent us from bringing the best up to the standards they could reach. Our most important task at the present is to check this waste.

---

[4] *Higher Education for American Democracy*, Report of President's Commission on Higher Education, I, p. **47** ff.

The way to do it appears simple enough. It is, says Dr. Aydelotte, "to give those students who are really interested in the intellectual life harder and more independent work than could profitably be given to those whose devotion to matters of the intellect is less keen. . . ." True, to encourage superior scholarship there have always been such inducements as cash awards, medallions, and keys in Phi Beta Kappa and other honorary fraternities. But aside from these tributes, little attention was given to the needs of the more-than-average intellectually potent. It is to meet the requirements of such students that Swarthmore inaugurated its honor courses. Under this plan students of special aptitude may become honors students at the end of their sophomore year. As such they are excused from course requirements and from ordinary examinations. They attend classes as they see fit. In return for this blessing, however, they are expected to devote two years to mastering a definite field of knowledge, in which they are examined at the end of their senior year. These examinations are comprehensive, of about a dozen three-hour papers, followed by an oral inquisition which, as might be expected, is most penetrating. When the student has traversed all these inquisitorial highroads without being felled, he receives an A.B. of the first, second, or third class—a distinction which he no doubt has earned. Should he fail to do work of a sufficiently high order, he is outfitted with a simple A.B., without honors.

Similar to the honors system at Swarthmore is that of special honors at Smith. Here, too, the student is given a great deal of freedom. As at Swarthmore, the Smith honors candidate may attend classes as she chooses. Her work is planned by a general director, who, however, gives heed to what the student actually wants. The Smith student for honors works in a special field in which she studies in six subdivisions, two each semester. Every fortnight or so she is required to organize her ideas into a short paper which is then discussed by instructor and student. During the last semester a longer paper is prepared and some time is now devoted to a general review. This is inspired by the purpose of preparing for a final examination, covering the field of the student's work of the last two years.

The honors system is no longer a rarity, and today many colleges are experimenting with some form of it. The most valuable aspect of the scheme, some believe, is that it encourages the gifted student to shoulder responsibility. But there are other benefits: it puts a premium on the student's initiative; it encourages individual thinking; it permits training in judgment; and it allows a student to work at his own pace.

11. Other developments

Besides the developments already described there are, of course, many others. There is, for example, a greater effort to guide the student in the solution of his many problems. Many colleges have installed what is known as Freshman Week, or Orientation Week, in which an attempt is made to help the incoming student get his bearings. Some institutions have a faculty adviser or dean for each class. The position of dean of men or dean of women is, of course, a familiar one.

Some colleges have begun to suspect that their instruction might be improved, and are beginning to give greater heed to instructional efficiency. The lecture method, which is as old as the universities themselves, is probably still the most widely used by college teachers. However, it has been vigorously criticized, especially on the ground that it is too "teacher-centered" and that as such it encourages student passivity. To stimulate greater learning interest and activity on the part of their students, progressive college teachers have leaned more and more to newer methods, employing variations of the project method, the workshop, and more recently, the panel discussion. Like teachers in the lower schools, college teachers have begun to make greater use of audio-visual aids, including the radio and the sound-film. At Princeton, Professor Ken-

neth Hechler has made a novel use of the telephone in his
class in American Political Parties. By connecting the telephone with a loudspeaker, the professor and his class have
been able to interview prominent American political men at
distant points all over the nation. Men like Senator Aiken of
Vermont, Carroll Reece, former chairman of the Republican
National Committee, Edward J. Flynn, former Democratic
National Committee chairman, have been interviewed in this
manner—and the students have not hesitated to ask them
searching questions.

Some colleges are also beginning to raise their standards of
scholarship. The question of athletics is still making the
welkin ring. On the one hand, there are those who would
de-emphasize sports, who feel that gigantic crowds and large
gate receipts are not for the best interests of the college. On
the other hand, there are those who see no dangers to the
college in big-time athletics. Under the impetus of a Carnegie
investigation, a number of evils in college football were revealed, with the result that some institutions began to de-
emphasize their athletics. If some colleges are beginning to
put less stress on intercollegiate athletics, many of them are
putting more emphasis on intramural sports.

The matter of the curriculum has already been discussed.
In general the trend in this domain seems to be to offer courses
which, though once deemed unworthy of collegiate recognition,
now are regarded as valuable and desirable. The tendency to
liberalize the college curriculum is relatively recent in origin.
The movement in part is due to the demands of the students
themselves. Another cause, no doubt, is the college's larger
concept of its reason for being. The old, restricted academic
motive, though still adhered to by many institutions, has
become considerably enlarged, and today America's higher
learning has harnessed itself in a growing way to the community and its needs. The movement has been criticized
particularly by those who feel that this "service idea" is putting out the flame of scholarship. Practical subjects, ranging

from courses in Millinery to Baseball Theory, they fear, will tend to get the preference. Or, to put it somewhat differently, the colleges will tend more and more to appeal to the mass appetite instead of concentrating on the development of leaders. In line with the new courses has come an army of new academic degrees. The simple bachelor's degree in arts or in science has been expanded into dozens of forms and has produced such offspring as the Master of Church Administration and the Bachelor of Science in Practical Arts and Letters.

The efforts to reorganize college programs and practices have increased perceptibly during the last fifty years. Many of these attempts, of course, have been chiefly of local and minor importance and in the long run will no doubt pass into limbo. A few, however, have evoked a rather widespread attention.

One of the first assaults on academic tradition in the present century was made in 1906 by the College of Engineering of the University of Cincinnati by means of the so-called "cooperative plan." Combining an academic program with one of practical work, the plan pairs students who share a full-time outside job. The two students alternate their time between the job and the classroom. Thus, while one of the pair attends classes for a period of six weeks or more, the other works for their common employer. At the end of the stipulated period the pair exchange their roles, the worker going to classes and the other going to work. By virtue of the cooperative plan students are able to supplement their book learning with practical experience, so necessary and withal so difficult to obtain; while at the same time, of course, they benefit economically. By utilizing their summer months they are generally able to complete a normal four-year program in about five years.

The cooperative plan has generated a flock of imitators, and it has found its way even into some of our high schools. Although the plan has been favored mainly by schools of engineering, it is adaptable to other fields. Early in the twenties it was adopted by Antioch College, at Yellow Springs, Ohio. Here the plan was designed to combine "a liberal college education, vocational training and apprenticeship for life." Antioch's cultural-vocational program was not intended to furnish the student an opportunity to work his way through college, nor was its primary purpose to teach students the rudiments of a trade or profession. All these it regarded as "incidental benefits" of a new kind of liberal education which, as in the days of ancient Athens, it sought to relate to actual living in an actual society.[5]

Several universities have established what is known as a "general" college for the benefit of such students whose educational interests and aptitudes do not fall into the conventional pattern of the kind of work which ordinarily leads to a bachelor's degree. Along this line St. Louis University has established a degreeless and creditless institution whose main reason for being is to further the personal development of its students. The University of Minnesota's General College admits any student who, in its estimation, may profit by its program. Designed to meet the personal interests of youths and to prepare them for the responsibilities which will inevitably invade their adult lives, Minnesota's program concerns itself not only with broad essentials of the humanities, the social and natural sciences, but also with the pressing needs of young people which involve such vital matters as health, sex, marriage, family relations, vocation, civic and social relations, and so on. The completion of the program, which covers two years, leads to a certificate; some of the courses, moreover, may be credited toward bachelor degrees in the university's other schools and colleges.

What is commonly known as the "Chicago plan" was

---

[5] In an address at Boston in January, 1923, Charles W. Eliot declared that "there are many hopes" that the Antioch plan "will result not only in developing trained senses, manual skill, and character-forming practices, but also in attaining as high a level of culture as can be obtained by giving the student's whole time for four years to cultural studies."

inaugurated in 1931 at the University of Chicago. Stressing the "broad fields of human knowledge," the Chicago program has organized general survey courses in the humanities, the social sciences, the physical sciences, and the biological sciences. Every student must be familiar with the content of these four major fields which he generally studies during his freshman and sophomore years. Upon passing comprehensive examinations in the four required fields, the student continues his education by specializing in any one of them or by attending one of the university's professional schools. Interestingly enough, a student may take his comprehensives whenever he feels ready; hence there is no compulsory class attendance. Another feature of the Chicago plan is its abolition of the conventional credit system.[6]

12. The depression and the second World War

As might be expected, both the depression and the second World War affected the American higher learning. Under the impact of the economic collapse of the late twenties and the early thirties, the colleges' expanding enrollments came to an end. Their incomes shrank, not only because they received less in tuition fees, but also because the return on their endowment funds diminished. The colleges' sad economic plight necessitated a general retrenchment in which teaching staffs were curtailed and salaries cut, and in which academic work as a whole was seriously hampered.

---

[6] Holding that the best age for basic general education is from fifteen to eighteen years of age, Chicago admits students after they have completed two years of high school work. The student's competency is determined on the basis of acceptable grades in high school, his principal's recommendation, and a battery of aptitude tests.

In addition to the foregoing innovations in the practices of the modern American college, there are of course many others. Notable among them are experiments of varying kinds at Goddard, Bennington, Sarah Lawrence, Bard, Rollins, Reed, and many others. For an analysis of some of these the reader is referred to the *National Society for the Study of Education,* 31st Yearbook, Part II, Bloomington, Ill., 1932; also Fraser, M., *The College of Tomorrow.* New York: Columbia University Press, 1937; and American Association of University Women, "Newer Aspects of Collegiate Education; a Study Guide," Washington, D. C.: 1936.

As the country came out of the economic slump, conditions in the college began to brighten. However as America launched its defense program and then assumed the role of a belligerent, the war's prehensile fingers were soon on the colleges everywhere. Thus, as more and more students entered the armed services, the college classrooms gradually emptied. Not only did the war play havoc with college enrollments, but it also depleted the faculty rosters. In time the loss of students was offset somewhat by the influx of soldiers and others sent by the government to the colleges for special training.

In the course of time colleges began to reshape their offerings to meet the special needs created by the emergency. Generally speaking, the demand for mathematics, physics, chemistry, and for various technical subjects whose value in modern warfare was great increased considerably, as did the demand for languages. Several colleges added Russian, Chinese, and Japanese to their linguistic offerings. Moreover, in order to teach these languages quickly and efficiently new and improved methods were devised.

Under war conditions accelerated courses became popular. Thus, where ordinarily a student would devote fifteen weeks to a thirty-hour course, he now telescoped the thirty hours into four weeks or even less. By foregoing the usual vacations, he was able to obtain his degree in much less than the usually required time. To some extent, of course, the idea of acceleration had existed even before the war. At New York University, and in a number of other institutions, the idea of operating for the greater part of the year has brought into being not only the conventional summer session, but also an intersession and postsession besides the regular session.

It should hardly be necessary to point out that the war enhanced the financial difficulties of the American college. With ascetic economy a few, like Harvard and Columbia, managed to weather their difficulties fairly well. Many offset

their financial losses to some extent by harnessing themselves
to the government's War Training Program. Through government contracts they made available their buildings, equipment, and even their instruction for young men and women
trained at government expense.

13. After the war

With the end of hostilities some of the colleges' war difficulties vanished. Where formerly their enrollments had
dwindled to a faint trickle, they suddenly burst into a torrent.
Everywhere the higher learning was flooded with applications,
especially from returning servicemen and women who were
anxious to avail themselves of their G. I. educational benefits.
As little colleges became big, and large ones grew larger, their
problems of readjustment mounted. Strangely enough, their
larger enrollments did not end their financial headaches. The
fact is that tuition fees cover only a part of the cost of a
student's college education; hence increased enrollments were
in many cases something of a dubious blessing. To meet their
rising costs of instruction, colleges throughout the country
raised their tuition fees. Others sought to replenish their
dwindling resources by staging fund-raising drives; some were
even obliged to borrow money in order to continue.

To meet the needs of their many new students, colleges and
universities were confronted by the task of expanding their
facilities. Housing, classrooms, and laboratories and all kinds
of equipment were required; but inflated costs and shortages of
critical materials made these acquisitions difficult to obtain,
and although large sums of money were spent for these purposes, progress was relatively slow.

Another postwar woe to afflict America's higher learning
was the difficulty of securing competent and experienced
instructors. During the war men of learning had left their
posts in large numbers; and though a good number had
returned to the teaching fold, many others had accepted

positions with the government or with private industry where their salaries were generally better than in the colleges.[7]

The American colleges find themselves confronted by pressing and perplexing questions. The present high enrollments are expected to recede. At the same time, however, we appear to be passing into an age in which higher education will become more and more the national style. "American colleges and universities," the President's Commission on Higher Education has declared, "must envision a much larger role for higher education in the national life. They can no longer consider themselves merely the instrument for producing an intellectual élite; they must become the means by which every citizen, youth and adult, is enabled to carry his education, formal and informal, as far as his native capacities will permit." [8] By 1960 the Commission envisions a "minimum of 4,600,000 young people . . . enrolled in nonprofit institutions for education beyond the traditional twelfth grade." Once the colleges embrace such a program, the issues underlying college expansion will become increasingly important. Just how large, for example, shall colleges permit themselves to become? Where does college expansion cease to be desirable? Shall the colleges—to use the jargon of commerce— cater to a quality market or shall they aim for a mass market? And above all, how shall a program of expansion be adequately financed? Where will the money come from beyond the tuition fees and the shrinking returns from endowments which will provide the necessary housing, the classroom space, the expensive laboratories, the libraries, and all the other equipment and facilities so essential to an efficient college? These things run into high figures. In fact, it has been estimated that by 1960 the operational expenses of America's

---

[7] Although college teachers received wage increases, these were relatively low, averaging less than 20 per cent in 1946 as against 60 per cent for the average employee over his 1940 income.

[8] *Higher Education for American Democracy,* p. 39. A Report of the President's Commission on Higher Education, Vol. I. Washington: Government Printing Office, 1947.

higher learning will approach some two billion dollars, exclusive of additional moneys spent on the necessary building program.

To meet these costs, at least in part, federal aid for the college has been suggested. Actually, of course, all higher education has been subsidized to some extent during the past score of years, either by state funds, by WPA and other assistance during the depression, and by substantial wartime contracts. Many colleges, however, fearing that federal aid might jeopardize their prized independence, look at federal subsidies with wary eyes. However, since the colleges' financial condition appears likely to become worse rather than better during the coming years, it is hardly conceivable that any important college can hope to get along without some kind of governmental aid. The real question, it has been suggested by some authorities, seems to be not so much whether or not there shall be federal aid, but rather how it shall be expended. At present there are those who urge that the money should go to the colleges directly, to be spent for the benefit of the students as the colleges see fit; but there are others who argue that a significant share of the money should go to the students themselves to be spent by them, as in the case of the G. I. Bill of Rights, at whatever college they may select.

Not all the colleges' problems are altogether financial, though a good many of them no doubt will cost money to solve in the end. The problem of providing adequate programs of adult education must be dealt with, as must the matter of developing the offerings in general education. More important than even these are the problems which deal with the equalization of educational opportunity and the elimination of discriminatory practices against racial and religious minorities. Regarding the inequality of educational opportunity which exists in America, the President's Commission has pointed out that "the greater number of children being born in the families and the regions of the country that are least able to provide them with a good education . . . is contributing to the spread of a meager cultural heritage, and that this may one day tip the balance in our struggle for a better civilization." The remedy suggested is the raising of the economic and cultural levels in the less fortunate areas, and at the same time the provision of outside assistance to "enable these areas to give their children equal educational opportunities with others in the Nation." Regarding discrimination, the colleges will assuredly have to come to grips with such manifestations of the problem as the quota system and segregation. The President's Commission has declared the quota system "a violation of a major American principle and contributing to the growing tension in one of the crucial areas of our democracy." As for segregation, not only is the system indefensible according to any honest democratic standard, but it is also economic idiocy, for obviously to maintain two systems of education "duplicating even inadequately the buildings, equipment and teaching personnel, means that neither can be of the quality that would be possible, if all the available resources were devoted to one system."

H. Adult Education

1. Meaning and scope

It must have been a cynic who suggested that if three educators got together and discussed adult education each would have something else in mind. One view on the subject is the following by a member of the People's Institute, a noted New York school for adults:

It is sought to make of adult education something which will broaden the interests and sympathies of people regardless of their daily occupations along with it; to lift men's thoughts out of the monotony and drudgery which are the common lot; to free the mind from servitude and herd opinion; to train habits of judgment and of appreciation of value; to carry on the struggle for human excellence in our day and generation . . . ; to enlist all men, in the measure they have capacity for it, in the achievement of civilization.

The following is still another view:

Adult Education: An educational movement for men and women, young and old, who no longer are in contact with formalized education, whose primary interest lies in a vocation, but who possess a secondary interest in their own educational improvement as a sustained and continuous process.

Although these words leave unrevealed the vastness and variety of the territory covered by adult education, they contain a few of its more prominent hallmarks. Adult education, thus, is usually a voluntary undertaking engaged in by persons old enough to be beyond the period of compulsory schooling. Unlike most college and university students, these volunteer learners concentrate their main efforts not on study but on earning their daily living. The efforts of such adult students, however, must be more than merely casual or haphazard; they must "be planned and have continuity."

2. Studies in adult learning

Time was when it was generally held that the ability to learn was a monopoly of youth. People of middle age and beyond, it was assumed, were at best slow in acquiring new knowledges and skills. In a way, this notion was reassuring for those adults who preferred the serenity of indolence to the quest for knowledge. But this refuge has vanished. After considerable experimentation, Edward L. Thorndike of Columbia University was convinced in 1920 that "the zenith of power for acquiring information, ideas and the more subtle skills" arrives in one's early twenties. The decade from twenty to thirty is held superior to any other, and the decade from thirty to forty is now held to be on a par with that of ten to twenty. In the words of Dr. Thorndike:

Even at forty-five a man can hold his own with his son at the presumably versatile and receptive age of fifteen. If middle age can equal youth at youth's own intellectual specialty, adulthood may continue doggedly to claim superiority in its field of alleged supremacy—general and practical judgment.

3. Types of adult education

Adult education in the United States falls into two main kinds—formal and informal; these, as usual, are split and split again into other varieties. The informal type of adult learning is more or less indirect. Under the informal banner march such agencies as public libraries, museums, lyceums, forums, drama leagues, women's clubs, the pulpit, the press, movies, and radio. Some of these dispense offerings of systematic study, but on the whole the education they give belongs to the unorganized variety. A distinguished place must be reserved in this informal group for the United States Department of Agriculture. This, under the provisions of the Smith-Lever Act of 1914, dispatches to the rural areas every year thousands of county, home, and agricultural agents whose chief duty is to dispense the latest findings in scientific farming, housekeeping, psychology, and so on.

The more organized or formal type constitutes the important division of adult education. Gracing its ranks are the correspondence schools and the university extension courses. In addition, there are the public evening schools and extension classes of noncollegiate rank besides those conducted by Rotary, Kiwanis, the Knights of Columbus, the various Y's, and workers' groups.

The institute. The institute generally concentrates on the lecture, and though the audience is composed of more or less mature minds, questions and discussions are not stressed. One of the first institutes, the Lowell Institute, was founded in 1839 in Boston. In its prime, Lowell attracted such lecturers as Agassiz, John Fiske, James Russell Lowell, Oliver Wendell Holmes, and Charles Eliot. Besides its regular lectures, Lowell conducts a number of technical and professional courses. During a season thousands of persons gather at Lowell to listen to lectures on such topics as "The Weather in Peace and War," "The Latin Kingdom of Jerusalem," "Intelligence Tests and Their Significance for School and Society," "History of the Recent Fauna of Siberia and Central Asia," and so on.

One of the most notable institutes is the Brooklyn Institute of Arts and Sciences. Founded in 1823, the Brooklyn establishment, more than a century later, boasted of an endowment of $2,000,000. Of this, the educational department, which sponsors most of the lectures, receives about half a million. In addition there are special grants, such as one for $10,000 for chamber music. The biggest part of the income, however, comes from the members themselves, of whom there are several thousand. Unlike the rank and file of institutes, Brooklyn concerns itself with many things. It is interested, for example, in the Brooklyn Botanical Garden, the Brooklyn Museum of Arts and Sciences, and the Children's Museum. For teachers, it offers courses in education. In music the Brooklyn Institute has for a long time held top rank, offering concerts by Kreisler, Rachmaninoff, the New York Philharmonic Symphony Orchestra, and many other eminent artists.

Schools for adults. One of the most popular forms of adult education flourishes not in institutes but in schools which have been especially organized to teach grownups. The oldest is the People's Institute, which was established in 1897 in New York. During its first score of years it did the work of a combined lyceum and forum, besides some social work. In recent years, however, the school has restricted its activity to adult education. Unlike some of the more prosperous institutes, the People's Institute is not blessed with a superabundance of money. Most of its work, in fact, has been carried out in the face of economic handicaps. The People's Institute has staged lectures by eminent headliners in their respective fields. But the Institute's most significant work is not these special talks but its regular courses. It is here also that for many years the Institute's director, the late Everett Dean Martin, was active. Ranging from "Democracy in the Light of Psychology" to "Nietzsche and the Spirit of Today," from the "New Liberalism" to "Psychology," Martin's courses constituted a strong magnet.

From the Institute's lecture work there has emerged a School of the Institute which aims at meeting the needs of small groups in specialized subjects. Such specialized work naturally presumes some previous training, though even here the People's Institute has set up no entrance requirements. The work of the School, like that of the Institute, is manned by well-known experts, most of whom are university professors.

New School for Social Research. Duplicating to some extent the work of the Institute is another Manhattan school for adults, known as the New School for Social Research. This is purely a twentieth century creation, coming into being in 1919. It seeks, according to its announcement, "to draw to its lecture rooms . . . persons of maturity with an intellectual interest, graduates of colleges engaged in professions or in business, and men and women who by reading and discussion have prepared themselves for the serious study of social problems." A fair share of the students who attend the New School are college graduates and some even have advanced degrees. To meet the needs of these students, the faculty must "be men who can speak the layman's language and understand his interests." At the same time, however, they must be something more than entertainers and popularizers. "They must," to quote the school's announcement, "have unimpeachable academic standing as men who not only recognize the academic canons of exactitude and adequacy, but who also are able to carry on and direct productive scholarship." True to these ideals, the New School has had on its staff such outstanding masters as Charles A. Beard, James Harvey Robinson, Roscoe Pound, Felix Frankfurter, Lewis Mumford, John Dewey, and others. The school moved into the national spotlight when it honored itself with the services of many notable foreign scholars who, because of their race or social or political credo, had been forced out of their native lands.

The courses offered at the New School are fairly advanced

and, as might be expected, they lean toward the social. There is work in behaviorism, anthropology, social psychology, in aesthetics, criminology, politics, in history, labor, mental hygiene, and so on. But letters and arts have not been overlooked. There was, for example, a course in contemporary letters conducted by Henry Wadsworth Longfellow Dana. At the same time Stark Young lectured on the art of the theater; and Lewis Mumford discoursed on architecture in American Civilization.[1]

4. The depression and after

With the coming of the depression adult education moved rapidly forward. Not only was there an increased demand for such education, especially from the vast legions of the unemployed, but to satisfy that demand various new agencies were created. Probably the most important single agency in the development of programs of adult education has been the federal government. Relating part of its relief program to education, the government hired many thousands of unemployed teachers, putting them in charge of classes of adults.[2]

The interest in adult education did not vanish with the passing of hard times. In fact, many localities have made adult education a permanent part of their school program. Increasingly, moreover, the American college has been giving the new field its serious consideration. A number of the larger universities have established divisions of adult education which offer non-credit courses ranging from physics and Russian literature to angling and photography. At the University of Chicago the Great Books have been brought into the field of adult education. There it is expected that within a few years the program will be reaching some 150,000 persons scattered in some 30 to 40 cities. With the aid of the Carnegie Corporation, a national association dedicated to

---

[1] Since its inception the New School has extended its work. Today it operates not only in the field of adult education, but it also confers degrees.

[2] According to figures released by the Advisory Committee on Education some 44,000 unemployed teachers taught about 1,725,000 persons.

promoting adult education and to the study of its requirements has been organized. More recently the President's
Commission on Higher Education gave its endorsement to
adult education. "Adult education," it declared, "along with
undergraduate and graduate education, should become the
responsibility of every department or college of the university.
It should be the duty of the English faculty or the physics
faculty, for instance, to teach English or physics not just to
those who come to the campus, but to everyone in the
community or the State who wants to learn, or can be
persuaded to want to learn, English or physics." The university, it went on to say, must broaden its concept of
education. It must cease "to be campus-bound." Instead it
must go to the people; "by every available and effective means
for the communication of ideas and the stimulation of intellectual curiosity" it must make itself available to the multitudes who desire the service it offers. Only thus will higher
education "play its social role in American democracy and in
international affairs successfully." [3]

5. Adult education abroad

Grundtvig and the Danish Folk High Schools. Though a
nineteenth century creation, the people's colleges or folk high
schools of Denmark are still significant. In fact, some of the
main features of modern adult education owe their origin to
the Danish schools. The founder of the folk high schools was
the Lutheran Bishop Nikolaij Grundtvig (1783–1872), who
was motivated by a desire to enlighten the masses. Indeed, it
was because of the masses that the folk high schools took on
their freedom of form and method. Inspired by the ideals of
Grundtvig, the prototype of folk high school came into being
in 1844 in the village of Rödding in northern Slesvig. Briefly,
this was an economic, cultural, and patriotic enterprise, and

---

[3] *Higher Education for American Democracy,* p. 97 ff. A Report of the
President's Commission on Higher Education, Vol. I. Washington: Government Printing Office, 1947.

was intended as an antidote for the formal education of the regular secondary schools. Four years after the founding of Rödding, Denmark and Prussia went to war, with ruinous results for the Scandinavians.

The work of Kristen Kold. It was about this time that the name of Kristen Kold made its connection with the folk high school. Trained for the teaching profession, Kold (1816–1870) had spent part of his early life as a schoolmaster. His pedagogical unorthodoxy, however, had vexed the authorities, who practically banned him from teaching in Denmark. With the establishment of a more liberal form of government after the war with Prussia, these obscurantists lost much of their power and Kold returned to schoolmastering. A disciple of Grundtvig, Kold established a school at Ryslinge where he bought a few acres of ground and built a small shack. At first there were some fifteen students, ranging from the late teens to the early thirties. Subsequently, Kold moved his school to another part of the island, and in 1862 he built a much larger school at Dalum where every year he continued to attract students in large numbers.

Kold's talent for lifting the heart and mind of the common people was extraordinary, as was also his gift for arousing a desire for a richer spiritual life. His teaching was oral, for he felt that the "living word" was the master-key that unlocked the student's desire to learn. When he first began to teach, he spoke on history, literature, and the Scriptures, and his talks were always followed by discussion. Kold was not interested in knowledge as such, and during his lectures he did not even allow his hearers to take notes. He once said:

If we lay a drain pipe, we mark the spot in order to find it again in case of necessary repair, but when we sow grain it is not necessary to mark the spot. And you may be sure what you have heard and enjoyed hearing will come forth again when it has taken root in your mind.

Recent developments. Today there are some 60 people's high schools in Denmark. In addition, similar schools are found in other Scandinavian domains as well as in Finland and some of the Teutonic countries on the continent. The folk high schools are private ventures. Attendance, of course, is strictly voluntary. Though the schools are private, the Danish state donates funds annually to help in their support, and some 9,000 men and women, between the ages of seventeen and thirty, attend during the year. Aiming to "enable pupils to return to their daily work with a deeper understanding of human life and its problems," these schools of twentieth century Denmark have kept close to the ideals of the founding fathers. In a sense, the folk high school is a home, the pupils, teachers, and the principal and his wife living together very much like a family. Besides the lecture and its ensuing discussion, considerable stress is put upon that incidental spontaneous education which comes from a learning situation. This may be on a hike, or it may emerge from a conversation. It may be in the classroom, or it may be when all are together at their meal. But whether it be lecture or discussion, within the four walls of a schoolroom or out in the woodlands or fields, learning proceeds in the grand manner, for its own sake, for pleasure and mental excitement, without social or economic rewards—indeed, even minus such academic ornaments as examinations, credits, degrees, and diplomas.

Twentieth century Denmark is, of course, different from the Denmark of Grundtvig and Kold. During the lifetime of these two the nation was predominantly agricultural; today less than half the population is engaged in farming. The original folk high schools catered primarily to the untutored; today the general culture of the masses is on a much higher plane. The folk high school naturally has not been unmindful of changing social and economic conditions. More stress is now put on the individual's creative efforts. There is a rising interest in aesthetics and art criticism. Before the second World War the majority of students in the folk high school showed little interest in social problems. This, Danish schoolmen have explained, is due to the fact that the larger part of the students come from the rural populace, which seems to have been fortunately blessed with relatively good social conditions. Gradually, however, it has become apparent that the folk high school should be an important force among the industrial working classes. At Copenhagen, notably, there is a large free folk high school, which since 1911 has been featuring what are known as *holiday* courses. Thousands of students have participated in this work, and most of these come from the homes of the workers. In the wintertime they are given the opportunity of renewing the relationship with their teachers by attending lectures and social gatherings at the Grundtvig House. The special needs of the urban learner have been further recognized by the establishment of a folk high school for the people of Copenhagen.

Fritz Wartenweiler and adult education in Switzerland. Descendants of the original folk high schools have arisen in many parts of the world; wherever they are and whatever their work, they have attained significance only where their leaders have caught a glimpse of the ideals which moved the school's pioneers, men like Grundtvig and Kold.

Such a leader is Fritz Wartenweiler who, for many years, has given himself to the cause of adult education in Switzerland. As a boy he was attracted to farming, but in time the idea of becoming a teacher beckoned. Eventually he went to Berlin, where he studied education and philosophy. Then his studies lured him to Copenhagen, where his interest in the folk high school was ignited.

To lift the Swiss peasantry and instill in it the spirit he had observed in Denmark, Wartenweiler set out to learn all he could, both about teaching and also about the people he wanted to teach. He accepted a teaching post in one of the public schools in his native canton of Thurgau, where he taught 70 pupils of all grades and all ages. Like Pestalozzi, his great countryman, Wartenweiler radiated a boundless enthusiasm. And again like Pestalozzi, he credits the final success to his students and associates. "What my pupils

learned from me during those years," he has said, "I don't
know; but what I learned from them is incalculable."

It was not until 1919 that Wartenweiler launched his own
educational enterprise. Beginning in a modest way with five
young men as his students, he discussed those questions which
interested and affected them. Some hours were given every
day to labor in the fields, and all practical work around the
house was done by the students themselves. Thus the enterprise continued from the dawn of spring to the end of fall,
winter being reserved by Wartenweiler for the teaching of his
own sons.

In time came growth. More ground was rented; more land
cultivated; a whole farm was leased. Then in 1925 Wartenweiler's lease was canceled and the school was closed.

Wartenweiler now set out to familiarize the populace with
his ideas. An entertaining speaker, who talked the language
of the common people, who understood their ways and sympathized with them, he attracted more and more listeners.
Meanwhile, three schools working along lines similar to his
were established. At one of them, in Neukirch, he became a
frequent guest and teacher. Then a number of people interested in Wartenweiler's work organized a society (The
Freunde Schweizerischer Volksbildungsheime) for the purpose
of aiding his project. In the summer of 1929 Wartenweiler
offered courses once more. This time the students flocked to
him. So encouraging was the venture that in the ensuing
winter he repeated it with the same good results.

In the course of time came special courses for older people.
Since most of them were tied down to their jobs, Wartenweiler
instituted special holiday courses for them. Two or three
times every summer men and women would gather at Neukirch for a week or so to discuss problems of common interest.
There was always some central theme around which these
talks were woven. Special stress was put on the study of the
world's great figures such as Pestalozzi, Vinet, Marx, Catherine
Booth, Gandhi, Lenin, and so on. Through lectures and panel

discussions, solutions to problems were sought, misconceptions cleared and confidence awakened. As might be expected among the Swiss, such occasions would be incomplete without plenty of music and singing.

Surviving hard economic and political storms, Wartenweiler's schools have grown in size, number, and influence. They are not quite as spiritual and religious as their Danish forerunners. Having no partisan ax to grind, they strive as far as possible to consider all points of view, with the result that at times they have reaped the furor of factions which are blind to all save their own particular way of saving the world. Another difference between Wartenweiler's schools and those of Denmark is that in the former the peasantry does not dominate. The vocational representation among Wartenweiler's protégés is varied, including plumbers, teachers, blacksmiths, nurses, mechanics, writers, and others.

Adult education in England. In England adult education is an old story. Originating more than a century ago, the movement is firmly rooted today. In its most common guise it appears as workers' education. And here, interestingly enough, academic strongholds like Oxford and Cambridge have lent a helping hand. Since 1907, because of cooperation between labor groups and the universities, several varieties of higher education are now available to workers. It was the talent and effort of a Britisher, Dr. Albert Mansbridge, and his colleagues that created the World Association for Adult Education. Founded in 1918, this organization seeks "the development of adult education throughout the world and the federation in one Association of individuals and institutions concerned with adult education in all countries." The Association has attracted members from more than 40 nations.

Adult education in Germany. In the Reich the interest in adult education goes back to 1871 with the creation of the *Gesellschaft für Verbreitung der Volksbildung,* which sought to spread education to the masses on a grand scale. This society was to serve as an antidote to what its backers called the "cultural monopoly" of the upper classes. Like many similar organizations this *Gesellschaft* taught mainly through lectures. Besides this phase of adult learning, the Germans, especially in the larger cities, developed an array of specialized technical and practical courses for grownups. By 1905 the Danish influence had begun to make itself felt in Germany, with the consequent establishment of several people's higher schools. After the first war, adult education developed rapidly, assuming, incidentally, many of the forms found in America. Especially significant was the florescence of the people's colleges. These institutes represented a welter of conflicting ideals. Thus there were those of a purely socialistic brand whose reason for being was mainly to augment the number of Marxians. On the other hand, there were the purely nationalistic folk colleges run to develop 100 per cent patriotic Germans. Besides these there were schools for adults run on denominational Christian lines and appealing particularly to the peasantry. Most of these schools were propaganda temples, dedicated to the furtherance of their own private causes. Less opinionated was the neutral type of folk school. In many ways it corresponded to the better types of American schools for adults. In the Third Reich, where propaganda and regimentation were accepted as essentials of education, such schools, of course, were put under the ban. Whatever adult education was found in Nazi Germany was closely related to the ideals of National Socialism.

Adult education in Soviet Russia. In the U.S.S.R. adult education is also getting considerable attention. Important phases of Russian adult education include a program of "political enlightenment" and a vigorous campaign against illiteracy. Between 1920 and 1923, according to Soviet statistics, some 2,400,000 men and women were made literate; and by the end of 1940 this roll of honor was augmented by many millions more. Besides the campaign for literacy the work of "political enlightenment" comprises most of the familiar features of adult education found in other lands.

Thus there are organized lectures, discussions, and debates, circulating libraries, reading rooms, aesthetic exhibits, concerts, and literary evenings. And, of course, much time is devoted to the indoctrination of communistic ideology. "The guiding principle of the work of practically all institutions of political enlightenment," says Pinkevitch, "is to integrate agitation, propaganda, and teaching with the proximate interests of the adult learner."

I. Workers' Education

1. Background

Labor's concern for education dates back for more than a century when American workers engaged actively in the fight for free public education. The idea, however, of a special educational program for workers, as distinguished from other types of citizens, is actually a child of the present century. It came into being shortly after the first World War. At that time much of its inspiration came from abroad, particularly from England, where workers' education was in vigorous bloom, and where, in fact, the trade union movement and its political arm, the Labor Party, had soared to high prestige. The impressive program on the part of English labor for social reconstruction stirred longings in the breast of American liberals and progressives. With visions of similar achievements for America, some of them tried to translate their hopes into actuality by way of workers' education. The early twenties saw the establishment of the Workers Education Bureau, the Brookwood Labor College at Katonah, New York, and the Bryn Mawr Summer School for Women Workers in Industry. The American Federation gave the new movement its blessing, extolling the new "trade union colleges" and supporting the Workers Education Bureau.

However, the high hopes of the liberals failed to materialize. Trade unions were not enthusiastic for "grand ideas," which they decried as impractical and intellectualistic, and even, occasionally, as radical. With the development, moreover, of a boom psychology in the prosperous twenties, reaction and apathy invaded organized labor, whose membership showed a marked decline. On the whole, labor seemed content with the *status quo* and its lush and easy wages and, like the bankers and the brokers, its leaders were disinclined to thwart its magic. Long-range programs aiming at an improvement of our social and economic system were not wanted. By 1925 James H. Maurer, president of the Workers Education Bureau, and a pioneer in the realm of workers' education, sadly conceded the movement's failure.

But his sorrow was a bit premature, for with the coming of the depression the situation changed. For one thing, many new unions came into being and with the expansion of many of the older unions, millions of workers joined the ranks of organized labor. For another thing, the social climate of the Roosevelt regime was generally favorable to labor. The New Deal brought the federal government into the field of workers' education. Through the WPA the government offered free education to those unions desiring it. Even so, the progress made by workers' education during this time was not too impressive. True, when compared with its sluggish record of the previous decade, it had moved ahead; but when its advance is placed against the enormous growth of organized labor, the number of unions dedicated to a strong educational program and the number of workers participating in such a program look pale and feeble.

2. Adult and workers' education

Although there is a kinship between adult education and workers' education, the two are not identical. The latter, true to its name, works in the domain of labor, concentrating on the particular problems and interests of the working people, and especially the organized working people. Its purpose is not "to give a bit of culture to the student; nor is its chief concern to pave his way to a better job. Workers' education strives to stimulate the student to serve the labor movement in particular and society in general and [is] not . . . to be used for selfish advancement." [1]

Basic to workers' education is the effort to help the worker to find his location upon the scale of our socio-economic setup, to gain a clear knowledge of all the facts relevant to his condition as a *wage-earner*. . . . Workers' education aims at equipping the worker with the kind of tools that will enable him to become a better wage-earner, and this means *to make him a union member* and ever a *better* union member.[2]

Thus conceived, workers' education is, as Theodore Brameld has succinctly put it, "first and last of, by, and for the members of trade unions, whether these workers are workers in factories who wear overalls or white-collared workers." [3]   In this respect workers' education differs from general adult education and from vocational training.

3.   Aspects of workers' education

Since the beginning of the New Deal in 1933, workers' education has revealed several characteristics.   Over the movement there still hovers the ultimate goal of liberals and progressives, which seeks the improvement of our socioeconomic order by having workers' education play a dynamic and creative part in the development of some form of democratic collectivism.   Furthermore, through a variety of social, cultural and recreational activities, an effort has been made to clarify and solidify the bonds between the member and his union.   As for education in the strict sense, classes and projects focusing on the worker's immediate interests and problems have developed increasingly.   Union members learn about such matters as collective bargaining, the nature of contracts between labor and management, conducting strikes, running a union meeting, labor-management relations, the political

---

[1] Adam, T. R., *The Worker's Road to Learning,* p. 24.   American Association for Adult Education, 1940.

[2] John Dewey Society, *Workers' Education in the United States,* p. 7. Brameld, T., Editor, Fifth Yearbook.   New York: Harper & Brothers, 1941.

[3] Brameld, T., "Workers' Education in America," *Educational Administration and Supervision,* xxx, 129 ff., March, 1947.

functioning of labor, as well as such problems of industry as unemployment, machine change, speed-ups, time, and motion studies, and so on. Besides courses designed to enhance the efficiency of the union and its member worker, background courses are offered in the history of the labor movement. More recently, moreover, there has been a growing consideration for sound and up-to-date educational procedures. It has been increasingly recognized that the principles and techniques which have been developed by professional students of education are in the main as applicable to workers' education as they are to the more general types of education.

4. Government sponsored programs

During the past two decades workers' education has been conducted in the form of (1) government sponsored programs, (2) union programs, and (3) programs sponsored by state-supported schools.

Early in the thirties, under the banner of the New Deal, governmental projects of all kinds were organized to carry on the war against unemployment. Under the Work Projects Administration a Workers' Education Project came into being. Seeking in the first place to provide work for jobless teachers, the project established classes and a field service for workers in more than 30 states, with the result that hundreds of teachers entered the sphere of workers' education. At its peak the Workers' Education Project embraced more than 2,000 workers' groups, enrolling as many as 75,000 men and women, of whom some 4,000 came from New York City. By the end of the thirties, however, Congress began to pare its appropriations with the result that the scope of the Project diminished considerably. To carry on what was left of the previous program, a Workers' Service Program was created as part of the Community Service Division, WPA. Despite formidable handicaps, among which a dearth of money loomed like the Alps, the new body carried on, though on a greatly diminished scale. The new body developed a program which included classes, workshops, and discussion groups for workers; conferences and forums; radio work, motion pictures, and exhibits; a library service; an advisory service in health, housing, employment, and other problems; an information service on new labor legislation; research studies of varying nature; and recreational activities.

5. Programs within unions

For more than a half-century some form of workers' education has been developing under union auspices. In the favorable social climate of the early thirties union educational activity had vigorous growth. Most ambitious among union-sponsored educational programs has been that of the International Ladies' Garment Workers Union—the ILGWU. With an annual outlay for educational purposes bordering on 500,000 dollars, the ILGWU has promoted a variety of educational enterprises throughout the United States and Canada. Its educational director, Mark Starr, has gained deservedly high renown for his many contributions to the cause of workers' education. Although classwork is the core of the garment union's educational program, woven into it are such features as excursions, lectures, forums, workshops, radio talks, and social activities ranging from club meetings to dramatic and musical productions. *Pins and Needles,* a musical written, acted, and directed by its members, won high praise from New York's front-line critics and went on to become a Broadway hit. Every member of the ILGWU who seeks election to any of the union's paid offices must first complete a course of special training; furthermore, all members are expected to be familiar with the union's history and functions. In addition there are courses in a variety of subjects including citizenship, English, public speaking, current events, parliamentary law, labor problems, economics of the garment industry, consumer problems, history of the American labor movement, and so on. Courses in the history of the ILGWU and the American labor movement have thus far drawn the highest attendance; next in popularity have been courses in current events and labor problems. Believing that sound education should have room for "fun" as well as "ideas," the ILGWU offers a rich assortment of recreational activities, from choral and instrumental music to swimming, bowling, baseball, soccer, basketball, and other sports. During the recent past the union has conducted a number of summer institutes in cooperation with representative labor colleges, such as the now defunct Brookwood Labor College and the Wisconsin Summer School for Workers. To encourage its members to participate in this work the union has appropriated a number of special scholarships.

Of similar nature, though somewhat less extensive in scope, has been the work of several other unions. Through its Department of Cultural Activities, the Amalgamated Clothing Workers (ACW) has sponsored workers' schools and officers' institutes in ten key cities of its territory. One of the specialties of the ACW has been its correspondence courses in which several thousand students annually enroll. The United Automobile Workers of America (UAW), reputed to be the largest union in the world, has organized an educational program with full-time experts in charge. In 1940 it voted to require its locals to use part of their funds to run classes, with special stress on "training-for-union service." In Detroit, where the UAW is naturally strong, a training school has been established. Like the Amalgamated Clothing Workers, the UAW has developed some first-rate correspondence courses. Moreover, with the American Federation of Hosiery Workers, the UAW has pioneered in making films and distributing them to its locals. Its film library is well stocked, and one of its productions, *United Action,* a documentary portrayal of one of its historic strikes, received critical acclaim.

On the reasonable premise that farmers are workers, the Farmers' Union has developed a program of workers' education designed to meet the many peculiar needs of its members. On the roster of its activities one will find such items as summer camps and winter institutes for the training of

junior and adult leaders; special courses to teach farmers
how to organize and run their local unions and cooperatives;
one-week training schools for officers; and schools to train
cooperative managers.[4]

6. National agencies

In the history of modern workers' education two national
agencies—the Workers' Educational Bureau of America
(WEB) and the American Labor Education Service (ALES)
—have played a significant part. Founded in 1921, the
Workers' Education Bureau aimed "to collect and to disseminate information relative to efforts at education on any
part of organized labor; to coordinate and assist in every
possible manner the educational work now carried on by the
organized workers, and to stimulate the creation of additional
enterprises in labor education throughout the United States."
Three years after its inception (1924) the Bureau was officially
blessed by the American Federation of Labor when it voted a
levy on its members to support the work of the WEB. Since
1929 the control and financing of the Bureau has been under
the AFL. Designated by William Green as "the educational
arm of the American Federation of Labor," the Bureau has
dipped into every conceivable phase of workers' education. It
has published books and pamphlets; run a news service;
promoted conferences, lectures, radio programs, week-end
institutes, and correspondence courses. It has participated in
international conferences of the workers' education international; it has brought eminent leaders of labor from here

---

[4] Besides the educational work of these unions many others, of course, have
also been educationally active. Among others have been unions representing
hosiery workers, hatters and millinery workers, oil workers, miners, electrical
and radio workers, rubber workers, machinists, teachers, architects, aluminum
workers, steel workers, fur workers, textile workers, office workers, professional
workers, technicians, engineers and chemists, mariners, upholsterers, ship-
builders, flat glass workers, railroad clerks, state, county, municipal, and federal
workers, and several others. Nonetheless, there are still many unions with no
program whatsoever.

and abroad before its audiences; and it has given helpful boosts to young and inexperienced unions.

The American Labor Education Service (ALES) began life in 1932 as the Affiliated Schools for Workers. Originally a loose union of workers' schools, the ALES has since then broadened its scope. Like the Workers' Education Bureau, it works with the AFL; unlike the Bureau, it also works with the CIO, thereby extending the bounds of its operation considerably. In the main its work resembles that of the Bureau.

7. Schools for workers

Besides the educational work carried on by the unions and the agencies cooperating with them, a number of schools scattered through the country have specialized in workers' education. Most of them have been of modest size, catering to a handful of students, and blessed generally with far more enthusiasm than capital assets. The fact seems to be that organized labor has not put much stock in the idea of an all-year school for workers. Unions, it is true, have sent some of their members to them as students; occasionally they have provided them with specially trained teachers for certain courses, and they have dipped into their tills to provide scholarships for deserving students. All in all, however, their financial support has never been adequate.

A few schools for workers were founded before 1900, but most of them are of the present century.[5] Through the efforts of a group of Socialists, the Rand School of the Social Sciences, with an educational program for workers, was established in

---

[5] About 1894 Avalon College was founded near Trenton, Missouri, by the Christian Socialists, Mr. and Mrs. McA. Miller. Subsequently the school's name was changed to Ruskin College in honor of the first residential labor college established in England. Destroyed by fire in 1906, the school was reorganized by the Millers, this time in Florida. Another nineteenth century school enrolling workers was Breadwinner's College, established in 1898 in New York City by Thomas Davidson. Emotionally, Davidson was often hostile to labor, and his educational views and practices would certainly not be acceptable to modern proponents of workers' education.

1906. Two years later, the Finnish people residing around Duluth, Minnesota, established the Work People's College, the pioneer residential labor college in the trade union field in this country. The Boston Trade Union College, sponsored by the Central Labor Union, was founded in 1919; and in the same year the Central Labor Council helped to organize the Seattle Labor College. The year 1921 marked the opening of two important workers' schools—Brookwood Labor College, at Katonah, New York, and the Summer School for Working Women at Bryn Mawr.

For many years Brookwood Labor College was the leading school for men and women desiring to prepare themselves for service in the labor movement.[6] Its founder and dean, A. J. Muste, a Presbyterian pastor and a man of liberal convictions, believed that workers' education should be something more than "pure and simple trade unionism"—a belief which was not universally shared by labor leaders of his day. His was the long-term view of the liberal who envisioned in workers' education the force which in time would bring forth a new and better social order. Brookwood, however, stressed the usual subjects of workers' education with offerings in parliamentary law, social psychology, social economics, history of civilization, history of the American labor movement, foreign labor, and the like. For a number of years the College received part of its support from the American Federation of Labor, but in 1929 the AFL's Executive Council voted to discourage further help on the ground of the College's alleged "disloyalty." The action aroused a storm of protest and criticism among liberals. "The College," declared John Dewey, "more than most institutions of whatever sort, has been truly educational in living up to its efforts to lead students to think —which means, of course, to think for themselves." [7] But the breach was never mended. Brookwood continued to function

---

[6] *Brookwood Labor College—Labor's Own School,* ALES, 1936, gives a brief account of this historic school.

[7] Dewey, J., "Labor Politics and Labor Education," *New Republic,* LVII, 2, January 9, 1929.

until 1937 when a combination of factors, accentuated by the
College's wretched financial condition, forced it to close.
During the 16 years of the school's activity, it struggled
constantly to keep alive; nonetheless its service to the cause
of workers' education was great. Some five hundred persons
were trained in its classes—a mere handful, to be sure; but of
this handful a significant number rose to distinguished and
responsible positions in social and labor movements. No less
significant—indeed, perhaps even more significant when
viewed in the panorama of the ages—was Brookwood's stalwart defence of academic freedom. For this principle, the
right to teach the truth without interference, it stood up
resolutely, defending it even with the full knowledge that its
action would assuredly bring it hardship.

The Bryn Mawr Summer School for Women Workers in
Industry was a cooperative enterprise between college women
and women in industry.[8] Speaking strictly, the school was not
a part of Bryn Mawr College, but a separate institution using
the Bryn Mawr campus and buildings. The school's purpose,
in the words of one of its announcements, was:

> to offer young women in industry an opportunity to study liberal subjects
> and to train themselves in clear thinking; to stimulate an active and con-
> tinued interest in the problems of our economic order; to develop a desire
> for study as a means of understanding and enjoyment of life. The school
> is not committed to any theory. The teaching is carried on by instructors
> who have an understanding of the students' practical experience in industry
> and of the labor movement. It is conducted in a spirit of impartial inquiry
> with freedom of discussion and teaching. It is expected that thus the
> students will gain a truer insight into the problem of industry and feel a
> more vital responsibility for their solution.

Eight weeks were offered for the realization of this program,
students coming from all parts of the country. One hundred
was the number set for capacity registration. Admission

---

[8] Instrumental in planning and bringing the new school into being were
President M. Carey Thomas of Bryn Mawr College; Mary Anderson, Chief of
the Women's Bureau; Hilda Worthington Smith, who became the school's
first Educational Director; and Ernestine Friedmann, Executive Secretary.

requirements were simple enough. One had to be an industrial worker, aged between twenty-one and thirty-five, with elementary schooling or its equivalent. Nonindustrial workers were not generally admitted, though exceptions were made in certain instances.

The subjects offered comprised economics, composition, and hygiene—all of which were required. In addition, the student had to choose one of the following: science, psychology, and literature. Added to all this were a half-dozen lectures on history, at odd hours, at which attendance was optional. The important subject was economics. Since the girls who graced the lecture rooms in this particular instance were of diverse attitudes and points of view, ranging from radical Bolsheviks to anti-union conservatives, the discussions which whipped the classroom air were often hot and frictional. To bolster its lectures and discussions, the Summer School for Working Women employed a variation of the tutorial system. By it, every instructor had at least one tutorial assistant who was expected to supplement in greater detail the work of his chief. This he did in part in an hour known as the tutorial period, of which there were two or three every week. In such a period the tutor met a group of about a half-dozen students, holding conference on the matter presented by the instructor to the class as a whole.

Historically, the Bryn Mawr school was the first in America to cater to the special needs of the woman industrial worker. Under Hilda Smith and her co-workers it gained a deserved renown. It was, in fact, widely imitated, and its work led directly to the creation of a number of other projects in workers' education. The school reached its heyday in the latter twenties; but like most schools of its kind, it fell upon lean years. In 1939 it was reorganized as the Hudson Shore Labor School and moved to new quarters at West Park, New York.

Though the Highlander Folk School has been justifiably lauded for its magnificent accomplishments as a community school, its name is perhaps of even greater importance in the annals of workers' education. Founded in 1932 by Myles Horton, the school's present director, on some 200 acres of land near Monteagle, Tennessee, Highlander has trained many thousands of workers and labor education leaders in its resident and extension courses.[9] Believing that the problems of the "isolated" mountaineer were in essence the same as those of all struggling people of the south, Highlander was convinced from the outset that "only through a strong labor movement could living conditions of all the people improve," and that "only through a strong labor movement could the people be guaranteed their democratic rights." The school, in other words, has become a dynamic part of the struggle to organize the south.

Cooperatively owned and managed by its teaching staff, Highlander is affiliated with no group or organization. Its policies are determined by an executive council composed of southern labor leaders, educators, and members of the staff. Specifically, the school seeks "to assist in the defense and expansion of political and economic democracy." To accomplish this, it believes that "the strengthening of the unions through education is the school's primary task."

Besides its community program, Highlander has embarked upon a full-fledged program as well as an extension program by which its teachers go to the mines and the farms. Its general sessions are open to all union members regardless of race or creed. At the special request of a particular union it also holds special sessions which are open only to the members of that union. Year round, moreover, the school is open to groups for conferences and institutes. The Hosiery Workers of the Tri-State Area hold a week-end recreational and

---

[9] Myles Horton's fine leadership has contributed in a major way to the success of the Highlander Folk School. His sympathy for the struggling people who are his neighbors was born in his own personal experience. The son of a sharecropper, Horton battled with poverty for a good part of his early life. "I never wore shoes till I was grown," is his way of illustrating hardship.

educational session every three months. Other progressive groups, such as the industrial YMCA, the Religion and Labor Foundation, the Southern Conference for Human Welfare, and Citizens Political Action Groups, have found that Highlander is one of the rare places in the south where all may meet, regardless of race, creed, color, or national origin.

What does one learn at Highlander? One may learn how to build a better union, how to prepare a case for arbitration, how to maintain order at a meeting. One may attend courses in political action, in the study of contracts, in publicity, in economics, the history of labor, or current events. One may even study music and singing. Indeed, Highlander students are encouraged to write songs, and every year their famous songbooks are enriched by contributions from the students.

For many the Highlander Folk School has come to symbolize the spirit behind the movement of the American working people. Yet it is much more than a shining ideal. Through it countless men and women have learned how to work and live cooperatively. Characterized as "a focal point for the new labor forces gathering in the South," [10] the school has reached thousands of unionists of all colors and creeds—a rarity in the south. To many thousands more it has given training for some form of leadership in the labor movement. A large proportion of its students hold important offices in their local unions; many have served significantly on grievance committees, negotiating committees, on interracial, safety, housing, transportation, and education committees; still others have served as delegates to city councils and state conventions. So the record continues, one of the most significant in recent educational history. It is, says John Dewey, "one of the most important social-educational projects in America." [11]

[10] Stevens, A., "Small-Town America," *The Nation,* 784, CLXIII, June 29, 1946.

[11] For an interesting digest of union education in the South see Lawrance, Mary, *Education Unlimited,* published under the imprint of the Highlander Folk School, April, 1945.

8. State and locally supported programs

Though the great majority of our junior and senior high school graduates will some day be confronted by the necessity of having to decide whether or not to be trade unionists, public elementary and secondary schools have evinced little interest in workers' education. This, however, should be no cause for great wonder, since most boards of education have no labor representation. On the whole, boards of education have been socially and economically conservative. Generally speaking, when the vital facts of the worker and his significant activities and relationships have managed to get into the school, it has not been through the main entrance of the school's total program, but through the side door of the social studies. Yet here and there one does come upon an occasional oasis. One of the most refreshing is Minneapolis, where, at the request of the unions, a series of units in the history of the labor movement and in the part played by American labor in American life was developed for the junior and senior high schools.

On the level of higher education the consideration accorded to workers' education by state authorities has been somewhat more generous. Historically, Wisconsin was the first state to make room for workers' education when, in 1924, it established the University of Wisconsin School for Workers, with a budget which is now provided by the University of Wisconsin under the joint control of university and labor officials.[12] Beyond administration costs, however, the major part of the school's support has come from organized labor. Political and reactionary winds have played havoc with the school, which, despite its frailty, has managed to keep going—though often under reefed sail. The larger portion of Wisconsin's program

---

[12] Before the founding of the Wisconsin School for Workers an attempt had been made in 1921 in California to develop a program of workers' education under the combined efforts of the state university and organized labor. The project reached the planning stage and even got as far as a committee composed of five members representing labor and four representing the university. That, however, was as far as the joint venture ever went.

has been carried on in its six-week summer school when workers from all over the country, but predominantly from the midwestern states, have come to study with the university's professors and with experts chosen and trained by labor for this purpose. Out of Wisconsin's successful summer school have come its winter institutes which have been conducted with the cooperation of the unions in various industrial centers. In 1937 the legislature dug into its treasury to appropriate a special grant to make possible the enlargement of the enterprise by the establishment of an extension program through which workers' education was to be carried out in any part of the state. A few years later, however, this auspicious development unfortunately came to an end when a reactionary state administration decided to cut down on its appropriations for workers' education.[13]

Not only is Wisconsin the pioneer state-supported program of workers' education on a university level, but in its field it is without a rival. Here and there one will find some spasmodic effort. In 1938, for example, the Virginia legislature appropriated $1,500 to finance a course in the history of the labor movement and a course in public speaking to be conducted in the university's extension division. More recently, Michigan made a modest entrance into workers' education through its extension division. Cornell University, which is a privately endowed institution, has held conferences between the representatives of labor and management in the hope of clarifying their common problems and thereby leading to better relationships. Goddard College, of Vermont, has sponsored meetings of farm and labor representatives to discuss common problems. Recently Harvard University began experimenting with a one-year program for small groups of labor leaders whose expenses are borne jointly by the university and the unions selecting them.

Such efforts, excellent and well-intentioned though they

---

[13] The School for Workers was continued by the University and is now operated on virtually a self-supporting basis.

generally are, are after all infinitesimal. Though the vast majority of the American people are workers in the sense that their income is derived from wages and salaries they receive from their employers, most universities have done little about it. Though the representatives of the higher learning will agree that in our industrial society a wise labor leadership is as fundamental as other kinds of leadership, yet no university has thus far established a vigorous, full-blown department of workers' education comparable to similar departments—or even schools—of law or engineering or business and finance.

J. Intercultural Education

Though intercultural education is a movement new to the American scene, its essence has been with us for some time. Whenever a teacher undertook to plant the seeds of tolerance and brotherly understanding in her protégés, she was moving in the sphere of intercultural education. If, now and then, she consciously organized her instruction, it probably appeared under such guises as International Understanding, the Race Question, Minority Problems, and the like. From such simple and faint beginnings, intercultural education has grown into a fairly stalwart movement, involving not only schools but many nonschool agencies as well. It recognizes the lamentable fact that large groups are still barred from full participation in the life of the community; and it "seeks to bring education to bear . . . on actual and possible intercultural tensions and on the evils of any and all bias, prejudice and discrimination against minority groups." [1] Its advocates are not endeavoring primarily to "reform" the prejudiced and the bigoted; for they realize full well that the clouds which shroud the inner man will not lift through logic alone. What they seek instead is to modify those conditions and processes in our society which

---

[1] Kilpatrick, W. H., and Van Til, W., Editors John Dewey Society, *Intercultural Attitudes in the Making*, p. 4. Ninth Yearbook. New York: Harper & Brothers, 1947.

breed bias and discrimination, so that children will no longer
be infected by the prejudices now sanctioned by their elders.

1. Background

Religious and social intolerance is an old story on this
continent. It began, in fact, with the earliest settlers. In the
eyes of the white-skinned immigrant, the Indian appeared of
low and inferior stock, and it wasn't long before he had to
suffer for the color of his reddish skin. Religious intolerance
was not uncommon even among those who had come to the
New World for religious freedom. Roger Williams and Anne
Hutchinson have become the classic examples of Puritan
intolerance. With the growth and development of our country
and the arrival of more and more immigrants, prejudice arose
not only among the diverse religious faiths but also among
nationalities. With the subsequent enslavement of the Negro,
racial and economic currents poured into the rising stream of
prejudice. During the Republic's first century, however, it
was possible for some of the oppressed to pull up stakes and
seek refuge in freer and more hospitable acres. Today the
frontier has all but vanished, and the victims of bias and
prejudice can find no ready exit.

Though America generally esteems itself as a land of tolerance and equal opportunity, its practice has fallen short of
its theory. Growth in population, with its accentuation of
differences in economic and social status, its consciousness of
differences in physical appearance and religious belief, has
spawned a colony of problems. At the moment America's
greatest racial problem is that of Negro-white relationships.
Discrimination against the Negro exists not only in the South,
where it is practiced openly and unashamedly, the ignominy
is found in the north, too, where Negroes have been refused
services in hotels and restaurants—where, in fact, they have
even been denied emergency treatment in some hospitals. In
large cities, like New York, residential segregation has obliged
the Negro to dwell in overcrowded sections. Such segregation

has in turn produced segregated Negro schools. Although many Protestant churches display "All Welcome" signs, the Protestant Negro knows full well that such ecclesiastic blandishments are not intended for him whose color is dark. Some churches drawing the color line seek to balance their account with the Lord by contributing money to the support of Negro schools, hospitals, and orphanages.

Close on the heels of the Negro-white problem is anti-Semitism, which many observers believe is on the rise. Though Jew-haters commonly speak of a Jewish race, anthropologists tell us there is no such thing. Many Gentiles are prejudiced against the Jew because of his religious practices, his social customs, and his economic competition.

Like the Jew, the Roman Catholic has been subjected to all sorts of bias and hostility. Along with Jews and Negroes, Catholics are on the active agenda of the Ku Klux Klan and similar organizations. The fact that Alfred E. Smith was a Catholic lost him many votes in the rural sections and especially in the southern Bible Belt when he ran for the presidency in 1928. Only in the cities, where their numbers have been large and where they have been economically strong, have Catholics been relatively free from discrimination.

Most of the latter-day immigrants came to this land to better their economic status. But since aliens competed for jobs with natives, the increase in our foreign populace inevitably made for tension. Fear of economic insecurity paved the way to antagonism and eventually to discrimination against the invader. Minority groups of Irish, Poles, and Italians, most of whom were unskilled and poorly educated, had to live in segregated quarters. They toiled as day laborers, eking out their paltry pay, and finding it almost impossible to belong to our society.

With the greater use of machinery and the consequent need for fewer hands, thousands of Negroes left the rural south to seek employment elsewhere. But the Negro's infiltration into the skilled industrial occupations has been slow. He has been employed in industrial undertakings usually when it has been clear that he can be kept subordinate. Race prejudice has bolted the door to full industrial advantage. Since the Negro has demonstrated his industrial ability, his potential competition for jobs has frightened some of the whites. His rising economic effectiveness has sparked dormant antagonisms, kindling them at times into riot and bloodshed. The difficulty has been intensified when the wages and working conditions offered the Negro have been below those of the co-laboring white man. Naturally the Negro resents any discrimination against his right to earn for himself the best possible livelihood; and the white man, for his part, dreading the looming competition from the Negro, drowns his economic fear in the acid of indeterminate prejudice, fortifying the growing tensions between Negroes and whites.

To some extent the war has benefited the minority. The great and consuming demand for manpower weakened barriers which hitherto have been impregnable. The greater strength of the labor unions, too, has been a boon to the Negro, who has begun to organize. But these are relatively small and they are mere externals. Fine though they are, they cannot of themselves dissolve the suspicions and the hatred planted in the plumbless depths of ignorant and fear-torn souls.

2. Agencies concerned with intercultural relationships

Despite the obvious need for definite programs of intercultural education, most state boards of education have been dilatory and even indifferent in meeting the need. Indeed, by 1945, only four states—California, Massachusetts, New York, and Texas—had developed programs for intergroup education.[2] At the same time Oregon and Pennsylvania reported themselves in the planning stage. The real advances in the intercultural domain have come locally through the efforts of teachers, principals, and superintendents, flanked

---

[2] Warren, J. E., "Intergroup Education Through State Departments of Education," *Harvard Educational Review*, XV, 111–116, 1945.

and supported by noneducational organizations. The number
of such bodies is significant and includes such organizations as

1906*	The American Jewish Committee
1909	The National Association for the Advancement of Colored People
1910	The National Urban League
1920	The National Civil Liberties Union
1920	Federal Council of Churches (Department of Race Relations)
1925	Institute of Pacific Relations
1928	The National Conference of Christians and Jews
1934	The Bureau for Intercultural Education
1938	The Southern Conference for Human Welfare
1941	The East and West Association
1944	The American Council of Race Relations
1944	The American Jewish Congress [3]

* Founding Date.

Besides these and other privately financed national agencies,
a number of privately financed state and local bodies concern
themselves in one way or another with the improvement of
human relations. Recently, moreover, a number of public
agencies have come into being, such as the Fair Employment
Practices Commission, organized during the second World
War. By the end of 1946, five states—New York, New Jersey,
Indiana, Massachusetts, and Wisconsin—had passed a Fair
Employment Practices Act designed to wipe out discriminatory practices in employment. In addition, several cities have
established a Mayor's Committee on Unity to deal with local
problems.

However, whatever the nature of the agency, there is nearly
always a twofold program: fact-finding functions, and educational functions.

3. The Bureau for Intercultural Education

A pioneer in the educational aspects of human relations is
the Bureau for Intercultural Education, which came into being
in 1934. Known originally as the Service Bureau for Inter-

[3] Compiled from Johnson, C. S., *Directory of Agencies in Race Relations*,
Rosenwald Fund, 1945.

cultural Education, the Bureau was in large measure the result
of the early trail-blazing of Rachel Davis-Dubois, who for
more than a decade had been developing materials designed to
give our school children a better understanding of the rich
and diverse cultures that comprise America. At the outset the
Bureau sought to help schools "to organize some of their
activities around this major social problem. . . ."

It provides first-hand contact for teachers and pupils with fine representative personalities of America's culture groups; it arranges courses for
teachers in Education in Human Relations; it makes available collections of
source books, posters and art materials, assembly programs and classroom
units; and is publishing a series of books on the participation of various
culture groups in American life.[4]

Three years after the Bureau's inauguration (1937) it joined
hands with the Progressive Education Association as a Commission on Intercultural Education. The Commission addressed itself to the task of acquainting the nation's youth
"with the cultural heritage of our various ethnic groups"
thereby encouraging the "growth of a richer American culture." It endeavored "to insure the continuance of our
democratic principles by developing appreciation of the unique
contributions of each national and racial group to our common
life"; and it hoped "to lessen individual maladjustments which
are a reflection of the increasing tensions and conflicts between
groups."

In 1939 the Bureau was reorganized with William H. Kilpatrick as chairman of its board and Stewart G. Cole, then
president of Kalamazoo Teachers College, as its head. The
reconstituted Bureau broadened its operations, which now

---

[4] *Annual Report 1934–35,* Service Bureau for Education in Human Relations,
in Report of the Committee for Evaluation to the General Education Board,
1939.

"The Service Bureau has held as basic the assumption that prejudices are
dispelled and attitudes of understanding and appreciation of various cultures
are built up through shared experiences around the cultural contributions of
these groups." The Bureau attempted to do this by working with teachers in
the public schools. "History of the Service Bureau," Report of the Committee
for Evaluation to the General Education Board, p. 7.

included the establishment of consultant relations with other educational agencies, editorial inquiry and publication of specialized social studies, professional guidance of schoolmen and women in intercultural education, and research in problems of group conflict and cultural democracy.

During the next few years the Bureau maintained a consultant service with a dozen school systems in New York's metropolitan area besides working with various civic councils and conferring with a number of state departments on education. To cover the nation it organized a guidance-by-mail service; conducted institutes in the larger cities from coast to coast; and cooperated with colleges and universities in directing workshops in intercultural problems. It was busy, too, with the printed word, some of its members publishing important books, and some confining themselves to short articles in the Bureau's periodical, the *Intercultural Education News*.

In 1944 the Bureau took soundings. A survey was conducted to tap information from organizations at work in the intercultural field, from a number of representative school systems, and from anthropologists, sociologists, psychologists, and social psychologists. Some 800 agencies, it was found, were engaged in one way or another in intercultural activities; yet all but a handful devoted most of their effort to speeches and publications; and few had more than a vague idea as to the effectiveness of their efforts. In addition, the survey trained its searchlight on 14 school systems, scattered from coast to coast and varying in size and type. It was found "that while problems were many, varied and difficult, even the most interested school administrators had only scattered and in some cases confused ideas as to what could be done." The survey revealed one fact very clearly—namely, what we actually know about prejudice, its causes, range, scope, and intensity, is very meager. In fact, we don't even agree on therapies and techniques for dealing with such problems.

To throw some scientific light on these matters, field centers were established in Detroit, Gary, Kalamazoo, Battle Creek,

East Chicago, and Philadelphia to work in cooperation with their school systems. They were to serve as laboratories for an intensive study of intercultural education. Their findings, it was hoped, would contribute to the development of a new and sounder program of intergroup education. In Philadelphia the work was restricted to the kindergarten and the first two grades of five schools, but in the other cities it was carried on on a city-wide scale. In each center the Bureau staff was "to stimulate democratic planning and administration, to encourage the collection and reporting of pertinent information, to help local personnel in finding resources for dealing with their problems." [5] Surveys delved into such matters as tensions, classroom practices, administrative practices, personnel, attitudes, local and national resources. Data were gathered on such items as community setting, school-community relations, special problems, special facilities, student activities, school organization, curricula, learning materials, techniques, and best practices. The work of the Bureau was reflected in the school systems themselves, through their adoption of new administrative policies, the development of new kinds of learning materials, and the consideration of new curricular proposals.

To develop skilled leadership in intercultural education, the Bureau addressed itself to the problem of developing a program of professional training. It organized professional seminars and scientific panels at colleges and universities, bringing to them the leading scholars in the field. It fostered the establishment of workshops at various colleges and universities, as Goddard, Columbia, Minnesota, Stanford, Ohio State, and New York. In the field it sought to come to grips with the real problems as they were felt by the local people; it strove to train people how to deal with these problems and to develop some kind of evaluation procedures.

Though the Bureau has worked assiduously and in the short time of its activity has accomplished much, the task still to be

---

[5] *A Report to the Board*, p. 9. Bureau for International Education, 1947.

done is monumental. "There is a dearth of trained leadership and there are still enormous areas needing further research. Hence, the idea of a Center for Human Relations Studies for these purposes was born. It reached fruition when the Bureau in cooperation with the School of Education of New York University joined hands to establish such a Center which opened in the fall of 1947." [6]

4. Intergroup education in cooperating schools

Established in 1928, the National Conference of Christians and Jews has endeavored to improve relations between religious groups. To accomplish this it has depended largely on interfaith conferences, with speakers representing the viewpoints of Catholics, Protestants, and Jews. It also developed the idea of Brotherhood Week. In the main its operations have been in the community. In 1944, with the assistance of the American Council on Education, it sponsored the Intergroup Project in Cooperating Schools, the main purpose of which was "to explore and to expand the effective programs of teaching intergroup relations." [7] Schools in 17 cities, representing every part of the country except the deep south, entered the project. [8] The schools taking part in the project were for the most part in "communities with heterogeneous racial, religious or ethnic populations which presented a variety of difficulties in democratic relations." Under Dr.

---

[6] Quoted from an unpublished report of Victor E. Pitkin, Director of the Bureau's work of Analysis and Research.

[7] The idea germinated at the Harvard workshop in the summer of 1944. Dr. Hilda Taba, the workshop director, took time out to make a study of the school systems of Milwaukee, Cleveland, Pittsburgh, and South Bend for the purpose of determining the nature of the problems to be encountered in intercultural education. She asked herself such questions as: What cultural groups are involved? What are the curricular problems? What are the administrative problems? Her preliminary survey led the NCCJ to support a study project which became the Intergroup Project.

[8] The cities represented were Cleveland; Pittsburgh; Hartford; Portland, Oregon; Denver; Providence; Milwaukee; Minneapolis; St. Louis; San Francisco; Newark, New Jersey; Oakland, California; Chicago; Los Angeles; South Bend; Wilmington, Delaware; and Shorewood, Wisconsin.

Hilda Taba of the University of Chicago, director of the enterprise, investigations were undertaken into the curriculum with a view to providing greater opportunities in it for intergroup education; guidance programs were reconsidered, especially in schools having a wide mixture of student population; special studies were made of children and adolescents of minority groups; communities were studied and plans developed for the improvement of school and community relations; and experiments were undertaken with school-wide programs in selected schools with special problems of group relations. In addition, spot experiments along special lines were carried on, such as a study of stereotypes in literature, vocational guidance for Negro children, coordination of English and history for teaching American culture. Unlike the Bureau for Intercultural Education, the Intergroup Project has concerned itself with a selected school or schools within a system rather than with an entire city system. Like the Bureau, however, it has recognized the importance of teacher training in the successful operation of intercultural education. Some of this training has occurred directly in connection with program planning, which involved the development of curricular materials, the study of children and the community, the exploring of resources, and working with the community. The Intergroup Project has made considerable use of workshops, sponsoring them at various universities, and encouraging teachers from the schools to come to the workshops to work out their problems with the help of the staff in charge.[9]

5.   The college study in intergroup relations

In 1944 a number of schoolmen met at Columbia University to consider education for improving intergroup relations on college campuses. Out of their deliberations came the College Study in Intergroup Relations, an undertaking which had the

[9] For a running account of the work and progress of the project on Intergroup Education, consult its Bulletin to Cooperating Schools, the first number of which appeared in September, 1945.

financial backing of the National Conference on Christians and Jews and the educational support of the Council on Cooperation in Teacher Education, an association of some of the nation's most important educational groups.[10] Headed by Lloyd Allen Cook, of Wayne University, the College Study was launched as a cooperative effort by a score of selected teacher education institutions seeking "to improve the education of young people going into teaching in respect to their knowledge about, concern for, and skill in good human relations in and about the school." Its prime stress was "on the nature, workings and effects on children of race, creed, immigrant heritages, and income levels." Believing that "young people of all age levels are entitled to treatment in terms of their personal worth," the study based its projects "on a democratic human relations philosophy," though it insisted that the "scientific method shall be used." Since its inception the College Study has engaged in more than a hundred diverse projects and activities. Some have delved into the attitudes and experiences of college students; others have concerned themselves with school children; still others have taken adults for their subject. Some of the participating colleges have stressed experimental teaching in the realm of race relations. Some have undertaken curricular surveys with the aim of bringing about course revisions. In a few instances combined college and community attacks were made on some individual intergroup problem, as for example, the relations of Spanish-Americans and Anglo-Saxons in Greeley, Colorado. The College Study in Intergroup Relations has stressed "action research" as against mere fact finding. It has explored

---

[10] The participating colleges included: Marshall College (W. Va.), Springfield College (Mass.), State College (N. Y.), State College (N. J.), University of Pittsburgh, West Virginia State, Central Michigan College of Education, Ohio State University, Roosevelt College (Ill.), State Teachers College (Moorhead, Minn.), State Teachers College (Milwaukee, Wis.), Lynchburg College (Va.), Southwest Texas State Teachers College, Talladega College (Ala.), Arizona State College, Colorado State College, San Francisco State College, University of Denver, State Teachers College (Eau Claire, Wis.), Wayne University (Detroit).

intergroup problems in teacher education, but "how to translate learning into day by day actions" has been its primary and ever-present concern. Its thinking has been along the following line:

> *Knowledge* is a way of effecting changes in behaviors. This is the fundamental assumption of all higher education, the chief reason why we read so many books. *Experience* is also a way of effecting behavioral changes: we learn, in Dewey's phrase, by "suffering and undergoing." Either without the other is incomplete, ineffective; so it would be pointless to choose between them. Hence the problem of ends in a sense is solved, we want both knowledge and experience in a realistic program of intergroup education. . . .[11]

It holds that "action research via the small group technique will bring about the greatest insight on how to educate for the kind of life every democratic person so earnestly wants for every child." To this and to knowledge and experience it adds the importance of studying the "personality structure and the community frame of life."

6. The Springfield Plan

Although organizations like the Bureau for Intercultural Education and the National Conference of Christians and Jews and enterprises like the College Study have played a great and leading part in the promotion of intergroup education, others, too numerous to consider here, have contributed substantially to the movement. In cities flung across America from Newark, New Jersey, to San Diego, California, as well as in countless remote and obscure hamlets, one may observe schoolmen and laymen giving earnest and conscientious thought to the improvement of human relations in schools and communities.

One of the first to glow in the national spotlight for its

---

[11] Quoted from a bulletin of the College Study on Intergroup Relations. These bulletins are mimeographed and present a running account of the development of the enterprise. See also *Improving Intergroup Relations in School and Community Life,* a study conducted and reported by the Sub-Committee on In-Service Education of Teachers, The North Central Association of Secondary Schools and Colleges, 1946.

work in the intercultural realm was Springfield, Massachusetts. Under the leadership of its superintendent of schools, Dr. John Granrud, Springfield organized a program for teaching democracy in its schools as early as 1940.[12] In the selection and promotion of its school personnel Springfield had acquired a high repute for its democratic practices, for its insistence on merit as the determining yardstick in such matters, and for its utter disregard of racial, religious, ethnic, or political considerations. Even in administration, where democracy is honored so often as a theory only to be maltreated as a practice, the Springfield school system had consistently sought to apply in its own affairs the democratic theories it was striving to inculcate in others. Decisions, for example, were generally made by a consensus rather than by a single administrative mind. Springfield's schools have approached the problem of intercultural relationships in two basic ways: they have sought to provide more and more stimulating experiences in democratic living; and they have made wide use of study units designed to give the child a background for his thinking about democracy—to show him "how it works, or how sometimes it does not work," and how he can do his share in sustaining and improving it. The young child learns to be a good citizen, not by studying about it in a book, but by being a good citizen of his school. He learns tolerance "without ever hearing the word, by accepting as a matter of course all children as comrades in work and play." Children of different ethnic groups are urged to bring in samples of their peoples' art; they dance the dances of the various nationalities; and they sing the different folk melodies. All year round they "work together without regard to the color of the skin or what church they may attend."[13]

---

[12] In 1939 the National Conference of Christians and Jews suggested to Dr. Granrud the starting of a program for teaching democracy in the schools. A committee representing all levels of education and thought in the city undertook the planning phase. Following this several months were devoted to working out procedures.

[13] Chatto, C. I., "The Springfield Program for Democratic Citizenship," *Intercultural Education News*, VI, 1, 1946.

The program varies from school to school, each one working out its own plans in accordance with its specific conditions. One school, for example, organized its pupils into committees of heterogeneous cultural makeup and entrusted them with all sorts of real responsibilities ranging from matters involving safety to conduct on the school playground and even to respect for neighbors' lawns. Another school developed an annual Festival of Lights by which it combined the observance of Christmas and the Jewish Hanukkah, the Feast of Lights.

In the secondary school the intercultural problem becomes more difficult since the adolescent is beginning to acquire some of the biases and faults of his elders as well as the virtues. Various student organizations and school publications have provided opportunity for cooperative effort. In the senior high schools class presidents represent almost as many national origins as there are classes. In the Trade School a Negro youth rose to the editorship of its paper; and subsequently he was chosen instructor in printing at the Springfield Boys' Club.

In the sphere of instruction specific units designed to educate for democratic citizenship have been introduced into the existing courses in English, the social studies, and the sciences. Beginning in the seventh grade and continuing through the senior high school, they involve studies of the contributions of other civilizations to our American democracy; the effects of governments upon people; the contributions of different ethnic groups to the building of America; the facts and fictions about the races of mankind; public opinion, prejudice, and propaganda. Eleventh graders learn to look upon American democracy as a "piece of unfinished business, with emphasis on the tasks still lying before this and succeeding generations." A feature of the twelfth grade is the High School Town Meeting, which is a discussion program intended to afford boys and girls "an opportunity to learn the methods of democratic procedure, to practice the processes of democratic group thinking, and to apply the principles of democracy to actual situations." [14]

Springfield doesn't halt its intercultural work at the close of the school day. In its evening schools for adults it continues to toil for better intercultural relations through group discussions and other stimulating activities. A link between the schools and the public is the Adult Education Council, which sponsors numerous community enterprises fostering cooperation and leading toward better mutual understanding. Even the schools' Placement Bureau has been put to work in combating employers' prejudices against certain races, religions, or nationalities.

Such is the essence of the Springfield program for intercultural education. Still in its experimental stages, it represents the first steps "toward the solution of the problem . . . of making fair-minded, intelligent citizens for tomorrow." Without doubt Springfield has demonstrated that the public school can do far more than it has in the past in the development of democratic attitudes and in the eradication of prejudices and biases which undermine our American life.

Side by side with the efforts of Springfield and numerous other cities and towns all over the United States to bring about improved democratic human relations, one must place the work of those who for many years have been making scientific probes into some of the manifold phases of intergroup relations. Such research groups as those headed by Arnold Gesell of Yale, the work in group dynamics conducted by Ronald Lippert of Michigan University, the studies in liberalism and conservatism conducted by Lentz at Washington University in St. Louis, the intensive interview techniques evolved by Likert when he was with the Department of Agri-

---

[14] "Most of the discussions of town meeting lead to some sort of appropriate action. One group, after spending several sessions in a consideration of the merits and defects of the rationing program, adopted a formal resolution pledging themselves as young Americans to abide conscientiously by the rules of rationing and to fight the black market wherever they found it, even in their own homes." *Ibid.*

culture, the use of projective techniques by psychologists, such as Murray of Harvard and Sanford and Levinson of California, the counseling work of Carl Rogers, the studies by Louis Raths of New York University's School of Education on the needs of children—all these have contributed to a clearer perception of the intercultural problem and have led to the development of new and more scientific attacks upon it.

K. International Education

1. Historical background

To bring about international accord and world peace through education is an old and persistent dream among schoolmen.[1] More than six hundred years ago, for example, Pierre Dubois advocated the establishment of international schools which, he hoped, might be financed by moneys saved through the elimination of war. Unfortunately this well-meaning man failed to tell us how war was to be abolished, and his proposal never went beyond the realm of fancy. Hardly less visionary was the suggestion made in the seventeenth century by the Moravian pastor and schoolmaster Comenius who urged the creation of a "Pansophic College" where scholars from all over the world were to work together to bring about eternal and universal peace. Early in the nineteenth century a Frenchman, Marc-Antoine Jullien, suggested the forming of a commission which was to gather and disseminate information about European education not only to improve education everywhere, but also to advance international peace. But hard-headed statesmen were not interested and so Jullien's proposal, like its predecessors, came to naught. Several other plans designed in one way or other to educate men for international understanding were put forth in the course of the century, but they never came to fruit either.

---

[1] Rossello, P., *Les Précurseurs du Bureau International d'Éducation.* Geneva: International Bureau of Education, 1943. An abridged translation was made by Marie Butts.

The first to come close to success was the Bostonian, Fannie Fern Andrews. A student of international law, with a doctor's degree from Harvard, she became interested in education for international peace. She must have been as persuasive as she was pertinacious, for in the course of time she gained the sympathetic ear of President Taft. By March, 1912, the Department of State had been induced to negotiate for an international conference to be held at The Hague. However, most nations turned a cold shoulder on the proposal, and instead of agreeing to send delegates to The Hague, they put all kinds of obstacles in the way of the proposed convocation. Delay, vacillation, an avalanche of technicalities, and, most important, a lack of any sincere interest in the project caused one postponement after another. When, in 1914, the stage for the meeting had at last been set, the outbreak of the first World War put an abrupt and ironic end to the venture.

The ideal persisted; and after the conflict it came out of seclusion. Still the driving force behind the movement, Mrs. Andrews, who by now had gathered a following, undertook to persuade the Allied leaders to incorporate an international office of education in the League of Nations. Specifically it was proposed that they should

endeavor to make the aims and methods of instruction accord with the guiding principles of the League of Nations and, for this purpose, they are to establish a permanent international bureau of education which shall form an integral part of the League.

The proposed bureau, however, never came into being. Not that the League's fathers were altogether unsympathetic. But at the moment healing the world's economic and political maladies seemed more urgent to them than the formulation of ways and means to forestall the recurrence of similar pestilences in the future.

2.   The commission on intellectual cooperation

A few years later the idea reappeared. In 1921, at the suggestion of Léon Bourgeois, the League recommended the formation of a commission of eminent educators and scientists to "study the questions of international cooperation and education" and to advise the League on what might be done to "facilitate intellectual exchange among the nations, especially as concerns the communication of scientific data and methods of education." But again there was hostility. Education, it was felt, was a national enterprise and not the business of the League. To allay such nationalistic fears the Geneva diplomats agreed to delete the word "education" from the original resolution; instead the League now proposed to deal with "intellectual cooperation." Yet even this honeyed phrase sent up the national blood pressure and it was not until 1926, after years of wrangling and parliamentary sleight of hand, that a Commission of Intellectual Cooperation was created.

The new body was weak, unloved by most of its makers who had no desire to provide more than a pittance for its support. With only consultative and advisory powers, the Commission —or as it came to be called, the CIC—had no official governmental status and hence it could do little more than shadow-box. Its members were selected for their scientific and scholarly distinction. On its rosters one will find the names of such notables as Madame Curie, Henri Bergson, and Gilbert Murray; but one can look in vain for the name of one who might be expected to be familiar with the ways of professional politicians and sagacious enough to cope with them.

To simplify its complex and far-reaching operations, the CIC worked through national subcommittees. Its enterprises included (1) the planning and organization of meetings to bring about greater international cooperation among the world's universities, libraries, museums, and teacher organizations; (2) the study of what schools were doing to familiarize children with the work and purposes of the League and the principles of international cooperation; (3) the examination of textbooks, particularly in the field of history, with a view to bringing about the elimination of superheated, nationalistic passages; and (4) the study of the media of mass communication, such as radio, film, and press, for the purpose of putting them into the service of international cooperation.[2] On occasion the Commission's help was sought by an individual government. At the request of China, for example, a special delegation went to that ancient land to assist in modernizing its schools. Despite the wide range of its activities and the value of much of its work, the CIC was not in high favor. The nationalist-minded, both within and without the League, continued to suspect its motives and to undermine its efforts, and because of their strength and influence the League was in no position to grant the Commission any real power. What further handicapped the CIC was its inadequate facilities, its lack of official status, insufficient personnel, and inadequacy of funds.

3. The International Bureau of Education

When it became apparent that the League had no real desire to come to grips with the world's important educational problems, a group of educators residing in Geneva organized the International Bureau of Education in 1925. Small, without many resources, and without the stamp of governmental approval, the Bureau began work as a private agency, collecting and distributing educational information throughout the world. The Bureau's renown grew steadily and in 1929 it was accorded recognition as an intergovernmental organization, controlled and partially supported by the member nations. Its membership was never large and the nations affiliated with it were little ones, like Switzerland and Ecuador. The larger powers, like the United States and Great Britain, vouchsafed the Bureau an occasional pat on the back, but they refused to associate themselves officially with it. On the

---

[2] On the recommendation of the CIC the League Assembly prepared an international agreement to regulate broadcasting. Subsequently 30 states ratified it. Another convention was drafted on the subject of tariff-exempt circulation of educational films.

assumption that education, like science, knew no frontiers and that a knowledge of foreign education was prerequisite to international understanding, the Bureau developed an ambitious program in comparative education. It organized annual international conferences; it published an educational yearbook and numerous studies in comparative education; it issued a quarterly bulletin containing reviews of important educational books from all over the world; it created a first-rate library; and it made available exhibits of public instruction. Although the Bureau performed primarily as an international educational clearing house, it hoped also that this might contribute to the furtherance of international understanding. In this of course it was overoptimistic. Yet in its failure there was at least a useful lesson; for in striving to steer a neutral and dispassionate course, the Bureau was in no position to criticize the aims and principles underlying national systems of education. Its political nonpartisanship, though necessary because of the nationalistic framework within which the Bureau was obliged to operate, nonetheless weakened its effectiveness as an agency for peace.[3]

4. International cultural relations programs

The League's Commission on International Cooperation and the Bureau of International Education were not the only groups concerned with international education. As a matter of fact, the number of agencies interested in this form of education is fairly large. For one thing, a number of governments, notably the United States, Great Britain, France, and Germany, organized what is known as a "cultural relations program" as an integral part of their diplomatic offices. The last of the large powers to adopt such a program, the United States, founded the Division of Cultural Relations in the

---

[3] Nazi propagandists took full advantage of the Bureau's good intentions. The information sent out by the office of the Nazi Minister of Education Rust, and published by the Bureau, was on the surface all very innocent; at bottom, however, Rust's handouts were nothing more than artful propaganda for Nazi ideology.

Department of State in 1939. Its first head, Dr. B. Cherrington, has summarized its aspirations thus:

1. International cultural relations should be reciprocal.
2. International cultural relations should serve mankind; they should not be perverted for some irrelevant purpose of the state.
3. Cultural exchanges should originate from the authentic centers of culture; they should involve the direct participation of the people and institutions concerned.

In the evolution of international cultural relations such ideals, however, have not always been paramount. Governments, in the main, have been too intent to advertise the virtues of their own cultures; on the other hand, they have been chary in their friendliness toward the cultures of other lands. Thus inspired, their programs commonly appeared in the form of nationalistic promotion. In 1931, for example, the German Republic, though wallowing in poverty, was spending some 15 per cent of the total budget of the Foreign Office to restore and inflate the Reich's cultural prestige abroad, and for this purpose it employed not only the press, the radio, and motion pictures, but it also established schools in other countries (the *Auslandsschulen*) and sent some of its schoolmasters abroad. With the coming of the National Socialists these activities were incorporated in the high-powered machinery of the Ministry of Propaganda and Public Enlightenment, and the campaign became more energetic and determined than ever.

Before Hitler's rise, Great Britain showed only a slight interest in the program of cultural relations. However, as Britain became more and more aware of the growing challenge of nationalism in several of the continental domains, the British Foreign Office, in 1934, helped to establish the British Council, a semi-official body financed in part with funds from the public cash till. Frankly nationalistic, it proposed to encourage English studies in foreign schools, especially, however, in those lands which were of strategic significance to British foreign policy, as Egypt, the Middle East, the Balkans, Portugal, and South America. By 1940 the program had outgrown its simple origins and the Council was incorporated under royal charter. Its function, more nationalistic than before, now undertook to develop "cultural relations between the United Kingdom and other countries for the purpose of benefiting the British Commonwealth of Nations."

The pioneer in the development of a cultural relations program is France. Soon after the first World War, when the national heat in France was high, one of her politicians, Raiberti, asserted that "intellectual and moral expansion is the best way to prepare for economic expansion"—a declaration which was vigorously applauded in France. Known as the *oeuvres françaises à l'étranger,* French cultural expansion abroad was carried on through the Ministry of Foreign Affairs. About one fifth of its total budget was poured into the work, which included not only the ordinary phases of education involving schools, libraries, the arts and letters, but also such cultural pastimes as travel and sport and the encouragement of such organizations as the *Alliance Française.*

5. Regional collaboration

Another development in international education took the form of regional collaboration. Notable here are the accomplishments of the United States and its neighboring Latin American Republics. Through federal agencies an extensive inter-American cultural program was worked out involving the exchange of students, teachers, films, and other educational materials.[4] In 1936 an inter-American agreement was reached at Buenos Aires for the promotion of inter-American cultural relations, and by 1943 sixteen nations had affixed their signatures.[5]

---

[4] They are long-named and include the Interdepartmental Committee on Cultural and Scientific Cooperation, the Office of the Coordinator of Inter-American Affairs, and the Division of Inter-American Relations of the United States Office of Education. See also Greene, D. and Esman, S. G., *Cultural Centers in the Other American Republics.* Pub. 2503, U. S. Department of State. Washington: Government Printing Office, 1945.

[5] Machinery for the exchange of students was created by agreement. A government nominating a student was responsible for travel expenses; the

The Department of State not only facilitated the exchange of students in accordance with the terms of the Buenos Aires Convention, but in time it did even more. In 1940, for example, it effected a reduction in transportation fares for self-supporting students traveling to the United States. In the same year Congress approved a budget for travel grants for students who could not otherwise come to this country; and a year later the legislature established maintenance grants for certain qualified Latin-American students.

In the exchange of professorships with Latin-American countries the United States, however, has displayed only a faint-hearted interest. The French, the Germans, and the English have been much more active; indeed, even during the war the European nations were more generous with governmental subsidies and maintained more visiting professors in the lands south of the Rio Grande than did the United States. The fact that an exchange professorship to Latin America was economically unalluring for most American men of learning no doubt contributed to this situation. Nor did the Buenos Aires Convention help to alter these matters. True, the Department of State became somewhat more energetic: it rendered assistance to a few carefully chosen lecturers; it helped to send a number of professors of English to our southern neighbors; and in response to requests from individual universities, it assisted a dozen professors to go to Latin-American universities—all of which, however, seems hardly more than a feeble accomplishment.

The cultural interrelationship program of the United States and the neighboring republics embraced several other features besides the exchange of students and teachers:

Assistance in the translation into Spanish and Portuguese of books published in the United States; and the translation of works in those tongues into English.

government receiving the student was required to pay his tuition, board, and lodging. In the case of an exchange professor all expenses were to be defrayed by the government nominating him.

Translation of summaries of significant writings on education published in the United States and Latin America.

Translation by the Department of State of suitable government publications and their distribution through our diplomatic and consular channels.

Preparation of materials for teaching inter-American subjects in thousands of schools.

Facilitating the exchange of art exhibits and the distribution of art publications.

Developing a program for the exchange of music.

Arrangement of exhibits of educational films, reaching an audience of more than two million persons a month in 42 countries.

The development and distribution of radio programs to further the program of cultural interrelationships.

Assistance to libraries.

Assistance to schools sponsored by American citizens residing in Latin America.

The maintenance by the Department of State of cultural centers in various Latin-American countries.

6. The Institute of International Education and the World Federation of Educational Associations

Standing out among the many private groups interested in international education are the Institute of International Education and the World Federation of Education Association. The former came into being soon after the first World War, largely through the efforts of Stephen Duggan, then affiliated with the College of the City of New York. Convinced, like many others, that education must be dealt with internationally if we are ever to attain international understanding, Dr. Duggan submitted a plan to the Carnegie Endowment for International Peace. His scheme met with favor and funds were put up to set it in operation. In the course of more than a quarter of a century the Institute has furthered the exchange of students, professors, and lecturers; [6] it has evolved a useful student counseling service; and it has developed the so-called Junior Year Abroad by which qualified American collegians are enabled to study abroad during their Junior Year. With the coming of Fascism and the wholesale

[6] Between the two world wars the Institute effected more than 5,000 student exchanges.

cashiering of "politically nonreliable" professors from the universities of Germany, Spain, and Italy, the Institute helped a number of these unfortunates to start anew in the United States. More recently it has undertaken to facilitate student exchanges between the United States and the former fascist countries.[7]

At the invitation of the National Educational Association some 600 educators from 60 countries assembled in 1922 in San Francisco to consider the formation of a world educational organization. Out of their deliberations came the World Federation of Educational Associations. Its aims were the familiar ones: international cooperation in education; the gathering and dissemination of significant educational information; and the promotion of international peace. In the pursuit of these goals the Association followed more or less in the path of similar organizations, such as the International Bureau of Education at Geneva. It published bulletins describing new and significant phases of education in various lands and it sponsored a number of biennial international conferences, the first in 1923 in San Francisco, and the last in 1937 in Tokyo.[8] Despite its laudable purposes and the importance of much of its work, the Association failed to draw adequate financial support. Financially anemic, perpetually understaffed, with voluntary rather than professional workers on its staff, it led a precarious life. During the war its treasury virtually evaporated, and with its members scattered all over the globe and some of them in enemy domain, the Federation passed into an eclipse. With the end of hostilities, however, and with the growing interest in some form of organized international education, it soon emerged from the shadows.

---

[7] Duggan, S., *Twenty-sixth Annual Report of the Director.* New York: The Institute of International Education, 1945. See also Elliot, R., *The Institute of International Education 1919–1944.* New York: The Institute of International Education, 1944.

[8] Other meetings were held in Edinburgh, 1925; Toronto, 1927; Geneva, 1929; Denver, 1931; Dublin, 1933; Oxford, 1935.

Reorganized in 1946, it is now known as the World Organization of the Teaching Profession.[9]

7. International education in colleges and universities

In the welter of organized effort dedicated to the advancement of international education, the occasional endeavor on the part of colleges and universities might readily be overlooked. Not only have many of them cooperated in the programs of student and professional exchange, but here and there a few have undertaken intensive studies of foreign cultures. Thus, in the uncertain days of the Weimar Republic the University of Munich established the field of *Amerikanistik* by which it proposed to make an extensive and integrated study of American culture in all its phases—its history, its letters, art and music, its people, and its ways of life. Less systematically the same thing has been attempted in a more limited way for other cultures in the conventional courses in history, language, and literature. More akin, however, to the integrated nature of Munich's *Amerikanistik* have been some of the projects undertaken recently by a few American universities. In 1945, for example, the summer school of the University of Wyoming offered an extensive program in the cultures of central Eastern Europe—the region lying between Germany and Russia. A year earlier Cornell had begun the intensive study of civilization of the Soviet Union. Under the direction of Professor Ernest Simmons, the program included courses on Soviet literature, history, government, economics, social institutions, and life. Supplementing this work was a series of workshop seminars on such specialized subjects as The Russian People, Medicine and Health, Jurisprudence, Military and Naval History, Scientific Achievements, Theater and Cinema, Agriculture, Art and Architecture, Music, and so on.[10]

---

[9] "Draft Constitution of the World Organization," *Phi Delta Kappan,* XXVII, 2, p. 67, October, 1946.

[10] Cornell's work evoked a great deal of interest. Though carried on at a time when the enrollments of American colleges were depleted because of

8. Comparative education

Closely related to the development of international education has been the work of students of comparative education. Theirs has been the unglamorous task of digging up the essential facts of foreign education and its cultural background without which no program of international education could function. The study of foreign education is of course not new. Since the conquest of Athens by the Romans and the conqueror's subsequent Hellenization, there have been many instances of international exchange of educational ideas and practices. The foundations of modern comparative education, however, were laid in the nineteenth century when Marc-Antoine Jullien urged the gathering of information on education in European countries. In its earlier form the study of comparative education was largely descriptive, offering an account of the main facts of foreign school systems such as their administration, organization, and practices. These were examined chiefly for their own sake, were seldom related to their national backgrounds, and had no real appreciation of the conditioning part played in education by differences in national environments. Today this academic approach to comparative education, though still lingering, has been generally discarded by experts in the field. No longer satisfied to study foreign education *per se*, modern comparative education stresses adaptation rather than assimilation in education. It considers problems which are common to most systems of education rather than those which are exceptional and esoteric. Students of comparative education today grapple with such questions as

What are the factors which determine the character of an educational system?
What is the meaning of nationalism?
What is the relation between education and nationalism?
What is the relation of the individual to society or the State?

---

wartime conditions, some 120 students registered for from one to five of the courses.

What is the meaning of freedom in a constituted society?
Who shall have control of the education of the child?
What is the place of private education and of private schools?
How far does the responsibility of society or of the State for the education of its members extend?
What is the scope of preschool education?
What is the scope of primary education?
What should be the curriculum in each type of school?
What is the meaning of culture?
What should be the relation between general and special education?
How are teachers prepared and what is their status?
Should the administration and provision of education be centralized or decentralized?
How can standards be maintained?
What should be the place of examinations?
Who shall formulate curricula and courses of study?
What are the essential elements of an educational system?
What is the meaning of equality of educational opportunity? [11]

In studying these problems, which are common to most modern nations, the student of comparative education looks for and then analyzes their causes; compares the differences between the various systems and tries to ascertain the reasons for them; and finally he studies and appraises the solutions made. To accomplish all this he considers not only externals, but all the forces, spiritual and material, which shape the national life, such as a nation's history and traditions, its economics and politics, the forces which fashion its social organization and those which shape its course of development; for in such comparative studies "the things outside the schools matter even more than the things inside the schools, and govern and interpret the things inside." [12]

Although comparative education originated in the nineteenth century, it is not until the twentieth—indeed, not until after the first World War—that it emerged full-fledged. With the great interest in the promotion of international educational cooperation, it was only natural that the study of

[11] Kandel, I. L., *Comparative Education*, p. xviii. Boston: Houghton Mifflin Company, 1933.

[12] Sadler, M. E., "How Far Can We Learn Anything of Practical Value from the Study of Foreign Systems of Education?" 1900.

foreign education should have provoked more attention at that time. Giving the movement its impetus and direction in the United States was the work of specialists like Paul Monroe, I. L. Kandel, Thomas Woody, Thomas Alexander, Harold Benjamin, and F. E. Farrington.[13] In the course of time the expanding interest in comparative education was reflected in the establishment of a number of organizations and in the appearance of publications specializing in the field. In the movement's vanguard in this country was the International Institute of Teachers College, Columbia University. Its *Educational Yearbook,* which was edited by the scholarly Dr. Kandel and which contained reports on education from educators all over the world, made its debut in 1925. Appearing regularly thereafter until it became a war casualty in 1944, the Yearbook has become a treasure chest of information for students of international education.[14]

9. UNESCO

The feeling that education should in some way help to forge enduring peace grew steadily during the second World War. It expressed itself most definitely in the United States, where various plans were put forth by individuals as well as organizations. Among the leaders was the NEA's Educational Policies Commission which urged the establishment of a permanent international body for education, with functions

---

[13] There are, of course, many others. Foreigners who have been active in comparative education include, among many, Peter Sandiford, Canada; Nicholas Hans and Sir Michael Sadler, England; Friedrich Schneider and Rudolf Lehmann, Germany.

[14] Other important yearbooks are the *Yearbook of Education,* London, and the *Internationale Jahresberichte für Erziehungswissenschaft* issued in Breslau in 1923 and 1928. The *Internationale Zeitschrift für Erziehungswissenschaft* was founded in 1931 by Friedrich Schneider. With articles in several languages it was an excellent periodical in the field until it became an organ for the Nazis. In 1947 the magazine reappeared under the editorship of its founding editor. What the nature of the *Zeitschrift* will be may perhaps be inferred from the words of its editor. The editor will, he says, "broadmindedly report on every significant publication in the field of education from the various nations, but at the same time will show with the utmost clarity, that the Review represents the idea of Christian education."

similar to those of the CIC but with greater power.[15] Another group to give active support to the idea of creating such an international body was the International Education Assembly. At meetings held between 1943 and 1945 attended by the unofficial representatives of most of the United Nations, the Assembly gave its attention to the looming problems of postwar education, and in particular to the need of some sort of international agency capable of dealing with them.[16]

Meanwhile the idea of creating an international office of education had penetrated into some of the governmental sanctums in Washington. By May, 1945, enough spadework had been done to make it possible for Assistant Secretary of State MacLeish to announce that the United States Government, with the advice of organizations interested in cultural exchange, had developed a charter for a United Nations agency to function along this line. During the same month Congress passed joint resolutions favoring the establishment of such an agency, but also declaring that such a body must not interfere with our domestic policies in education.

From these preliminaries evolved the United Nations Educational, Scientific and Cultural Organization, or, as it is called, UNESCO. The new organization was founded in 1945 in London when 43 nations signed its constitution. Russia, however, did not join. UNESCO is dedicated to the idea that education can advance international peace. "Since wars begin in the minds of men," declares the preamble of its constitution, "it is in the minds of men that the defenses of peace must be constructed." To condition the minds of men UNESCO believes that a wide diffusion of culture is essential, and that man must have access "to the unrestricted pursuit of objective truth and the free exchange of ideas and knowl-

---

[15] Educational Policies Commission, *Education and the People's Peace*. Washington: National Education Association, 1943.

[16] The recommendations and conclusions reached at these meetings have been printed in *Education for International Security* (1943), *Education for a Free Society* (1944), *Education in the United Nations* (1945), and *International Education through Cultural Exchange* (1945).

edge." To give some reality to this view UNESCO has proposed a world-wide program in fundamental education. Specifically, this will embody:

1. An international student exchange on a far larger scale than heretofore.

2. An exchange of ideas through the dissemination of reports through all the modern media of communication and dealing with the educational, scientific and cultural advances of the nations everywhere.

3. A world-wide exchange of books and educational materials with special emphasis on works in such languages as the Slavic tongues, Chinese, Japanese, Malayan, and others not too well known in this country.

4. The reduction of illiteracy especially in backward nations.

5. Assistance to the war-wrecked nations of Europe and Asia in the work of restoring their schools and universities, their laboratories and libraries.

In some measure this program is now in progress; [17] what its ultimate form will be is not yet clear. One thing, however, has been recognized—that peaceful and friendly relations among men can only be created if there is general stability and well-being. "Such conditions," declares the Charter of the United Nations, "imply advances in economic and living standards as well as the universal acceptance of fundamental human rights and freedoms. . . ."

On the credit side of its ledger UNESCO displays a number of entries. To begin, no one will deny that its basic premise is desirable. The fact, moreover, that during the short period of its existence it has been able to carry out a modest program, under conditions which have at times been difficult and even discouraging, will certainly have to be recorded as a credit. The strength of UNESCO, such as it is, lies in the fact that from the outset it has had the support of the governments that comprise it, and also that its place in the structure of the United Nations has been clearly defined. In these respects

---

[17] For contributions which various subjects can make toward international understanding see Royce H. Knapp, Editor *UNESCO and Nebraska Secondary School Youth,* University of Nebraska. For materials, audio-visual aids, etc., see *Handbook on UNESCO Projects,* as developed by the UNESCO Committee, Kansas State College, Manhattan, Kansas, 1947.

its status would appear to be better than that of its predecessor in the League, the impotent CIC.

Nonetheless, UNESCO has revealed a number of disquieting weaknesses. By its constitution the organization may not intervene "in matters which are essentially within the domestic jurisdiction" of member nations. Thus, as in the past, the doctrine of unlimited national sovereignty has been set down as a major principle. "Just what matters are essentially within their domestic jurisdiction," comments Stephen Duggan, "is a question." For example, "were the teachings of the Nazis in the German schools propagating hatred against neighboring countries 'essentially domestic'? No provision is made in the UNESCO constitution to take cognizance of such a condition." [18] Yet even if it were clear what matters lie within and without a country's domestic jurisdiction, UNESCO could do very little about anything it might consider undesirable. It may not establish control commissions which would enable it to report any objectional practices. Theoretically, UNESCO has the power to submit a case to the Security Council; but obviously the effectiveness of such a presentation would depend in large measure on the evidence it offers to substantiate any charges it may make. Under the present circumstances, however, UNESCO cannot readily obtain such evidence.

Another flaw in UNESCO as it now is constituted is the absence of Soviet Russia from its membership. There seems to be little possibility, however, of bringing Russia into the fold, for in the opinion of the Russians, UNESCO does not provide adequately for the operation of the Soviet philosophy of dialectic materialism. In the judgment of the Communists, participation in UNESCO would be meaningless.

The great hurdle which UNESCO will have to clear, if ultimately its mission is to be successful, is that of nationalism.

---

[18] Duggan, S., "UNESCO: A Critique," *Journal of Educational Sociology,* XX, 7, 1946.

It was selfish national interest which tripped the CIC, and unfortunately that same spirit is looming large again.

10. Teaching for international understanding

Although the dominant note in education throughout the world is still highly nationalistic, and the general efforts to educate for better international relations are still feeble, even before the outbreak of the second World War a number of educators dedicated themselves to the task of running schools to effect better international understanding. Two such pioneers are Kees Boeke of Holland and Paul Geheeb of Switzerland. Kees Boeke has for several years been operating the Children's Workshop Community at Bilthoven, Holland. In its organization, methods, and curricula this is a typical progressive school. Greatly interested in the international aspects of education, Boeke is seeking to extend the work of his school on an international basis, with pupils in the Children's Community coming from many lands.

As creator of the *Odenwaldschule* in pre-Nazi Germany (see p. 145), Geheeb performed magnificently in the field of progressive education. With the advent of National Socialism, his teaching freedom was greatly curtailed and finally he closed his school and migrated to Switzerland, where in 1937 he established his *École d'Humanité* (School of Humanity) not far from Geneva. Two years later he moved to Morat, in the canton of Fribourg.[19] Geheeb's new school is simply the logical continuation of the work he launched in Germany. At the original *Odenwaldschule* the pupils came from many countries, with the result that there was a definite international atmosphere about the place. This idea Geheeb has now deliberately incorporated in the School of Humanity. "Nothing would please me more," he once said, "than to have a half-a-dozen Chinese children, a number of Hindu youngsters, as well as pupils from all over the world in my school." In Geheeb's new venture all cultures and civilizations are to

---

[19] In the fall of 1939 the school moved to Schwarzsee, Fribourg.

be represented not only in the student body but also in the teaching staff. All these cultures are to contribute to the furtherance of international goodwill and understanding.

From the experiences of those who have labored in the field of international education, both in this country and elsewhere, several useful principles have emerged. In the first place, teaching for international understanding is not the province of any one level of education. It should start as early as the kindergarten and it should continue through the university. Furthermore, it should not be restricted to a subject or group of subjects; it should pervade the entire curriculum, no field being excluded. Teaching for international understanding, like all good teaching, is most effective when it occurs naturally and spontaneously. It is not something which can be memorized from a textbook. Nor is it something which can be "promoted" through preachings. Psychologists have suggested that in teaching about foreign peoples and their cultures, teachers would do well to stress similarities, to explain differences understandingly, and to dismiss oddities as such. Teaching for international understanding calls for a hard and effortful realism which seeks to get at all the pertinent facts. Teachers must make it their business to be familiar with all aspects of controversial questions, and teacher education has a tremendous obligation in the development of such an attitude. In the teaching of national history and geography, care should be taken not to magnify the ethnocentrism found in every group, nor to exaggerate the worth of the accomplishments of one's own group over those of other groups. The interdependence of living in one world, the common aspirations of human beings, their common problems and dangers, should be emphasized. Finally, to teach for international understanding our schools must become aware of something which up to now they have utterly neglected, namely their own great potentialities as a factor for peace.

Selected References

The following materials have been selected to provide a working bibliography for further reading and study. The first part comprises a list of general references which may be used in connection with the whole of this volume. The second part includes materials of a more specialized character. Needless to say, the lists are not exhaustive.

General Books

The History and Culture of the Western World

Barnes, H. E., *An Intellectual and Cultural History of the Western World*. New York: Random House, Inc., 1937.

Beard, C. A., and M. B., *The Rise of American Civilization,* revised edition. New York: The Macmillan Company, 1933.

Bogart, E. L., and Kemmerer, D. L., *Economic History of the American People,* revised edition. New York: Longmans, Green & Company, 1942.

Curti, M., *The Growth of American Thought*. New York: Harper & Brothers, 1943.

Hacker, L., *The Shaping of American Tradition*. New York: Columbia University Press, 1946.

Hicks, J. D., *The American Nation*. Boston: Houghton Mifflin Company, 1941; *A Short History of American Democracy*. Boston: Houghton Mifflin Company, 1943.

Miller, H., *An Historical Introduction to Modern Philosophy*. New York: The Macmillan Company, 1947.

Parrington, V. L., *Main Currents in American Thought*. 3 volumes. New York: Harcourt, Brace & Company, 1927–1930.

Sarton, G., *Introduction to the History of Science*. Baltimore: Williams & Wilkins, 1937.

Schlesinger, A. M., and Hockett, H. C., *Political and Social History of the United States*. 2 volumes. New York: The Macmillan Company, 1941.

Schneider, H. W., *A History of American Philosophy*. New York: Columbia University Press, 1946.

Seligman, E. R. A., and Johnson, A. (editors), *Encyclopedia of the Social Sciences*. 15 volumes. New York: The Macmillan Company, 1930–1935.

Thorndike, L., *History of Magic and Experimental Science*. Volumes 1–2. New York: The Macmillan Company, 1929; volumes 3–6. New York: Columbia University Press, 1934–1941; *A Short History of Civilization*. New York: Appleton-Century-Crofts, 1948.

Tschan, F. J., Grimm, H. J., and Squires, J. D., *Western Civilization.* 2 volumes, revised edition. New York: J. B. Lippincott Company, 1945.

The History of Western Education

Brubacher, J. S., *A History of the Problems of Education.* New York: McGraw-Hill Book Company, Inc., 1947.

Butts, R. F., *A Cultural History of Education.* New York: McGraw-Hill Book Company, Inc., 1947.

Cubberley, E. P., *The History of Education.* Boston: Houghton Mifflin Company, 1920; *Readings in the History of Education.* Boston: Houghton Mifflin Company, 1920; *Public Education in the United States,* revised edition. Boston: Houghton Mifflin Company, 1934; *Readings in Public Education in the United States.* Boston: Houghton Mifflin Company, 1934.

Eby, F., and Arrowood, C. F., *The Development of Modern Education.* New York: Prentice-Hall, Inc., 1934.

Edwards, N., and Richey, H. G., *The School in the American Social Order.* Boston: Houghton Mifflin Company, 1947.

Elsbree, W. S., *The American Teacher.* New York: American Book Company, 1939.

Good, H. G., *A History of Western Education.* New York: The Macmillan Company, 1947.

Hart, J. K., *A Social Interpretation of Education.* New York: Henry Holt & Company, 1929; *Creative Movements in Education.* New York: Henry Holt & Company, 1931.

Kandel, I. L., *History of Secondary Education.* Boston: Houghton Mifflin Company, 1930.

Knight, E. W., *Education in the United States,* revised edition. Boston: Ginn & Company, 1941.

Monroe, P. (editor), *Cyclopedia of Education.* 5 volumes. New York: The Macmillan Company, 1911–1919.

Mulhern, J., *A History of Education.* New York: The Ronald Press Company, 1946.

Noble, S. G., *A History of American Education.* New York: Farrar & Rinehart, Inc., 1938.

Reisner, E. H., *Nationalism and Education since 1789.* New York: The Macmillan Company, 1922; *Historical Foundations of Modern Education.* New York: The Macmillan Company, 1927; *The Evolution of the Common School.* New York: The Macmillan Company, 1930.

Ulich, R., *History of Educational Thought.* New York: American Book Company, 1945.

Woody, T., *A History of Women's Education in the United States.* 2 volumes. Lancaster, Pa.: Science Press, 1929.

Twentieth Century Europe

Boas, G., *Our New Ways of Thinking*. New York: Harper & Brothers, 1930.

Ebenstein, W., *Fascist Italy*. New York: American Book Company, 1939.

Hayes, C. J. H., *Essays on Nationalism*. New York: The Macmillan Company, 1926.

Heiden, K., *A History of National Socialism*. New York: Alfred A. Knopf, 1935.

Hitler, A., *Mein Kampf*. New York: Reynal and Hitchcock, 1939.

Johnson, F. E. (editor), *Religion and the World Order*. New York: Harper & Brothers, 1944.

Langsam, W. C., *The World Since 1914*, revised edition. New York: The Macmillan Company, 1943.

Leighton, J. A., *Social Philosophies in Conflict*. New York: D. Appleton-Century Company, 1937.

Merriam, C. E., *The New Democracy and the New Despotism*. New York: McGraw-Hill Book Company, Inc., 1939.

Northrop, F. S. C., *The Meeting of East and West*. New York: The Macmillan Company, 1946.

Schuman, F. L., *Germany Since 1918*. New York: Henry Holt & Company, 1937; *Soviet Politics at Home and Abroad*. New York: Alfred A. Knopf, 1946.

Siegfried, A., *France: A Study in Nationality*. New Haven: Yale University Press, 1930.

Spahr, M., *Readings in Recent Political Philosophy*. New York: The Macmillan Company, 1935.

Steiner, H. A., *Government in Fascist Italy*. New York: McGraw-Hill Book Company, Inc., 1938.

Whitehead, A. N., *Science and the Modern World*. New York: The Macmillan Company, 1925.

Wolf, J. B., *France, 1815 to the Present*. New York: Prentice-Hall, Inc., 1940.

Books Dealing With Specialized Subjects

Education in Twentieth Century Europe

Alexander, T., and Parker, B., *The New Education in the German Republic*. New York: The John Day Company, 1929.

Becker, H., *German Youth: Bond or Free*. New York: Oxford University Press, 1946.

Campbell, O. D., *The Danish Folk School*. New York: The Macmillan Company, 1928.

Counts, G. S., and Lodge, N. P. (translators), *"I Want to be Like Stalin"* (from the Russian *Pedagogika*, by Yesipov, B. P., and Goncharov, N. K.), New York: The John Day Company, 1947.

Englemann, S. C., *German Education and Re-education.* New York: International Press, 1945.

Gaus, J. M., *Great Britain: A Study of Civic Loyalty.* Chicago: University of Chicago Press, 1929.

Gentile, G., *The Reform of Education.* New York: Harcourt, Brace & Company, 1922.

Hans, N., *History of Russian Educational Policy.* London: P. S. King and Son, Ltd., 1931.

Hart, J. K., *Light from the North.* New York: Henry Holt & Company, 1926.

Hayes, C. J. H., *France: A Nation of Patriots.* New York: Columbia University Press, 1927.

Kandel, I. L., *Comparative Education.* Boston: Houghton Mifflin Company, 1933; *The Making of Nazis.* New York: Teachers College, Columbia University, 1935; (editor), *Educational Yearbooks of the International Institute.* New York: Teachers College, Columbia University, 1924–1944.

Kotschnig, W. M., *Slaves Need No Leaders.* New York: Oxford University Press, 1943.

Learned, W. S., *The Quality of the Educational Process in the United States and Europe.* New York: Carnegie Foundation, 1927.

Marraro, H. R., *The New Education in Italy.* New York: S. F. Vanni, 1936.

Merriam, C. E., *The Making of Citizens.* Chicago: University of Chicago Press, 1931.

Meyer, A. E., *Modern European Educators.* New York: Prentice-Hall, Inc., 1934.

Minio-Paluello, L., *Education in Fascist Italy.* London: Oxford University Press, 1946.

Ministry of Education, *A Guide to the Educational System of England and Wales.* London: His Majesty's Stationery Office, 1945.

Pinkevitch, A. P., *The New Education in the Soviet Republic.* New York: The John Day Company, 1929.

Richter, W., *Re-educating Germany.* Chicago: University of Chicago Press, 1945.

Shore, M. J., *Soviet Education.* New York: Philosophical Library, 1947.

Washburne, C., and Stearns, M., *New Schools in the Old World.* New York: The John Day Company, 1926.

Wilson, J. D. (editor), *The Schools of England.* London: Sidgwick & Jackson, Ltd., 1928.

Woody, T., *New Minds: New Men?* New York: The Macmillan Company, 1932.

Zink, H., *American Military Government in Germany.* New York: The Macmillan Company, 1947.

Twentieth Century America

Beard, C., and M. B., *American in Midpassage.* New York: The Macmillan Company, 1939.

Brown, F. J., and Roucek, J. S. (editors), *One America.* New York: Prentice-Hall, Inc., 1945.

Brown, W. A., *Church and State in Contemporary America.* New York: Charles Scribner's Sons, 1936.

Burke, C., *The Roots of American Culture.* New York: Harcourt, Brace & Company, 1942.

Cargill, O., *Intellectual America.* New York: The Macmillan Company, 1941.

Chase, S., *The Proper Study of Mankind.* New York: Harper & Brothers, 1948.

Counts, G. S., *The Prospects of American Democracy.* New York: The John Day Company, 1938.

Dewey, J., *Human Nature and Conduct.* New York: Henry Holt & Company, 1922; *Freedom and Culture.* New York: G. P. Putnam's Sons, 1939; *Problems of Men.* New York: Philosophical Library, 1946.

Ellwood, C. A., and others, *Recent Developments in the Social Sciences.* Philadelphia: J. B. Lippincott Company, 1927.

Gray, G. W., *The Advancing Front of Science.* New York: McGraw-Hill Book Company, Inc., 1937.

Harris, H., *American Labor.* New Haven: Yale University Press, 1939.

Hofstadter, R., *The American Political Tradition and the Men Who Made It.* New York: Alfred A. Knopf, 1948.

James, W., *Pragmatism.* New York: Longmans, Green & Company, 1907.

Linton, R. (editor), *The Science of Man in the World Crisis.* New York: Columbia University Press, 1945.

Lynd, R. S., and H. M., *Middletown: A Study in Contemporary American Culture.* New York: Harcourt, Brace & Company, 1929; *Middletown in Transition: A Study in Cultural Conflicts.* New York: Harcourt, Brace & Company, 1937.

Mead, G. H., *Mind, Self, and Society.* Chicago: University of Chicago Press, 1936.

Mead, M., *And Keep Your Powder Dry: An Anthropologist Looks at America.* New York: William Morrow and Company, 1941.

Merriam, C. E., *Systematic Politics.* Chicago: University of Chicago Press, 1945.

Mumford, L., *Technics and Civilization.* New York: Harcourt, Brace & Company, 1934; *The Culture of Cities.* New York: Harcourt, Brace & Company, 1938.

Rugg, H., *Culture and Education in America.* New York: Harcourt, Brace & Company, 1931.

Sutherland, R. L., *Color, Class and Personality.* Washington, D. C.: American Council on Education, 1941.

Warner, W. L., and others, *Color and Human Nature, Negro Personality Development in a Northern City*. Washington, D. C.: American Council on Education, 1941.

Whitehead, A. W., *Science in the Modern World*. New York: The Macmillan Company, 1932.

Education in Twentieth Century America

Aikin, W. M., *The Story of the Eight-year Study*. New York: Harper & Brothers, 1942.

Alberty, H. B., and Bode, B. H., *Educational Freedom and Democracy*, Second Yearbook of the John Dewey Society. New York: D. Appleton-Century Company, 1938.

American Council on Education, Commission on Teacher Education, *The Improvement of Teacher Education*. Washington, D. C.: American Council on Education, 1946.

American Historical Association, *Commission on the Social Studies in the Schools, Conclusions and Recommendations*. New York: Charles Scribner's Sons, 1934.

Axtelle, G. E., and Wattenberg, W. W., *Teachers for Democracy*, Fourth Yearbook of the John Dewey Society. New York: D. Appleton-Century Company, 1940.

Bagley, W. C., *Education and Emergent Man*. New York: Thomas Nelson and Sons, 1934.

Beale, H. K., *Are American Teachers Free?* New York: Charles Scribner's Sons, 1936.

Beck, II. P., *Men Who Control Our Universities*. New York: King's Crown Press, 1947.

Bell, H. M., *Youth Tell Their Story*. Washington, D. C.: American Council on Education, 1938.

Berkson, I. B., *Preface to an Educational Philosophy*. New York: Columbia University Press, 1940; *Education Faces the Future*. New York: Harper & Brothers, 1943.

Bode, B. H., *Modern Educational Theories*. New York: The Macmillan Company, 1927; *Democracy as a Way of Life*. New York: The Macmillan Company, 1937; *Progressive Education at the Crossroads*. New York: Newson and Company, 1938.

Brameld, T. (editor), *Workers' Education in the United States*, Fifth Yearbook of the John Dewey Society. New York: D. Appleton-Century Company, 1941; *Minority Problems in the Public Schools*. New York: Harper & Brothers, 1946.

Breed, F. S., *Education and the New Realism*. New York: The Macmillan Company, 1939.

Brubacher, J. S., *Modern Philosophies of Education*. New York: McGraw-Hill Book Company, Inc., 1939; (editor), *The Public Schools and Spiritual Values*, Seventh Yearbook of the John Dewey Society. New York: Harper & Brothers, 1944.

Butts, R. F., *The College Charts Its Course*. New York: McGraw-Hill Book Company, Inc., 1939.

Carr, W. G., *Only by Understanding*. New York: Foreign Policy Association, 1945.

Cartwright, M. A., *Ten Years of Adult Education*. New York: The Macmillan Company, 1935.

Caswell, H. L., *Education in the Elementary School*. New York: American Book Company, 1942.

Childs, J. L., *Education and the Philosophy of Experimentalism*. New York: D. Appleton-Century Company, 1931.

Clapp, E. R., *Community Schools in Action*. New York: The Viking Press, 1937.

Cole, S. G., *Liberal Education in a Democracy*. New York: Harper & Brothers, 1936.

Counts, G. S., *Dare the School Build a New Social Order?* New York: The John Day Company, 1932; *Education and the Promise of America*. New York: The Macmillan Company, 1945.

Cunningham, W. F., *The Pivotal Problems of Education*. New York: The Macmillan Company, 1940.

Deferrari, R. J., *Vital Problems of Catholic Education in the United States*. Washington, D. C.: Catholic University of America, 1939.

De Young, C. A., *Introduction to American Public Education*. New York: McGraw-Hill Book Company, Inc., 1942.

Dewey, J., *Democracy and Education*. New York: The Macmillan Company, 1916; *Experience and Education*. New York: The Macmillan Company, 1938.

Everett, S. (editor), *The Community School*. New York: D. Appleton-Century Company, 1938.

Fine, B., *Admission to American Colleges*. New York: Harper & Brothers, 1946; *Our Children Are Cheated*. New York: Henry Holt & Company, 1947.

Flexner, A., *Universities, English, German, American*. New York: Oxford University Press, 1930.

Gallagher, B. G., *American Caste and the Negro College*. New York: Columbia University Press, 1938.

Gulick, L. H., *Education for American Life, Report of the Regents Inquiry*. New York: McGraw-Hill Book Company, Inc., 1938.

Harvard University, *Report of the Harvard Committee, General Education in a Free Society*. Cambridge: Harvard University Press, 1945.

Henderson, A. D., and Hall, D., *Antioch College*. New York: Harper & Brothers, 1946.

Horne, H. H., *The Philosophy of Education*, revised edition. New York: The Macmillan Company, 1927; *The Democratic Philosophy of Education*. New York: The Macmillan Company, 1932.

Hutchins, R., *The Higher Learning in America*. New Haven: Yale University Press, 1936.

Jones, B., *Bennington College.* New York: Harper & Brothers, 1946.

Judd, C. H., *The Psychology of Social Institutions.* New York: The Macmillan Company, 1926.

Kandel, I. L., *Twenty-five Years of American Education.* New York: The Macmillan Company, 1924; *Conflicting Theories of Education.* Boston: Houghton Mifflin Company, 1938; *United States Activities in International Cultural Relations.* Washington, D. C.: American Council on Education, 1945.

Kilpatrick, W. H., *The Project Method.* New York: Teachers College, Columbia University, 1918; *Foundations of Method.* New York: The Macmillan Company, 1925; *Education for a Changing Civilization.* New York: The Macmillan Company, 1926; *Education and the Social Crisis.* New York: Horace Liveright, 1932; (editor), *The Educational Frontier.* New York: D. Appleton-Century Company, 1933; (editor), *The Teacher and Society,* First Yearbook of the John Dewey Society. New York: D. Appleton-Century Company, 1937; (with Van Til, W. A.), *Intercultural Attitudes in America,* Ninth Yearbook of the John Dewey Society. New York: Harper & Brothers, 1947.

Koos, L. V., *The Junior College.* Minneapolis: University of Minnesota Press, 1924.

Kotschnig, W. M., and Prys, E. (editors), *The University in a Changing World.* London: Oxford University Press, 1932.

Maritain, J., *Education at the Crossroads.* New Haven: Yale University Press, 1943.

Mayhew, K. C., and Edwards, A. C., *The Dewey School.* New York: D. Appleton-Century Company, 1936.

Mciklejohn, A., *The Experimental College.* New York: Harper & Brothers, 1932; *Education Between Two Worlds.* New York: Harper & Brothers, 1942.

Millet, F. B., *The Rebirth of Liberal Education.* New York: Harcourt, Brace & Company, 1945.

Morrison, H. C., *The Curriculum of the Common School.* Chicago: University of Chicago Press, 1940.

Morrison, J. C., *The Activity Program, The Report of a Survey of the Curriculum Experiment.* Albany: New York State Department of Education, 1941.

National Education Association, Educational Policies Commission, *The Purposes of Education in American Democracy.* Washington, D. C.: National Education Association, 1938; *Education and Economic Well-being in American Democracy.* Washington, D. C.: National Education Association, 1940; *Education for All American Youth.* Washington, D. C.: National Education Association; *Federal-state Relations in Education.* Washington, D. C.: American Council on Education, 1945.

National Society for the Study of Education, *Philosophies of Education.* Bloomington, Ill.: Public School Publishing Company, 1942.

Newlon, J. H., *Education for Democracy in Our Time*. New York: McGraw-Hill Book Company, Inc., 1939.

Parkhurst, H., *Education on the Dalton Plan*. New York: E. P. Dutton and Company, 1922.

Pierce, B. L., *Civic Attitudes in American School Textbooks*. Chicago: University of Chicago Press, 1930.

Prall, C. E., *State Programs for the Improvement of Teacher Education*. Washington, D. C.: American Council on Education, 1946.

Progressive Education Association, *Progressive Education Advances*. New York: D. Appleton-Century Company, 1938; *New Methods versus Old in American Education*. New York: Teachers College, Columbia University, 1941.

Ragsdale, C. E., *Modern Psychologies and Education*. New York: The Macmillan Company, 1936.

Raup, R. B., *Education and Organized Interests in America*. New York: C. P. Putnam's Sons, 1936.

Rugg, H., *American Life and the School Curriculum*. Boston: Ginn & Company, 1936; (editor), *Democracy and the Curriculum*, Third Yearbook of the John Dewey Society. New York: D. Appleton-Century Company, 1939; *Foundations for American Education*. Yonkers-on-Hudson: World Book Company, 1947.

Russell, J. D., and MacKenzie, D. M., *Emergent Responsibilities in Higher Education*. Chicago: University of Chicago Press, 1946.

Spain, C. L., *The Platoon School*. New York: The Macmillan Company, 1923.

Taba, H., and Van Til, W. (editors), *Democratic Human Relations: Promising Practices in Intergroup and Intercultural Education in the Social Studies*. Washington, D. C.: National Council for the Social Studies, 1945.

Thayer, V. T., *The Passing of the Recitation*. Boston: D. C. Heath & Company, 1928; *American Education under Fire*. New York: Harper & Brothers, 1944; with Zachry, C. B., and Kotinsky, R., *Reorganizing Secondary Education*. New York: D. Appleton-Century Company, 1939.

Van Doren, M., *Liberal Education*. New York: Henry Holt & Company, 1943.

Warner, W. L., Havighurst, R., and Loeb, M. B., *Who Shall Be Educated?* New York: Harper & Brothers, 1944.

Woelfel, N., *Molders of the American Mind*. New York: Columbia University Press, 1933.

Wrightstone, J. W., *Appraisal of Newer Elementary School Practices*. New York: Teachers College, Columbia University, 1938.

Index

597